COPING WITH DROUGHT IN KENYA

• FOOD IN AFRICA SERIES •

Series Editor: *Art Hansen*
Center for African Studies
University of Florida

- Africa's Agrarian Crisis: The Roots of Famine •
  Stephen K. Commins, Michael F. Lofchie, and Rhys Payne, editors

- Food in Sub-Saharan Africa •
  Art Hansen and Della E. McMillan, editors

- Agricultural Prices, Policy, and Equity in Sub-Saharan Africa •
  Dharam Ghai and Lawrence D. Smith

- Coping with Africa's Food Crisis •
  Naomi Chazan and Timothy M. Shaw, editors

- The Policy Factor: Agricultural Performance in Kenya and Tanzania •
  Michael F. Lofchie

- Coping with Drought in Kenya: National and Local Strategies •
  Thomas E. Downing, Kangethe W. Gitu, and Crispin M. Kamau, editors

COPING WITH DROUGHT IN KENYA

National and Local Strategies

edited by
Thomas E. Downing, Kangethe W. Gitu,
and Crispin M. Kamau

Lynne Rienner Publishers • Boulder & London

Published in the United States of America in 1989 by
Lynne Rienner Publishers, Inc.
1800 30th Street, Boulder, Colorado 80301

and in the United Kingdom by
Lynne Rienner Publishers, Inc.
3 Henrietta Street, Covent Garden, London WC2E 8LU

©1989 by Lynne Rienner Publishers, Inc. All rights reserved

Library of Congress Cataloging-in-Publication Data
Coping with drought in Kenya : national and local strategies / edited by Thomas E. Downing, Kangethe W. Gitu, and Crispin M. Kamau.
(Food in Africa series)
Bibliography: p.
Includes index.
ISBN 1-55587-151-8 (alk. paper)
1. Droughts—Kenya. I. Downing, Thomas E. II. Gitu, Kangethe.
III. Kamau, C. M. IV. Series.
QC927.D8C665 1989
363.3'492—dc19   89-30952
                                                              CIP

British Cataloguing in Publication Data
A Cataloguing in Publication record for this book
is available from the British Library.

Printed and bound in the United States of America

The paper used in this publication meets the requirements of
the American National Standard for Permanence of Paper for
Printed Library Materials Z39.48–1984.

Contents

- List of Figures, Tables and Appendixes ... ix
- Foreword *A.K. Kiriro* ... xv
- Acknowledgments ... xvii

PART 1 OVERVIEW OF THE 1984/85 DROUGHT ... 1

1 • Drought in Kenya *Thomas E. Downing, Crispin M. Kamau, Kangethe W. Gitu, and John Borton* ... 3
2 • Overview of the 1984/85 National Drought Relief Program *John Borton* ... 24

PART 2 DROUGHT FORECASTING AND MONITORING ... 65

3 • Synoptic Features Associated with the Failure of the 1984 Long Rains in Kenya *Michael W. Macodras, Philip N. Nthusi, and John Mwikya* ... 69
4 • Rainfall Variability in Tropical Africa and Kenya *Graham Farmer* ... 82
5 • Agricultural and Livestock Monitoring Using Aerial Photography *H. Mwendwa* ... 94
6 • Surveys and Activities of the Central Bureau of Statistics Related to Food Monitoring *B. F. Maganda* ... 106
7 • Food Crop Monitoring and Reporting by the Ministry of Agriculture *Duncan N. Mwanjila* ... 119
8 • Agricultural Yields, Production, and Monitoring Methods of the National Cereals and Produce Board *F. G. Murage* ... 122
9 • The Tanzanian Crop Monitoring and Early Warning System *D. A. R. Kashasha* ... 131

PART 3 DROUGHT VULNERABILITY, IMPACTS, AND COPING STRATEGIES — 139

10 • Drought and Its Implications for Water Supply in Northern Kenya *Gernot Bake* — 141

11 • Reconstructing Gabbra History and Chronology: Time Reckoning, the Gabbra Calendar, and the Cyclical View of Life *Paul W. Robinson* — 151

12 • Drought Vulnerability in Central and Eastern Kenya *George J. Anyango, Thomas E. Downing, Carolyn Getao, M. Gitahi, Charity Kabutha, Crispin M. Kamau, Mary Karanja, Sabina W. Maghanga, Simon K. Mbarire, Simeon Munene, Wycliffe Mutero, Harun R. Muturi, B. Mwangi, Margaret Wainaina, and F. Were* — 169

13 • Case Studies of Drought Impacts and Responses in Central and Eastern Kenya *Crispin M. Kamau, George J. Anyango, M. Gitahi, Margaret Wainaina, and Thomas E. Downing* — 211

14 • Impact of the 1984 Drought on Food Intake, Nutritional Status, and Household Response in Embu District *Charlotte G. Neumann, N. O. Bwibo, E. Carter, S. Weinberg, A. A. Jansen, D. Cattle, D. Ngare, M. Baksh, M. Paolisso, and A. H. Coulson* — 231

15 • Drought, Resource Distribution, and Mobility in Two Maasai Group Ranches, Southeastern Kajiado District *Barbara E. Grandin, Peter N. de Leeuw, and P. Lembuya* — 245

16 • Food Acquisition by the Samburu Herders During the Drought of 1983/84 *Louise Sperling* — 264

PART 4 INSTITUTIONAL EXPERIENCES IN DROUGHT MANAGEMENT — 281

17 • World Food Programme Emergency Food Aid for Drought Victims in Kenya *World Food Programme* — 283

18 • Nutrition and Health Activities of the Ministry of Health *Monica A. Okoth and Valerie S. Wambani* — 289

19 • Effect of the 1984 Drought on Education *J. B. M. Bukusi and Simon K. Mbarire* — 299

20 • Planning Against Drought and Famine in Turkana: A District Contingency Plan *Jeremy Swift* — 306

21 • Drought Assistance to NGOs Provided by CARE-Kenya *Robin Needham* — 329

22	• Drought Relief Activities of the Kenya Freedom From Hunger Council *Moses G. Mbugua*	337
23	• Relief and Recovery for Pastoralists: Oxfam's Experience *Eliud Ngunjiri*	344

PART 5 DROUGHT AND FOOD POLICY 353

24	• Drought and Food Policy in Kenya *J. B. Wyckoff*	355
25	• Drought and Food Policy in the African Context *Philip Ndegwa*	369

References	379
Abbreviations and Units of Measure	391
List of Contributors	395
Index	400

Figures, Tables, and Appendixes

FIGURES

1.1	Administrative boundaries	14
1.2	Agricultural livelihood systems	15
1.3	Distribution of population	16
1.4	Normal rainfall in the short and long rains	17
1.5	Seasonal rainfall in 1983–1984	18
1.6	Foreign-exchange reserves	19
1.7	Overview of the 1984/85 food crisis in Kenya	20
2.1	NCPB maize stocks by month	51
2.2	NCPB maize transactions	51
2.3	NCPB stocks of yellow and white maize	52
3.1	Percent of normal for February to June 1984 long rains	76
3.2	Daily pressure values in the southwest Indian Ocean	77
3.3	Surface winds on 10 April 1984	78
3.4	Surface winds on 11 April 1984	78
3.5	Surface winds on 12 April 1984	78
3.6	Tropical cyclone Helene	79
3.7	Tropical cyclone Honorine	79
3.8	Tropical cyclone Gladys	80
3.9	Tropical cyclone Kamisy	80
3.10	Streamline analysis for 10 April 1984	81
4.1	Mean normalized rainfall anomaly series for tropical Africa	88
4.2	Location map of stations in Kenyan analyses	89
4.3	Mean normalized anomaly time series for long rains	90
4.4	Mean normalized anomaly time series for short rains	91
4.5	Mean normalized anomaly time series for annual data	92

5.1	Areas surveyed by KREMU in the 1984/85 drought	100
6.1	Areas surveyed by the Central Bureau of Statistics	113
6.2	Monthly average prices for maize and beans	114
9.1	Spatial coverage of rain gauges in Tanzania	135
9.2	Maize phenology at the end of March 1985	135
9.3	Condition of maize at the end of March 1984	136
9.4	Condition of maize at the end of March 1985	136
10.1	Variability of annual rainfall at Marsabit	146
10.2	Average monthly rainfall and threshold values for rainfed agriculture	147
10.3	Probability of annual rainfall at Marsabit and Marsabit/3	148
10.4	Variation of starts and duration of rainy seasons at Marsabit	149
11.1	Location of Gabbra rangelands	163
11.2	Gabbra calendar, 1983–1984	164
11.3	Gabbra rainfall seasons	165
11.4	Gabbra oral rainfall data	166
11.5	Gabbra mean oral rainfall data and meteorological records	167
11.6	Gabbra perceived climatic cycles	168
12.1	Location of central and eastern Kenya study area	190
12.2	Terrain	191
12.3	Agroecological zones	192
12.4	Reliability of rainfall in the first rains	193
12.5	Reliability of rainfall in the second rains	194
12.6	Trends in seasonal rainfall	195
12.7	Trends in seasonal rainfall variability	196
12.8	Maize yields for scenarios of a good season and a moderate drought season	197
12.9	Soil water-holding capacity	198
14.1	Agroclimatic zones in the CRSP study area of Embu District	240
14.2	Kilocalories consumed by household, 1984–1985	240
14.3	Changes in adult body weight during the 1984 drought	241
14.4	Toddler classification changes in 1984	242
14.5	Pregnancy weight gain and percent of low birth weight	242
14.6	Land owned and cultivated in Embu District	243
15.1	Location of group ranches in southeastern Kajiado District	260
15.2	Range quality in southeastern Kajiado District	261

16.1 Location of Samburu District and Wamba Division   277
16.2 Samburu food sources by season   278

18.1 Weight-for-age chart   296

20.1 Cycle of pastoral terms of trade during drought conditions 326

TABLES

1.1 Scales of Drought Hazard   21
1.2 Droughts in Kenya   22
1.3 Production of Food Crops   23
1.4 Sales to Marketing Boards   23
1.5 Quantity, Prices, and Values of Tea and Coffee Exports   23

2.1 Food Import Requirements Reported by the
     Government of Kenya   52
2.2 Food Imports: September 1984 to June 1985   53
2.3 Beneficiaries of Food Relief from the Office of the President 54
2.4 Monthly Distribution of U.S. Title II Maize   55
2.5 Principal Known Donations to the Kenyan Relief Program   56

4.1 Rainfall Correlations for Long and Short Rains   93
4.2 Spectral Analyses of Area-Averaged Rainfall Series   93

5.1 Yield and Projected Maize Harvest in 1984   101
5.2 Comparison of Projected Maize Harvests in 1984   101
5.3 Livestock Numbers in the 1985 Census Compared to Average 102
5.4 Animal Populations in Baringo District, 1982–1985   102
5.5 Animal Populations in Garissa District, 1977–1985   103
5.6 Animal Populations in Isiolo District, 1977–1985   103
5.7 Animal Populations in Laikipia District, 1981–1985   104
5.8 Animal Populations in Mandera and Wajir Districts,
     1978–1985   104
5.9 Animal Populations in Marsabit, Samburu,
     and West Pokot Districts   105

6.1 Crop Forecast Survey Schedule   114
6.2 Crop Forecast Survey Results, 1983–1985   115
6.3 Maize Yield Estimates for 1985   118

8.1 NCPB Geographic Zones   128
8.2 Harvest Results from Two Maize Fields   128

8.3	Regression Equations for Cob Size and Weight	128
8.4	NCPB Maize Yield Survey for Machakos and Kitui	129
8.5	Results of the NCPB Maize Yield Survey by Zone	129
8.6	Expected and Actual Maize Purchases by the NCPB	130
10.1	Monthly Drought Threshold Values of Rainfall	150
10.2	Monthly Rainfall Probabilities for Marsabit/3	150
10.3	Seasonal Rainfall Probabilities for Marsabit/3	150
12.1	Agroclimatic Zones	199
12.2	Area of Agroecological Zones	199
12.3	Population Projections to the Year 2000	200
12.4	Population Density and Growth Rates by Agroclimatic Zone	200
12.5	Population by Age and Sex, 1979	201
12.6	Seasonal Drought Probabilities	201
12.7	Trends in Crop Production	202
12.8	Agricultural Responses to the 1984 Drought	202
12.9	Livestock Losses by Agroclimatic Zone	203
12.10	Ratio of Household Maize Purchases to Consumption	203
12.11	Sources of Household Income	204
12.12	Household Characteristics in the CBS/NES Survey of Drought Responses	205
12.13	Market Prices in 1984	205
12.14	Famine Relief in Kiambu, Murang'a, Kirinyaga, and Kitui Districts	206
12.15	Food Relief Distributed by the GOK/USAID Program	207
12.16	Nutritional Status by Agroclimatic Zone	208
12.17	Vulnerability to Hunger: Chronic Conditions and Severe Drought	208
12.18	Assessment of Smallholder Drought-Coping Strategies	209
13.1	Characteristics of the Four Communities	226
13.2	Drought Impacts in the Four Community Case Studies	227
13.3	Drought-Coping Strategies in the Four Community Case Studies	227
13.4	Food Trade in the Four Community Case Studies	228
13.5	Attendance at Adult Education Classes, Mutomo Division, Kitui	229
13.6	Use of Weather Information in the Four Community Case Studies	229
13.7	Food Distributed by the Chief of Mutithi Location, Kirinyaga	230
13.8	Famine Relief Provided by the Assistant Chief, Kawelu	230
13.9	Food-for-Work at Selected Sites in Kawelu	230

14.1	Adult Weight Change During the 1984 Drought	243
14.2	Anthropometric Status in Children from August to December 1984	243
14.3	Anthropometric Screening of Non-CRSP Households	244
14.4	Annual Drought Probabilities for Embu	244
15.1	Characteristics of Olkarkar and Mbirikani Group Ranches	262
15.2	Seasonal Rainfall in Southeastern Kajiado, 1981–1984	262
15.3	Distribution of Cattle in late September 1984	262
15.4	Annual Livestock Inventory Change, 1981–1983	263
15.5	Livestock Inventory Change During Drought in Olkarkar Group Ranch	263
16.1	Human and Cattle Populations in Samburu District, 1915–1984	279
16.2	Goat Prices at Wamba Town, 1984	279
17.1	World Food Programme Shipments and Distribution of Food Aid	287
17.2	World Food Programme Emergency Food Assistance Distributed by the GOK	287
17.3	World Food Programme Emergency Food Assistance Distributed by NGOs	288
18.1	Stunted Children in 1977, 1979, and 1982	297
18.2	Indicators of Childhood Health	297
18.3	District Feeding Programs for Children Under the Age of Five	298
19.1	Enrollment at Kanyiri Primary School, Embu, in 1984	304
19.2	Financial Aid to Government Secondary Schools in 1984/85	304
19.3	Schools Covered by the School Feeding Programme, 1981–1985	304
19.4	Pupils Covered by the School Feeding Programme, 1981–1985	305
19.5	Food Distributed by the Supplementary Food Program	305
19.6	Loans from ActionAid, Kagio	305
20.1	Annual Probability of Wet and Dry Years According to a Weighted Ecological Index	326
20.2	Main Disaster Years According to Turkana Chronologies	327
20.3	Sample Checklists for the Turkana District Early Warning System	327
20.4	Warning Stages and Planned Responses	328
21.1	NGO Participation in the OFDA Grant for Transport Costs	336
21.2	CARE-Kenya Monthly Grant Dispursements for Transport	336

22.1	Duration of Food Assistance Provided by the KFFHC	343
22.2	Distribution of Seed by the KFFHC	343
22.3	Tool Distribution by the KFFHC	343
23.1	Oxfam's Restocking Projects	351
25.1	Production and Imports of Cereals in Africa	378

APPENDIXES

2.1	Chronology of the Drought in Kenya	57
2.2	Estimated Production, Stocks, Trade, and Use of Maize	63
2.3	Estimated Production, Stocks, Trade, and Use of Wheat	64
9.1	Codes Used to Report Weekly Crop Data	137

Foreword

A. K. KIRIRO

The 1984 drought in Kenya was the most severe since 1930. There was an almost complete failure of the long rains except in the coastal areas and most of Western and Nyanza provinces. Consequently, agricultural production was sharply reduced, creating food shortages. Yet, the timely response of the government preempted potentially serious famine conditions in much of the country.

As the realities of the drought in 1984 became apparent, the National Environment Secretariat (NES) formulated a project with two main objectives: to document the effects of drought in six districts of central and eastern Kenya, and to record the response of governmental and nongovernmental organizations in the face of widespread drought. Funding for this work was provided by the Ford Foundation with technical assistance from Clark University. The project also contributed to an international assessment of the impact of climatic variations on agriculture (Parry, Carter, and Konijn 1988).

In May 1986, a workshop entitled "Drought in Kenya: Lessons from 1984" was held in Gigiri, Kenya. The workshop, sponsored by the National Environment Secretariat and United Nations Environment Programme (UNEP), was intended to focus research efforts upon the complex problem of drought in Kenya. The idea for this book grew out of the discussions among the participants in the workshop, who offered to write about their experiences pertinent to the drought situation in Kenya during 1984. The purpose of this book is to collect the lessons learned in the 1984/85 drought and make them available to researchers, planners, and managers who will be called upon to reduce vulnerability to famine and respond to drought in Africa and elsewhere.

The book is comprised of five parts, each introduced with a brief review by the editors. The introduction (Part 1) provides an overview of the 1984 drought and national responses in Kenya. The first chapter identifies major themes discussed throughout the text, while Chapter 2 reviews in detail the national response to the drought. The majority of *Coping with Drought in Kenya* assesses drought forecasting and monitoring (Part 2), documents famine vulnerability and household coping strategies (Part 3), and extracts lessons from institutional drought management (Part 4). The final part (5) discusses drought and food policy in Kenya and Africa. Most of the chapters cite examples and case studies from the Kenyan experience in 1984, yet it is clear that the observations contribute significantly to the wider understanding of drought.

I would like to thank the editors and authors for their contributions to this book, including the substantial revisions made to the original workshop presentations. Thanks are also extended to the government of Kenya, the Ford Foundation, UNEP, Clark University, and the National Center for Atmospheric Research[1] for their financial and technical support. Finally, the advice and cooperation of officials in the government of Kenya and non-governmental organizations, as well as the people of Kenya, are gratefully acknowledged.

The authors have written in their personal capacity—their interpretations and conclusions do not necessarily represent the policies of their agencies or the institutions that have supported their work.

---

1. The National Center for Atmospheric Research is sponsored by the National Science Foundation.

Acknowledgments

Chapter 2

The author would like to express his thanks to those personnel from the government of Kenya, donor agencies, and NGOs that gave him their time and access to documentation. The research was conducted during a four-week visit to Kenya in March and April 1987 and during two earlier visits to Kenya in September 1984 and March 1986. This chapter is based upon two earlier reports (Borton and Stephenson 1984, Borton 1987), the first funded by the Ford Foundation and the second prepared as part of a research project funded by an Economic and Social Research Grant from the Overseas Development Administration (ODA). The financial support of the ODA and the Ford Foundation is gratefully acknowledged. Particular thanks are due to A. K. Kiriro, director of the National Environment Secretariat, and his staff; Thomas Downing of Clark University; and Sue York of the Relief and Development Institute. The views expressed do not necessarily represent the views of the government of Kenya, the ODA, or the Ford Foundation. Any errors or omissions are solely the responsibility of the author.

Chapter 3

The authors are grateful to the director of the Kenya Meteorological Department for giving permission to use the available rainfall, cyclone, and surface- and upper-air data of the Kenya Meteorological Department. They also want to thank Serah W. Kirega for typing the manuscript.

Chapter 4

While any views and opinions offered are personal, this chapter and associated travel to Nairobi were funded by the Overseas Development Administration, to whom grateful thanks are due. Thanks are also due to colleagues in the Climatic Research Unit, particularly T. M. L. Wigley, and to members of the international scientific community, especially those of the Kenya

Meteorological Department and the National Environment Secretariat. *Asanti sana.*

Chapter 5

This chapter would not have been possible without the permission and encouragement of the director of the Kenya Rangeland Ecology Monitoring Unit (KREMU), D. K. Andere. The author wants to thank all KREMU staff members who contributed in one way or another toward the experimental design, data collection, and analysis.

Chapter 11

The fieldwork upon which this research is based was conducted between 1977 and 1981 and during several subsequent visits to northern Kenya. The research was funded by grants from the Fulbright Hays Doctoral Dissertation Research Abroad fellowships and by the Ford Foundation. The *Gabbra Historical Texts* that are referred to in the book are the transcripts of verbatim interviews conducted with Gabbra elders. Copies of these interviews are on deposit in the Kenya National Archives (Robinson 1985a).

Chapter 13

The authors are grateful for the support of the National Environment Secretariat and the Ford Foundation, and for the cooperation of the Central Bureau of Statistics, district administration, local chiefs, and residents.

Chapter 14

This research was supported by USAID Research Grant Number DAN 1309-G-SS-1070-00. The authors wish to acknowledge the assistance of E. K. Njeru (data manager), W. Martin (project administrator), T. Silverman and R. M. Trostle (editorial and manuscript assistance), and B. Browdy (programmer).

Chapter 15

The data presented were collected as part of the International Livestock Centre for Africa's (ILCA) interdisciplinary research on contemporary Maasai livestock production. Barbara E. Grandin conducted anthropological field research in Olkarkar from mid-1981 to mid-1983, while also supervising formal socioeconomic survey data collection. Occasional field visits were made between June 1983 and December 1984 to supervise formal and informal data collection related to the drought and post-drought recovery. Peter N. de Leeuw conducted ecological research at the ILCA study sites from 1982, including studies using remote sensing, low-level aerial survey, and ground investigations. P. Lembuya was the on-site fieldwork supervisor in

1983. He conducted in-depth interviews regarding decision-making strategies and livestock mortality during the drought, while also supervising several enumerators. Comments by Michael Ole Maki and Paul Chara of ILCA and Subhash Morzaria of the International Laboratory for Research on Animal Diseases are gratefully acknowledged.

Chapter 16

This work was undertaken while the author was a research associate at the Institute for Development Studies (IDS), University of Nairobi. Special thanks go to the Office of the President for granting the necessary research clearance, and to Kabiru Kinyanjui and Shem Migot-Adholla, both of IDS, for providing encouragement and insightful critique. Steven Lekutai served as an invaluable research assistant throughout the fieldwork. Dan Aronson and John Galaty offered useful comments on earlier drafts. Finally, Roy Larick's support was indispensable to all stages of this research and writing, and Michael Loevinsohn honed many of the final arguments. This research was supported by the Social Science Research Council and the American Council of Learned Societies. Funds were also provided by the Wenner-Gren Foundation for Anthropological Research, The Friends of McGill, and The Quebec Ministry of Education.

Chapter 25

This chapter draws upon a presentation made to the International Food Policy Research Institute board of directors in Nairobi in 1986 (see Ndegwa 1986).

·PART 1·
Overview of the 1984/85 Drought

Rainfall during the March to May 1984 rainy season in Kenya was well below normal, resulting in one of the worst meteorological droughts in the twentieth century. Maize production for 1984 was a third less than the average for the previous three years. In June, the government of Kenya appealed to donors for assistance, ordering imports of yellow maize in July at world market commercial rates. Grains sold to millers and traders, distributed through local markets, accounted for over two-thirds of all maize and wheat imports. Widespread famine was averted primarily due to the government's early response and commercial imports, which were later supplemented with food aid. This book draws upon the 1984/85 drought to compile lessons relevant to food policy in Kenya and elsewhere in Africa:

1. To prevent famine, the government of Kenya demonstrated the capacity to respond to drought in a timely fashion by importing food on commercial terms and mobilizing a large-scale distribution effort.
2. The drought was readily apparent. The rainy season was delayed and dry, as opposed to having poorly distributed rainfall. The widespread drought was centered on Nairobi, rather than fragmented and in remote areas. The established food monitoring systems were not well utilized. Improvements are required to cope with moderate or isolated droughts.
3. The government's successful response is due, in part, to economic policies promoting the export sector (resulting in large reserves of foreign exchange), a well-developed infrastructure, and a skilled and extensive administrative bureaucracy, including district officials.
4. The initial response was partly triggered by rapidly increasing sales by the National Cereals and Produce Board (NCPB), the government grain marketing parastatal. In the event government controls on the grain market in Kenya are reduced, the NCPB's share of grain trade

will be reduced and more variable. NCPB trading will be a less-reliable indicator of food shortages, and other food-monitoring systems will need to be strengthened.
5. *The food imports were at the very edge of timeliness. A delay of a month or lower stocks at the beginning of 1984 would have led to serious famine and, possibly, social unrest. A strategic reserve of six months appears to be the minimum required.*
6. *Distribution of imported food for sale through local markets proved an efficient strategy, stabilizing prices. There was no widespread failure of effective demand since most households in rural areas were able to purchase food when it was available.*
7. *The emergency work program was difficult to mobilize; it suffered from a lack of supervisory capacity to screen projects, provide technical assistance, deliver inputs and food, and monitor progress.*
8. *The lack of a systematic preparedness plan and comprehensive food-monitoring system resulted in some delays in food relief programs, shortcomings in making the best use of nongovernmental organizations (NGOs), lack of preparedness for recovering from the drought (most notably a shortage of seed), and costly excess stocks of yellow maize after the food crisis had ended.*
9. *Three projects stand out as being innovative: the grain-for-livestock scheme and restocking projects supported pastoralists' access to food and long-term drought-coping strategies; the U.S. grant to CARE for transport costs assisted many NGOs in providing food aid in remote areas; and the World Food Programme, through credit arrangements with the National Cereals and Produce Board, provided food to NGOs early in the drought at a critical stage for many households.*

· 1 ·

Drought in Kenya

THOMAS E. DOWNING   KANGETHE W. GITU
CRISPIN M. KAMAU   JOHN BORTON

Drought is a characteristic element of the environment of Kenya and has affected agriculture, the economy, social organization, and, ultimately and sometimes tragically, people in Kenya many times. This book brings together a diverse set of chapters, all related to the experiences and lessons learned in the 1984/85 drought in Kenya. The purpose of the book is to provide a history of the drought: to characterize the underlying vulnerability to drought, to document the impact of and responses to the 1984/85 drought, and to assess the lessons learned in response to the food crisis. In many ways, the people and government of Kenya responded admirably to the drought, and widespread famine was avoided. Kenya's successful experience has important implications for food policy in Africa, as well as in Kenya.

This chapter presents a framework for discussion of drought, followed by an introduction to the geography of Kenya as it relates to vulnerability to drought and hunger. The last two sections describe the impacts of the 1984/85 drought and summarize the major themes and conclusions of this book. The following chapter reviews the responses to the 1984/85 drought and presents the most important lessons learned at the national level in coping with the drought.

DROUGHT HAZARD FRAMEWORK

A rigorous definition of drought has not been adopted in this book, although many exist (Hounan et al., 1975). Instead, several chapters provide specific definitions. For example, in Chapter 10, Bake refers to the lower variability threshold; in chapter 12, Anyango et al. define severe drought as seasonal rainfall that's less than the 0.02 cumulative probability (or one-in-fifty-year episode). Drought primarily refers to a change in weather that results in a deficiency in available moisture below levels that are normally expected. The implicit reference is to weather, a short-term event, rather than climate, and deficiency relative to normal expectations (however they may be defined) required for specific uses of land and water. Drought, in this sense, almost always affects agricultural and livestock production to some extent, and this leads to the major impacts in Kenya. The impact of drought on the hydrological cycle and water supplies is important in many locales, but historically is less serious than changes in the food system.

While it is certain that drought will recur, its impact depends on a number of factors, the most obvious being the nature of the moisture deficiency. The duration, spatial extent, and magnitude of meteorological drought influence which regions and sectors of the country are affected. Within the drought-affected areas, the nature of the agricultural and economic systems determines the distribution of impacts. In addition, there are a number of trends in environment, population, and economy that are important in considering the likely effect of future droughts. The sum total of these factors may be termed the vulnerability to drought.

Drought-induced changes in agricultural production affect people in different ways. It may be useful to conceptualize the impact of drought on food supplies by considering the sources of food and the scale of impacts (Table 1.1). The cells of the table suggest the most important factors influencing food availability at each level.

Sen (1981) has characterized vulnerability to drought according to the methods by which people are able to procure food (entitlements). In Kenya, the major food sources are agricultural production, marketed exchanges, and donations. These sources differ in their relative importance, depending on the nature of the consumer.

For most rural households, on-farm production is the most important food source, often dependent on available labor and cash income for investment in soil conservation, improved seeds, and other inputs. The extent of cash cropping affects food production, while also enabling households to purchase inputs for food production. Local markets are important sources of staple and other foods. Households regularly sell a portion of their produce, knowing they will purchase food later in the year. In the 1984/85 food crisis, government efforts to provide food through the local market channels were critical in averting famine.

Given communities or districts may be food-surplus or food-deficit areas, depending on land quality, rainfall, and the agricultural infrastructure. Trade with other districts, controlled by the government (at least for the formal markets), is essential to ensure adequate district food supplies and to support the local market prices. In the 1984/85 food crisis, maize price differentials between districts were larger than within districts, indicating the imbalance between supplies and demand and the influence of government restrictions. Famine relief at the household and community/district levels is a last resort, subject to access to political influence, including the government and nongovernmental organizations (NGOs).

The nation is usually self-sufficient in maize but not in wheat, which it regularly acquires on the international market or through concessionary programs. Price incentives and the availability of inputs are the most important short-term factors, while agricultural research and extension are critical to maintain growth in agricultural production. National storage capacity and import facilities enable storage from one year to the next, as well as enabling international trade to dispose of surplus stocks or to make up for food deficits. International politics play an important role, influencing access to concessionary and free food aid.

The world supply of grains is fixed in any given year, affecting how much food is available in the international markets. The International Monetary Fund (IMF) operates an emergency credit for countries requiring extraordinary imports. If global demand is unusually high, as it was in 1972, world prices may be inflationary and supplies not available, at least on a time scale and in amounts required to prevent famine. While international trade is an efficient component of national food security, it entails some dependency on factors often beyond the control of national policies.

GEOGRAPHY OF DROUGHT IN KENYA

Kenya is a country of great diversity, located on the equator between Lake Victoria and the Indian Ocean (Figure 1.1). The capital is Nairobi, the largest city, while Mombasa and Kisumu are important regional urban centers. The 8 provinces and 41 districts (including Nairobi) cover over 580,000 sq km.

Agriculture

Most of the country—the northern districts, southern Rift Valley, and the dry areas between the coast and the eastern highlands—is used by nomadic and seminomadic pastoralists (Figure 1.2). The prime agricultural lands, comprising about 10 percent of the land area, are in the central and western highlands. For smallholders, the dominant sector in agriculture, maize is the staple food crop, and coffee and tea are the main cash crops. About three-fourths of the agricultural holdings are less than 2 ha, while large holdings account for 2 to 3 percent of the cultivated area (FAO 1984a). Smallholders (less than 8 ha of land) grow three-fourths of the national maize crop. Large-scale production is concentrated in the western highlands and interspersed with settlement schemes in the productive areas of the Rift Valley. Commercial ranching and the raising of livestock in smallholder areas are major land uses in the margins between pastoral and intensive agricultural lands. About 5.5 percent of the land area is devoted to national parks, reserves, and forests (Central Bureau of Statistics [CBS] 1983a).

Population and Economy

The distribution of the country's population (estimated at close to 20 million in 1986) reflects the concentration of agricultural lands (Figure 1.3). Average district densities over two hundred people per sq km are found near Nairobi and in western Kenya. Individual locations in these areas often have densities of over 500 people per sq km. The national population growth rate approaches 4 percent per year, while some urban areas have growth rates exceeding 10 percent per year (Central Bureau of Statistics 1981b, Downing, Lezberg et al., 1988).

The economy has been vigorous, growing at 3 to 5 percent per year since the mid 1970s (Gross Domestic Product [GDP] at constant prices), but only barely keeping pace with population growth (CBS 1983a). Agriculture, the largest sector in the economy, comprises 33 percent of GDP and over 50 percent of exports. The manufacturing sector (13 percent of GDP) has benefited from Kenya's prominence in East Africa, as have the trade and service sectors.

Drought Vulnerability

Drought has been a recurrent phenomenon in Kenya (Table 1.2). Traditionally, two areas have been the most drought-prone. The Eastern Plateau, roughly coincident with Eastern Province, is comprised mostly of semiarid, low-lying land that extends in an arc to the east and north of Mt. Kenya. These areas were formerly known as marginal lands due to their low rainfall and border with the wetter, more productive lands of the central highlands. The pastoral areas of northern and southern Kenya have long been recognized as drought-prone. Recently, attention has been given to climatic variability in the dry areas near Lake Victoria (South Nyanza); settlement schemes in the Rift Valley, where land holdings are often too small to support a household in dry years; and in Coast Province, where too much or too little rainfall and poor soils compound the problems.

THE 1984/85 DROUGHT

Rainfall Patterns

The average annual rainfall in the country varies from under 100 mm to over 2,000 mm on Mt. Kenya. Most of the country experiences two rainy seasons, the long (or first) rains from March to May or later and the short (or second) rains from October to December (Figure 1.4). Except for the pastoral areas, most of the country is suitable for maize production (over 300 mm of rain) during the long rains, while the short rains are generally lighter, except in southern Eastern Province. About two-thirds of the national maize production is grown during the long rains (Ray 1984).

The drought began with the 1983 short rains in northern and eastern Kenya (Figure 1.5). Only the central and western highlands received enough rain to produce maize. The following season, the 1984 long rains almost completely failed, except in a narrow strip along the coast and in the western highlands. The drought, however, was short-lived due to the abundant and widespread 1984 short rains. Rainfall in 1985 was also above normal.

Food Production

The poor rains in the northern and eastern areas during 1983 did not have a significant impact on aggregate production since these areas are semiarid and contribute little to national production. During 1984, all major food crops recorded large reductions in aggregate production. In percentage terms, the most dramatic fall was for beans, which is an important source of protein in rural areas and for low-income urban consumers. Aggregate bean production during the 1984/85 agricultural year was one-fourth of the average for the previous three years (Table 1.3). Potato production was half its normal level, and wheat, consumed primarily by urban consumers and more wealthy rural dwellers, had its production down by 39 percent. The production of maize, the primary staple grown by 90 percent of smallholders, was reduced by 34 percent from the average for the previous three years (CBS 1986).

Provincial production estimates, made in August 1984 by the Food and Agriculture Organization (FAO 1984a), show that the fall in production was most severe in Central and Eastern Provinces, where the estimated production for 1984/85 was 85 percent and 75 percent, respectively, below the average for the previous six years. For national supplies, the 11 percent reduction in production in the Rift Valley was more serious, as this province normally accounts for 41 percent of national production.

Livestock

With the majority of the livestock being kept in the arid and semiarid zones, the onset of the drought in the northern and eastern areas in 1983 meant that many pastoralists were affected during 1983, as well as in 1984. National data on the effects of the drought on livestock are not available. A number of surveys, however, were carried out in different parts of the country, all of which indicate that the drought had a severe effect on livestock (see also Chapter 5).

One survey, carried out in July 1984 by the UNESCO Integrated Project in Arid Lands, included forty-five communities in Garissa, Isiolo, Mandera, Marsabit, Samburu, and Wajir districts. This study concluded that up to 80 percent of the cattle, sheep, and goats had died in almost all of the surveyed communities (Field and Njiru 1985). Another survey, conducted in September 1984 by the Ministry of Finance and Planning's Baringo Pilot Semi-Arid Area Project, involved a 10 percent sample of stock owners in a large area of Baringo District. Between January and September 1984, overall losses (deaths and sales) for cattle, sheep, and goats were approximately 50 percent.

The most detailed survey was carried out in February and May 1985 by the National Range Research Station at Kiboko and studied a sample of 67 ranchers in Kajiado District and 106 farmers in the southern part of Machakos District (Mukhebi et al., 1985). In Kajiado, the off-take of cattle amounted to 76 percent of the pre-drought herd, with mortality accounting for 92 percent and sales for 8 percent of the losses. In southern Machakos, the total off-take was 61 percent, with 75 percent attributed to mortality and 25 percent to sales.

To cope with the dramatic increase in the numbers being offered for sale, the Kenya Meat Commission (KMC) had increased the rate of slaughtering at its two plants from 7,000 head of cattle per month to 23,000 head by August 1984. Average carcass weight fell from 130 kg to 80 kg (FAO 1984a). Cattle sales to the KMC were 222,000 in 1984, compared to 84,000 the year before (Table 1.4).

Coffee and Tea

The coffee harvest in Central Province, which in normal years accounts for two-thirds of the national production, begins in December. Thus, the effect of the drought on aggregate production was not recorded until 1985. The 1984 harvest, from growth in 1983, was actually the highest ever recorded (118,500 mt). Due to the drought, production fell in 1985 by 18.5 percent, down to 96,600 mt (Table 1.4).

Despite the fall in production, exports increased to a record level in 1985 (Table 1.5). This was attributable to the record harvest in 1984 and the International Coffee Organization (ICO) quota, which had led to a buildup of stocks during previous years (World Bank 1986a). Prices in 1983 were 22.5 percent higher than the previous year, 1984 prices were up 18.5 percent, and 1985 prices were 5 percent higher. The combination of increased prices, large stocks, and the suspension of the ICO quota resulted in substantial increases in export earnings before, during, and after the drought. Since coffee is Kenya's most important export commodity, accounting for 25 percent of all export earnings in 1983, this dramatic increase in the value of coffee exports was a significant factor in enabling commercial grain imports by the government in response to the drought.

Tea production in 1984 was 2.6 percent below that of 1983, yet it was still well above production during 1981 and 1982 (Table 1.4). Due primarily to the temporary withdrawal of Indian exports from the world market during 1984, the drought in Kenya coincided with a temporary boom in the world price of tea. Kenya benefited from a 68 percent increase in the prices received for its tea exports during 1984, which increased the value of tea exports by 53.5 percent despite the fall in production (Table 1.5). With tea exports accounting for 14 percent of all export earnings in 1983, the dramatic rise in earnings further contributed to increased foreign exchange reserves.

The combination of above-normal 1984 short rains and 1985 long rains and the response by growers to the 1984 tea boom resulted in a record production level, 26.5 percent higher than the previous year. India's return to the world market resulted in a substantial fall in prices during 1985, but the increased production ensured that the value of tea exports remained above the record 1984 level (Table 1.5).

Impact on the Economy

A comprehensive, quantified assessment of the impact of the 1984/85 drought on the Kenyan economy is not available. A rough measure of the drought's effect is that Gross Domestic Product (GDP) in 1984 grew by only 0.9 percent, compared to an average of 3.8 percent for the previous three years, although this cannot be attributed entirely to the drought (CBS 1986). Agricultural production, which normally accounts for one-third of the GDP, fell by 3.7 percent in 1984. Had tea and coffee exports not performed so strongly, the GDP would have declined further.

During 1984, foreign exchange reserves increased, exceeding the target reserve (set at a value equivalent to four months of imports) for the first time in several years (Figure 1.6). This occurred despite the expenditure on commercial food imports during 1984/85 (393,000 mt of maize imported from Thailand cost about $65 million). Much of the increase can be attributed to the increased value of tea and coffee exports during 1984. Had foreign exchange reserves not been so healthy, it is quite possible that the government might not have been able to purchase substantial food imports (see Chapter 2).

COPING WITH DROUGHT: REVIEW OF THEMES

The chapters in this book have been divided into five parts. Each part is introduced with a concise summary of the chapters, intended to highlight the principal lessons learned. Part 1 provides an overview of the drought, focusing on the national level. The rest of the volume amplifies the overview. Drought forecasting and monitoring are discussed in Part 2, followed, in Part 3, by case studies of drought vulnerability, impacts, and coping strategies in selected locales. Part 4 reviews institutional experiences in responding to the drought, while Part 5 summarizes drought and food policy issues in Kenya and Africa. The references for all the chapters are collected in one section, and the index facilitates access to specific subjects.

The experiences in Kenya in coping with drought enlighten several issues of hazard management and food policy. These are discussed in various chapters, and introduced below.

Part 1: Overview of the 1984/85 Drought

Rainfall between March and May 1984 was well below normal, resulting in widespread drought that affected agriculture and livestock. National food production declined, unprecedented sales were recorded by the National Cereals and Produce Board (NCPB), and massive food imports were required (Figure 1.7). Widespread famine was averted primarily by early government response and commercial imports, supplemented later with food aid.

Five major issues are introduced in Part 1: characterization of *vulnerability* to drought; effective *national response* to drought and government *preparedness*; the role of *early warning systems*; the use of *food aid* and targeted interventions; and *collaboration* between the government, nongovernmental organizations, and the commercial sector in preventing famine.

Vulnerability to drought, or hunger as the major consequence of drought in Kenya, is characterized above by food entitlements (subsistence production, market exchanges, and donations) and the scale of the consumer. These concepts of vulnerability are further developed in Part 3 with an analysis of long-term issues and coping strategies of pastoralists and smallholder agriculturalists.

The successful *national response* to the drought was largely due to three factors: the drought was readily apparent, with the dramatic failure of the rainy season centering on Nairobi; economic policies promoting the export sector resulted in large reserves of foreign exchange that enabled prompt imports of food; and a well-developed infrastructure and a skilled and extensive administrative bureaucracy facilitated the reporting of food shortages and delivery of commercial and relief food. Part 5 discusses the long-term issues concerning economic development.

The lack of a systematic *preparedness* plan, however, resulted in delays in food-relief programs, shortcomings in making the best use of nongovernmental organizations, lack of preparedness for recovering from the drought (most notably a shortage of seed), and costly excess stocks of yellow maize after the food crisis had ended. Part 4 provides case studies of several institutions, including a detailed proposal for district preparedness.

The established *early warning* and *food monitoring* systems were not well utilized. Improvements are required to cope with moderate or isolated droughts and to facilitate targeting food interventions for groups vulnerable to either chronic hunger or a severe drought. Chapter 2 and Part 2 provide some insight into who should provide early warning information, the demand for information on food security, and the level of responses triggered by different warnings.

The *collaboration* between government programs, nongovernmental activities, and the utilization of commercial markets resulted in a mix of strategies that worked well on the whole. The role of the NGOs and initial problems of cooperation with the government are discussed in Chapter 2 and elaborated in Part 4. The NGOs were able to mobilize *food aid* early in the drought and with greater targeting when the U.S. shipments arrived. Three projects stand out as being innovative: the grain-for-livestock and restocking projects supported access to food by the pastoralists and long-term drought-coping strategies; the U.S. grant to CARE for transport costs assisted many NGOs in providing food aid in remote areas; and the World Food Programme, through credit arrangements with the National Cereals and Produce Board, provided food to NGOs early in the drought at a critical stage for many households. Indirect intervention, however, was the major relief strategy, through food imports and their stabilizing effect on food prices.

Part 2: Drought Forecasting and Monitoring

Part 2 reviews efforts in drought forecasting and monitoring in Kenya and provides detailed data on the impact of the 1984 drought. The first two chapters cover meteorological aspects of drought in general and the failure of the 1984 long rains in particular. The chapters focus on various methods of monitoring agricultural and livestock production, including an example from Tanzania.

Five separate groups (Department of Meteorology, Kenya Rangeland Ecological Monitoring Unit [KREMU], Central Bureau of Statistics, Ministry of Agriculture, and the National Cereals and Produce Board) monitor aspects of food security. The urgent need is for increased cooperation, including field comparisons and validation of the different methods, and a strategy for monitoring household food security and national food flows, both as ongoing efforts and in preparedness for drought emergencies. Each system requires further testing and development to establish its reliability.

The initial response to the drought, in June, was based on weather reports, informal observations, and visual indicators of crop failure that were provided by the Ministry of Agriculture. The CBS, KREMU and NCPB data were not available until September or later, after commercial food shipments had begun to arrive. The monitoring system did not produce an early assessment of the abundant short rains, which might have alerted the government to the excess stocks of yellow maize. It appears that no one institution has clear responsibility for monitoring food security on a routine basis; there is not a consistent demand for information on household food security.

Part 3: Drought Vulnerability, Impacts, and Coping Strategies

The background resource, social, and economic conditions that affect regional or household vulnerability to the impact of drought are illustrated in the seven chapters of Part 3, with four examples from the pastoral areas and three chapters on smallholder agriculturalists.

A key component of pastoralist coping strategies is the ability to move herds to make the best possible use of vegetation reserves (fallback zones), water resources, and sporadic rainfall. Drought impacts in these areas are influenced by access to food markets; ability to purchase food with income from livestock sales, wage labor, or remittances; and the ability to recover from the drought by restocking.

Despite substantial differences in resources, almost all the households surveyed in four communities noted hunger as the major impact of the drought. The nutritional data from Embu documents the dramatic decline in weight for newborn infants, toddlers, and adults.

The range of practicable coping mechanisms has narrowed, shifting from agricultural to monetary activities. Participation in the monetary economy has reduced vulnerability to drought for smallholders, at least in the short term. The 1984 drought was known as *ni kwa ngweta*, or "I could die with cash in my pocket." Households have diversified their income sources to include off-farm wage employment in response to the need for cash to pay school fees, taxes, and medical expenses, and to purchase supplementary foods and consumer items. Local markets usually perform well in purchasing and selling food, alleviating the need to store food from one season to the next or as a drought reserve.

Since the government controls interdistrict grain trade, rural household reliance on local food markets implies a shift in the burden of coping with drought toward the national government. The government channeled about 80 percent of the food imports through commercial markets in 1984 and 1985. Without such an effort, price inflation would have resulted in widespread famine.

Part 4: Institutional Experiences in Drought Management

Part 4 reviews institutional experiences in dealing with the drought. These seven chapters are case studies of individual agencies, including one international program, two central government ministries, a district drought-contingency plan, and the experiences of three NGOs.

The World Food Programme was instrumental during the critical period in mid-1984 in providing NGOs with food from the NCPB. The maize, credited against future shipments of wheat, enabled many NGOs to begin timely emergency relief programs. The provision of transport funds, provided by the U.S. Office of Foreign Disaster Assistance and coordinated by CARE, enabled NGOs to continue and expand emergency relief activities. The grain-for-livestock exchange demonstrated the potential to support the efforts of pastoralists to procure food from their traditional source of wealth. A subsequent restocking project assisted in drought recovery.

There were shortcomings in the institutional responses. The health monitoring system was inadequate, and it has subsequently been expanded and improved to include nutritional assessments. Agreement was never reached on appropriate rations. Many programs started late due to inadequate preparedness for drought responses. While many NGOs distributed seed and other inputs following the drought, the amounts were often inadequate and distribution delayed. To date, it appears that the food crisis was treated as an isolated episode—drought emergency responses and recovery and rehabilitation projects have not been included in regular programs.

Part 5: Drought and Food Policy

Part 5 includes two chapters that extend the analysis of drought responses to issues of food policy in Kenya, placing Kenya's experience in the context of African food policy and economic development. Urgent lessons for improving food production and food security include expanded storage; food security planning in advance of food crises; coordinated early warning systems; a contingency plan for food imports, distribution, and logistics; planning recovery measures; and the reduction of long-term vulnerability. In many respects, the Kenyan experience is a positive anomaly, an example of the direction in which effective drought-coping strategies might be pursued. The importance of the interaction of food production and development, food aid, the financial implications of droughts and food surpluses, and the Asian experience in preventing famine are assessed. Drought should be seen as a warning of the desperate African food crisis to come if research and policy fail to address the mix of economic, food security, and population problems in Africa.

Figure 1.1 Administrative boundaries.

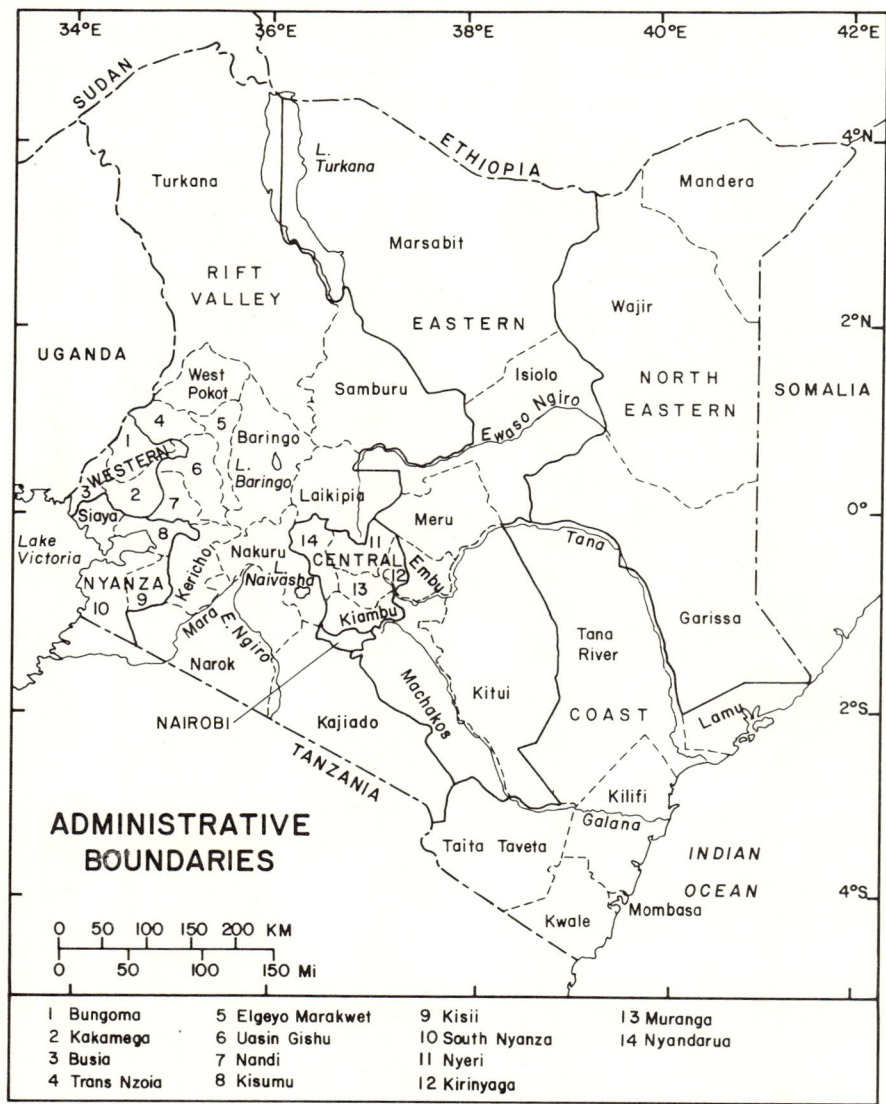

OVERVIEW OF THE 1984/85 DROUGHT • 15

Figure 1.2 Agricultural livelihood systems. Most of Kenya is suitable for pastoralism and ranching. The smallholder agricultural lands are located in the central and western highlands and along the coast. Source: Berry et al. (1980).

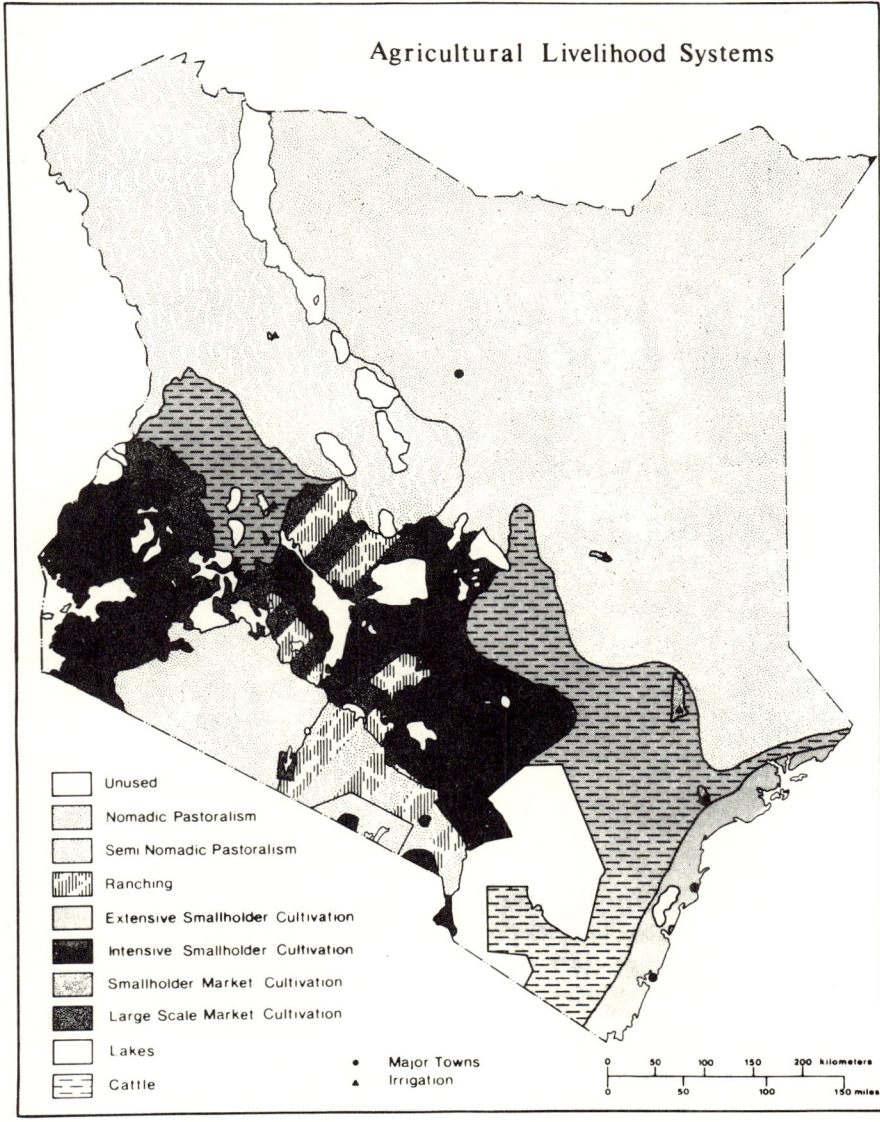

Figure 1.3 Distribution of population. Based on the 1979 census, population densities are highest in central and western Kenya, often over 400 people per sq km. Source: Central Bureau of Statistics (n.d.).

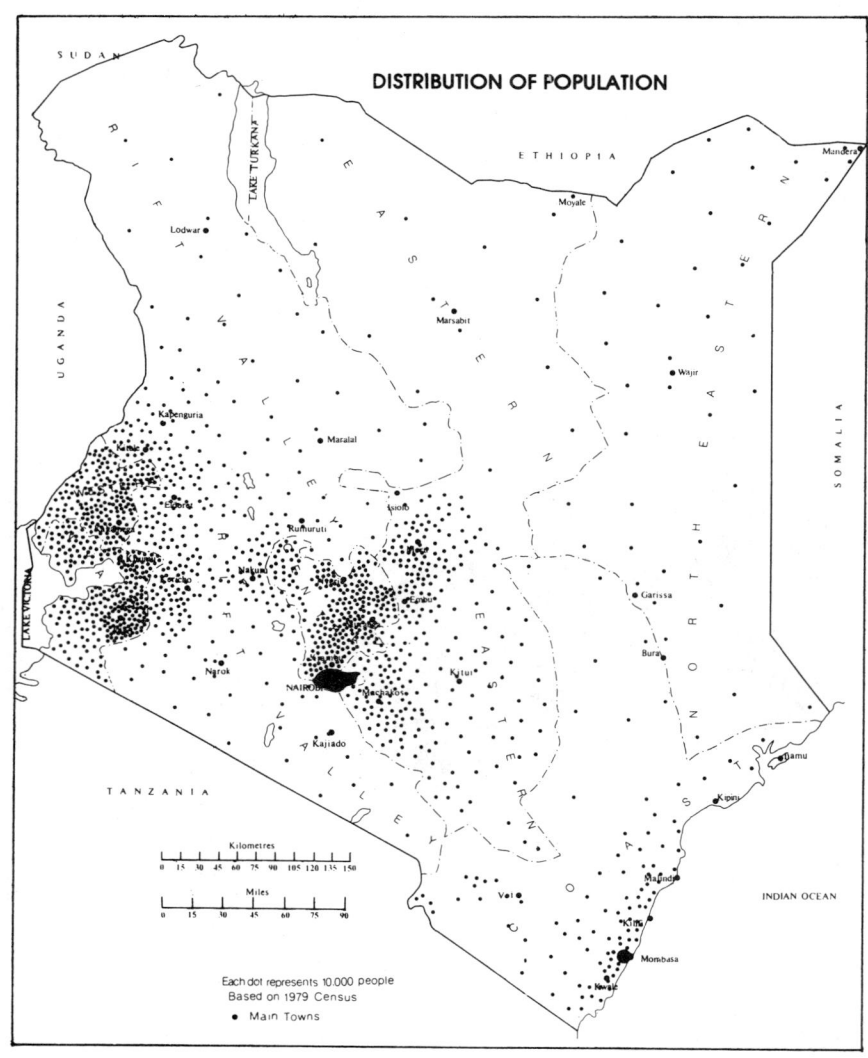

OVERVIEW OF THE 1984/85 DROUGHT • 17

Figure 1.4 Normal rainfall in the short and long rains. The long rains are generally wetter and more reliable, except in parts of Eastern Province. Source: Prepared by the Kenya Meteorological Department.

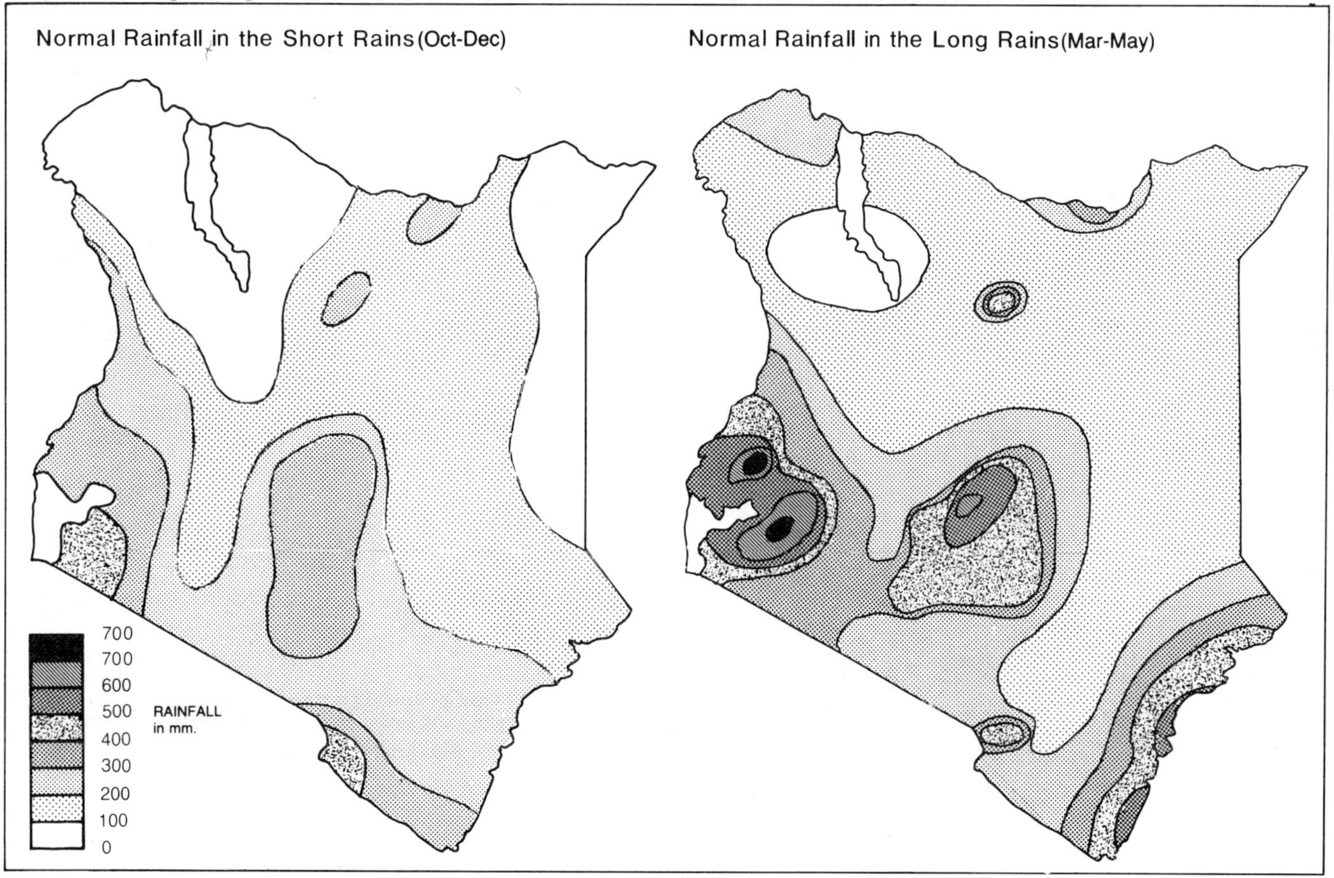

18 • COPING WITH DROUGHT IN KENYA

Figure 1.5 Seasonal rainfall in 1983-1984. The meteorological drought began in northern and eastern Kenya in the short rains of 1983 and ended with the above-average 1984 short rains. Source: Prepared by the Kenya Meteorological Department.

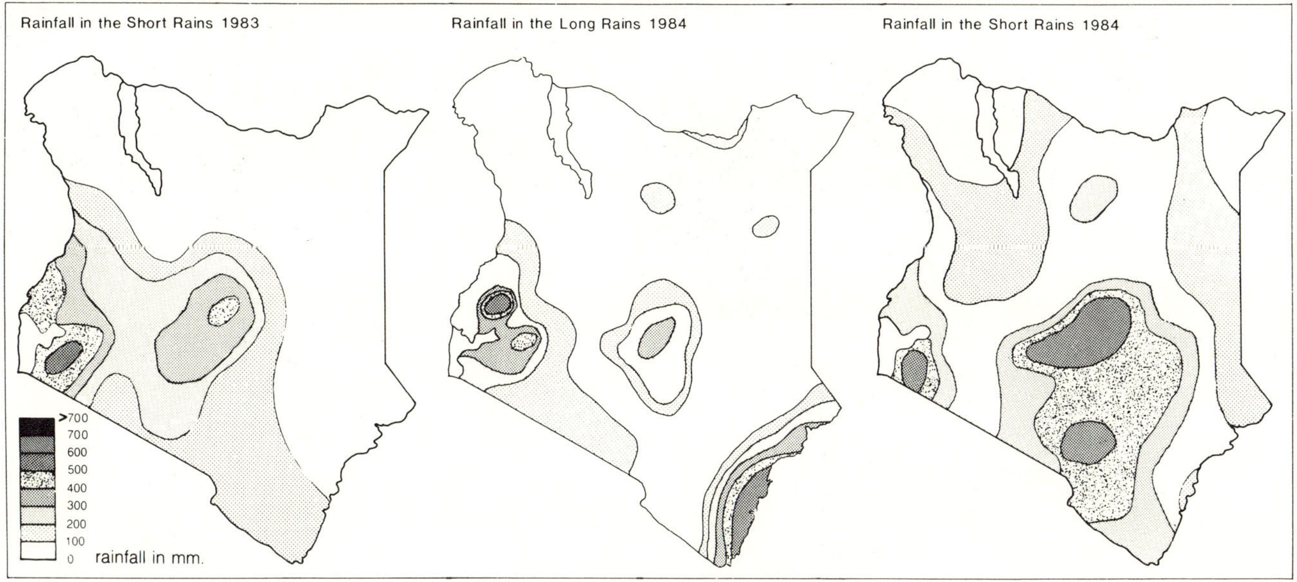

Figure 1.6 Foreign exchange reserves. The dashed line represents Central Bank holdings in foreign reserves in million Ksh. The solid line is the statutory guide of the cost of four months of imports (the average of the previous three years). Source: Central Bank of Kenya, Customs and Excise Department.

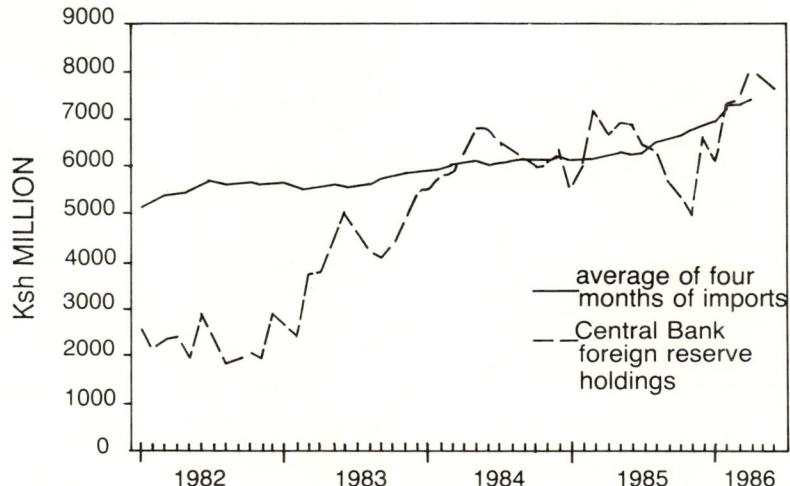

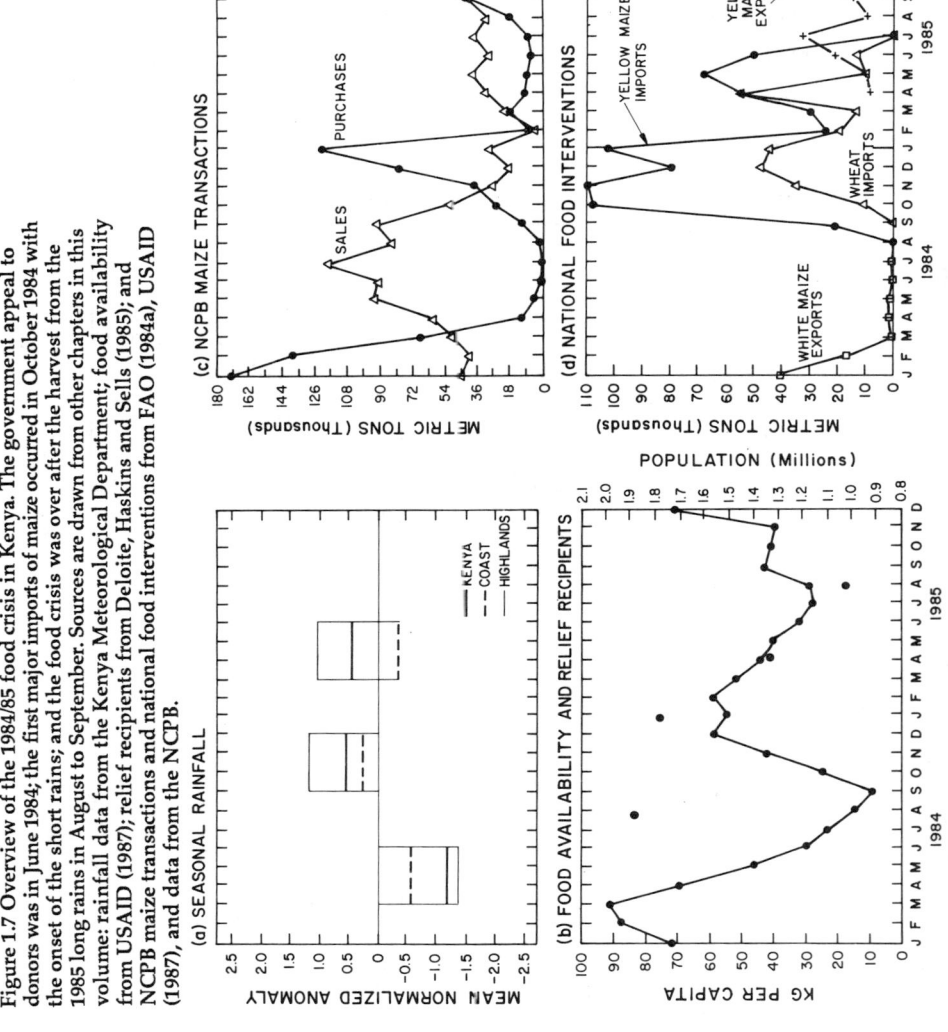

Figure 1.7 Overview of the 1984/85 food crisis in Kenya. The government appeal to donors was in June 1984; the first major imports of maize occurred in October 1984 with the onset of the short rains; and the food crisis was over after the harvest from the 1985 long rains in August to September. Sources are drawn from other chapters in this volume: rainfall data from the Kenya Meteorological Department; food availability from USAID (1987); relief recipients from Deloite, Haskins and Sells (1985); and NCPB maize transactions and national food interventions from FAO (1984a), USAID (1987), and data from the NCPB.

Table 1.1 Scales of Drought Hazard

	Scale of Food Procurement			
Food Source	Individual/ Household	Community/ District	National	International
Agricultural Production	On-farm Cash/food crops Soil cons. Labor Inputs Prices Credit Irrigation	Local Rainfall Agricultural infra- structure	National Prices Inputs Agricultural research & extension	World National policies
Marketed Exchanges	Local mrkt Price changes Supplies within district Supplies from NCPB Sources of cash	District mrkt Transport Inter- district trade Surplus or deficit area	National Credit Storage capacity Import facilities	International mrkt IMF facility Demand from other countries
Donations	Famine relief Access to: political leaders & NGOS	Famine relief Access to: political leaders & NGOS	Concessionary Food supplies Standing with major donors	

Table 1.2 Droughts in Kenya

Years	Region	Causes and Impacts
1883	coast	Drought: worst famine in 30 years, followed by smallpox.
1889–1990	coast	One year of drought: famine, along with rinderpest.
1894–1895	coast	Drought, locusts, intermittent warfare.
1896–1900	Kikuyu and Kamba lands, coast, much of East Africa	Failure of 3 consecutive rains; rinderpest, locusts; thousands died (est. 25 to 75% of population in some places); smallpox, war, famine, railway construction added to food shortages.
1907–1911	Lake Victoria area, Machakos, Kitui, coast	Minor food scarcities in various locales.
1913–1919	Ethiopia, Kamba lands, coast	Coincided with Sahelian drought. Impacts along coast exacerbated by warfare, restrictions on planting and livestock, influenza and locusts.
1921	coast	Record dry year.
1925	Kerio Valley, coast	Local food shortages.
1933–1934	coast, Kikuyu lands	Drought, crop losses, locusts; large livestock losses (50%) in Baringo District, soil erosion & overstocking recognized as problems.
1936	?	Minor drought and locusts.
1942–1944	Kenya, Uganda	Drought, locusts, smallpox & military demands caused food shortages; deaths under 200 people.
1947–1950	Kikuyu lands, coast	Rains failed; good harvests in Nyanza and Rift Valley provinces. One of most severe famines at coast.
1952–1955	Kitui & other districts	Drought reduced exports by 20 to 25%.
1960–1961	Widespread: Maasai lands, Machakos, Kitui, Rift Valley, northern districts	Drought followed by floods caused famine. U.S. aid sent. Cattle mortality among Maasai 70 to 80%. Widespread crop failure. Ten million Kenya pounds spent on food relief in 1961.
1974–1976	Kajiado, Kitui, lower Meru, Machakos, Tana River, Turkana	Government projects (food storage, drought-resistant crops, livestock improvement schemes) averted worse impacts. Maasai cattle losses as high as 80%.
1981	Eastern Province	Known as "famine with cash in my pocket." Large imports required, partly due to depletion of maize reserves by early exports.
1983	coastal hinterland, Kitui, Machakos, Meru, Kakamega, Nyanza	Poor long and short rains; high prices in local markets, some water shortages; cattle and human migration.
1984	Central, Rift Valley, Eastern and Northeastern provinces	Severe drought in long rains over all Kenya except Western and Coast provinces. Large food imports averted famine. Short rains normal.

Sources: Ambler (1988), Berry et al. (1980), Downing, Akong'a, et al. (1988), Downing (1982), Herlehy (1984), Odingo (1986), Ojany and Ogendo (1973), Wisner (1977).

Table 1.3 Production of Food Crops

	1981/82	1982/83	1983/84	1984/85	1985/86
Maize	1,967	2,349	2,178	1,422	2,430
Wheat	214	248	251	144	194
Beans	199	288	270	68	177
Potatoes	382	549	459	233	531

Sources: CBS (1986, 1988).
Note: Units are 1,000 mt.

Table 1.4 Sales to Marketing Boards

	1981	1982	1983	1984	1985
Coffee	90.7	88.4	95.3	118.5	96.6
Tea	90.9	95.6	119.3	116.2	147.1
Maize	472.9	571.3	636.0	560.2	582.9
Wheat	203.4	234.7	242.3	135.4	582.9
Milk	222.9	260.3	274.2	189.9	231.4
Cattle	61.0	71.0	84.0	222.0	116.0

Sources: CBS (1986, 1988).
Notes: Units are 1,000 mt, except for milk (million liters) and cattle (thousand head); milk is production recorded by the Kenya Cooperative Creameries; and cattle are intake of cattle and calves by the Kenya Meat Commission.

Table 1.5 Quantity, Prices, and Values of Tea and Coffee Exports

	1982	1983	1984	1985
Quantity, mt				
Coffee	100,995	90,457	96,914	104,662
Tea	80,413	99,938	91,198	126,086
Export Prices, Ksh/kg				
Coffee	28.64	35.40	42.03	44.07
Tea	19.30	24.70	41.55	30.36
Value of Exports, Kenya pounds				
Coffee	144,564	160,086	203,662	230,600
Tea	77,593	123,420	189,477	191,409

Sources: CBS (1984, 1985, 1986).

· 2 ·
Overview of the 1984/85 National Drought Relief Program

JOHN BORTON

CHRONOLOGY OF EVENTS AND GOVERNMENT RESPONSES

An overview of the national response to the drought is provided in this chapter. Due to the sensitive nature of the subject, access to government officials and internal documentation was limited. In addition, many key personnel had been transferred by 1987, and it was not possible to interview those individuals. As a result, the study provides a perspective of the crisis and response, focusing on the central government, donors, and major issues concerning the NGO community. It must be regarded as providing a provisional assessment of the relief program. Ideally, this chapter should be complimented with a thorough review by the government and studies of district and local responses.

The impact of the 1984 drought on agriculture and the economy has been described in the previous chapter (see Figure 1.7). The following section reviews the national responses, including early warning, preparing for food relief, implementing the relief program, and drought recovery. The responses by donors and NGOs are summarized, with further detail provided in subsequent chapters for several of the projects. The final section presents conclusions and lessons for Africa and Kenya.

The national response to the drought emergency can be divided into four phases: early warning, preparing for food relief, implementing the relief program, and drought recovery (see the chronology presented in Appendix 2.1, and Appendices 2.2 and 2.3 for a detailed assessment of the national food balance for maize and wheat). As noted in the previous chapter, the drought actually began in some parts of Kenya in 1983. The major government response, however, began in May 1984. An appeal for donor assistance was launched in June 1984, along with orders for commercial maize imports. The major food-relief efforts lasted from October 1984 to early 1985, when drought-recovery programs began in earnest, following the 1984 short rains and in preparation for the 1985 long rains.

EARLY WARNING PHASE: 1983 TO JUNE 1984

There was little government response to the deteriorating situation in the northern and eastern areas of Kenya prior to early 1984, when the drought spread. There was a slight increase in the numbers of destitute who regularly receive food through the Office of the President (OP). Presumably, information on the poor rains in these areas was available to the government, and district officials had reported on the situation by the end of 1983. A number of factors may explain why the government did not appreciate the severity of the situation in the northern and eastern areas until well into 1984:

1. Maize stocks held by the National Cereals and Produce Board (NCPB) had been at record levels throughout 1983 (Figure 2.1). At the national level, the country had a surplus of maize and was pursuing a vigorous export policy (41,000 mt of maize were exported in January 1984).
2. Rainfall in the arid and semiarid areas of Kenya is subject to considerable seasonal variation, and stress induced by below-normal rains is fairly common (Ojany and Ogendo 1973). Pastoral communities have evolved a range of response strategies that traditionally have enabled them to cope with short-duration droughts without external intervention (Hogg 1985).
3. Pastoral communities in northern Kenya are becoming more integrated into the national economy, but they have relatively less economic and political power than other groups (Hogg 1987). The history of banditry and conflict since the 1960s has tended to adversely affect the access these areas have to national development resources.

The delayed 1984 long rains and their failure in April were abundantly clear over most of the country, and the fact that Nairobi was located in the affected area was significant. The government was aware of the problem by the end of April.

The government began a concerted response to the drought at the end of April, when the president requested papers analyzing the implications of the poor rains from the Ministry of Agriculture, Ministry of Finance and Planning, and the Office of the President (Borton and Stephenson 1984). Thus, one month before the CBS Area Planted Survey commenced and two months before it reported a reduction in the area planted in 1984 and confirmed the slightly lower harvest in 1983 (see Chapter 6), the government was aware of the drought and had called for more information. The situation of a government pre-empting its formal early warning system in this way is unusual. The early warning system in operation in 1984 was therefore not put to the test. In comparison to a less clear-cut situation, where initial recognition of a problem might depend upon the results of the CBS surveys, the government had at least an additional two months of lead time to prepare to implement a relief program.

Confirmation of the seriousness of the situation was given during May by a dramatic 36 percent increase in the monthly sales of maize by the NCPB, to the unprecedented level of 93,000 mt (see Figure 2.2). Such an increase so far in advance of an actual harvest failure was probably the result of hoarding by consumers, industries, and/or traders in the expectation of future supply difficulties.

Appeal to Donors. On 13 June, the president of Kenya inaugurated the National Famine Relief Fund as a vehicle for mobilizing and channeling private donations to the affected communities. The fund was controlled by the Office of the President and operated as a trust fund, making grants to specific projects and community groups. A total of Ksh 40 million was donated by 1987.

On 19 June, the government made a formal appeal for assistance to all donor agencies represented in the country. The appeal estimated food import requirements of over 2.0 million mt (Table 2.1). The requirements for July to December 1985 were included as a precautionary measure in case the 1984 short rains and the 1985 long rains were poor. The estimates were based on an aggregate food balance-sheet approach, using preliminary forecasts of the shortfall in production. The Ministry of Finance and Planning considered an alternative approach based on estimates of the numbers of people who would experience a food deficit and their average individual nutritional requirement, though this approach was dropped in favor of the simpler method (Cohen and Lewis 1987).

By way of comparison, the Food and Agriculture Organization (FAO) Multidonor Mission, which assessed the situation in August 1984, estimated the total *cereal* import requirement for June 1984 to July 1985 at approximately one million mt. No estimate was made for possible requirements in the period between July to December 1985. The reasons for the lower estimate by the FAO mission are as follows:

1. A lower closing stock figure was used in the mission's calculations (maize: 100,000 mt; wheat: 30,000 mt) than was used by the government (maize: 240,000 mt; wheat: 117,000 mt).
2. The mission apparently had access to more recent and less pessimistic crop forecasts than those available in June.

It is not clear from the FAO report whether account was taken of the structural deficit implicit within the government calculations of the import requirements for wheat.

These figures are considerably higher than the amounts that were actually imported between September 1984 and June 1985 (Table 2.2). Thus, 858,000 mt of cereals were imported between September 1984 and June 1985, and this was in excess of demand by as much as 200,000 mt, as discussed below.

Gearing-up Phase: July to September 1984

The Government Relief Strategy. The government had agreed upon the principal elements of its strategy for coping with the crisis by the time the appeal was made to the donors on 19 June. Priority was to be given to maintaining essential food supplies within the existing marketing system. It was assumed that the majority of the population, especially those outside the eastern and northern areas experiencing a prolonged drought, had sufficient reserves of cash and assets to continue to purchase food as long as prices were kept at reasonable levels. The crucial task was to ensure that the system was kept sufficiently well supplied to ensure that shortages did not develop, resulting in queues, dramatic price increases, and possible social unrest.

Food relief was to be provided in the affected areas, but the government was anxious to limit the scale of free handouts. Therefore, second priority was given to job-creation schemes that would create temporary employment opportunities on public works, such as dam construction, soil conservation projects, and roadworks. These would be implemented through the Rural Development Fund of the Ministry of Finance and Planning, which disburses funds to districts to carry out labor-intensive infrastructure projects.

Third priority was to be given to free food distributions to portions of the community unable to work or draw on past savings (Office of the President 1984). Those eligible for the free food distributions were to be selected locally by chiefs and village-level famine relief committees and lists submitted through the district commissioner to the Office of the President. The free food distribution component of the program (often referred to as "straight famine relief" in government documents) was to be overseen by the Office of the President, while responsibility for implementation rested with the district commissioner.

Of the 858,000 mt of cereals imported between September 1984 and June 1985, evidently approximately 62 percent (around 530,000 mt) was distributed through existing marketing channels and 15 percent (125,000 mt) through the free distribution systems implemented by the Office of the President and NGOs. The remainder, approximately 23 percent, was either exported, used as livestock feed, destroyed because of quality problems, or used in food for work projects implemented after the relief program had formally ended.

One of the main problems experienced with the strategy concerned government capacity to implement large-scale public works programs at short notice. By the end of September, when the first projects had been approved and funds disbursed, the scale of the job-creation component was considerably smaller than had been originally intended. The U.S. Agency for International Development (USAID) consultant who had reviewed the situation in August had been given the impression that income generation was the hub of the government famine-relief strategy (Ray 1984). Guidelines for district officials prepared by the Office of the President optimistically spoke of up to 250,000 newly created job opportunities (Office of the President 1984). The reality, however, was less impressive. Limits set by the Ministry of Finance and Planning on the number of projects in each district at one time implied a national total of around 25,000 jobs. Although the success of the rural works program has not been evaluated, problems of monitoring and subsequent controversies over the nature of the program (cash or self-help) surfaced. As it turned out, not all the famine-relief distributions were free. By early 1985, when the real crisis period was over, local officials reportedly put a significant number of recipients to work on locally designed food-for-work projects.

Other features of the relief program should be mentioned. A slogan emphasized by the government in its initial discussions with donors and NGOs was "Planning, not Panic" (Ray 1984). The situation was to be treated as a serious problem, but not as a crisis; wherever possible, existing administrative structures and systems were to be used. Furthermore, the program was to be managed by Kenyans, rather than expatriate crisis-management advisors (Cohen and Lewis 1987). In the early part of the crisis, the press reported very little of the drought impacts or details of the government response, except for the calls for contributions to the Relief Fund. In 1985, the government sponsored a tour of the relief projects. Thus, a vehicle of communication was not used, although, by the same token, the press was not essential in motivating government response, and the potential for increased provocation and social unrest was lessened.

Organizational Structure. By the time the appeal was made to donors, the government had begun establishing an organizational structure for managing the response to the drought. A senior-level interministerial committee provided overall coordination and advised the cabinet on key policy issues. The Steering Committee, as it was called, was chaired by the influential chief secretary to the cabinet, and membership was composed of permanent secretaries of the Ministry of Finance and Planning, Office of the President (in charge of the provincial and district administration), Ministry of Agriculture, and other key ministries.

Beneath the Steering Committee, the Task Force on Food Supply and Distribution was established and was to report directly to the Steering Committee. The chairman and secretary were drawn from the Office of the President, with membership from the Ministry of Finance and Planning, NCPB, Ministry of Transport, Kenya Railways, Kenya Ports Authority, and other relevant institutions. A subcommittee of the Task Force addressed more directly the logistics issues associated with the port of Mombasa and road and rail transport inland.

Responsibility for coordinating the NGOs assisting in the relief program was assigned to the Kenya National Council of Social Services (KNCSS), a small unit separate from, but under the auspices of, the Ministry of Culture and Social Services. It was established some years before the drought to act as a coordinating forum for the large number of NGOs active in Kenya and to some extent to monitor and regulate their activities.

Those districts that did not already have District Relief Committees (also known as District Food Security Committees) were instructed to form them. These committees were chaired by the district commissioner and included senior district representatives of the relevant ministries. NGOs were instructed to form their own district-level coordinating committees and to nominate a representative to attend the meetings of the district relief committees.

The structure involved the creation of two new bodies at a time when many important decisions had to be made quickly. It would be surprising if members of the Steering Committee and the Task Force had not taken some time to work out the precise nature and boundaries of their new roles. Furthermore, the relationship of the two new bodies to the existing committees responsible for import decisions (such as the Cereals and Sugar Finance Committee) and other government matters appears to have been ambiguous. Whether import decisions could be taken by the Steering Committee or had to be referred to the Cereals and Sugar Finance Committee is not known.

The USAID consultant who carried out an assessment of the situation in August 1984 suggested that the organizational structure contained too many layers, and delays in making decisions would therefore inevitably result (Ray 1984). Nevertheless, the overall success of the program would suggest that the structure worked reasonably well. In practice, the chief secretary played a crucial role. As secretary to the cabinet, chairman of the Steering Committee and readily accessible to the Task Force by virtue of his location within the Office of the President, he was well placed to ensure that important decisions were dealt with as quickly as possible.

The Planning Department of the Ministry of Finance and Planning played a crucial role during the gearing-up phase by preparing estimates of import requirements; projecting when NCPB stocks would be exhausted; identifying potential logistics bottlenecks; planning and coordinating the arrival of imports; and briefing donors and NGOs about government plans, among other functions. Cohen and Lewis (1987) report a highly productive working relationship emerged between the Planning Department and the Office of the President. The capacity of the Planning Department to manage large amounts of information and provide timely analyses was aided by the use of microcomputers and long-term technical assistance projects that trained Kenyan planners and provided qualified expatriates.

Food Stocks and Imports. Crucial to the success of the government strategy was the ability to ensure sufficient food in the country to maintain supplies within the marketing system and for the operation of the Office of the President distribution system. At the beginning of May, maize stocks held by the NCPB were just over 540,000 mt, well above the level of 360,000 mt set as a target for a food security reserve by the National Food Policy paper (Government of Kenya 1981). Working on the assumption of a monthly drawdown of 90,000 mt, government planners estimated that the stocks would last until at least the end of September. The estimate of 90,000 mt appeared conservative, since monthly sales by the NCPB had never gone above 55,000 mt during the 1979/80 food crisis.

In fact, maize sales from May to September exceeded 90,000 mt; in July, they were above 110,000 mt (Figure 2.2). This rapid drawdown in stocks introduced the distinct possibility that stocks would run out before any food aid arrived. Furthermore, the sheer scale of the import requirements made it unlikely that the deficit would be covered by food aid alone. Thus, by the time of the appeal to donors in June, the government was preparing to tender for substantial imports. It is understood that the first tender for maize and wheat was made on 8 July, with additional tenders being made during August and September. It is not known whether or not the government deliberately waited until after the appeal to gauge the level of the food aid that might be expected.

Yellow maize from Thailand proved to be the cheapest and most readily available maize, and the Kenyan government purchased 386,000 mt from Thailand at a cost of $159 to $162 per mt (cost, freight, and insurance included), for a total cost of approximately $62 million. In addition, it purchased some 8,000 mt of maize for animal feed and 105,000 mt on a concessional purchase from the U.S. Commodity Credit Corporation. Most of the 74,000 mt of wheat was purchased from Australia or the EEC.

In order to cover the additional costs incurred by the NCPB in its cereals purchases and the higher transport costs incurred by having to move the food from Mombasa to consumers, the government increased the consumer price of maize by more than the producer price (in absolute and percentage terms) in September 1984 (World Bank 1986a).

The type of maize to be imported was of critical importance since Kenyan consumers strongly prefer white maize to yellow maize. However, very little white maize was available for export from outside Africa. At that time, white maize apparently also commanded a 30 percent premium on the world market (Cohen and Lewis 1987). Knowing that any maize coming as food aid would be yellow, the government decided to purchase yellow maize.

This choice encouraged informal rationing. Consumers who could afford to buy the remaining domestic supplies of white maize would be able to do so, while those willing to put up with the taste of yellow maize would be prepared to register for the Office of the President famine relief and remain on the register once the drought ended. However, there was the distinct risk that as soon as more preferred foods became available when the drought ended, demand for yellow maize would drop off dramatically, possibly leaving the government with stocks of yellow maize that it could not sell domestically. This did indeed occur (see below).

The first shipment of 21,000 mt of Thai maize, originally scheduled to arrive at the end of August, docked at Mombasa on 27 September. The NCPB closing stocks for the fourth week of September were 108,446 mt. With the newly arrived maize in transit during the first week of October, the closing stocks fell even lower to 96,026 mt (these figures are from NCPB weekly stock records). This took stocks below the FAO estimate of the safe minimum level for working stocks (100,000 mt).

Inevitably, the unprecedented sales and the approach of dangerously low stock levels had an effect on maize availability in the country. A crude rationing of maize sales took place from about July onwards, though details of the way the system operated are not known. As early as June, several NGOs operating small feeding schemes in the north and east reported difficulty in drawing maize and beans for which they had already paid. Beans became particularly scarce, continuing to be in short supply until mid-1985. Problems with maize supplies were experienced through November, when yellow maize stocks and distribution were rapidly increased. In the weeks immediately prior to the arrival of the first shipment, a number of NCPB depots completely exhausted their supplies.

It is clear that Kenya came very close to exhausting the stocks of its primary staple in September. Had the government delayed its decision to purchase maize abroad, or chosen to await the arrival of donor shipments, the country would most certainly have run out of food. This close call vindicates the government decision to act decisively on its own behalf once it recognized that it had a severe crisis on its hands. The NCPB sales and stock levels alerted the government to the severity of the food crisis, rather than the results of the early warning system and a national food-balance approach.

Logistics Issues. According to government estimates, around one million mt of cereal imports were required over a nine-month period (September to June). This would mean about 3,300 mt would be moved through Mombasa and inland daily. The ability of the port and the inland transport system to cope would be central to the success of the relief program and was the primary concern of donors, as well as the government, in the months following the government appeal.

The FAO mission carried out an assessment of the capacity of the port and the inland transport system. Of the sixteen dry-cargo berths at Mombasa, six were preferred for receiving grain imports because they were accessible by road and rail. Using an estimate of 1,500 mt unloaded each day from each ship at berth, the mission estimated that three berths would have to be specifically allocated to the grain imports. Additional berths would be needed if bunching occurred in the arrival of shipments.

The extent to which the continuous use of three berths for the cereals imports might disrupt Kenya's other import/export trade, as well as that of its neighbors served by Mombasa (Uganda, Rwanda, Burundi, Zaire, and Sudan), were not addressed by the mission, though it was of concern to some donors.

Initially, Kenya Railways estimated it could move 2,500 mt/day inland from the port; however, by the time of the FAO mission's visit, the estimate was reduced to 2,000 mt/day. The chief constraint was the availability of heavy locomotives. According to the FAO assessment, 35 to 50 percent of the ninety main-line locomotives were out of action at any one time. The main problems were the lack of spare parts and disorganized management (FAO 1984a).

In order to maintain the daily movement of 3,300 mt, road transport clearly had to play a significant role in helping clear the port and in the bulk movements between the port and the up-country NCPB depots. The FAO mission was generally optimistic of the capacity of the public and private road transport fleets to handle the predicted requirements. The Kenya Transport Association (KTA, an association of around 180 companies) estimated that its members could make available vehicle capacity of 1,000 to 1,300 mt/day without seriously disrupting other traffic. It was estimated that this could be increased to between 1,600 and 2,000 mt/day if government restrictions on night movements of trucks were lifted. The use of road transport offered the government a flexible way to supplement bulk movement by rail. However, road transport involved significantly higher costs. Whereas the Kenya Railways rate for moving grain was around Ksh 0.5 per mt/km, the KTA rate was Ksh 0.95 per mt/km; in October 1984, the KTA rate increased to Ksh 1.36 per mt/km (FAO 1984a).

Implementation Phase: October 1984 to Early 1985

Cereals Imports. The first commercial shipment of Thai maize arrived on 27 September and the first food-aid maize (a small consignment for WFP of 1,870 mt) arrived on 11 October. The degree to which the government was correct in not waiting upon donors for the maize imports is clearly shown by the small proportion of food-aid maize that arrived during the first months of imports. Between the end of September and the end of January, a total of 420,232 mt of maize was imported, of which only 28,814 mt (less than 7 percent) was food aid.

Since a significant portion of the Thai maize purchased by the government had high levels of aflatoxin (associated with cultivation and storage under humid conditions) or was spoiled, it had to be dumped at sea. One source outside the government, in a position to make a realistic estimate, suggested that approximately 25,000 mt (worth $4 million) had to be disposed of in this way. Presumably, the contract with the supplier enabled the government to be reimbursed.

The first shipment of emergency wheat imports was 10,000 mt donated by the Netherlands, which arrived on 24 October. The first commercial imports arrived at Mombasa at the end of the year.

Logistics. Detailed information on unloading rates at the port was not available. It appears that FAO estimates were exceeded by a significant margin. In November, the government informed the FAO that between three and five berths were being used, and up to 3,000 mt/day were being off-loaded (footnote added to FAO 1984a). Labor productivity rates well above the typical rates used in the FAO calculations may well have been the main reason for this difference. A few days before the arrival of the first shipment, the port workers union undertook to ensure the expeditious unloading of the grain shipments (Cohen and Lewis 1987). It is also understood that additional incentives were introduced for the port workers. It was perhaps inevitable that maintaining an orderly schedule for the arrival of ships presented difficulties; there were periods of bunching, when ships were lying offshore waiting to be brought alongside the dry berths.

The movement of grain inland from Mombasa has not been documented. By and large, it appears that the system succeeded in maintaining the necessary rate of around 3,300 mt/day, although there were periods when road and rail transport did not keep up with the port. However, at no time did this result in ships having to halt discharging in order to clear the backlog.

The railways apparently performed even less well than was feared during the planning period and were not able to sustain a rate of even 1,500 mt/day for long periods. The lack of sufficient heavy locomotives, the slow turnaround of rail wagons in Uganda, and competition from other bulk imports (notably fertilizers) all contributed to the poor rail performance. Deficiencies in the rail system were compensated for by road transport, which handled an average of around 2,000 mt/day, reaching 3,000 mt/day at times. As suggested by the FAO mission, members of the Kenya Transport Association were awarded the contract to transport grain from Mombasa to the main NCPB depots. The rate paid is not known. To enable trucks to transport grain around the clock, the government lifted its night time ban on truck movements. As many as one thousand trucks were involved in the operation, including vehicles involved in distributions from secondary depots (Cohen and Lewis 1987).

Because of its closer proximity to Mombasa, most of the food destined for the severely affected areas of Eastern Province was transported by road. With some of the food-distribution centers set up under the Office of the President in Eastern Province handing out rations to as many as seven thousand people in one day, it was decided to allow district commissioners to consign trucks arriving in Mombasa to proceed to the distribution centers without having to unload into the district stores.

Office of the President Distribution System. According to available data, approximately 114,000 mt of food (95,000 mt of maize, 6,500 mt of beans, 9,300 mt of milk powder, 1,400 mt of butter oil, and 1,800 mt of vegetable oil) were distributed by the OP between October 1984 and November 1985. Distribution began in late August, using 4,000 mt of WFP maize, and was increased in December, using the U.S. Title II donations.

The two U.S. Title II donations made up nearly all of the food distributed. Had the United States not made these donations, it is uncertain whether the government would have implemented such a large free-distribution component. The two Title II donations involved a total of 147,000 mt of maize, 2,700 mt of beans, and 1,800 mt of milk powder. Of the maize, 40,000 mt was rejected by the government (see below); 20,000 mt was intended to be sold to defray inland transportation costs, but it was eventually used in food-for-work programs in 1986. Thus, 87,000 mt of maize was available for use in the free-distribution system, together with the beans and milk powder.

The Office of the President free-distribution system operated in twenty-five of the forty-one districts. By October 1984, when the program began, the numbers of people on the lists compiled by the village relief committees, chiefs, district officers, and district commissioners had reached 1.57 million (Table 2.3). Of these, 75 percent were in Eastern Province, 3 percent in Central Province, 5 percent in Coast Province, 3 percent in Northeastern Province, and 15 percent in Rift Valley Province (Office of the President n.d.). Machakos (496,000), Kitui (326,000), and Meru (187,000) in Eastern Province accounted for 64 percent of the national total.

Some of those acquainted with the program felt that the selection of beneficiaries in some districts was too generous, and a figure of about 1.2 to 1.3 million people was a more accurate estimate of those actually in need. The Embu nutrition research project (CRSP) prepared a list of needy households from its research data on food intake and nutritional assessment. The number of people identified as requiring food relief was similar to the estimate prepared by the district administration; in fact the two lists coincided by 60 percent in the actual names of individuals (see chapter 14 by Neumann et al.).

The number of potential relief recipients began to decrease from about January 1985 onwards, when crops grown during the short rains became available in the eastern areas of the country. Unfortunately, there are discrepancies between the numbers given in the two source documents, so it is not possible to give a definitive picture of when the most significant reductions took place. The process by which the numbers were reduced is thought to have varied. In some areas, people stopped attending the distribution centers of their own accord, while in others the village and district committees decided to halt distributions in those areas judged not to require more free food. As the pressure on the distribution system was reduced, some areas introduced food-for-work activities for people remaining on the lists. This discouraged some of those on the lists from appearing for the distributions.

An analysis of the number of recipients and the food received in each district was carried out by the team that was monitoring the U.S. Title II donation (Table 2.4). In comparison with the target monthly ration of 10 kg per person, the average monthly ration actually achieved was 11.3 kg, with a maximum of 20.1 kg in Isiolo, Marsabit, and Laikipia (grouped together because they were served by the same NCPB depot) and a minimum of 4 kg in Elgeyo Marakwet. The worst affected districts received about the target level: Machakos (10.9), Kitui (11.6), and Meru (9.9). For a distribution system set up so quickly and covering such a wide area, the attainment of the target ration in virtually all the districts was an impressive achievement.

Recovery Phase: Early 1985 to Late 1985

From a national crisis in September 1984, the food situation recovered with a speed that took many by surprise. The short rains maize crop in Eastern Province was harvested from December to February and, despite the apparent shortage of seeds during late 1984, the harvest was good. The total short rains maize crop was over 10 percent above average (825,000 mt compared with an average of 740,000 mt for 1970-1986 [USAID 1987]). In March, the long rains began early and were above normal in most locations. The 1985 long rains harvest was a record one, over 20 percent above average (2,010,000 mt compared with the 1970–1986 average of 1,640,000 [USAID 1987]). By the end of 1985, the NCPB was making record purchases (e.g., 245,000 mt in January 1986).

In many aspects of the relief program, the winding-down process began in early 1985. The numbers of recipients of the Office of the President distribution system began falling off around this time. Within the emergency program of the Catholic Relief Services, the Diocese of Marsabit and Kitui unilaterally reduced the ration size back to regular levels in March. In April, the Government/Donor Agricultural Sub-Committee produced a joint paper entitled "Lessons from the 1984 Drought" (see below) and then turned its attention to longer-term planning issues. A variety of programs, however, continued for much of 1985 and some into 1986. The OP supplied food to some 540,000 recipients in October 1985, and agreement to use 20,000 mt of Title II maize in food-for-work projects was not reached until July 1986.

Maize Stocks. During January 1985, the maize stock position had improved dramatically, to just over 450,000 mt, a level that was more or less maintained until the end of the year, when it rose to over 600,000 mt.

January is traditionally when the NCPB makes its largest monthly purchases, as the long rains harvest from the west of the country becomes available. In January 1985, the NCPB recorded purchases of 120,000 mt. Sales from the 1984 long rains (in the west) and short rains (in the central and eastern regions) harvests were somewhat higher than had been expected in mid-1984. The stock position was assisted by the continued arrival of maize imports.

As the situation improved and local white maize became available, consumers switched to purchasing this preferred staple. The U.S. Title II yellow maize continued to be distributed through the Office of the President distribution system, but sales of yellow maize fell off sharply. With the continued arrival of shipments, particularly of the U.S. Commodity Credit Corporation (CCC) purchase, destined for sale through the NCPB, stocks of yellow maize increased to 265,000 mt in May 1985 (Figure 2.3). The disposal of these stocks became a significant problem for the government. By the end of the year, when NCPB domestic purchases of white maize had begun to reach record levels, stocks of yellow maize had only come down to 230,000 mt. By April 1986, these remained at 214,000 mt (NCPB data).

As a result, the government decided to export 126,000 mt of yellow maize, at prices well below the original purchase price (World Bank 1986a). Exports began in May 1986. Presumably, all the exported maize was from the Thai purchases. All the U.S. Title II maize appears to have been distributed, and export of the 105,000 mt purchased from the CCC was not permitted under the terms of the purchase. The amount exported was about one-third of the original Thai purchase.

The price at which the maize was resold was about $60 to $70 per mt. Using an import price of $160 and a resale price of $65, the loss to the government of the exported maize was on the order of $12 million. This figure does not include the storage and handling costs during the fifteen or so months that the maize was in Kenya. An interesting question, then, is whether the government could have avoided this situation by halting maize imports earlier.

The last of the Thai maize shipments arrived during the third week of January. During February, March, and most of April, the only maize shipments arriving were from the second U.S. Title II donation, for the Office of the President. In the third week of April, the first shipment of a large concessional purchase by the government from the CCC arrived. This purchase originated in late 1984 when the Whitten amendment was approved by the U.S. House of Representatives; it was to enable drought-affected African countries to purchase U.S. agricultural commodities at prices well below the world price. Kenya was one of the twenty-eight eligible countries and the government bid for large amounts of wheat and maize. The wheat bid was unsuccessful. The 105,000 mt of maize was purchased for about one-third of the prevailing world price.

By the end of January 1985, the government would have been aware of NCPB purchases during that month and the increase in its stock levels. It would also have been aware of the above-average short rains in the eastern half of the country. The CBS Crop Forecast Survey was delayed that year due to a change in the sample frame. It is not known when the results for the predicted short rains harvest became available. Quite possibly, therefore, the government could still have been uncertain about the higher-than-average short rains harvest because of uncertainty over the effect on production of the seed shortages experienced during late 1984.

With the long rains season accounting for around 85 percent of maize production, the key question for government planners was the production forecast for the 1985 long rains. As the results of the CBS Crop Forecast Survey are not normally available until June (for area planted) and August (for the harvest), the necessary information may not have been available until after the U.S. CCC shipments had arrived (see Chapter 6 for details of the CBS surveys).

By April, it must have been clear that the long rains were above normal and that a good harvest could be expected if the rains did not finish early. By this time, however, it was almost certainly too late to cancel the entire U.S. CCC contract. Nevertheless, with a sailing time of around three weeks from the U.S. Gulf of Mexico ports to East Africa, it is conceivable that the last two shipments (containing 50,000 mt), which arrived in the first week of June, could have been cancelled. However, no attempt was made to do so.

A sequence of events that might have been associated with the buildup of yellow maize stocks and the failure to cancel part of the U.S. CCC contract concerned the last of the U.S. Title II shipments, which arrived off Mombasa on 20 May aboard the MV Cove Trader. At 40,000 mt, this was the largest shipment of the USAID donation. An assessment of the quality of the grain by port authorities resulted in the shipment being declared unfit for human consumption. The assessment was disputed by USAID, supported by the results of independent surveys. Unable to resolve the dispute, USAID eventually sold most of the shipment on the world market, and the maize was not replaced.

With no consumer demand for the yellow maize stocks that had built up principally as a result of the U.S. CCC contract, much of it remained in store throughout 1985 and most of 1986. However, some was apparently used in the brewing industry and some in manufacturing glucose for the domestic confectionery industry. The most significant attempt to utilize the stocks came in September 1986, when 60,000 mt was offered to the milling industry for use in livestock feeds.

Rehabilitation Programs. The Office of the President was still supplying food to 540,000 recipients in October 1986, and several NGOs continued with limited feeding programs and/or food-for-work programs until the end of the year. As is the case in many relief programs, it is difficult to determine the degree to which the programs were continued in Kenya because of the availability of food or because of the continuation of genuine need.

Throughout late 1984 and early 1985, there was generally perceived to be a serious shortage of maize (particularly of the drought-resistant Katumani variety) and bean seed for use in the 1984 short rains and the 1985 long rains. In response, the government used irrigated land on the Bura irrigation scheme to produce some 720 mt of Katumani seed in time for use in the 1985 long rains.

The National Famine Relief Fund set up by the president in June 1984 proved to be a significant vehicle for rehabilitation efforts. The following rehabilitation activities were funded: 760 mt of maize seeds were distributed in about twenty districts during 1984 and 1985; 340 ox plows were distributed in five districts; a beekeeping program was aided in Baringo; and various water projects were carried out (Office of the President n.d.).

The high stock losses in the pastoral areas presented a more severe and longer term rehabilitation problem than aiding recovery in arable areas. Recovery of herds would take several years, and some herders had lost their entire stock. A variety of small projects were implemented by NGOs and other groups in these areas to provide alternative income sources and improve basic services.

RESPONSE BY DONORS AND NGOS

Donors

Known donations toward the relief program by bilateral and multilateral donors are shown in Table 2.5. Most donors confined their emergency assistance to food-aid donations. Apart from the USAID Title II and WFP donations, all cereals food aid was wheat to be sold by the NCPB, with various arrangements for use of the proceeds. Of the total amount of cereals imported between September 1984 and the end of June 1985, food aid accounted for 33 percent and commercial purchases for the remainder. As Kenya was already receiving program and project food aid for development purposes, some wheat would have been provided as food aid in the absence of the drought, so not all of this amount can be attributed as a direct response to the drought.

Similarly, the £1.5 million balance-of-payments support provided by the United Kingdom represented bringing forward to the 1984/85 financial year an amount that would have been provided in the following year whether or not there had been a drought. The funds were provided to enable the importation of equipment and supplies for the natural-resources sector from British suppliers to assist recovery from the drought during early 1985. In addition, the Disaster Unit of the Overseas Development Administration made grants for just over £370,000, principally to the African Medical Relief and Education Foundation (AMREF) and Catholic missions in the northern and eastern areas. Interestingly, grants of over £100,000 had been made to NGOs operating in northern Kenya before the government appeal of June 1984.

Due to the number of donors involved and differences in their procedures for making commitments and signing agreements with the government, it is not possible to give a full picture of the timing and response by donors to the government appeal. Some donors awaited confirmation of the import requirements by the FAO multidonor mission that visited the country in August.

Relations between the donor community and the government were marred on two particular occasions during 1984. By the end of April 1984, the failure of the rains was apparent to donors, as well as to the government. However, from that time until the appeal to donors in mid-June, the donor community was unaware of the preparatory measures being taken within the government to cope with the drought and misinterpreted the government's silence as signifying inactivity.

In August 1984, the government rejected an offer of technical assistance to help strengthen logistical management capacity. The assistance had been recommended by the FAO mission and supported by several donors. Indeed, for a time, one bilateral donor tried to make its wheat donation conditional upon the implementation of the recommendation.

This section focuses on the activities of donors and NGOs that have not contributed to this book and on issues of coordination. Part 4 details the activities of the World Food Programme, CARE, Kenya Freedom From Hunger Council, and Oxfam.

U.S. Agency for International Development. The donor response was dominated by the scale of the U.S. commitments. Of the 285,674 mt of cereals food aid delivered (and accepted) between October 1984 and the end of June 1985, 136,414 mt (48 percent) was U.S. food aid. Of this, 29,998 mt was Title I wheat, and 106,414 mt was Title II maize. An additional 105,287 mt of maize was provided on highly concessional terms by the U.S. Commodity Credit Corporation. The total value of the Title II food aid and transport costs was $54.9 million. The Title II donation made up nearly all the food distributed by the Office of the President.

An interesting feature of the Title II donation was the monitoring arrangements. Independent management consultants (Deloitte, Haskins and Sells) were hired by USAID to monitor food distributed from the port to a sample of final distribution points. Regular reporting of the results to USAID were shared with the Office of the President. The reports complimented the information reaching the Office of the President from district officials and enabled improvements to be made to the distribution system during 1985.

World Food Programme (WFP). WFP activities during the emergency program are described in Chapter 17. Some additional points are worth highlighting:

1. The credit arrangement between the WFP and NCPB, whereby WFP wheat imports were exchanged for domestically produced maize and beans, considerably increased WFP operational flexibility in responding to the emergency. Thus, the WFP was allowed to draw on its maize credits and commence the expansion of the Primary School Feeding Programme and the food-for-work activities in Turkana, and to issue maize to NGOs in advance of the arrival of the shipments approved by WFP Rome in August.
2. By distributing additional food through the Primary School Feeding Programme, especially in some of the most affected areas before large-scale distributions by the Office of the President, the WFP contribution to relieving hunger was considerably greater than suggested by the size of its program.
3. Of the 18,000 mt of maize provided, approximately 70 percent was distributed by NGOs to their own emergency food-distribution programs and the remainder through the OP. The project was of great importance to the NGO community. Had WFP not supported them, their role in the relief effort would have been greatly reduced.
4. The country representative personally played a highly positive role in assisting the NGO community to respond to the drought by providing advice and representing their concerns to the government.

UN Children's Fund (UNICEF). UNICEF responded to the emergency by implementing a specially designed program of approximately $750,000. The program was unusual in several respects:

1. It was planned in conjunction with the Ministry of Finance and Planning; UNICEF's willingness to design its program around the needs as perceived by the ministry was commented upon favorably by government officials.
2. Due to pressures on the UNICEF Kenya program, it was decided at the outset that the emergency program would be administered separately, with a heavy reliance on short-term personnel and consultants.
3. UNICEF was unique among the donor community in being given permission by the government to deal directly with the district administration in the four severely affected districts of Machakos, Kitui, Meru, and Embu.

Among the activities funded were the donation of ten trucks in July 1984 to the Ministry of Education to assist the expansion of the Primary School Feeding Programme proposed by WFP; assistance to the Ministry of Health in the collection and analysis of nutritional and health data; technical assistance to district commissioners offices in the four districts; distribution of 210 mt of mixed seed in the four districts (implemented in conjunction with CARE and Oxfam, using FAO technical advice); provision of oral rehydration salts and an associated education program to control the incidence of diarrhea; provision of inner tubes, tires, and batteries to rehabilitate trucks in the four districts; assistance to district medical officers in the four districts to implement a preventative and therapeutic feeding program; support for the NGO coordination efforts of the Kenya National Council of Social Services and organization of seminars for NGOs on technical subjects; and airfreighting and stockpiling of the most commonly required supplies in nutritional emergencies in case serious nutritional deterioration occurred. An internal review was critical of several aspects of the program's management, including poor coordination, a lack of involvement of the senior country program staff, and the misuse of expatriate consultants (Silverman 1985).

Nongovernmental Organizations (NGOs)

Only a limited number of the NGOs participating in the relief operation have reviewed or documented their activities and experiences. It is not possible, therefore, to give an accurate assessment of the relative contribution of the NGO community. A reasoned guess is that between 25,000 and 30,000 mt of food were distributed by NGOs to NGO-run feeding programs. Perhaps an additional 15,000 mt were transported by NGOs to government feeding programs.

Kenyan Red Cross Society. Together with AMREF and Oxfam, the Kenyan Red Cross Society (KRCS) became involved in localized relief efforts around Wajir town following an incident in February 1984. As the seriousness of the drought became apparent, the area involved and the number of beneficiaries expanded. Distribution of food began in May 1984, with 10,000 recipients. Oxfam, which already had nurses working in the area, took responsibility for supplying and managing the wet-feeding operation, with KRCS being responsible for the dry, take-home rations. The KRCS appealed to the League of Red Cross and Red Crescent Societies in Geneva for material assistance, and the first overseas supplies (beans, milk powder, vegetable oil, and high-energy biscuits) arrived in July. The scale of the program increased throughout the year as outlying communities were incorporated. By the end of the year, there were approximately 20,000 recipients. KRCS purchased a total of four trucks to help with the distributions because of the difficulties of hiring transport locally. In 1985, an additional distribution center was set up in Garissa town.

World Vision. Before the drought, World Vision was involved in a large number of community development projects around Kenya. As the situation in the northern and eastern areas worsened, some of the communities appealed to the World Vision office in Nairobi for assistance. Initially, World Vision responded, using its own resources to purchase food from NCPB, and free distribution began as early as April 1984. The programs grew rapidly using WFP food; by September 1984, 27,000 families were receiving rations. Initially, the majority of recipients were located in Marsabit and Samburu districts, but in August, a large program was set up in the severely affected areas of Eastern Province. According to World Vision documents, a total of 3,900 mt of food was distributed to 126,000 families (assumed to be equivalent to around 800,000 people) in eighteen districts (World Vision 1985).

Catholic Relief Services. The Catholic Relief Services (CRS) supplied food (primarily U.S. Title II food) to 130 Mother and Child Health (MCH) centers around the country before the drought. Most of the centers were run by the Catholic church and administered through the diocesan structure. Nondrought supplementary rations were provided through these centers to around 90,000 mothers and children. In addition, CRS supplied food to a small number of destitutes and food-for-work projects. By virtue of having an existing program and food stocks within the country, CRS was able to assist other NGOs with limited food supplies early in 1984 (e.g., in Wajir) and to accommodate an increase in the destitute category from as early as February 1984. However, its emergency program was seriously delayed.

In June 1984, CRS submitted a request to USAID to expand its program by increasing the numbers of beneficiaries in the affected areas and increasing the size of the MCH ration (bulgur wheat, powdered milk, and vegetable oil) from 10 kg/month to 28 kg/month. USAID proposed that the additional in-country transport costs should be borne by counterpart funds raised by previous Title I donations to the government. In any event, the government did not make these funds available to CRS, and the agency had to await the approval of $1.09 million by the Office of Foreign Disaster Assistance in September 1984. As a result, the emergency program shipment did not arrive until January 1985. CRS was able to introduce the larger drought-emergency ration in October, however, using 900 mt on credit from the WFP. In all, 3,500 mt was distributed to around eighty centers implementing the emergency program.

African Medical Research and Education Foundation (AMREF). AMREF had been involved in long-term health programs in southern Machakos (Kibwezi), Narok, and Kajiado districts before the drought. Nutritional status of preschool children in these areas was found to be worsening in mid-1984; following the government appeal in June, AMREF decided to launch an emergency program. Funds were raised from a wide variety of local and overseas sources. Food distribution began in Kajiado and Narok in September 1984 and in November in Kibwezi. Distribution was through eighty-five centers run in conjunction with local church groups or through clinics run by AMREF. In all, 1,600 mt (1,100 mt of which was WFP maize) were supplied to approximately 43,000 preschool children between September 1984 and July 1985 (AMREF 1985).

Coordination Between the Government and NGOs

Kenya National Council of Social Services. As part of the plans prepared in June 1984, the government appointed the Kenya National Council of Social Services to coordinate the relief activities of the large number of NGOs operating in Kenya. The first meeting of the NGO Relief Coordinating Committee, chaired by the KNCSS, took place on 19 June (the same day as the government appeal to donors) and was addressed by the director of planning, who outlined the proposed role for KNCSS. The KNCSS was to act as the representative of the NGOs, though it was not clear at that point whether it would have a seat on the Task Force or whether it would have to deal with the Task Force through the Ministry of Finance and Planning.

The lack of clarity over the proposed role, KNCSS's small staff and lack of experience in the management or coordination of large-scale relief programs, and NGOs' sensitivity over possible threats to their independence and relationships that they had built up for years with officials in some of the ministries resulted in open skepticism among some of the larger NGOs toward the government proposals. This skepticism was reinforced by the poor support given to the KNCSS during July and August. Apart from some support from UNICEF, KNCSS was not strengthened to cope with its new role. It was not given a seat on the Task Force; only after repeated requests did a representative of the Task Force attend a meeting of the NGO Coordinating Committee.

The government appeared slow to address an issue that was crucial to most NGOs, i.e., whether they would be given access to government food supplies or whether they should import their own. If they were to follow the latter course, they needed to know whether the government would assist them in funding the transport costs inland from Mombasa. By August, it had still not been decided whether NGOs would have access to the U.S. Title II food that was provided to the Office of the President, and it remained unclear whether the NCPB would charge transport costs on a swap arrangement proposed by the government for NGOs importing their own supplies (Ray 1984).

The government may have been slow in providing information on the details of its program because it was still working them out. Thus, its

"Guidelines on Food Supply and Distribution" for district officials were not distributed until 21 August (Office of the President 1984). Given the pressure on a few key officials, there simply may not have been enough time to deal speedily with the many issues that were not central to the government's main concerns. Whatever the reasons, there seemed to be general agreement among donors and NGOs that the government did not make full use of the resources available within the NGO community.

For the KNCSS, the situation appears to have begun to improve during September. With the help of the WFP representative, the Coordinating Committee adopted a more focused strategy in its dealings with the government. Issues requiring immediate decisions from the government were agreed upon by the Coordinating Committee, and a small group of representatives (including the WFP representative) met with officials in the Office of the President. Only one issue was tackled at a time. The first meeting apparently dealt with procedures for NGOs to draw WFP credit maize from NCPB stores, while the second was concerned with the simplification of the procedures required for the importation of food commodities and emergency supplies by several NGOs.

In addition, pressure on the KNCSS to obtain decisions on food supplies and government transport funding was reduced by the approval of the WFP emergency project that provided food for NGOs and the donations of transport funds through the EEC and CARE. The EEC gave 500,000 ECUs to four NGOs (AMREF, the Kenyan Red Cross Society, the Kenya Freedom From Hunger Council, and the National Christian Council of Kenya) and, at the end of September, the U.S. Office of Foreign Disaster Assistance gave CARE $1.9 million to cover NGO transport costs (see Chapter 21).

By October, most NGOs were preoccupied with commencing the implementation of their programs. The KNCSS was no longer the focus of attention, and it concentrated on providing a forum for the exchange of information. This it did fairly well, the meetings of the Coordinating Committee being well attended, not only by NGOs, but also by such donors as UNICEF, WFP, EEC, FAO, and, occasionally, the World Bank. Attempts were made to obtain monthly reports from each of the NGOs as to the amount of food distributed and the number of beneficiaries reached, but the response was never complete. With the assistance of UNICEF, a workshop was held on ration composition, and there was some agreement on the need to standardize ration sizes and composition between NGOs. In January 1985, the KNCSS arranged a meeting between the district commissioner of Machakos and the NGOs active in the district in order to iron out some of the problems experienced by the NGOs. The meeting was seen as a success, and a similar meeting took place in Kitui District the following month.

Food Distribution by NGOs and the Office of the President. By mid-December 1984, the WFP announced that its maize supplies available to

NGOs were running low, and the issue of NGO access to government food stocks resurfaced. Agreement was reached between KNCSS, WFP, and the Office of the President that NGOs would submit requests for the amount of food they required to the local district commissioner, who would then authorize drawings from the NCPB stores. The way in which this agreement was implemented, however, varied among districts.

There was some initial confusion between the Office of the President and the district commissioners regarding who had the authority required to make the allocations to NGOs. The Office of the President claimed that it had devolved authority to the district commissioner, while the district commissioners in many districts refused to make any allocations until specific authorization had been received (CARE 1985). By January, no allocations had been made to NGOs in Machakos, apparently because the district commissioner was still waiting for information from some of the NGOs (KNCSS 1984-1985). Presumably, the required information was the location of NGO activities and their capacities. At that time, there were reportedly 8,500 mt of Title II yellow maize in the district stores (KNCSS 1984-1985).

In some districts, NGOs that had been operating in the district before the drought and had formed working relationships with the district commissioner had little difficulty in being given access to the Title II supplies. In contrast, some of the NGOs that had only begun working in the district as a result of the drought were refused access. In many districts, there was apparently some overlap between the catchment areas of feeding programs implemented by the government and those of the NGOs. When NGOs began applying to use food belonging to the government in centers close to those being supplied through the Office of the President, some district commissioners rationalized the situation by closing the NGO centers and adding the beneficiaries to those of the government centers. In districts where NGOs had their programs discontinued, the NGOs were often requested to assist the government with transportation. An NGO might thus have its own program closed down, while still continuing to make distributions and claim reimbursement from the CARE project.

The effectiveness of many NGO relief programs and the smooth running of the relief system as a whole must have been affected by the confusion over the relationship between NGO and government feeding programs. Some of the confusion and variation in practice can presumably be explained in terms of unsatisfactory communication between the center and the districts and within the districts themselves. Perhaps fewer problems would have been experienced between the NGOs and the government if clearer procedures had been made available earlier and the government been more responsive to the concerns of NGOs. Other factors may help to explain the apparently distant relationships with some NGOs. Instances were reported of some religious NGOs selecting recipients on the basis of their affiliation rather than their degree of need. The operation and sensitivity of some NGOs was not beyond question, and reports were heard of feeding programs being started before the district commissioners had been approached for support or approval.

CONCLUSIONS AND LESSONS

While the government may have underestimated the deteriorating situation in the northern and eastern areas in 1983 and early 1984, it responded decisively when faced with a crisis of national proportions. The single most significant action of the relief operation was the purchase of 386,000 mt of maize from Thailand at a cost of about $62 million. Had it delayed making this purchase (possibly as a way of encouraging a more generous response from the donor community) by even four weeks, it is likely that there would have been serious food shortages and social unrest toward the end of October 1984.

Nevertheless, the government's good fortune should not be forgotten. First, the early warning system was not tested since the failure of the rains was apparent to officials in Nairobi as early as April. Had the drought not been so apparent, valuable weeks may have been lost while waiting for the results of the crop forecasting system.

Second, maize stocks in early 1984 were unusually high, well above the security reserve level set by the National Food Policy paper of 1981. This effectively bought more time for the imports to arrive.

Third, foreign exchange reserves were higher than at any time in the previous three years due in part to the fortuitous action by the government of India in halting its tea exports. Had India continued to export tea or if the drought had struck one or two years earlier, the government of Kenya might literally have been unable to afford to be as decisive as it was in 1984.

This last point, however, needs to be placed in context. Though it may have been somewhat fortuitous that foreign exchange reserves were high, the fact remains that Kenyan agricultural policy has consistently stressed the development of a strong commodity export sector, which has been based on coffee and tea. This strategy has resulted in a more diversified economy, making it more able to withstand the effects of drought on domestic staple-food production.

The importation of 858,000 mt of cereals between the end of September 1984 and June 1985 was a massive logistics operation. Its success clearly owes a great deal to Kenya's comparatively well-developed transport infrastructure. The government does deserve credit for the way it planned the logistics operation and mobilized the necessary resources in what many donors had initially regarded as the Achilles' heel of the relief system.

In terms of its timing, the free-distribution component of the government program was late. Sufficient distribution did not commence until December 1984, fully eight months after the failure of the long rains had become apparent, four months after the critical shortages of September, and two months after the onset of the short rains that signaled the end of the drought for many areas. Its lateness may be explained by the inadequate food supplies in the country until the flow of maize imports commenced; the priority accorded to maintaining supplies in the marketing system; and the government's decision to base the program on food aid, principally the large Title II donation that first arrived in October 1984. Considering the degree of suffering experienced in late 1984, particularly by the people of Eastern Province for whom the drought had begun eighteen months earlier, the delay in commencing this component of the program was regrettable, even if partly understandable.

Nevertheless, once the program of free distribution commenced, it proved to be a substantial effort, reaching up to 1.5 million recipients on a regular basis in twenty-five districts. In terms of its organization and implementation, this program represented a significant achievement. Kenya's ability to mount such a large program owed a great deal to its comparatively effective administration, with its hierarchical structure, clear lines of authority, and strong presence in rural areas.

The response by donors was good, but not massive. USAID made a large Title II donation, which constituted most of the supplies used in the free-food-distribution program. It is difficult to know what the other donors would have contributed had the government been less decisive in its actions. The WFP and the OFDA transport grant to CARE made a very positive contribution to the effectiveness of the overall relief program and to the efforts of the NGO community in particular.

The NGO community made a valuable contribution to the overall relief efforts. Some responded to the situation in the northern and eastern areas of the country several months before the government did so. In the final analysis, however, it appears that the government could have made better use of the experience and outreach afforded by the large NGO community in Kenya. That it did not may have been partly due to the lack of a strategy detailing the respective roles of the government and the NGOs. The fact that so few NGOs have evaluated their relief activities suggests a lack of willingness to learn from their experiences and a certain lack of professionalism.

The above-normal short rains at the end of 1984 and the good long rains of 1985 brought a rapid end to the crisis, producing an unusually quick transition from a problem of national food shortage at the end of 1984 to one of a national food surplus at the beginning of 1986. The speed of the recovery and the extent to which consumers switched from buying yellow maize to other foods when they became available in early 1985 resulted in large stocks of yellow maize that could not be sold domestically. About one-third of the maize purchased from Thailand in 1984 was exported in 1986 at great embarrassment and considerable financial loss to the government.

It is tempting to look toward the early warning system to account for this unfortunate ending to an otherwise successful program. However, it is the conclusion of this review that the situation was unavoidable, as it would have been a very courageous official to have canceled even part of the concessional purchase from the US Commodity Credit Corporation before the likely outcome of the 1985 long rains harvest was known.

A final point is that for much of the country, the drought was short, though severe. Indeed, it lasted for just one season in the main arable areas. Without a doubt, the imports averted the complete exhaustion of staple food supplies within the national marketing system and, most likely, social unrest in urban areas and drought-affected districts as well. It does not necessarily follow, however, that the relief program averted famine in the rural areas. Substantial free food distribution by the government only began in December 1984, just one or two months ahead of the short rains harvest in Eastern Province. In the absence of food relief, mortality rates would have increased through the harvest season, but may not have developed into widespread famine.

Lessons for Kenya

Though rare, droughts as severe as that of 1984 will inevitably recur. While the relief program was a comparative success, there are a number of lessons that need to be absorbed by the government, donors, and NGOs.

The government has taken the first steps necessary to learn the lessons from the drought. Toward the end of 1985, the Office of the President carried out a substantial review of the relief program. Unfortunately, this document is confidential, and it seems unlikely that it will be released for some years to come. It is not known what recommendations were made, how extensive the review was among the ministries, or what steps the government has taken to implement the findings.

In April 1985, the newly formed Government/Donor Agricultural Sub-Committee produced a paper entitled "Lessons From The 1984 Drought" (Agricultural Sub-Committee 1985). The paper synthesizes earlier papers produced separately by the government and donors, papers that apparently differed little in their analyses of the strengths and weaknesses of the relief program. In summary, the main recommendations of the joint paper are:

1. *Early warning*: earlier and more reliable information on the weather and the likely production of minor food crops, as well as the major crops; better coordination and the clearer definition of responsibilities between all the bodies involved in the crop forecasting system.
2. *Food security planning*: review of the desirable level of food stocks; better integration of export, import, and stock level decisions.
3. *Food distribution*: contingency plan or manual laying down the role, authority, and responsibilities of the different parties (including NGOs) from the Task Force down to the district level; preparatory work so that food-for-work and rural works programs can be initiated

at an early stage of a relief program and funds channeled to the districts more rapidly.
4. *Drought recovery*: contingency planning for recovery to start at the same time as relief measures; greater flexibility in the price of animal feeds to encourage farmers to maintain herds; contingency planning for widespread destocking schemes in pastoral areas; better coordination of livestock marketing.

This review and the contributions to this book support most of these recommendations.

To what extent have these lessons actually been learned by the government? There are encouraging signs that the government is more sensitive to issues regarding national food security as a result of the experiences of 1984. For example, in April 1987, maize exports were abruptly halted when it was feared that a three-week delay in the start of the long rains might signal the start of another drought.

However, since the joint government/donor paper was prepared, there appears to have been little progress in implementing the recommendations. Some improvement has been made to the early warning system since the drought through the Kenya Rangeland Ecological Monitoring Unit (KREMU) and the Central Bureau of Statistics (see Chapters 6 and 7). Such improvements still have a long way to go before an effective and integrated early warning system is established.

In early 1986, USAID offered to support the Office of the President in organizing a workshop of district administration staff involved in implementing the relief program. It was hoped that the workshop would offer the opportunity to set down the valuable experiences acquired by these officials during the relief program and possibly to act as a first step in the development of contingency plans. Such a post-hoc review is routine in India, facilitating the evolution of effective national and local response plans (McAlpin 1987). Unfortunately, the workshop did not materialize.

The apparent lack of progress may be partly attributed to the government's preoccupation, since the beginning of 1986, with managing maize surpluses. The problem of governments' not according greater priority to disaster-preparedness measures when they are overwhelmingly preoccupied with short-term issues is not peculiar to Kenya. In addition, the drought and the management of the response to it remains a sensitive issue for the government. It is difficult to predict when or how the government may begin to take additional steps to address the acknowledged weaknesses in the relief program.

Lessons for Other Countries in Africa

Kenya's ability to purchase much of the necessary food imports was crucial to the comparative success of the relief program. This ability was due in general to its comparatively strong economy and in particular to its policy of encouraging a strong commodity export sector. In preparing agricultural development strategies, other countries would do well to acknowledge the positive contribution that a strong export sector can make to improving the ability to cope with droughts.

The high maize stock levels at the beginning of 1984 gave the government a valuable breathing space (which was almost exhausted) in which to import maize and plan its relief program. Kenya's experience is a useful case-study contribution to the debate over the appropriate size of strategic grain reserves in African countries.

The ability of the logistics systems to cope with the massive import program, particularly the capacity of the port and inland transport routes, is again a reflection of a comparatively strong economy in which international trade plays a significant role. The infrastructure was not designed with sufficient capacity to cope with occasional large-scale food import programs. Thus, once again, Kenya's success may be attributed not to conscious disaster-preparedness efforts, but to the benefits that have accompanied its particular economic development strategy.

An object lesson of Kenya's experience was the decisiveness of government action once it recognized the seriousness of the situation. This carried with it certain costs, such as the later need to export surplus yellow maize after the program ended. Such costs were far outweighed by the benefits of the government's decisiveness.

The comparatively effective, centrally directed administration, with its strong presence in rural areas, was another major strength of the program. This enabled fairly accurate identification of those in need of direct assistance and the implementation of a substantial program of free food distribution. Maintaining or developing a strong district administration is a useful lesson for other countries in drought-prone areas of Africa.

The difficulty in mounting a substantial job-creation program at short notice is an experience shared by other governments in Africa. Such programs require prior planning and investment in the development of technical and supervisory personnel if they are to result in more than just "make work" projects. While such investments may not necessarily represent an appropriate use of scarce resources, other countries need to decide the emphasis they wish to place on job-creation schemes well in advance of a relief program.

Kenya's less-than-successful experience in making effective use of the NGO community also holds lessons for other countries, both the governments and NGOs. Effective structures for NGO coordination and clear delineation of responsibilities between NGO and government relief efforts need to be drawn up in advance. This requires a great deal of trust and information sharing between the two groups, both before and during a program.

OVERVIEW OF THE 1984/85 DROUGHT • 51

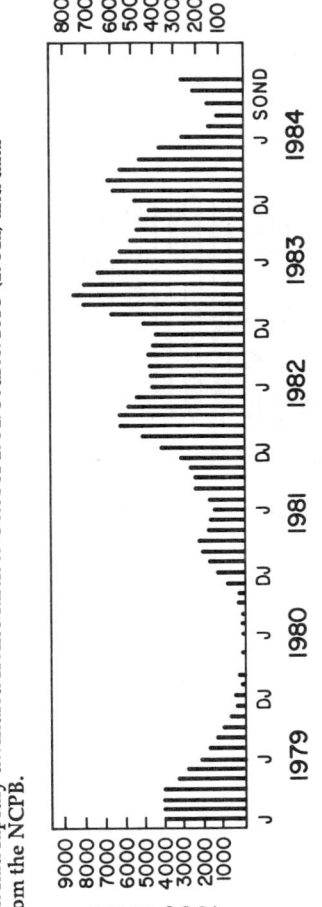

Figure 2.1 NCPB maize stocks by month. Stocks had built up after the 1980 food crisis but had rapidly dwindled from March to October 1984. Source: FAO (1984a) and data from the NCPB.

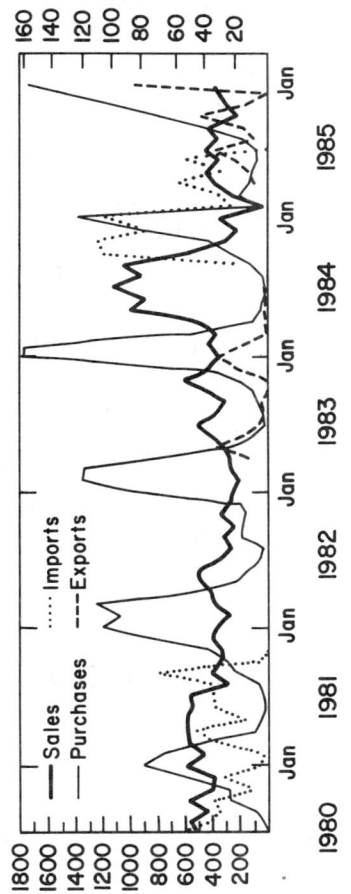

Figure 2.2 NCPB maize transactions. Purchases in early 1984 were higher than in previous years, but sales escalated from March onward, thereby triggering national concern about the drought. Sources: FAO (1984a) and data from the NCPB.

Figure 2.3 NCPB stocks of yellow and white maize. Yellow maize arrived in Kenya in September. At certain times in 1985, stocks of yellow maze were greater than those of white maize. Source: Data from the NCPB.

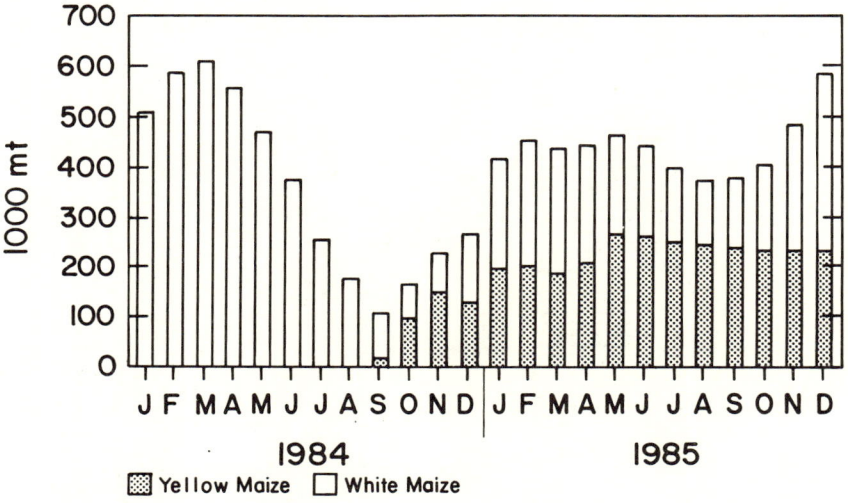

Table 2.1 Food Import Requirements Reported by the Government of Kenya

Commodity	June 1984–July 1985	July 1985–Dec 1985
Maize	900,000 – 1,100,000	424,000
Wheat	426,000	84,000
Milk Powder	10,000	—
Beans	Unspecified	—

Source: Borton (1987).
Note: Figures are in mt.

OVERVIEW OF THE 1984/85 DROUGHT • 53

Table 2.2 Food Imports: September 1984 to June 1985

Date/Source	Maize Commercial	Maize Food Aid	Wheat Commercial	Wheat Food Aid
September 1984				
27 Thailand	21,002			
Total	21,002	0	0	0
October				
4 Canada[1]				965
11 WFP		1,870		
20 Thailand	20,000			
21 Thailand	20,497			
21 Title II		10,509		
23 Thailand	20,979			
23 Thailand	15,000			
24 Netherlands				10,000
28 Thailand	13,592			
28 Title II		5,000		
Total	90,068	17,379	0	10,965
November				
4 Thailand	12,439			
4 Australia				4,879
9 Title I				12,000
10 Thailand	14,531			
11 Thailand	14,995			
15 Thailand	13,862			
17 Thailand	21,226			
20 Title I				17,998
22 Thailand	13,377			
24 Thailand	19,176			
Total	109,606	0	0	34,877
December				
1 Thailand[1]	6,324			
3 Thailand	21,819			
9 Canada				16,000
10 Thailand	21,200			
16 EEC				10,123
22 EEC			21,698	
23 Title II		11,435		
30 Thailand	19,049			
Total	68,392	11,435	21,698	26,123
January 1985				
4 Thailand	19,716			
6 Thailand	13,285			
9 Thailand	21,218			
13 Thailand	14,277			
14 EEC			16,625	
16 Thailand	14,055			
21 Thailand	19,799			
25 France				1,000
25 Unknown				564
25 Canada				12,050
28 Australia				15,000
Total	102,350	0	16,625	28,614

54 • COPING WITH DROUGHT IN KENYA

Table 2.2 Continued

	Maize		Wheat	
Date/Source	Commercial	Food Aid	Commercial	Food Aid
February 1985				
15 WFP				9,319
25 Title II		24,241		
28 EEC				11,000
Total	0	24,241	0	20,319
March				
3 Title II		30,000		
15 WFP				13,318
Total	0	30,000	0	13,318
April				
5 Australia			20,640	
5 WFP				14,672
7 US CCC	22,138			
13 Title II		20,400		
20 US CCC	7,149			
22 FRG				5,000
25 Title II		4,831		
25 Australia			14,620	
Total	29,287	25,231	35,260	19,672
May				
12 US CCC	26,000			
20 US CCC[2]		40,000		
28 US Feed[1]	2,000			
31 WFP/India				5,000
31 EEC				5,000
Total	28,000	40,000	0	10,000
June				
2 US CCC	30,000			
4 US CCC	20,000			
7 Sweden				10,000
15 WFP				3,500
Total	50,000	0	0	13,500
Grand Total	498,705	148,286	73,583	177,388

Source: USAID (1987).
Notes: Figures in mt.
[1]for animal feed.
[2]Cove Trader shipment, which was rejected.

Table 2.3 Beneficiaries of Food Relief from the Office of the President

Month		Monitoring Team	Office of the President
1984	August	1,391,900	na
	October	na	1,575,300
1985	January	1,288,500	na
	April	835,800	na
	August	530,900	na
	October	319,400	544,800

Source: Deloitte, Haskins and Sells Management Consultants (1985).

Table 2.4 Monthly Distribution of U.S. Title II Maize

District	Jan. 85	Feb. 85	Mar. 85	Apr. 85	May 85	Jun. 85	Jul. 85	Aug. 85	Sep. 85	Oct. 85	Nov. 85	Totals	Av. Mo. Ration kg/head
Baringo	475.6	339.1	1,912.5	985.3	2,561.2	943.8	1,666.0	1,345.8	417.1	197.4	18.6	10,862.4	16.3
Elgeyo Marakwet	362.9	177.4	87.7	272.1	—	388.4	189.5	245.9	42.6	4.0	—	1,770.5	4.0
Embu	890.3	206.2	31.8	440.8	204.7	381.0	462.0	—	277.7	—	—	2,894.5	12.0
Narok	—	—	104.4	804.2	378.5	—	71.2	50.0	—	—	—	1,408.3	20.1
Isiolo	—	2,538.2	2,274.4	3,536.7	203.5	297.0	4,310.1	1,498.7	160.0	—	—	18,231.4	20.1
Marsabit	1,103.7				1,696.2					250.0			
Laikipia						362.9							
Kajiado	503.8	700.8	414.2	231.3	198.9	—	150.0	—	—	—	—	2,316.3	11.5
Kiambu						50.0			67.3				
Muranga							—						
Kitui	3,698.7	350.5	7.9	494.2	2,178.9	—	710.0	1,000.6	750.0	220.0	1,772.6	11,183.4	11.6
Lamu	1,105.1	—	—	885.7	—	—	732.9	502.0	252.0	311.5	—	5,626.7	9.9
Tana River				741.3		551.2	545.0						
Machakos	1,106.8	2,877.5	729.5	1,627.3	3,645.6	1,212.9	1,760.2	—	230.0	—	—	13,198.8	10.9
Meru	2,692.9	866.8	588.0	81.8	456.9	247.0	68.7	151.9	—	—	—	5,424.0	9.4
Garissa, Wajir Mandera	—	1,590.0	—	—	378.0	—	—	—	—	—	—	1,968.0	5.3
Nyandarua	1,978.3	1,172.7	—	—	927.2	271.3	1,292.3	201.8	—	—	—	8,018.0	11.2
Samburu			1,572.6							360.6	241.2		
Nyeri	57.2	124.3	389.0	—	—	—	—	—	—	—	—	570.5	13.0
Taita Taveta	—	—	—	—	1,225.0	—	258.0	58.0	52.0	—	—	1,593.8	12.3
Turkana	—	931.0	846.4	1,116.2	—	—	1,436.4	727.6	171.9	144.0	141.5	5,965.0	4.0
West Pokot	—	—	—	—	—	450.0	—	—	—	—	—		
TOTAL (mt)	14,245.3	11,874.5	8,958.4	11,216.9	14,055.4	5,155.5	13,652.3	5,782.3	2,420.6	1,487.5	2,173.9	91,022.6	

Source: Deloitte, Haskins and Sells Management Consultants (1985).
Note: Total quantity dispatched for distribution, per NCPB was 86,886 mt. Dashes indicate no distribution. Blanks indicate data not available.

Table 2.5. Principal Known Donations to Kenyan Relief Program

Donor	Food Aid Commodity	mt	Financial Assistance and Purposes
USA	Maize	107,000	Free distribution, US $1.9 million
	Beans	2,700	grant for NGO transport costs
	DSM	1,800	
Germany	Wheat	5,000	For sale
EEC			UK £1.4 million for inland transport costs
UK			UK £10 million balance-of-payments support; UK £0.37 million grant to NGOs and purchase of pesticides
Australia	Wheat	20,000	For sale
Canada	Wheat	18,000	For sale
Netherlands	Wheat	10,000	For sale
France	Wheat	1,000	For sale
Denmark			UK £1.05 million rural works program
WFP	Maize	25,270	Free distribution
	Beans	1,070	
	DSM	7,400	Kenya Cooperative Creameries
	But. oil	1,500	
	Veg. oil	240	
UNICEF			US $750,000 for transport and various relief projects
World Bank			12 lorries for School Feeding Programme

Sources: USAID (1987), FAO (1984a), data from the Ministry of Finance and Planning.

OVERVIEW OF THE 1984/85 DROUGHT • 57

Appendix 2.1 Chronology of the Drought in Kenya

Time	Events
Early Warning	
Pre-1984	Food assistance was provided by the World Food Programme (WFP) (Turkana Rehabilitation Project, Primary School Feeding Programme in thirteen districts, resettlement areas, dairy development), African Medical Research and Education Foundation (AMREF), Catholic Relief Services (CRS), and the Office of the President (OP).[1,2]
	Tea and coffee prices were high, and the trade deficit in 1983 was the lowest in four years.[3]
	The short rains were poor in Eastern Province and other areas. The National Cereals and Produce Board (NCPB) exported maize due to cash flow problems and high stock levels. The contracts had been signed much earlier than the data of shipment. The government of Kenya (GOK) succeeded in canceling some obligations for exports after the drought was recognized. Estimates of private stocks (among smallholders) were not available and a major (continuing) uncertainty in food monitoring.[4]
1984	
January	The GOK increased producer prices, effective in July: maize prices increased 8.3 percent over 1983 levels; wheat, 7.5 percent; milk, 10.4 percent.[3]
February	The Meteorological Department seasonal forecast indicated below-normal long rains, and the OP was briefed in a confidential memo.[5]
	The Central Bank noted improvement in the economy since the austerity measures of 1982; the International Monetary Fund (IMF) endorsed Kenya's economic performance.[3]
	Conflict over water supplies in Wajir dramatized the impact of the drought in Northeastern Province. The Kenyan Red Cross Society (KRCS), AMREF, and Oxfam provided food assistance to 10,000 people, beginning in May 1984, and to 20,000 recipients by the end of 1984.[1]
March	The long rains failed in most of country, and the drought, including its presence in Nairobi, was apparent in April.[5]
	USAID/Kenya monitored the drought through a mission-wide committee. This early response and a permanent agriculture section facilitated monitoring in advance of other donors. Periodic Situation and Outlook Reports were distributed.[6]
April	USAID encouraged the GOK to organize a drought-response committee, but the government did not want to signal a crisis situation that might lead to hoarding.[6]
	The president requested analysis of the drought's implications from the Ministry of Agriculture, Ministry of Finance and Economic Planning, and the Office of the President. The Ministry of Agriculture surveyed agricultural production in April and May, while the Central Bureau of Statistics Crop Forecast Survey results were not available until about August.[1]
	World Vision began free food distribution, which accelerated, using WFP maize, to include 27,000 families by September.[1]
May	Coffee production in 1983/84 was higher than in 1982/83, with prices 25 to 30 percent higher. Tea prices increased 80 percent over 1983, although India began exporting again. The tea crop was 119,700 mt in 1983, and exports were 32 percent greater than in 1982. Production in the first quarter of 1984 was about 13 percent lower than in 1983 due to the drought.[3]
	Water restrictions were announced for Nairobi.[3]

Appendix 2.1 Continued

Time	Events
June	The president inaugurated the National Famine Relief Fund and established the interministerial Steering Committee and Task Force for Food Supply and Distribution.[3] The government appeal to donors on 13 June requested food aid due to a shortfall in grain supplies as a result of the failure of the 1983 short rains and 1984 long rains. Food-import needs identified by the GOK totaled about 1.5 million mt of maize, 510,000 mt of wheat, 10,000 mt of milk powder, and an unspecified amount of beans. Emphasis was placed on market distribution and food-for-work, rather than free distribution. The Director of Planning briefed NGOs regarding the role of the Kenya National Council for Social Services (KNCSS), a unit with little food-relief experience. The NGOs were skeptical regarding the competence and role of the KNCSS.[1] CRS requested assistance from USAID to expand the emergency program, but funds were not made available until September.[1]
Gearing-Up	
June	The Planning Department assessed import requirements using two methods: estimating the population-at-risk and calculating their food deficit based on nutrition requirements; and using the shortfall in national production as an indicator of import requirements. The second method, judged to be simpler and more reliable, was used. The Planning Department and Ministry of Agriculture circulated monthly summaries of stocks, imports, and forecast requirements.[7] The CBS crop survey results confirming the 1983 short rains harvest, 1984 long rains area planted, and food prices in selected markets were reported. The increase in prices of maize and, particularly, beans was noted.
July	The GOK began organizing district relief committees (or district food security committees). NCPB depots in several areas ran out of maize between July and September, even though surplus supplies were kept in western Kenya. The GOK feared the rapid drawdown of NCPB stocks would completely deplete stocks, after sales increased from 600,000 bags per month to over one million. Rationing was subsequently imposed. The government ordered the first commercial imports of yellow maize, which cost 30 percent less than white maize, and would encourage the switching to secondary foods. Additional contracts were let in August and September. Transport needs were assessed. The Kenya Railways estimated it could unload 2,500 mt per day in Mombasa, and subsequently revised the figure to 2,000 mt per day because 40 to 50 percent of the locomotives were not operating. The OP distributed only 22,000 bags of maize in July due to a lack of local transport.[1] Foreign-exchange reserves were sufficient for 4-1/2 months of average import expenditures, and economic indicators were positive, although revenue estimates for 1984/85 were reduced by 30 percent due to the drought. Commercial maize imports required the revision of the budget. Tea production in January to July was over 10 percent below 1983 levels, although good short rains later in 1984 resulted in an average 1984 crop. Immature and less drought-resistant bushes of smallholders were most affected. Tea factories worked fewer days, while one in Kiambu almost closed. The coffee crop for 1984/85 was estimated at 1.1 million bags, about half of the 1983/84 crop, but carryover from the previous year was sufficient to meet the International Coffee Organization (ICO) quota for Kenya. The price support level was exceeded in July, resulting in free pricing and higher coffee revenues.[3]

Appendix 2.1 Continued

Time	Events
July continued	Hoarding and black marketing were alleged: forty-three trucks of maize were unaccounted for from one NCPB depot. Parliament questioned earlier exports of beans.[3] The Kenya Power and Lighting Co. (KP&L) assured consumers that electricity would not be affected and rates would not increase.[3] From March to November, there was little public political involvement in relief planning, identifying the needy, or establishing guidelines. There was little news-media coverage of the drought except for official announcements of GOK officers.[3] The UNESCO report on drought in Eastern and Northeastern provinces noted up to 80 percent mortality of livestock, except for camels. The northern Rift Valley was also suffering losses.[8] USAID/Kenya alerted Washington of the drought situation. The USAID administrator visited Kenya and pledged assistance, in context of implementing grain market reforms. The visit was scheduled before the drought, but it ensured a timely response by USAID.[6] UNICEF began its emergency program of $770,000, including a donation of ten trucks to the School Feeding Programme in July.[1] Oxfam began the grain-for-livestock program, following a pilot scheme in May. Extremely weak cattle were exchanged for 45 kg of maize from the WFP. Meat was dried locally.[1] The KNCSS and NGOs endured an awkward period, with little information from the government and the lack of help in procuring food relief.[1]
August	Guidelines were sent to the district administration for identifying the needy and organizing food relief. The district administration identified 1.1 million needy people, 70 percent of whom were in Machakos, Kitui, Meru and Embu.[1,10] The FAO Multilateral Mission assessed the GOK request for food aid from 9 to 25 August. The long rains maize crop was estimated to be 1.25 million mt (62 percent of the five-year average); bean production was gauged at half of normal in the Rift Valley, Central and Eastern provinces; and prices were two to three times the norm. Food assistance was recommended.[9] The USAID/Kenya Food for Peace Officer prepared a report on food requirements and agencies involved. The document was given a limited circulation, but it exceeded any comprehensive assessments provided by the GOK. The report highlighted the government approach: "Planning, not Panic" and "Food Imports/Employment Generation." It noted the drought impacts and potential problems in defining rations, food-for-work proposals, coordination, funding transport, logistics, and rehabilitation. The situation in Eastern Province was judged desperate for 700,000 to 800,000 people.[10] The Nutrition CRSP project in Embu estimated that 30 percent of the population in the study area as severely affected and 30 percent moderately affected. Three hundred households had no food. Data were regularly sent to the government to encourage a rapid response.[10] USAID commitments for September to December totaled $16 million and comprised 54,000 mt maize, 77,000 mt wheat, and some beans and milk. Most was scheduled to arrive in October and November.[10] The Kenya Meat Commission worked two shifts and slaughtered 20,000 cattle per month at Athi River and 3,000 per month at Mombasa, compared to an average of 7,000 per month at both plants in normal years. The average liveweight was 80 kg, compared to 130 kg for a normal animal. Prices were as low as Ksh 1.45 per kg liveweight.[1]

60 • COPING WITH DROUGHT IN KENYA

Appendix 2.1 Continued

Time	Events
August continued	The Kenya Cooperative Creameries milk intake was 400,000 liters per day, half of normal. Milk powder stocks were 900 mt (about six weeks of supply, including expected liquid sales), due to the drawdown since March. School milk and UHT processing stopped in May. Commercial and WFP shipments were expected in September and October.[10]
	The USAID/Office of Foreign Disaster Assistance approved $6 million to transport food aid in Africa. CARE coordinated the Kenya funds for twenty-five NGOs. UNICEF helped rehabilitate and operate trucks.[6]
	The WFP emergency projects to expand the School Feeding Programme, Turkana Rehabilitaiton Project, support the dairy industry, and provide assistance to NGOs were approved. Other NGOs also began or accelerated activities.[1]
	The Director of Planning chaired two meetings (one with donors and one with NGOs) regarding the organization of food relief operations.[1]
September	From June to September, about 10 percent of the needy people received food aid (about 2,000 mt per day) through the OP.[11] District lists of needy people totaled 1.6 million.[11] Fourteen NCPB depots were low or without food, but expected to be supplied by the end of September.[1] The president reported the famine relief fund totaled over $1 million.[3]
	The CBS crop forecasts for the 1984 long rains yielded initial projections from interviews in July. Confirmation of the projections was included in the November surveys of area planted in the 1984 short rains.
	The GOK contracted with the Kenya Transport Association to transport 1,600 to 2,000 mt of grains per day from Mombasa to NCPB depots.[7] Consumer maize prices were increased (more than producer prices) to defray increased transport costs.[1]
	Proposals for rural works projects were submitted by fifteen districts and Authority to Incur Expenditures issued by the end of September. Reduced targets, due to a limited supervisory capacity, were three projects per district per ministry (Agriculture, Environment and Natural Resources, Livestock, Transport, Works) and three months of work, resulting in assistance for 25,000 people. Preexisting proposals with 75 percent labor costs were given priority. DANIDA donated Ksh 25 million to the Rural Development Fund for tools and materials to assist the program. Not yet decided was how laborers would be paid (cash, vouchers, or food).[1]
	Stock losses (including sales) in Baringo between January and September 1984 were: cattle (49 percent); sheep (52 percent); and goats (47 percent).[1]
	USAID approved $11 million for the relief program, with deliveries scheduled for October to December. Approval of an additional $60 million was expected soon, making the U.S. contribution one third of the import requirements.[1]
	The GOK prohibited maize sales to CPC Industrial Products, the supplier of 90 percent of Kenya's industrial starch and all of its glucose, with an annual maize requirement of 0.4 percent of an average harvest. CPC laid off two hundred workers as a result.[1]
	The KNCSS, with help from UNICEF and WFP, adopted a more focused approach, including weekly appointments with OP officials and single-purpose meetings. As WFP food became available, NGOs cooperated more fully.[1] The School Feeding Programme was expanded with assistance from the WFP to Machakos, Kitui, Meru, and Embu (147,000 children).
	AMREF began food distribution in Narok and Kajiado; in November, it began to distribute food in Kibwezi.[1]

Appendix 2.1 Continued

Time	Events
September continued	The first maize (commercial) shipment from Thailand arrived, and 4,600 mt per day were unloaded. Dock workers pledged to ensure prompt grain handling. Subsequently, the port often operated at more than design capacity.[7] Initial distribution of the imported maize was delayed in NCPB stores for almost a month while the OP and district administration arranged for transport to distribution centers.[1] Closing stocks of maize in the first week of October were 96,000 mt, about three weeks of national consumption requirements.[12]

Implementation

October	The short rains began early and were above average in most of Kenya.[3] The first emergency wheat supplies began to arrive.[3] Flour shortages caused Elliott's Bakeries to close for a few days. Unga Ltd. was unable to procure its wheat requirements of 1,000 mt per day. These two incidents illustrated the low food stocks and narrow margin between shipments and deliveries. Wheat producer prices were increased 29 percent to boost production in the next season.[3] Approximately 114,000 mt of free food was distributed by the OP between October 1984 and November 1985, but substantial distribution only began in December.[1] UNICEF distributed 210 mt of seed in Machakos and Kitui in October and November. Many other NGOs were unable to purchase enough seed in the 1984 short rains and 1985 long rains for effective assistance in recovering from the drought.[1]
November December	Wheat donated by Australia, originally destined for Uganda, arrived.[3] The president's Jamhuri Day speech noted the current food situation: 290,000 mt of maize had been imported (90 percent commercial) and 110,000 mt of wheat (45 percent commercial) since August; 2,000 mt of beans and 1,800 mt milk powder were imported as food aid. Additional imports of 260,000 mt of food were planned.[3] Commercial imports were estimated to cost the GOK $80 to 120 million since July. Distribution through commercial markets was admired by donors, although distribution troubles in Northeastern and Eastern provinces and the pastoral areas were noted.[3] The KP&L spent K£ 5 million to generate electricity in 1984 due to the increased use of fuel oil. While demand (units sold) increased by almost 6 percent, expenditure on fuel oil was 65 percent higher than in 1983. Profits for KP&L were less than half of those in 1983, but the company paid a dividend.[13] An additional K£ 8 million would have been spent if the short rains had failed, and rationing may have been required.[3]
1985 January	Over 1.2 million people were eligible for relief.[11] Donors had pledged a total of 364,000 mt of food aid.[3] The CBS crop surveys for area planted in the 1984 short rains and confirmation of the 1984 long rains harvest were reported—somewhat late due to problems in conducting the survey, including the switch to a new sample frame. The GOK increased producer prices: maize, 12 percent; wheat, 9 percent; and milk, 11 percent. K£ 13 million credit was reserved for the long rains season. Fertilizer supplies and distribution were inadequate, but improvements were promised, as over 190,000 mt were imported. Consumer prices were also raised, but less than producer prices.[3]

Appendix 2.1 Continued

Time	Event
February	Purchase of food aid from the US CCC (120,000 mt) was agreed upon: 40,000 mt were to be sold to millers to pay for transport and distribution costs, along with $3 million granted for the remainder of the handling costs.[3]
	The WFP estimated 30,000 mt of cereals and 4,500 mt of supplementary foods were needed for the most vulnerable groups; 60,000 mt of cereals were needed for food-for-work projects; and 220,000 mt were required for normal consumption. World commodity prices were high in 1984, resulting in a 42 percent increase (over 1983) in the value of marketed agricultural production in Kenya.[3]
April	835,800 people were identified as eligible for famine relief.[11]
Recovery	
May	The Cove Trader shipment of 40,000 mt of yellow maize from the United States was rejected by the GOK due to fragmented grains. The ship was too large to dock at Mombasa and was first off-loaded onto smaller ships, resulting in a higher percentage of broken grains. The large stocks of yellow maize, well beyond needs, were also a factor in the rejection. The maize was sold on the international market after attempts failed to have it sent to other drought-stricken countries.[1,4]
June	The 1985 long rains were about average, and the drought emergency was considered over, although food aid was required during the recovery phase and until the next harvest.[3]
	Rehabilitation programs were not well defined, and there were no plans to hand over food-aid projects to development agencies.[7]
August	Over 530,000 people were eligible for food relief.[11]
October	319,000 were eligible for food aid.[11]
	Grain import requirements were normal and foreign exchange reserves sufficient for three months of average imports. Wheat production was estimated at 144 percent of the 1984 crop, and wheat import requirements were 47 percent less than in 1984.[3]

Notes and Sources: Adapted from Downing, Berry et al. (1987). Original sources are:
[1]Borton (1987)
[2]Kliest (1985)
[3]Economist Intelligence Unit (1984, 1985, 1986)
[4]Ray (personal communication in 1987)
[5]Kenya Meteorological Department (personal communication in 1987)—see also chapters 1 and 3
[6]Interviews by Jeanne Downing with USAID, U.S. State Department and UN officials in 1987
[7]Cohen and Lewis (1987)
[8]Field and Njiru (1985)
[9]FAO (1984a)
[10]Ray (1984)
[11]Deloitte, Haskins and Sells Management Consultants (1985)
[12]Assuming 0.25 kg per person per day requirements and a population of 19 million, 96,000 mt would last twenty days. This does not include stocks held by intermediary traders and consumers.
[13]Kenya Power and Lighting Co. (1985).

OVERVIEW OF THE 1984/85 DROUGHT • 63

Appendix 2.2 Estimated Production, Stocks, Trade, and Use of Maize

	July-Dec. 1984	Jan.-Mar. 1985	April-June 1985	1984/85 Total	July-Sept. 1985	Oct.-Dec. 1985	Jan.-Mar. 1986	April-June 1986	1985/86 Total
Supply									
Beginning stocks	545.5	687.4	1,032.3	545.5	641.9	862.1	1,445.7	1,549.7	641.9
Domestic production[1]	900.0	795.0	30.0	1,725.0	770.0	1,240.0	720.0	20.0	2,750.0
Commercial imports[2]	289.0	102.4	107.2	498.6	0.0	0.0	0.0	0.0	0.0
Food aid[2]	33.1	54.2	25.2	112.5	0.0	0.0	0.0	0.0	0.0
Total supply	1,767.6	1,639.0	1,194.7	2,881.6	1,411.9	2,102.1	2,165.7	1,569.7	3,391.9
Utilization									
Exports	0.0	0.0	0.0	0.0	0.0	0.0	0.0	39.6	39.6
Seed use[1]	13.0	28.0	8.3	49.3	0.0	17.0	28.0	8.3	53.3
Feed and waste[3]	93.7	55.1	15.6	164.4	46.0	69.5	43.5	8.5	167.5
Food total	973.5	523.6	528.9	2026.0	503.8	569.8	544.6	550.0	2,168.3
Per capita (kg)	50.0	26.5	26.5	103.0	25.0	28.0	26.5	26.5	106.0
Total utilization	1,080.2	606.7	552.8	2,239.7	549.8	656.3	616.1	606.4	2,428.7
Ending stocks[4]									
NCPB	295.4	466.7	474.3	474.3	388.0	586.5	859.6	769.7	769.7
Private	392.0	565.6	167.6	167.6	474.1	859.4	690.1	193.6	193.6
Total private stocks	687.4	1,032.3	641.9	641.9	862.1	1,445.7	1,549.7	963.2	963.2
Consumption deficit[5]									
mt	63.6	0.0	0.0	63.6	0.0	0.0	0.0	0.0	0.0
Percentage of normal	93.9	100.0	100.0	97.0	100.0	100.0	100.0	100.0	100.0
Population (thousands)	19,463.0	19,760.0	19,958.0	19,661.0	20,154.0	20,350.0	20,550.0	20,756.0	20,450.0

Source: USAID (1987).

Notes:

[1] USAID/Agr Econ estimates based on MALD, CBS, FAO, and USDA databases, agroclimatic and market price analyses as well as regular and periodic field trips.

[2] Source: NCPB, USDA, and USAID/FFP.

[3] Feed is estimated to be 2,500 mt/month and waste 5 percent of supply attributed as the maize enters the system.

[4] Source: NCPB stock reports through 23 August 1985. Private stock is calculated as a residual. The model employed assumes a minimum pipeline of 90,000 mt for NCPB and 75,000 mt for the private sector.

[5] Deficit is calculated as population estimate multiplied by the moving average monthly consumption rates minus the available food supply. Expected consumption rates are: July-Sept. 25 kg, Oct.-Dec. 28 kg, Jan.-June 26.5 kg.

Appendix 2.3 Estimated Production, Stocks, Trade, and Use of Wheat

	July-Dec. 1984	Jan.-Mar. 1985	April-June 1985	1984/85 Total	July-Sept. 1985	Oct.-Dec. 1985	Jan.-Mar. 1986	April-June 1986	1985/86 Total
Supply									
Beginning stocks	100.0	80.8	78.5	100.0	32.5	99.6	208.1	156.8	32.5
Domestic production[1]	75.7	7.0	2.3	85.0	105.0	119.8	7.5	2.7	235.0
Commercial imports[2]	21.7	16.6	35.3	73.6	74.1	0.0	0.0	0.0	74.1
Food aid[2]	72.0	62.2	43.2	177.4	4.2	88.0	11.0	22.0	125.2
Total supply	269.4	166.6	159.3	436.0	215.8	307.4	226.6	181.5	466.8
Utilization									
Exports	0.0	0.0	0.0	0.0	0.0	0.0	0.0	0.0	0.0
Seed use[1]	2.0	0.0	7.0	9.0	0.0	1.0	0.0	7.2	8.2
Feed and waste[3]	10.0	5.1	4.8	20.0	11.0	12.5	1.1	1.5	26.1
Food total	176.6	83.0	114.9	374.5	105.2	85.8	68.8	89.3	349.0
Per capita (kg)	9.07	4.20	5.76	19.03	5.23	4.22	3.34	4.30	17.09
Total utilization	188.6	88.1	126.7	403.5	116.2	99.3	69.9	98.0	383.3
Ending stocks[4]									
NCPB	35.9	43.6	12.5	12.5	79.7	152.1	111.6	51.8	51.8
Private	44.9	34.9	20.0	20.0	19.9	56.0	45.2	31.8	31.8
Total private stocks	80.8	78.5	32.5	32.5	99.6	208.1	156.8	83.6	83.6
Consumption deficit[5]									
mt	-1.5	-7.9	23.1	13.7	12.5	-7.8	-28.1	-8.6	-32.0
Percentage of normal	98.9	91.4	125.2	103.5	110.8	89.5	71.0	91.3	90.6
Minimum stock surplus/deficit	-4.2	-6.5	-52.5	-52.5	14.6	123.1	71.8	-1.4	-1.4
Population (thousands)	19,463.0	19,760.0	19,958.0	19,612.0	20,154.0	20,340.0	20,550.0	20,756.0	20,450.0

Source: USAID (1987).

Notes:

[1] USAID/Agr Econ estimates based on MALD, CBS, FAO, and USDA databases, agroclimatic and market price analyses as well as regular and periodic field trips.

[2] Source: NCPB, USDA, USAID/FFP.

[3] Feed by-product is estimated to be 1 percent, waste is estimated to be 5 percent of supply attributed as wheat enters the system.

[4] Source: NCPB stock reports through November 1986. Private stock is calculated as a residual. The model employed assumes a minimum pipeline of 20,000 mt for the private sector.

[5] Consumption deficit is calculated as population estimate multiplied by the monthly average consumption rate of 1.533 kg/capita in 1985 and 1.5713 kg/capita in 1986.

·PART 2·
Drought Forecasting and Monitoring

In Kenya, five separate groups have developed aspects of a food-monitoring system. The urgent need is for increased cooperation, including field comparisons and validation of the different methods, and a strategy to monitor household food security and national food flows, both as ongoing efforts and in preparedness for drought emergencies. Each system described in the following chapters requires further testing and development to establish its reliability.

The Department of Meteorology collects and analyzes rainfall and agrometeorological data (Chapter 3). Although it has a dense network of stations, relatively few report on a timely basis that is useful for operational monitoring. Research on synoptic systems, teleconnections, and circulation dynamics is promising, but it has not led, as yet, to significant improvements in forecasts. The 1984 drought is clearly a random, unique episode in the region. Unlike western Africa, rainfall in Kenya does not show a long-term downward trend (Chapter 4).

The Department of Resource Surveys and Remote Sensing (formerly the Kenya Rangeland Ecological Monitoring Unit [KREMU]) has demonstrated the utility of aerial surveys to monitor maize yields and areas planted (Chapter 5). These surveys are instrumental in research (as a systematic check on ground-based estimates) and during drought crises.

The Central Bureau of Statistics (CBS) maintains a large field staff to carry out a variety of rural surveys, including crop production, household budgets, and nutritional assessments (Chapter 6). They have the greatest potential to provide accurate data, drawn from a representative sample, concerning household food security and its many determinants. At the moment, their methods are based on farmer responses, rather than measurements, and are biased toward smallholders, rather than systematic national coverage. The pastoral areas are excluded. A recent survey, however, has shown farmer responses at the time of harvest to be fairly accurate estimates of actual production. A project to synthesize food-security information within the government was initiated by the CBS in the early 1980s. It developed data-processing methods, analyzed background information on food security, and produced a pilot monthly bulletin on the food situation.

The Ministry of Agriculture maintains the largest field staff of any government agency. As such, it is able to monitor crop production in any part of the country through the hierarchy of the district administration (Chapter 7). While the ministry compiles food production reports, the methods are not documented and have not been validated against other field surveys. Detailed results are often not available.

The National Cereals and Produce Board (NCPB), the central marketing agency, provides valuable data on food flows, particularly purchases, stocks, and sales (Chapter 8). As in the CBS surveys, the NCPB field assessments of crop yields, based on sample crop measurements, tend to be compiled rather late in the season. They are useful as a check against earlier indicators.

In 1984, little of the potential crop-monitoring information was used. In June, the initial response to the drought was based on weather reports, informal observations, and visual indicators of crop failure provided by the Ministry of Agriculture. The CBS, KREMU, and NCPB data were not available until August or later—after commercial food shipments had begun to arrive. The monitoring system did not produce an early assessment of the abundant short rains, which might have alerted the government of the excess stocks of yellow maize.

The nascent effort within the CBS to synthesize information on food security has not been entirely successful. The monthly bulletin was not officially approved, and it is no longer being produced. The difficulty of developing a reliable and timely early warning system in Kenya raises questions about the demand for data on food security. It appears that no one institution has clear responsibility for monitoring food security on a routine basis; there is not a consistent demand for information on household food security. At the national level, only very general information on food production, consumption, and stocks is required in most years to gauge levels of imports and exports. This is the concern of the NCPB. The Ministry of Agriculture and CBS monitor production and prices, more as routine surveys than as a concerted effort to identify households or groups vulnerable to hunger. Rural households are expected to care for themselves in all but the most extreme situations.

This book does not propose specific improvements in Kenya's food-monitoring system. Three general models exist and would be useful to consider in developing more integrated assessments in Kenya:

1. The current situation is characterized by multiple agencies and independent surveys. Results can be collected during a food crisis, but the surveys otherwise operate within the goals and limitations of their host agencies. The advantage of such an approach lies in the strength of independent collaboration of an emerging crisis and the ability to make use of flexible administrative capabilities. During a food crisis, ad hoc committees can be operationalized to coordinate data and responses. A detailed preparedness plan would formalize this approach and reduce some of the confusion and delays experienced in 1984.

2. The Tanzania model (summarized in Chapter 9) typifies the aims of the CBS food-monitoring project. This approach requires the local monitoring of an integrated food balance, including supply (often utilizing meteorological information as an early indicator), demand, and prices, all collected in one place for systematic comparison with time series, other locales, and as national aggregates. While this yields the most thorough assessment of household and national food security, it requires considerable data and analytical skills and the cooperation of the several agencies generating the constituent parts of the system (meteorological, agricultural, livestock, health, water, and economic indicators).

3. An entitlement approach divides the information requirements into two streams. Monitoring the commercial food sector (national purchases, sales, and stocks) would assist national planners in scheduling imports, exports, and an adequate strategic reserve. At the local level, monitoring would focus on food entitlement by identifying vulnerable groups and their sources of food. This would involve indicators of prices, wages, and income, in addition to on-farm production. An open-market system would encourage private trade to make up most of the local food-supply deficits and to reduce the burden on the government of scheduling interdistrict trade.

Improvement in the current monitoring capabilities are justified to monitor droughts or food crises that might not be apparent from the current, coarse resolution systems because they occur in small areas or reflect a complex of factors, such as a poor distribution of rainfall during the season, pest infestation, and price inflation; and to facilitate targeting food interventions for groups vulnerable to either chronic hunger or during a severe drought. In the context of anticipated global climate changes due to greenhouse gases, it is ever more important that national weather and agricultural forecasting and monitoring efforts be improved. The value of timely and reliable information, in preventing hunger and famine, planning agricultural imports and exports, and ameliorating the worst social and economic effects of variations in climate, agriculture, and the economy is likely to outweigh the cost.

No early warning system is guaranteed to succeed. Perhaps more effort should be focused on early response systems—identifying the range of appropriate actions at national and local levels, the required information, and the responsible agencies.

· 3 ·

Synoptic Features Associated with the Failure of the 1984 Long Rains in Kenya

MICHAEL W. MACODRAS
PHILIP N. NTHUSI
JOHN MWIKYA

Most of Kenya experiences two rainy seasons a year, which generally occur from March to May (long rainy season) and October to December (short rainy season). The rains are associated with the northward and southward movement of the Intertropical Convergence Zone (ITCZ). The intensity and location of the ITCZ in this region is controlled by the Azores and Arabian highs in the Northern Hemisphere and by the Atlantic and Mascarene highs in the Southern Hemisphere (Anyamba and Ogallo 1984, Ogallo and Okoola 1985, Agumba 1984, Ogallo and Anyamba 1985).

In 1984, Kenya experienced widespread failure of the long rains (Kinuthia et al. 1984). Dry conditions were not confined to Kenya, but were experienced in other African countries, suggesting large-scale atmospheric anomalies during this period. This chapter investigates the anomalous climatological situation of 1984. Graphical representation, coupled with surface synoptic and upper-air charts, are displayed to facilitate understanding of the meteorological situation. The following section first describes the rainfall-monitoring activities of the Kenya Meteorological Department (KMD).

RAINFALL MONITORING

The Kenya Meteorological Department supports a well-developed network of rainfall and meteorological stations. As of 1984, over 1,800 stations were recording daily rainfall on cards provided by the KMD. About half of the stations regularly reported to Nairobi at the end of each month. As such, the data may be useful for historical purposes, but are not available for timely monitoring unless a special request is made. There were thirty-two synoptic stations reporting daily, if not hourly, data that are more useful for monitoring. Of the synoptic stations, thirteen report agrometeorological information. Data from the synoptic stations are summarized every ten days in the *Decadal Crop and Weather Review*, and as many as

900 stations with monthly reports are included in the monthly *Farming Weather*.

In addition to decadal and monthly monitoring, the KMD forecasts seasonal rainfall, usually two months before the season begins. Analogue and trend analyses are utilized in a qualitative fashion (Okoola 1986). Beginning during the short rains of 1983, a map of the expected seasonal rainfall departures from normal was prepared. The 1984 maps were circulated within the government. The February forecast for the 1984 long rains noted the weak ITCZ and its lack of progression, which would likely result in delayed and below-normal long rains.

During the 1984 drought, the KMD prepared cumulative seasonal rainfall maps that were included in briefings prepared by the Ministry of Agriculture and distributed to the interministerial Task Force on Food Supply and Distribution.

MAJOR SYNOPTIC FEATURES INFLUENCING PRECIPITATION IN KENYA

Many studies have been conducted to determine the major synoptic features influencing precipitation in Africa (Kidson 1977, Kanamitsu and Krishnamurti 1978, Newell et al. 1984, Nicholson 1981b). In East Africa, studies have related the weather to the large-scale atmospheric circulation (Agumba 1984, Ogallo and Okoola 1985, Ogallo and Anyamba 1985, Ogallo 1987). Some of the major synoptic features that influence the weather in this region include the Intertropical Convergence Zone, easterly waves, tropical storms, low-level troughs, jet streams, and extratropical weather systems (Ogallo and Anyamba 1985).

In sub-Saharan Africa, Kidson (1977) and Kanamitsu and Krishnamurti (1978) found that drought years were accompanied by increased subsidence and decreased low-level convergence over sub-Saharan Africa, decreased moisture flux, and reduced upper-level easterly flows into the region. In East Africa, anomalies in the wind field were related to the abnormally wet conditions of 1961 and abnormally dry 1984 (Anyamba and Ogallo 1984). Agumba's (1984) study of the fluctuations of the long rains in Kenya in relation to the large-scale circulation noted that the long rainy season in Kenya seems to depend greatly on moisture advection encouraged by circulation systems in the Indian Ocean and Central Africa, as well as convective processes brought about by the ITCZ and unstable conditions from the west.

The two rainy seasons in Kenya (March to April and October to December) are controlled by the northward and southward movement of the sun. The area of greatest heating and the lowest pressure occurs where the sun is approximately overhead, and is known as the Intertropical Convergence

Zone. The movement of the ITCZ follows the sun, but normally lags four to six weeks behind the time of the sun's maximum elevation. A narrowing of the breadth of the ITCZ shortens the wet season at any particular point. Likewise, if the ITCZ is delayed, it passes over Kenya more rapidly, resulting in a shorter, drier season.

The sun is approximately overhead in Kenya at the end of March; the ITCZ is expected to be most effective about a month later (April/May), during the long rainy season. At these times, the pressure is high in the subtropical latitudes of the Sahara and South Africa, and there is a general movement of air mass from the high-pressure belts toward the trough of low pressure in the equatorial region. This may result in organized southeasterly and northeasterly winds meeting in a zone of convergence, or, more often, winds that are not well organized converging locally. Both types of convergences result in the vertical upward motion of the air, leading to condensation and precipitation. There are frequently considerable jumps, however, in the position of the rain belt and hence large day-to-day variations in the amounts and distribution of rain caused by changes in the area of convergence.

The seasonal rainfall patterns dependent on the ITCZ are usually modified by anomalies in the semipermanent anticyclones (Azores, Mascarene, and the South East Atlantic highs). Abnormal development of tropical storms may introduce such anomalies. Tropical cyclones typically occur from November to April in the southern Indian Ocean. These rarely come within 10 degrees of the equator, and the tracks normally curve southward in the area of Mauritius and Madagascar. As such, East Africa is seldom directly affected. The anomaly in 1984, with cyclones persisting late in the long rains close to the equator, is discussed below.

RAINFALL IN 1984 COMPARED TO NORMAL

The normal distribution of rainfall for the long and short rainy seasons is discussed in Chapter 1 (Figure 1.4). Average rainfall during the long rains of March to May is 100 to 400 mm for most parts of the country; western and coastal areas usually receive over 600 mm of rainfall. Maximum precipitation during the short rains is 400 mm, with most agricultural areas receiving 200 to 400 mm.

During the 1984 long rains, a severe meteorological drought (rainfall below the climatological normal) existed in most of Kenya. The meteorological drought actually began in much of eastern and northern Kenya with the short rains of 1983 (see Figure 1.5). Rainfall was below average in almost all parts of Kenya during the long rains of 1984. The deviation from the long-term rainfall mean exceeded 60 percent in a number of stations (Figure 3.1). The areas most affected by the low rainfall were the dryland agricultural areas of Eastern, Central, and Rift Valley provinces. Most of the highlands west of the Rift Valley and near Lake Victoria received adequate or almost normal rainfall, partly due to the influence of Lake Victoria as a moisture source and occasional influxes of the Congo air mass. Stations within this area generally reported lower-than-average amounts of precipitation, yet rainfall was within 0.5 standard deviations from the mean. The meteorological drought ended with the 1984 short rains, which were unusually wet and widespread (Figure 1.5). The following 1985 long rains were also abundant.

The areas that suffered the most from drought are those that depend on the Indian Ocean as their primary moisture source. In order to explain the rainfall in Kenya during March to May 1984, therefore, it is necessary to recognize the synoptic disturbances that caused reduced precipitation over this region.

PRESSURE PATTERNS AND TROPICAL CYCLONES IN 1984

This section documents the pressure patterns and tropical cyclone tracks of 1984 compared to selected dry and wet years. Data were obtained from the National Meteorological Centre, Climatological Section, and the Library of the Meteorological Department. Daily pressure values in hPa over 8 grid points were averaged to compute the areal pressure average for the southwest Indian Ocean. The grid points included both island stations and ship reports. Where data were missing, the values were interpolated from the pressure analysis.

1984 Pressure Patterns over the Indian Ocean

By the beginning of the first week of April 1984, the features in the Southern Hemisphere were fairly well organized (Figure 3.2). In particular, the ridge over the Mozambique Channel had a central value of 1,026 hPa from 1–5 April and extended up to 5 deg S of the equator. By the second week of April, however, very weak pressure patterns dominated the southwest Indian Ocean due to the formation of tropical cyclone Kamisy on 5 April. This cyclone steered to the east, resulting in the collapse of the East African ridge.

By 22 April, the ridge through the Mozambique Channel was reestablished with a central pressure of 1,030 hPa and extending up to 4 deg N. This situation was more or less maintained for the rest of the month.

During 1984, the areal pressure means were low, averaging about 1,012 hPa during the first half of April (Figure 3.2). Between 16 and 17 April, the value surged upward to an average of about 1,016.5 hPa, indicating a strong build up that could have led to a swift migration of the ITCZ through Kenya, resulting in the failure of the long rains.

Although the Arabian ridge was a weak feature during April 1984, it generated an easterly to northeasterly flow during the second week of April (Figures 3.3 to 3.5). However, by the beginning of the second week (8 April), the ridge collapsed, forming a belt of weakness that linked the dynamic trough and the low-pressure system over the Indian subcontinent. This situation was maintained for the rest of the month, with an exception occurring at the beginning of the fourth week (22 to 23 April).

Though pressure values in the Northern Hemisphere (Arabia) were not studied, they would provide a more detailed picture of the north-south pressure gradient.

During 1982, which can be regarded as a normal year, pressure values in the southwest Indian Ocean behaved differently compared to 1984. Low values dominated during April and May; the average pressure over the two months was about 1,013 hPa. This indicates the ITCZ remained in East Africa with few fluctuations, resulting in good rains in 1982.

In 1982, vertical wind studies show that, despite the low pressure values, the presence of deep westerlies could also have contributed to moisture influx. The periods of deep westerlies were 3 to 7 April and 11 to 17 April 1982, based on data from the Nairobi synoptic station.

Pressure Patterns Over the South Atlantic

The pressure patterns over the South Atlantic were generally weak, owing to the formation of deep low-pressure and frontal systems (Figure 3.2). Consequently, the ridge emanating from the quasi-permanent anticyclone over the South Atlantic was, on the whole, weak from 1 to 7 April 1984, with a central pressure of 1,022 hPa. However, from 8 April on, there was a remarkable increase in pressure that reached 1,032 hPa by 17 April. For the remainder of the month, the central pressure of the anticyclones fluctuated between 1,026 and 1,024 hPa.

Tropical Cyclones in Selected Years

Tropical cyclone tracks have been investigated since 1941, with emphasis on the last tropical cyclones in each season. The dry years of 1974, 1976, and 1984 were highlighted and compared to several wet years, including 1969. A few days, 10 to 12 April 1984, were chosen for streamline analysis.

In 1969, eight tropical cyclones were formed. The last cyclone (Helene) and one formed during March were located at 9 deg S and 72 deg E by 18 March (Figure 3.6). Helene steered to the west and curved southward by 22 March to avoid Madagascar. It lasted nine days.

Eight tropical cyclones were formed during the 1974 season. The tropical cyclone Honorine was formed on 12 April, lasting eleven days (Figure 3.7). It steered to the west and landed on the African mainland.

Eight tropical cyclones were also formed in 1976, another dry year.

Tropical cyclone Ello was formed on 9 March, decaying by 12 March at 10.5 deg S and 55 deg E. It had a direct hit over the African mainland. Gladys was formed on 27 March and steered to the west, hitting the African mainland (Figure 3.8). The last tropical cyclone formed on 3 April and filled by 12 April. It was formed at 9 deg S and 81 deg E, and lasted fourteen days.

In 1984, eleven tropical cyclones were formed, although there were no tropical cyclones during March. Tropical cyclone Kamisy was formed on 3 April and filled on 16 April. It steered to the west, passing through the Mozambique Channel and hitting Madagascar (Figure 3.9).

In 1985, a wet year, eight tropical cyclones were formed during the season, only one of which occurred during March, at 18 deg S and 60.5 deg E. It steered to the west, but missed Madagascar. The last tropical cyclone, Helisaonina, was formed on 10 April and filled by 18 April. It steered to the west, close to Madagascar, and lasted only six days.

Streamlines

Streamlines describe the direction of wind patterns for selected time periods. The streamlines of 10 to 12 April 1984 show tropical cyclone Kamisy as an area of convergence over Madagascar (Figure 3.10). There was a diffluent southwesterly and southeasterly flow pattern off the Indian Ocean coast that was feeding into the cyclone. Consequently, a moisture deficit existed over Kenya during this period, since the only other major air mass affecting the region was dry, from the northeast, and following a continental track. There was, however, some convergence between the Lake Victoria airflow and the southeasterlies over western Kenya during this period. The influence of Kamisy extended to higher altitudes (see the 200 hPa streamline analysis in Figure 3.10) and was maintained to the beginning of the third week of April. Although there was a fairly deep trough over the Mozambique Channel, the flow pattern over Kenya remained easterly with little indication of diffluence.

CONCLUSION

The drought during the 1984 long rains was related to a number of synoptic conditions. It is not possible to assign causality, although an understanding of the relationship between the general circulation and rainfall may assist in future forecasts.

In the first half of 1984, high-pressure cells in southern Africa were weaker than normal. For example, the average strength of the Mascarene high was about 1,030 hPa in April. During a normal year, a strong, well-defined ridge is seen in the south. In 1984, numerous and massive cold fronts with equatorward extensions passed over southern Africa and eroded the high-pressure cells.

Tropical cyclones during drought years tend to steer to the west and directly hit the African mainland, persisting longer than normal. For example, Kamisy persisted well into April, when, in a normal year, the ITCZ would have been established over Kenya.

The weak pressure systems in the south and the persistent cyclones delayed the northward progression of the ITCZ. The long rains in Kenya exhibit less variability in their termination than in their onset; a delayed ITCZ and delayed onset of the rains is associated with a shorter and drier long rain season.

The regional wind patterns were characterized by diffluent southeasterly flows along the coast, preventing inland advection of moisture from the Indian Ocean. The diffluent coastal winds prevailed through May. The other major air masses were continental from the northeast and limited incursions from Lake Victoria and the Congo basin. The upper levels of the atmosphere inhibited convective development, with an abnormal lack of diffluence aloft.

The occurrence of drought in Kenya depends on events in March and April in both hemispheres. The anomalies in 1984 suggest a reduction in the strength of the meridional circulation. The causes of the Southern Hemisphere oscillations and their relationships to the global general circulation are not clear, therefore warranting additional research.

The KMD, recognizing the need to accurately forecast and monitor seasonal rainfall, has promoted more extensive research, some of which was reported at the First Technical Conference on Meteorological Research in Eastern and Southern Africa (January 1987). In addition, the KMD plans to upgrade its synoptic and agrometeorological station network and to contribute to the development of more refined agrometeorological monitoring systems.

Figure 3.1 Percent of normal for February to June 1984 long rains. Sources: Kenya Meteorological Department (1984), Agumba (1984), and data from the KMD.

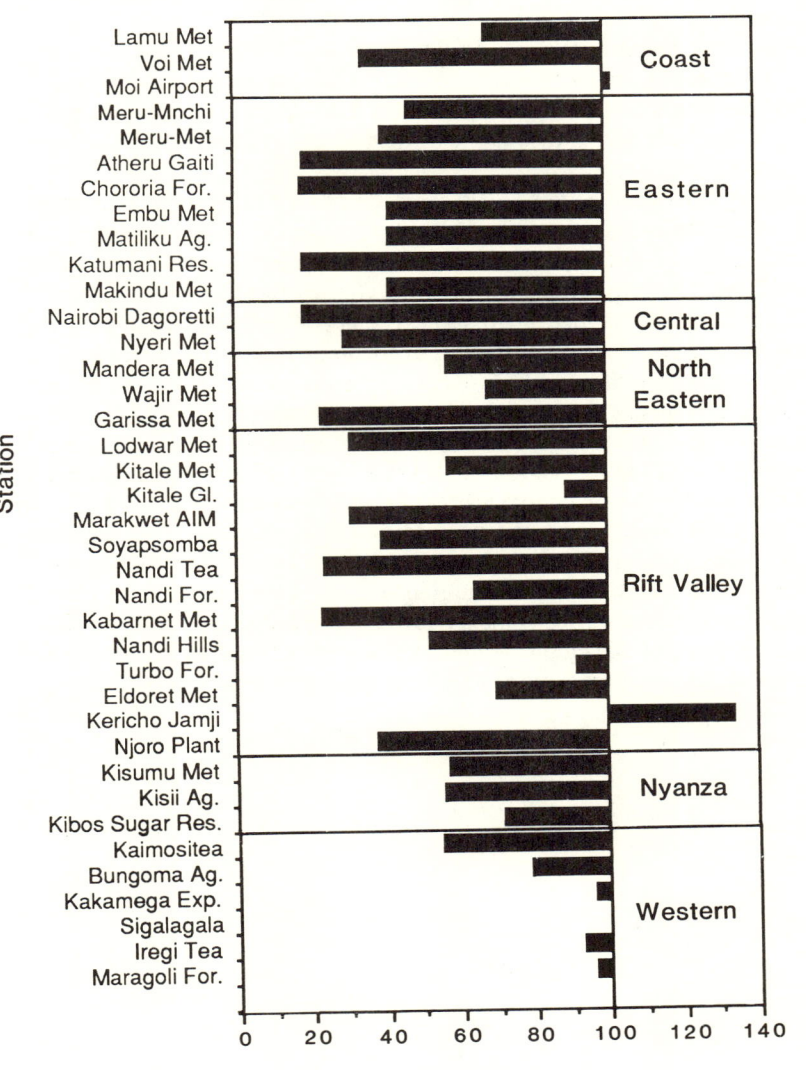

FORECASTING AND MONITORING • 77

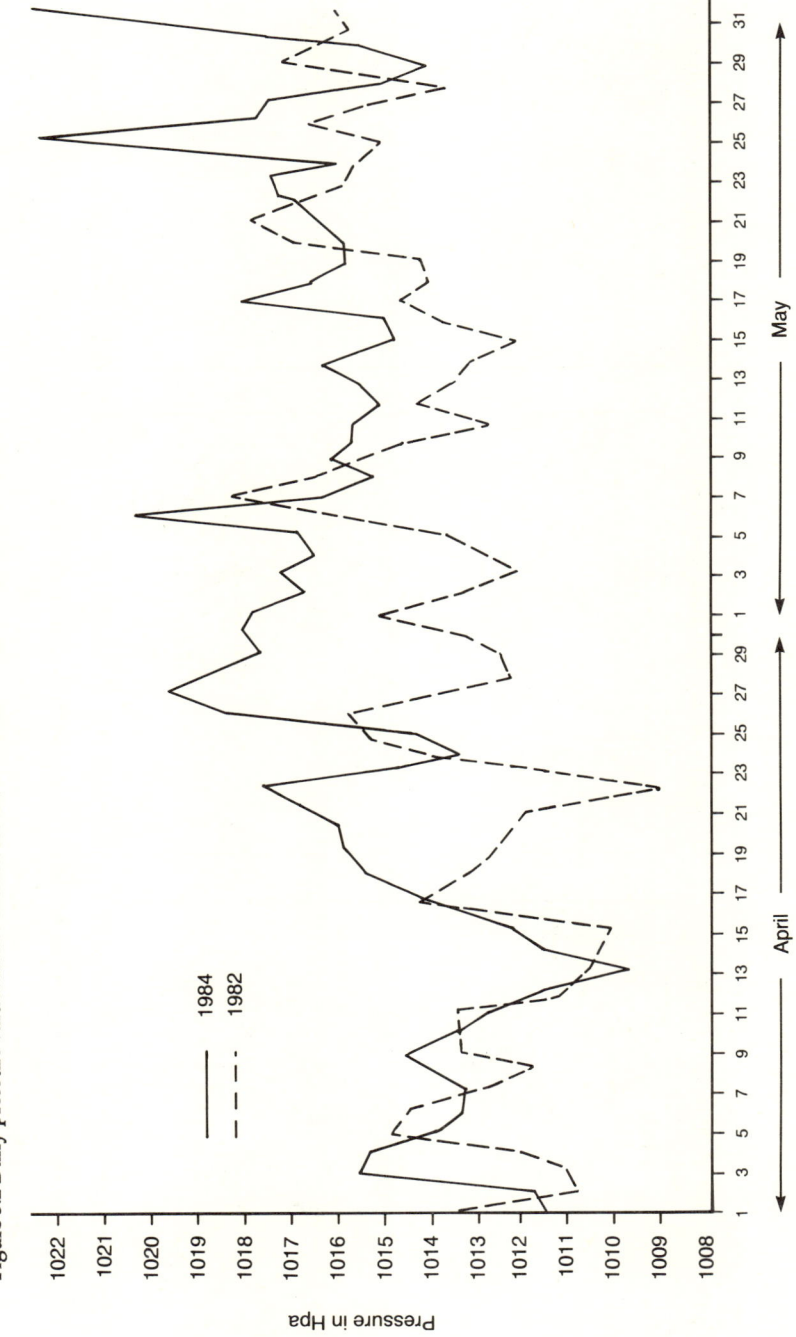

Figure 3.2 Daily pressure values in the southwest Indian Ocean. Source: Data from the KMD.

Figure 3.3 Surface winds on 10 April 1984.

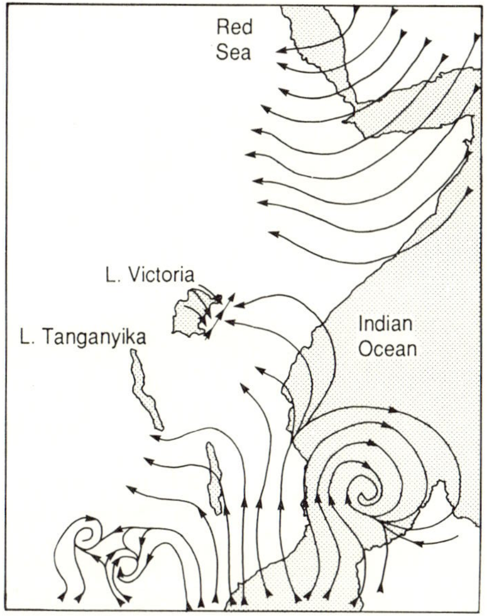

Figure 3.4 Surface winds on 11 April 1984.

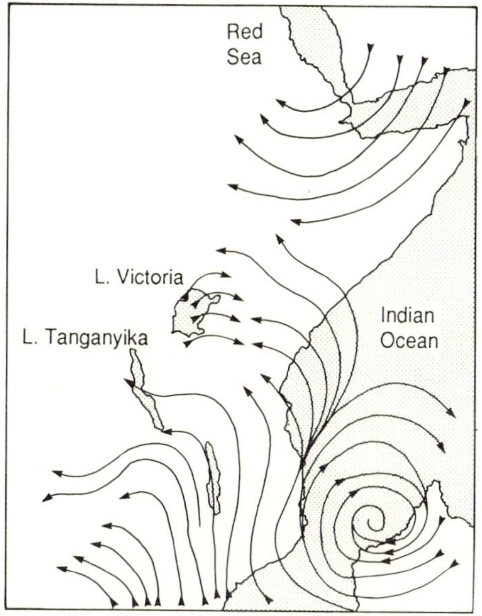

Figure 3.5 Surface winds on 12 April 1984.

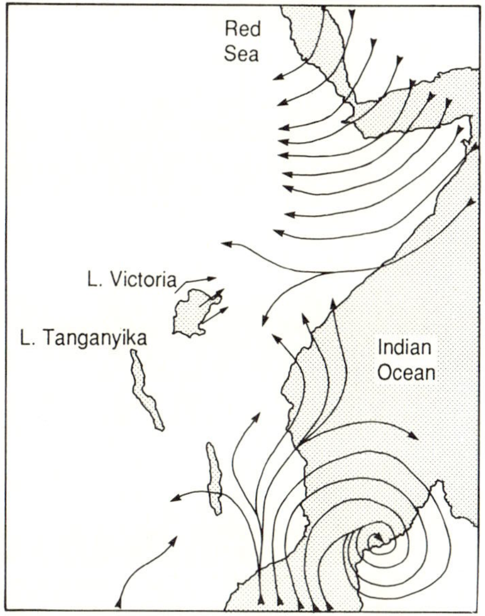

Measurement for Figures 3.3, 3.4, 3.5 and 3.10 is at noon (1200Z). Source: Data from the KMD.

FORECASTING AND MONITORING • 79

Figure 3.6 Tropical cyclone Helene. Source: Data from the KMD.

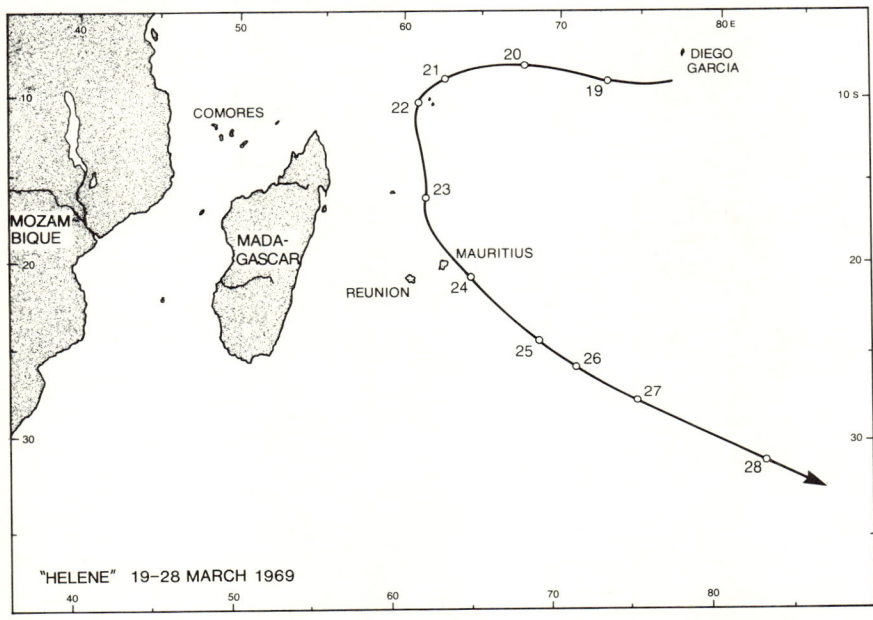

Figure 3.7 Tropical cyclone Honorine. Source: Data from the KMD.

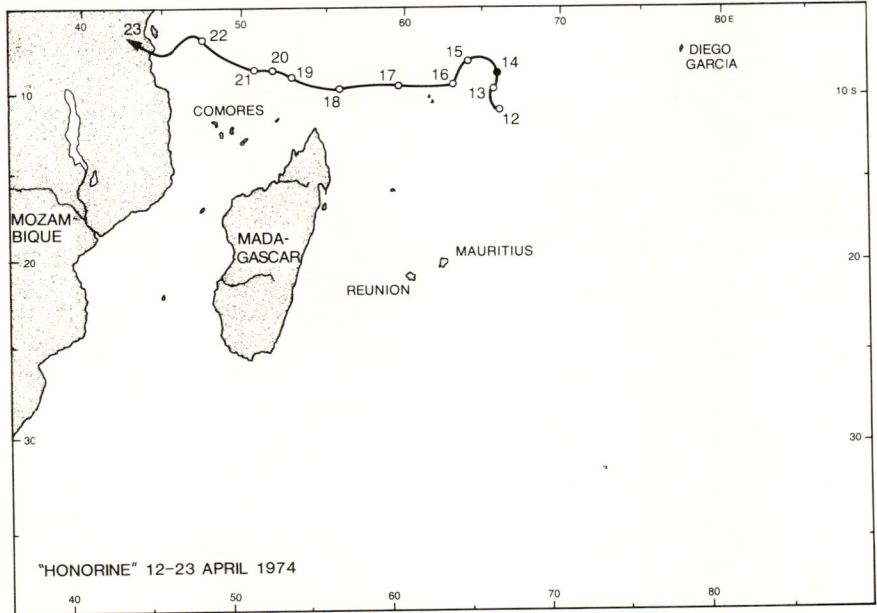

80 • COPING WITH DROUGHT IN KENYA

Figure 3.8 Tropical cyclone Gladys. Source: Data from the KMD.

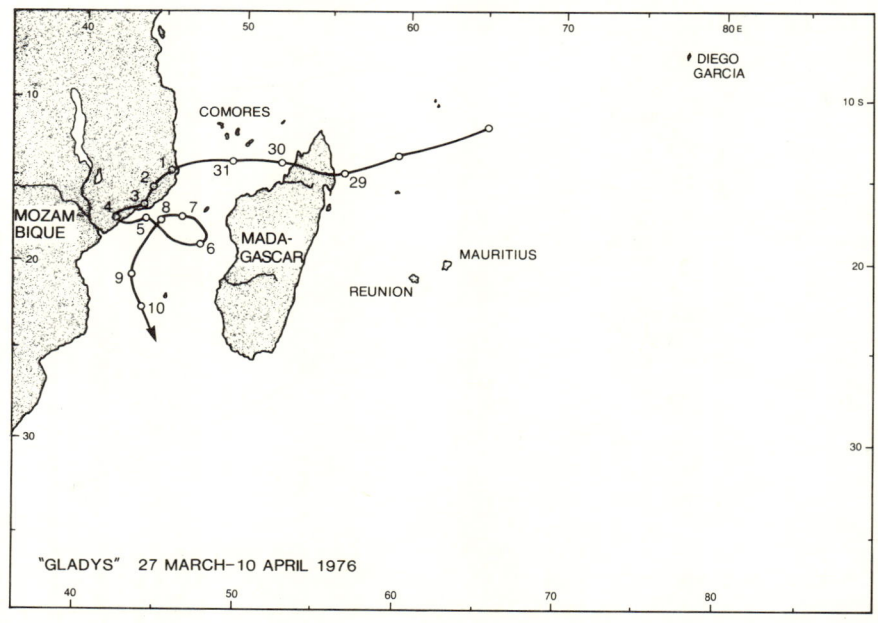

Figure 3.9 Tropical cyclone Kamisy. Source: Data from the KMD.

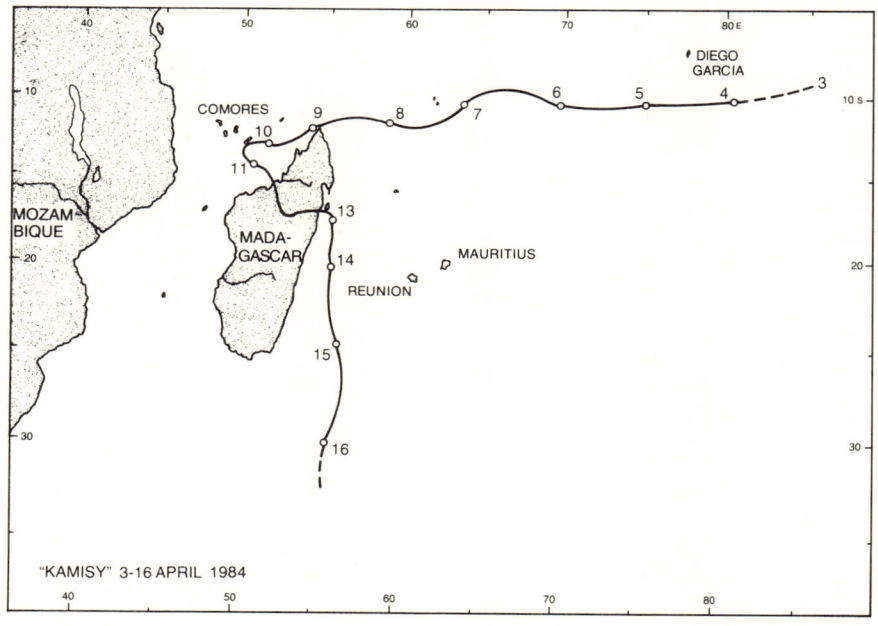

Figure 3.10 Streamline analyses for 10 April 1984. (a) 700 hPa; (b) 200 hPa. Source: Data from the KMD.

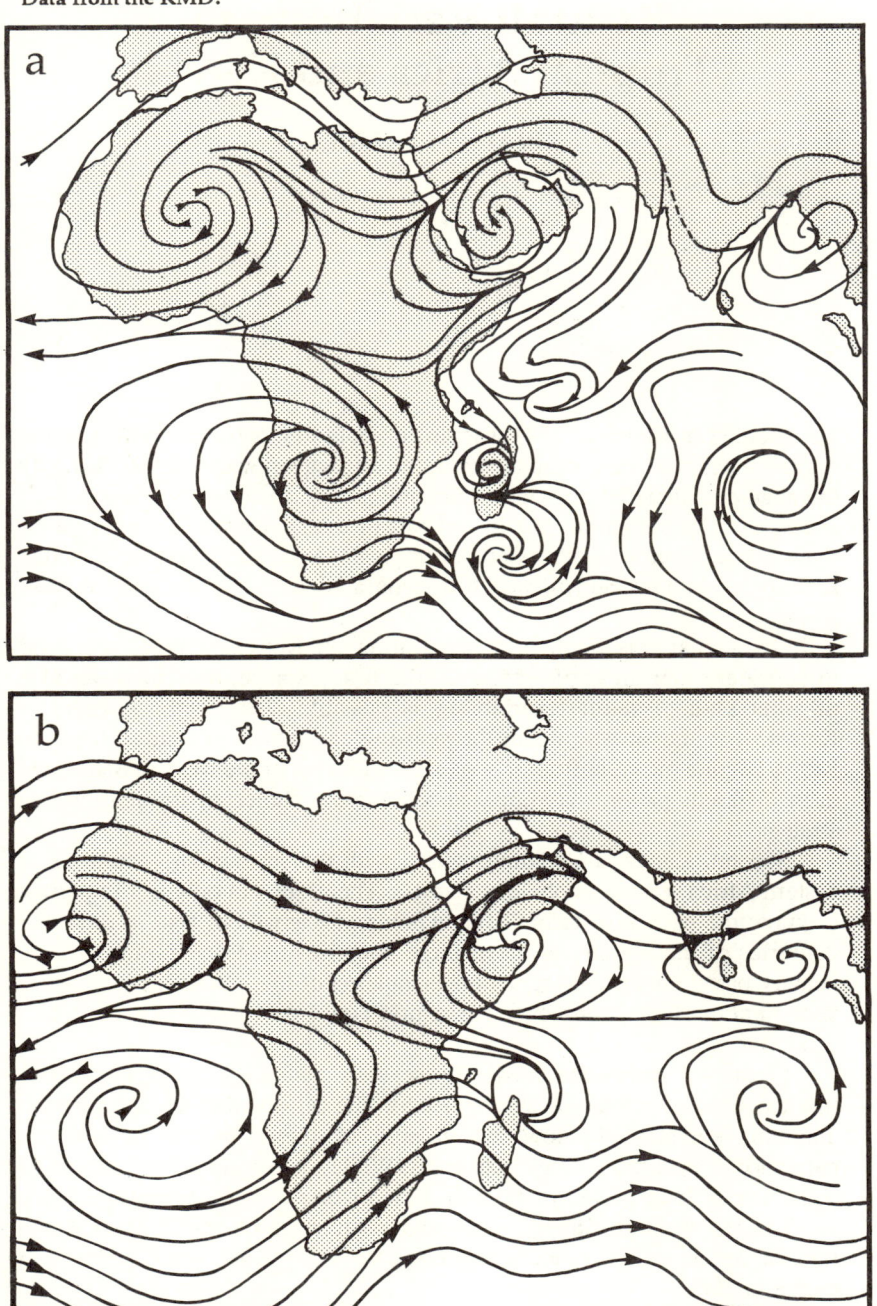

· 4 ·
Rainfall Variability in Tropical Africa and Kenya

GRAHAM FARMER

The drought in Kenya in 1984 was severe, both in the extreme nature of the rainfall deviations from normal and in the impacts on water and food supply (detailed elsewhere in this book). Climatologically, the drought was a one-off event, with no indication that it was part of a longer run of drought years. Such is not the case in other parts of tropical Africa, including the Sahelian regions of western Sudan, which is geographically not that remote from Kenya.

Given that this book is concentrating on Kenya, why do we need to consider other areas of Africa? In the first instance, it gives us an idea of what kind of rainfall variability is possible close to the borders of Kenya. It is shown below that the year-to-year pattern of rainfall totals in Kenya is quite different from that of western Sudan or the western Sahel, and each different pattern has implications for the choice of drought-coping strategies.

Second, Kenya is a trading nation, with the surrounding countries of eastern Africa serving as obvious markets. Therefore, not only is it important to know the pattern of rainfall fluctuations in Kenya, but also in the other countries of the region. As all of these countries have economies that are heavily based on agriculture, an understanding of the intricacies of year-to-year rainfall fluctuations over the region could prove to be an important economic tool.

Figure 4.1 shows time series for seasonal rainfall in different parts of tropical Africa (Farmer and Wigley 1985). The construction method for such diagrams is explained below, but the point of interest here is the different patterns of longer time-scale fluctuations. While some regions have suffered a significantly long period of rainfall deficit (for example, every year since 1970 in the western Sahel), other regions have more statistically stable rainfall series, with a random scattering of drought years and years with excess rainfall.

FORECASTING AND MONITORING • 83

RAINFALL DATA AND GRAPHICAL METHODS

The rainfall data used for this study are monthly totals. Data for 1900 to 1983 have been compiled by the National Center for Atmospheric Research (NCAR) at Boulder, Colorado, United States, and, to a larger extent, in the case of Africa, by S. E. Nicholson (SEN) of Florida State University, Tallahassee, Florida, United States (Nicholson 1981a, 1981b). A problem associated with this readily available database is that many of the stations compiled by Nicholson have a last year of record in the database of around 1973. For this chapter, additional data have been kindly provided by the Kenya Meteorological Department (KMD). These data update the stations in Kenya to include 1985.

For the Kenyan analyses presented here, twenty-two stations were available in the NCAR/SEN database. The station distribution is spatially biased toward the agricultural highlands, particularly with the three Nairobi stations (Figure 4.2). The analyses have, therefore, been subdivided into a crude division of the highlands and coast (Figure 4.2).

It should be noted that the full NCAR/SEN database is not guaranteed with regard to verification and homogeneity. For example, two sources of error are the mistranscription or inaccurate computer coding of the monthly returns and homogeneity problems due to site changes and the consequent amalgamation of data from two locations (see Farmer and Wigley [1985] for details). Note also that the NCAR/SEN database does not contain an excess of errors relative to other databases; all databases have the potential to contain many errors.

The time series presented and analyzed here have been derived in the following manner. All stations in a given region are normalized with respect to the individual station's long-term mean and standard deviation. This means that for any particular station, the appropriate long-term mean is subtracted from each monthly, seasonal, or annual value, which is then divided by the long-term standard deviation. The mean and standard deviation are computed from 1931 to 1960 to avoid problems caused by a high 1961 value (see below). Normalization means that stations with different means and standard deviations are easily compared. Once the data have been normalized, each value in the time series, as in Figure 4.1, is the average of the number of stations that have data in that year. It is thus the mean normalized anomaly. Additional details of the merits and problems of this kind of approach can be found in Katz and Glantz (1986).

KENYAN ANALYSES

The long rain (March to May) series for all of Kenya, the highlands, and the coast are given in Figure 4.3. Data are shown for the period 1920 to 1985, with 1920 chosen as a year when the recording network had built up to almost full density. Implications for policy and planning are discussed below, but the first stage is to set out some of the statistical characteristics of these series.

The Kenya long rains series shows that 1984 was the lowest value, and the first to exceed minus one standard deviation from the mean since 1933. Another important feature of the series is that there are no particularly extended runs of drier, or wetter, than normal years. This is in marked contrast to the pattern in neighboring Sudan, and raises interesting questions about why such marked differences exist. When the Kenya series is broken down into the two geographical areas, it is the highlands series that shows the deficit in 1984 (the worst since 1933), while at the coast the 1984 long rains mean value is drier than normal, but not exceptionally so.

For much of Kenya, the 1984 short rains, defined here as September to November, were, in contrast to the long rains, much wetter than normal. Taking the Kenya short rains graph first (Figure 4.4), the outstanding feature is in the short rains of 1961, when the very high seasonal total exceeded three standard deviations from the long-term mean. This feature is also very strong in the highlands graph, but is not as large in the coastal series. It is, nevertheless, the highest value for this century. All three graphs show that the 1984 short rains were indeed wetter than normal, around the one standard deviation range.

The annual series for all three geographical regions are presented in Figure 4.5. It is obvious that the calendar-year totals are composed of at least two rainy seasons; in western regions, there is a significant amount of rainfall during June, July, and August (Farmer 1981, Davies et al. 1985). Given the results in Figures 4.3 and 4.4, it is not surprising that 1984 comes out different from normal. This illustrates well the need for data more detailed than at the annual level in the Kenyan case. Even the seasonal data used here can hide the agriculturally important factor of the frequency and amount of rainfall within a season (a Kenyan example is described in Farmer and Wigley 1985). It is therefore important to recognize the limitations of any data set, and to apply those limitations to the results of any analysis of those data.

Given the above data series, further analyses relevant to the discussion below were carried out. First, can a long rains seasonal total be predicted by the previous short rains and/or vice versa? Table 4.1 shows the correlation matrix based on data for the period 1920 to 1985.

The correlation between the long rains and the short rains in the same calendar year is not significant for all three regions (Kenya, highlands, and coast), ranging from 0.00 to 0.10. When the data were lagged to "predict" the long rains from the preceding short rains, the results showed no significant improvement. It would appear that the total amount for a rainy season cannot be predicted simply from the total amount of the previous season.

Another correlation of interest is between the highlands and the coast for the long rains or the short rains on a year-to-year basis. Table 4.1 shows that the highlands and the coast "move together" in both seasons, as represented by correlations of 0.34 for the long rains and 0.82 for the short rains. This has implications for the planning of spatial compensation zones (discussed below).

Spectral analysis was applied to the area-averaged series described above to identify statistically significant peaks (or cycles) that could be used to forecast future cyclic trends in the series provided they are stable (Table 4.2) (Mitchell et al. 1966).

Two general and statistically significant spectra can be seen. Peaks with a wavelength around 3.4 to 3.5 years are prevalent in all three highlands series and in the Kenya series. Such peaks explain a moderate amount of the variance in the series, but the peaks around five years explain much more; they are present in the coastal series, as well as in the highlands and, because of duplication, the Kenya series. Such findings are in good agreement with previous work on periodicities in East African rainfall as noted by Mutulu et al. (1988), Rodhe and Virji (1976), Ogallo (1978), and Nicholson (1985).

Having identified the spectral peaks, the next step is to identify the mechanism, because without a physical cause to back up the frequency of the peak, there is the possibility that the peak is spurious, a statistical artifact. Cycles around five years are of the right periodicity to match the El Niño/Southern Oscillation (ENSO) phenomena. The peaks around 3 to 3.5 years may also be related to ENSO related events, e.g., such a peak exists in the Atlantic Ocean (Farmer and Wigley 1985). African rainfall and its links to ENSO are discussed in Ogallo (1987), Nicholson and Entekhabi (1986), and Ropelewski and Halpert (1986). ENSO analysis of the Kenyan series presented here are discussed in Farmer (1987, 1988).

RESULTS AND POLICY

The production of the rainfall series and their analysis is standard scientific analysis. The next step is to consider the implications of the climatological results in terms of planning for droughts and their impact. The first observation concerns the nature of the rainfall series. Figure 4.3 shows that the 1984 long rains drought in the highlands region was a statistical one-shot event and not part of a run of dry years. However, Figure 4.1 shows that extended runs of "below normal" rainfall years can occur, and indeed have occurred, in parts of eastern Africa that neighbor Kenya. (While this begs the immediate question of why such a pattern has not shown itself in Kenya, the answer, even if it were known, would not be central to the point raised here.) If it is suspected that a drought year is in fact part of a prolonged run of deficit years, it may be a prudent coping strategy to grow crops with shorter growing seasons. They would then be able to cope more easily with reduced totals or an effective shortening of the rainfall season (Dennett et al., 1985; Hutchinson 1985). However, shorter-season crops are generally associated with lower average yields. If the rainfall series were more stable and droughts were one-off in nature, it may not be beneficial to change the crop type just to cope with a possible drought. Obviously, there are other reasons to develop short-season crops, such as moving into more marginal areas, which could then give the potential for some return in a season that started late.

In the Kenyan case, it may make more sense to concentrate on improving the infrastructure ready to cope with the next drought, although it must be pointed out that the response in 1984 to the drought was efficient when compared to the situation in some other countries. Possible areas of improvement might include transport facilities, storage of crops on the farm and in regional facilities, and improving the techniques of storage itself in order to reduce the amount of crop losses.

Another possible coping strategy could be the identification of spatial compensation zones (Palutikof et al., 1982; Palutikof 1986). These are areas that are regularly unaffected by drought during drought episodes in other areas. Planting portions of crops in each area would then ensure some return in most years. An obvious choice for such zones in Kenya would be between the highlands and the coast, although, as Table 4.1 shows, the two areas are positively correlated and are more likely to be similarly affected. A more sophisticated analysis, such as factor analysis (Farmer 1981, Ogallo 1987) could identify spatial compensation zones within Kenya, no doubt an area for future research.

More work must be carried out on forecasting seasonal rainfall totals, as this holds the greatest potential agricultural reward. Simple correlations between the long rains and the short rains do not help. The KMD has had success in using cycles in forecasting, but more work needs to be carried out on identifying the mechanisms behind the cycles. If the mechanisms can be identified, not only does it give the method a greater physical reliability, but it may be possible to make an earlier correlation between the mechanisms and the seasonal rainfall total. Obviously, the earlier a forecast, the better, particularly for drought, because it gives more time to plan relief efforts.

Other areas of research relating to seasonal forecasting are being pursued. These include the sea-surface temperature anomaly approach developed in western Africa (Lamb 1978, Lough 1981, Folland et al., 1986) and the analysis of the relationship between seasonal rainfall totals and Indian Ocean cyclone activity (see Chapter 3).

CONCLUSIONS

This chapter has provided an introduction to the variability of seasonal rainfall totals in tropical Africa, and particularly Kenya, in the twentieth century. Having placed the 1984 long rains drought in context, some questions have been raised concerning the implications of the rainfall variability for the planning of coping strategies for the next drought. Time series of seasonal rainfall totals show that marked deviations from normal can occur, and indeed have occurred within the last forty years in the Sahelian regions. In the Kenyan case, however, the rainfall series show themselves to be statistically more stable; while Kenya has avoided the direct effects of a run of drought years, it has nevertheless experienced indirect effects due to the other countries in the region suffering such runs.

The area averages presented here show the extreme nature of the 1984 drought, the worst since 1933 in the agricultural highlands area, though not as marked on the coast. While individual years may lack agreement, there is a general year-to-year tendency for the coast and the highlands regions to move in the same direction (i.e., experience the same rainfall anomaly sign for both the long and the short rains). Analysis of the above series also suggests that seasonal totals cannot be predicted from the total of the previous rainy season. The data contain some significant series that could be used to develop forecasting seasonal totals. However, it would be better if the underlying mechanism could be identified.

On the policy side, the 1984 drought was statistically a one-off event, and as such is random and not predictable. Random events in a stable rainfall series do not warrant the adoption of coping strategies, such as wholesale switching to shorter-growing-season crops, because those crops tend to have lower yields in wetter years. It may be beneficial to concentrate on improving the infrastructure in such regions (transport and food storage), improving drought awareness and planning, and conducting further research on spatial compensation zones and seasonal forecasting.

Figure 4.1. Mean normalized rainfall anomaly series for tropical Africa. Actual data have been computed from the NCAR/SEN data base. Asterisks indicate missing data. The smooth line is a padded nine-term binomial filter. The base period for normalization is 1931 to 1970. A contrast can be seen between Region 1, the West African Sahel, with an extended run of deficit years, and Region 5, where the dry and wet years are more randomly distributed in time. The more constant series for Kenya, which lies across the boundaries of Regions 5 and 7, are detailed in Figures 4.3 to 4.5. Source: Farmer and Wigley (1985).

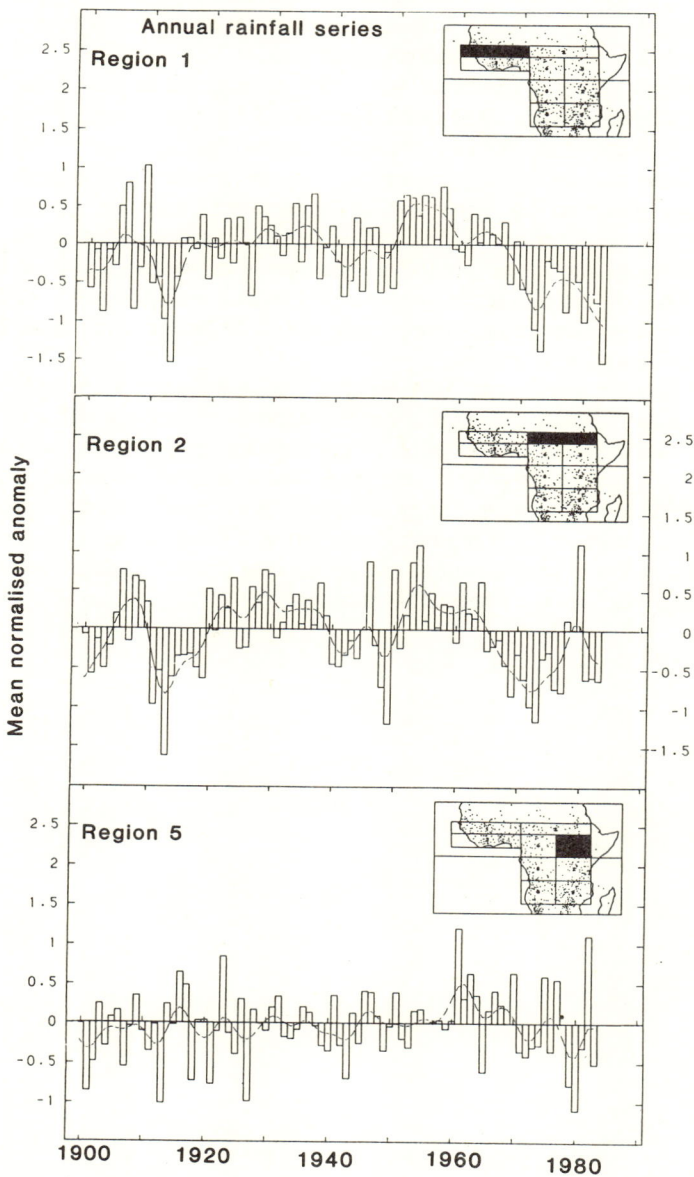

Figure 4.2. Location map of stations in Kenyan analyses. Stations shown are from the NCAR/SEN database, with at least twenty years of records in the 1931-1970 base period. The highlands, of central and western Kenya, and the coast are the main agricultural areas.

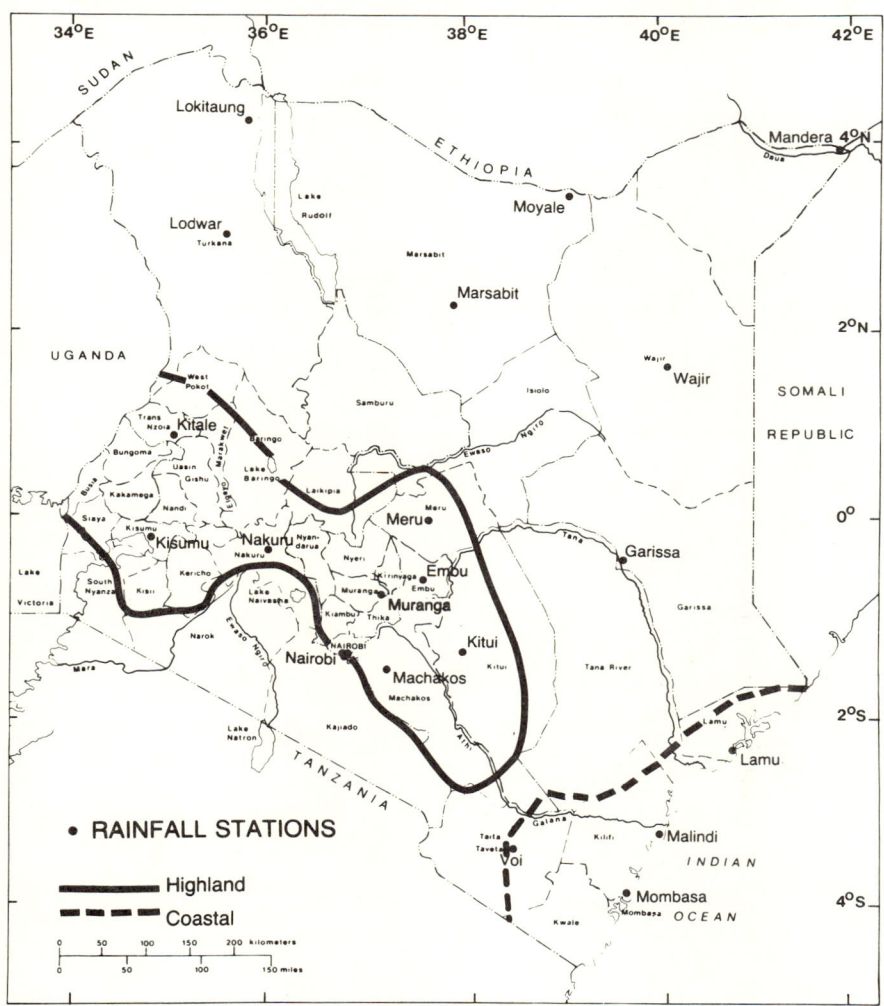

Figure 4.3. Mean normalized anomaly time series for long rains. Period is March to May, 1920–1985. The drought in 1984 is clearly evident in the national series, but the two regional series show its concentration in the highlands area. There is a slight reduction in the number of stations going into the average in recent years. Note that the NCAR/SEN database contains no Kenyan data for 1928, although the data are recorded in the KMD. Source: NCAR/SEN database and data from the KMD.

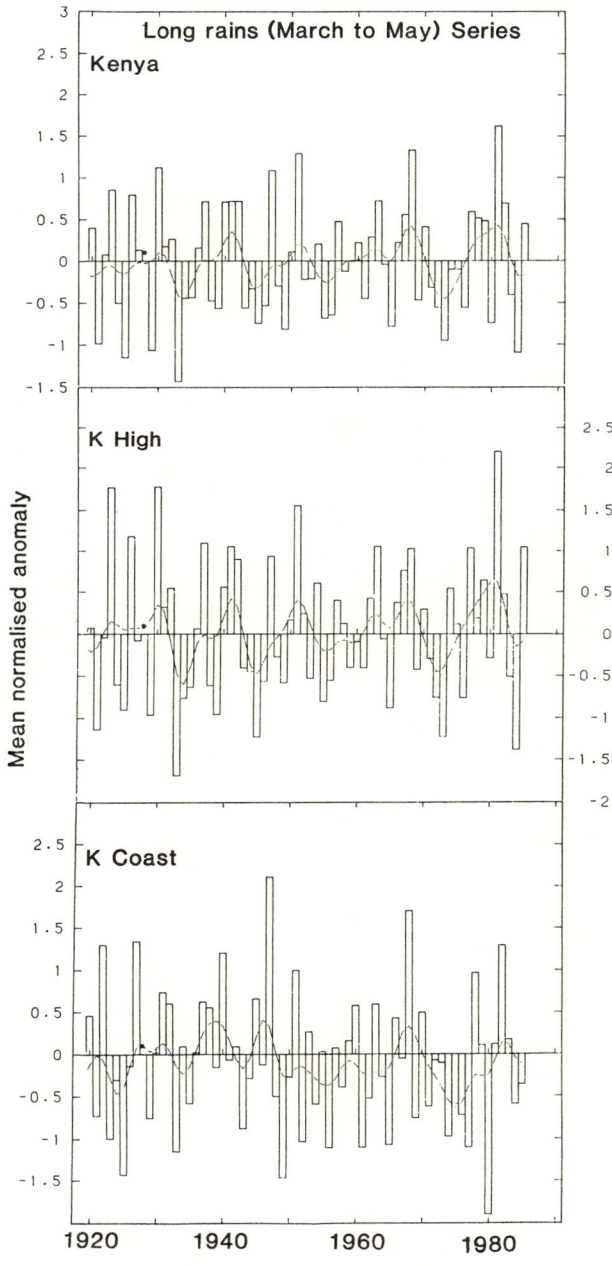

Figure 4.4. Mean normalized anomaly time series for short rains. Period is September to November, 1920–1985. Regions and method as in Figure 4.3. The very extreme values in all three series in 1961 represent a true event. Excessive rains in 1961 and 1962 caused many problems, including a two-meter rise in the level of Lake Victoria (Farmer 1981). Source: NCAR/SEN database and data from the KMD.

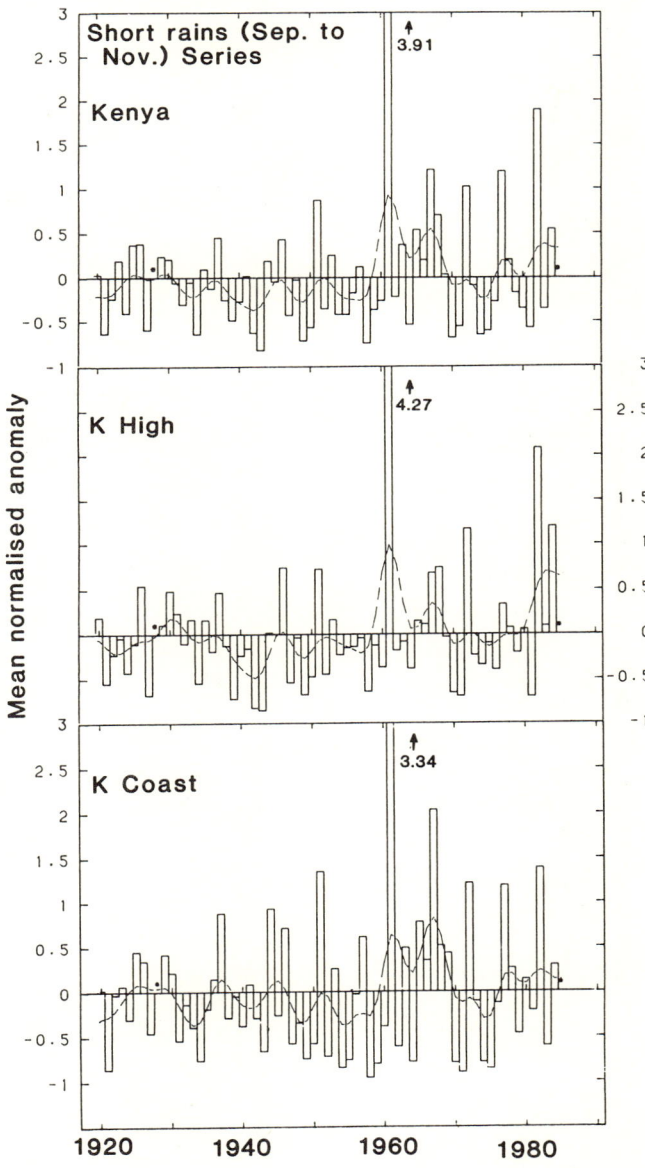

Figure 4.5. Mean normalized anomaly time series for annual data. Period is January to December, 1920–1985. Regions and methods as in Figure 4.3. These illustrate the compensating effect of the above-average short rains of 1984 after the long rains deficits. Annual rainfall totals in areas of bimodal, or even trimodal, seasonal distributions must always be used with caution. Source: NCAR/SEN data base and data from the KMD.

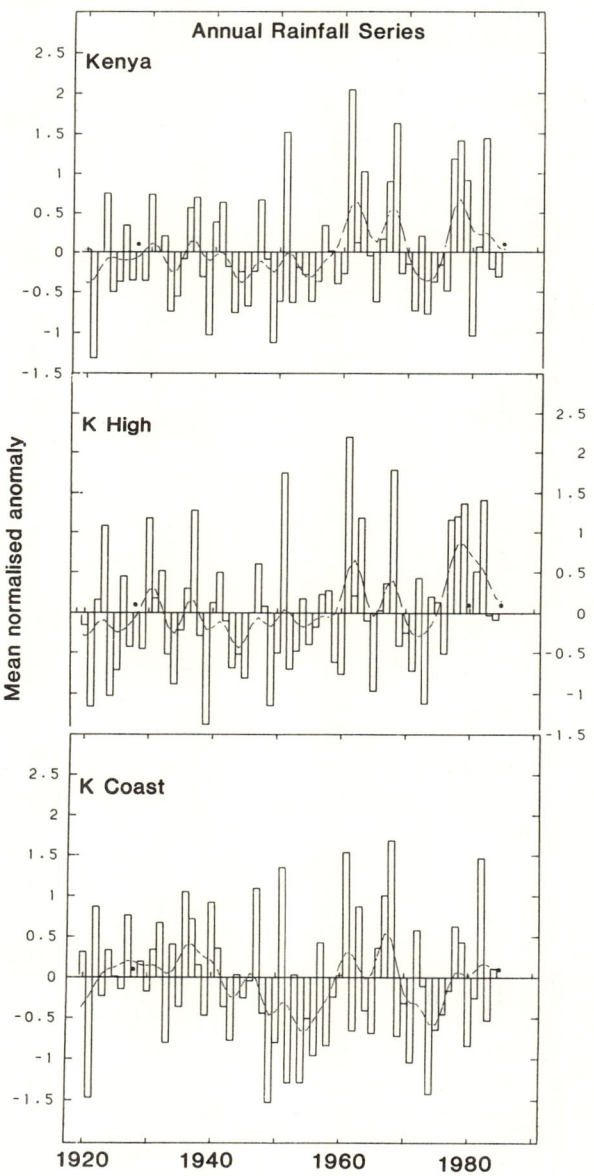

Table 4.1 Rainfall Correlations for Long Rains and Short Rains

	Long Rains			Short Rains		
	Kenya	Highlands	Coast	Kenya	Highlands	Coast
Long Rains						
Kenya	1.00					
Highlands	0.94	1.00				
Coast	0.59	0.34	1.00			
Short Rains						
Kenya	0.10	0.07	0.02	1.00		
Highlands	0.05	0.01	0.04	0.95	1.00	
Coast	0.14	0.13	0.00	0.92	0.82	1.00

Notes: Based on 1920–1985 data, for March to May (long rains) and September to November (short rains) seasonal rainfall in the same calendar year.

Table 4.2. Spectral Analyses of Area-Averaged Rainfall Series

Area\Season	Annual	Long	Short
Kenya	3.3 to 3.5 14%	3.4 to 3.5 13%	
	4.9 to 5.3 26%	5.1 to 5.3 14%	5.1 to 5.3 17%
Highlands	3.4 to 3.5 14%	around 3.4 8%	around 3.5 9%
	4.9 to 5.3 25%	5.1 to 5.3 15%	
Coast	5.1 to 5.3 17%	no sig. peaks	5.1 to 5.3 18%

Notes: The first figures show the range of the peaks identified. Use of the term "around" indicates a more pronounced peak. The second value is the amount of variance explained by the peak.

· 5 ·
Agricultural and Livestock Monitoring Using Aerial Photography

H. MWENDWA

The objectives of monitoring land use, including crop harvest and livestock numbers, are:

1. To provide baseline resource data inventories to planners and decisionmakers that will enable them to prepare economically viable and ecologically sound development programs
2. To provide planners and decisionmakers with knowledge regarding land use changes in various administrative and planning units

The Department of Resource Surveys and Remote Sensing (formerly the Kenya Rangeland Ecological Monitoring Unit [KREMU]) in the Ministry of Planning and National Development uses aerial photography as an inexpensive, yet effective, means to accomplish these objectives. Photographic analysis of land use can generate satisfactory data quickly and at low cost to determine cropping patterns and animal numbers over large areas. This chapter describes the results of monitoring for estimates of maize yields and livestock during the recent drought.

MAIZE YIELD ESTIMATES

Study Area and Methods

The severe drought that affected most of Kenya in 1984 pointed out the need for accurate methods of forecasting crop harvests to ensure that adequate national food supplies are available. The methods used prior to the drought tended to be slow and often unreliable. No standard set of procedures used to forecast crop harvest has been documented and made readily available so that independent workers can repeat and verify the forecasts.

The study area covered a total land area of approximately 38,160 sq km, including most of the main cereal-growing districts of Kenya—Bungoma, Elgeyo Marakwet, Kakamega, Nakuru, Nandi, Trans Nzoia, Uasin Gishu, and West Pokot districts in western Kenya (Figure 5.1). The topography undulates with high areas, including Mt. Elgon, Cherangani Hills, Nandi Hills, Mau ranges, Longonot Crater, Elgeyo Escarpment, and Kerio Valley. The general elevation of the area falls between 1,000 m and 4,000 m. The soils and climate generally have a high potential for agricultural production. Rainfall varies greatly from less than 500 mm/year in the arid areas of West Pokot District to 2,345 mm/year in Nakuru District. The temperature also shows a large range that is related to elevation.

KREMU developed two procedures to provide reliable early crop harvest forecasts (Peden and Mwendwa 1984, Peden et al., 1985; Agatsiva et al., 1984). These procedures include the use of aerial photography to estimate area planted and radiometry to estimate yields. Radiometry, using reflectance of near infrared (800 nm) and red (670 nm) light, has proven effective for estimating crop production based on green biomass (Pearson et al., 1976). The amount of green plant biomass is closely related to the ratio of infrared to red light reflected during daytime by the crop. High and low ratios characterize large and small amounts of green plant material, respectively.

The country was stratified into agricultural and nonagricultural land based on information derived from the 1984/88 development plan. Using a 35 mm camera, sample aerial photographs were taken at an approximate height of 457 m above ground level in the agricultural areas. A photograph was taken every 5 km in transects spaced 5 km apart along the Universal Transverse Mercator (UTM) grid. The photographs covered approximately forty-five hectares on the ground. In Bungoma, Nandi, Uasin Gishu, and Trans Nzoia, the photography was done in July 1984; in Kakamega, it was conducted in April 1984; in Nakuru, West Pokot, and Elgeyo Marakwet it was done in October 1984; and Kitui and Machakos districts were surveyed in January 1985, following very good 1984 short rains.

Each photograph was projected on a screen containing one hundred evenly and systematically spaced dots. The number of dots falling on maize fields was a direct estimate of the percentage of the area covered by maize in that photograph. Photographs were taken early (prior to planting) in Kakamega; hence, dots falling on bare soil were assumed to be maize fields. This was verified in subsequent field checks. Maize cover as a percentage of the total agricultural portion of each district was computed as a simple average of the cover estimates obtained in all the photographs taken in that district. The actual area of maize in each district was calculated by applying the percentage value to the actual area of the agricultural land, except in Kakamega, where it was applied to the entire district.

Airborne radiometer measurements were taken over each field. Two separate radiometers simultaneously measured near infrared (800 nm) and red (67 nm) light. The ratio of the two wavelengths is a measure of green biomass. The maize had tasseled and cobs had started to form, but it had not as yet lost its green color. The aircraft was flown over the fields at about 70 m above the ground. At this height, each probe covers an area of about 75 sq m on the ground. Measurements were made over the approximate center of the field.

The aerial transects were spaced 10 km apart, and the pilot endeavored to fly over at least two maize fields every 2.5 km. Prior to the photography and radiometer measurements, the maize-growing districts in this study were stratified, using Landsat imagery, experience, and aerial reconnaissance, and maize-growing areas were delineated on 1:250,000 topographic maps.

Results and Discussion

The KREMU estimates of maize harvest depend on two independent surveys: the area planted and the yield per hectare. Estimated areas planted with maize in Bungoma, Elgeyo Marakwet, Kakamega, Nakuru, Nandi, Trans Nzoia, Uasin Gishu, and West Pokot ranged from 51 to 757 sq km (Table 5.1). The radiometer measurements estimated yields ranging from 13.1 to 33.0 bags/ha. Predicted harvest for each district ranged from 62,220 to 1,676,000 bags. The average yield in the 5 by 10 km transects, referenced to UTM coordinates, was derived from measurements using airborne digital photometers. Maize production ranged from near zero bags/ha in drought-affected eastern Uasin Gishu District to more than 40 bags/ha in Nandi District.

Using aerial photography to estimate the area planted and radiometry and ground samples to estimate yields has proven to be cheap, quick, and efficient. There are three other approaches to estimating maize yield in Kenya (see the following chapters by Maganda, Mwanjila, and Murage). The Central Bureau of Statistics (CBS) relies on trained enumerators who interview a large sample of farmers. The second method relies on sales to the National Cereals and Produce Board and estimates of yields based on sample cob measurements. The third method relies on visual estimates of the area planted to maize and of yields expected, as collected by the agricultural extension staff from travels through their area of operation. It is subjective and difficult for many officers in different areas to make consistent observations. Comparison of the KREMU, Ministry of Agriculture, and CBS estimates indicates close agreement for the total of the eight districts (Table 5.2). Estimates of total production for individual districts differ by a factor of three, although the yield estimates are more consistent. The crucial variable appears to be area planted to maize.

The initial KREMU survey of three hundred maize fields required about nine hours of flying time, whereas a ground survey team would have taken up to five weeks. The use of aircraft also gives access to otherwise inaccessible areas. Now that the method has been standardized, consistent and reliable results are expected. It is important that the photography and radiometry measurements be conducted at a time when the maize has passed the critical stage in growth but is still green. As a follow-up, KREMU is trying to improve the efficiency of timing the aerial photography and radiometer measurements. Doing so involves a critical look at the growing calendar of maize in various districts and ecological zones, and should help to improve acreage and yield results.

There are many sources of error that affect production estimates, including the definition of the maize strata, estimate of percent cover of maize, and estimate of yield. The most critical of these is the definition of maize strata, because small areas where maize is grown are overlooked. This is particularly so in arid areas and in the high potential areas like Bungoma and Trans Nzoia districts, where it is difficult to define a sharp boundary between the forest and maize-growing areas.

LIVESTOCK AND WILDLIFE IN NORTHERN KENYA, 1985

Study Area and Methods

Livestock and wildlife are very important natural resources. After the 1984 drought, KREMU attempted to determine how many animals died as a result of the drought. The study results give animal censuses from 1977 to 1985 by administrative units (Figure 5.1). The results, however, do not give a complete picture of what happened to livestock during the drought. For example, Tana River District was not surveyed at the same time, but was occupied by pastoralists migrating from neighboring districts. A decrease in livestock numbers was also caused by sales to markets. Sales and migration mask the estimates of livestock mortality due to the severe drought.

KREMU's methods of censusing animal populations follow Norton-Griffiths (1978). Between 1977 and 1984, all surveys were conducted using systematic reconnaissance flights (Mbugua 1986) oriented in an east-west direction, with transects spaced 10 or 5 km apart and a flying height of 91 or 122 m. Where terrain prevents east-west flights at low altitude, north-south flights were undertaken. In 1985, the districts surveyed were stratified according to animal distributions and concentrations based on information from the district livestock officers and previous KREMU surveys (Mbugua 1986). During the surveys, observers in the aircraft photographed animal herds exceeding ten in size.

Results and Discussion

Compared to previous censuses, livestock numbers were substantially lower in all the districts except West Pokot and Baringo districts (Table 5.3). The total change for the nine districts was almost 1.5 million animals or over a 30 percent decrease in the livestock population. The largest percent decreases were in Mandera, Isiolo, Wajir, Marsabit, and Garissa districts.

Tables 5.4 to 5.9 show livestock and wildlife population estimates for each census. Data for the period 1977 to 1983 have been reported and fully discussed by Peden and Mwendwa (1984). The livestock numbers in all the districts under study have continued to decline since 1977.

Between 1977 and 1978, livestock numbers declined in all districts except Wajir and Marsabit. In Laikipia, there was a 65 percent decline in cattle numbers between the 1978 and 1985 censuses. In 1977/78, Marsabit, Isiolo, and Mandera districts recorded an increase in livestock, but the 1985 census indicates Isiolo and Mandera lost up to 50 percent of the cattle population. Sheep and goat populations show little variation between 1977 and 1985 in the districts considered; all the districts recorded a higher goat and sheep population in 1985 than in previous years. The camel population seemed to decrease over the study period (Mbugua 1986). Mandera, Laikipia, and Wajir showed a reduction in camel population in the 1985 census, while Garissa District recorded an increase of 17 percent in the camel population between 1977 and 1985. Donkey numbers increased between 1977 and 1985 in Isiolo and Garissa districts, but declines were recorded in Samburu, Marsabit, and Laikipia.

On the average, wildlife species may have been less affected by drought than livestock. The censuses reveal fewer losses, except for elephants and rhinoceroses. In Isiolo and Garissa, there was a sharp decline in the elephant population between 1978 and 1985—overall 80 and 96 percent, respectively (Mbugua 1986). The black rhinoceros has continued to decline, both in range and numbers, since 1977 (Stelfox et al., 1981). Though observed in very small numbers in southern Garissa in 1977 surveys, none have been seen in subsequent surveys. The high concentration of Burchell's zebra occurred around Maralal in Samburu and in the southern parts of Laikipia and Garissa districts. A large decline in Burchell's zebra occurred in Isiolo and Garissa during the survey period. Garissa and Laikipia were the only districts showing an increase in zebra population between 1977 and 1985.

Whereas the 1977/78 census was conducted during the dry season, the 1981 and 1985 censuses were undertaken during the wet season. The results, therefore, should be treated with caution. During the dry season, pastoralists move their livestock from Marsabit into Ethiopia (Kufwafwa 1985, Field et al., 1976), from Samburu into the Buffalo Springs and Shaba game reserves (Stelfox et al., 1979), and from Garissa District to Tana River, Isiolo, and Meru districts (Kufwafwa 1985). The effect of transhumance must be studied before making clear conclusions about livestock losses or gains in northern Kenya. Decreases in numbers could also have been caused by sales. It is therefore difficult to give a precise estimate of the animals that died as a result of the drought, since no surveys were conducted just prior to the drought.

CONCLUSION

Maize is the most important cereal in Kenya. The severe drought of 1984 substantially reduced the national harvest of maize. National planners and policymakers need advance knowledge of projected harvests to arrange for imports if there is a shortfall, or exports if there is a surplus and the strategic reserves are full. KREMU's methods of area and acreage estimation are capable of providing valuable and timely information. A more rigorous validation of the four maize monitoring systems would be beneficial to all concerned.

Since livestock is a crucial resource during times of drought, used for both food and cash, its numbers, mortality rates, and migrations are critical in regional drought preparedness and responses. Aerial reconnaissance is the only cost-effective method of assessing these trends.

Figure 5.1 Areas surveyed by KREMU in the 1984/85 drought.

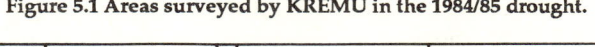

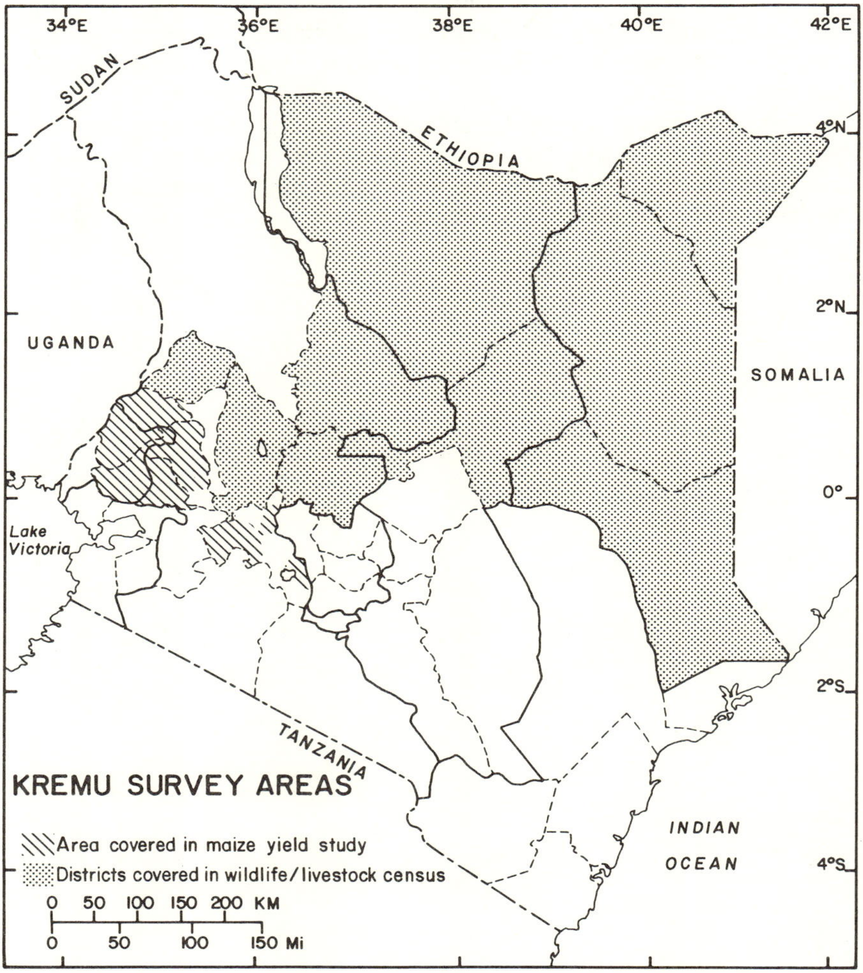

Table 5.1 Yield and Projected Maize Harvest in 1984

District	Total Area (km)	Agric. Area (km)	Number of Photos	Area planted Maize (km)		Yield (bags/ha)		Predicted Harvest (bags)
				Mean	SE	Mean	SE	
Bungoma	3,074	2,527	57	616	57	25.0	1.9	1,540,000
Elgeyo Marakwet	2,810	2,094	60	51	1	12.2	1.2	62,220
Kakamega	3,497	3,288	538	635	30	26.4	1.2	1,676,400
Nakuru	5,769	4,312	142	421	10	13.1	1.4	551,510
Nandi	2,745	2,405	119	384	37	33.0	1.8	1,267,200
Trans Nzoia	2,468	1,997	79	485	52	30.3	1.3	1,469,550
Uasin Gishu	3,784	3,137	158	757	56	14.4	1.8	1,090,080
West Pokot	9,100	801	15	65	3	24.2	1.2	157,300
Total	33,247	20,561	1,168	3,414	107	22.9 *	1.5	7,814,260

Source: Data from the Kenya Rangeland Ecological Monitoring Unit.
Note: * Average yield for total area was weighted by area planted in each district; SE is standard error.

Table 5.2 Comparison of Projected Maize Harvests in 1984

District	KREMU			MOA			CBS		
	Area (km)	Yield (bags/ha)	Total Harvest 1,000 bags	Area (km)	Yield (bags/ha)	Total Harvest 1,000 bags	Area (km)	Yield (bags/ha)	Total Harvest 1,000 bags
Bungoma	616	25.0	1,540	788	25	1,970	218	57.0	1,242
Kakamega	635	26.4	1,676	730	25	1,825	323	40.4	1,305
Nandi	384	33.0	1,267	550	32	1,760	539	27.2	1,464
Trans Nzoia	485	30.3	1,470	536	32	1,715	405	30.1	1,217
Uasin Gishu	757	14.4	1,090	396	10	396	320	29.5	911
Nakuru	421	13.1	552	480	3	144	375	11.6	436
Elgeyo Marakwet	51	12.2	62	190	16	304	—	—	—
West Pokot	65	24.2	157	145	30	435	89	67.9	604
Total	3,414	22.9	7,814	3,815	22	8,549	2,269	35.4	7,179

Source: Data from KREMU, CBS, and MOA.
Notes: MOA is Ministry of Agriculture; CBS is Central Bureau of Statistics. The average yield for total area was weighted by area planted in each district. CBS yield per hectare has been calculated using the information provided on crop area and total harvest. See Table 7.3 for a comparison of aggregate estimates of production.

Table 5.3 Livestock Numbers in 1985 Census Compared to Average

District	Livestock Population		Absolute Change	Percent
	Average from Previous Censuses	1985 Census		
Baringo	281,054	309,302	+ 28,248	+ 10
Garissa	671,990	441,681	− 230,309	− 34
Isiolo	619,396	375,104	− 244,292	− 39
Laikipia	363,911	299,633	− 64,278	− 18
Mandera	516,776	109,800	− 406,976	− 79
Marsabit	762,530	494,809	− 267,721	− 35
Samburu	406,385	328,912	− 77,473	− 19
Wajir	726,785	447,343	− 279,442	− 38
West Pokot	180,890	275,623	+ 94,733	+ 52
Total	4,529,717	3,082,207	− 1,447,510	− 32

Source: Data from KREMU; see *KREMU Newsletter* 2(1 and 2), 1985.
Notes: Total livestock includes estimates of cattle, sheep, goats, camels, and donkeys.
Average is of previous censuses by KREMU.

Table 5.4 Animal Populations in Baringo District, 1982–1985

Animal type	Sept. 1982		Oct. 1984		Mar.–Apr. 1985	
	Number	SE	Number	SE	Number	SE
Livestock	279,453	22,806	266,885	19,710	309,302	25,089
Cattle	97,453	11,397	89,924	8,976	102,690	11,660
Sheep and goats	177,537	19,739	173,981	17,537	201,488	22,048
Camels	1,562	504	1,637	537	3,818	1,678
Donkeys	2,901	583	1,343	316	1,306	418
Wildlife	3,876	870	1,807	455	1,039	496
Buffalo	—	—	—	—	—	—
Giraffe	25	25	—	—	—	—
Burchell's zebra	1,227	430	695	330	480	400
Elephant	—	—	—	—	—	—
Impala	603	244	—	—	—	—
Thomson's gazelle	—	—	—	—	—	—
Grant's gazelle	1,136	645	679	217	469	280
Oryx	145	127	46	33	—	—
Lesser kudu	120	57	93	67	—	—
Eland	376	253	201	135	—	—
Waterbuck	95	67	—	—	—	—
Gerenuk	122	82	31	21	90	87
Ostrich	27	26	62	59	—	—
Greater kudu	—	—	—	—	—	—
Total animals	283,329	22,823	268,692	19,715	310,341	25,094

Source: Data from KREMU; see *KREMU Newsletter* 2(1 and 2), 1985.
Note: SE is standard error.

Table 5.5 Animal Populations in Garissa District, 1977-1985

Animal type	Feb.–Aug. 1977 Number	SE	Feb.–Sept. 1978 Number	SE	Apr.–May 1983 Number	SE	March 1985 Number	SE
Livestock	713,853	120,799	671,674	68,726	630,222	58,569	441,681	48,829
Cattle	382,315	98,717	306,769	52,813	282,913	24,821	184,626	30,899
Sheep and goats	279,674	69,450	322,617	43,561	298,018	45,658	194,399	35,979
Camels	50,808	14,168	40,820	5,997	47,250	11,522	59,553	11,577
Donkeys	1,056	481	1,468	722	2,041	688	3,103	1,022
Wildlife	71,778	7,629	101,563	7,997	85,370	9,735	24,132	2,836
Buffalo	—	—	96	85	6,269	3,464	—	—
Giraffe	9,635	2,038	11,268	1,356	13,527	2,651	9,576	2,057
Burchell's zebra	2,730	1,858	3,543	1,527	4,733	2,114	1,250	694
Grevy's zebra	660	312	650	233	568	182	1,018	687
Elephant	6,511	2,211	7,673	2,216	3,661	1,330	292	294
Kongoni	837	432	1,735	817	589	424	—	—
Hunter's Hartebeest	2,778	1,404	8,243	2,064	9,320	3,706	917	410
Topi	4,482	2,050	18,453	5,033	24,740	7,095	2,250	927
Impala	495	331	553	449	1,241	755	—	—
Grant's gazelle	17,671	5,355	21,631	4,368	5,386	1,474	1,726	578
Oryx	4,435	1,701	6,830	1,562	3,198	1,036	1,740	782
Lesser kudu	5,287	1,154	4,865	945	2,735	437	833	353
Eland	2,215	1,679	231	169	168	164	—	—
Waterbuck	—	—	656	234	252	107	667	344
Gerenuk	11,688	1,795	10,110	993	6,753	952	2,285	587
Rhinoceros	44	41	—	—	—	—	—	—
Ostrich	2,310	442	5,026	929	2,230	517	1,578	470
Total animals	785,631	121,040	773,237	69,190	715,592	59,373	465,813	48,912

Source: Data from KREMU; see *KREMU Newsletter* 2(1 and 2), 1985.
Note: SE is standard error.

Table 5.6 Animal Populations in Isiolo District, 1977-1985

Animal type	Aug.–Sept. 1977 Number	SE	Aug.–Oct. 1978 Number	SE	Apr.–May 1985 Number	SE	Average Number	SE
Livestock	646,471	144,693	592,321	79,744	375,104	64,047	537,966	59,064
Cattle	115,908	37,996	159,652	27,891	69,948	20,304	115,169	17,107
Sheep and goats	371,853	82,521	389,940	74,405	278,326	60,536	346,707	42,177
Camels	154,996	112,597	38,363	6,593	20,922	4,368	71,427	37,624
Donkeys	3,714	2,144	4,366	1,266	5,908	2,453	4,663	1,165
Wildlife	90,774	32,905	59,684	6,397	30,364	5,174	60,273	11,306
Buffalo	2,501	2,593	467	367	—	—	989	582
Giraffe	3,175	1,222	2,217	360	1,511	698	2,301	484
Burchell's zebra	979	605	945	344	242	162	722	238
Grevy's zebra	3,280	2,079	1,894	626	1,440	410	2,205	737
Elephant	828	511	1,722	1,340	165	122	905	480
Grant's gazelle	61,820	32,564	38,871	5,902	17,029	448	39,240	11,131
Oryx	4,757	1,764	2,078	626	4,343	2,216	3,726	967
Lesser kudu	212	140	340	142	319	215	290	98
Eland	1,522	1,284	1,020	909	—	—	847	349
Waterbuck	256	226	144	134	—	—	133	59
Gerenuk	6,005	1,136	4,008	505	2,407	813	4,140	496
Ostrich	5,439	1,746	5,978	1,415	2,470	768	4,629	792
Impala	—	—	—	—	438	288	146	96
Total animals	737,245	148,387	652,005	800,000	405,468	64,256	598,239	60,136

Source: Data from KREMU; see *KREMU Newsletter* 2(1 and 2), 1985.
Note: SE is standard error.

Table 5.7 Animal Populations in Laikipia District, 1981–1985

	Sept. 1981		May 1982		Mar.–Apr. 1985	
Animal type	Number	SE	Number	SE	Number	SE
Livestock	392,149	23,642	329,997	40,587	299,633	28,888
Cattle	237,271	16,829	168,611	22,795	92,193	12,543
Sheep and goats	151,298	16,589	159,819	33,571	206,501	25,021
Camels	2,869	668	61	66	313	261
Donkeys	711	294	1,506	807	626	194
Wildlife	105,649	12,347	65,271	8,999	58,688	5,101
Buffalo	2,024	1,203	833	506	1,987	1,150
Giraffe	4,623	863	3,134	960	1,895	527
Burchell's zebra	46,655	11,569	23,592	7,756	19,373	2,619
Grevy's zebra	37	22	240	156	386	330
Elephant	1,786	687	707	522	2,097	1,719
Kongoni	10,514	1,731	6,771	1,643	3,569	751
Impala	6,740	1,135	5,509	1,360	8,794	2,230
Thomson's gazelle	3,169	884	5,203	1,753	6,366	2,372
Grant's gazelle	10,648	1,727	4,565	884	6,384	1,110
Oryx	1,822	576	1,843	811	1,398	705
Eland	14,002	2,703	11,386	3,190	5,519	1,237
Waterbuck	682	163	381	195	37	35
Ostrich	2,801	467	1,003	268	883	261
Lesser kudu	62	44	30	21	—	—
Gerenuk	84	46	75	55	—	—
Total animals	497,798	26,672	395,268	41,573	358,321	29,335

Source: Data from KREMU; see *KREMU Newsletter* 2(1 and 2), 1985.
Note: SE is standard error.

Table 5.8 Animal Populations in Mandera and Wajir Districts, 1978–1985

	Mandera District				Wajir District			
	Jul.–Sept. 1978		Feb. 1985		Jul.–Sept. 1978		Feb.–Mar. 1985	
Animal type	Numberer	SE	Number	SE	Number	SE	Number	SE
Livestock	442,387	67,198	109,800	39,819	902,713	70,677	447,343	55,409
Cattle	37,799	7,063	18,227	11,940	197,805	29,352	70,323	15,654
Sheep and goats	286,597	65,513	48,322	26,085	502,442	61,725	242,542	48,048
Camels	117,135	13,178	43,251	8,134	199,502	17,923	133,103	22,719
Donkeys	847	294	—	—	2,964	1,591	1,375	580
Wildlife	9,375	933	3,058	737	95,130	6,633	41,187	10,071
Giraffe	3,168	427	561	414	7,971	770	6,690	1,702
Elephant	342	213	—	—	93	88	—	—
Gazelle	192	131	—	—	60,498	6,183	4,576	1,619
Oryx	790	225	289	170	6,315	1,483	4,576	1,619
Lesser kudu	1,575	349	489	276	2,272	635	1,226	453
Gerenuk	2,576	3,048	941	416	13,344	1,323	3,637	813
Ostrich	732	576	778	309	4,637	905	3,170	1,075
Zebra	—	—	—	—	—	—	223	221
Total animals	451,753	67,204	112,858	29,828	997,843	70,988	488,530	56,317

Source: Data from KREMU, see *KREMU Newsletter* 2(1 and 2), 1985.

Table 5.9 Animal Populations in Marsabit, Samburu, and West Pokot Districts

	Marsabit District				Samburu District				West Pokot District			
	Feb.–Apr. 1981		Feb. 1985		Feb.–Mar. 1981		April 1985		Mar.–Apr. 1981		Mar.–Apr. 1985	
Animal type	Number	SE	Number	SE	Number	SE	Number	SE	Number	SE	Number	SE
Livestock												
Cattle	504,741	52,874	494,809	99,114	322,020	33,312	328,912	26,684	95,343	12,110	275,623	80,702
Sheep and goats	78,225	14041	100,689	25,975	105,247	14,273	92,018	14,472	53,596	9,316	79,096	16,721
Camels	377,118	50,696	347,548	92,956	198,835	29,727	229,267	22,319	41,436	7,736	195,486	78,949
Donkeys	46,553	5,271	45,645	22,530	13,460	4,597	5,339	1,969	—	—	771	488
Wildlife	2,845	801	927	809	4,478	1,060	2,288	767	311	111	270	197
Buffalo	66,322	4,225	55,446	11,868	24,164	2,989	25,721	3,473	391	159	1,426	595
Giraffe	646	557	1,347	832	698	397	1,182	716	24	23	270	261
Burchell's zebra	3,107	585	3,084	1,718	2,420	378	2,583	332	—	—	—	—
Grevy's zebra	600	458	—	—	7,201	1,959	6,630	2,163	—	—	—	—
Elephant	3,285	718	1,588	710	1,880	962	398	194	—	—	—	—
Impala	231	113	532	467	935	536	1,449	630	192	125	154	149
Grant's gazelle	105	89	456	281	1,274	680	3,538	1,864	—	—	—	—
Oryx	41,493	3,486	29,381	8,392	3,233	882	5,412	1,466	—	—	—	—
Lesser kudu	9,830	1,914	12,151	7,676	1,702	582	1,002	377	—	—	77	76
Eland	610	144	253	126	64	30	72	30	—	—	—	—
Gerenuk	30	25	—	—	1,524	859	627	474	—	—	462	295
Ostrich	3,561	414	4,235	1,191	789	184	1,832	409	—	—	39	37
Greater kudu	2,824	665	2,384	930	241	86	627	313	—	—	—	—
Water buck	—	—	35	32	25	22	—	—	175	96	—	—
Zebra	—	—	—	—	486	386	37	36	—	—	424	413
Thomson gazelle	—	—	—	—	1,692	1,037	332	259	—	—	—	—
Total Animals	571,063	53,043	550,255	99,822	346,184	33,446	354,633	26,909	95,734	12,111	277,049	80,704

Source: Data from KREMU; see *KREMU Newsletter* 2(1 and 2), 1985.
Note: SE is standard error.

· 6 ·

Surveys and Activities of the Central Bureau of Statistics Related to Food Monitoring

B. F. MAGANDA

During 1983 and 1984, Kenya experienced drought conditions that resulted in three successive crop failures in parts of the country. The drought emphasized the urgent need for timely and reliable information on the food situation in Kenya. The food-sector monitoring program of the Central Bureau of Statistics (CBS), developed with assistance from the Oxford Food Studies Group (FSG), seeks to establish a nationwide forecasting and monitoring system for the major food crops in Kenya; this program combines information and expertise from many different sources and provides timely information to planners and policymakers. A fundamental component of the program is to strengthen the capacity within the CBS for the rapid processing and use of the information. The monitoring system includes an agroclimatic crop-yield model, processing of data collected in crop forecast surveys, monitoring market prices, analysis of trends in health and nutrition, and analysis of food flows reported by the National Cereals and Produce Board (NCPB). Information is formally presented to the Interministerial Food Forecasting Committee. This chapter describes these activities, with a particular focus on the 1984 drought.

CROP FORECAST SURVEY

The Crop Forecast Survey (CFS) is a periodic survey based on the National Sample Survey and Evaluation Programme (NASSEP) sample frame. The first NASSEP frame was used between 1980 and 1984; a revised frame was developed in late 1984 and was first used in the long rains 1985 CFS. The sample frame covers twenty-four districts in Kenya, including all the key cereal-growing areas, namely Trans Nzoia, Uasin Gishu, Nakuru, Kericho, Nandi, Bungoma, Kakamega, and South Nyanza (Figure 6.1, Table 6.1). The CBS maintains a staff of enumerators, supervisors, and district statistical officers in each district included in the sample frame. The pastoral areas are excluded from the sample frame due to the problems of defining a sample and the expense in conducting regular surveys. Within each district, twenty-seven clusters have been selected, each containing one hundred households on the average. The sample permits district-level estimates, with varying degrees of error, depending on the number of returns. Ten percent of the households in each cluster are interviewed in each survey.

The Crop Forecast Survey is carried out four times a year—at the beginning and end of each of the long rains and short rains seasons (Table 6.1). The first survey, at the beginning of the season, establishes the area that has been planted with maize, beans, potatoes, millet, and sorghum. The survey at the end of the season determines the forecast of expected production for the same crops, as well as confirming the production of the previous season. The questionnaire is relatively simple, but it does include some information on the intended disposal of the crop (consumption and sales) and how much of it is currently retained on the farm. The survey relies on household responses for area and production, while yields are calculated from the area and production estimates. The second NASSEP sample frame measures field sizes, which provide more reliable estimates of area planted and, hence, the yields. A recent study compared farmers' estimates of maize production, sample measurements of the harvest, and the total harvest on 118 smallholders' farms (Verma et al., 1988). The average of the sample crop cuttings (using random squares) overestimated the harvest by 38 percent. Farmers' initial estimates of the maize harvest on average underestimated production by 6 percent, while the average pre-harvest and post-harvest farmers' estimates were 2 percent and 1 percent, respectively, higher than the actual measured harvest. This indicates that farmers' reports may be very good indicators of the actual harvest.

Results from the Crop Forecast Survey are supplemented by estimates from the Large Farms Survey (when available), which gives estimated yearly maize and wheat production on the large farms.

The results of the Crop Forecast Surveys from the 1983 short rains to the 1985 long rains are presented in Table 6.2. The response rates vary considerably, but they are generally quite good during the long rains: Over 95 percent of the districts (or district groups where more than one district is combined for sampling purposes) had household response rates of over 80 percent. During the short rains, few of the districts had household response rates over 95 percent, and about half had 80 to 95 percent response rates. For various reasons, not all the districts are included in each CFS, an omission that leads to errors in interpreting the results. For instance, the response from the 1985 long rains CFS was inadequate, and this, combined with the lack of experience with the new sample frame, led to a misleadingly low estimate of national production.

The data confirm the magnitude of the drought in the affected areas of Central, Eastern, and Rift Valley provinces. Machakos, for example, produced four times more maize in the 1985 long rains compared to the long rains of 1984. The onset of the drought in Eastern Province in the 1983 short rains is clear, as is the end of the drought with the surplus production in the 1984 short rains.

The use of the CFS data is described below. One major obstacle is the timely processing of the survey returns. The 1984 long rains area measurement, 1983 short rains harvest confirmation, and 1984 long rains harvest confirmation were delayed. Even if all the data had been prepared on schedule, reliable estimates of household production would not have been available until the end of the current season or the start of the following one. Thus, the CFS data are important on an annual basis and to provide a database for comparing trends and other monitoring estimates. They are less useful in making decisions about the current season.

AGROMETEOROLOGICAL CROP FORECASTING

The Central Bureau of Statistics has continued to work toward improving crop monitoring and forecasting by venturing into new areas of research that incorporate weather influences on crop growth, development, and yields. The methods currently being developed, following the FAO model (see Chapter 9), are based on a cumulative ten-day water balance established over the entire growing season for the given crop. The agrometeorological forecasts provide timely indications of the cropping season, which can be verified from other sources as the season progresses.

The forecasts use actual rainfall data and available climatological data for the calculation of the water requirements of crops. The water balance is the difference between precipitation received by the crop and the water lost by the crop and the soil. The model, using ten-day time periods, requires calculation of the following parameters:

1. Normal precipitation
2. Actual precipitation
3. Number of days of rainfall
4. Potential evapotranspiration (i.e., maximum quantity of water that may be evaporated by a uniform cover of dense short grass when the water supply to the soil is not limited)
5. Crop coefficients at each stage of crop growth (i.e., real evapotranspiration of the crop)
6. Water reserves in the soil

The CBS estimates these parameters with the assistance of the Kenya Meteorological Department. Eventually, the CBS hopes to come up with crop indices that indicate the cumulative percentage of the crop water requirements that have been satisfied at any stage of the crop's growing period. The index can be directly related to yields, giving a satisfactory, timely, and qualitative appreciation of the yield, or at least the change in the yield. Initially, it is hoped that the index will be used to adjust the forecast of yield derived from the Crop Forecast Survey. While the method allows good qualitative assessments, the quantitative forecast depends on historical statistics of yields and production. Although the method can be used to demonstrate the utility of calculating cumulative water balances for a ten-day period and to show the yield losses due to water stresses in the plant during its growing cycle, it is also evident that other factors contribute to yield reduction. These elements may be physical, such as strong winds or floods causing water logging; biological, such as locusts, birds, fungi, or insects; or managerial, such as the availability and use of fertilizers and seed. The final yield forecast probably will be strongly related to the water balance, but it should also take into account other factors. Information must be completed on all aspects of crop development for the establishment of a good crop-monitoring and forecasting system.

MARKET PRICE SURVEY

The Market Price Survey is carried out on a weekly basis by the CBS in a number of rural and urban markets, where average market prices are recorded for nine major crops: maize, beans, potatoes, tomatoes, cabbages, kale (*sukuma wiki*), finger millet, sorghum, and bananas. The prices gathered from this survey are important in monitoring food supplies and demand, particularly for the informal markets and local food supplies. The trend of market prices measures food availability and affordability. This information is also provided to the Interministerial Food Forecasting Committee.

In 1984, Embu was greatly affected by the drought, and the prices of both maize and beans were high. In contrast, Trans Nzoia is in a food surplus area, and maize prices did not inflate to the same degree (Figure 6.2).

HEALTH AND NUTRITION INFORMATION

As part of the Child Health and Nutrition Information System (CHANIS) the Ministry of Health receives child-nutrition data from health facilities. Nine pilot districts were reporting in January 1986, and others have since been added. This data provide information at the facility level of children in age groups, 0–11 months, 12–35 months, and 36–59 months. The weight and age of each child is noted. If the child has made no weight gain in the preceding three months or if the weight for that age is below the third percentile of the World Health Organization's reference weight, then that information is also noted (see Chapter 18). The CBS receives this data every month from the Ministry of Health. In principle, the CHANIS data can be used to confirm the human impact expected from changes in crop production and price.

USE AND PROCESSING OF FOOD-SECTOR MONITORING INFORMATION

The processing of the crop forecast and market price surveys on microcomputers has resulted in the availability of a large amount of good quality data. These two surveys are central to the development of monitoring and forecasting activities and can be linked to data from the NCPB, Ministries of Agriculture and Health, and the Meteorological Department. The monitoring value of this data has been further enhanced by the analysis of forecast estimates of crop production in past years compared to confirmed estimates, and the analysis of trends in market prices, for example, to compare dry and wet years.

Work in progress intends to combine price information (both officially and in the local markets) with household-level production and disposal information. This will improve the ability to forecast food availability at both the national and local levels. Continuing analysis of the Household Budget Survey will provide information regarding the relationships between nutrition and socioeconomic factors. A systematic comparison of the field-level results of the various food-monitoring approaches (including KREMU, NCPB, and the Ministry of Agriculture) would make an important contribution in the refinement of the different approaches.

The food sector is complex, and its monitoring requires the compilation of data from as many sources as possible. For example, a particular group or the poor in a certain district may be vulnerable to retail-market price fluctuations; their vulnerability becomes more acute prior to the harvest when retail prices are high and opportunities for wage labor are low. The assessment of the food sector monitoring project might note:

1. that market prices are above the seasonal norm
2. that the cropped area is below the seasonal norm (i.e., providing a likely fall in demand for hired labor)
3. that the crop water balance index is low; this is later confirmed by the crop forecast survey, likely resulting in low food stocks within the household

The incidence of malnutrition would increase at this time, which the results of the CHANIS survey may help to confirm. If the NCPB stocks in the area are also low, the system may advise the government that an abnormal demand for purchased foods can be expected. The emerging situation should be targeted for verification by other ministries that collect relevant information. For instance, the Meteorological Department could provide more rainfall data, and the Ministry of Agriculture could request additional crop information from its field staff.

The formal mode of collaborating in monitoring the food sector is through the Interministerial Food Forecasting Committee (IMFFC). The members of this committee are from:

1. Central Bureau of Statistics (CBS)
2. Food and Nutrition Planning Unit (FNPU)
3. Kenya Rangeland Ecological Monitoring Unit (KREMU)
4. Ministry of Agriculture
5. National Cereals and Produce Board (NCPB)
6. Office of the President

The director of the CBS convenes and chairs quarterly meetings of the committee. Members present their independent survey reports or estimates of production and crop areas of major food crops, (maize, beans, potatoes, sorghum, millet, and rice). A food forecasting working group is concerned with coordinating the different forecasts and developing methods to predict yields. The committee harmonizes results or estimates presented by each department or ministry, and then decides on national estimates of area, production, and yield of the above crops. For example, after the 1985 long rains, very different national estimates were made by the four organizations monitoring maize production, reflecting differences in methods and samples (Table 6.3). The committee discussed each estimate and agreed on a national estimate of 29 million bags for the year. The CBS estimate is generally believed to be low, as the Crop Forecast Survey underreports the production from large farms.

The committee provides a forum to discuss the development of the monitoring system. Its major purpose is to inform the government of expected production so that rational decisions may be taken. For example:

1. If the production is lower than expected consumption, the government will need to decide whether to import food.
2. If production is more than expected, the government can decide on adequate storage facilities, as well as provide funds to the NCPB to purchase the surplus from the farmers.
3. Food-deficit districts can be identified and transport arrangements made to have food transferred to these districts at the appropriate time.

The committee has suffered in the past from a lack of full member participation. A recurrent problem is having all the information from the various members ready in a final state for discussion. In addition, the committee has no statutory power to enforce cooperation. During the drought emergency, the committee continued to meet, but much of its synthesizing role was taken over by the Task Force on Food Supply and Distribution in the Office of the President, which required more detailed and frequent information than the committee normally handles.

CONCLUSION

The CBS has played a lead role in developing a systematic food-monitoring system. Its continuing development requires collaboration between all the parties involved. A pilot Food Sector Bulletin was prepared in 1986 in order to present decisionmakers with a periodic synopsis of the food situation in Kenya. The benefits of reliable and timely information far outweigh the costs, both economic and human, if decisions on imports, exports, and food relief are made on the basis of faulty or incomplete data.

Figure 6.1. Areas surveyed by the Central Bureau of Statistics. Shaded areas were included in NASSEP I.

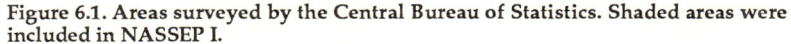

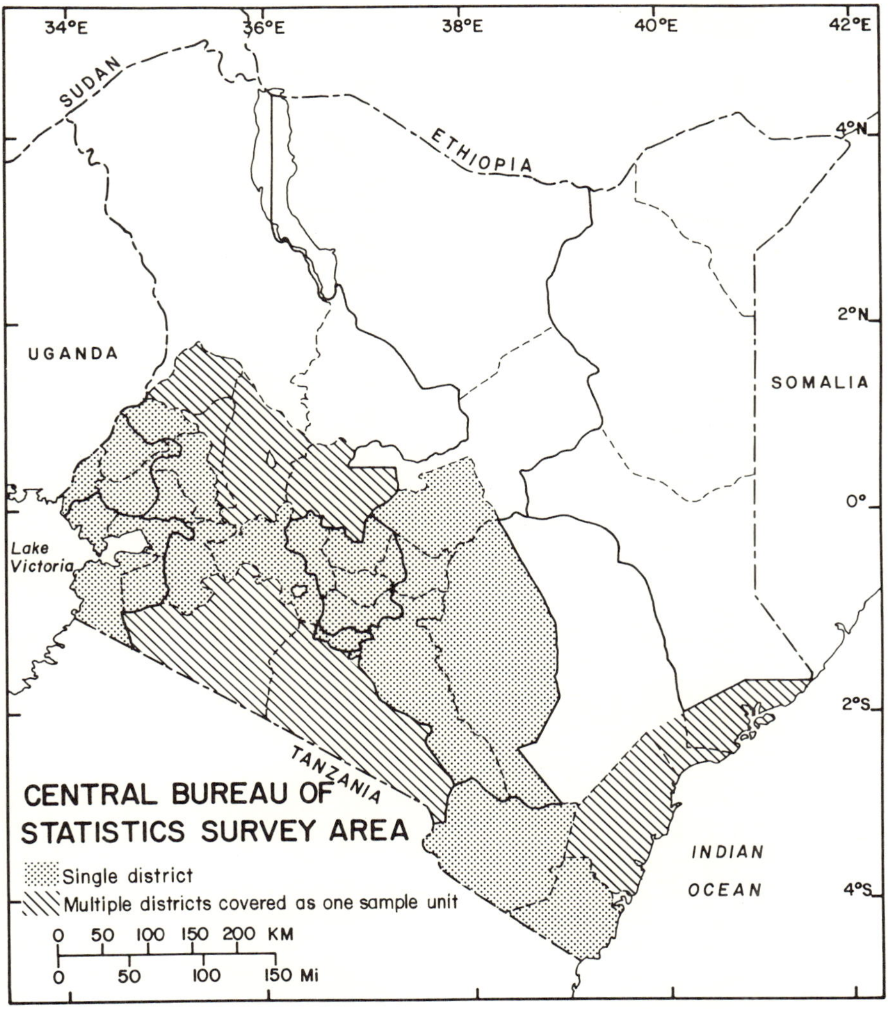

Figure 6.2 Monthly average prices for maize and beans. Source: data from the CBS.

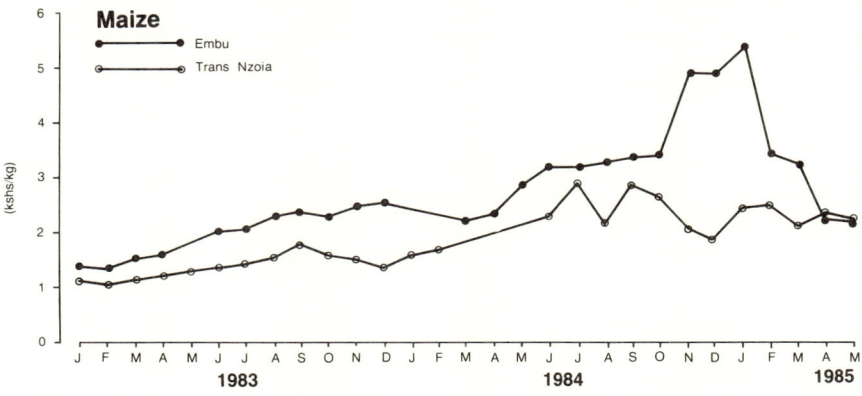

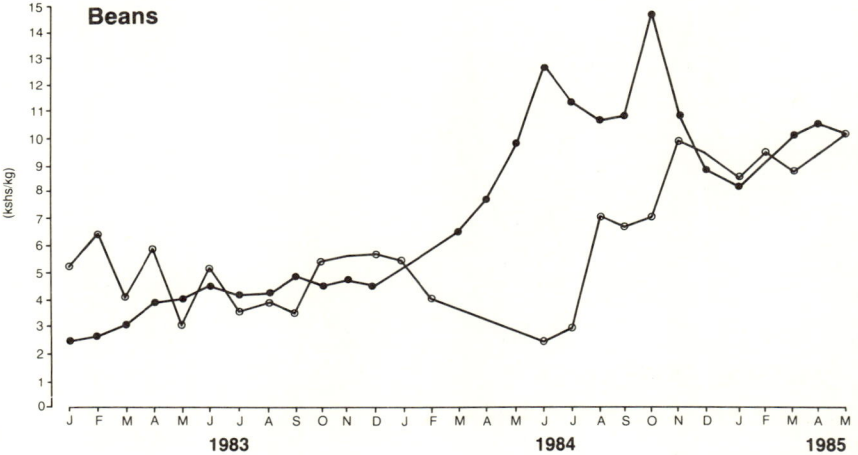

Table 6.1 Crop Forecast Survey Schedule

Month	Survey	Launching Date	Report Due
Long Rains (LR)			
April/May	Estimate of LR area planted; Confirmation of previous SR harvest	15 April	15 June
July/August	Forecast of LR harvest	15 July	15 September
Short Rains (SR)			
October/November	Estimate of SR area planted; Confirmation of previous LR harvest	15 October	15 December
December/January	Forecast of SR harvest	15 December	15 March

Note: The short rains surveys are not carried out in the Rift Valley since it has only one primary season.

Table 6.2 Crop Forecast Survey Results, 1983–1985

District	Maize - Confirmed Harvest Estimates (1,000 bags)			
	1983 SR	1984 LR	1984 SR	1985 LR
Kil/Lamu/Tana	54.2	302.0	273.9	19.8
Kwale	33.7	155.4	244.9	87.1
Taita/Taveta	22.0	22.9	162.0	110.4
Machakos	311.4	98.1	554.1	396.4
Kitui	57.0	6.8	486.0	284.9
Meru	312.5	43.1	525.8	309.7
Embu	53.0	43.1	215.6	90.2
Nyeri	49.5	76.9	196.7	143.4
Murang'a	167.1	76.0	346.6	267.3
Kirinyaga	40.0	46.1	170.9	280.4
Kiambu	104.7	32.3	254.5	248.7
Nyandarua	4.8	126.3	230.1	3.5
Nakuru	—	653.5	—	1,369.8
Nandi	—	955.4	—	—
Narok/Kajiado	—	105.8	—	—
Kericho	—	1,377.1	—	1,897.3
Uasin Gishu	—	133.4	—	—
Trans Nzoia	—	979.4	—	—
Baringo/Laikip.	—	326.0	—	—
Marakwet/Pokot	—	433.8	—	—
S. Nyanza	177.2	301.3	641.1	404.5
Kisii	319.5	549.5	953.6	630.0
Kisumu	28.1	33.6	153.1	68.2
Siaya	—	186.7	209.8	172.4
Kakamega	—	620.2	1,355.1	321.6
Bungoma	—	394.1	1,371.5	231.7
Busia	40.3	113.9	134.0	85.9
Total	1,775.1	8,192.7	8,479.3	7,423.3

Notes: Bags are 90 kg. LR is long rains; SR, short rains. District error estimates for the 1983 short rains range from 13 to 96 percent (8.8 percent for the total); from 14 to 68 percent (6.6 percent for the total), for the 1984 long rains from 11 to 38 percent (6.4 percent) for the 1984 short rains, and from 14 to 75 percent (11.2 percent) for the 1985 long rains. Dashes mean either the district was not surveyed or no returns were compiled; they are not included in the error estimates.

Table 6.2—Continued

District	Maize - Area Planted Estimates (1,000 ha)		
	1984 LR	1984 SR	1985 LR
Kil/Lamu/Tana	92.8	167.7	52.3
Kwale	43.0	99.5	29.2
Taita/Taveta	11.4	1.4	15.7
Machakos	—	2.7	126.1
Kitui	57.8	1.4	114.5
Meru	43.0	0.7	55.4
Embu	26.4	4.4	13.9
Nyeri	14.6	14.0	20.6
Murang'a	22.6	12.1	38.5
Kirinyaga	10.9	16.9	25.2
Kiambu	17.3	0.3	41.2
Nyandarua	8.2	18.3	19.7
Nakuru	9.8	22.0	38.9
Nandi	21.9	690.2	28.6
Narok/Kajiado	10.2	71.7	—
Kericho	33.0	806.0	58.9
Uasin Gishu	13.1	68.7	23.9
Trans Nzoia	11.6	310.5	42.1
Baringo/Laikip.	5.9	2.7	—
Marakwet/Pokot	14.6	359.3	—
S. Nyanza	35.6	33.6	61.6
Kisii	50.8	195.7	72.1
Kisumu	20.0	1.8	48.0
Siaya	32.6	51.5	40.6
Kakamega	100.5	245.7	86.6
Bungoma	75.5	296.5	53.4
Busia	25.0	48.4	17.6
Total	808.1	3,543.9	1,124.3

Notes: Areas are for pure and mixed stands. Results for the 1983 short rains were not available. Errors for each district estimate range from 12 to 51 percent (5.5 percent for the total) for the 1984 long rains, 12 to 100 percent (8.2 percent for the total) for the 1984 short rains, and 13 to 34 percent (5.5 percent) for the 1985 long rains.

Table 6.2—Continued

District	Beans - Confirmed Harvest Estimates (1,000 bags)			
	1983 SR	1984 LR	1984 SR	1985 LR
Kil/Lamu/Tana	0.1	—	0.3	—
Kwale	—	1.3	4.9	0.3
Taita/Taveta	1.4	3.7	7.0	9.8
Machakos	78.0	29.9	98.9	60.6
Kitui	10.8	2.2	81.6	88.2
Meru	111.6	13.4	114.6	145.8
Embu	16.4	12.8	40.0	50.9
Nyeri	43.2	27.6	50.5	41.7
Murang'a	39.1	17.4	66.6	69.4
Kirinyaga	37.6	7.7	39.9	57.5
Kiambu	17.0	2.7	27.9	44.6
Nyandarua	—	0.4	0.5	0.1
Nakuru	—	61.3	—	48.7
Nandi	—	16.0	—	0.9
Narok/Kajiado	—	14.2	—	—
Kericho	—	40.1	—	50.9
Uasin Gishu	—	1.4	—	—
Trans Nzoia	—	30.2	—	—
Baringo/Laikip.	—	42.7	—	—
Marakwet/Pokot	—	20.4	—	—
S. Nyanza	19.1	39.4	76.4	56.3
Kisii	51.7	79.5	121.0	97.9
Kisumu	0.5	2.2	8.4	3.1
Siaya	—	21.8	27.8	28.9
Kakamega	—	70.3	156.3	47.5
Bungoma	—	63.9	125.1	50.6
Busia	1.8	7.8	9.6	6.7
Total	428.1	630.0	1,057.3	960.5

Notes: District errors for 1983 short rains range from 12 to 100 percent (total is 7.8 percent), from 19 to 100 percent (8.1 percent) for 1984 long rains, from 20 to 100 percent (9.0 percent) for the 1984 short rains, and from 14 to 100 percent (10.1 percent) for the 1985 long rains.

Table 6.2—Continued

District	Beans - Area Planted Estimates (1,000 ha)		
	1984 LR	1984 SR	1985 LR
Kil/Lamu/Tana	1.9	—	0.4
Kwale	0.0	0.2	1.7
Taita/Taveta	5.0	5.1	5.1
Machakos	—	64.6	49.6
Kitui	34.4	35.9	56.2
Meru	45.9	42.0	53.7
Embu	11.9	7.0	8.7
Nyeri	11.8	20.6	16.9
Murang'a	15.6	25.9	30.4
Kirinyaga	7.6	20.3	17.3
Kiambu	10.5	13.6	22.5
Nyandarua	2.0	0.6	5.5
Nakuru	5.2	—	13.6
Nandi	4.9	—	9.0
Narok/Kajiado	2.3	—	—
Kericho	2.8	—	15.4
Uasin Gishu	6.6	—	5.9
Trans Nzoia	7.4	—	17.8
Baringo/Laikip	3.5	—	—
Marakwet/Pokot	5.1	—	—
S. Nyanza	3.5	22.0	12.7
Kisii	46.5	42.1	52.2
Kisumu	5.5	3.3	8.8
Siaya	20.1	22.1	25.0
Kakamega	83.2	27.9	69.2
Bungoma	50.4	17.5	30.1
Busia	7.8	4.3	5.6
Total	401.3	374.8	533.2

Source: Data from the Central Bureau of Statistics.
Notes: Area is for pure and mixed stands. Estimates for 1983 short rains are not available. District errors for the 1984 long rains range from 14 to 100 percent (total is 7.9 percent); for the 1984 short rains, from 12 to 100 percent (6.4 percent); and for the 1985 long rains, from 14 to 100 percent (7.2 percent).

Table 6.3 Maize Yield Estimates for 1985

Organization	1985 LR	1985 SR	1985 Total
CBS	22.9	5.0	27.9
KREMU	25.4	3.5	28.9
Ministry of Agriculture	23.6	5.0	28.6
NCPB	27.0	8.1	35.1

Source: Data from the Central Bureau of Statistics (CBS), Kenya Rangeland Ecological Monitoring Unit (KREMU), Ministry of Agriculture, and National Cereals and Produce Board (NCPB).
Note: Units are bags/ha using 90 kg bags. Estimates as of October 1985, assuming a normal short rains. See Table 5.2 for district comparisons between KREMU, Ministry of Agriculture, and CBS estimates.

· 7 ·

Food Crop Monitoring and Reporting by the Ministry of Agriculture

DUNCAN N. MWANJILA

In Kenya, the Ministry of Agriculture has staff from the sublocation to the national level, in parallel to the government administrative system of subchiefs, chiefs, district officers, district commissioners, and provincial staff. This means that the ministry is one of the best-established institutions, having a wide base that enables it to monitor the crop situation throughout the country.

The frontline staff, agricultural advisors at the location and sublocation levels, was previously appointed through the district administration. The staff was composed of people who could command authority and enforce order in their local areas and whose advice would be readily adopted. In most cases, they were very close to the location chiefs. Once appointed, the staff was trained in basic agriculture and then returned to work as junior technical assistants within their locations or sublocations. Currently, this cadre is being replaced by a more educated and qualified staff.

In addition to the technical assistants, the field staff includes a locational extension officer, divisional extension officer, district crops officer, and provincial crops officer. These staff members form a direct line of authority to the headquarters staff: the minister and permanent secretary, director of agriculture, and chief of the crop production division.

FOOD AND CROP MONITORING AND REPORTING

The key to the monitoring and reporting system is the District Agricultural Office. It is at the district level that action reports are prepared and made available to district and national decisionmakers. For any given season, the following activities are part of the monitoring system:

1. Production targets based on previous performance
2. Programs for the implementation of production targets (e.g., land preparation, inputs availability and distribution, and the processing of credit facilities)

3. Crop condition in the field, stage of growth, and the effects of weather and other natural hazards, pests, and diseases
4. Achievements and the realization of production targets
5. Pre- and post-harvesting procedures
6. On-farm and national storage facilities
7. Marketing progress from farmers to consumers
8. Food situation: the prices of foodstuffs in local markets and the areas experiencing food shortages

A food and crop monitoring report is prepared on a monthly basis, or fortnightly when serious conditions prevail. This report provides continuous monitoring of the major crops, especially the major food crops. Forecasts of deficits and surpluses are given to the appropriate authorities for necessary action. The report is prepared by every extension worker, and reviewed, updated, and aggregated at the location, division, and district levels. The district report is submitted to the provincial office and headquarters. The reports are discussed at staff meetings at each level before being forwarded to the next level. The reports represent an estimate of crop conditions based on visual indicators and past history, rather than a statistical sample or measurement. The strength of the monitoring system is its coverage of almost all the agricultural areas. In most areas, good communications between the district offices and Nairobi allow emerging problems to be checked and regular updates made of the crop situation.

EFFECTS OF THE REPORTING SYSTEM DURING THE 1984 DROUGHT

The food and crop monitoring and reporting system has been in use for a long time and has helped the government to identify and rectify problems affecting farmers. For example, periods of food shortage following a drought are easily identified, such as in 1965, 1970, 1975, 1980, and 1984. The government developed and published the National Food Policy in 1981 as a result of the serious food shortage in 1980 (see Chapter 24).

This policy was operational in 1984. The monitoring and reporting system, operating fortnightly, provided the early information that enabled the government to take quick action in 1984 by importing food in time, banning the exportation of food, launching the National Famine Relief Fund, and mobilizing the relevant organizations to ensure that importation and transportation of food progressed smoothly.

Through the reporting system, the government was made aware of the need to:

1. Have adequate strategic food reserves embracing a wide range of foods, including maize, beans, wheat, and milk powder

2. Encourage on-farm storage and reduce post-harvest losses
3. Give farmers production incentives (i.e., inputs, credit facilities, extension services, price reviews, market outlets, and an infrastructure for transport)

One of the most important activities of the ministry during the drought was to coordinate combined efforts by the National Irrigation Board and the Kenya Seed Company to produce seed maize at the Bura Irrigation Scheme on the Tana River. This greatly increased the availability of maize seed (especially Katumani and hybrids 511 and 512), which was scarce during the 1984 short rains.

CONCLUSION

The district agricultural officers continuously monitor the weather and food and crop situation in their districts. They have access to information from their own staff, as well as reports from other ministries and the district administration. The system is comprehensive and reliable, although it could be improved with additional training for the field staff.

· 8 ·
Agricultural Yields, Production, and Monitoring Methods of the National Cereals and Produce Board

F. G. MURAGE

The National Cereals and Produce Board (NCPB) is a government parastatal, with responsibility for marketing cereals (maize, sorghum, wheat, millet, and rice) and other produce (notably, beans) throughout the country. In 1981, it maintained ten major storage facilities in the country, with a capacity to hold 7.5 million bags (675,000 mt) of food crops (Government of Kenya 1981). Storage needs for 1983/84 were projected to be 11.5 million bags (1,035,000 mt), although little progress was made to expand storage facilities until after the 1984/85 drought. The NCPB is usually a monopoly agent and controls interdistrict trade; however, in 1987, milling companies were allowed to purchase maize directly from producers. The NCPB also handles imports and exports in liaison with the Ministry of Agriculture and Ministry of Finance. As a result of its monopoly position, the NCPB has accurate data on food stocks in the formal market, but it does not collect information on private household retentions or sales to local traders in the informal market.

The NCPB has two methods to estimate national production as an indicator of the amount of produce the NCPB may be offered to purchase: a sample survey of maize yields and estimates by the NCPB field staff, called area managers. This chapter describes the maize yield survey in some detail (see also Murage 1985). The estimates by area managers are discussed in the last section.

MAIZE YIELD MONITORING

In the crop-monitoring exercise, projection of maize output is of cardinal interest. Projecting output involves forecasting the area planted with the crop and the average yield per unit area. It is difficult to forecast annual yields because many factors that affect yields, such as weather and diseases, are beyond the farmers' control. Forecasting yields is more difficult than forecasting area planted.

Sampling Method

A number of facts about the biological characteristics of maize and the physical characteristics of Kenya and its people have influenced the selection of the sampling method. The most important of these facts are:

1. Maize yields vary with rainfall, temperature, and soil conditions.
2. Maize yields vary with different amounts of input and with differences in husbandry.
3. Available hybrid seeds have been bred to suit different sites in Kenya.

The geographical differences in yield are of most importance. To facilitate comparisons between groups of farmers and to reduce variations in yields, the sample is first stratified in nine different ecological zones (Table 8.1). Using the UTM grid on 1:250,000 topographical maps, the zones were delineated to the nearest 10 x 10 km square. Each zone (1 to 9) consists of a series of numbered squares used as the basis for a random sample.

Within each zone, a random sample is drawn on a geographic basis, with each place in a zone given an equal chance of being included. A sample of at least twenty-five squares was drawn for each zone (with the exception of zone 7, in which individual farms were selected, and zone 8, in which there were only fifteen segments). The target is at least 120 cases from each zone. A 1 x 1 km "segment" was selected from each 10 x 10 km square and marked on 1:50,000 maps. These areas are the primary sampling units (PSU). This randomization also has the purpose of sampling the variation occurring from differences in soils and climate.

In each PSU, a cluster of four individual farmers were selected at random from a list of fields compiled by the leader of the survey team after visiting the PSU. A condition for inclusion on the list was that a field must be at least a quarter of an acre. A secondary purpose of the study is to relate various husbandry habits and input levels to yields.

For the larger farms, a different method was necessary, because the 100 ha contained in a sq km was usually only a fraction of the total farm size. From a register of large farms obtained from the Central Bureau of Statistics (CBS), all farms that had reported growing maize in the year before 1975 were extracted. From this set, a subsample of 20 percent was drawn, giving a total of about 140 farms distributed over the zone.

The survey is conducted when the cobs are ripe, from June to January for the first rains (the major maize crop, planted in March to April) and November to January for the second rains (Table 8.1). The survey data are processed on an IBM-PC. It takes about a month after the returns from each zone are received to produce a yield estimate for the zone. Since the crop calendar is different in each zone, the survey lasts between six and seven months, using two teams conducting a total of about one thousand interviews.

Measurements

Maize yields depend on the number of cobs per ha and on the weight of the grain on the cobs. There is a direct relationship between the size of a cob and the weight of its grains. A regression analysis of volume against weight indicated that about 92 to 94 percent of the variation in weight was explained by diameter and length, using the equation:

$$w = d^2 \times l$$

where

w = weight of grain at 13 percent moisture content
d = diameter of cob, measured outside of husks
l = length of cob, measured outside of husks

In the survey, thirty cobs were selected at random in each field. Each of these cobs had its diameter and length measurement recorded. Cob populations were estimated using two different methods, depending on whether or not the maize was planted in rows.

Maize Husbandry

Apart from cob populations, size measurements, and the geographical and climatic information implicit in the sample, a number of questions about farm husbandry are asked at each visit. Agronomic research on maize in Kenya has shown that yields are related to various combinations of inputs and to different husbandry techniques employed by the farmer. The following questions are asked (for each question, a hypothesis is indicated about the effect of the factor on yields):

1. Did you use purchased hybrid seed? Hybrid seed will produce higher yields than local seed.
2. How did you prepare your land? Plowing is assumed to coincide with improved husbandry in general and to be positively correlated with higher yields.
3. What planting method did you use? More elaborate methods are assumed to be correlated with improved husbandry and higher yields.
4. Time of planting? Early planting increases yield.
5. Was the maize planted in rows? Row planting is assumed to be positively correlated with better husbandry and with higher yields.
6. What type of hybrid seed did you plant? This question is used to cross-check question (1) above.
7. Did you use fertilizer? Fertilizer increases yields and is correlated with improved husbandry.
8. Did you use insecticide? Insecticide decreases losses and is correlated with improved husbandry.
9. Was the maize thinned? When performed to achieve the correct plant population, thinning increases yield and is correlated with improved husbandry.

10. Was the field clean from weeds? Good weeding increases yields.
11. Was the maize interplanted with other crops? Interplanting reduces the plant population and reduces the maize yield (regardless of what happens to the interplanted crop).
12. Was there any lodging of the maize? Lodging before the crop matures may reduce the yields, and animals and vermin may destroy the lodged mature crop.
13. Was hail damage noticed? Serious hail damage may reduce yields.
14. Was insect damage noticed? This question cross-checks (8) above. Insect damage is known to reduce the yields.
15. Was there any other damage observed? Other damage, such as monkeys at the Coast, elephants at Nyahururu, and pigs, may reduce the yields considerably.

Validation of Model

The quality of the yield estimates depends on the accuracy of the cob population estimates, the cob size measurements, and the model used to convert volume to weight. The various methods used in the survey have been tested in a number of ways to establish what errors are likely to occur.

The estimates of the cob population are critical. An analysis of variance showed no significant differences between the enumerators in estimates of the number of cobs (in fields not planted in rows) or distance between rows and number of plants (in fields planted in rows). In spite of this, significant differences have been observed between actual measurements for fields not planted in rows. In seventy-two separate fields, the overall average was 13.26 cobs per square, with a standard deviation of 3.86. It is likely that the tendencies to overestimate or underestimate cancel each other out, and no adjustments have been made for enumerator effects in the yield calculations. An investigation of cob sizes for 106 farms and four interviewers revealed no significant differences in the size measurement for different interviewers.

In order to check the results from measurements with actual yields, two different methods have been used. The first was the complete harvesting of a sample of maize cobs from fields in Githunguri and near Kerugoya. In both cases, eight measurements were performed using the yield survey method. The area of the field was carefully measured, and all the maize was removed and weighed in the field. A random sample of one hundred cobs was dried and shelled, and the dry weight determined (Table 8.2). For Githunguri, the two methods give consistent estimates, but the results are not satisfactory for Kerugoya. The harvested yield was 2,074 kg/ha, one-third less than the estimate based on the cob measurements. The explanation for the large error is that the Kerugoya field was extremely difficult to measure. The error is due to large variations in the plant population estimate since the rows were irregular, a number of plants had fallen, and germination had failed in large areas. In Githunguri, the field was planted in straight rows, well weeded, and easy to measure.

A number of maize cobs were measured for length and width, both outside and inside the husks. The cobs were then dried and shelled, and the weight of the grain was recorded for each cob. Regression analyses for the inside and outside measurements were 0.95 and 0.93, respectively, and the improvement from dehusking the cobs was judged as marginal. Since outside measurements are simpler, all measurements are taken for the outside of the cobs. The cobs were left on the standing plant so as not to interfere with the farmer's field.

During the survey, samples of maize cobs were collected from several farms in each zone. These cobs were measured and weighed, and a regression analysis was performed on the samples from each zone. The regression equations differed slightly, probably due to the different amounts of local maize in different zones and the varying shapes of the most common hybrid in each zone. Short and thick cobs give a different regression equation than do long and thin ones. The regression equations used to estimate yields in the different zones are given in Table 8.3.

Results

The yields calculated from the survey are biological yields in a standing crop. The measurements do not allow for diseased cobs, rotting, damage by pests or insects in the field, harvesting losses, or losses after harvest. Post-harvest losses have been studied rather extensively in various African countries; from previous work, losses of 10 to 15 percent in Kenya can be expected. Pre-harvest losses, however, have not been studied comprehensively in Kenya, but it is likely that they are of a similar magnitude.

The Central Bureau of Statistics estimates the area planted to maize (see Chapter 6). The yield rates from the NCPB survey are multiplied with the area estimates in order to estimate production. The calculated yields and the available data on past purchases by the NCPB are used to predict expected purchases. Table 8.4 provides the results of several years of zone 6 (Machakos and Kitui), which has the lowest average yields, with almost no yields in 1984.

Table 8.5 shows the results of the survey for the first (long) rains for 1981, 1983, and 1984 by zone. The variation in yield between zones is considerable. The most productive zones are in western Kenya (1 and 7), where high yields were recorded even during the drought. Although the sample size and its geographic distribution varies each year, the national average in 1984 was considerably lower than that of the previous drought in 1981.

Most of the farmers reported purchasing some seed, thinning their fields, clear weeding, and interplanting maize. Less than half used fertilizer or insecticide. The effect of the 1984 drought is also indicated by the lower rates of improved husbandry. Farmers abandoned fields that did not germinate or promise a satisfactory return to their efforts.

AREA MANAGERS' ESTIMATES

NCPB area managers are stationed at the field depots (each of which have a defined area) in order to oversee the purchase and distribution of produce. To aid the NCPB in determining its budget requirements, area managers estimate the amount of produce they expect to purchase in each season. Estimates by district for 1984/85 and 1985/86 are provided in Table 8.6. The estimates are usually provided at the start of the season and before the yield survey; they are updated based on observations of the crop and the volume of purchases during the season.

The field reports from the depots are most useful in monitoring the level and flow of food stocks. As noted in Chapter 2, the high volume of sales from depots in drought-affected areas prompted the government's timely response. Expected purchases for the 1984/85 agricultural year differed substantially from actual purchases, indicating the lack of systematic effort by the area managers in monitoring crop production. In May 1984, they underestimated total purchases by 10 percent.

CONCLUSION

The NCPB has a critical role in monitoring the production, sales, and stocks of food in Kenya. It has the potential to combine a field sample survey with other data concerning projected yields and area planted, such as that collected by the Central Bureau of Statistics and KREMU, and integrate these projections with its regular monitoring of food trade.

Table 8.1 NCPB Geographic Zones

Zone No.	Approximate Area (District)	Approximate Altitude Range	Average Rainfall	Survey Period
1	Bungoma, Kakamega, Kisii, Kericho	1,500–2,800	over 1,500 mm	Aug–Sep
2	Bungoma, Kakamega, Kisii	1,200–1,500	1,200–1,600	Jul–Aug
3	Nyanza Province, except Kisii	1,100–1,400	1,000–1,200	Jun–Jul
4	Lower parts of Meru, Embu, Kirinyaga, Murang'a, Kiambu	1,100–1,500	800–1,000	Aug–Sep
5	Upper parts of Meru, Embu, Kirinyaga, Nyeri, Murang'a, Kiambu	1,500–2,400	1,000–1,500	Sep–Oct
6	Machakos, Kitui	1,000–1,400	500–800	Jun–Jul
7	Large-scale farming areas, Uasin Gishu, Trans Nzoia, Nakuru	1,500–2,000	over 1,000	Sep–Nov
8	Highlands in Nyandarua	1,800–2,400	800–1,200	Dec–Jan
9	The Coastal Belt	0–500	900–1,200	Jul–Aug

Source: Murage (1985).

Table 8.2 Harvest Results from Two Maize Fields

	Githunguri	Kerugoya
Size of field, sq m	2,670	3,965
Harvested Yield, kg/ha	4,662	2,074
Estimated yield from cobs	4,632	3,119
Standard deviation, measured yield	568	1,135
Coefficient of variation, %	12	36

Source: Data from the NCPB.

Table 8.3. Regression Equations for Cob Size and Weight

Zone	Average Size	Average Weight	Constant	Coefficient	r^2	n
1	485	176	–3	.335	.96	78
2	534	181	–2	.305	.95	65
3	405	124	–1	.280	.89	69
4	482	154	4	.280	.94	97
5	476	156	–10	.315	.94	46
6	345	81	4	.225	.81	40
7	511	178	4	.304	.92	100
8	—	—	1	.300	—	—
9	420	143	32	.245	.95	—

Source: Data from the NCPB.
Notes: Size = $d^2 \times l/1000$ (d = diameter, l = length). The regression equation is $y = a + b \times$ size, where y = weight, a = constant, and b = regression coefficient.

Table 8.4 NCPB Maize Yield Survey for Machakos and Kitui (Zone 6)

Year	Average Yield	
	kg/ha	bags/ha
1975	661	7.3
1976	146	1.6
1977	396	4.4
1978	468	5.2
1981	848	9.3
1983	37	0.4
1984	17	0.2
1985	855	9.4

Source: Data from the NCPB.
Notes: Measurements were not done for 1979, 1980, and 1982. Bags are 90 kg.

Table 8.5 Results of the NCPB Maize Yield Survey by Zone

Zone	Avg. Yield	Farms	Seed	Fert	Insect	Thinned	Inter	Weeded	Insectd
1981									
1	3509	51	51	38	19	42	30	43	25
2	2589	25	23	7	7	13	14	18	0
3	1514	49	30	13	5	39	14	37	2
4	1658	58	43	20	13	46	35	54	6
5	2372	39	34	22	11	32	26	36	27
6	823	101	26	12	10	48	90	99	4
7	4095	84	76	62	34	50	39	69	68
8	3734	34	23	16	5	26	24	17	26
Total	2405	441	306	190	104	296	272	373	158
1983									
1	3463	59	57	42	8	44	29	46	28
2	2136	55	55	11	3	44	29	40	31
3	1609	23	9	6	1	22	11	18	7
4	1672	56	14	22	16	28	32	49	14
5	3031	88	71	59	22	57	52	81	5
6	1075	4	1	0	1	1	3	4	0
7	4030	89	88	78	53	61	40	64	44
8	3103	27	22	19	0	20	17	21	14
Total	2908	401	317	237	104	277	213	323	143
1984									
1	3211	22	20	20	10	17	19	15	10
2	2791	52	48	12	0	37	26	37	30
3	835	69	14	2	1	21	12	25	16
5	608	93	17	15	11	8	2	17	0
8	891	42	21	15	6	22	16	22	23
9	1700	24	6	1	1	3	13	19	13
Total	1352	302	126	65	29	108	88	135	92

Source: Data from the NCPB.
Notes: Variables are: Avg. Yield - Average yield for zone, kg/ha; Farms: number of farms surveyed; Seed: number of farmers who purchased seed; Fert: number of farmers who applied fertilizer; Insect: number of farmers who applied insecticide; Thinned: number of farmers who thinned the field; Inter: number of farmers who interplanted the field; Weeded: number of farmers who clear weeded the field before planting; Insectd: number of fields with insect damage in the field. Total is the average yield weighted by the number of farms and the sum across zones for each variable.

Table 8.6 Expected and Actual Maize Purchases by the NCPB

District/Region[1]	1983/84 Actual	1984/85 Expected[2]	1984/85 Actual	1985/86 Expected
Nakuru	509,614	293,313	18,713	827,426
Baringo	124,194	71,644	—	—
Uasin Gishu	1,064,304	614,366	394,756	1,013,754
Trans Nzoia	1,082,952	623,580	1,298,396	2,013,904
West Pokot	69,198	39,972	54,512	
Elgeyo Marakwet	112,255	64,844	23,457	182,169
Kericho	534,058	308,454	295,019	698,782
Nandi	593,433	226,897	372,313	620,423
Kajiado	18,724	10,760	124,056	140,976
Laikipia/Samburu	128,010	73,868	4,819	270,825
Narok	127,410	72,547	61,712	228,239
Rift Valley	4,164,152	2,401,245	2,647,753	5,996,498
Busia	10,073	11,463	16,502	100,704
Bungoma	503,682	573,163	803,872	820,300
Kakamega	318,872	362,859	465,739	689,995
Western	832,627	947,485	1,286,113	1,610,999
Kisii	185,228	145,959	78,537	351,714
Kisumu	3,321	2,629	354	9,116
Siaya	—	—	370	2,096
So. Nyanza	320,929	251,415	84,238	353,073
Nyanza	509,478	400,000	163,499	715,999
Meru/Marsabit	126	—	42,270	121,200
Embu	27	—	5,631	40,000
Kitui	12	—	35,919	100,000
Machakos	239	—	27,671	200,000
Isiolo	—	—	—	—
Eastern	404	—	111,491	461,200
Nyeri	35	—	—	3,000
Kirinyaga	62	—	1,329	97,000
Murang'a	30	—	4,890	43,000
Nyandarua	21,492	20,000	3,305	77,000
Kiambu	100	—	—	500
Central	21,719	20,000	9,524	220,500
Kwale	—	—	529	400
Kilifi	—	—	—	—
Taita	—	—	—	—
Lamu	—	—	—	—
Mombasa	—	—	—	—
Coast	—	—	529	400
Total	5,528,280	3,768,730	4,218,909	9,005,596

Source: Data from the NCPB.
Note: Units are 90 kg bags. Dash indicates no data reported.
[1]Regions (italicized) are not identical to provinces, and regional totals are as reported by the NCPB—they may not be the sum of the district estimates.
[2]1984/85 expected purchases are as of 11 May 1984.

· 9 ·

The Tanzanian Crop Monitoring and Early Warning System

D. A. R. KASHASHA

Tanzania encompasses a variety of agroecological zones, including semiarid soda flats and tropical rain forests. Rainfall tends to be bimodal, with a dry season in February. In some years, the dry season is short and crops are not affected. Crop failures in such a diverse country seldom cover more than two contiguous regions (of twenty regions in the country). Serious food problems normally affect areas less than a district (about 10,000 sq km) in size, but they may affect several districts at once. Years completely free of food problems in some areas are exceptional.

The Tanzanian Crop Monitoring and Early Warning Systems Project (CMEWSP) was one of the first in Africa to provide operational forecasts of food production to decisionmakers. The experience gained in developing and running this project over the last decade is relevant to planners in Kenya as they consider improving the various food-forecasting mechanisms.

The project was started in October 1978, with funds from the Dutch Government, and executed by the Food and Agriculture Organization (FAO). The budget for the second phase of the project (January 1982 to December 1984), was $1,385,293 by the donor government and Tsh 2,138,400 by the host government. This chapter summarizes the methods and operation of the project, while additional detail is provided in Frere and Popov (1979), FAO (1986), and Gommes (1985).

The purpose of the project is to provide advance information on cereal food-crop production and supply and to alert all those concerned well in advance of an impending food shortage or surplus so that suitable remedial action can be taken. This is achieved by:

1. Collecting, analyzing, and disseminating data on the food situation
2. Preparing early forecasts of food crop production
3. Recording the availability of agricultural inputs, including diesel fuel, relating such data to demand, and assessing probable effects on food production

132 • COPING WITH DROUGHT IN KENYA

The FAO provides a team leader (an agronomist or economist) and an agrometeorologist or agronomist. The Ministry of Agriculture and Livestock Development (KILIMO) provides one agronomist, one agricultural economist, and two agricultural field officers, while the Directorate of Meteorology provides one agrometeorologist. Other support staff are drawn from KILIMO or may be employed directly by the project.

The project has its own headquarters which is under the auspices of the Ministry of Agriculture and Livestock Development. However, it cooperates with the Directorate of Meteorology and other relevant agencies.

DATA COLLECTION, ANALYSIS, AND REPORTS

Data on crop parameters (phenology and condition), daily rainfall, and rural prices are received from about four hundred stations operated by agricultural extension officers and volunteers, primarily from schools, missions, and hospitals (Figure 9.1). A number of new stations were opened to fill gaps. Data are exchanged with Zambia to cover the border area. Crop parameters are also supplied monthly by over eighty district agricultural development officers (DADOs).

Regional food security officers (one in each region) report monthly on crop purchases by cooperatives from peasants and by the National Milling Corporation (NMC) from cooperatives. They also report on food stocks and inputs in their respective areas. The National Milling Corporation reports weekly and monthly on the food-stock position for the nation as a whole, including food imports.

All observers attend training seminars on observing and reporting. These seminars are organized and funded by the project in collaboration with the Directorate of Meteorology. This is the only direct expenditure on observers by the project. The project provides rain gauges and measuring cylinders, and it maintains constant correspondence with the observers through a prepaid reply service so that there is no need to procure stamps. Inspection tours are made by project staff. The importance of maintaining the network cannot be overemphasized.

Appendix 9.1 lists different codes that observers use on the weekly reporting card and that DADOs use on monthly forms. Regional food security officers report a summary of the official marketed output and input position. (Some produce is retained and not included in the marketed output figures.) If the forms are posted as soon as they are filled, returns at the project are generally over 70 percent within two weeks. There are only a few areas, which have peculiar transport constraints, where returns are delayed. A primary network of about fifty stations can be contacted by radio or telephone.

The data were initially computerized on Hewlett Packard microcomputers, which were later replaced by Olivetti personal computers. Before data entry, some quality control is done. For routine operations, programs have been developed by Dr. Gommes, a former project agrometeorologist (1980 to 1985). There are four groups of programs, most of which are written in a version of BASIC. RAINS and CROP manage the rainfall and crop data. AGRO estimates crop yields, based on the FAO crop-specific soil-water balance approach. The AGRO model uses daily data to compute a water satisfaction index, based on potential evapotranspiration (derived from Penman), rainfall, crop coefficients, and soil water-holding capacities. A weighted multiplier, indicating the amount of real data compared to probabilistic data for the rest of the season, is used to make predictions of the season's performance. The model was calibrated with district averages from district agricultural reports. LONGTERM compares long-term climatic data with the current season.

Computerization enables reports to be prepared for different purposes. The most frequent printouts are rainfall summaries for every region for any desired period, total rainfall maps for a desired period, crop phenology and the condition of various crops in a desired week, and rural prices for various crops in a given week. For example, the maize phenology at the end of March 1985 is mapped in Figure 9.2. Given the diversity of agroecological zones, the phenology is important in determining regional food supplies. Two seasons are contrasted in Figures 9.3 and 9.4. Crop conditions are mapped relative to the local average conditions. A good crop in one region may not be better than an average crop in a more productive zone. In 1983/84, most of the country was fair or worse than average, while in 1984/85, only one area reported crop failure while most of the country reported fair to good yields.

Interim production estimates are obtained for each district and crop by multiplying the area planted by yields. Yields are given by DADOs and by the crop specific soil-water balance calculations. These estimates are issued monthly from March until the national staple food supply projection is produced in July.

Ad hoc reports are prepared for senior officials in KILIMO on the most recent crop and food situation. The *Farming Weather Bulletin*, which is produced monthly in conjunction with the Directorate of Meteorology, focuses on rainfall and crops; it has maps of precipitation, crop stage and condition, and longest dry spells. It is distributed to the farming community. The *Consolidated Assessment of the National Staple Food Situation*, produced monthly, covers all aspects of the food situation, including crop condition to production estimates, stocks and supply projections, prices, and local grain purchases and imports. It is intended for senior officials in government and national parastatal organizations.

The *Consolidated Assessment of the National Staple Food Situation* follows crop performance throughout the season. It thus enables problem areas to be detected early in the season. The *Interim Production Estimates* further strengthen the identification of problem areas, as well as the expectations of good harvests. The *National Staple Food Supply Projections* give a clearer picture of the overall food situation in Tanzania for the year ahead.

CONCLUSION

The Tanzanian Crop Monitoring and Early Warning Systems Project is well established and seems to be achieving the desired results. It gives advance information to higher authorities, who are to take appropriate steps. It is not costly to operate, especially given the benefits of avoiding either famine or the overimportation of food. However, the project needs external finances for the procurement of computer spare parts, rain gauges, and measuring cylinders.

In the opinion of the author, such projects would benefit by being under the auspices of the meteorological services rather than the ministry of agriculture, since most of the data are meteorological or agrometeorological.

Figure 9.1 Spatial coverage of rain gauges in Tanzania. Shading indicates rural population (in thousands) per rain gauge in the CMEWSP network. The average spatial coverage of agricultural areas may be approximated by dividing the population density by five, assuming each person grows 0.2 ha. Source: Gommes (1985).

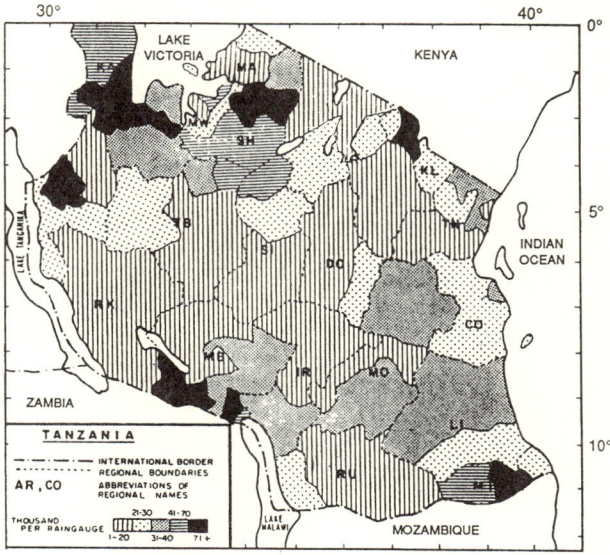

Figure 9.2 Maize phenology at the end of March 1985. N = no crop in the fields; A = planting; B = vegetative; C = flowering; D = "ready for harvest," or complete maturity, and E = harvest ongoing. Source: Gommes (1985), from the March 1985 *Farming Weather Bulletin*.

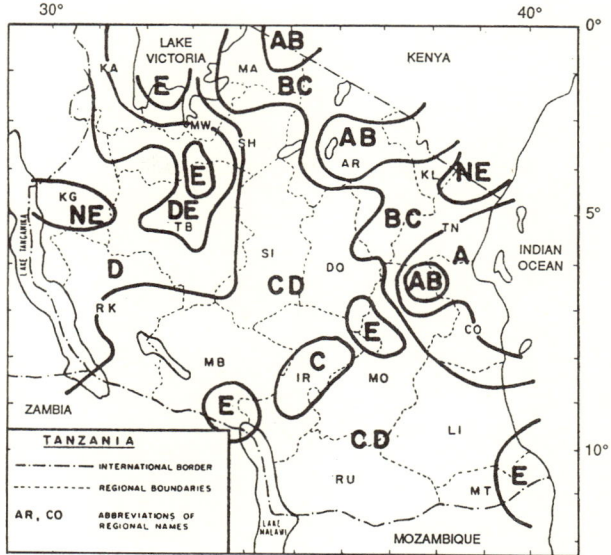

136 • COPING WITH DROUGHT IN KENYA

Figure 9.3 Condition of maize at the end of March 1984. Maize condition is expressed on a descriptive scale: 1 = failure; 2 = poor; 3 = normal or average; 4 = good; and 5 = excellent. Failure and excellent represent extreme conditions, i.e., a complete crop failure and a bumper harvest. The scale refers to local conditions; the same crop condition may describe crops in different states in different parts of the country. Source: Gommes (1985).

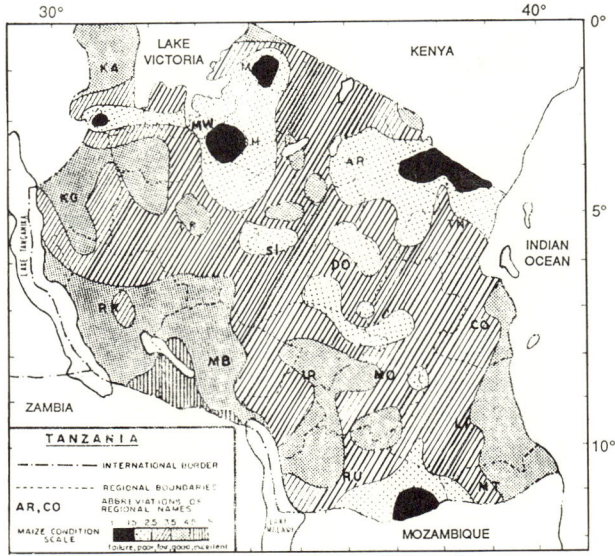

Figure 9.4 Condition of maize at the end of March 1985. Legend and notes as in Figure 9.3. Source: Gommes (1985).

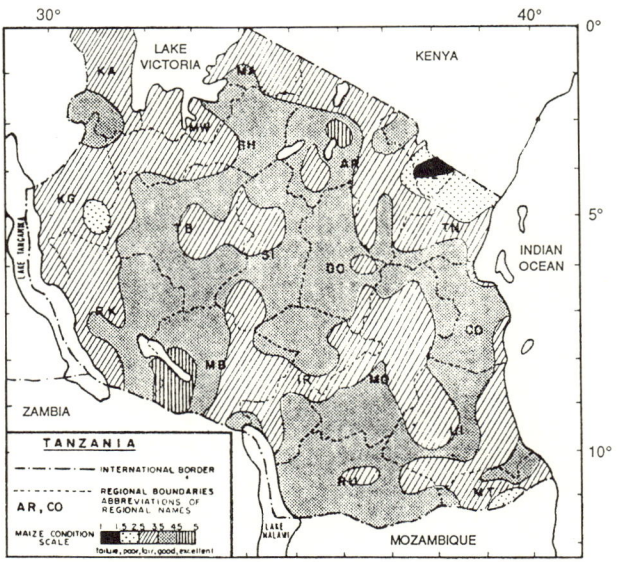

Appendix 9.1 Codes Used to Report Weekly Crop Data

Crop Condition

1 failure	Plants are very weak; almost no harvest is expected.
2 poor	Crop condition is below normal.
3 fair	Corresponds to a normal or "average" crop growth.
4 good	Crop condition better than normal.
5 excellent	Indicates a bumper harvest.

Crop Stage

A emergence	Planting is underway; crops have not exceeded a height of 10 cm.
B vegetative	Covers all the stages from "A" to the appearance of flowers (for cereals) or the corolla (beans).
C flowering	Appearance of flowers (for cereals) or the corolla (for beans).
D maturity	Full ripeness has been reached, and the crop is ready for harvesting.
E harvest	Farmers have started harvesting. Stages "D" and "E" have been distinguished since many farmers leave their crop in the field for some time after the full ripeness has been reached.

Adverse Effect During the Current Week

0	no adverse effect
1	insufficient rain or "too much sun"
2	excessive rainfall
3	hail, wind, or storm
4	army worms (*Spodoptera exempta*)
5	other insects
6	birds, mainly *Quelea quelea*
7	other animals (baboons, wild pigs, buffalos, elephants)
8	diseases, mainly maize streak virus
9	excessive weed growth
10	other (to be specified in the comments)

Production Compared with the Previous Season

--	less than half
-	between half and the same
=	about the same
+	between the same and twice as much
++	more than twice

· PART 3 ·
Drought Vulnerability, Impacts, and Coping Strategies

Aspects of vulnerability to drought are discussed in the first three chapters of Part 3, followed by four case studies of coping strategies in specific locales during the 1984/85 food crisis. Vulnerability to drought among pastoralists and their coping strategies are assessed in Chapters 10 (water resources in northern Kenya), 11 (Gabbra), 15 (Maasai), and 16 (Samburu); see also Chapter 20 for information on the Turkana District drought-monitoring plan. Detailed data on the impact of the drought among smallholder agriculturalists are presented in Chapter 14 (Embu), while Chapters 12 and 13 assess drought vulnerability and coping strategies in Central and Eastern provinces as part of the National Environment Secretariat project on climatic variability.

Deep aquifers in northern Kenya appear to be recharged every ten years, while the surface water resources are ephemeral. Large areas of rangelands are not accessible during times of drought because of the lack of water. Concentration of herds around existing sources furthers the impact of the drought.

A key component of pastoralist coping strategies is the ability to move herds to make the best possible use of vegetation reserves (fallback zones) and sporadic rainfall. Drought impacts in these areas are influenced by access to food markets (in competition with markets closer to the principal NCPB stores); ability to purchase food with income from livestock sales, wage labor, or remittances; and the ability to recover from the drought by restocking (see also Chapter 23). The role of indigenous weather prediction and support for local resource management are stressed.

Among agriculturalists, a number of observations appear to be widespread. However, the 1984 experience must be generalized with caution. The drought in most of the agricultural areas lasted only one season, followed by the plentiful and early 1984 short rains. There was little time or necessity to consider the adoption of new coping strategies or the most drastic ones: the drought impacts were most severe between July and November, while the short rains began in October and food aid was initiated in August. In addition, the bimodal distribution of rainfall reduces drought risk, since the two rainy seasons are independent, i.e., drought in one season does not change the probability of drought in the subsequent season. Food storage, which affects the amount of food that households typically store and the choice of coping strategies, is not needed for the entire year.

Despite substantial differences in resources, almost all the households surveyed in four communities noted hunger as the major impact of the drought (Chapter 13). The nutritional data from Embu document the dramatic decline in weight for newborn infants, toddlers, and adults (Chapter 14). The drought resulted in serious malnutrition very quickly—developing in one to three months. In this case, nutritional status was an early indicator of the severity of the drought and the vulnerability of rural households. Following the targeted food relief, nutritional recovery was also fairly rapid—on the order of two to eight months.

The range of practicable coping mechanisms has narrowed, shifting from agricultural to monetary activities. Land subdivision and consolidation, reduced common lands, and limited markets for surplus production have constrained such traditional coping strategies as farming in diverse agroecological zones and sending livestock to distant lands.

Participation in the monetary economy has reduced vulnerability to drought for smallholders, at least in the short term. The 1984 drought was known as ni kwa ngweta, or "I could die with cash in my pocket." Households have diversified their income sources to include off-farm wage employment in response to the need for cash to pay school fees, taxes, and medical expenses, and to purchase supplementary foods and consumer items. Local markets usually perform well for purchasing and selling food, alleviating the need to store food from one season to the next or as a drought reserve.

Since the government controls interdistrict grain trade, rural household reliance on local food markets implies a shift in the burden of coping with drought toward the national government. The government channeled about 80 percent of the food imports through commercial markets in 1984 and 1985. Without such an effort, price inflation would have resulted in widespread famine.

Of the many issues concerning vulnerability to drought, perhaps two require the most urgent research in order to improve policy. The sexual division of labor is a common theme in development studies, but more research is required as to how development efforts might focus on women's strategies for coping with food crises and hunger. Community storage projects are now being undertaken in many areas. These efforts require continued monitoring, as the decisions to invest in agriculture versus off-farm employment and to store or sell food lie at the center of household functioning in an economy devoted to both commercial and subsistence agricultural production.

· 10 ·
Drought and Its Implications for Water Supply in Northern Kenya

GERNOT BAKE

The frequency of drought in northern Kenya and its implications for water supplies are explored here. The area under study is composed of about 22,500 sq km in southwestern Marsabit District (Eastern Province). The region is located east of Lake Turkana toward Mt. Marsabit, and between the Hurri Hills in the north and the Ndoto and Njiru mountains in the south. It is inhabited by the Rendille, Samburu, Gabbra, and Borana tribes.

The main area is an endorheic basin that drains toward the Chalbi Desert, except for a smaller area in the southeast, which belongs to the Milgis system. The Chalbi depression has a base level of around 400 m above sea level. Surrounding mountains include Mt. Kulal (2,100 m), Mt. Marsabit (1,428 m), and the Hurri Hills (1,500 m). The mountains in the south rise even higher. The lower parts of the area are almost flat, with some inselbergs in the south. The plains are of polygenetic origin, with sediments from both the basement and the volcano systems. The Chalbi Desert is an old lake bed, most likely dated in the early quaternary, which gives evidence of a former wetter climate in the northern part of Kenya. Under exceptionally wet conditions, the old lake bed can be flooded for a few days.

There are a number of drainage lines in the area (see maps in IPAL 1984, Bake 1984). Most of these lines are directed from south to north. They often form interior deltas, where all of the runoff infiltrates and hence does not reach the base level. Under wet conditions, however, such as experienced in November 1982, a consecutive flow from the south to the Chalbi Desert can be observed. Wider runoff systems in northern Kenya are called *lagas*.

NATURE OF DROUGHT

The definition of drought depends on the application (see Chapter 1). Often it is not precisely defined. King (1983, p. 54) refers to drought as "a serious deficiency of water for herbage production caused by the cumulative effect of above average evaporation and/or below average rainfall." The year in northern Kenya is divided into two wet and two dry seasons. By their nature, dry seasons already have a deficiency of water. They cannot be classified as drought episodes, because they are a regular feature of the arid climate. Drought is a permanent climatic feature of the drylands of northern Kenya. It is not yet possible to predict long-term droughts, either because the period of observation is too short or the climate is too variable.

Drought is here classified as rainfall less than the *mean lower variability limit*. The drought threshold values of monthly rainfall are given in Table 10.1, with the annual values for Marsabit shown in in Figure 10.1. The data for Marsabit/3 are tentative, since only six years of rainfall records were available, a sample too small for statistical analysis. A comparison of the available data, however, shows that there is a correlation between the trend and amount of rainfall. Therefore, it seems justifiable to use the Marsabit/3 data as representative of rainfall patterns for the vast lowlands west of Mt. Marsabit.

In northern Kenya, the years 1919–1922, 1934, 1945, 1949, 1975–1976, and 1980 were drought years (Figure 10.1). The distribution of the average monthly rainfall is shown in Figure 10.2. Oltorot (with an annual rainfall of 265 mm) represents the dry lowlands; Marsabit (849 mm) and Gatab near Mt. Kulal (826 mm) represent the wetter highlands in the east and west, respectively. The threshold value of rainfall indicates the minimum requirements for rain-fed agriculture (calculated according to Schreiber's methodology; see Bake [1983]). Rain-fed agriculture is only possible in the upper oasis regions of the mountains.

Combined with average monthly rainfall, monthly and seasonal rainfall probabilities may give some indication of the probability of drought years (Table 10.2). The annual probability of a drought year in northern Kenya has been statistically determined to be 0.25, which means that one year in four can be expected to be a drought year (Figure 10.3). The rainfall pattern during a season is also important. The probability of one month of the March to May rains being less than 25 mm is 0.80 (Table 10.3). The start of the rainy seasons is also variable (Figure 10.4).

EFFECTS OF DROUGHT ON THE WATER SUPPLY

Water supplies for human and animal consumption are primarily derived from surface and subsurface water. During the wet seasons, livestock and people traditionally use open surface water in natural water courses (*lagas*) and ponds; during the dry seasons, they rely on hand-dug wells that reach as deep as 20 m. Several bore holes with motor pumps have recently been installed, drastically altering this picture. Perennial water can only be found on Mt.

Marsabit's crater lakes and at Lake Turkana, where the water is slightly alkaline. *Lagas* have water only immediately after a significant rainfall.

There are various aquifers in northern Kenya (Bake 1984). The main aquifer, which is also the deepest, varies in depth, depending on the depth of the submiocene level. Local aquifers are situated mainly around *lagas*; these are often very shallow and have low yields. There is a constant flow of subsurface water from the surrounding volcanic mountains that recharges the aquifers of the lowlands.

The recharge rate of an aquifer was determined by calculating the infiltrated water in the rainfall area between the 150 and 400 mm isohyet. An average infiltration rate of 40 percent was used in this formula. This figure seems to be justified since most of the soils and bedrocks are of low consistency and low volcanic origin, and have high infiltration rates. The amount of infiltrated water was calculated at 1.996×10^9 cu m per year for an area of around 22,600 sq km. Even with an infiltration rate of only 25 percent, this amount would be 1.247×10^9 cu m per year, thus giving the area a good recharge rate for its aquifers. During drought years, however, the situation changes. Rainfall is then about 40 percent less than normal, decreasing the above figures to 1.2×10^9 cu m per year for a 40 percent infiltration rate and 7.482×10^8 cu m per year for a 25 percent infiltration rate. At first glance, these figures seem very high, as they are valid for the entire area. Infiltration rates during droughts are lower than those under normal or wet years because the soil is encrusted (algae crust or silt crust). Further research on this point is absolutely necessary.

Observations of water infiltration have implications for the effects of drought on hydrology. The surface water that is usually available during the wet season will be reduced. Episodic or seasonal rivers might carry runoff less frequently or not at all, thus reducing the recharge of local aquifers around these *lagas*. Normally reliable water ponds or springs will dry out, thus forcing tribal movements. Shallow wells (less than 10 cm) around the *lagas* will also dry out, depriving people of another water source. The extent to which these wells are dependent on the actual recharge from the runoff in the nearby *lagas* is detailed in Bake (1984). Nomads and their animals have fewer reliable water sources during the traditional wet season when there is a drought. In the dry season of a drought year, the situation gets worse as no water is stored during the wet season. Nomads then move to reliable water sources like bore holes (e.g., at Kargi and Korr), Lake Turkana, or to Ethiopia, where higher rainfall is common in the south (Borana). The concentration of livestock, however, destroys the sparse drought vegetation around the reliable water sources, thereby contributing to desertification.

The water needs of various livestock species are different; thus, the maximum distance tolerable between water sources will vary according to the animals herded. Cattle require the most water, while camels can go without water for over eleven days. During drought periods, cattle are the first to die, followed by smallstock, whereas camels die only in prolonged droughts (lasting two or more years). Camels die due to lack of forage rather than the lack of water.

The effects of drought conditions on aquifers is not easily judged, as it requires such expensive and time-consuming measurements as observation wells and fixed transects. Nevertheless, it is known that the shallow and local aquifers will react first, sometimes within days and sometimes after a somewhat longer time period. The deeper aquifers, like the ones tapped by various bore holes, have the longest reaction times. They will still produce adequate water yields at the end of the drought, although the water table might drop. This depends very much on the characteristics of the bedrock. Therefore, it is necessary to determine the age of the pumped ground water. This has only been done for a few bore holes in northern Kenya. The age of the aquifer waters around Korr is between sixteen and forty-three years. It will take decades for these waters to be affected by drought, although overpumping might reduce the available water.

PRECAUTIONS FOR DROUGHT IN MARSABIT DISTRICT

Droughts are a common feature in arid and semiarid lands. Traditional nomadic strategies were adjusted to climatic challenges, and gave the people a fair chance to survive. Today, increasing human population and livestock numbers, and the tendency toward sedentarization make the pastoralist increasingly vulnerable to this natural phenomena. During the last drought, livestock died, and people were fed from external sources.

Drought affects the hydrology of the area. With decreasing rainfall, surface runoff water becomes sparse, and subsurface water is not recharged. The deep regional water table may be unaffected, but the local aquifers will become almost dry. These perched water tables cannot supply enough water for all the livestock. In periods of drought, the new wells will also become dry because they merely tap the local aquifer. The reaction of the nomads is then to concentrate near reliable water sources, such as bore holes. These areas are already under a high grazing pressure; consequently, there is not enough forage available near the wells during drought conditions.

Two deep bore holes have been proposed for the central Hedad area. These would tap the regional, reliable water table and would take part of the grazing pressure off other areas. These bore holes should not be used unless there is a longer drought period in the area. Instead, they should be sealed and the necessary equipment (pumps and storage tanks) stored in Marsabit. The equipment used should be easily transportable. The bore holes should not be used when there is just a breakdown since they should only be put to use during drought emergencies.

From the climatic point of view, analysis of drought is often an analysis of the past. Drought prediction and monitoring, however, have to be an analysis of the future or, at least, the present. Reliable warning systems are still far from operational on the global, regional, and local levels (see Chapter 20 for a model district contingency plan).

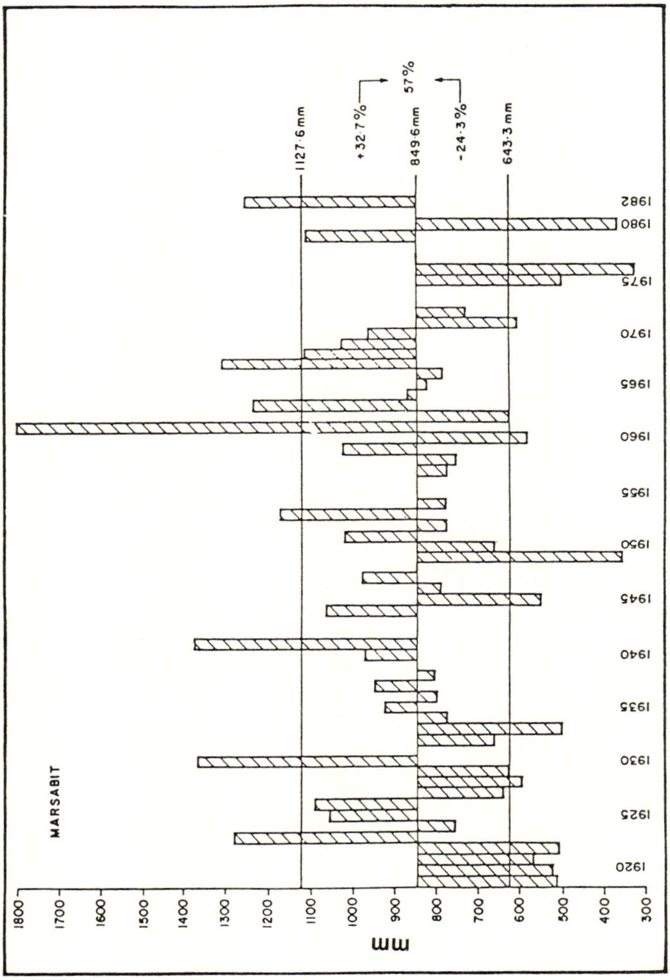

Figure 10.1 Variability of annual rainfall at Marsabit. Annual mean is 849.6 mm. The upper (lower) line is the average of the wet (dry) years, or the mean variability. The mean upper variability is 32.7 percent greater than the mean, and the mean lower variability is 24.3 percent less than the mean, giving a total variability of 57 percent.

Figure 10.2 Average monthly rainfall and threshold values for rainfed agriculture. The one humid month (November) at Oltorot represents a singular event in the station records.

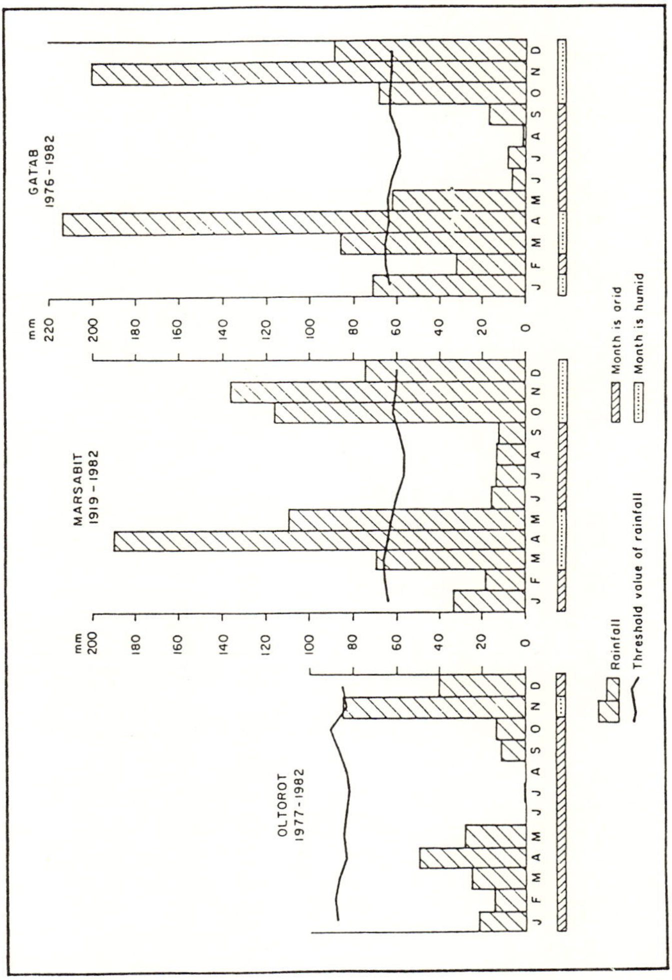

148 • COPING WITH DROUGHT IN KENYA

Figure 10.3 Probability of annual rainfall at Marsabit and Marsabit/3.

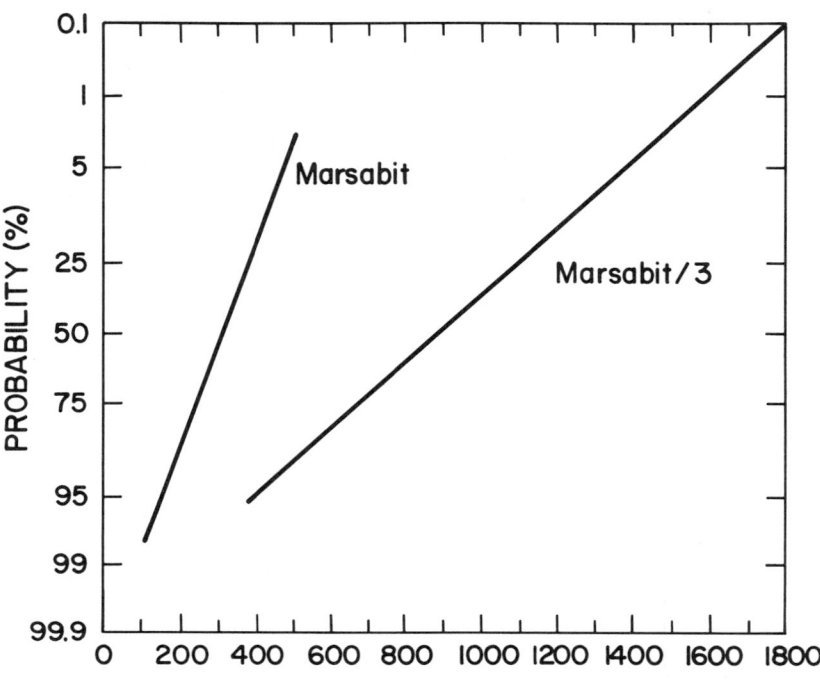

Figure 10.4 Variation of starts and duration of rainy seasons at Marsabit.

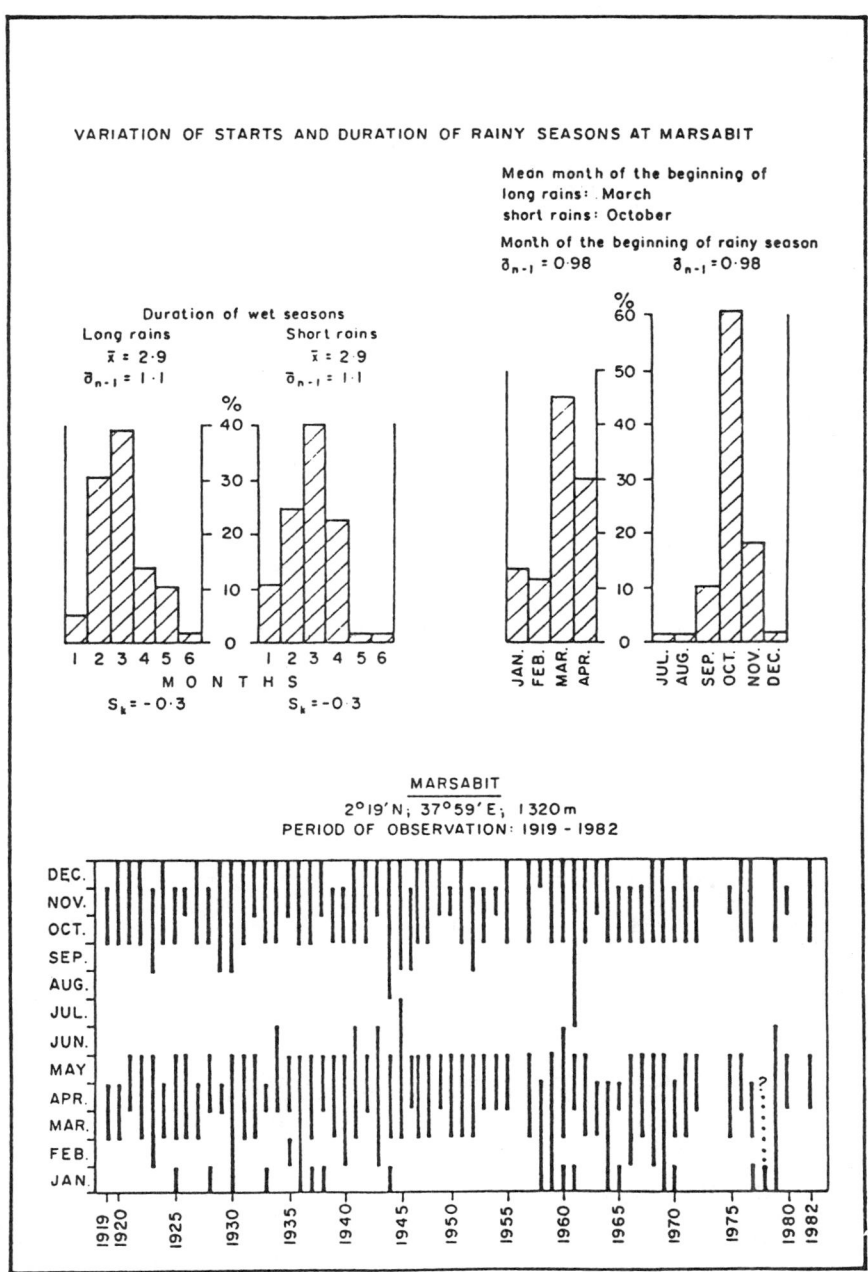

Table 10.1 Monthly Drought Threshold Values of Rainfall

Month	Marsabit	Marsabit/3	Season
January	7.4	2.5	dry*
February	2.9	1.0	dry*
March	25.3	8.4	wet
April	63.0	21.0	wet
May	34.6	11.5	wet
June	3.6	1.2	dry*
July	4.6	1.5	dry*
August	5.7	1.9	dry*
September	3.1	1.0	dry*
October	47.9	16.0	wet
November	73.9	24.6	wet
December	26.0	8.7	wet

Note: Monthly drought threshold value is the minimum rainfall (in mm) below which a drought occurs. Values marked * are only of theoretical meaning, as the dry seasons are not periods of forage production or plant growth.

Table 10.2 Monthly Rainfall Probabilities for Marsabit/3

	J	F	M	A	M	J	J	A	S	O	N	D
Median	6	1	14	70	23	1	2	2	2	34	39	16
Probability of receiving												
<25mm	.26	.93	.63	.14	.52	1.00	.98	.96	1.00	.38	.36	.65
>50	.05	.02	.12	.66	.28	0	0	0	0	.29	.28	.13
>100	0	0	0	.26	0	0	0	0	0	.04	.09	0
>200	0	0	0	.02	0	0	0	0	0	0	.01	0

Source: ILCA (1979).
Notes: Years of record, 50; median, 250 mm per year.

Table 10.3 Seasonal Rainfall Probabilities for Marsabit/3

	Monthly Drought Threshold			
	25 mm		50 mm	
Sequence of Wet/Dry Months	MAM	OND	MAM	OND
WWW	.05	.09	.02	.01
WWD	.04	.05	.06	.10
WDW	.28	.16	.01	.02
WDD	.26	.09	.03	.16
DWW	.03	.15	.16	.04
DWD	.02	.08	.42	.23
DDW	.17	.26	.08	.06
DDD	.15	.14	.22	.38

Source: Bake (1986).
Notes: MAM = March-May wet season; OND = October-December wet season; W means month wet, D means month dry (i.e., WWD in first season means that rainfall in March and April exceeded the drought threshold, while May was below the drought threshold). For example, the probability of receiving more than 25 mm in every month (WWW) of the MAM season is 0.05, while the probability of receiving less than 50 mm in every month (DDD) of the OND season is 0.38.

· 11 ·
Reconstructing Gabbra History and Chronology: Time Reckoning, the Gabbra Calendar, and the Cyclical View of Life

PAUL W. ROBINSON

> If they get grass there, if there is no grass here, [camels] can drink water here and go back there and stay for ten days. . . . That is how camels can stay far from [water].
>
> But cattle cannot go away from water as far as this mountain and be able to stay for two days. Cattle are not able to go far away from water. So it is with goats and sheep; they cannot go far away from [water] except during the rains. During the rains, when there is water everywhere on the surface of the ground, they drink.
>
> *Yatani Tocha* (Gabbra Historical Texts [GHT] 007)

THE ROLE OF HISTORY IN GABBRA SOCIETY

In a harsh and demanding environment, such as is utilized by the Gabbra pastoralists of the Kenya-Ethiopian frontier region (Figure 11.1), that which is unnecessary for survival and which adds unnecessary encumbrance and weight must be discarded. In Gabbra society, this functionalism pervades every aspect of corporate and individual life. The material goods that people possess are essential and have purpose. The sum total of a family's possessions, including dwelling tent, beds, utensils, containers for water, milk and fat, and clothing, must all be fully transportable and not exceed the carrying capacity of several camels. Mobility is a key to survival, and all that inhibits mobility is deemed extraneous.

Gabbra social organization has been developed to retain those mechanisms that allow communication and dissemination of information, that facilitate wide bonds of kinship, mutual obligation, and assistance, and that permit societal cohesion while allowing for necessary independence. Unnecessary regulation of life-style, centralization of power, and trappings of political authority that would inhibit the flexibility and independence required for survival are not employed. Strategies for management of rangelands and water are designed to facilitate efficient utilization of those resources by livestock so as to increase productivity and minimize negative effects of a harsh and relentless environment. Migration of households and livestock is calculated to place productive units in optimal locations (where rangelands occur in proximity to water resources) and to carefully manage and conserve all resources of long-term survival.

The Gabbra, who are not literate, must retain all accumulated knowledge within the collective memories of individuals; for them, history must be relevant, functional, and integral to survival. History for the Gabbra is a means of recording events, of locating those events in a cyclical framework and cosmology, of unifying society, and of anticipating the future. History is a topic that preoccupies the interests and the time of Gabbra elders, and a knowledge of and expertise in matters of history and its ramifications are significant measures of a man's stature and success. It is not uncommon to see groups of elders under their favorite tree, discussing for hours matters of the past (*wan wan durri durri*) and the ways in which the past affects current climate, grazing strategies, relationships with other peoples, and the fortunes of individuals or groups within pastoralist society.

A correct interpretation of history and the cyclical return of events, together with a thorough knowledge of genealogic history and the linkages for assistance that genealogy can provide, can give a man and his dependents a significant edge in all matters of livestock management. Further, historical competence allows the maximization and optimization of strategies in the intricate maneuvering of people and livestock for survival and prosperity.

For the Gabbra, remembered history is of two general types: genealogical and cyclical/chronological. Genealogical history serves to integrate members of society through descent and kinship and provides lineages for purposes of marriage, residence, and the solicitation, sharing, and transfer of livestock. Genealogical linkages facilitate a sense of corporate identification and responsibility among small (usually less than seventy persons), widely diffused, and fairly independent settlements. Bonds of descent, blood, and marriage dramatically increase one's options for survival in times of crisis by extending links of assistance and obligation.

Chronological history is deemed by the Gabbra to be cyclical in nature; what is crucial is that history will recur with regularity. For the Gabbra, understanding the nature and length of cycles (daily cycles, seasonal cycles, yearly cycles of longer duration, and life cycles) allow one to predict environmental changes and maximize management of livestock, rangeland, and water resources, thereby minimizing hazards.

Cyclical/chronological history is remembered in minute detail, but the time-depth is relatively shallow. Once the longest recognized cycle (*athial*) of eighty years has repeated itself, all that came before is rapidly forgotten since it becomes a redundant and unnecessary encumbrance.

GABBRA CYCLES: UNDERSTANDING AND RESPONDING TO ENVIRONMENTAL VARIATION

The Gabbra note that time passes in a cyclical manner. Days cycle from sunset to sunset, with the sun and moon repeating their daily movement with regularity. The passages of night and day are marked by the Gabbra with those repeating cycles, and they are associated with the daily events cycling in unison with them. Events that occur on a daily basis (such as the morning milking of livestock, taking the stock to pasture, the return of the animals from pasture, and the evening milking) all take place in harmony with the sunrise, passage of the sun through the heavens, sunset, moon rise, and the passage of the moon, planets, and stars.

The Gabbra observe that days cycle in groups of seven and therefore identify a week (*torban*) as a set of seven days that cycle. The nomenclature of Gabbra days follows both the Somali and Arabic forms. The Gabbra also identify their days with specific animals or events.

Monthly lunar cycles (*jia*) occur with precise regularity, and social and ritual events are predicated on the absolute regularity of lunar cycles. The Gabbra meticulously record each day of both the light and dark of the moon, and there is a certainty to the lunar cycle that is evidenced by celebrations each month on the new moon's appearance. Ritual events take place in a lunar context; as such, each member of society, no matter how widely dispersed spatially, can know precisely when ritual celebrations are to occur. The Gabbra recognize a cycle of twelve lunar months that roughly correspond to a year; the Gabbra, however, do not base their annual calendar on these lunar cycles. Lunar months are associated with ritual; for the Gabbra, each month either has specific ritual duties or is free from ritual obligation.

Seasonal cycles of wet and dry, although irregular from year to year, are also recognized and form the basis for the calculation of their yearly (*ganna*) calendar (Tablino 1974, 1980).[1] The long rains of the southeast monsoon (*ganna*) fall between April and June; a long, dry, but relatively cool season (*adolessa*) follows and lasts until early October; the short rains (*agaya*) commence with the onset of the northeast monsoon in October and last into December; and a hot and dry season (*bon agaya*) with attending high winds lasts until the onset of the *ganna* rains.

Ganna is calculated on the basis of a strict counting of the number of days between successive *almando*, or new year, celebrations. Gabbra years are exactly 365 days in length; hence, each year begins on the day of the week following the day that the previous year began. If one year begins on a Friday, the following year begins on a Saturday, and so forth until a week-cycle of years is completed (Ganya Hurri, GHT/001/8):

---

1. Asmarom Legesse first informed me of this calendar's existence. Father Paul Tablino, of the Catholic Mission, Maikona, first outlined the Gabbra calendar and chronology. His assistance has been invaluable on all questions concerning Gabbra time reckoning.

The name of a year is the same as the name of a day. The day of which one asks, "what day is this," is the same as that. It becomes seven and in the eighth, eight years. It comes back in a cycle in the eighth year. It is that way. Even the days are so: *Alsinin, Talassa, Arba, Kamis, Gumat, Sabdi, Ahad*. Even the names of the years are these.

The years thus take on a cycle of their own. Because the Gabbra make no allowance for leap years, this cycle repeats itself indefinitely and comprises a week-cycle of years (*bara*).

What makes this calendar unique and invaluable to the historian is that, in addition to giving each year the name of a day of the week, the Gabbra also say that each year has an event that gives that year its name. Each year then is associated with an event of importance that occurred during that year. For example, a *Sabdi* (Saturday) year in which malaria was particularly severe would be named *Sabdi bini*, or the Saturday year of malaria. Often, more than one event will be associated with a given year, and events may vary with the specific geographical location of individuals and their phratries during that particular year. Individuals usually are able to recount the name of the year and its event, as well as the climatic conditions during the year, and where they and their herds moved during that year. When taken as a whole, the calendar provides the historian with a comprehensive record of events throughout the Gabbra area on a yearly basis.

Many Gabbra herders interviewed between 1977 and 1985 could remember each year, together with its event(s), as far back as the turn of the twentieth century. Several exceptional historians were able to recount the years in succession as far back as circa 1870, during the lifetimes of their fathers (see Robinson 1985b for a reconstructed Gabbra *ganna* calendar). Using the *Arba* (Wednesday) year, which began on 2 November 1983 and ended on 31 October 1984, as a model, Figure 11.2 summarizes the methods whereby the Gabbra calculate a year. In addition to summarizing the *ganna* enumeration, the figure also summarizes the lunar calendar for the same year. With the sighting of the new moon on the night of 4 November 1983, the lunar month of *Raggal* commenced. Each lunar month constitutes twenty-eight days, and each new month is heralded by the sighting of a new moon. The Gabbra have only twelve lunar months in their calendar, and the year both begins and ends with the month of *Raggal*.

Because the Gabbra calendar does not make provision for leap years, over time the seasons have become skewed from the nomenclature and so do not exactly parallel the *ganna* calendar. The actual correlations of rainfall, based on available rainfall figures from Marsabit, North Horr, and Sabarei, are presented in Figure 11.3. Throughout the area, rainfall seasons are primarily bimodal (Barako Goma, GHT/001/2; see also Chapter 10), although there is some evidence of fairly regular out-of-season rainfall during the *adolessa sorara* season.

On Marsabit Mountain, which represents traditional highland areas utilized by the Gabbra, the *agaya* rains begin during the month of October, peak, and then rapidly taper off in November. The *ganna* rains on Marsabit begin during the month of March, peak in April, and drop off considerably in May. Average monthly rainfall during *agaya* is significantly less than during the *ganna* season. The figures for North Horr represent the lowland areas utilized by the Gabbra. Although rainfall figures for the lowlands have not been recorded for long time periods, the *agaya* season appears to be significantly larger in quantity than the *ganna* rains (Barako Goma, GHT/011/9).[2] In this region, rainfall begins in November and drops off slightly in December. The *ganna* rains fall predominantly in April, but the average amounts are not enough to generate significant vegetation growth. A clear pattern of *adolessa sorara* out-of-season rains emerges during the month of August.

The figures for Sabarei, located on the Kenya-Ethiopian frontier, just west of Dukana, represent those areas utilized by the Gabbra during drought periods. Here again, the figures do not represent a long period of time, but seasonal patterns emerge. The *agaya* rains appear to be distributed over three months (October, November, and December), with the greatest amount occurring in November. The *ganna* rains also fall significantly earlier than at North Horr or Marsabit, beginning in March and continuing through April. A very clear *adolessa sorara* season is evident in July. The *agaya* rains at Sabarei are significantly wetter than those in the North Horr region.

While these figures must be used with a great deal of caution, there are several items worth noting: (1) with the exception of the *adolessa sorara* season, the enumeration of seasonality on the *ganna* calendar and the actual recorded seasons of the year appear to be misaligned by approximately two months, especially in those regions inhabited by the majority of the Gabbra for the past 150 years—namely the region encompassing North Horr in the south and the Ethiopian frontier region in the north; (2) in the lowland rangelands and along the Ethiopian frontier, the *agaya* rains appear to be of greater quantity when they do fall, while figures from Marsabit Mountain appear to be the reverse; and (3) the Chalbi lowlands, represented by the figures from North Horr, receive considerably less rainfall than either the highland massif of Marsabit in the south or the frontier region to the north.

The *ganna* calendar is important, not just for its recording of events, but also as a method of keeping a close record of climate and grazing strategies over time. Gabbra elders are usually not only able to recount the name of the years and events of significance during those years, but they are also able to recount the climatic conditions of each year and to remember where they and

---

2. Gabbra historians concur that when the *agaya* rains fall, they tend to be heavier than *ganna*. *Agaya* rains, however, are more unreliable, and *ganna* rains more regular and of longer duration. There is likely to be inaccuracy in the figures due to the few numbers of years for which there is data, but the general patterns are confirmed by Gabbra accounts.

their herds moved each year. Taken as a whole, the calendar provides the historian with a comprehensive record of events throughout the Gabbra areas on a seasonal and yearly basis. Figure 11.4 reconstructs the climate in the Gabbra rangelands for the period between 1903 and 1981, using Gabbra oral testimonies. Independent accounts from five Gabbra elders (Yatani Tocha, Mamo Dadu, Boru Alle, Mamo Adano, and Yatani Rassa) concerning their perceptions of rainfall and rangeland conditions are presented. The perceptions of the elders have been arbitrarily placed on a five-point scale, in which the years are identified as being very wet, wet, average, dry, or very dry. Factors used to determine the scale rating include assessments made by each informant as to rainfall quantities, lengths of rains, location of rainfall, rangelands utilized by the Gabbra in that particular year, and the quality of the rangelands. Each elder's testimony was assessed independently, and the mean value of the four independent testimonies was then graphed.

The degree of consistency between the elders is remarkable. There are significant differences in only three of the seventy-nine years for which there is evidence. In those cases, an elder will report a year as having been wet while another will report the same year as having been dry. The three years are 1924, 1928, and 1958. In each of these cases, the difference is in the testimony given by Yatani Tocha, who, during his lifetime, has occupied the rangelands in the north, along the Ethiopian frontier. The other informants consulted have tended, for the most part, to occupy the southern rangelands, which tend to receive significantly less rainfall.

Figure 11.5 shows strong similarities between Marsabit and Moyale rainfall figures and the mean Gabbra oral rainfall data. As is the case with historical traditions of many other nonliterate societies throughout Africa, the traditions of the Gabbra are proving to be highly reliable and consistent. The correlation also shows the coherence between rainfall in the lowlands (reconstructed from oral records), on the rangelands utilized by the majority of the Gabbra, and rainfall recorded by meteorological stations in the highlands of Marsabit and Moyale. Although rainfall is likely to be higher and more reliable in the highlands, the relative annual fluctuations appear to be consistent with the variations recorded by Gabbra oral historians. Such broad correlations between two independent sources located in two distinctly different ecological zones have broad implications for the study of both regions.

For the purpose of this study, probably the most important feature of the rainfall figures correlated from both sources is the appearance of cyclical climatic patterns. The most recent analysis of climatological data from the region inhabited by the Gabbra concluded that there are no regular climatic cycles (Bake 1983). The Gabbra, however, not only recognize seasonal and annual cycles of time, but they also recognize that events recur in cycles of longer duration (Halake Guyo, in Sora Ade and Bagaja Bidiru GHT/015/23; see also Yatani Sorale GHT/024/20 and Dabasso Idho GHT/025/1):

There are some [cycles] which come back in 8 years, there are some which go as far as 40. There are some which do not come back to us, even as far as 50 years. We just count in this way.

At least four longer cycles are recognized: *ogolti*, the cycle of seven years; *dachi*, the cycle of thirty years; *kontomat*, the cycle of seventy years; and *athal*, the cycle of eighty (or one hundred) years (Yatani Sorale GHT/033/2ff). These cycles of longer duration are associated with such events as recurrent droughts, periods of heavy rainfall, life-cycles, warfare, insecurity, and the recurrence of diseases. The Gabbra expect the events of those years to repeat in their cycles.

The Gabbra *perceive* cycles and in turn *predicate* their resource management strategies on a certain predictability that they recognize in the climatic patterns. For example, in the short term, a three-year cycle has immediate implications. The Gabbra observe that if two years have good rainfall, then the third year will be a poor rainfall year.

One of the most important cycles for the Gabbra is the seven-year cycle (*bara*), the cycle upon which the *ganna* calendar is based. The Gabbra believe that there is a predictability for specific years within the seven-year cycles as to whether they will be good or bad in terms of climate (Figure 11.6).

If the year is *Gumat* (Friday), then the Gabbra expect that it will have average or above average rainfall (Yatani Tocha GHT/027/40). Between the years 1895 and 1979, which had nineteen *Gumat* years, only three years have been dry. Significantly, these three years have been the last *Gumat* years: 1965, 1972, and 1979. In the 1986 *Gumat* year, the rains fell throughout the Gabbra grazing areas, and were considered to be very good.

If the year is *Sabdi* (Saturday), the Gabbra believe it will be one of drought, unless the *Sabdi* falls into a thirty-five-year cycle, in which case the year will be a wet one. Between 1889 and 1980, or for fourteen *Sabdi* years, all the years have been either dry or of drought, with two exceptions. The exceptions are the years 1917 and 1952, years that are separated by thirty-five-year intervals. The Gabbra expect the *Sabdi* year of 1987, which will be the thirty-fifth year since 1952, to be unusually wet.

If the year is *Ahad* (Sunday), a drought year is expected, unless it occurs outside a sixty-three-year cycle. There appear to be fourteen-year periods that are separated by sixty-three years, and these years are generally wetter. Thus, the fourteen-year period between 1890 and 1907 constituted a wet phase for *Ahad*, while those *Ahad* years between 1911 and 1960 were dry or drought years; 1967 to 1981 signified another wet phase. This cycle is less recognized and understood than those of other years.

If the year is *Alsinin* (Monday), the Gabbra anticipate that it will be very wet (Dabasso Idho GHT/025/5, Yatani Tocha GHT/027/5). In the fourteen consecutive *Alsinin* years between 1891 and 1982, all had very good rainfall, the exception being 1933, during which time drought conditions were reported.

During *Talassa* (Tuesday) years, the Gabbra expect sufficient rains. In every case, for the eleven *Talassa* years between 1892 and 1983, the years are remembered as actually having sufficient rains. The year 1934 is remembered as having had spectacular rains, and it is significant for the Gabbra that those heavy rains followed an unusual drought in the *Alsinin* year that preceded it.

If the year is *Arba* (Wednesday), the Gabbra expect it to be dry unless it falls within a forty-two-year cycle. In thirteen recorded *Arba* years between 1893 and 1977, ten were dry or drought years; however, the years 1893, 1935, and 1977, which are exactly forty-two years apart, were very wet. When this research was conducted, the Gabbra correctly anticipated the 1984 drought.

Finally, if the year is *Kamis* (Thursday), the Gabbra expect it to be dry unless it falls within a forty-two-year cycle and follows good *Arba* years; in such a case, it will be wet. The years 1894, 1936, and 1978 were forty-two years apart, followed good *Arba* years, and are remembered as having been wet. All other *Kamis* years are remembered as having been dry or very dry. Again, when this research was conducted, the Gabbra correctly anticipated that 1985 would be dry.

Further trends can be observed from the evidence. It appears that droughts lasting for two seasons (one year) occur on the average of every fifth year. Hence, the years 1918, 1922 to 1924, 1928, 1933, 1938, 1943 to 1945, 1950, 1955, 1960, 1965, 1970 to 1972, 1976, 1980, and 1985 are all drought years. During major back-to-back drought periods (1922 to 1924, 1943 to 1945, and 1970 to 1972), two-year long droughts occur with only one or two seasons of rainfall in between.

Periods of abnormally heavy rainfall also appear to cycle, and are separated by an average of fourteen to fifteen years of dry conditions. Generally, drier periods can be noted for 1917 to 1930, 1937 to 1951, and 1958 to 1973. The periods of abnormally heavy rains and generally wetter climate average seven years in duration, e.g., the years 1930 to 1937, 1951 to 1958, and 1974 to 1981.

THE 1984/85 DROUGHT

In 1984, the Gabbra rangelands were in the throes of a devastating drought that had begun with a failure of the *ganna* rains of April to May 1983. By September 1984, virtually no rain had fallen in the lowlands south of the frontier for a period of twenty-two months. Nearly all of the pastures in the lowlands had been exhausted by the livestock or were located too far from water resources to be utilized; even the usually verdant Hurri Hills with an abundance of perennial grasslands were brown, dusty, and barren.

In the Gabbra chronology, 1983 was a *Talassa* year, a year in which conditions are normally expected to be dry, but not critically so, and which was to be followed by *Arba*. *Arba* years are also considered to be on the dry side usually, but they are known to have good rains on occasion. However, 1983 was perceived as being quite different, for the year was believed by the Gabbra to be cycling with 1920 (i.e., a sixty-three-year event cycle). Those Gabbra who recognized this long cycle believed that several years of continuous drought would probably ensue.

The rationale for this line of thought was that if the year was indeed cycling in a sixty-three-year cycle, then 1983 was going to be the equivalent of 1920, and 1984 would then exhibit the same characteristics as 1921, a year remembered as having been a drought year. The drought was so severe in 1921 that people had to collect dry grass from birds' nests to feed their livestock.

To further compound the problem, 1985 would be the cycle of 1922, which was named the year of *Kamis golbo agari*, or the year of famine in the lowlands. In addition, this *Kamis* was due to revert to dry conditions in the pattern of its own seven-year cycle.

A few elders, among them the most highly revered Gabbra historians, Yatani Sorale and Kushi Roba (the latter died in the drought of 1984), both saw additional ominous signs. Each historian observed that the *athlal* cycle of eighty to one hundred years was also returning and that the climatic conditions of the 1890s would also prevail. Hence, Sorale and Roba were very concerned that the region was entering into a prolonged drought that would only be relieved by minor, insufficient, and intermittent rains. Both were convinced that a disease similar in intensity and severity to the rinderpest panzootic of the 1890s would again ravage the livestock of the Borana and Gabbra.

In the later half of 1983, the nomadic camps (*ola*) associated with these elders moved from the environs of the Hurri Hills toward Lake Turkana and into areas the Gabbra traditionally reserved for drought periods. By the time the *agaya* rains (October to November 1983) were expected, there were considerably fewer Gabbra left in a position to move onto the Hurri Hills, provided the rains did fall. For the most part, Gabbra herd owners who continued to occupy the lowlands in the Chalbi region were those who did not hear, recognize, or heed the warnings of the historians. Herd owners interviewed in March to April 1984 were unable to answer questions regarding the cycle of the time. When asked where one could locate those individuals who did know matters concerning cycles and history, informants consistently replied that those individuals had gone in November 1983 to the Lake Turkana rangelands.

As no rain had fallen by early 1984, the rangelands in the Lake Turkana region began to be seriously depleted, and a number of Gabbra elected to return to the Chalbi region in anticipation of what was thought would be the *ganna* rains of March to April 1984. Conversely, however, those in the company of Yatani Sorale and several other sages began to make the arduous and dangerous trek over hot, parched, and insecure terrain toward the

Ethiopian border near Sabarei and then further north to Gorai and Tertalle. They were following the strategy of those who had survived the droughts of the 1890s and 1920s with a significant percentage of livestock intact. In April to May 1984, there were light rains north of the frontier, but there was no rain whatsoever in the Chalbi lowlands and on the Hurri Hills.

By this time, those people who had elected to remain in the lowlands were in critical condition. Most of their livestock had perished, and the specter of famine loomed. In May 1984, livestock losses in the Chalbi area were estimated to be 95 percent of the cattle, 60 percent of the goats, 40 percent of the sheep, and 5 percent of the camels. At this time, the government of Kenya, several nongovernmental organizations, and missionaries began to distribute relief aid; in the Kalacha area alone, more than 7,000 people were on famine relief by August 1984.

In November 1984, the expected *agaya* rains fell briefly on the Hurri Hills and sporadically in the lowlands. The vegetation generated by these poor rains did not significantly alleviate the crisis, and it was not until the *ganna* rains of April to May 1985 that conditions improved dramatically. Significantly, those who most closely followed the traditional regime did not elect to return toward the Hurri Hills; rather, they continued to trek north and east onto the Megado Escarpment and toward the Borana highlands. They did this in September to October 1984, in full recognition that the Ethiopian highlands of Sidamo Province were also experiencing protracted drought and that most of the Borana cattle had perished.

There appear to have been adequate rains in the Borana area in November 1984, and the Gabbra who moved to that region appear to have found ample browse for the camels, sheep, and goats. The Gabbra remember that during the 1890s they had assisted the Borana, who had lost most of their cattle to rinderpest, with gifts of camels. Reports filtering south from Ethiopia indicate that the Borana once again made official pleas in 1984 to the Gabbra for camels and that a number of Gabbra herd owners responded affirmatively to these requests. It is also evident from reports that those Gabbra anticipating the current drought conditions who took the very difficult and dangerous strategies outlined above did not lose nearly as high a percentage of their livestock as those who elected to remain in the Chalbi lowlands.

Those Gabbra who recognized the cyclical recurrence of climate anticipated correctly that the drought would continue through 1985 (*Kamis*) and would break either in the *agaya* rains of November 1985 or in the *ganna* rains of April 1986. Further, they predicted that both 1986 and 1987 would be very wet years. What makes this prediction even more interesting is that 1987 is a *Sabdi* year. On only two occasions since 1889 have *Sabdi* years been wet (1917 and 1952), and these have been at precisely thirty-five-year intervals. The Gabbra expect that the thirty-five-year *Sabdi* cycle will be stronger than the sixty-three-year event cycle of the 1920s, and so 1987 will yield very good rains.

CONCLUSIONS

It has been the central theme of this discussion that, over time, the Gabbra have developed strategies that have enabled them to successfully utilize one of the harshest and driest environments in eastern Africa. By examining Gabbra historiography, the Gabbra have observed that there are cyclical patterns to the recurrence of events and that survival depends on the accuracy and interpretation of their perceptions.

Even if Gabbra oral testimonies are not empirically verifiable, it nonetheless remains true that the Gabbra perceive certain phenomena to be occurring and then base their actions on the anticipation of events recurring with regularity. It is similarly true that those Gabbra herd owners who consistently emerge from crisis situations with the greatest percentage of their herds intact are precisely those who most closely recognize and follow the Gabbra cycles.

It here becomes necessary to ask of what importance and relevance this is in the latter decades of the twentieth century. In 1984 to 1985, a significant percentage of Africa was caught in a devastating drought, and famine has stalked portions of the continent virtually without abate since the 1970s. The areas that are the most seriously affected and that take the longest to recover are the marginal areas, such as those occupied by the Gabbra. The threat of widespread desertification is real throughout much of the Sahel and northeast Africa, with the distinct possibility that those areas will not be able to support even much smaller populations. Many pastoralist groups have ceased to be a part of the food-production strategy within the nations in which they live; instead, they have become a seemingly permanent part of the food crisis that debilitates those nations.

Until 1985, the Gabbra have been a notable exception to this rule. Despite occupying a very harsh environment, which has not really had adequate rainfall on a regular basis since the late 1960s, they have managed to survive, and, in many cases, to prosper. The Gabbra are perhaps unique, at least in Kenya, in that they are still able to utilize most of the rangelands they occupied at the turn of the century, having lost only the northern slopes of Marsabit Mountain and the dry-season grazing areas near the Lorian Swamp to permanent settlement, agriculture, or other pastoralist groups.

Strategies developed by the Gabbra to utilize their traditional rangelands closely follow the pattern of resource distribution that allows for the widest possible spread of human population and livestock. Moreover, the Gabbra seem to be able to anticipate ecological and climatic events, as well as changes in the environment. Here, they seem to have a significant edge over contemporary meteorologists, climatologists, and government planners since they are able to place themselves and their livestock in positions where adversity will have the least negative impact on them.

There are, however, disturbing trends as trading centers such as Maikona, Kalacha, and North Horr develop. These centers tend to become focal points for the delivery of services (medical, educational, developmental, and aid) and have come to be considered places of refuge during crisis. During the past fifteen years, there has been considerable growth in the human populations of these and other centers, attended by the growth in livestock populations that are more or less permanently based in proximity to these centers. Year-round use of the lowland pastures surrounding the Chalbi basin, for example, has in effect denied those rangelands to the traditional Gabbra, who require those pastures during the dry season. This has severely inhibited the viability of the overall resource-management strategies developed over time by the Gabbra and has therefore increased dependency during the most recent crisis periods.

It is the stated intention of the government of Kenya to ensure the survival of pastoralists, such as the Gabbra, and to bring the arid and semiarid areas of the country into the national food-production economy. The following is indicative of the government development plans for these regions during the 1984–1985 five-year development plan (Government of Kenya 1983, p. 56):

> The pastoralists derive a meager livelihood from the care of livestock in dry areas *requiring* [italics mine] a nomadic existence. The Government seeks to improve their income-earning opportunities.
> . . . It is preparing the younger generation in arid and semi-arid areas to improve the productivity of their nomadic style.

In the case of the Gabbra, the role of historiography can be critical in determining the nature and design of development strategies. An understanding of the full scope of Gabbra traditional resource management practices, Gabbra society, and of Gabbra understanding of the environment and history can lead to the incorporation of that body of information and understanding into development strategy.

Thus, history becomes a method of reducing dependency and fostering independence, self-respect, and self-assertion for Gabbra society. It becomes a framework for understanding the parameters of the successful utilization of an unforgiving environment that periodically strains their system of production to its limits. By understanding Gabbra history and cycles, it becomes appropriate to talk about improving the quality of life of the Gabbra through an enhancement of traditional range and water management and utilization practices. Such practices would be based on the assumption that these traditional resource management and utilization practices and livestock economy comprise the most effective resource management system with the least deleterious impact on the environment of any strategy known for the area.

As nomadic pastoralists, the Gabbra are highly adapted to the harsh environment in which they live; hence, development initiatives can attempt to restore a sense of value in the survival strategies that many have been abandoning. Development can then include the provision of mechanisms with which they can more productively and securely utilize the resources of their environment.

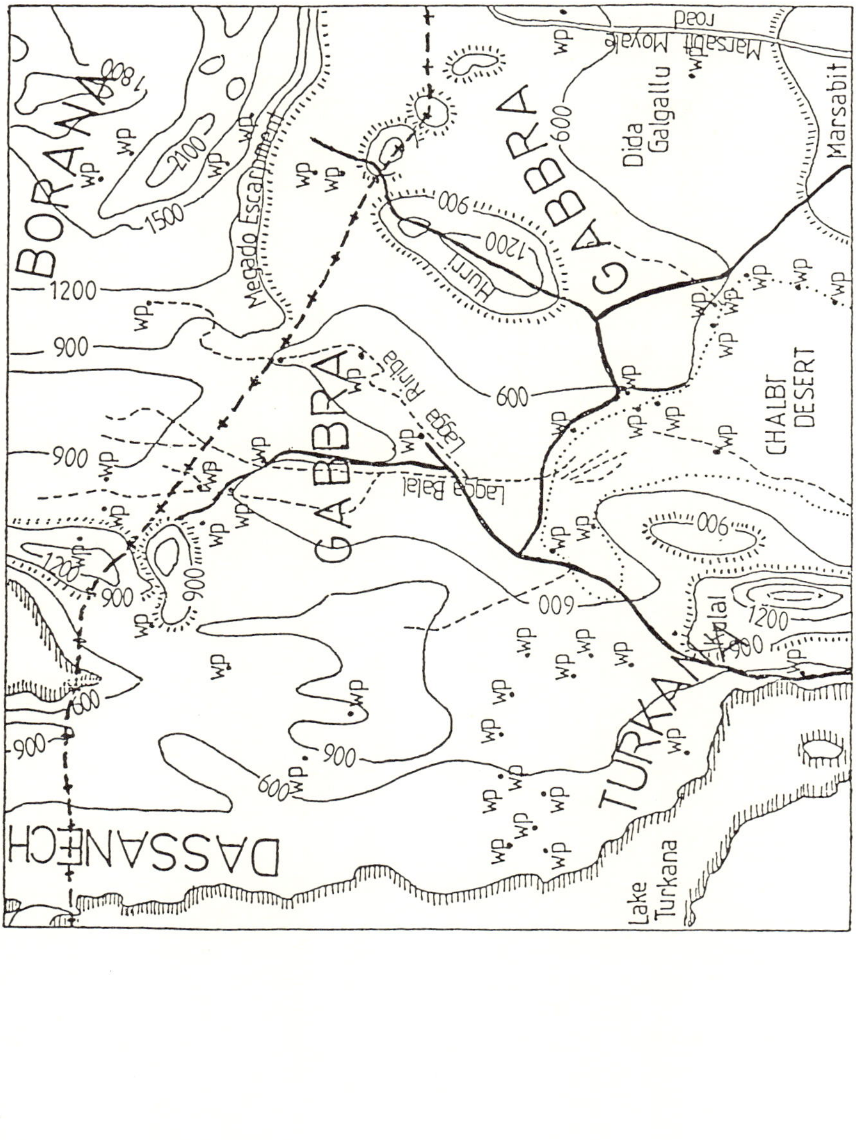

VULNERABILITY, IMPACTS, AND COPING • 163

Figure 11.1 Location of Gabbra rangelands. Area shown is northwest of Marsabit Town, along the Kenya-Ethiopia border (+++ in figure). Source: Robinson (1985b).

164 • COPING WITH DROUGHT IN KENYA

Figure 11.2 Gabbra calendar, 1983–1984. The two rainy and dry periods are shown, given their Gabbra names in the outer ring and the distribution of expected rain on the inner ring. The year starts with the *bon agaya* season on the full moon of 2 November 1983, in the *Raggal* lunar month. Source: Based on Robinson (1985b).

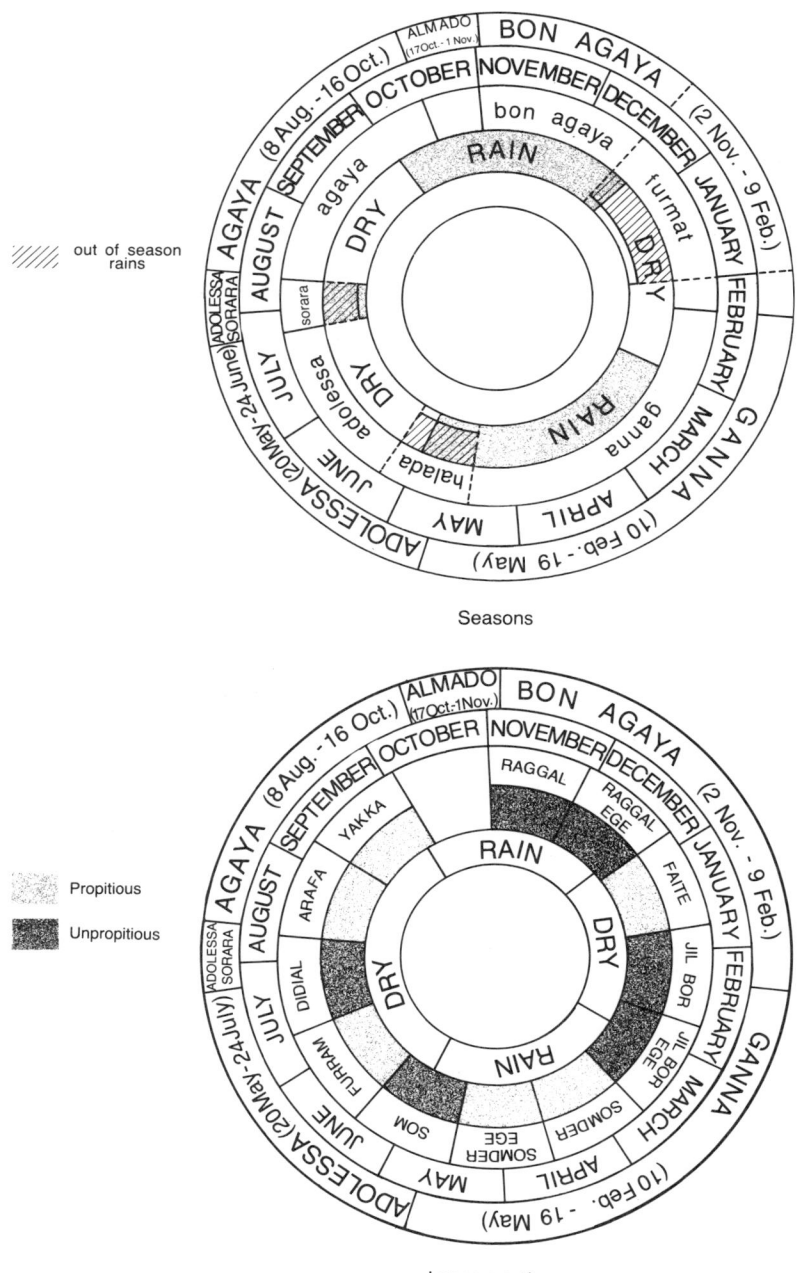

Seasons

Lunar months

Figure 11.3 Gabbra rainfall seasons. Arcs in the figures give the average monthly rainfall totals in mm, indicating a bimodal distribution: October to December and March to April. Gabbra seasons are named on inner circle. The Marsabit data are for 1918–1975, although some data are missing for 1931–1935, 1939, 1942–1943, and 1973–1974. The North Horr data are for 1960–1964. The Sabarei data are for 1948 to part of 1950 and 1960–1964. Source: Based on Robinson (1985b).

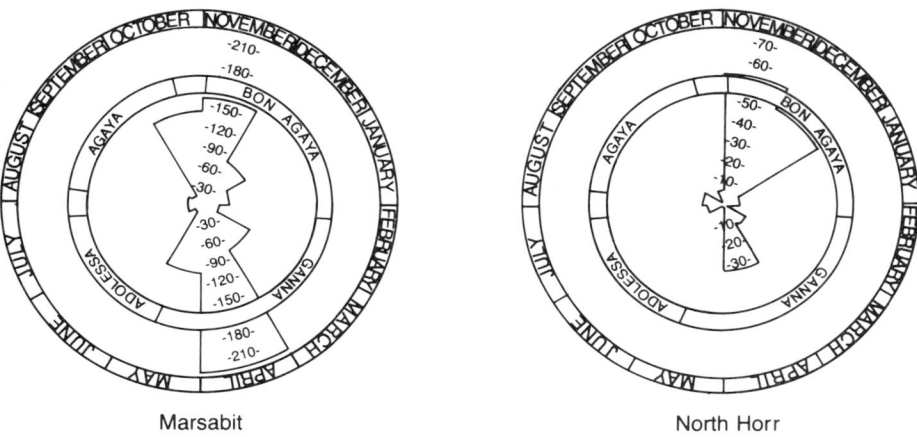

Marsabit North Horr

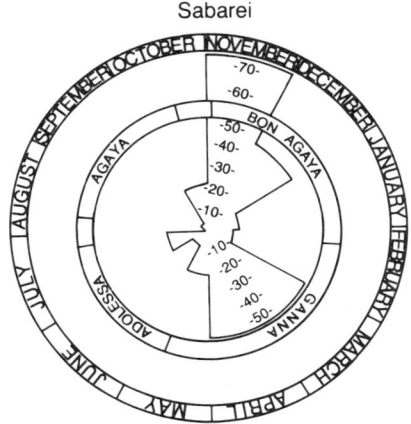

Sabarei

166 • COPING WITH DROUGHT IN KENYA

Figure 11.4 Gabbra oral rainfall data. Annual rainfall, rated on a five-point scale, is reconstructed based on oral records (Gabbra Historical Texts/027, 028, 030, and 031). The average of the four records is shown at the bottom. Source: Based on Robinson (1985b).

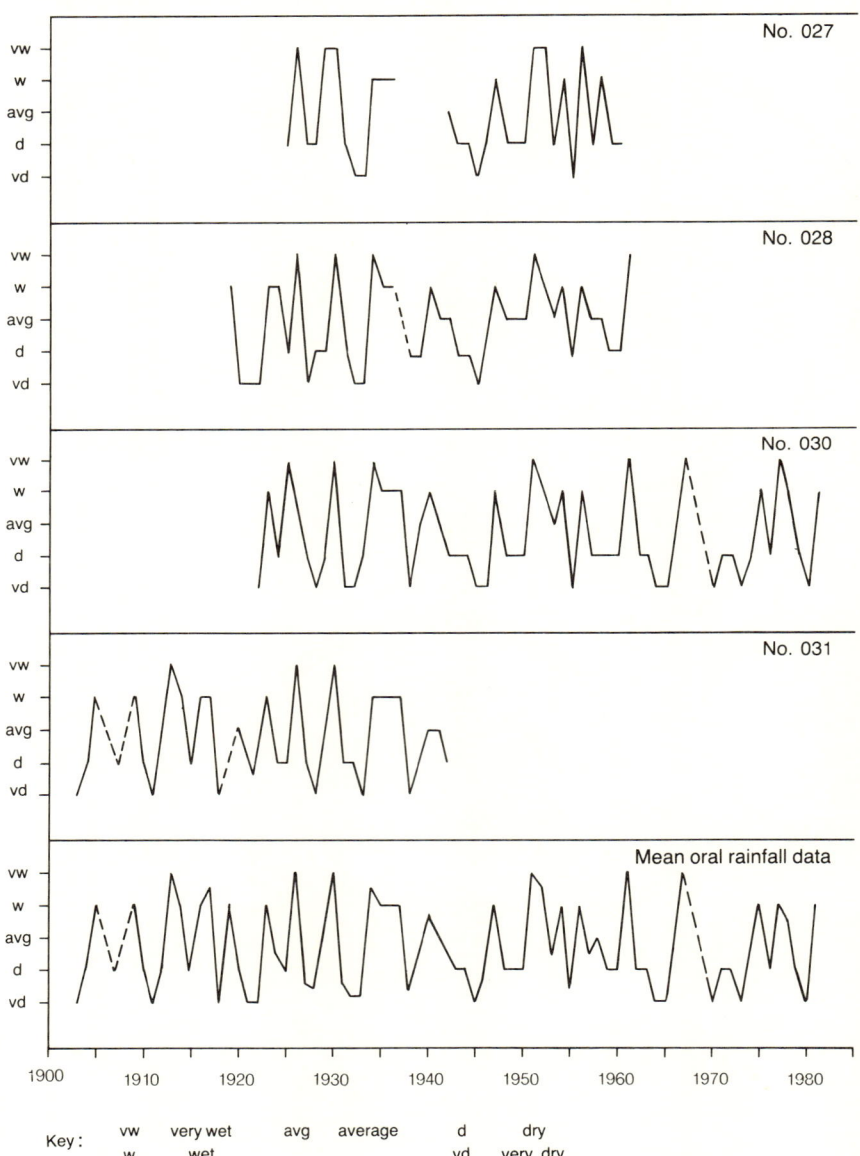

VULNERABILITY, IMPACTS, AND COPING • 167

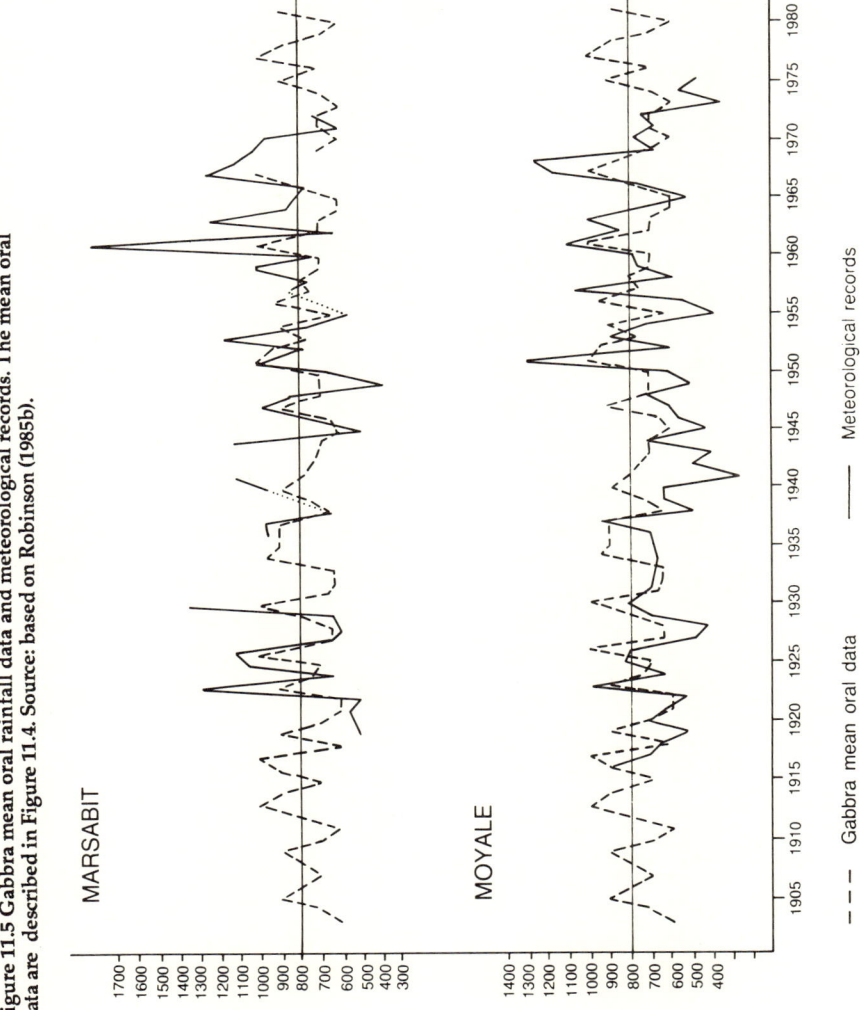

Figure 11.5 Gabbra mean oral rainfall data and meteorological records. The mean oral data are described in Figure 11.4. Source: based on Robinson (1985b).

Figure 11.6 Gabbra perceived climatic cycles. Each year is named according to its place in the climatic cycle. For example, 1970 to 1973, very dry years, were, respectively, *Arba, Kamis, Gumat,* and *Sabdi* years. 1974 (average) was *Ahad,* 1975 (very wet) was *Alsinin,* 1976 (dry) was *Talassa,* and 1977 (wet) was *Arba,* completing the 7-year cycle. In addition, there are longer cycles that produce anomalies in the 7-year cycle, e.g. the 35-year wet cycle in *Sabdi* years. Source: Robinson (1985b).

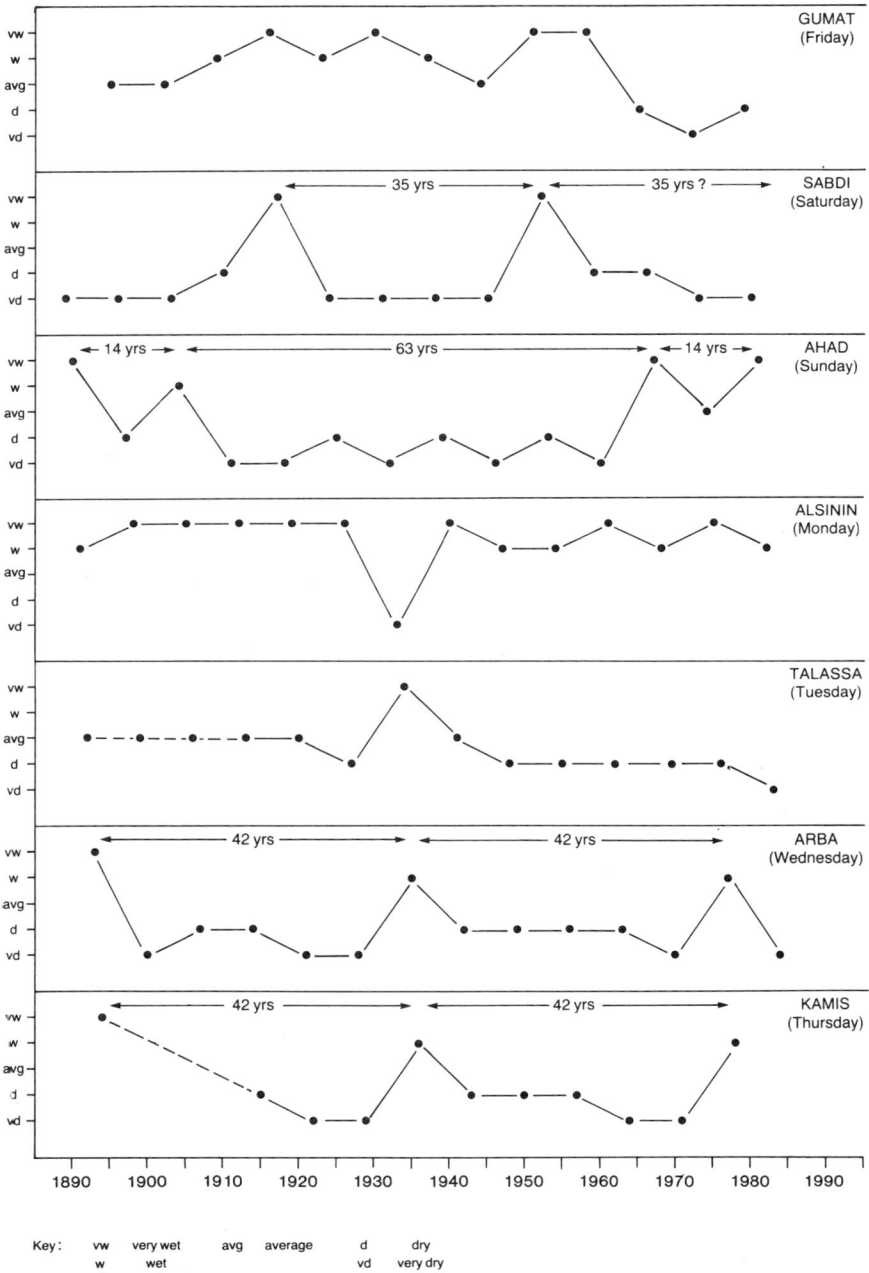

· 12 ·

Drought Vulnerability in Central and Eastern Kenya

GEORGE J. ANYANGO
THOMAS E. DOWNING
CAROLYN GETAO
M. GITAHI
CHARITY KABUTHA
CRISPIN M. KAMAU
MARY KARANJA
SABINA W. MAGHANGA

SIMON K. MBARIRE
SIMEON MUNENE
WYCLIFFE MUTERO
HARUN R. MUTURI
B. MWANGI
MARGARET WAINAINA
F. WERE

The 1984 drought affected large areas of the country, but it was most readily apparent in the agricultural lands surrounding Nairobi. Chapter 1 discusses vulnerability to drought in terms of food sources (or entitlements) and the scale of the affected area, ranging from the individual to the nation. This chapter describes vulnerability to drought experienced by smallholder agriculturalists in the six districts of central and eastern Kenya (Kiambu, Murang'a, Kirinyaga, Embu, Machakos, and Kitui). It is based on research carried out by the National Environment Secretariat (NES) during the 1984/85 drought episode. (The following chapter provides additional details regarding four community case studies undertaken by the project.)

Definitions of hunger and vulnerability to drought are introduced in this chapter, which also includes information on the six districts. The following sections treat vulnerability to three aspects of hunger: food shortage, food poverty, and food deprivation. The final section presents estimates of the numbers of people vulnerable to hunger in an average year and during the 1984 food crisis.

VULNERABILITY TO DROUGHT

While drought may result in water shortage, episodic diseases, and economic losses, the major impact for rural smallholders in Kenya is decreased food security. Hunger spans a variety of causes and consequences, related principally to three aspects: food shortage, food poverty, and food deprivation (Kates et al., 1988).

Food shortage refers to the availability of food relative to consumption requirements. It may be aggregated at a regional, national, community, or household level. In the context of this study, it refers to the ability of households to provide for their food consumption from on-farm agricultural production. It is most directly affected by the natural resources available to the household, in addition to labor, technology, and economic incentives.

170 • COPING WITH DROUGHT IN KENYA

Food poverty refers to the ability of households to purchase food, primarily in local markets. Permanent employment is relatively insensitive to climatic fluctuations, while sales of farm produce (crops and livestock) and casual agricultural wage income are more directly affected. Price changes mean that a secure income or access to credit is important in enabling households to purchase adequate food supplies.

Food deprivation implies that hunger is ultimately experienced by individuals who have insufficient food due to the failure of production, social, economic, or political systems. At the individual level, pregnant and lactating women and children under the age of five are the most vulnerable to food shortages either because they require more food or have less capacity to cope with deprivation.

Underlying these characteristics of hunger are two resource dimensions: temporal persistence and resource endowment. Chronic hunger persists over time, perhaps accentuated by seasonal fluctuations. It is related to poverty rather than drought. During food crises, larger numbers of people, and additional socioeconomic groups, are vulnerable to episodic hunger and even famine if extraordinary measures to procure food fail. Resource endowment refers to available natural resources and socioeconomic infrastructure. These resources are not equally available to households. In this study, vulnerability to hunger is described according to an agroclimatic zonation (outlined below), which captures the variations in resources better than administrative entities.

BACKGROUND ASPECTS OF CENTRAL AND EASTERN KENYA

Location, Terrain, Geology, and Soils

The six districts (52,642 sq km) mentioned above are located in Central and Eastern provinces of Kenya (Figure 12.1). The proximity of Nairobi in the western portion of the area and Mombasa to the southeast contributes to the pattern of development, labor migration, and off-farm income. The terrain is diversified, but with a general trend from the higher elevations of the Aberdares (almost 4,000 m) and Mt. Kenya (over 5,000 m) in the north and west to the lower elevations in the east and south (Figure 12.2). The nature of the terrain can constrain food production, as the very steep slopes inhibit the use of ploughs or tractors and contribute to soil erosion. The rivers vary from those capable of producing hydroelectric power and large-scale irrigation (such as the Tana, Athi, Thiba, and Nyamindi) to seasonal rivers located in the southern parts of Embu, Kirinyaga, Murang'a, Kiambu, and most of Kitui and Machakos districts.

The geology of the study area strongly influences the farming environment. The best soils for farming have developed over the tertiary and quaternary volcanics of the Aberdares and Mt. Kenya. The basement system rocks and sedimentary formations, covering most of the lowlands, have resulted in shallow sandy soils. There are no mineral deposits of economic importance in the study area except for building materials, including sand taken from river beds.

The soils vary from the rich, deep, well-drained, volcanic soils on the slopes of Mt. Kenya to the poor, shallow, poorly drained soils as found in the southern parts of Embu and Kirinyaga and in the lowlands of Machakos and Kitui. Mountain soils occur in broad zones from west to east, skirting the Aberdares and Mt. Kenya. They have clay soil textures and are very deep. The soils at lower altitudes are more variable, with higher sand content. In numerous areas, black cotton soils are found. Agriculture in the study area is dependent on the nature of the soils, in particular their ability to store water, although poorly drained soils may not be suitable for farming.

Agroecological Zones

For agricultural planning and to classify environmental conditions, it is useful to divide the six districts into agroclimatic or agroecological zones. The Kenya Soil Survey, or KSS (Sombroek et al., 1982), prepared an agroclimatic zone map of Kenya using the ratio of average annual rainfall to average annual potential evaporation, E_o. Agroecological zones were developed in the Farm Management Handbooks, or FMH (Jaetzold and Schmidt 1983), based on the results from a water balance crop production model. The two classifications result in similar map units. The zones are briefly described below (Tables 12.1 and 12.2 and Figure 12.3). They are named according to the most suitable or distinguishing agricultural land use, although specific crops are grown in many of the zones.

The alpine zones comprise small areas of the six districts and are almost entirely devoted to national forests or parks. The fringe of the escarpment in Kiambu is suitable for high-altitude livestock and pyrethrum or wheat.

The three zones on the fringe of the national forests that comprise the productive highlands are the tea/dairy, coffee/tea, and main coffee zones. Average farm sizes are small, averaging one to three hectares per household. Dairy livestock, tea, and coffee are the primary cash enterprises, while maize, beans, and potatoes are the main food crops. The marginal coffee zone is similar to the tea and coffee zones, except that the return from the coffee is less and food production is more risky.

The sunflower/maize zone is suitable for maize cultivation, but it lacks a productive cash crop. Farm sizes are somewhat larger than in the wetter zones, 1.5 to five hectares. The next two, drier zones, the cotton and marginal cotton zones, have similar characteristics. Although maize is still cultivated, good years are less common than bad ones. Cotton can be a profitable crop, but it is plagued with marketing problems.

The driest zones in the six districts are the livestock/millet and ranching zones. Population densities are much less in these zones, with farm sizes averaging eight to ten hectares and sufficient common grazing land to support additional livestock. Sorghum and millet are the only reliable grain crops.

The tea/coffee zones (I and II) rarely experience drought. The 1984 event was anomalous in its severity in these zones, and even then had few serious consequences (loss of dairy livestock being the most critical). The drier zones are all vulnerable to drought. In the livestock/millet zone (V), droughts are frequent, but households are somewhat better adapted (larger holdings, drought-resistant crops) than those in the wetter zones (III and IV), where the reliance on maize production increases the risk that on-farm production may be insufficient for household needs. Households with little land devoted to food production are particularly at risk, and must depend on off-farm sources for income.

Population

The Kikuyu are the predominant ethnic group in Kiambu, Kirinyaga, and Murang'a, comprising over 95 percent of the total population in these districts in 1979. The Embu comprise over 60 percent of the population of Embu, while the Kamba comprise over 96 percent of the total population of Machakos and Kitui (CBS 1981a). Kiambu had the highest population density among the six districts in 1979: 280 persons per sq km. Kitui district had the lowest density (fifteen persons per sq km). High population growth rates exist for all six districts. Growth rates between the 1969 and 1979 censuses range from 3.08 percent per year in Kitui to 4.6 percent per year in Embu. The high population growth rates have been attributed mainly to high fertility rates and declining mortality rates resulting from improved nutrition and better health facilities. High growth rates are expected to continue for at least the next decade. Table 12.3A shows the size of the population expected by the year 2000 if current population growth rates continue. Table 12.3B shows the expected population if fertility rates are reduced 50 percent by the year 2000. Population growth will expand the demand for food and may outstrip the national food supply in the near future.

Perhaps more indicative of the changing population/land resource balance in the six districts is an assessment of the population growth rates and densities by agroclimatic zone. The change in population density for rural sublocations from the 1969 and 1979 census was calculated (Downing et al., 1988); see Table 12.4. The highest growth rates were in the tea and coffee zones, indicating an absorptive capacity of these productive areas, and in the livestock/millet zone, due to migration from the highlands and expansion of the agricultural area. The low growth rates in the maize zone (III) indicate that this area had already reached its "carrying capacity" by 1979. Unless the increasing population is used for more intensive agriculture, which appears to be neither substantial nor prevalent at present, the population growth rates indicate increased vulnerability to drought in most of the zones, particularly in the lower zones where off-farm employment possibilities are limited.

The age structure at the time of the 1979 census reveals the very high dependency ratio of 57 percent (Table 12.5). In times of drought, providing adequate food to the dependent population is more difficult. Also, families with young children and few adults have less labor available for cultivation or wage employment (see Tanner 1987 for an example of household life-cycle issues related to malnutrition in Brazil). The high dependency ratio will be more critical in future droughts if the current high population growth rates continue.

FOOD SHORTAGE:
SELF-PROVISIONING FROM ON-FARM PRODUCTION

Household agricultural production, the level of self-provisioning from on-farm production, is principally related to climatic and edaphic resources and agricultural and livestock practices. These are discussed below.

Climatic Patterns and Trends

The annual average rainfall varies between 2,000 mm on the upper slopes of the Aberdares and Mt. Kenya to less than 400 mm in eastern Kitui. The gradient of rainfall is generally from north and northeast to south and southeast, with notable pockets of higher rainfall in the hilly areas. The most important local controls over the climate of the area are topography and aspect. Rainfall increases with altitude, although aspect, exposure to moisture-bearing winds, is also important (Nieuwolt 1980, Porter 1976).

Air temperature and evaporation are also correlated with altitude. Annual average temperatures range between 20 to 24 deg C at lower elevations, with monthly averages between 15 and 30 deg C. Temperatures at higher elevations are 1 to 2 degrees cooler. July is usually the coolest month, with overcast skies. March is the warmest, with clear skies before the onset of the rains. Minimum temperatures in the upper zones are seldom below 10 deg C, a critical temperature for maize cultivation. Average annual potential evaporation, E_o, ranges from less than 1,200 mm on Mt. Kenya to over 2,500 mm in the lowlands of the study area; in most of the area, it exceeds average annual rainfall.

The most important source of moisture is the Indian Ocean. A secondary source, of more importance in western Kenya, are Lake Victoria and Central Africa. To some extent, the variability in the rainfall of central and eastern Kenya can be attributed to the distance of the area from these two sources of moisture, and the mechanisms by which the moisture is advected inland (see Chapter 3 for more detail on the synoptic situations resulting in drought).

Since the rainfall pattern is bimodal, a more accurate picture of the usefulness of climate as an agricultural resource is found in Figures 12.4 and 12.5, which depict the amount of rain expected to be exceeded in six out of ten years for each rainy season. The March to May (long)[1] rains begin in mid- to late March, and last through the end of April in the drier zones or late May in the wetter ones. Almost 1,000 mm can be expected in the upper zones of Kiambu, Murang'a, Kirinyaga, and Embu. Toward the south of the study area, the March to May rains become lighter and less reliable than the October to December rains. The October to December rains have the same general pattern. They begin in late October and end in early December. The uplands of Kiambu, Murang'a, Kirinyaga, and Embu are drier than during the March to May rains, averaging 500 to 600 mm. Conversely, the hills of Machakos and Kitui are somewhat wetter, expecting 350 to over 500 mm. Most of the lowlands receive over 200 mm during this season.

Maize production on suitable soils requires a minimum of 300 mm of rainfall during the season. Areas expecting less than 300 mm in six out of ten seasons, unshaded in Figures 12.4 and 12.5, may be considered particularly prone to drought, at least in regard to maize cultivation. Locations on the 300 mm isohyets have a 40 percent probability of drought (with rainfall less than 300 mm). The wetter areas would have a lower probability of drought, and the drier areas a higher probability (see also Braun 1977). Using this simple definition, almost all of the lowlands would be considered drought-prone. Seasonal drought probabilities for four rainfall stations were calculated based on cumulative probabilities for the entire station record (Table 12.6). A mild drought, or worse, is expected to occur in about one out of three years for the long rains and almost one in two years for the short rains. The effect of these rainfall anomalies will be markedly different at the four stations due to different temperature regimes and soil types, as indicated below.

Several stations with long records were analyzed for trends in seasonal rainfall and interannual variability of seasonal rainfall. In contrast to west Africa, where a notable decrease in rainfall has occurred during the last two decades (Farmer and Wigley 1985, Lamb 1982, Nicholson 1985), there is no evidence of a persistent trend in either the seasonal rainfall (Figure 12.6) or its variability (Figure 12.7) in the six districts.

Agriculture

The wide variety of crops in the study area reflects the diverse climates and soils. The main cash crops are tea and coffee for the high and medium potential zones, and cotton and tobacco in the lower potential areas. The

---

1. In general, the first rainy season (March to May) is colloquially called the long rains and is the dominant season in the highlands and western Kenya. The second season (October to December) is known as the short rains. The October to December rains, however, are more reliable in southern Machakos and Kitui than the March to May season, where they are known as the long rains. In this book, the national terminology is followed, i.e., the March to May rains are referred to as the long rains and the October to December rains as the short rains.

main food crops are maize and beans for all zones, while sorghum, millet, cow peas, and pigeon peas are widely grown in the drier areas; potatoes are common in the wet highlands. Tomatoes, cabbages, and kale form the bulk of horticultural produce (Table 12.7).

Cash crops. Cash crops are important to the small-scale farmer. Apart from earning money for expenses like school fees, they play an important part in securing farm inputs. A farmer who earns some money from cash crops has access to rural credit, and may use some of the profits for fertilizers, pesticides, and other farm inputs. This may increase on-farm yields and food production, and improve household food security. Food can be stored and household financial needs met from the sales of cash crops; household financial needs would otherwise require the sale of food crops.

Both tea and coffee areas have been expanding, partly into less-suitable areas. Cotton production continues to suffer due to marketing problems. As a result, farmers have opted to grow other cash crops, particularly in Kiambu, Murang'a, Embu, and Kitui districts. Tobacco, grown in the drier zones, is restricted by the availability of wood fuel for tobacco curing.

Food crops. Maize is the staple food in the study area. The National Dryland Farming Research Station has developed varieties of maize that are suitable for low-rainfall areas. Katumani (Composite B) maize needs 120 days to mature, while Makueni Composite (recently released) requires 95 days. The Katumani composites need at least 250 mm of rainfall for a crop and 350 mm for average yields compared to 400 to 500 mm for local maize.

Katumani Composite has been widely adopted by farmers in the dry areas, although many also plant local maize. The larger grain of local maize is preferred to the smaller, harder Katumani grain. Otherwise, Katumani maize tastes like other maize and is of comparable nutritional value. Since Katumani is a composite, farmers can plant it for successive seasons, using seeds harvested from the first crop. If the largest cobs are saved, the seed stock drifts toward longer maturing plants, and subsequent generations are similar to local varieties. Given that Katumani competes with traditional drought-resistant crops in areas of Kitui and Machakos, the small area per household devoted to Katumani, and the drift in the seed stock, the effect of Katumani as a drought-coping strategy is diminished.

Beans, pigeon and cow peas, and green grams are important food crops. In the lower zones, cow peas and pigeon peas are allotted more area than beans and are often interplanted with other crops, especially maize. They are mixed with maize and cooked together to flavor the maize and increase the protein content of the largely starchy maize grains.

Traditional crops that either resist periods of drought or evade drought by maturing early include pigeon peas, cow peas, cassava, sweet potatoes, sorghum, and millet. They have been widely grown in the past, but recently neglected. The reasons for the conversion to maize include taste preferences; an unfashionable association with traditional foods, such as cassava or sorghum *ugali*; the lack of a well-developed market for these crops; and a shortage of labor, particularly to scare birds away from sorghum fields. However, these crops are still planted, and the area in which they are planted is gradually increasing, though it is negligible compared to that of maize. Agricultural research has also produced better varieties of many of these crops, and attempts have been made to increase the urban demand.

Constraints to agricultural production. Low annual rainfall and its low reliability are major constraints to expanding agricultural production. The importance of rainfall is illustrated in the results of a dynamic crop production model (Konijn 1988); see Figure 12.8. The model uses climatic and edaphic variables, and was run for good and moderate drought seasons at representative rainfall stations: Kerugoya (tea/coffee zone), Embu (maize/cotton zone), Machakos (marginal cotton zone), and Makindu (livestock/millet zone). In the long rains at Kerugoya, the difference in maize production between good and drought seasons was very small—less than 20 percent. At Makindu, in the short rains (the more reliable for maize), a good season might produce over 1,000 kg/ha, while little would be harvested during a drought. Embu and Machakos had similar variations between seasons, but they produced some harvest in the drought scenario. In terms of maize production, Kerugoya is not drought prone, Embu and Machakos are subject to considerable drought impacts, and Makindu is not suitable for maize cultivation.

Most farmers have to rely on rain-fed agriculture. The several irrigation schemes in the study area (Mwea, Kibirigwi, Yatta Furrow, and along the Tana and Athi rivers) grow commercial horticultural crops or rice.

In the highlands, soils are generally well suited for agriculture, especially if soil erosion can be controlled. In the lower areas, soils are sandy and shallow, with lower water-holding capacities than the deep, clay soils. In a region where rainfall is often sporadic, occurring in discrete events separated by several days or more, soil water-holding capacities are critical to plant growth. The soils were assessed for their water-holding capacity using data from the Kenya Soil Survey. For each soil type, the soil list (Sombroek et al., 1982) provides a range of typical depths and a breakdown of the range of soil textures. The soil textures were ranked according to their water-holding capacities, using available site tests and expert opinion (Weeda and Mungai, personal communication, 1985). Soil texture is the major determinant of soil water-holding capacity (Weg and Mbuvi 1975). The productive available moisture (pam) is an estimate of the amount of water the soil could hold that would be available for extraction by plants. It is defined as the amount of water in 10 cm of soil between field capacity (a water suction value of 330 mb or pF 2.5) and permanent wilting point (15,000 mb or pF 4.2). At pressures lower than 330 mbar, the water is lost to deep infiltration by gravity; at pressures greater than 15,000 mb, the plant cannot extract the water from the soil. The pam was estimated for each soil texture. For each soil type, the most common soil textures were used, and total productive available moisture was estimated by multiplying the soil depth by the pam. The result was usually a range of values for each soil type. The average value (taking the average of the lowest and highest estimates) is mapped in Figure 12.9. The greater potential of the highlands, with over 200 mm of water-holding capacity, is clear, compared to the low (25 mm or less) capacities of the lowlands.

The difference in average maize yields due to high and low assumptions of soil water-holding capacity was assessed with a crop water model (Downing and Porter 1987). In the Machakos lowlands, complete crop failure may be expected with low soil-water capacities, while in the highlands of the Aberdares and Mt. Kenya, rainfall is sufficient and soils deep enough so that soil-water capacities are not very important. While the 1984 drought severely affected agriculture in this area, it should be considered a rare event in the wet highlands having deep, clay soils.

Farmers often prepare or plant their land after the rains have started, due to labor bottlenecks, a lack of draught animals, or a lack of cash or credit for seed. Delayed planting results in lower yields, particularly in the lower zones. Simulations of the effect of planting delays on maize yields were made using a crop water balance model (Downing and Porter 1987). At Kerugoya, each day that planting was delayed beyond the onset of the rains (as determined according to a threshold value) resulted in a 0.7 percent reduction in yield for the first four weeks. By comparison, the average daily reduction at Makindu was 12.2 percent for the first four weeks. At this rate, a delay of half a week would reduce the crop yield by half.

As the Kenyan population grows, the size of holdings is reduced as a result of land subdivision and the development of infrastructure, such as schools, roads, hospitals, and markets. Land/population pressure is especially notable in the tea/coffee and maize/sunflower zones (see below). More people have to be supported within a small area, and this entails diminishing marginal return to labor.

In areas where cash crops are grown, land under food crops is diminishing. Coffee and tea occupy about 25 to 35 percent of the land-holding, generating higher incomes than food crops.

Livestock

Livestock keeping is a deeply rooted custom in the study area. Before the introduction of a monetary economy, wealth was gauged by the number of livestock owned. Although conditions have changed, almost every small-scale farmer owns, or aspires to own, a cow, goat, or sheep.

In the highlands, most households keep one or more milk cows, often an improved breed. Milk is an important part of the diet in these zones, and may also be a profitable cash enterprise. Many households also have a few small stock, primarily sheep. On-farm grazing is limited, and livestock is usually stall-fed with crop residues and fodder. An average situation is 2.5 to 4.0 livestock units of 400 kg grade animal on three ha, of which one ha is in forage or grazing.

In the lower zones, the livestock situation shifts toward beef production using local, zebu cattle and smallstock (goats and sheep) and toward greater reliance on off-farm grazing. In the maize and cotton zones, the average situation is 8 livestock units of 300 kg zebu animal on 5 ha, of which 1.5 ha is forage and grazing. In the sorghum, millet, and livestock zones, a representative situation is a stocking rate of 3 ha per 300 kg zebu animal, with 100 ha in natural grazing/browse available to the household. In the ranching zones, nomadic pastoralism and commercial ranching are practiced; in eastern Kitui, they are limited by access to reliable water supplies.

The impact of climatic variability on livestock production varies with the agroecological zone and livestock situation (Potter 1988). Using the average situations noted above, in average to good years in the highlands, considerable milk production may be realized (2 to 10 kg/day). In a moderate drought (10 percent probability of occurrence), no milk would be produced, but the animals would live. In a severe drought (as in 1984), animals in the lower highlands, typical of Embu, would starve. This is what happened in 1984, when 30 to 40 percent of all the grade cattle in Eastern and Central provinces were estimated to have died (Nkanata 1985). In the maize/cotton zone, typified by data from Katumani, little milk would be produced from on-farm forage or grazing, even in a very good year. Successful livestock enterprises require feeding with crop residues, off-farm grazing, or commercial feeds. In severe and prolonged droughts, there will be no crop residues, and off-farm grazing will be scarce. Animal mortality rates of over 50 percent can be expected. Many farmers in 1984 had to purchase fodder at exorbitant prices to keep their few animals alive. In the sorghum/millet/livestock zone, livestock enterprises are probably more reliable than crop production. The key determinant is the quality of the vegetation and the ability of the animal to chose its diet. In average or good years, a gain of 50 kg/year/ha or more is possible. In a drought, liveweight gain is less, about 30 to 35 kg/year/ha, but it is dependent on the previous state of the grazing land and access to water supplies. Only in a prolonged drought are significant livestock deaths expected.

There are a number of other constraints to increasing livestock production in the six districts. In the highlands, the most pressing constraint is land, either for grazing or fodder production. Commercial feeds are too expensive for most small farmers. Overgrazing of common lands and a lack of fodder crops are problems in the lower zones. Marketing of livestock products is constrained by a lack of suitable transportation, irregular supplies, and improper management. The government parastatals have been particularly inefficient. Extension services are geared toward the small-scale farmer, but they have not been particularly effective.

Agricultural Impacts of the 1984 Drought

Crop production following the failure of the long rains was reduced (see Chapter 6). Very low production was realized in such staple food crops as maize, beans, cow peas, and sorghum, resulting in acute seed shortages during the short rains from October to December.

An essential aspect of planning for drought episodes is to prepare for recovery from crop failure. Bean seed was particularly scarce in the six districts; almost half or more of the households reported a shortage of seed for planting in the short rains (Table 12.8). White maize seed was more widely available, except in the lower zones, where, along with sorghum and millet seed, about two-thirds or more of the households reported shortages. The government and NGOs provided free seed to needy households, which was critical, but often late in arriving. The very good rains in late 1984 and in 1985 ensured above-average harvests. If they had been less plentiful, requiring replanting of crops, the seed shortages would have been more acute. As it was, many farmers planted seed varieties ill-suited for the agroclimatic zones. Even some of the yellow maize from the imported relief food was planted.

There did not seem to be strong evidence that farmers increased the area planted in food crops in the short rains after the drought (Table 12.8). Given the lack of seed, cash for buying seed, labor if someone had left the household, and the predominant small plots in the six districts, there was little ability to expand the acreage devoted to agriculture, at least over a short time scale of one year.

The improvement of agricultural production in these districts must rely on making better use of the good and poor years, rather than expanding the agricultural frontier into less-suitable lands.

During the short rains of 1984, some of the lowlands were attacked by army worms, which caused damage to both crops and pasture. The crops had grown to a stage where they could not be severely damaged by worms, and the total damage ranged between 5 and 7 percent.

Due to drought, water levels were low, and crops under irrigation were affected. In some instances, the area cultivated was reduced. At the Mwea irrigation settlement scheme, some people were forced to irrigate at night as water was rationed. As a result, rice production was reduced by over 2,000 mt. In Machakos and Kitui, irrigation was halted along the Yatta Furrow to ensure adequate water supplies for domestic uses.

Following the drought, the remaining draught animals were emaciated. Some people had moved from their farms to towns in search of employment, leaving behind the aged, women, and young children. For example, in the Mwea settlement scheme, 50 percent of the draught animals used to level the paddy fields died. Some paddy fields were abandoned as the farmers went back to their original homes and relatives in other areas.

One of the major impacts was the loss of livestock. Many of the animals were sold or slaughtered rather than having died as a result of the drought. However, prices were very low due to the market surplus, the inadequacy of the Kenya Meat Commission's buying and processing facilities, and the poor state of the animals. In the CBS/NES Survey of Drought Responses, 32 to 45 percent of all households surveyed (including those that never had livestock before), sold, slaughtered (for home consumption), or lost cattle (Table 12.9). The respective figures for goats are 14 to 42 percent. The average number of cattle per household in April 1984 varied from 2.3 to 7.3 for the five agroecological zones. The average number in January 1985 was 1.5 to 3.6, a reduction of 26 to 51 percent. The numbers of goats declined by 23 to 57 percent. The marginal cotton and livestock/millet zones experienced the largest decreases. Embu District alone lost 22,558 (21 percent) cattle in 1984, and Kirinyaga District lost 25,598 (26 percent) cattle.

The loss of livestock is a major impact, particularly in cases where the livestock was composed of improved breeds and earned income to the farmer through milk sales. In the upper zones, smallholders realized how vulnerable the grade cows are to drought when fodder and grazing land are scarce. In the drier zones, livestock is a reserve capital that helps buffer the effects of drought. Over a year after the drought, most households had not recovered from the losses and were buying animals, if available and affordable. If another drought comes before households are able to restock, they will have little to sell to buy food.

FOOD POVERTY:
ACCESS TO FOOD IN LOCAL MARKETS

With the failure of on-farm production, the major source of food during drought is through marketed exchanges, which depend on access to the monetary economy. The patterns of household cash incomes and market conditions are described below.

Cash Incomes

Throughout the study area, households participate in the monetary economy. Cash is required to pay school fees and medical expenses, to purchase household commodities, to buy essential and supplementary foods, and to purchase farm inputs. Probably the most urgent need in normal times is to pay for school fees, as Kenyans have invested heavily in education (see Chapter 19). Even in average years, households purchase a significant proportion of their food in the local market (Table 12.10; see also CBS [1981c]). In the event of crop failures, this proportion increases dramatically.

The CBS/NES survey asked households what were their usual sources of cash income. The six districts are primarily agricultural, as indicated by the importance of farm produce as a source of income (Table 12.11). In 62 percent of the households, sale of farm produce was a source of income. There are notable variations in sources of income between the zones. While farm produce was a source of income to 90 percent of the households in the tea/coffee zone, only 50 percent cited this as a source in the maize/cotton and livestock/millet zones. The importance of farm produce declines in the drier zones, while the livestock sector gains.

In the event of crop failure, families with off-farm income would be better off than those fully dependent on the farm. The survey results indicate that just over 50 percent of the households interviewed (except in the marginal coffee zone) had at least one member in the nuclear family of the head of the household in permanent employment (Table 12.12). The highest percentage (61 percent) was in the maize/cotton zone.

Agricultural casual labor, remittances, and permanent employment were sources of income to just over 30 percent of all the households. The percentage is higher in the drier zones. As productivity declines, off-farm income becomes a necessity.

Business as a source of income is of little significance in the survey area, being a source to only 15 percent of the households. Likewise, nonagricultural casual labor is an income source to only 10 to 25 percent of the households, except in the livestock/millet zone, where over one-third of the households reported this as a source of income.

Local Food Markets

Farmers sell much of their produce before the next crop is harvested. In normal years, the sales provide cash and may be more efficient than storing food due to the cost of storage facilities and pesticides. When crops fail, farmers have little food in their stores. Reliance on marketed food places the household in a vulnerable position with regard to the organization of the market and fluctuations in market prices.

After farmers deliver their cash crops to the marketing bodies, it usually takes between one and two seasons to receive the full payment. In 1984 and 1985, farmers received money during the drought from their previous harvests and were able to buy food, when it was available. Income from cash crops mitigates the effects of drought as long as food is available in the market. Some of the cooperative societies organized to promote cash crops also provided food relief and rescheduled loan payments.

Impact of the 1984 Drought

During the drought period, essential food commodities, such as maize, beans, and flour, were scarce and sold at exorbitant prices. In retail shops, consumers were forced to buy other commodities, such as sugar or tea, before buying food. Table 12.13 shows average retail prices of maize and beans for a sample of markets. White maize prices increased by 149 to 299 percent between the beginning and end of 1984, while bean prices rose from 154 to 274 percent (see Chapter 6).

The National Cereals and Produce Board (NCPB) stores and distributes food to registered agents only. In the study area, there are five NCPB depots: Sagana, Embu, Mwingi, Machakos, and Kitui. The depots store produce for sale and famine relief. The NCPB sales are regulated by the government, but sales of local produce are not. The large-scale provision of yellow maize through commercial channels helped stabilize prices, even that of the preferred white maize.

There was an oversupply of animals at the few slaughtering facilities in the area. Local demand for meat was limited, as people had to purchase basic food grains. The two slaughterhouses near Nairobi were also taking animals from other areas of Kenya. No effort was made to provide mobile abattoirs that could at least process the hides and bones. As a result of the market failure, livestock prices collapsed. In one area, a goat sold for Ksh 40, not enough to purchase 2 kg of yellow maize. A year later, goats were selling for over Ksh 400, if they could be found for sale.

The CBS/NES survey did not assess the actual level of household income; it assessed whether the sources changed from normal during the 1984 drought, and, if so, whether income increased or decreased. The level of farm produce is a function of climate, inputs, and labor. A major change in any of these factors could adversely affect production. The 1984 drought resulted in crop failure, as reflected in a reduced number of households depending on farm produce as a source of income—only 40 percent as compared to 62 percent during normal years—and the lower receipts compared to normal years. Livestock sales gained in importance, both in the number of households reporting livestock income and in the increase in livestock income compared to normal. Casual labor and business income declined. Permanent employment and remittances increased in amount of income, but not in the percentage of households receiving them. In the case of permanent employment, the increased amount was due to annual increments. Remittances decreased in the upper zones, but increased in the lower zones. As the other income sources did not increase dramatically during the drought, the agricultural losses must have contributed to deprivation in 1984.

The survey results indicate that some zones were more adversely affected than others. The tea/coffee and marginal coffee zones were the least affected. The other three zones are drier and therefore more vulnerable to agricultural drought, as reflected in the decline in agricultural production. For instance, in the maize/cotton zone, the number of households depending on farm produce declined from 50 percent to 34 percent, a decline that was similar in the marginal cotton and livestock/millet zones. The importance of livestock increased slightly but not enough to compensate for the agricultural losses. As no source of income seems to have gone up significantly in the marginal zones, it can be concluded that the drought had its heaviest toll there. The majority of households, especially in the marginal zones, reported a decrease in income during the drought.

FOOD DEPRIVATION: NUTRITION AND HEALTH

Pregnant and lactating mothers and children under five are the most vulnerable to food deprivation. The general nutritional status of the population affects its ability to withstand short-term food shortages. In the absence of reliable food supplies during the drought, serious malnutrition may result.

Nutrition and Health

Diarrhea, malaria, diseases of the skin, eye and ear infections, and rheumatism are common in all six districts. Other diseases, like bilharzia, anemia, and malnutrition (as reported at clinics) are not widespread. Malaria is the "king of diseases," representing between 15 and 30 percent of reported cases in all the districts, except Kiambu, where the rate was 5 percent (CBS 1983).

Background data on nutrition in Kenya are presented in Chapter 18. The highest rates of stunted children (0-4 years) in the Third Rural Child Nutrition Survey were found in Kitui (30 percent), Murang'a and Kirinyaga (25 percent), Machakos (23 percent), and Embu (22 percent). Kiambu had the lowest rate (18 percent).

Impact of the 1984 Drought

Changes in diet. While white maize, either whole or ground, is the usual staple food of the region, diets changed after the 1984 long rains crops failed (Table 12.12). Over two-thirds of the households in all the zones reported a shift in the major food consumed. The highest percentages were in the upper zones. For most of the households, the shift was from white to yellow maize. From 31 to 87 percent of the households in each zone (or 63 percent of all households) relied on yellow maize as their staple food for at least three months between April and December 1984. Much of the yellow maize was purchased; all of it had been imported by the government or other relief agencies in 1984 to prevent widespread famine. It was widely available and crucial to the well-being of the rural households.

Famine relief in 1984/85. As noted in other chapters, the government was able to avert famine by importing sufficient maize to keep the commercial markets relatively well supplied (which dampened potentially extreme price increases) and by organizing a massive food-relief program. Given the seriousness of the drought and the vulnerable agricultural and economic systems, famine relief was required by many people in the six districts, especially in Machakos and Kitui, where crops failed almost completely and people had fewer alternatives. The number of people receiving famine relief and the amounts distributed are listed in Tables 12.14 and 12.15 (see also Chapter 2). Approximate figures obtained from the district administration show that the following percentages of the total population were given famine relief aid: Murang'a (3 percent); Kiambu (7); Kirinyaga (4); Embu (0.7); Machakos (35); and Kitui (95). These figures are not necessarily complete since, in many cases, the records were not available. With many organizations operating relief projects, usually in more than one area, it was impossible to obtain and reconcile all the relief aid provided in a given district.

In most districts, food aid began in August to October, although the supplies in the months before the yellow maize arrived (late September to November) were erratic and inadequate. Assistance by the Office of the President comprised about 10 kg per capita of yellow maize (Table 2.4 in Chapter 2). The "rule of thumb" estimate of maize consumption in Kenya is two 90 kg bags per year per person. Using this estimate and the GOK/USAID average monthly ration, the food relief averaged 5 to 10 percent of individual requirements. Many households received very little assistance. The distribution of yellow maize in commercial markets was overall more important than the food-relief efforts. The estimates of famine-relief recipients began to drop rapidly as the 1984 short rains crop was harvested.

In the CBS/NES survey, only 14 percent of the households in the tea/coffee zone received famine relief, while 67 percent and 77 percent of the households in the marginal cotton and livestock/millet zones, respectively, received assistance from some institution. These data do not indicate how much each family received. In many cases, the relief was irregular, but at least it was available.

Nutritional impacts. Although there is a pilot program to register births and deaths, no information was available on changes in fertility or mortality rates during the drought. The health-reporting system during 1984 did not record malnutrition if the patient had another condition. Thus, it is difficult to assess the vulnerability of the population to climatic variability on the basis of the health data available. The data presented in Chapter 14 indicate the rapid rise in malnourished children in the marginal cotton and livestock/millet zones.

To assess the nutritional effects of the drought, measurements of mid-arm circumference (MAC) of 527 children were taken in January 1985 as part of the CBS/NES survey. The timing of the survey was after the drought had been broken by the short rains, but before all of the short rains crop had been harvested. In assessing the nutritional status, a World Health Organization age-specific standard for MAC was used, with the measurements expressed as a percentage of the standard (Table 12.16). A negative score refers to a case below the reference standard for the child's age. The MAC is an easy method of nutritional surveillance, as it is fairly independent of age. It indicates nutritional status primarily for wasting (short-term deficiency) and some stunting (long-term or chronic problems). The method is not entirely reliable, however. In comparison with other indicators used in Kenya, MAC may falsely indicate severe, short-term malnourishment in 15 percent of the cases (CBS 1983b). Thus, the interpretation of the MAC data described here must be done with some care.

Nutrition is a complex variable, governed by a number of factors, such as economic well-being, sociocultural factors, and education. Lack of food is, therefore, a major factor in causing malnutrition, but it is not the only one. The survey data reveal a poor state of health in the study area (Table 12.16). Only 22 percent of the children were recorded as healthy, while over 50 percent were either marginally or severely malnourished (less than 80 percent of the standard). The nearly 14 percent of the survey group that fall in the severe category are the most worrisome.

Although zonal comparisons reveal no simple trend, some notable differences do emerge. The maize/cotton zone had the highest proportion of unhealthy children (only 14 percent healthy with 64 percent either marginally or severely malnourished). Although it is not possible to fully explain this scenario, a few contributing factors, such as low productivity, scarcity of cash crops, and fairly dense populations, should be noted. In this zone, most of the food has to be purchased.

The proportion of children at risk and those slightly malnourished is fairly similar in all zones. However, there is one notable trend: the proportion of severely malnourished children rises as one moves from the high-potential to the low-potential zones. With much less diversification in household access to food, these marginal areas are vulnerable to drought.

Migration. To cope with the ravages of drought in the badly hit marginal areas (crops failed and the demand for agricultural labor declined), some family members moved away to look for work or live with relatives. Family life was most disrupted in the drier zones. In the livestock/millet zone, at least one household member in 38 percent of the households moved (only those household members who were away for more than one month were counted) due to the drought (the reason for leaving the household as given by the respondent). This compared to only 7 percent in the marginal coffee zone and 20 to 26 percent in the other zones. Given the degree of hardship caused by the drought, the number of households from which people felt constrained to leave appears rather low. The rural households are basically stable in that they do not need to migrate to survive hardship. Certainly, the government food-relief efforts contributed a great deal in reducing the number of migrants.

CONCLUSION: VULNERABILITY TO HUNGER AND HOUSEHOLD COPING STRATEGIES

In closing, this section estimates the number of people vulnerable to chronic and episodic hunger and reviews the range, prevalence, and effectiveness of household strategies for coping with drought.

Vulnerability to Chronic and Episodic Hunger

The estimates of vulnerability to hunger are based on the characteristics of the population, socioeconomic circumstances, and data from the CBS/NES Survey of Drought Responses (see Downing 1988 for details). They are provided only for zones I to V, which include most of the settled agricultural areas and for which data are available. Based on projections from the 1979 census, over 3.5 million people resided in the five zones in 1984.

Average conditions are the socioeconomic conditions prevalent before the 1984 drought and a climatic regime based on median rainfall probabilities for each zone. Episodic hunger is based on the 1984 drought experience, corresponding to a rainfall probability of 2 percent (98 percent of the years are expected to be wetter). Vulnerability is characterized by the three definitions of food shortage, food poverty, and food deprivation as discussed above.

Household food shortage is measured by expected productivity in average and severe drought (as in 1984) years for cropping systems typical of the five zones. The area cropped and household composition are drawn from the CBS/NES survey data. Food-short households are defined as those that produce less than two-thirds of their consumption requirements (using the FAO recommended caloric intake). The food-short households expand from 27 percent of the population in an average year to 82 percent during a drought (Table 12.17).

Probably the most important determinant of vulnerability to hunger is access to reliable off-farm income: food poverty is a more telling indicator of drought impacts than food shortage. Households were deemed vulnerable to food poverty unless a member of the household or its nuclear family (son or daughter of the head of household) had permanent employment. This indicator of food poverty is appropriate in the absence of data on household budgets. Other sources of income, such as sales of produce or livestock, casual wage employment, handicrafts, small businesses, and donations, would be vulnerable to climatic variations. Donations, either from relatives or official food relief, are uncertain and difficult to predict. Effective food relief may avert famine; it is premature to assert that the recent, successful experience reduces long-term vulnerability to hunger in Kenya. The food poor (without reliable off-farm income) among the food short are 10 and 30 percent of the population in average and drought years.

There were over 943,000 children under the age of five and pregnant and lactating women in 1984 in the six districts (27 percent of the population). They are the most vulnerable individuals, subject to food deprivation, because they require more energy (per body weight) and have less capacity to cope with deprivation. These individuals with special nutritional needs, within households that are partially self-provisioning (food short) and without reliable income (food poor), are 2 and 8 percent of the population in average and drought years.

The totals provided here are illustrative of how the factors influencing vulnerability to hunger may be combined, and should not be interpreted as absolute figures. The estimates are likely conservative. While the most vulnerable group comprised almost 300,000 children and women in vulnerable households, others would also need food assistance due to low wages in some occupations and the poor distribution of income within the household. These estimates are based on categories of households, not a household budget survey. The categories and definition of vulnerable groups change over time, with population growth and different states of the economy, and with differing assumptions about resource endowment, nutritional health, and access to the monetary economy.

Household Drought-Coping Strategies

There have been dramatic changes in the household economy of rural smallholders in central and eastern Kenya, beginning after World War II with colonial policies and then accelerating after independence with land consolidation, population growth, and expansion of the monetary economy. These underlying forces have shaped major changes in the range and prevalence of coping strategies available to smallholders. The assessment of drought-coping strategies (Table 12.18) is drawn from available rural surveys and case studies of specific locales (more detail is provided in Downing 1988). However, the ratings are subjective. The categories correspond to the three dominant food entitlements: subsistence production, monetary activities, and donations.

Subsistence production. Subsistence production may be improved through soil conservation, water conservation, irrigation, cropping in diverse areas and agroecological zones, inter- or relay cropping, dry planting, mixed livestock herds, dispersed grazing, fodder production, and the planting of drought-resistant crops. In the last decade, soil conservation and drought-resistant maize have been widely adopted (Rukandema et al., 1981, 1983). For example, over 9,000 km per year of terraces were constructed in

Machakos in the early 1980s (EcoSystems Ltd. 1986). However, other traditional coping strategies, such as cultivating plots in separate zones and using distant grazing lands, have diminished with reductions in on-farm labor and due to the consolidation and subdivision of holdings. There has been a dramatic shift from traditional drought-resistant crops (e.g., sorghum and millet) to maize. Most of the agricultural strategies are effective in a moderate drought, but have limited benefit in a severe drought.

The agricultural strategies do not impede recovery from drought. Though largely unavailable to smallholders, irrigated seed production is effective for seed companies and government agencies in meeting the extreme demand for seed after a drought.

Constraints to improving subsistence production have been land, labor, and capital (particularly with respect to its alternative investments in the monetary economy). Technology and information are probably lesser constraints for most of the strategies. Efforts to make the best use of good seasons are constrained by the lack of a guaranteed market for surpluses in the good seasons, lack of credit to purchase inputs, a limited agricultural labor market, and conflicting demands from off-farm employment (see de Wilde 1984, Schmidt 1979, and Chapter 24).

Market exchanges. Most of the strategies involving market exchanges are highly effective in normal years and during moderate droughts. In severe droughts, the effectiveness depends on food prices and whether the drought affects employment and prices of capital assets (e.g., land and livestock). Land sales were not common in the 1984 drought in the study area, perhaps since they are constrained by administrative procedures that require the approval of the local elders and government.

The more extreme measures to secure cash (migration and selling capital assets) greatly constrain recovery from drought. Conversely, access to cash can strengthen the household's ability to purchase sufficient seed and resources to make the best use of the next season.

Labor and education are the major constraints to participation in the monetary economy: wage workers must have sufficient training and capabilities, with few domestic responsibilities. Land resources are important in cash-cropping, while capital is needed for investments in businesses and cash crops.

Donations. Remittances and donations are highly effective in coping with drought, but uncertain in their prevalence and magnitude. Although these are considered transfer payments, they likely entail enduring social and economic obligations. For instance, loans and credit are included in this category, although repayment requires access to cash incomes, and in the long term are entitlements through monetary exchanges. The extent of rural, informal credit facilities in times of drought is important, but not documented.

Donations of seed may be a major element in recovering from drought and an opportunity to influence the cropping patterns.

The constraints to securing remittances and donations are primarily social, depending on networks of relatives and institutions. In most cases, the effectiveness of this group of coping strategies is correlated to household status. The truly destitute are major beneficiaries only in severe droughts. Capital may be required to secure some loans. For example, some coffee cooperatives gave loans and food to their members during the 1984 drought.

Trends in coping strategies. In summary, trends in coping strategies in the last several decades encompass (see Downing 1988):

1. Decreased numbers of livestock per household, decreased availability of off-farm grazing lands, and increased labor costs to manage livestock herds
2. Maize: it has become the dominant food crop in much of the semiarid areas, replacing such traditional drought-resistant crops as sorghum and millet, and increasing the sensitivity of agricultural production to climatic variations
3. Some investment in agriculture, particularly soil conservation
4. Ineffectiveness of most agricultural strategies in a severe drought, particularly in the drier zones
5. A reduced range of practicable coping strategies, particularly related to on-farm agricultural production
6. Increased household autonomy or responsibility for food security at the expense of traditional kin-based networks
7. Expansion of the monetary economy, and efforts by smallholders to diversify off-farm income; Investment in education is seen as a primary strategy for securing reliable off-farm income

The reduction in the range of coping strategies, the shift toward diversifying sources of income, and a greater reliance on local food markets has increased the government's responsibility to maintain adequate food supplies in each district.

Figure 12.1 Location of central and eastern Kenya study area. Source: Downing (1988), after Berry et al. (1980).

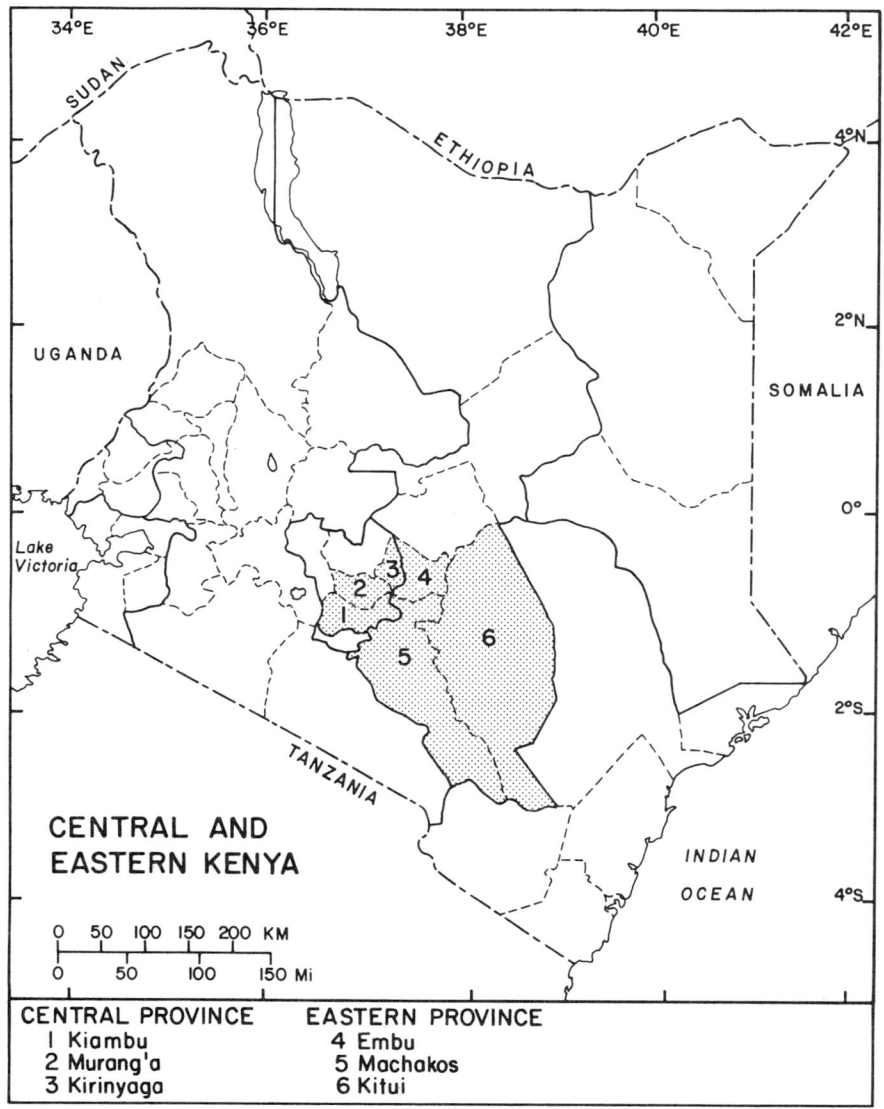

VULNERABILITY, IMPACTS, AND COPING • 191

Figure 12.2 Terrain. Source: Downing (1988), based on Survey of Kenya (1970).

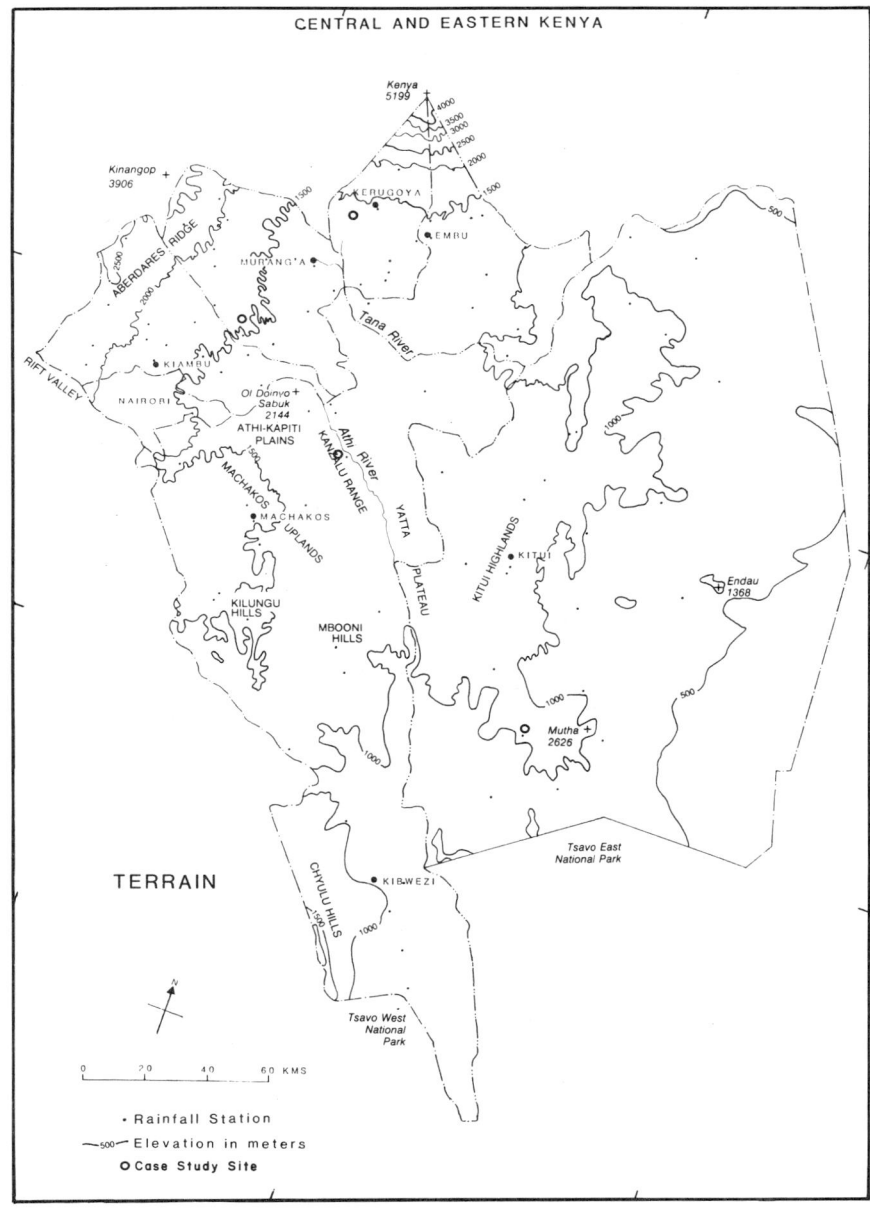

192 • COPING WITH DROUGHT IN KENYA

Figure 12.3 Agroecological zones. The Farm Management Handbook classes are mapped, and the corresponding Kenya Soil Survey units are shown in the key. Source: Downing (1988), based on Jaetzold and Schmidt (1983).

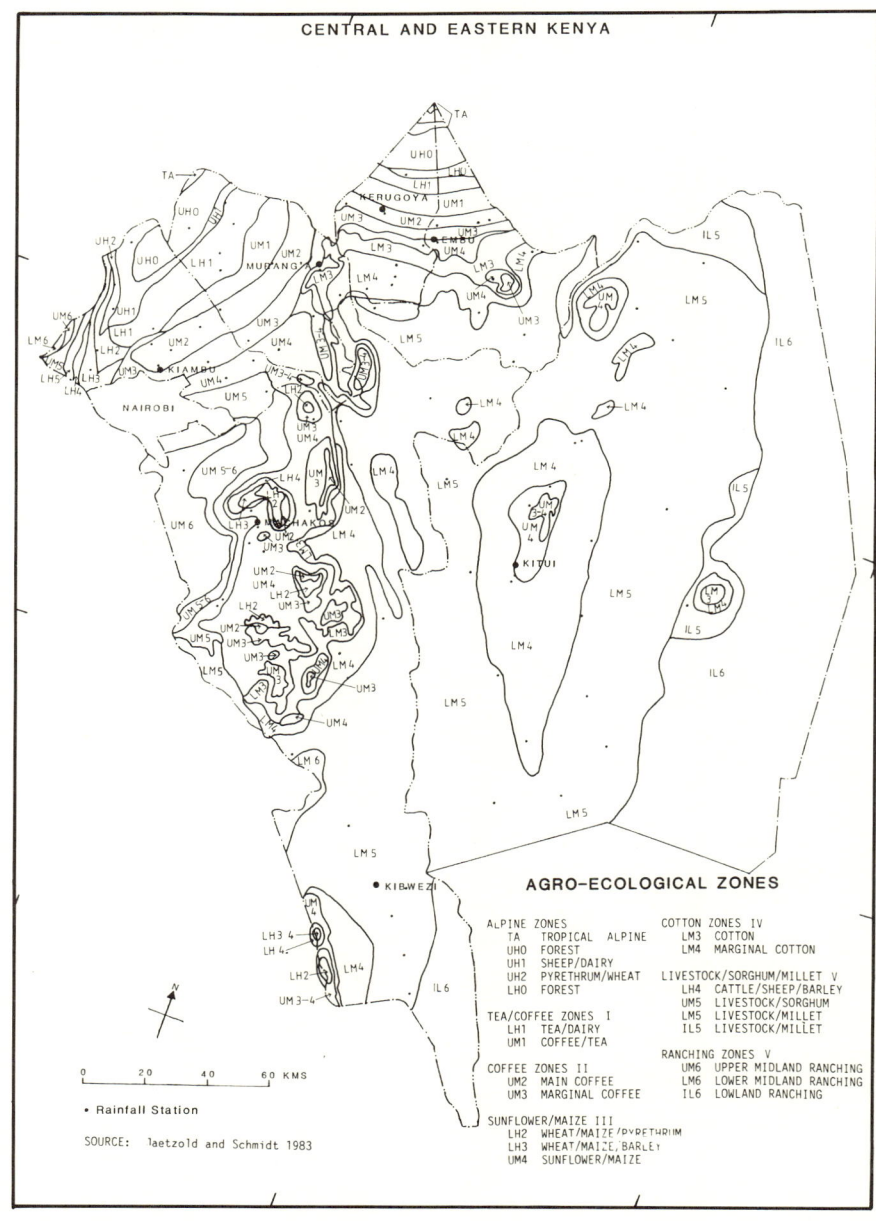

Figure 12.4 Reliability of rainfall in the first rains. Isohyets indicate amount of seasonal rainfall expected to be exceeded in 60 percent of the years. Shaded area receives more than 300 mm, a critical threshold for maize. Source: Jaetzold and Schmidt (1983).

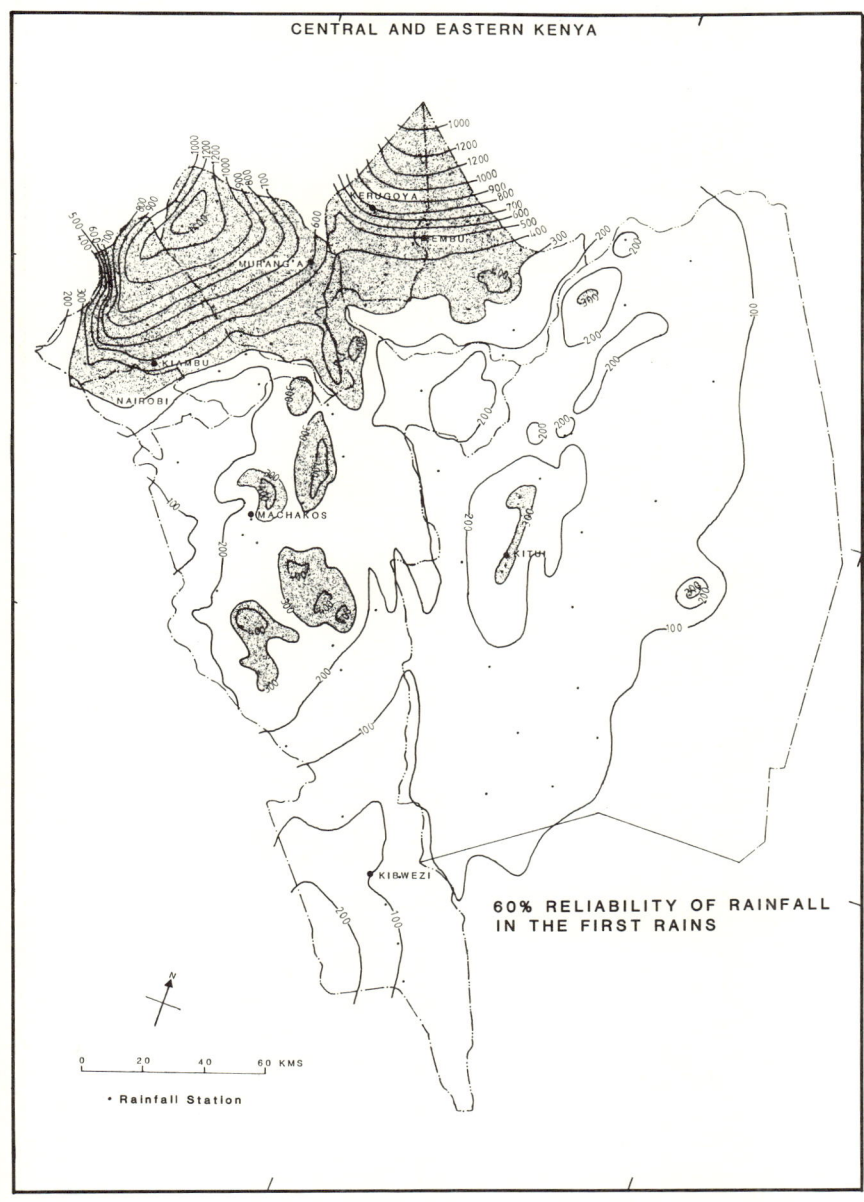

Figure 12.5 Reliability of rainfall in the second rains. Notes as for Figure 12.4. Source: Jaetzold and Schmidt (1983).

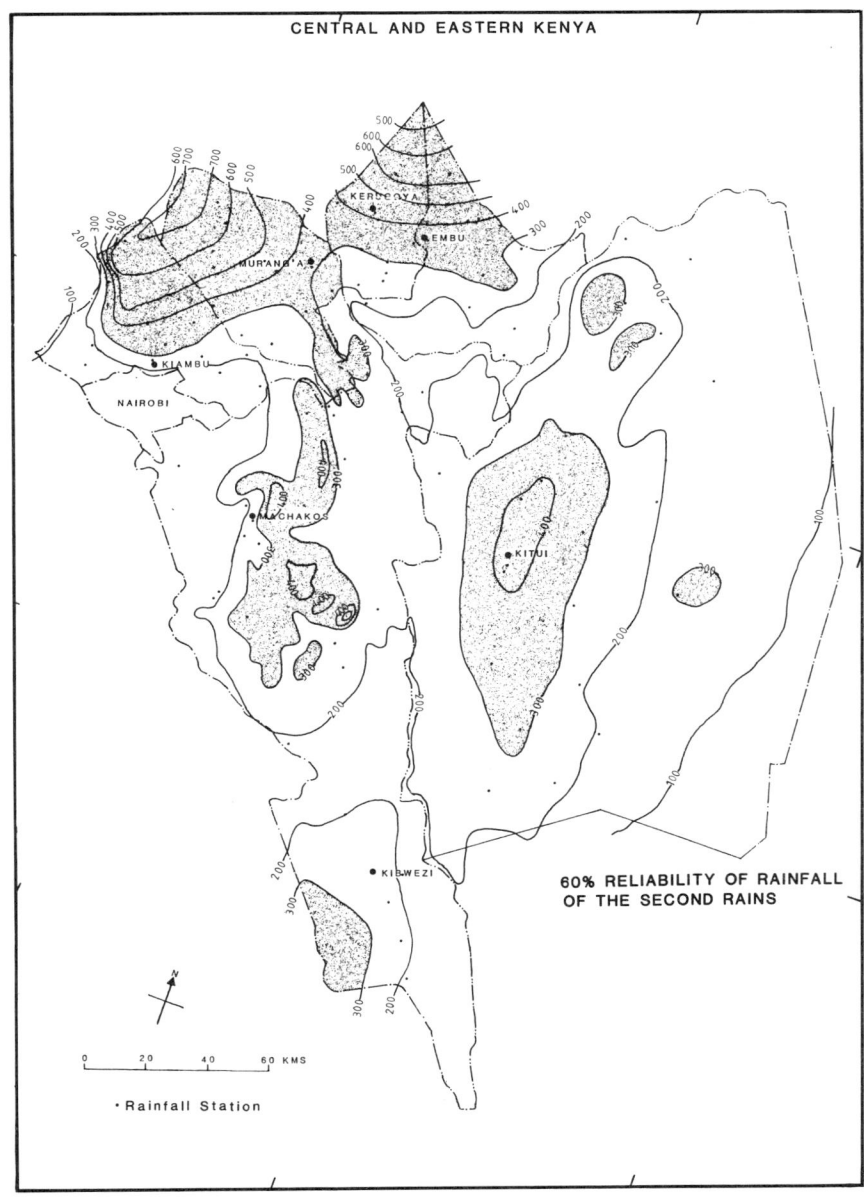

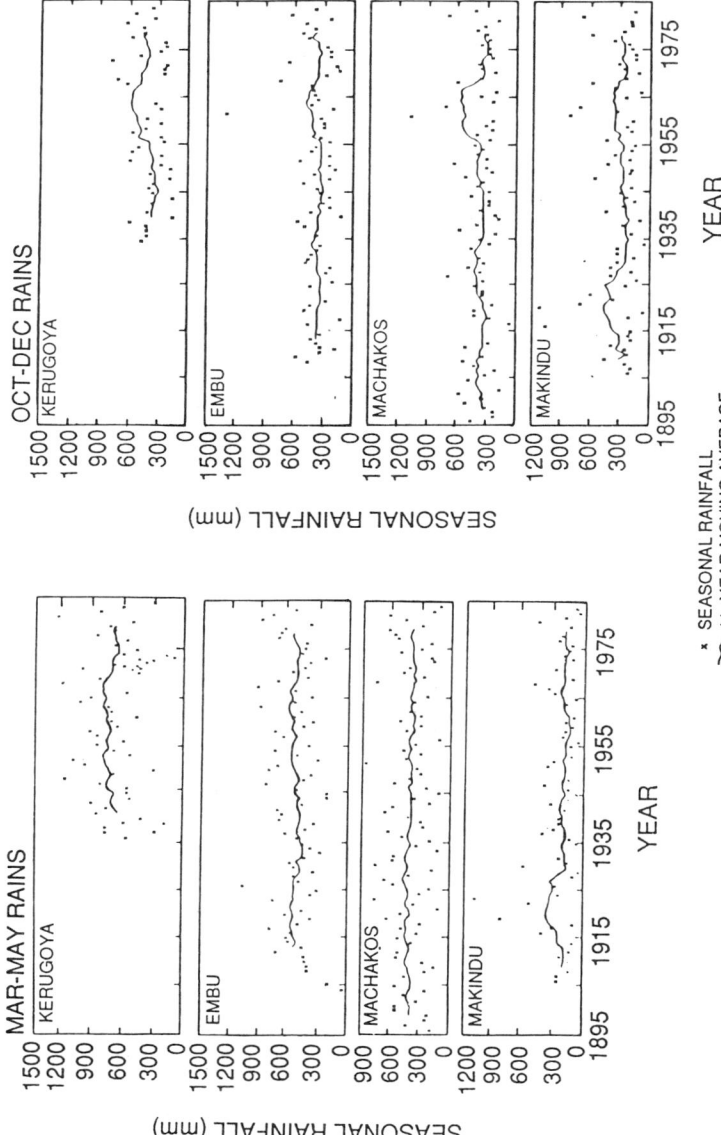

Figure 12.6 Trends in seasonal rainfall. The moving averages of seasonal rainfall show no long-term trends. Source: Downing, Mungai, and Muturi (1988).

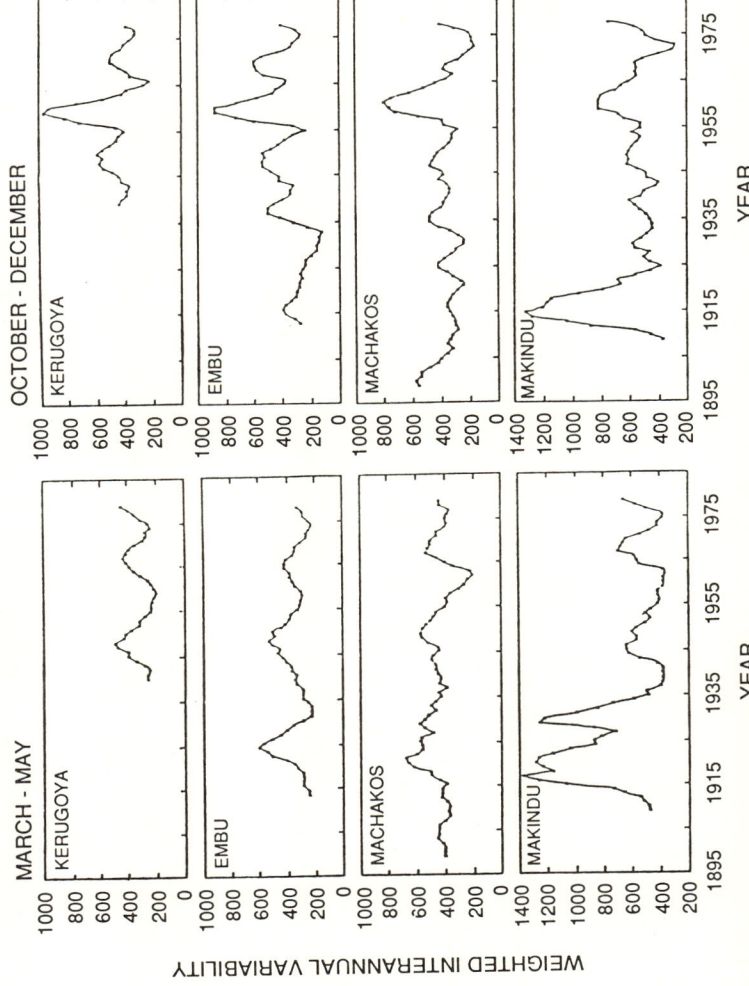

Figure 12.7 Trends in seasonal rainfall variability. Interannual variability is defined as: IAV = [Sum (|X^i-$X^{(i-1)}$|)]/(n-1)/X^a, where: X = seasonal rainfall; i = year; n = averaging period, eleven years, and X^a = average seasonal rainfall. A binomial weight was applied to the IAV statistic to reduce the large fluctuations caused by anomalous events, as in the Makindu series in the 1910s and the wet seasons in the early 1960s. Except for the anomalous wet seasons, the series show no long-term trend. Source: Downing, Mungai, and Muturi (1988).

Figure 12.8 Maize yields for scenarios of a good season and moderate drought season. The results from the crop production model indicate the highest variability in yields at Machakos and the relative food security in zones I/II, typified by Kerugoya. Source: Konijn (1988).

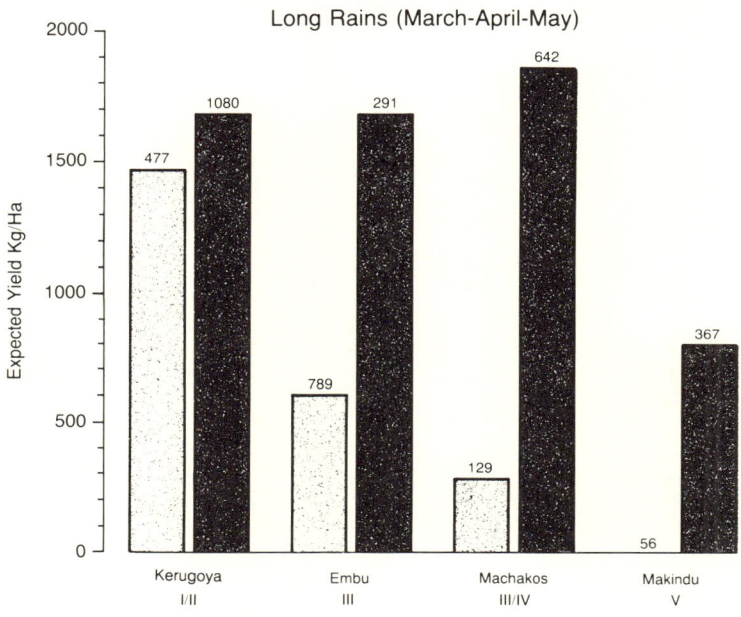

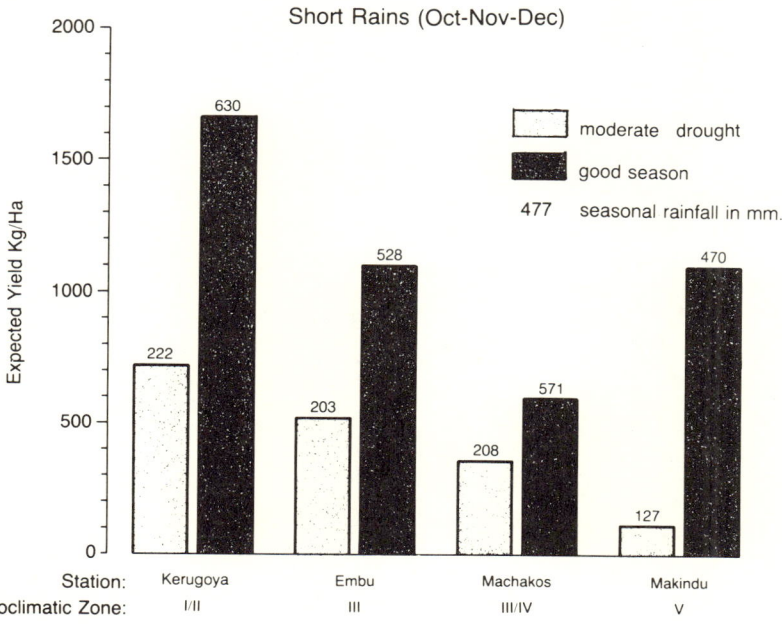

Figure 12.9 Soil water-holding capacity. The productive highlands, with water-holding capacities two or three times the soils in the lowlands, are shaded. Source: Downing (1988), based on soil descriptions in Sombroek, et al. (1982), Jaetzold and Schmidt (1983), and data from the Kenya Soil Survey.

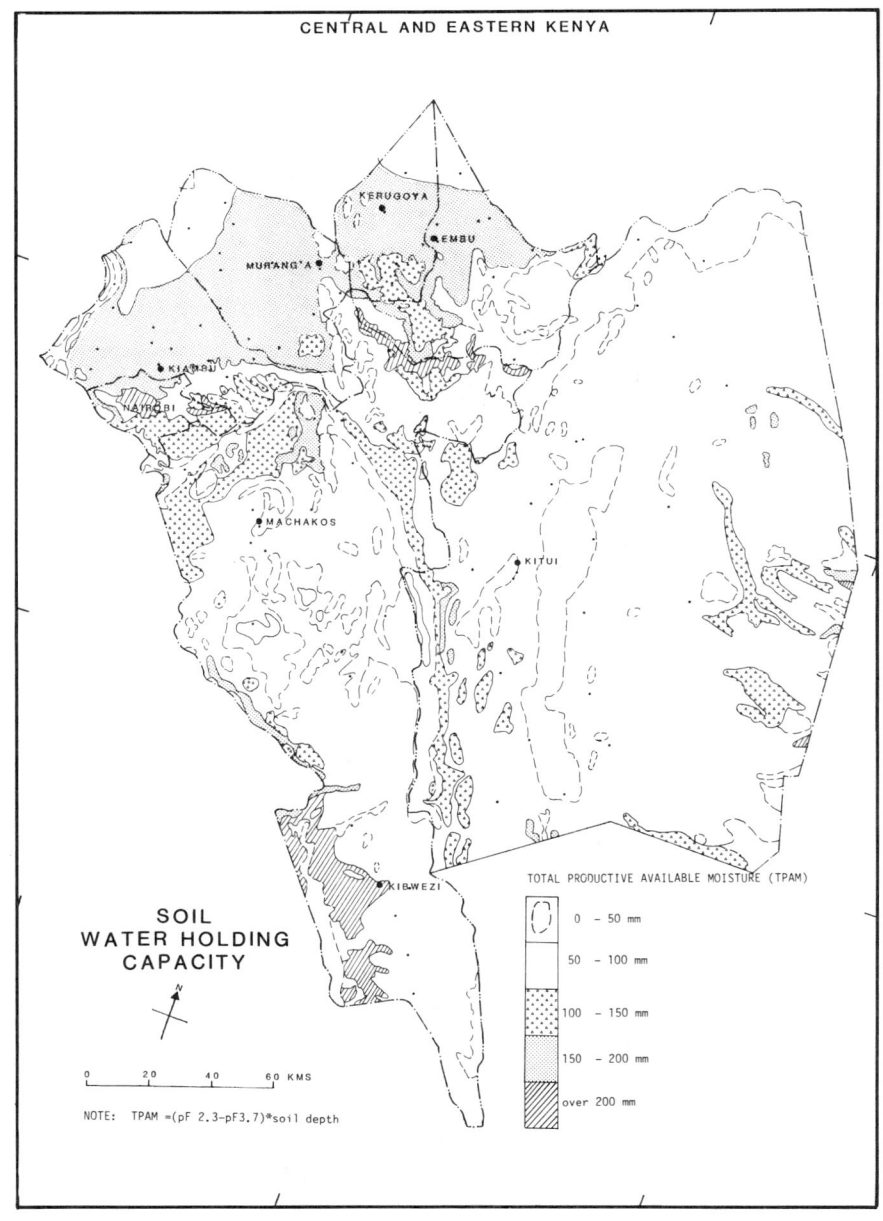

Table 12.1 Agroclimatic Zones

Description	Agroclimatic Zone Number	r/E_o %	Growing Days
Tea/Coffee	I	>80	365
Marginal Coffee	II	65–80	290–365
Maize/Cotton	III	50–65	235–290
Marginal Cotton	IV	40–50	180–235
Livestock/Millet	V	25–40	110–180
Ranching	VI	15–25	75–110
Arid Ranching	VII	<15	<75

Source: Sombroek, et al. (1982).
Notes: Zone VII is not found in the six districts. r/E_o is ratio of average annual rainfall to evapotranspiration.

Table 12.2 Area of Agroecological Zones

Zone	Kiambu	Murang'a	Kirinyaga	Embu	Machakos	Kitui	Total
Highlands (I)	84	49	—	—	—	—	133
Tea/Dairy (I)	182	344	38	11	—	—	575
Coffee/Tea (I)	120	261	124	84	—	—	589
Main Coffee (II)	304	307	123	66	3	—	803
Marginal Coffee (II/III)	179	241	102	59	68	69	718
Sunflower/Maize (III)	363	442	63	83	188	344	1,483
Cotton (III/IV)	—	51	158	198	34	25	466
Marginal Cotton (IV)	—	113	338	247	250	2,533	3,481
Livestock/Sorghum/Millet (V)	164	—	9	1,266	282	10,166	11,887
Ranching (VI)	27	—	—	—	—	6,996	7,023

Source: Jaetzold and Schmidt (1983).
Notes: In sq km. Zone designations are: Upper Highlands (UH1, UH2, UH3) Tea/Dairy (LH1), Coffee/Tea (UM1), Main Coffee (UM2), Marginal Coffee (UM3), Sunflower/Maize (LH2, LH3, UM3-4, UM4), Cotton (LM3), Marginal Cotton (LM4), Livestock/Sorghum/Millet (LH4, UM5, LM4-5, LM5, IL5), and Ranching (LH5, UM6, LM6, IL6). Roman numerals in parentheses are the Kenya Soil Survey equivalent zones.

Table 12.3 Population Projections to the Year 2000

A. Constant Fertility and Mortality up to the Year 2000

Age	Kiambu	Kirinyaga	Murang'a	Embu	Machakos	Kitui
0–14	835.0	351.2	783.7	324.9	1,268.8	550.2
15–59	738.5	307.2	678.6	298.6	1,162.8	486.2
60 +	47.5	21.3	46.7	19.2	76.2	37.4
Total	1,621.1	679.8	1,509.0	642.7	2,507.6	1,073.5
Annual Growth Rate (%)	4.02	3.98	3.94	4.18	4.21	3.92

B. 50 Percent Reduced Fertility by the Year 2000, Constant Mortality

Age	Kiambu	Kirinyaga	Murang'a	Embu	Machakos	Kitui
0–14	533.8	224.4	501.7	207.9	811.5	352.9
15–59	696.3	289.7	640.0	282.0	1,098.0	458.1
60 +	47.5	21.3	46.7	19.2	76.2	37.4
Total	1,277.8	535.5	1,188.4	509.2	1,985.8	848.3
Annual Growth Rate (%)	2.79	3.74	2.71	2.98	3.00	2.71

Source: National Environment Secretariat.
Note: Totals may differ from column sums due to rounding.

Table 12.4 Population Density and Growth Rates by Agroclimatic Zone

A. 1979 Density

District	I	II	III	IV	V	VI	Total
Machakos	—	—	333.3	130.9	45.0	36.8	70.4
Kitui	—	—	231.3	103.3	25.9	3.2	19.9
Embu	433.4	462.9	88.1	66.0	30.2	—	99.7
Murang'a	347.3	469.8	252.8	49.0	—	—	290.7
Kirinyaga	512.7	361.3	227.2	113.7	151.4	—	261.3
Kiambu	204.2	515.1	430.5	160.5	75.6	—	295.6
Total	333.0	468.4	275.2	110.8	35.5	5.1	70.9

B. Change in Density from 1969 to 1979

District	I	II	III	IV	V	VI	Total
Machakos	—	—	0.0098	0.0714	0.0290	0.0784	0.0344
Kitui	—	—	0.0359	0.0320	0.0449	0.0250	0.0388
Embu	0.0393	0.0541	0.0077	0.0388	0.0579	—	0.0412
Murang'a	0.0425	0.0428	0.0328	0.0200	—	—	0.0385
Kirinyaga	0.0459	0.0398	0.0419	0.0120	0.0011	—	0.0311
Kiambu	0.0153	0.0350	0.0170	0.1025	0.0540	—	0.0436
Total	0.0349	0.0417	0.0249	0.0549	0.0382	0.0545	0.0398

Source: Downing, et al. 1988, based on data from the Central Bureau of Statistics.
Notes: Density in people/sq. km. Rates are average annual growth rates. Dashes indicate zones not in the district or for which the area is too small to have representative data.

Table 12.5 Population by Age and Sex: 1979

		Kiambu	Murang'a	Kirinyaga	Embu	Machakos	Kitui
Male	0–4	63	64	27	25	95	42
	5–9	57	58	24	22	89	41
	10–14	49	49	22	19	74	35
	15–59	160	119	65	54	208	84
	60+	15	21	7	7	26	14
	Total	344	311	143	128	493	216
Female	0–4	62	63	27	25	94	42
	5–9	57	58	24	22	89	41
	10–14	49	48	22	19	73	34
	15–59	154	145	66	61	249	117
	60+	19	23	10	7	23	15
	Total	342	338	148	135	530	249
Total	0–4	125	127	53	51	189	85
	5–9	114	116	49	44	178	82
	10–14	98	97	43	38	147	70
	15–59	315	264	132	115	457	201
	60+	34	44	17	14	49	28
	Total	686	648	291	263	1,023	464

Source: Central Bureau of Statistics (1981).
Note: Population in thousands. Totals may differ from column sums due to rounding.

Table 12.6 Seasonal Drought Probabilities

	Kerugoya	Embu	Machakos	Makindu
March–May (Long) Rains				
No. Years	49.	76.	91.	81.
Mild drought	0.31	0.36	0.25	0.43
Moderate drought	0.22	0.22	0.20	0.23
Severe drought	0.06	0.08	0.05	0.06
October–December (Short) Rains				
No. Years	50.	76.	90.	80.
Mild drought	0.46	0.41	0.49	0.56
Moderate drought	0.32	0.29	0.26	0.40
Severe drought	0.14	0.18	0.11	0.11

Source: Akong'a, et al. (1988).
Notes: Probabilities based on a normalized drought index:
  No drought $DI > -0.2$
  Mild drought $DI \le -0.2$
  Moderate drought $DI \le -0.5$
  Severe drought $DI \le -0.8$
where, $DI = (P - X)/S$
  P = seasonal precipitation
  X = long-term average for that season
  S = seasonal standard deviation of P
Drought is defined on a cumulative basis, such that "mild drought" incorporates all years where the Drought Index (DI) is less than or equal to –0.2. Thus, the probabilities do not total to unity.

Table 12.7 Trends in Crop Production

Crop	Unit	1980	1981	1982	1983	1984
Coffee	ha	49,639	52,181	53,762	55,584	—
	mt	149,234	144,211	132,378	186,014	—
	kg/ha	3,006	2,764	2,462	3,347	2,746 [1]
Tea	ha	18,277	18,763	19,293	19,675	20,873
	mt	59,977	64,900	73,707	85,650	99,271
	kg/ha	3,281	3,459	3,820	4,353	4,756
Cotton[2]	ha	44,385	42,841	44,382	46,285	48,252
Maize	ha	308,084	321,770	365,010	347,587	316,358
	mt[3]	178,483	231,410	451,331	321,285	213,204
	kg/ha	579	719	1,236	924	674 [4]
Beans	ha	141,975	178,729	189,660	187,870	149,956
	mt[3]	53,147	138,184	141,325	126,211	46,433
	kg/ha	374	773	745	672	310
Sorghum and Millet	ha[5]	56,996	54,900	69,007	60,774	69,749
Potatoes[6]	ha	8,957	10,275	15,522	14,562	12,913
	mt	78,592	66,015	65,617	—	24,615
	kg/ha	8,774	6,425	4,227	—	1,906

Source: Data in annual agricultural reports from the Ministry of Agriculture.
Notes: The crop data are incomplete and not consistent between years and districts. The available data are reported here for all six districts, aggregated to indicate the levels of production and trends.
[1] Does not include yields in Kirinyaga and Machakos.
[2] Yield data not available or not reliable.
[3] Production in Kitui is estimated from Machakos yields up to 1984.
[4] Data are aggregated for the entire year. The drought in Kirinyaga, for example, resulted in a yield of 360 kg/ha for the long rains and 1,980 kg/ha for the short rains.
[5] In Embu and Machakos, sorghum and millet data are reported together. Kiambu and Murang'a not included, as little sorghum or millet is grown there.
[6] English or Irish (not sweet) potatoes. Potatoes are not grown in Machakos and Kitui.

Table 12.8 Agricultural Responses to the 1984 Drought

	I Tea/ Dairy/ Coffee	II Coffee	III Maize/ Sunflower/ Cotton	IV Marginal Cotton	V Livestock/ Millet	Total
No. of households	91	58	164	124	128	565
Did not have enough seed in the 1984 short rains for planting (% of Households):						
Maize	28	28	39	63	75	50
Sorghum or millet	—	—	—	65	66	29
Beans	47	46	63	82	86	68
Planted a larger area in 1984 short rains than in 1983 short rains (% of Households):						
Maize	24	19	28	33	26	27
Sorghum or millet	—	—	33	29	34	24
Beans	9	28	18	16	19	17

Source: CBS/NES Survey of Drought Responses.
Notes: Sorghum and millet are not grown in the upper zones. The CBS/NES Survey of Drought Responses was conducted in January and February 1985, after the plentiful short rains but before the short rains harvest. The CBS national sample frame was used to select ten to twelve clusters (sublocations) in each district, stratified by agroecological zone. The final sample was 565 households: Kiambu (95), Murang'a (96), Kirinyaga (106), Embu (64), Machakos (91), and Kitui (113), representing 3,424 people. The total column data are percent of the total sample.

Table 12.9 Livestock Losses by Agroclimatic Zone

	I Tea/ Dairy/ Coffee	II Coffee	III Maize/ Sunflower/ Cotton	IV Marginal Cotton	V Livestock/ Millet	Total
Cattle						
Avg. per household:						
April 1984	2.3	2.3	2.8	4.8	7.3	4.1
January 1985	1.7	1.5	2.0	2.6	3.6	2.4
% Decrease	26	35	29	46	51	58
% Households that slaughtered, sold, or lost animals	41	45	33	44	32	38
Goats						
Avg. per household:						
April 1984	1.4	0.9	2.7	6.2	11.8	5.1
January 1985	1.0	0.6	1.6	3.3	5.1	2.6
% Decrease	29	23	41	47	57	50
% Households that slaughtered, sold, or lost animals	24	14	21	42	20	25

Source: CBS/NES Survey of Drought Responses.
Notes: Includes all households, regardless of whether or not they had any livestock. Excludes cattle owners with more than fifty-four head of cattle. Twenty-seven percent of the households had no cattle in April 1984, 36 percent had no cattle in January 1985, and 51 percent did not lose any cattle between April and January. Excludes goat owners with more than fifty goats. Forty-six percent of the households had no goats in April 1984, 53 percent had no goats in January 1985, and 58 percent did not lose any goats between April and January.

Table 12.10 Ratio of Household Maize Purchases to Consumption

		Province	
Cycle	Dates	Central	Eastern
14	16.5–12.6	.34	.14
15	13.6–10.7	.44	.33
16	11.7–7.8	.88	.30
17	8.8–4.9	.33	.37
18	5.9–2.10	.25	.43
19	3.10–30.10	.30	.49
20	31.10–27.11	.17	.60
21	28.11–25.12	.36	.71
22	26.12–22.1	.24	.53
23	23.1–19.1	.19	.28
24	20.2–19.3	.24	.13
25	20.3–16.4	.18	.12
26	17.4–15.5	.28	.14

Source: Central Bureau of Statistics (1982).
Notes: In 1,000 mt. Based on the Integrated Rural Survey (IRS4), May 1978 to May 1979. Dates are day/month.

Table 12.11 Sources of Household Income

	I Tea/ Dairy/ Coffee	II Coffee	III Maize/ Sunflower/ Cotton	IV Marginal Cotton	V Livestock/ Millet	Total
Farm Produce						
Usual source	90	71	50	67	50	62
1984 drought	88	80	34	19	14	40
Incr/same	51	31	14	11	33	28
Decreased	43	69	86	89	67	68
Livestock						
Usual source	14	17	14	19	57	29
1984 drought	14	20	23	38	61	33
Incr/same	30	20	73	73	51	57
Decreased	70	80	27	27	49	43
Agricultural Casual Labor						
Usual source	27	25	31	35	31	31
1984 drought	23	24	29	34	21	27
Incr/same	52	14	11	29	34	27
Decreased	48	86	69	71	66	67
Nonagricultural Casual Labor						
Usual source	20	10	18	25	37	23
1984 drought	20	10	16	21	30	20
Incr/same	18	13	46	28	55	39
Decreased	82	88	54	72	45	61
Businesses						
Usual source	10	14	15	12	22	15
1984 drought	7	8	15	15	20	14
Incr/same	50	40	50	62	21	42
Decreased	50	60	50	38	79	66
Remittances						
Usual source	35	25	41	46	42	39
1984 drought	30	25	37	49	40	38
Incr/same	38	33	55	69	49	53
Decreased	62	67	45	31	51	47
Permanent Employment						
Usual source	24	24	32	29	35	30
1984 drought	22	19	34	31	29	29
Incr/same	79	75	59	90	81	73
Decreased	21	25	41	10	19	27

Source: CBS/NES Survey of Drought Responses.
Note: Percent of households.

Table 12.12 Household Characteristics in the CBS/NES Survey of Drought Responses

	I Tea/ Dairy/ Coffee	II Coffee	III Maize/ Sunflower/ Cotton	IV Marginal Cotton	V Livestock/ Millet	Total
Avg. household size	6.03	5.73	5.86	6.23	6.16	6.02
Household member moved (% of Households)	23	7	21	26	38	25
Nuclear household member permanently employed (% of Households)	58	47	61	54	54	56
Remittances (% of Households):						
Usually rec'd	34	28	40	51	40	40
Rec'd in 84	34	28	40	57	46	43
Incr in 84	7	4	14	27	15	15
Decr in 84	21	14	16	16	20	18
Received food relief (% of Households)	14	35	25	67	77	45
Yellow maize a major food in 1984 (% of Households)	31	34	60	81	87	63
Major food changed in 1984 (% of Households)	84	78	76	67	67	73

Source: CBS/NES Survey of Drought Responses.
Note: Percentages are for all households interviewed.

Table 12.13 Market Prices in 1984

	I Tea/ Dairy/ Coffee	II Coffee	III Maize/ Sunflower/ Cotton	IV Marginal Cotton	V Livestock/ Millet	Total
White Maize						
Jan–Mar Ksh	3.98	3.25	2.80	2.94	3.49	3.24
Oct–Dec Ksh	5.94	5.50	6.20	7.22	10.24	6.85
Increase %	1.5	1.7	2.2	2.5	3.0	2.1
Beans						
Jan–Mar Ksh	10.01	7.58	6.33	6.09	8.72	7.57
Oct–Dec Ksh	15.41	14.33	14.32	16.68	17.23	15.49
Increase %	1.5	1.9	2.3	2.7	2.0	2.1
Yellow Maize						
Jan–Mar Ksh	4.10	—	—	5.72	5.26	5.36
Oct–Dec Ksh	4.10	—	—	6.29	5.74	5.82
Increase (%)	1.0	—	—	1.1	1.1	1.1

Source: CBS/NES Survey of Drought Responses.
Notes: Increase is ratio of Oct–Dec prices to Jan–Mar prices. Number of markets surveyed are: white maize: zone I, 11; zone II, 6; zone III, 15; zone IV, 11; zone V, 7; total, 50; beans: zone I, 10; zone II, 6; zone III, 15; zone IV, 11; zone V, 9; total, 53; and yellow maize flour: zone I, 1; zone IV, 4; zone V, 5. In 1984, $1.00 = Ksh 16.00. Survey was conducted in January 1985 by asking women vendors in open-air markets what they sold maize and beans for in 1984 (and shop keepers for yellow maize flour), for January to March, April to June, July to September, and October to December.

Table 12.14 Famine Relief in Kiambu, Murang'a, Kirinyaga, and Kitui Districts

District/Division	Maize (kg)	Beans (kg)	Milk (gh)	Families (no.)
Kiambu/Kikuyu	72,290	2,666	2,644	1,322
Lari	63,000	1,980	2,662	1,200
Limuru	196,560	5,400	3,520	3,500
Thika	236,660	0	5,280	2,500
Total	568,510	10,046	17,106	8,522 *
Murang'a/Kandara	36,450	450	220	
Kangema	33,950	1,800	440	*
Kiharu	67,750	2,700	660	680
Kigumo	62,100	2,700	660	*
Makuyu	193,950	6,840	1,760	1,734
Total	394,200	14,490	3,740	2,414 *
Kirinyaga/Mwea	244,530	16,200	12	14,920

Kitui District	Maize	Beans	Other	Recipients
Food				
Maize & Beans	1,664,050	1,636,920		
Castor Oil			485,900	
Recipients				295,000
Seed				
Maize & Beans	221,000	105,300		
Sorghum			17,180	
Green Grams			26,390	
Cow Peas			7,760	
Pigeon Peas			90	
Millet			450	
Total	1,885,050	1,742,220	537,770	295,000

Source: Interviews with district officers.
Notes: Units in kg, except as noted. For Kiambu and Murang'a: milk is milk powder. For Kirinyaga: milk is in packets, assumed to be 0.5 kg per packet, and maize and beans were converted from bags, assuming 90 kg per bag. For Kitui: maize converted, assuming 50 kg per bag (this was the common bag used for yellow maize, and underestimates the amount of maize distributed since some was white maize from the NCPB); beans (both food and seed) converted, assuming 90 kg per bag; green grams converted assuming 50 kg per bag.
* incomplete total due to missing data on number of families aided.

Table 12.15 Food Relief Distributed by the GOK/USAID Program

	Kiambu	Murang'a	Kirinyaga	Embu	Machakos	Kitui
Estimates of number of relief recipients						
Aug 84	15,000	4,000	5,000	40,234	308,220	295,000
Jan 85	9,700	2,000	—	40,234	308,220	200,000
Apr 85	5,000	2,000	—	24,900	100,000	88,200
Aug 85	3,000	1,000	—	15,000	80,000	40,000
Oct 85	3,000	1,000	—	10,000	35,000	30,000
Yellow maize food relief, mt						
Jan 1985	1[1]	1[1]	4[4]	890.3	1,106.8	3,698.7
Feb	2[2]	2[2]	—	206.2	2,877.5	350.5
Mar	—	—	—	31.8	729.5	7.9
Apr	—	—	—	440.8	1,627.3	494.2
May	—	—	—	204.7	3,645.6	2,178.9
Jun	—	50.0	—	381.0	1,212.9	—
Jul	—	—	—	462.0	1,760.2	710.0
Aug	—	—	—	—	—	1,000.6
Sep	3[3]	3[3]	—	277.7	230.0	750.0
Oct	—	—	—	—	—	220.0
Nov	—	—	—	—	—	1,772.6
Total	—	—	—	2,894.5	13,189.8	11,183.4
Average monthly ration of yellow maize, kg						
	11.5[5]	11.5[5]	—	12.0	10.9	11.6
Pinto beans food relief, mt						
Total	6[6]	6[6]	6[6]	1,960	16,074	17,777
Non-Fat dried milk food relief, mt						
Total	7[7]	7[7]	7[7]	1,700	16,820	12,565

Source: Deloitte, Haskins and Sells M.C. (1985).
Notes: In many cases, the records for Kiambu, Murang'a, and Kirinyaga are combined, so district estimates are not possible.
[1]Kajiado, Kiambu, and Murang'a received 503.8 mt in January and
[2]700.8 mt in February.
[3]Kiambu and Murang'a received 67.3 mt in September.
[4]Yellow maize data were not reported for Kirinyaga, evidently not one of the targeted districts.
[5]Kajiado figures are probably higher than the Kiambu and Murang'a figures.
[6]Kiambu, Murang'a, and Kirinyaga are combined, in some cases with Kajiado as well. The total for the four districts is 80 mt.
[7]As in note [6]; the total for the four districts is 133 mt.

Table 12.16 Nutritional Status by Agroclimatic Zone

	I Tea/ Dairy/ Coffee	II Coffee	III Maize/ Sunflower/ Cotton	IV Marginal Cotton	V Livestock/ Millet	Total
Healthy	24	10	20	36	25	115
	29.6	24.4	13.8	28.1	18.9	21.8
At-Risk	25	11	32	30	32	130
	30.9	26.8	22.1	23.4	24.2	24.7
Marginal	28	18	56	51	57	210
	34.6	43.9	38.6	39.8	43.2	39.8
Severe	4	2	37	11	18	72
	4.9	4.9	25.5	8.6	13.6	13.7
Total	81	41	145	128	132	527
	100	100	100	100	100	100

Source: CBS/NES Survey of Drought Responses.
Notes: First line is the absolute number of cases; second line in each row is the column percentage. Categories are: *healthy*, positive MAC score or less than 5 percent below the standard; *at-risk*, scores 5 to 10 percent below the age-specific standard; *marginal*, 10 to 20 percent below the standard; and *severe*, over 20 percent below the standard.

Table 12.17 Vulnerability to Hunger: Chronic Conditions and Severe Drought

Vulnerable Group	Agroclimatic Zone					Total
	I	II	III	IV	V	
Population	564.4	365.0	853.3	894.6	876.8	3,554.1
Food Shortage						
Chronic	24.2	25.4	39.7	37.0	5.8	26.7
Drought	35.1	43.6	91.6	100.0	98.7	81.6
Food Shortage and Food Poverty						
Chronic	12.5	19.0	14.3	9.7	0.2	9.9
Drought	20.7	25.4	34.9	30.1	33.3	30.0
Food Shortage, Food Poverty, and Food Deprivation (Special Needs)						
Chronic	2.5	6.5	2.7	2.5	0.0	2.3
Drought	4.3	7.3	7.9	8.4	9.1	7.7

Source: Based on Downing (1988) from CBS/NES Survey of Drought Responses.
Notes: Population is in thousands. Numbers are percent of column total, i.e., percent of population in each agroclimatic zone.

Table 12.18 Assessment of Smallholder Drought-Coping Strategies.

A. Prevalence, Effectiveness, and Impact on Recovery

Coping Strategy	Prevalence	Effectiveness			Impact on Recovery
		Average Year	Moderate Drought	Severe Drought	
Subsistence Production					
Soil and water conservation	H	H	M	L	0
Irrigation	L	M	H	H?	+
Multiple farms	L	M	M	L	0
Inter/relay planting	H	H	H-L	L	+
Early planting	M-H	M	H	L	0
Drought-resistant crops	H	L	H	M	+
On-farm storage	L	L	M	H	+
Mixed livestock herds	M-H	H	H	M	+
Dispersed grazing	L	H	H	M	+
Fodder production[1]	M	H	H	M	+
Monetary Activity					
Local wage labor	M	H	H	H	+
Migrant wage labor	M	H	H	H	−
Permanent employment	M	H	H	H	+
Local businesses	L	M	M	L	0
Cash crops[2]	M-H	H	M	L	+
Sell capital assets	L	H	M	M-L	−
Livestock sales	M-H	H	M-H	M-L	−
Remittances/Donations					
Relatives/friends	M-H	M	H	H	+
Government & official[3]	M-H	?	H	H	?
Loans/credit[4]	L?	H	H	H	+

Prevalence: H   High   >50 percent
              M-H Moderately high 30-50
              M   Moderate   15-30
              L   Low   0-15

Ratings: − Negative, impedes recovery
           + Positive, aids recovery
           0 Neutral, no effect on recovery
           ? Uncertain

Table 12.18—continued

B. Constraints to Adoption

Coping Strategy	Constraints				
	Labor	Capital	Technology	Education/ Information	Land
Subsistence Production					
Soil and water conservation	X	X			X
Irrigation	X	X	X	X	X
Multiple farms	X				X
Inter/relay planting	X			X	
Early planting	X		X		
Drought-resistant crops	X				
On-farm storage		X	X	X	
Mixed livestock herds					X
Dispersed grazing	X				X
Fodder production[1]			X	X	X
Monetary Activity					
Local wage labor	X			X	
Migrant wage labor	X			X	
Permanent employment	X			X	
Local businesses	X	X			X
Cash crops[2]	X	X	X	X	X
Sell capital assets		X	X		X
Livestock sales		X		X	
Remittances/Donations					
Relatives/friends					
Government & official[3]				X	
Loans/credit[4]		X		X	

Source: Downing (1988), revised from Akong'a and Downing (1987), based on author's qualitative analysis.

Notes: X indicates a constraint; blank indicates not a constraint.
[1] Very common in upper zones, almost nonexistent in lower zones.
[2] Does not include food crops, as in [1].
[3] More common in the upper zones.
[4] Includes both formal and informal credit.

· 13 ·

Case Studies of Drought Impacts and Responses in Central and Eastern Kenya

CRISPIN M. KAMAU
GEORGE J. ANYANGO
M. GITAHI

MARGARET WAINAINA
THOMAS E. DOWNING

The 1984 drought was severe in much of Kenya, yet not all areas were equally affected nor were all households within the same area affected to the same extent. To investigate the broad range of impacts and responses to the drought, the National Environment Secretariat (NES) conducted a sample survey in six districts of central and eastern Kenya (see Chapter 12). This chapter describes the results of four case studies undertaken a year after the drought (February 1986) in order to provide more detail concerning smallholder drought-coping strategies and to specifically inquire what people thought (in retrospect) they could do to prevent drought or ameliorate its impacts. In addition to interviews with members of selected households, field teams sought the views of community leaders, such as the representatives of the Kenya African National Union (the political party in Kenya), district and local administration, extension workers, teachers, businessmen, and health-care staff. Their recall of the effects of the drought corroborated the household interviews.

The topics addressed in the survey were: number of household members, size of landholding, major drought impacts, drought-coping strategies, use of weather information, agricultural coping strategies, sales and purchases of food and seed, general problems of food storage, storage and marketing of farm produce, and off-farm income. Community leaders were specifically asked about lasting effects of the 1984 drought, impacts on health and education, and food relief. The four communities (Githunguri, Kombuini, Mbiuni, and Kawelu) were chosen to correspond to clusters surveyed previously; many of the households surveyed in January 1985, in the midst of the drought, were resurveyed in February 1986.

CHARACTERISTICS OF FOUR COMMUNITIES

The four communities are located in areas representative of agroclimatic zones (Figures 12.2 and 12.7, Table 13.1). The wetter zones in Central and Eastern provinces were excluded, as previous studies indicated that drought there was rare and its impacts relatively less severe. As documented in Chapter 12, the four communities lie along an altitudinal and moisture gradient from the humid highlands of the Aberdares and Mt. Kenya to the semiarid lowlands bordering Tsavo National Park. There are two rainy seasons, the long rains (March to May) and the short rains (October to December). The first season is the main growing season in Githunguri, Kombuini, and Mbiuni, while the short rains are more reliable in Kawelu. In many respects, patterns of population and economy correspond to this gradient.

Common trends in each community include population growth, subdivision of landholdings (Table 13.2), conservation of soil, forests and water basins, access to off-farm employment (Table 13.3), and participation in the monetary economy (Table 13.4).

Githunguri Sublocation, Murang'a District

At an altitude of about 1,700 m, Githunguri Sublocation (Gaicanjiru Location, Kandara Division) is situated in agroclimatic zone III (labeled the maize/sunflower/cotton zone, but on the margin for coffee production). There is a relatively high population density and small holdings per household, between 0.1 to 2.0 ha for the sample households (Table 13.2). The average household farm is less than 1.0 ha. Even where the land has not been officially subdivided, relatives often have divided the land between themselves, since each married son is entitled to the use of a portion of his father's land.

All the households in Githunguri grow the staple food crops of maize and beans; English potatoes are also widely grown. Other common food crops are cow peas, pigeon peas, and sorghum, but they are grown on a limited scale and are not staple foods. Households produce little surplus food; few (33 percent) sell maize or beans, and even fewer sell potatoes (Table 13.4). Coffee is a recent crop in the area, but it is planted by an increasing number of farmers. Most of the households own one or two cattle and/or a few goats.

All households purchase food crops for both consumption and planting. Sales and purchases of foodstuffs are primarily between individuals at home or in local markets. Income for the purchase of food is derived from the sale of other produce (coffee and, in a few cases, French beans, cabbages, and kale), employment (over two-thirds of the households had income from permanent or casual employment), and remittances from members of families employed outside the area (Table 13.3). Income from off-farm sources plays an important role in sustaining the welfare of rural households.

Kombuini Sublocation, Kirinyaga District

Kombuini Sublocation (Mutithi Location, Mwea Division) is a generally flat plain (about 1,500 m), spanning agroclimatic zones III and IV (sunflower/

maize/cotton and marginal cotton zones); see Table 13.1. The population density (348 people per sq km in 1979) is comparable to that of Githunguri, but in a less productive zone. Landholdings in the survey were under 3.6 ha, with an average of 1.9 ha.

Maize, beans, sorghum, and millet are the dominant crops, grown by 75 to 95 percent of the respondents. Over half the households have cattle (65 percent), while 45 percent have sheep and/or goats. Drought-resistant crops, such as Katumani maize, cassava, and sweet potatoes, are grown in small quantities. A few farmers have planted coffee, but with little success.

Agriculture is generally the most important source of household income. Respondents sell their produce (however little) to pay school fees and, in order of importance, to buy some basic home items, food, clothes, and cattle feed. Eighty percent of the respondents sell maize, 55 percent beans, 45 percent pigeon peas, and 35 percent sorghum and/or millet. They sell mostly through the local markets and rarely to the National Cereals and Produce Board. Only three households (15 percent) had income from permanent employment, although almost all had income from off-farm labor in the nearby rice scheme, the Kimbimbi research station, or elsewhere.

Mbiuni Sublocation, Machakos District

Mbiuni Sublocation (Mbiuni Location, Northern Division) lies between 790 and 1,220 m in the marginal cotton zone (IV). The population density was 135 people per sq km in 1979. Although some farmers in Machakos have large ranches and estates, the average holding in the survey was 2.6 ha, with some households owning as little as 0.5 ha.

Smallholders in Mbiuni are primarily subsistence farmers, cultivating maize, beans, cow peas, millet, cassava, and fruits, among other crops. Cow peas, millet, cassava, and Katumani maize (a quick-maturing variety developed for the dry areas) do well in the area. All the households had cows and goats.

Households produce little surplus food due to the small holdings and unreliable rainfall. Less than one-third of the households reported that they regularly sold food crops. In fact, they buy food both for consumption and resale. People buy food from the local markets supplied from outside the area. Over three-fourths of the households rely on income from permanent employment or off-farm casual labor. Livestock sales are also important.

Kawelu Sublocation, Kitui District

Kawelu Sublocation (Mutomo Location, Southern Division) is in the semiarid livestock/millet zone (V). The sublocation had about 1,200 people in the 1979 census (34 people per sq km). There is a high dependency ratio, since many adult males leave the area in search of wage employment due to a lack of suitable conditions for agricultural activities in the area. Most of the farms are small, considering the climatic conditions (about 2 to 6 hectares).

Agriculture is mostly subsistence in nature. The range of crops is limited by climatic conditions: maize, millet, sorghum, beans, cow peas, green grams, cotton, and pigeon peas are grown. Cattle reared in the area are the local zebus, raised mainly for meat production. Indigenous sheep and goats are also common, with the latter performing well.

Most of the households (89 percent) received income from permanent or casual employment, which was the major source of income for food and to pay for school fees. Almost all households purchase food, such as maize, beans, cow peas, and pigeon peas. Livestock sales are also important, as all households sell livestock.

IMPACT OF THE 1984 DROUGHT

In each area, the drought was severe; rainfall for the long rains was 27 to 67 percent of the 60 percent reliability level (Table 13.1). There was not enough rain to produce a maize crop in any of the communities, or even sorghum or millet in Kitui.

In February 1986, respondents were asked how the drought affected them. The interviewers tried to compile a complete list of impacts, without going through a checklist of potential impacts. Even a year after the drought, hunger was the most common impact (85 to 100 percent of the respondents), ranking as the most important impact (70 to 84 percent of the respondents); see Table 13.2.

Githunguri

The major effect cited by households and community leaders was the general shortage of food from June 1984 to February 1985: 95 percent cited hunger as a major impact, 68 percent said food was more expensive, and 37 percent said that food was in short supply. People looked generally weak, and there were general complaints due to insufficient food intake that were not related to diagnosed ailments. Households had to rely on yellow maize, the less desirable, imported grain.

Half the households lost cattle, which either died or were sold to avoid death or for cash for food and/or school fees. Most of the cattle were grade milk cows. Their loss was a considerable loss of assets, as well as lost income and nutrition from the milk.

There were cases of children leaving school because money for a building fund could not be raised or because they were hungry. At other times, children missed school to look for work to supplement family incomes.

The effects of the drought were not, however, as severe as in some parts of Kenya. One beneficial result of the drought was an increase in vegetable-growing along the Kabuku River using water drawn from the Kabuku. The community leaders did not think the drought had lasting negative effects in the area.

Kombuini

The most important short-term effect of the drought was the shortage of food supply. People had no food in their stores; all of the respondents said food was short and they had to buy food, which was very expensive at this time. Respondents quoted prices between Ksh 6 and 8 per kg of maize flour, two to three times the usual price. Hunger was noted by 85 percent of the respondents. Over half of the households received some food relief.

The recipients reportedly had problems cooking some of the beans and experienced general stomach upsets, probably due to the maize or beans. Ninety-five percent of the respondents spent many hours finding food either to purchase or to receive from relief centers. They ate less-desirable foods, such as yellow maize and some local green leaves that are normally not eaten.

Livestock losses were cited by almost half of the respondents. Sixty-five percent of the respondents had cattle and/or goats and sheep. Half lost all their livestock either through death (40 percent) or by being forced to sell their almost-dying livestock at very low prices. The respondents reported that prices ranged between Ksh 20 and 50 per full-grown cow. Three respondents suffered greater losses than the others. One lost 28 cows.

Only a few sources of water, which are of little significance, dried up. Thirty percent of the respondents traveled farther than normal in search of water, while only 25 percent reported using less water.

A fourth of the households said children were absent from school due to sickness, hunger, or lack of fees. Few children, belonging to one-fourth of the respondents, left school, and the children from only two households never went back after the drought. According to one of the teachers interviewed, a third of the school population at Kangai Primary School left school temporarily because of hunger, poor health, or shortage of money (which was required for the self-help development fund or for school uniforms during the drought).

Forty percent of the respondents left the area, though temporarily, to look for food either from relatives or friends in the upper zones of the district.

Mbiuni

Household members and community leaders concurred that there was an acute shortage of food between May 1984 and early 1985; and 93 percent went hungry; over a third cited food shortage or food poverty as important drought impacts.

Many of the livestock (cows and goats) died, while others had to be sold to avoid death or for cash for food or school fees (two-thirds of the households suffered livestock losses); fish were also reported to have died in large numbers in the Athi River. Many households in the area received famine-relief food.

Some children had to leave school because of a lack of school fees. Household members spent more time looking for food and water. Increases in malnutrition, ringworm, and rickets cases among the younger children in the lower primary school were reported. The area chief noted that his routine work had also been hampered by his inability to assemble people easily.

Long-term impacts cited in the interviews included livestock losses: over 90 percent of the people had not recovered their former livestock holdings, and there was a general feeling that it might not be possible to do so for a long while. Trees had also died and would take a long time to replace. Respondents felt that many people were poorer than they were prior to 1984, and many headmasters in secondary schools reported that some students had not yet paid their fees. Lack of money to buy farm inputs and implements was largely felt to be the reason for low food production. The *miethya* groups, women's cooperatives that make contributions and help individual women in turn, were in difficulty because regular contributions were not possible.

Kawelu

In Kitui District, the 1984 drought was a continuation of the drought of the preceding two years, and Mutomo Division experienced acute hardship. After poor harvests in the preceding years, many people went hungry because their grain stocks had already been depleted. All respondents suffered hunger; 72 percent said food was short, and half of that available was more expensive. Many found it very difficult to get food even though they had the means to buy it. There were even cases of hoarding by shopkeepers to influence prices, and people were required to buy other items, such as sugar, in addition to the basic foods.

The Tiva and Ngunga rivers dried up, with the water table so low that even shallow wells in the riverbeds yielded little water. Consequently, there was little water in the area as the surface dams, rock catchments, and bore holes were also dry. Vendors sold water at two or more times the usual rate.

Livestock losses were experienced by 72 percent of the respondents. Many people had no choice but to sell their livestock at throwaway prices. Goats and sheep fetched as little as Ksh 40 per head, while cattle sold for Ksh 100. There was about one-third less livestock in 1984 than in 1983. Traders from outside the division took advantage of the situation, although the national market was also overwhelmed. The more drought-resistant animals, such as donkeys, endured the drought; donkeys were valued for transporting water. In some instances, people sold cattle and goats to buy donkeys. Records show an increase of about 14 percent in the number of donkeys in 1984 over the previous year. Many of the donkeys come from outside Kitui District, mainly from Northeastern Province.

The local primary school registered a marked fall in attendance. Older students had to interrupt their learning to join their parents in food-for-work projects or to look for wage employment elsewhere. Projects run on a self-help basis also experienced interruptions. About three hundred to four hundred adults in the adult literacy program missed school in 1984 in Mutomo Division, a drop in attendance of about 56 percent. The division normally experiences a boom in attendance after International Literacy Day, when there is a campaign to lure more people into adult literacy classes. In 1984, however, there was a drop in attendance despite the campaign (Table 13.5). In 1983, the drop in attendance between the beginning and end of the year was about 25 percent, while it increased to 50 percent in 1984.

Malnutrition and diseases related to hunger increased. About 4 percent of the total admissions at Mutomo Hospital in 1984 were due to malnutrition. There were four cases of adult deaths and twenty-eight cases of child deaths due to diseases possibly related to malnutrition. Of 4,377 patients admitted in 1984, 11 percent were due to anemia. Generally, however, total admissions that year were very low due largely to the fact that the hospital requires patients to pay before they are admitted. June to July was the worst period of the year, resulting in 706 admissions, 115 of which were directly due to famine cases. There were also cases of indigestion in people who had eaten local fruits.

COPING STRATEGIES

Food relief differed markedly between the four communities. In Kawelu, it was widespread and essential; in Githunguri, few households received assistance; and in Kombuini and Mbiuni, it was sporadic, although helpful.

The household and community leaders were queried as to how they would cope with future droughts (Table 13.3). Responses were recorded and later categorized: no suggestions, agricultural practices, livestock practices, storage, and diversify income. Most respondents suggested at least a few coping strategies.

Two sets of coping strategies were investigated further. One solution to food shortage is to store enough food to last a season or a year. Patterns of food trade and constraints to increased storage were investigated (Table 13.4). Most households reported little surplus food to store, although the constraints did not seem unsurmountable.

Another group of coping strategies seeks to make the best use of information about the weather and improve responses to imminent good or poor seasons (Table 13.6). Most people suggested a few responses, but they were either occasionally the same strategies for both good and poor seasons or they were ambiguous in their possible efficacy. The results are not encouraging in regard to the prospects for adapting farming systems to timely prediction or monitoring seasonal weather.

Githunguri

In all of Githunguri Sublocation, only 11 of about 550 households received famine-relief food during the drought, as it was not a targeted area for the government or NGOs.

Two-thirds of the suggested coping strategies to reduce the impact of future droughts were agricultural. Early planting, planting drought-resistant crops (sorghum, cassava, sweet potatoes), improving agricultural technology and yields, and the use of river water to grow vegetables could be undertaken during drought conditions. Several respondents suggested the storage of fodder in order to provide for their livestock. Cash is a constraint, although few identified looking for work or other income-generating activities as specific drought-coping strategies.

Community leaders were aware of government activities to decrease the impacts of droughts, including soil conservation; agricultural, forestry, and livestock extension services; and the encouragement of on-farm storage.

Marketing and storage problems often discourage farmers from producing food in large amounts and storing adequate amounts for emergencies. In the case of Githunguri farmers, the most important constraint to increased storage is the low level of production due to small holdings and low yields. Sorghum, pigeon peas, and cow peas are stored for only about a month, while maize, beans, and potatoes are stored for two to three months. Inadequate or inappropriate storage space is not a major problem in the opinion of Githunguri farmers. Household members consider insects, such as weevils (94 percent of respondents) and pests, such as rats (67 percent) a threat to stored maize and beans. Many households (44 percent) also expressed concern about theft.

Since there are inadequate supplies of local foodstuffs, farmers did not think there were marketing problems, nor did they see the need to join a storage or marketing cooperative if one were established. Only those who grew French beans for the export market expressed the need for cooperative action to ensure the sale of their produce and increase their returns. Only a third of the farmers usually sell maize or beans. Basic foods are purchased from off-farm income or the return to cash crops, such as coffee.

Most of the people interviewed did not think it is possible to predict when the rains will come or whether a season will be bad or good. Weather was mentioned, however, as the major cause of poor harvests in the area. Perhaps due to the 1984 drought and the poor 1985 short rains, the majority of the respondents expected crop failure year after year in some areas.

Among the activities that would be undertaken in response to late rains (indicating a poor season) were the planting of vegetables using river water, application of fertilizers, planting of such drought-resistant crops as sorghum, sale of livestock, and a search for employment. Fewer practicable activities were suggested to increase production in response to a favorable season. Water conservation during droughts, increased application of fertilizers, and the hiring of extra labor during good seasons are limited by the availability of cash and the small land holdings.

Kombuini

According to the community leaders interviewed, people got food relief from the Consolata fathers, the Church of the Province of Kenya (CPK), Catholic Relief Services (CRS), and the government. Needy people were selected by famine-relief committees. It was not easy to select the needy, but the disabled, aged, landless, and those with large families and no formal employment were generally given priority.

Of the households interviewed, 65 percent received some food relief, although 40 percent received only 2 kg of yellow maize. Although aggregate figures are not complete, one organization gave food aid to eighty households, while six hundred were in food-for-work programs. Since the supply was not regular, the households received at least one kg of maize or beans per person per unit time (either weekly, biweekly, or monthly, depending on availability). Other foods that were supplied included maize flour, rice, and dry skimmed milk (DSM). A church group aided sixty-four households by providing 10 kg of maize and beans and one packet of maize flour per week. Salad oil (3 to 4 liters per family per month) and maize and bean seeds for planting were also supplied. The chief of Mutithi Location supplied food aid to 1,841 people (Table 13.7). Community leaders felt that too little aid was supplied.

According to community leaders, people can be well prepared to cope with future droughts if they would improve storage facilities; increase production by growing a variety of quicker maturing crops; keep a variety of fewer and high-quality animals; form more active self-help groups to keep bees, chickens, or other small animals and help market farm produce; and grow cash crops like sunflower and cotton to diversify household sources of income.

Half of the coping strategies suggested by household members were agricultural, while over a third involved off-farm employment. Three-fourths of the respondents use tree planting, terraces, or grass strips to conserve soil. All agreed that the methods are effective, but wider implementation is limited by finance, labor, or the age of the household members.

Most of the respondents use oxen for cultivation and planting, though few farmers actually own them. Many farmers lost their oxen during the 1984 drought and have not been able to purchase others. Therefore, some farmers without working oxen tend to plant late, further restricting their ability to recover from the drought.

Thirty percent of the casual laborers indicated that they usually have no difficulty in finding employment. All the respondents who were working as casuals (both agricultural and nonagricultural), however, indicated that they had problems finding jobs during the 1984 drought. The shortage of casual work was due to the lack of institutional jobs and because households were spending to purchase food money that was normally used to hire labor.

Most of the households (70 percent) store food from one season to another, but the storage time varies since it is dependent on the amount of crop harvested and the financial situation of the household. Maize, beans, pigeon peas, sorghum, and millet are stored as food and/or seed by over 50 percent of the respondents.

Many households also buy the same types of food that they store. For example, all the respondents grow maize, yet 95 percent also buy maize or beans for food or seed. Maize or beans are sold by 75 percent of the respondents. This implies an apparent lack of stored foods a few months after harvest, the length of time being variable from one household to another. More vulnerable households (with smaller holdings and little off-farm income) store less food for shorter periods, often doing so inside the house. Over 50 percent of the households did not have a well-built store. The most common storage problems are due to insects (63 percent of respondents) and pests (58 percent). Other problems, such as sprouting, rotting, space, and theft, affect fewer households and are not significant constraints. Ninety percent of the respondents dust their produce with insecticides (if cash is available) or use local methods of food preservation.

Forty percent of the respondents indicated that they expected crop failures in the area every other year. The respondents attributed poor harvests to rainfall, insects, birds, lack of tools, and lack of inputs, in order of importance. Most of the respondents (80 percent) did not know of someone in the area who can tell whether the rains will come or whether a season will be good or bad.

If they thought the rains would be late and/or would not be sufficient, 90 percent of the respondents would plant a variety of drought-resistant crops, 85 percent would also plant early, and 30 percent would irrigate. To supplement their income, 70 percent would look for employment (if available), and 35 percent would try to save cash. Twenty percent of the respondents would rely on food aid, either from official or private sources. None indicated that they would take a loan. Two-thirds of the suggested coping strategies were agricultural, and a quarter were related to wage income.

Conversely, if respondents thought the rains would be good, 75 percent would apply fertilizers, 55 percent would apply pesticides, 50 percent would plant new or larger areas, and 25 percent would hire extra labor for weeding to increase production. Forty percent would also improve their livestock quality, while only 5 percent would increase livestock numbers.

Mbiuni

In addition to the government and some local groups, World Vision, Christian Children's Fund, Church of the Province of Kenya, and Catholic Relief Services provided food relief in Mbiuni. Identifying the needy was reported to have gone smoothly through the famine-relief committees. About 4,000 people received food aid in the sublocation. The most crippling problem was the lack of transportation to distribute the food when it was available.

In the future, respondents said they would plant drought-resistant crops, practice conservation, look for off-farm employment, apply fertilizer, plant fruit trees, plant early, and destock. Other coping strategies were to ask their children to help more on the farm, irrigate where possible, preserve maize stalks for livestock, leave some land fallow for animals, plant more bananas (to give to livestock), and make more use of draught animals. Almost all of the suggestions related to agriculture (79 percent) or livestock (18 percent).

Well over half the respondents buy basic foods: maize, beans, cow peas, or pigeon peas (87 percent); sorghum or millet (53 percent). Less than one-third of the households usually sell food. Livestock sales and off-farm income are the predominant sources of income to purchase foods. The livestock market is seen as a major problem. Not many of the respondents were members of a marketing cooperative, but most agreed there were many benefits to be reaped from joining.

Insects and pests were the major problems facing increased storage of food. Suggestions for improving storage included well-ventilated granaries to facilitate free-air circulation, mixing the harvest with ashes when a farmer could not afford fertilizers, and keeping produce in the house to avoid theft.

Many people felt there was no way to tell when the rains would come or whether the season would be good or poor. Half of the respondents expected crop failure every year or two. The most common reason for poor harvest was the poor infrastructure, including lack of labor and inputs and poor management (such as planting late). Three-fourths of the suggested responses to both good and poor seasons were agricultural or concerned livestock.

Kawelu

In early 1984, people tried to cope with the drought, hoping it would soon end. By June 1984, they resorted to eating unusual foods, such as baobab and other wild fruits that were crushed and cooked, some of which were even sold in the markets. Some leaves of trees were also cooked as vegetables.

When the situation became serious, a number of agencies besides the government provided famine relief, including the Catholic church, DANIDA,

AIC church, World Vision, USAID, World Food Programme, and Action-Aid (in Ithumba Primary School). Initially, the food was given to the disabled and elderly, but it became necessary to provide almost everyone with food as the situation deteriorated. All the households in Kawelu Sublocation received famine relief.

The government formed famine-relief committees at the district, division, location, and sublocation levels to monitor the distribution of famine-relief food (Table 13.8). The government machinery ensured that the most deserving cases were not ignored, as the assistant chiefs made personal contact with such people. Most of the food distributed was yellow maize. Because of the poor harvest in the 1984 short rains, the situation did not improve in 1985, and relief food was provided throughout 1985.

The government, the Catholic Mission and DANIDA promoted food-for-work programs for soil and water conservation, and bee and goat improvement projects. Mutomo Division had over ninety water conservation projects, thirty-four of which are in Kawelu Sublocation. There were about thirty-one soil conservation projects, including five in Kawelu Sublocation. During the 1984 drought, 3,919 kg of maize was distributed as food-for-work in the soil conservation sites in the division. Other food distributed included beans (9,360 kg) and oil (5,240 l); see Table 13.9. About a fifth of the food aid went to Kawelu Sublocation. Almost all the able-bodied people participated in the food-for-work program to supplement the food aid from the government. There were occasional problems transporting food from the district headquarters to the distribution points.

All of the respondents had suggestions for coping with future droughts. Efforts are being made to expand the production of Katumani maize and other drought-resistant crops, such as sorghum, millet, and pigeon peas. There is also a need to prepare fields early in order to enable planting at the onset of the rains. A third of the suggestions concerned livestock, including ways to store fodder.

Conservation is also important. The natural canopy cover is not dense. The area's aridity limits forest growth, and overgrazing, excessive tree cutting, and cultivation without fallow destroy the vegetation. Fuel wood requirements are causing extensive tree cutting in most of the area, often leaving areas virtually barren of trees. In the absence of vegetation, the high intensity of the rainfall causes massive runoff and increased soil loss and degradation. Terracing and contour plowing would conserve rainfall and increase yields in all years.

Over half of the households usually sell maize, beans, sorghum, or millet, and all sell livestock. Almost all households also buy basic foods and livestock. Problems of storage are one reason why people sell their produce. Most of the crops are grown for subsistence and are not stored for long periods. All of the respondents mentioned insects and pests as problems, while over half cited sprouting, rotting, lack of space, and theft as additional constraints to storing food. Many farmers smoke their produce to control pests and insects. All felt a cooperative society would help in marketing and storing food. Several women's groups (*miethya*) in the area help their members with farm work, storage facilities, and marketing.

Another reason people sell food is the lack of alternative sources of income. Of the households interviewed, only 20 percent had at least one member permanently employed, although 89 percent had some wage income from off-farm employment. Most of the households used the cash income for food purchases, but over half sold livestock or cash crops in exchange for food. A fifth sold food crops to purchase other food or to buy staples later in the year.

Most of the respondents thought it was possible to predict seasonal rainfall using such measures as observing the behavior of the vegetation (flowers bloom just before the rains). Half expected crop failures every one or two years, due primarily to the weather (100 percent of the respondents) and inadequate infrastructure (71 percent). A variety of agricultural and livestock-related coping strategies were suggested in response to either a good or poor season.

CONCLUSION: LESSONS FROM THE 1984/85 DROUGHT

The most striking result of the community case studies is that June to September 1984 was a critical period, a time when many people had already exhausted their resources and simply went hungry. By October, some yellow maize had started to arrive in the markets, and food-relief projects began to gear up. Once provided with relief capabilities (food and funds for transport), the relief operations seemed to have gone forward fairly well.

The survey did not attempt to calculate an aggregate measure of the drought's impact for each community. Hunger was prevalent throughout the area. A rough ordering of the impacts, however, can be made based on the amount and duration of food relief required. The rainfall deficit was most severe and prolonged in Kawelu, where almost the entire population was involved in food relief or food-for-work projects. Kombuini and Mbiuni were probably equally affected. The impacts in Githunguri were somewhat less since fewer people required external food assistance and some crops were grown using hand irrigation. The impacts were primarily economic (lost livestock and reduced savings).

The lingering impacts of the drought were the diminished resources of vulnerable households, particularly the loss of livestock. In 1986, many people had less livestock or none at all. In the highlands, this resulted in lower milk production and loss of income. In the lower zones, households are now more vulnerable to future droughts. Rebuilding herds will either take a long time or a considerable cash investment.

There were several lessons learned. In several areas, small-scale irrigation is possible. Particularly in the drier zones (IV through V), soil and water conservation was observed to be a critical factor in coping with climatic variability. The importance of trees as a reserve of fodder was also noted in some places.

Farmers in each community are net buyers of food. Even after the food shortages experienced during 1984, most farmers are not able to be self-sufficient in food production. Agricultural coping strategies can only reduce the impact of drought, not eliminate the need for food from other parts of Kenya. Given the small holdings, land devoted to cash crops, and the existing farming practices, farmers are not going to be self-sufficient in the near future. The welfare of smallholders requires regular supplies of food from the local markets and shops, especially during droughts.

Members of many households with small holdings have to find casual employment to supplement the returns from agriculture, even in normal years. Since, in times of drought, employment becomes difficult to find and there are few credit facilities, targeted famine-relief assistance will be required periodically. Even areas such as Githunguri, which may not appear to require assistance, have households where members cannot work for one reason or another and require assistance.

There is a need to address the issue of climatic variability more seriously to identify viable alternatives should agriculture fail. The relationships between rural and urban areas and between the food surplus and deficit areas were highlighted during the drought.

Many households survived because of relatives working in the urban centers. The service center strategy, through the district focus for rural development, should be strengthened in order to enhance regional development. This can be achieved by establishing viable small-scale enterprises. The scope of agricultural cooperatives can be broadened to serve members more effectively, by ensuring punctual delivery of seeds, fertilizers, and insecticides, as well as the elimination of the long delays in payments. The cooperatives in some areas were vehicles for distress loans, and even bought food for their needy members. Many community groups in the rural areas can be tapped to promote local initiatives in development.

The local markets were extremely important in providing food to rural households, and more efficient than famine relief in ensuring access to food (provided it was not too expensive). Dependence on the local market for food, even in usual years, expands the burden of coping with drought beyond the community or district to the national level. In a good year, Murang'a District will produce a surplus of food that the government must purchase in order to maintain production incentives. In a usual year, the district may be self-sufficient, while in a poor season, large imports will be required. In lower Kirinyaga, Machakos, and Kitui, households may be self-sufficient only in good years and will otherwise depend on food surpluses from other districts or the national stores. In turn, the national food balance depends, in part, on international prices, availabilities, and terms of trade.

People have increasingly changed their eating habits from such traditional, drought-resistant foods as sorghum and millet. These crops should be encouraged, perhaps by promoting them in the national food demand. Sorghum flour can easily be mixed with wheat flour in bread.

Table 13.1 Characteristics of the Four Communities

	Githunguri	Kombuini	Mbiuni	Kawelu
District	Murang'a	Kirinyaga	Machakos	Kitui
Agroclimatic zone	III	III/IV	IV	V
Altitude, m	1,500	1,260	1,260	850
Soil type and texture	nitisols, clay	nitisols & vertisols, clay	cambisols & acrisols, sandy clay loam, sandy clay to clay	luvisols & ferralsols, sandy clay to clay
Major crops	maize, beans, potatoes, vegetables, coffee	maize, beans, sorghum, millet	maize, beans, cow peas, millet, fruit	maize, beans, cow peas, pigeon peas, green grams, sorghum/millet, cotton
Mean monthly temperature, deg C				
Maximum	22–27	25–30	22–28	26–31
Minimum	12–15	13–16	12–16	14–18
Rainfall reliability[1], mm				
Long rains	500	400	300	150
Short rains	300	300	325	300
Average annual rainfall, mm	1,100	1,000	800	750
1984 long rains, mm	185	135	200	40
Population density, 1979 (people per sq km)	455	348	135	34

Sources: Jaetzold and Schmidt (1983), Central Bureau of Statistics (1981a), Sombroek et al. (1982), and East Africa Meteorological Department (1975).

Notes: [1] Amount of rainfall that is expected to be exceeded in 60 percent of the seasons.

Table 13.2 Drought Impacts in the Four Community Case Studies

	Githunguri	Kombuini	Mbiuni	Kawelu
Households interviewed	19	20	15	18
Landholdings, ha				
Average	1.9	1.9	2.6	4.8
Range	0.1–9.5	0.5–3.2	0.5–6.4	2.3–9.1
Average household size	8.3	5.7	8.7	10.2
Drought impacts[1], %				
Hungry	95	85	93	100
Food shortage[2]	37	100	40	72
Food poverty[3]	68	100	33	56
Food relief	0	65	13	39
Increased sickness	16	20	27	22
Lost livestock	47	45	67	72
Water shortage[4]	11	45	33	11
Absent from school[5]	11	25	7	0
Hunger most important drought impact[6], %	84	70	80	83

Source: NES Survey of Household Coping Strategies.
Notes: [1]The following responses are to the question: How did the 1984 drought affect your family? They are not a checklist of impacts.
[2]Food difficult to get, had to spend more time looking for food, or had to buy more food.
[3]Food more expensive or lacked cash.
[4]Used less water or had to travel further to get water.
[5]Children absent from school due to hunger or lack of school fees.
[6]Ranked first of the cited impacts.

Table 13.3 Drought-Coping Strategies in the Four Community Case Studies

	Githunguri	Kombuini	Mbiuni	Kawelu
Households with permanent or casual employment, %	68	85	80	89
Difficult to find work, %				
Usually	37	40	47	78
During 1984	68	45	53	56
Took out loans[1], %	37	45	40	56
Coping with future drought, %				
Nothing[2]	11	0	7	0
Agricultural practices[3]	66	51	79	56
Livestock practices[3]	21	10	18	30
Store food or feed[3]	13	1	7	13
Diversify income[3]	13	39	4	14

Sources: NES Survey of Household Coping Strategies.
Notes: [1]Either cash or food, e.g., from cooperatives.
[2]Percent of households responding.
[3]Percent of the first six suggestions, e.g., of 57 suggested coping strategies for Mbiuni, 45 (79 percent) concerned possible agricultural practices. Storage coping strategies overlap agricultural and livestock practices.

Table 13.4 Food Trade in the Four Community Case Studies

	Githunguri	Kombuini	Mbiuni	Kawelu
Usually sell[1], %				
Maize or beans	33	75	27	50
Cow or pigeon peas	0	45	27	39
Sorghum or millet	0	55	33	61
Livestock	28	45	67	100
Uses of cash[2]				
Food	21	50	53	6
School or medical fees	16	40	47	6
Usually buy[1], %				
Maize or beans	100	95	87	94
Cow or pigeon peas	44	40	87	94
Sorghum or millet	44	70	53	72
Livestock	11	50	60	94
Source of cash for food or livestock purchases[1], %				
Food sales	12	45	7	18
Livestock or cash crops	22	25	60	59
Wages, gifts or remittances	89	80	67	88
Problems in marketing livestock[3], %	21	45	80	100
Storage problems[4]				
Insects	94	63	93	100
Pests	67	58	40	100
Sprouting or rotting	56	26	7	56
Space	17	26	7	56
Theft	44	16	7	61
Suggestions for improving:[5], %				
Food storage	47	95	93	83
Livestock or food marketing	26	65	47	44
Communal group membership[6]	53	90	87	100

Source: NES Survey of Household Coping Strategies.
Notes: [1]Percent of households, e.g., half of the respondents in Kawelu sold either maize or beans, and 94 percent bought maize or beans.
[2]Use of income from sales of maize, beans, cow peas, pigeon peas, sorghum, millet, cattle, sheep, goats, or donkeys, e.g., half of the respondents in Kombuini used the cash from sales of the above for food, and 40 percent used the cash for school or medical fees. In Kawelu, the interviews revealed only a general use of the cash—other household items.
[3]Percent of respondent with problems in marketing their livestock.
[4]Percent of households reporting problems storing maize, beans, cow peas, pigeon peas, sorghum, or millet.
[5]Percent of respondents with suggestions.
[6]Either a member or willing to join a cooperative to facilitate marketing food.

Table 13.5 Attendance at Adult Education Classes, Mutomo Division, Kitui

	1983			1984			1985		
Month	Men	Women	Total	Men	Women	Total	Men	Women	Total
Jan.	120	828	958	63	599	662	98	549	647
Feb.	111	765	811	68	654	722	52	521	573
Mar.	151	1,072	1,223	81	668	759	68	564	632
Apr.	105	861	966	68	662	730	53	422	475
May	123	1,082	1,205	45	381	426	75	666	741
June	133	945	1,078	56	473	529	69	616	685
July	135	989	1,124	68	542	610	93	525	618
Aug.	155	1,256	1,411	68	542	610	70	527	597
Sep.	140	1,090	1,230	81	604	685	71	642	713
Oct.	140	109	1,239	42	463	585	76	576	655
Nov.	89	784	873	58	303	361	106	701	807
Dec.	92	613	723	21	272	293	138	1,030	1,168

Source: Kitui District Education Officer.

Table 13.6 Use of Weather Information in the Four Community Case Studies

	Githunguri	Kombuini	Mbiuni	Kawelu
Weather information, %				
Expected crop failure every				
1–2 years[1]	53	45	53	56
Causes of crop failure				
Weather or soils[2]	100	100	73	100
Infrastructure[3]	26	45	87	71
Infestation[4]	5	45	0	12
Able to predict season	68	25	33	89
Response to late rains[5], %				
Nothing	5	0	7	0
Agricultural	80	69	58	58
Livestock	10	8	26	32
Store food or feed	15	2	3	6
Diversify Income	10	23	16	10
Response to good season[6], %				
Nothing	21	0	20	0
Agricultural	96	89	55	76
Livestock	4	6	26	18
Store food or feed	4	5	6	12
Diversify Income	0	5	19	6

Sources: NES Survey of Household Coping Strategies.
Notes: [1]Percent of households responding.
[2]Percent of respondents who ranked either weather or soils as the first or second most important cause of crop failure.
[3]As in previous note, but including lack of tools, inputs or labor, or improper management, e.g., late plowing.
[4]As in previous note, but including damage from insects, diseases, birds, and animals.
[5]Responses to the question: If you thought or realized the rains would be late, what *could* you do to avoid hardship? Responses are percent of the first six suggestions, as in above notes.
[6]Responses to the question: If, during the season, you find the rains are very good, what *could* you do to increase your production? Responses coded as in above notes.

Table 13.7 Food Distributed by the Chief of Mutithi Location, Kirinyaga

Sublocation	Maize (kg)	Beans (kg)	DSM (kg)	No. of Recipients
Kathiga	7,326	363	91	249
Kombuini	7,326	408	91	22
Mathigaini	11,862	363	91	231
Kabiriri	7,326	408	45	29
Kinyaga	7,326	363	45	253
Rukanga	7,326	408	91	19
Kiandegwa	7,236	408	45	396
Total	51,192	2,721	499	1,841

Source: Chief, Mutithi Location.
Notes: Period of time is October 1984 to May 1985. DSM is dried skim milk.

Table 13.8 Famine Relief Provided by the Assistant Chief, Kawelu

	Month	Yellow Maize	Katumani Maize	Sorghum	Beans
1984	April–August	1,785	—	—	—
	August	4,848	—	—	—
	November	645	90	30	—
	December	733	—	—	—
1985	August	15,836	—	—	—
	September	5,277	—	—	—
	October	559	—	—	65

Source: Assistant Chief, Kawelu Sublocation.
Notes: Units in kg.

Table 13.9 Food-for-Work at Selected Sites in Kawelu

Site	No. of People	Maize	Beans	Oil	Cow Peas
Katewi	60	2,340	—	—	—
Kyasio	91	9,000	90	130	450
Kasundu	56	—	—	—	—
Ithasya Ngua	—	450	—	—	—

Source: Kitui District administration.
Notes: Original data in bags, converted to kg using 90 kg bags for maize, beans, and cow peas, and 10 kg tins for oil.

· 14 ·
Impact of the 1984 Drought on Food Intake, Nutritional Status, and Household Response in Embu District

CHARLOTTE G. NEUMANN
N. O. BWIBO
E. CARTER
S. WEINBERG
A. A. JANSEN

D. CATTLE
D. NGARE
M. BAKSH
M. PAOLISSO
A. H. COULSON

Embu District includes high-potential agricultural land not usually subject to serious drought or severe food shortages. A failure of the short rains in 1983 and the long rains in 1984, however, resulted in very poor harvests of maize, beans, and millet in the upper zone, and almost complete crop failure in the more drought-prone lower zone. Traditional coping strategies soon proved incapable of avoiding serious nutritional problems, and the community found itself in a precarious position. Outside assistance played a critical role in famine survival, and much was learned about how households and communities respond to food crises. This chapter documents the impact of the drought, as well as the lessons learned from monitoring the nutrition situation at the time of the drought.

The study area comprises two zones in Kyeni South Location, Embu District, Eastern Province: an upper zone (II) over 1,300 m, and a lower zone (III) between 1,000 and 1,300 m (Figure 14.1). The upper zone has an average rainfall of over 1,000 mm per year, while the lower zone receives about 550 mm annually. Zone II is characterized by loamy and clay soils that are best suited to coffee production. Zone III, the maize/cotton zone, is more sandy, which suits the cash crops of tobacco and cotton. Most residents of this region are small-scale agriculturalists. Maize and beans are the food staples, with sorghum, millet, sweet potatoes, and cassava grown to a lesser degree.

Through periodic data collection regarding household and individual food intake, anthropometry, agricultural production, socioeconomic status, market conditions, and rainfall, the Kenya Nutrition Collaborative Research Support Program (CRSP) was able to document the occurrence and effects of the drought from its onset. The government of Kenya first became aware of the situation in Embu as a result of information supplied by the Nutrition CRSP project. Even many district government officials were unaware that famine conditions existed in their area until they were presented with the evidence documented by CRSP data.

The Nutrition CRSP Project, funded by USAID, studied the functional effects of marginal malnutrition in developing countries. Kenya, Egypt, and Mexico were selected to investigate the effects of chronic deficits in energy intake on such functional areas as disease resistance, reproductive performance, physical growth, work performance, socioeconomic performance, and cognitive development. The Nutrition CRSP-Kenya Project was jointly conducted by the University of Nairobi and the University of California at Los Angeles.

The project consisted of a pilot phase (February 1983 to December 1983) and a main study phase (January 1984 to March 1986). Households (247 total) were selected from a preliminary survey of 1,600 households for participation in the two-year study. The households selected were chosen to provide a full range of food (energy) intake and nutritional status. The target groups evaluated included nonpregnant women, pregnant women (followed from the third month of pregnancy to term and through the first six months of lactation), infants (from birth to six months of age), school-age children (seven to nine years), and adult males.

The data collection was carried out by trained enumerators who made regular home visits to collect data on food intake and functional performance variables. The data is currently being analyzed to allow testing of a number of hypotheses that relate food intake to function.

IMPACT OF THE DROUGHT

Food Intake

Quantitative food-intake information was obtained on each study household, as well as target individuals within those households. The field staff spent eight hours per day twice a month within a given household to weigh and measure all ingredients of prepared dishes and beverages, as well as to measure individual intakes. Meals or food eaten away from the household or eaten when the field-worker was not in the house were recalled using standard recipes (average ingredients were based on multiple recipes taken from the study household).

Through a combination of several sources of food tables of nutrition values and selected food-nutrient analyses carried out by a commercial laboratory for the CRSP project, energy values and proximate analyses (carbohydrate, protein, and fat) for the ingested food were calculated (Platt 1962, FAO 1969, Paul and Southgate 1978, Watt and Merrill 1975). Preliminary calculations for energy intake (kcal) revealed that from April through November 1984, there was an overall steady decline in household and target individual energy intake (Figure 14.2). In the case of the toddlers (eighteen to thirty months), it was noted that the amount ingested tended *not* to increase with increasing age. The food intake enumerators also noted that there was an increase in the consumption of wild plants and insects, as well as more processed purchased foods, such as refined maize meal.

The project staff estimated that approximately 30 percent of the population was severely affected, with another 30 percent moderately affected by the drought (total population in the target area was about 12,000). The lower, more arid zones were the most severely hit by the famine. Starting in June and July 1984, CRSP field staff reported that many households were without food and lacked the resources to obtain any. Stored food was nonexistent within the homes, and there were no community stores or granaries. Some foods were available in local markets, but prices had escalated; households usually did not have sufficient money to purchase this food. CRSP Activity Observation Teams reported that more adults and school-age children were leaving home to look for food, including collecting food from common lands.

Nutritional Status

The primary methods of assessing nutritional status were monthly anthropometry (height, weight, and fat folds) and periodic home visits for physical inspection of young children for signs of severe protein energy malnutrition (PEM). This was defined as weight for age less than or equal to 60 percent of the median, and/or weight for height less than or equal to 75 percent of the median (National Child Health Survey reference data). Most striking during the famine period was the shift from a prevalence of 2 percent severe PEM to 6 percent among children. In addition, obvious clinical cases of wasting, edema, and other signs of kwashiorkor were noted.

As a group, adult males and females showed considerable weight loss (Table 14.1 and Figure 14.3). Among school-age children and toddlers, 65 to 70 percent did not gain any weight from August to December 1984, and 24 percent experienced weight loss during that time (Table 14.2). There was also an increase in the level of stunting among toddlers during this same period (Figure 14.4).

Pregnancy Outcome

Preliminary analyses show that women in their last trimester of pregnancy during the drought experienced, as a group, decreased pregnancy weight gain and an increase in the percent of infants born with low birth weights of less than 2,800 g (Figure 14.5). Hospitals and the health center in the study area reported a decrease in the number of deliveries for early 1985, which they attributed to food shortages.

RESPONSE TO THE DROUGHT

Role of the Nutrition CRSP Project

For humanitarian and ethical reasons, the Nutrition CRSP project entered into famine-relief efforts to offset the impact of the severe food shortages in the area. These efforts were channeled through local community famine-relief committees formed throughout the drought stricken areas by the Office of the President. The Nutrition CRSP Program was able to obtain maize and other food aid with a relatively short lag time through the World Food Programme, UNICEF, the Netherlands Embassy, and various relief organizations. The rapid response time of the mobilized food assistance was a critical factor in reducing the impact of the drought. This quick response was made possible by the close monitoring of the food intake and nutritional status data made available by the CRSP project.

Local committees, chiefs, and subchiefs identified families at greatest risk in the affected areas. Criteria included household size, land productivity, and the economic situation of the household. The Nutrition CRSP project examined research data on food intake and nutritional assessment and then prepared a list of households that appeared to be in greatest need. The listing prepared by the community leaders coincided by 60 percent with that of the CRSP project. In addition to those identified with special needs in the general area, all households under study in the nutrition project were included in the famine relief efforts.

Estimate of Household Rations

Households were provided with emergency subsistence rations and seeds for planting. The relief objective was to provide an average of 1,500 kcal per person per day, or about 50 kg of maize per household per month (based on an average household size of six). The main assumptions were that little else other than relief food would be available, the situation would continue for at least six months, the distribution of food within the household would most likely not be equitable, and that even this ration could probably not supply a nutritionally adequate level of energy intake. To meet this intake objective for the Embu area would require about 309 mt of maize over a six-month period. In spite of the tremendous efforts by all those involved, CRSP allocations averaged less than the desired 50 kg per household per month.

Distribution Activities

Famine-relief distribution commenced on 15 September 1984. Nine different locations were selected as famine-relief distribution centers. These sites included the project field offices in each of the four clusters and markets of Kathanjure, Kinthithe, Kathanguri, and Karurumo, and at special sites in Kasafari and Kigumo (areas that were assisted but were not part of the CRSP study area). The distribution centers were supervised by senior project personnel and staffed by project field workers and community volunteers. Initially, maize was distributed to 277 study households and 869 other households. Each household received a ration of 12 to 16 kg of maize at the first distribution.

The date of the second distribution was 9 October 1984. Since total supplies of maize were of limited quantity, rations were allocated according to the number of persons per household. Households with two or fewer persons received 5 kg, households with three to six persons received 10 kg, and households with over six persons received 15 kg of maize. In late October, the maize rations were increased slightly for all households. By this time, 1,269 households were receiving allocations.

In December 1984, plans were made to continue famine-relief distribution through February 1985. An anthropometric screening of non-CRSP households in Kyeni South Location and in contiguous sublocations in the drier areas was held in order to identify additional families with malnourished children to be registered for famine relief. All children under ten years of age were screened. Households were selected for assistance if one or more of the children were at least moderately wasted and/or severely stunted. This criteria was set at less than or equal to -1 standard deviation of weight for height and/or less than or equal to -2 standard deviations of height for age (Table 14.3).

Beans, dehydrated skim milk, and oil were added to the maize rations to supplement the nutritional value of maize and because a large number of households were totally dependent on relief for all food supplies. These goods were usually purchased locally at very high prices, with only a small amount being donated. Rations of each of these items were distributed just prior to Christmas and at two- to three-week intervals through February 1985. During this phase of the distribution effort, 1,538 households received allocations.

Seed Distribution

The second strategy of the relief effort was the distribution of seeds for planting once the rains returned in October 1984. During the drought, seeds were eaten, and replacement seeds in the local markets were prohibitively expensive or not available. Therefore, to allow families to begin to generate their own food supplies, it was critical that seed replenishment be included in the relief program.

Seed needs for Embu District were calculated based on the following assumptions:

1. Average household size = 5.21, from the Nutrition CRSP Project Census Survey
2. Average land per household = 5 to 8 acres, from the Nutrition CRSP Project Socioeconomic Status Survey

3. Seed requirements and cost, from the Nutrition CRSP Project Seed Planting Questionnaire and Market Survey:
   maize = 10 kg/acre at 7 Ksh/kg
   beans = 20 kg/acre at 12 Ksh/kg
   millet = 10 kg/acre at 12 Ksh/kg
4. Affected households = 1,500-1,600 households

In order to produce enough food from the short rains to allow a family to survive until the long rain harvest, a six-month (March to September) food supply was necessary. On the basis of an average household size of five and a daily requirement of 1,500 kcal per person, each household would need 1,350,000 kcal from the short rain harvest. If the average household yield of cereal and grain legumes is 1,500,000 kcal per acre, then each household would need enough seed (cereal and/or legumes) for one acre.

The Nutrition CRSP project requested seed from BARAC (Black Americans in Response to African Crisis) and World Vision. Bean seeds for planting were obtained and distributed, with households receiving between 6 and 10 kg each. A total of 1,269 households received seeds just as the short rains started in October 1984. An additional shipment of Katumani maize and bean seed was received from World Vision in 1985. Katumani maize is a composite variety, which is shorter and relatively drought-resistant compared to the local variety. In October 1985, 5,000 kg of bean seed were distributed; in March 1985, an additional 2,000 kg of maize were distributed.

The CRSP famine-relief program came to a close in March 1985. By that time, the rains had returned, and Embu households were again becoming self-sufficient in their food-production capacity. Between September 1984 and March 1985, the assistance program had distributed food relief totaling 193,524 kg of maize, 35,946 kg of beans, 4,092 liters of oil, and 5,696 kg of dehydrated skim milk. In addition, the program distributed 5,000 kg of maize seed and 15,900 kg of bean seed for planting.

Rehabilitation Unit

In addition to the food- and seed-relief activities, a low-cost, temporary rehabilitation unit was set up at the Mission Hospital to treat children suffering from severe protein energy malnutrition (both kwashiorkor and marasmus). A large tent with sufficient space to house thirty mothers and their children and infants was erected. Mothers carried out the feeding and care of their children under the supervision of the physician and nurses. With the aid of food relief, the hospital was able to serve three nutritious meals per day to the children and mothers. The average stay of a child was about three weeks.

COPING WITH DROUGHT

Drought is a recurring problem for much of Embu District and Kenya as a whole. Table 14.4 shows the expected probabilities for various levels of drought in this area, based on the assumption that the minimum amount of rainfall required for dryland agriculture is 300 mm per growing season. For the long rains, these probabilities mean that a mild drought will occur every 2.8 years, a moderate drought every 4.5 years, and a severe drought every 12.5 years. For the short rains, the frequencies are 2.4 years for a mild drought, 3.4 years for a moderate drought, and a severe drought will occur every 5.6 years (Downing, Mungai, and Muturi 1988).

Drought does not necessarily translate into famine. Agricultural and economic systems (the sharing of food supplies within family networks, cultivation of drought-resistant crops, some reliance on off-farm employment, and the production of cash crops) have been developed that enable families to overcome the effects of reduced rainfall. The problem occurs, however, when the survival strategies these systems offer cannot cope with the scale or duration of the food shortages. This was the situation in Embu during the 1984 drought, where food shortages had adverse effects on health and nutritional status to the point where external assistance became necessary.

The coping strategies that were employed had an effect on famine survival and therefore provided some positive outputs. These strategies, however, also carried negative consequences that often were unavoidable. While assuring immediate survival, many of these strategies increased the level of poverty for the household in the long term. Some of the coping strategies and their limitations are described below.

Food sharing. It was common for households to share food with other households while food was available in adequate quantities. The spatial dimension of the drought, however, inhibited the utility of this strategy in 1984 since food production was reduced over a wide area. Families that had members integrated into the cash economy (through salaried employment or businesses) had better access to still adequate, but expensive, food supplies.

Foraging for food. Family members would forage for whatever food supplies could be found in the area. Diets were supplemented with local plants, insects, and rodents. This is a traditional response to famine in Kenya and elsewhere. The Kithioro famine in 1918 was imported into Embu from Gikuyu when the Agikuyu came in search of food. At this time, they so depleted local food supplies that Embu was soon engulfed in the famine (Mwaniki 1975).

Food reserves. Very few families had stored food. Therefore, this option was not a central strategy for survival. Food storage needs to be assessed in light of several factors: capacity for excess production, need for conversion of excess production into cash, physical capability of food storage, and ability to protect against losses from food storage structures (through rodents, insects, or wetness).

Purchase of food. Various staple foods were sporadically unavailable in the markets. At times, families were forced to purchase and consume more expensive and less nutritious processed foods (such as refined flour and bread) to supplement their diets. The cash necessary to purchase food was not always readily available to households in need. Since the purchase of food was often the only remaining source of food, families were forced to seek cash through means such as: (1) selling animals (particularly goats)—this had an immediate effect of flooding the market and lowering prices, as well as the long-term effect of reducing farmers stock; (2) seeking employment—this was a difficult strategy given the scarcity of jobs; (3) selling possessions—this was not a very successful approach since most families had very little to sell (selling of tools or farm implements had severely negative long-term effects since doing so reduced a farmer's ability to grow food when more favorable climatic conditions returned; furthermore, as with animals, the selling prices were low during this time, and farmers could not get a fair price for their possessions); (4) loans—this was mainly an option only for farmers who were members of organizations, such as coffee cooperatives; few farmers owned enough land to support an adequate loan (Figure 14.6; CRSP surveys showed that nearly a third of all farmers owned no land); in most cases, these farmers were cultivating borrowed land; and (5) other income-generating activities—this included an increase in the production of baskets, sisal rope, and some carpentry work (these activities, however, were also subject to the depressed economy of the area, and their impact was therefore marginal).

Other sources of food. The primary alternative source of food was to eat the seed that had been set aside for planting when the rains returned. While this strategy was useful in addressing the immediate problem, it carried the danger of prolonging the hardship period. When the rains did come, there was insufficient seed to plant full crops. Since cash reserves had been spent in order to buy food there was no money available to replace the seed.

The Embu drought of 1984 demonstrates the need to better understand the nature of such events and the full impact of responses to those events. From the experiences and observations of the Nutrition CRSP project, some valuable lessons have been learned. These include the need for:

1. Household and community food-storage facilities and practices

2. Shifts in agricultural practices to increase the number and quantity of drought-resistant crops and varieties grown (especially millet and sorghum), and the willingness and ability to switch to famine crops (such as cassava) during a period of marked food shortages
3. Household and community seed banks
4. Increased income generation, cash availability, or credit schemes to allow farmers to purchase food and seed during emergencies
5. A central government to move food produced in one area to areas where food shortages exist
6. A simple, but valid, information-gathering system to monitor community markets, household food supply and availability, crop yields, rainfall, and nutritional status in order to provide an early warning of potential food problems
7. Small water schemes to protect farmers against a complete reliance on rainfall for their crops

Embu farmers are vulnerable to even temporary climate changes that can precipitate severe health problems. In order to reduce their vulnerability, it is necessary to understand the changing patterns of social, economic, and cultural relationships that define the feasibility of coping with drought and famine. The lessons learned as a result of the CRSP project serve as a partial step in attaining that level of understanding. The refinement of these approaches, however, remains a substantial challenge for all concerned with the impact of famine.

Figure 14.1 Agroclimatic zones in the CRSP study area of Embu District. Source: Based on Mungai and Muturi (1988).

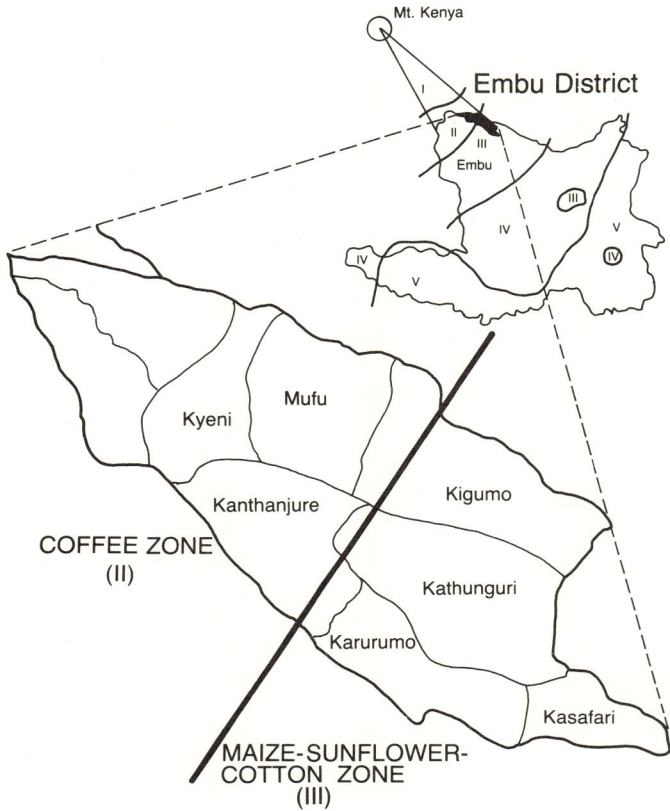

Figure 14.2 Kilocalories consumed by household, 1984-1985. Source: CRSP Food Intake Surveys.

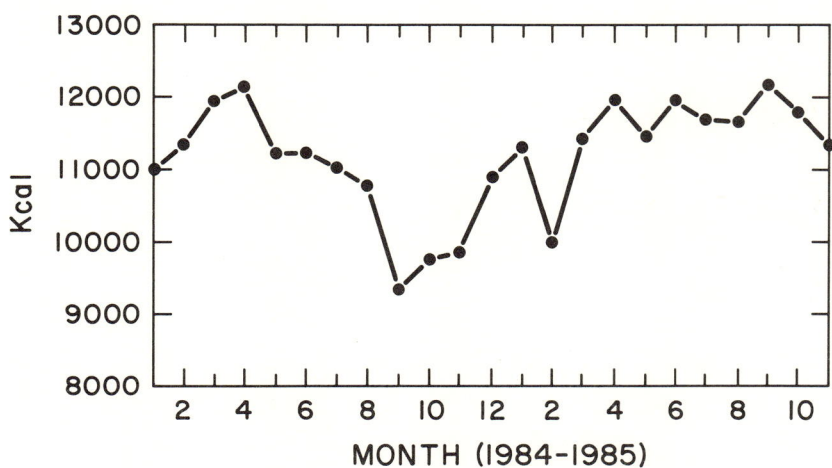

Figure 14.3 Changes in adult body weight during the 1984 drought. Source: CRSP Anthropometric Survey.

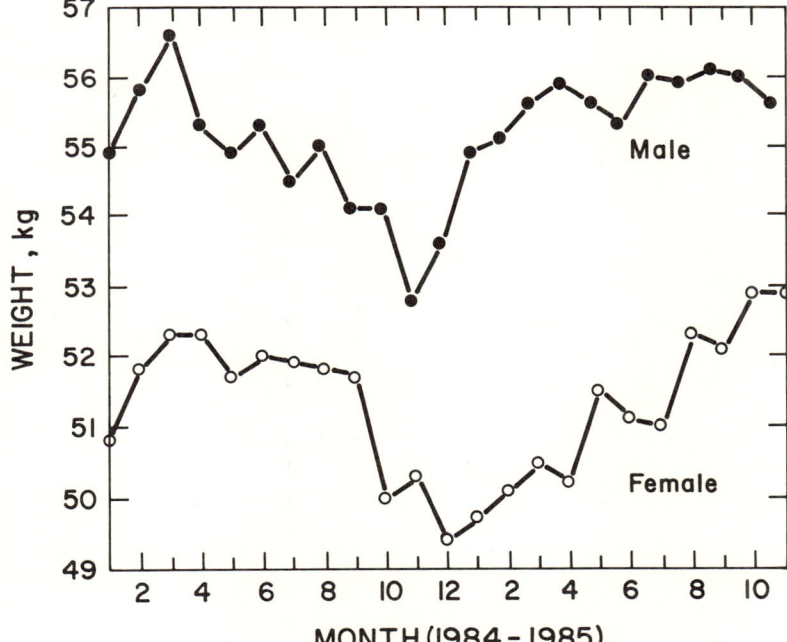

242 • COPING WITH DROUGHT IN KENYA

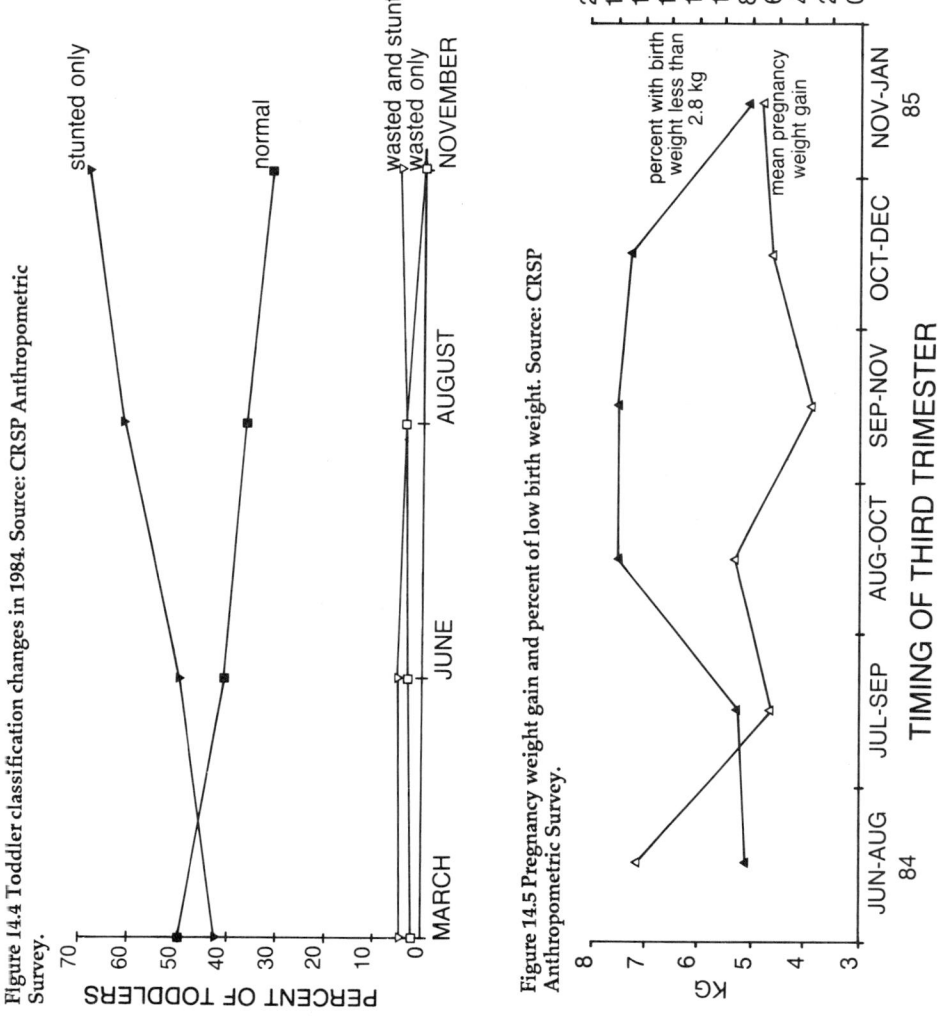

Figure 14.4 Toddler classification changes in 1984. Source: CRSP Anthropometric Survey.

Figure 14.5 Pregnancy weight gain and percent of low birth weight. Source: CRSP Anthropometric Survey.

Figure 14.6 Land owned and cultivated in Embu District. Source: CRSP Socioeconomic Survey.

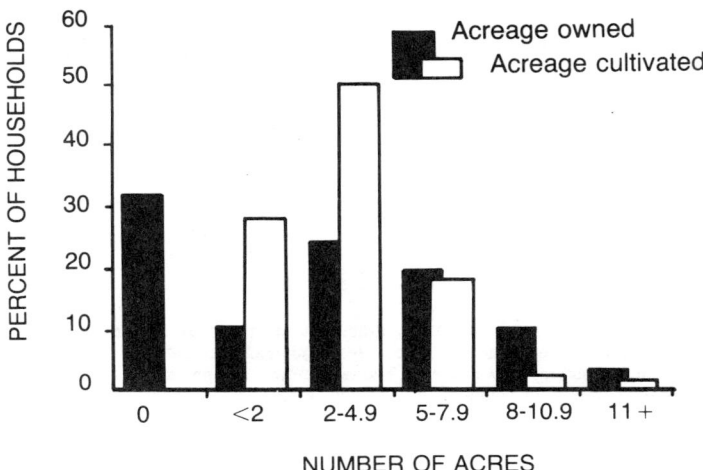

Table 14.1 Adult Weight Change During the 1984 Drought

	Lead Males ($n = 236$)	Lead Females ($n = 269$)
Mean weight loss (kg)	3.4	3.5
Range (kg)	0.1–7.9	1.2–6.7
% with weight loss	41	38

Source: CRSP Anthropometric Survey.

Table 14.2 Anthropometric Status in Children from August to December 1984

	Number	Percent Showing Weight Loss	Percent Showing No Weight Gain
Infants (0–6 months)	103	10	24
Toddlers (18–30 months)	114	24	69
School age (7–9 years)	137	14	65

Source: CRSP Anthropometric Survey.

Table 14.3 Anthropometric Screening of Non-CRSP Households

Sublocation	Severe Malnutrition (W/H ≤ –2 SD)	Moderate Malnutrition (W/H ≤ –1 SD)	Severe Stunting (H/A ≤ –3 SD)	Total Screened
Kigumo	94 (17.2%)	—	192 (35.0%)	548
Kasayari	7 (8.0%)	33 (37.9%)	31 (35.6%)	87
Karaumu	18 (6.8%)	86 (32.7%)	111 (42.2%)	263
Kathanguri	43 (14.6%)	118 (40.1%)	105 (35.7%)	294

Source: CRSP Data Survey.
Notes: Data are for children under ten years of age. The sample is not from a representative sample survey. Rather, people were encouraged to come to an examining center where the measurements were taken. The raw number and percent of total screened are shown. W/H = weight for height, W/A = weight for age, SD = standard deviation.

Table 14.4 Annual Drought Probabilities for Embu

	Level of Drought		
	Mild	Moderate	Severe
Long rains	.36	.22	.08
Short rains	.41	.29	.18

Source: Downing, Mungai, and Muturi (1988).

· 15 ·

Drought, Resource Distribution, and Mobility in Two Maasai Group Ranches, Southeastern Kajiado District

BARBARA E. GRANDIN
PETER N. DE LEEUW
P. LEMBUYA

East African rangelands are marked by extreme variability in rainfall. Traditional pastoral production systems are characterized by high rates of opportunistic mobility to respond to varying fodder and water resources. With increasing population densities, changing land use and tenure, and altered sociopolitical systems, however, grazing resources have diminished and will continue to do so. In many areas, possibilities for mobility have been particularly hampered. During periods of drought, limited mobility has severe consequences for pastoral production.

Land tenure change was a major component of several recent livestock development projects (in Kenya, Botswana, and Sudan, for example). Tenure change was instituted primarily for technical reasons unrelated to the traditional pastoral mode of production and access to resources. Developers hoped to confine small groups of people to small, fixed areas of land. In Kenya, this was a major consideration in the formation of group ranches in Maasailand. A group ranch is an organizational structure through which a group of people jointly hold freehold title deed to an area of land. While developers considered the ecological viability of the group ranches to be important, it was not an overriding concern; relatively little attention was paid to the existing, traditional herd management system and the need for mobility in times of drought. Management and planning for group ranches has placed little attention on helping the Maasai on group ranches to develop drought-coping strategies that are superior to their traditional strategy of mobility. Nor have efforts been made to determine the utility and viability of continued drought-related mobility.

A case study from two quite different group ranches in southeastern Kajiado District is presented here (see also Grandin and Lembuya 1987 and ILCA 1981). The ranches differ in a number of ways, including ecological potential, date of incorporation as group ranches, Maasai subtribe affiliation, and degree of sedentarization. The chapter focuses on the mobility response of semisedentary Maasai producers, with information from a more nomadic group presented for comparison.

TWO GROUP RANCHES: OLKARKAR AND MBIRIKANI

Olkarkar group ranch in the Kaputiei subtribe area was incorporated in 1970 under the initial phase of the Kenya Livestock Development Project; it covers approximately 10,000 ha, with about forty households normally resident (Table 15.1 and Figure 15.1). It receives an average of 600 mm of rainfall per year, bimodally distributed. The production system focuses on cattle, with smallstock having gained importance only in the last twenty years. Also in the last twenty years, production in the Kaputiei subtribe area has become increasingly sedentary, with producers often staying in the same *boma* location for more than five years. Kaputiei producers do not routinely divide their herds by sending animals to distant grazing areas in dry seasons. The whole family and the animals stay together in the same location in times of average rainfall. Residential units have declined from five households per compound in the early 1960s (Njoka 1979) to two households per compound in the early 1980s (Grandin 1986a).

Mbirikani group ranch was not incorporated until 1981; it covers approximately 135,000 ha, with over two hundred households normally resident. Much of the ranch is in the rain shadow of the Chyulu Hills and receives only 400 mm of rainfall or less; the southeastern hills (far from permanent water), however, receive 600 mm. As in Olkarkar, cattle are the mainstay of the pastoral system, although smallstock are important for home consumption and drought security. There is some indication that members of the Kisongo subtribe have become more sedentary in the last twenty years, yet their production system is still seminomadic, with the mean length of stay in the same compound being less than one year. Residential unit size has declined to 3.5 households per compound, but cooperation in production is the norm. Kisongo producers routinely split their herds in the dry season, often sending smallstock to special grazing sites. Unlike the Kaputiei, they have retained both the capability to move easily (by using donkeys and acquiring fewer material possessions) and the ability to acquire labor for splitting herds (by engaging in large-scale cooperative production).

In normal times, residential compounds in Olkarkar are found in an arc within a 7-km radius around the sole permanent watering point near Simba. Most Mbirikani residential sites are found clustered along the water pipeline, a few are in the southwestern corner near the river, and fewer still are located in the southeastern corner, which is near temporary water but over 15 km from permanent water.

Drought is a fairly common phenomenon; in the last thirty years, serious droughts occurred in 1954 to 1956, 1960 to 1961, and 1973 to 1976 (see Campbell 1984 for an assessment of the impact of the 1970s drought). During these periods, there were heavy livestock losses and movement of animals across subtribal boundaries, even to places distant from Maasailand. Mbirikani also experienced moderate drought conditions in 1966/67 and 1981/82; these necessitated increased mobility, primarily within the subtribal boundaries.

Subtribe identification continues to be important in Maasailand. Producers cross subtribe boundaries only under the most difficult of circumstances. The severity and extent of a drought can be seen in the degree to which producers will cross subtribal boundaries.

NEIGHBORING AREAS AND DROUGHT FALLBACK AREAS

Fallback area refers to an area that has relatively better grass cover than the usually grazed areas at the time of a drought onset. Although the distribution of pockets of fodder will vary with the specific rainfall conditions in each drought, there are areas that are consistently more likely to have fodder available. Some of these areas, though not all, are within Maasai control. Fallback areas usually have one or more of the following characteristics that cause them to be relatively underutilized:

1. Disease problems (especially tick-borne disease and trypano–somiasis)
2. Far from water (and to a lesser extent from shops)
3. Difficult to graze due to steep slopes or rockiness
4. Relatively unproductive vegetation types
5. Restricted access (national parks, research stations, or forests)

Movement to fallback areas sometimes occurs in waves, with one Maasai group moving into an area that another group has just vacated. This movement occurs for several reasons. First, access to many fallback areas and their associated water supplies is acquired through social relations, the strength and extensiveness of which decline with distances. Second, producers may be reluctant to move their animals too far due to the stress of trekking and changing ecological zones. Third, the fallback area for a poorly endowed area might include a better endowed part of Maasailand that other producers have vacated in search of even greener pastures.

Fallback Areas for Olkarkar

Olkarkar is bounded on the north by the railway line separating Maasailand from Wakamba farmers in Machakos District, and on the other three sides by group ranches (Figure 15.1). Under the traditional grazing system, Olkarkar was part of a locality that is now divided and includes Kiboko group ranch to the east and parts of two other group ranches to the south and west. At the time of demarcation, proportionately more of the common users of the locality opted to register in Olkarkar rather than in Kiboko due to a higher incidence of trypanosomiasis and tick-borne disease in Kiboko.[1] Kiboko thus had about 25 percent more land per registered member than Olkarkar. The central eastern area of Kiboko, known as Normao, is relatively underutilized because of perceived disease threats and difficulty in obtaining acceptable water. It is the first major drought fallback area of the nearby producers.

Kiboko group ranch is bordered on the east by Machakos District. The northern part of this Machakos area includes the Kiboko National Range Research Station (which was a game conservation area open to the Maasai prior to the late 1960s). During the 1974 drought, Maasai had been allowed to graze on the research station. The southern part includes the northern Chyulu Hills, a steep, hilly area that is normally utilized only by honey gatherers. The area is difficult to access, far from water, and reported by Maasai to be ridden with tick-borne disease and trypanosomiasis. On the southwestern edge of the Chyulu fallback area is a hill called Oldoinyo Sampu, which is in Maasailand near the borders of Kaputiei section, Kisongo section, and Machakos District. All these areas serve as a second level of fallback area for local Maasai, as well as those from other parts of Kajiado District.

Water in these fallback areas of Olkarkar is available from two sources. Of these, the Kiboko River is said to be unhealthy; the water is stagnant in places, leaches abound, and tsetse flies are common between the river and the hills to the east. The second source is the shallow, dry riverbed wells near Ilkilonyeti. These produce a slightly salty water at a great labor cost since the water is lifted from the wells by hand. Between 1981 and 1983, there were six wells in the Kilonyeti area. By September 1984, many new wells had been dug to accommodate the vast increase in the cattle population. Even so, lines were long, and much grazing time was lost.

Further from Olkarkar into Machakos District, across the Chyulu Hills, lies the Kibwezi forest, the Kaambo Hills, and surrounding agricultural lands, which were used extensively as a fallback area during the drought of the mid-1970s, but were used little in 1984. The few producers who went there reported difficulty in gaining access to the forests and having to pay the residents for access to grazing on agricultural land.

---

1. The Maasai in the study area use the term *oltikana* to describe a number of tick-borne diseases: East Coast fever, anaplasmosis, heartwater, and babeseosis (redwater). Ethnoveterinary research indicated that Maasai producers are good diagnosticians; their recognition of clinical symptoms is excellent (unpublished data collected by Grandin). Multilingual Maasai from the area believe East Coast fever, rather than other tick-borne diseases, is the most important drought-related *oltikana*. In serological studies in 1982 to 1983, low incidences of anaplasmosis and East Coast fever were found (Waghela et al., 1983). Incidence of East Coast fever was greatest in Mbirikani animals that had shifted during the minor drought of 1982, lending support to Maasai verbal reports of East Coast fever.

Fallback Areas for Mbirikani

Mbirikani is bounded on the north by Kaputiei group ranches, on the east by the very steep, unoccupied southern Chyulu Hills of Machakos District, and on the south and west by other Kisongo group ranches. Mbirikani group ranch, like all Kisongo ranches, is large and includes several different neighborhoods (each of which has its own traditional grazing area). Traditional grazing patterns, however, have been disrupted in the last thirty years by the construction of a water pipeline in 1955 that provides permanent water at a number of points, the granting of individual title deeds to largely non-Maasai farmers on the foot slopes of Kilimanjaro in the 1960s, the gazetting of Amboseli as a national park in 1973 (thus precluding legal Maasai use of the extensive swamp system), and the adjudication of group ranches among the Kisongo in 1980. It is not clear how the boundaries of group ranches were determined, but these boundaries clearly cut off areas traditionally used by Mbirikani producers, particularly to the west (Campbell 1981; Peacock et al., 1982; Peacock 1984).

There are several intermediate and two main, ultimate fallback areas for Mbirikani residents. The intermediate areas are necessary, in part, because of the long distances traveled. These are used when conditions are less severe. The first is Oltiasika, which provides access to southern Chyulu grazing but is relatively underutilized in normal times. It is said to be a disease focus, especially for tick-borne disease and, to a lesser extent, trypanosomiasis; it is also very far from shops (where maize meal is purchased). The Oldoinyo Sampu area is also used by Kisongo producers, although the nearby water sources are controlled by the Kaputiei. Mbirikani producers historically moved toward the Kilimanjaro foot slopes, but much of this area is now under the control of farmers, most of whom are not Maasai. Several of the group ranches south of Mbirikani beyond the Chyulu rain shadow tend to have better conditions; these are therefore a destination for early drought mobility.

The two ultimate fallback areas are Risa (near the border of Amboseli National Park) and Iltilal (near the border of Tsavo West National Park). The Risa area is serviced by water pumped from Amboseli and provided to the Maasai as compensation for their loss of access to the Amboseli swamps. The government is responsible for providing diesel fuel to run the pump; watering is free of charge. Located in the extreme southeast of Kisongo territory, Iltilal is within a neighboring group ranch. It is relatively underutilized because, although close to Tsavo Park, it is far from park water resources. Water at Iltilal is derived from riverbed wells. Trypanosomiasis is reported to be a significant problem when East Coast fever occurs, but it is less common.

DROUGHT ONSET IN OLKARKAR AND MBIRIKANI

The range conditions of Olkarkar and Mbirikani just prior to the 1984 drought differed due to the rainfall patterns of the previous few years. Rainfall records were available for several locations near the study sites (Table 15.2). The degree of green cover in early January 1984 has been derived from the National Oceanic and Atmospheric Administration's Advanced Very High Resolution Radiometers (NOAA/AVHRR) satellite imagery, supplied by B. Holben of the National Aeronautic and Space Administration. The data gauge the resources available in the area at the beginning of the dry period, which lasted an additional ten months (Figure 15.2).

In Olkarkar, difficulties began in March 1983, when a fire swept through dense standing hay (from the November to December 1982 rains) in the major dry-season grazing area of southeastern Olkarkar. The rains of early 1983 were poor and grass regrowth was minimal, particularly over the burnt area. Beginning in April, grazing patterns within the ranch changed, becoming concentrated at the northern and southwestern parts of the ranch. As the Olkarkar resources were depleted, off-ranch grazing became necessary, and producers began shifting to Normao in Kiboko ranch. This movement occurred as early as July 1983 for producers who normally relied on the burnt area, and as late as October for others. Although the total rainfall in late 1983 was average, it fell primarily in the last three weeks of December, leading to much less herbaceous growth than the rainfall figure alone would suggest. Nevertheless, there was sufficient grazing to enable Olkarkar producers to return to their homes in December. Subsequently, the April to May long rains failed completely. By the end of May 1984, when no rain had fallen, it became increasingly clear that a major drought was in progress, and that no rain could be expected for five to six months.

The beginning of the 1984 drought in Mbirikani should be dated even earlier (Table 15.2). Dry conditions prevailed in much of Mbirikani in 1981 and 1982; during this period, there was substantial movement within the ranch, as well as to Kisongo ranches south of Mbirikani, where more rain fell in April to May 1982 (Peacock et al., 1982). A number of producers suffered serious cattle losses, largely from tick-borne diseases contracted in the fallback areas (Grandin 1984). In late 1982, the rains in Mbirikani were quite heavy, and producers were able to return to their home compounds. In the south, however, smallstock had contracted Nairobi sheep disease (a tick-borne virus endemic to that area). This virus was carried back north with the animals, where an epidemic gradually spread through the ranch and into Kaputiei. The rains of April to May 1983 were average, but the rains of late 1983 fell over a short period and only in a few scattered locations; much of Mbirikani received no rainfall at all. There was no green cover in most of Mbirikani in January 1984 (Figure 15.2). In April to May 1984, a little rain fell to the south of Mbirikani, but none in the ranch itself.

MOBILITY PATTERNS IN OLKARKAR

Mobility was the primary strategy used to cope with the fodder shortages. In Olkarkar, the two major periods of movement occurred first in July to October or November 1983 and again in April to November 1984.

July to October or November 1983

The first households to shift out of Olkarkar were those from the burnt southern part of the ranch. However, as there was no rain in October and very little in early November, more households continued to shift. Sixteen Olkarkar households moved the bulk of their cattle toward Normao, while twelve others scattered to neighboring group and individual ranches.

There are seventeen permanent compounds in the Normao/Kilonyeti area, eleven of which took in friends and relatives from other group ranches. In addition, one temporary compound was built to accommodate a rich man with over five hundred cattle. Over three thousand head of cattle had converged on the area by mid-December 1983, doubling the number normally resident. About 80 percent of the cattle were from Olkarkar, while the rest came from six other households (each with far fewer animals) that belonged to three other neighboring ranches and three households normally resident elsewhere in Kiboko.

As the duration of stay was expected to be short, only a few people from each household moved with the animals. Ideally, the animals went with a *moran* (warrior), who managed and watered the animals, two children to herd, and a woman or older girl, who did domestic chores and helped to water the animals. Conditions were not very serious; intensive labor was mainly required for watering if wells rather than the river were used. Limited accommodation was available in existing compounds.

At the same time that Olkarkar people were seeking better pastures toward Kilonyeti, people from Mbilin, the group ranch to the west of Olkarkar, were flooding into Olkarkar. By mid-December 1983, almost 2,500 cattle had shifted into Olkarkar group ranch (about as many as had shifted out). Sixty percent of these were from Mbilin, with the rest from other nearby group and individual ranches. This situation represents an example of a common sequence of pastoral movement during drought. Producers first move to nearby areas where they have close social ties and where the stress on the animals is not severe (as distances to trek and ecological changes are small). Frequently, the producers from those areas are themselves moving to a slightly better, nearby area.

When the rain came in December, the people started to return home. By mid-January, the situation had largely returned to normal, although the vegetation resources were relatively scanty for that time of year.

April to November 1984

The failure of the April to May rains was a harbinger of a very difficult period in southeastern Kajiado, as was to be the case for much of Kenya. The Maasai acknowledged that a major drought was in progress and began to plan their movements, knowing that rain would not fall for at least five months.

Most producers first went to Normao and then to the north Chyulu and Oldoinyo Sampu areas. They used those areas in that order, first shifting animals into Normao, while building new compounds between the Kilonyeti wells and the grazing areas in Machakos District. The labor required to build compounds in uninhabited areas was considered worthwhile since it put the cattle in a better location; it was also necessary in order to accommodate the increased numbers of people who would have to shift. Whereas in the earlier movement only a few people shifted with each herd or group of herds, most household members moved during the severe drought period largely due to increased labor demands. Adult men were needed for watering, lifting weak animals, and herding; women helped to water cattle, skin dead animals, and do domestic work; and children were needed for herding and helping with livestock work in the compound. In addition, management supervision and family provisioning is easier if the whole household is in one location. Because grazing resources in Olkarkar were so poor, producers were reluctant to leave cattle behind. Most households split, however, leaving only a few lactating cattle at the home compound to feed the people who remained behind. Smallstock also remained in home compounds. Splitting households was particularly common in households with pregnant women or women who had recently given birth—as it was in larger, richer households.

Most households in Olkarkar shifted southeast toward the Chyulu Hills. Data is available on thirty-four of the households normally resident in Olkarkar: eighteen moved to the Normao/north Chyulu area, three went to northeastern Kiboko group ranch, three moved long distances to Kibwezi, five went west to the neighboring group ranch, and five stayed in Olkarkar. The eighteen households that went to Normao/north Chyulu were grouped into fifteen herding units. In late June, there were forty herding units in the vicinity. By August, there were over ninety herding units with the following origin: Olkarkar (15), Kiboko (14), Merueshi (17), other nearby group ranches (27), north Kaputiei (2), Matapato and Ildalalakutuk subtribes in central Kajiado (more than 13), and one individual rancher from Kiboko. It is estimated that there were over 12,500 head of cattle in these ninety units.

After households left Normao, the North Chyulu location was the first to be settled; it was the most heavily used, having thirteen *bomas* and about fifty households. Olorien had two *bomas* used by nine households, Ildonyo Sampin had six *bomas* and about thirty households, Eluaai was settled by only three households in one *boma*, and Oldoinyo Sampu, which was the final place of settlement, had seven *bomas* and nineteen households from

Kaputiei (some of which had earlier been in the other locations), and one unenumerated *boma* of households from Kisongo and Matapato sections.

There also was some sequential movement within the fallback area. This occurred as a result of four major factors:

1. *Heavy grazing pressure.* Grass in Normao was quickly consumed due to the heavy grazing pressure. Producers then moved their animals to Chyulu *bomas* to graze the empty hills and into the range research station, especially at night. Their presence at the station was increasingly unwelcome, and the strategy was finally abandoned.
2. *Animal diseases.* Tick-borne disease and trypanosomiasis appear to be endemic in Western Kiboko and the north Chyulu fallback area. Many Olkarkar producers complained that cattle died more from disease than hunger. By September, some producers had moved their animals from north Chyulu toward Oldoinyo Sampu; many others returned home, preferring hunger to disease.
3. *Human health and comfort.* Animals began to die in large numbers mainly after mid-August; from then on, the number of carcasses increased with each passing day until the stench became unbearable.
4. *Wild animals.* Wild buffalo and, to a lesser extent, lion were problematic in north Chyulu. At least one *moran* (an unmarried adult male) was attacked by a buffalo, causing people to fear for the safety of their herding children.

By late September, half of the Olkarkar producers had returned home. The animals were by then considered too weak to trek to distant places, such as Kibwezi, where fodder might still be available. Skins had become an important source of income; if cattle died in distant, rocky places, it would be difficult for women to find and skin them. By bringing the animals home to die, more of the skins would be saved. The psychological factor of despair must also be included as an incentive to return home.

The rains that ended the drought started uncommonly early in October. Most of the producers who had remained in the Chyulus returned home several weeks after the onset of rains, after allowing their surviving animals to gain some strength. A few herders delayed until late November or December.

MOBILITY PATTERNS IN MBIRIKANI

Mobility in Mbirikani differed from Olkarkar, due to ecological factors and the social conditions of production. Compared to Olkarkar producers, Mbirikani producers moved more often, covered greater distances, and simultaneously had animals in more places. The nine households from

Mbirikani that were closely monitored during the period from May to December 1984 stayed in an average of seven different locations in those seven months, while most Olkarkar producers stayed in only two or three locations (including home) during the same period. While producers in Olkarkar rarely split animals into more than two compounds (one at home, one away), producers in Mbirikani often had animals in three or more compounds. In Olkarkar, virtually all smallstock stayed in the home compound; in Mbirikani, most smallstock were moved, sometimes with cattle, though more often independently.

Movement in Mbirikani is greatly facilitated by the stronger tradition of cooperative management among the Kisongo. It was quite common, for example, for brothers to join forces, each taking some animals in different directions, and/or having one assume most livestock management responsibilities so the other could engage in trading to help support the family. Even after the drought, a number of previously independent households continued joint management to facilitate household provisioning and engagement in nonpastoral labor. Mbirikani producers have retained their ability to move by keeping the materials necessary (donkeys and carriers), which the bulk of the Kaputiei producers no longer have. Olkarkar producers frequently hired vehicles or begged for assistance from ILCA in order to move.

The overwhelming majority of Mbirikani households shifted cattle in an easterly direction, first stopping at Oltiasika. As the grazing became depleted, they moved south to the Iltilal well area, from where they could graze east into Tsavo West National Park. A small splinter group went from Oltiasika across the Chyulu Hills toward Kaambo, where they encountered disease problems and drug shortages. They then returned to Oltiasika and proceeded with the others to Iltilal. Although the Maasai knew that difficulties would ensue with park authorities, they saw no alternative. In mid-August, the Maasai grazed the relatively underutilized western part of the park secretly. Trouble soon ensued with some park officials, but it was temporarily smoothed over with periodic gifts and the promise not to penetrate too deeply into the park where much wildlife (and tourists) are found. Inevitably, the grass cover was depleted as more herds congregated, and the Maasai were forced to abrogate this agreement. Men and cattle pushed deeper into the park while leaving their families at Iltilal. Toward the end of September, they were forced to leave the park altogether, with many returning to Iltilal and Oltiasika, where it soon started to rain. As soon as the rains were well established, herders left Oltiasika because of problems with disease and the purchase of food. Many went to the Ilmao Hills, where rains had been heavy.

The second most commonly adopted strategy was to move in a southwesterly direction toward Risa water tank and Amboseli National Park. In April, some rain fell at Risa, which caused a number of producers to move in that direction. Problems ensued, however, as the government failed to supply water to the Risa tank due to a lack of diesel fuel. For a couple of weeks, animals were trekked over 20 km back to the pipeline to water; watering was done every third or fourth day. Finally, the Maasai were allowed to move into the park to water. Many stayed there, while others who had claimed that the swamps were polluted with carcasses of wildebeest and zebra that had died from an unidentified disease scattered to other areas. In late September, the remaining Maasai were chased out of the park. As there was no grazing or water nearby, they spread out to many different locations.

Several households, with only a few cattle, living near the rivers and swamps on Mbirikani's southern border did not move their animals; a few went northeastward to Oldoinyo Sampu. In May to June 1984, there were difficulties between the Kaputiei and the Kisongo, as the former tried to prevent the latter from using their water. The Kisongo retaliated by preventing the Kaputiei from entering their subtribal territory. Although this dispute benefited no one, it was resolved only when the Kaputiei apologized after several months of negotiations. The few Kisongo having close family ties with Kaputiei were able to avoid this restriction.

In Olkarkar, many producers returned to their homes in September before the rains fell, while in Mbirikani most producers were away from their home areas until December. They followed the rains, while making use of the surface water and initial flushes of green grass.

LIVESTOCK DISTRIBUTION AT THE END OF THE DROUGHT

An extensive (9,400 sq km), systematic reconnaissance survey was conducted by EcoSystems Limited on 24-26 September on behalf of ILCA in order to determine the distribution of livestock in the study sites and their surroundings (Table 15.3, based on the survey units mapped in Figure 15.2). The survey confirms the patterns expected on the basis of the field work. In the north, large concentrations of animals (fifty-one cattle per sq km) were found in Unit 2, which covers the northern Chyulu fallback area as well as Kiboko group ranch. The Olkarkar area had a density of twenty-six head of cattle per sq km, reflecting the fact that a number of producers from Olkarkar and elsewhere had returned, having already left the fallback area. Machakos District to the east (including part of the research station), Kibwezi forest, and mixed farming areas had an average density of twenty-five cattle. In the south, Mbirikani and its neighboring Kisongo group ranches were almost devoid of cattle. Great concentrations of cattle were found around Amboseli and Tsavo West national parks (with densities of thirty-one and forty cattle per sq km, respectively). The foothills of Kilimanjaro, which are primarily agricultural land, had a density of fifteen per sq km. It is not known to what extent these were animals of resident farmers or pastoralists.

LIVESTOCK-HOLDING CHANGES
BEFORE AND DURING THE 1984 DROUGHT

Livestock mortality, which affects both the immediate and long-term subsistence of pastoral populations, is the foremost result of drought. Assessments of livestock mortality and other offtake (such as forced sales, slaughter, gifts, and loans) are difficult to obtain. Production units can be fluid in composition, and mobile populations are difficult of access. In the course of its research, ILCA conducted a number of censuses, which were much easier to conduct accurately in semisedentary Olkarkar than in seminomadic Mbirikani; Olkarkar producers rarely split herds, and since the individual household tends to be the unit of production, the unit of enumeration was fairly stable.

Climatic conditions from mid-1981 to mid-1983 were average in Olkarkar, but below average in Mbirikani (Table 15.2). During this time, Olkarkar producers experienced a substantial net increase in livestock holdings, while those in Mbirikani experienced a slight net decrease (Table 15.4). ILCA sample households had been stratified into three wealth groups based on livestock unit (LU) to people ratios in 1981. Poor households had less than 5 LU/capita, average households had 5 to 13 LU/capita, and rich households had more than 13 LU/capita (one LU is equivalent to 250 kg liveweight). In Olkarkar, rich producers generally experienced higher rates of accumulation than average or poor producers. The exception occurred in cases wherein poor producers received a number of cattle as gifts from richer kinsmen, but the number actually accumulated by poor producers is insignificant compared to that of rich producers. In Mbirikani, changes of livestock inventory across wealth rank are less clear. Campbell (1984) found proportionately fewer losses among large herds compared to small herds in the 1972-1976 drought in the Mbirikani area.

In Olkarkar, only a few households experienced a net loss of cattle, while about a third lost smallstock (due largely to Nairobi sheep disease). In Mbirikani, almost all households showed a decline in both cattle and smallstock holdings, although the actual rates of decline varied tremendously. Losses were due to drought, disease, and the high voluntary offtake necessary to sustain the human population as milk yields declined.

Between May 1983 and January 1985, cattle and smallstock holdings for Olkarkar households decreased considerably, in reverse of the earlier trend (Table 15.5). On the average, cattle holdings declined over 40 percent between the two censuses. There was, however, significant variation across households, due to several interrelated factors:

1. Access to market outlets
2. Wealth of the producer
3. Fallback area chosen
4. Ability to afford and gain access to veterinary drugs

Several Olkarkar producers, mainly those of average wealth and rank, are also livestock traders. As such, they had access to the necessary channels for livestock sales. They used these channels to sell some of their own animals, rather than buy those of other producers. In contrast, by the time it was clear that a serious drought was in progress, the average producer had little possibility of selling animals. The three biggest traders in the ILCA sample showed only a 4 percent decline in herd size between the two censuses since they had been able to sell animals early in the drought and purchase animals after the rains began. At early signs of a drought, commercial producers can afford to divest themselves of their livestock more readily than pastoralists (for whom these animals are the only source of security). Hence, pastoralists tend to wait until a drought has clearly begun before selling animals, by which time market outlets are not available. There were some opportunities, albeit limited ones, for cattle sales throughout this period. While prices of live animals plummeted, however, the price of cattle hides soared (up to Ksh 120). By late July, the price for a live animal was only Ksh 50 to 100 higher than the price of a hide. As it is not possible to predict whether a given animal will live or die, producers felt it was more sensible to keep an animal than to sell it. A large-scale skin trade was carried out by both Maasai and Kamba traders, some of whom had been livestock traders. Others were young men with spare capital.

Drought-related cattle inventory changes also differed across wealth status. Although the reasons are not entirely clear, several contributing factors have been identified:

1. At the beginning of the drought, the livestock of the wealthy producers were in better condition and health than those of poor producers, largely due to lower rates of milk offtake in wealthy households (Grandin 1986b) and better veterinary care.
2. Whereas cattle of most poor households are normally watered daily, cattle of rich households in Olkarkar are watered every other day, a process that slightly depresses milk yield, but enables a wider radius of grazing (Grandin 1986b). As the drought progressed, cattle of wealthy producers did not have a period of stressful adjustment to two-day watering that was necessitated by poor range conditions, as did animals of poor producers.
3. Richer households could more readily afford to purchase drugs and acaricide.
4. A few of the richer households split their herds and sent them to several locations during the drought, using both hired and socially recruited labor, thereby decreasing site-specific risks.

Rich producers averaged a net decline in cattle numbers of about 40 percent (ranging from 18 percent for a trader to 60 percent), while poor producers averaged 70 percent (ranging 30 to 90 percent).

Reports from producers indicate that there was variation in cause and extent of mortality across the different fallback locations. It is difficult to estimate location-specific mortality rates based on the available census data. On the whole, more cattle were reported to have died of disease than of starvation, although there is a strong interaction between poor body condition and the effect of disease incidence.

Large-scale mortality did not occur until late August 1984. Old cows and suckling calves died first, followed by pregnant and lactating cattle and young weaners. Older immatures and adult males were reported to have the highest survival rates. Mortality continued until just after the onset of the rains in early October. In the first week of rain, there was a peak in mortality, which the Maasai report to be a common post-drought phenomenon.

Unfortunately, reliable quantitative data are not available on cattle losses in Mbirikani. On the basis of reports by producers and field assistants, it is believed that losses were more severe than those of Olkarkar. In over half the cases, producers report disease rather than starvation as the primary cause of death. Tick-borne disease, probably East Coast fever, was said to be the most common disease problem.

Starvation was not reported to be a problem for smallstock in Olkarkar. Several flocks, however, contracted Nairobi sheep disease; over 50 percent died as a result. The function of smallstock as drought security was clear, as Olkarkar households slaughtered mostly sheep for home consumption, primarily selling goats at quite high prices to meet essential cash needs. Smallstock mortality was also low in Mbirikani, where many smallstock were slaughtered for consumption.

SUGGESTIONS FOR POLICY AND FURTHER RESEARCH

On the basis of this case study, a number of areas for further research and analyses can be suggested to assist the government in preparing drought initiatives for pastoral areas marked by extreme fluctuations in carrying capacity.

As animals move into new locations and their nutritional state declines, normal disease resistance will diminish. Local-level research on disease incidence and tick distribution in both normal pastures and fallback areas is needed. Mechanisms to ensure supplies of essential drugs must be researched and developed.

Many drought fallback areas for southeastern Kajiado have fodder, yet they are normally underutilized due to disease incidence (mainly ECF and trypanosomiasis). The possibility of a large-scale campaign of prophylaxis for trypanosomiasis when drought is certain should be investigated. As fallback areas are far from dips, yet tick-ridden, the prevention of tick-borne diseases is particularly important. In the case of East Coast fever, control by infection and treatment (Radley et al., 1975) in the early stages of drought might be possible and cost effective.

Reclamation of disease-ridden locations could, however, have serious implications. Many fallback areas already have been removed from pastoral control for game parks and agriculture. Were the major tick-borne diseases and trypanosomiasis controlled and the remaining areas opened to full-time utilization (especially by nonpastoralists), an essential element of pastoral production would be lost, with serious limitations to the productivity of the land remaining under pastoral control.

By the end of May, producers realized that a major drought was in progress. Since the cattle were still in reasonable condition at that time, their meat yield would have been substantial. Further analyses are needed to determine to what extent it would be in the long-term interests of the government to develop slaughter facilities (either stationary or portable) to cope with periodic oversupply. This should be accompanied by schemes to restock after the drought.

Meteorological data (in combination with remote sensing) should be used to forecast and monitor times and locations of drought and oversupply.

Major mortality did not begin until late August 1984. This has important implications for strategies for supplying supplementary feed, as only two to three months of a maintenance diet would have been required for survival. If a nucleus of breeding females could have been kept alive, particularly for poorer households, the households would regain independence more quickly, thereby lessening the need for government welfare. The possible mechanisms for targeted supplementary feeding and their cost effectiveness require investigation.

Mobility, the most important strategy adopted during the drought, was essential for animal survival. As an aid to long-term land-use planning, it would be useful to examine possibilities for permitting and encouraging mobility across group ranch, subtribe, and district boundaries.

Figure 15.1 Location of group ranches in southeastern Kajiado District.

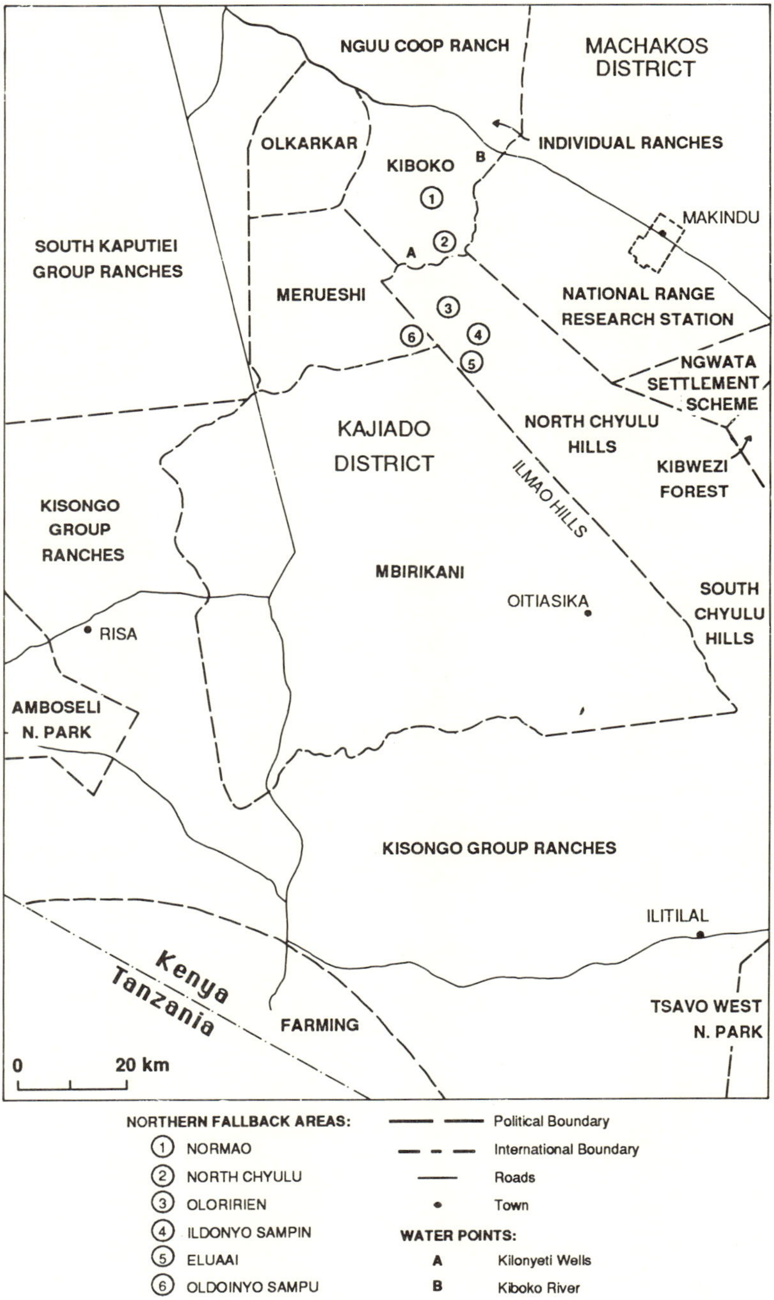

NORTHERN FALLBACK AREAS:
① NORMAO
② NORTH CHYULU
③ OLORIRIEN
④ ILDONYO SAMPIN
⑤ ELUAAI
⑥ OLDOINYO SAMPU

———— Political Boundary
— — — International Boundary
———— Roads
• Town

WATER POINTS:
A Kilonyeti Wells
B Kiboko River

VULNERABILITY, IMPACTS, AND COPING • 261

Figure 15.2 Range quality in southeastern Kajiado District. Lower figure shows area covered in rangeland survey (dashed line) and survey units. Data are based on NOAA/AVHRR imagery for early January 1984.

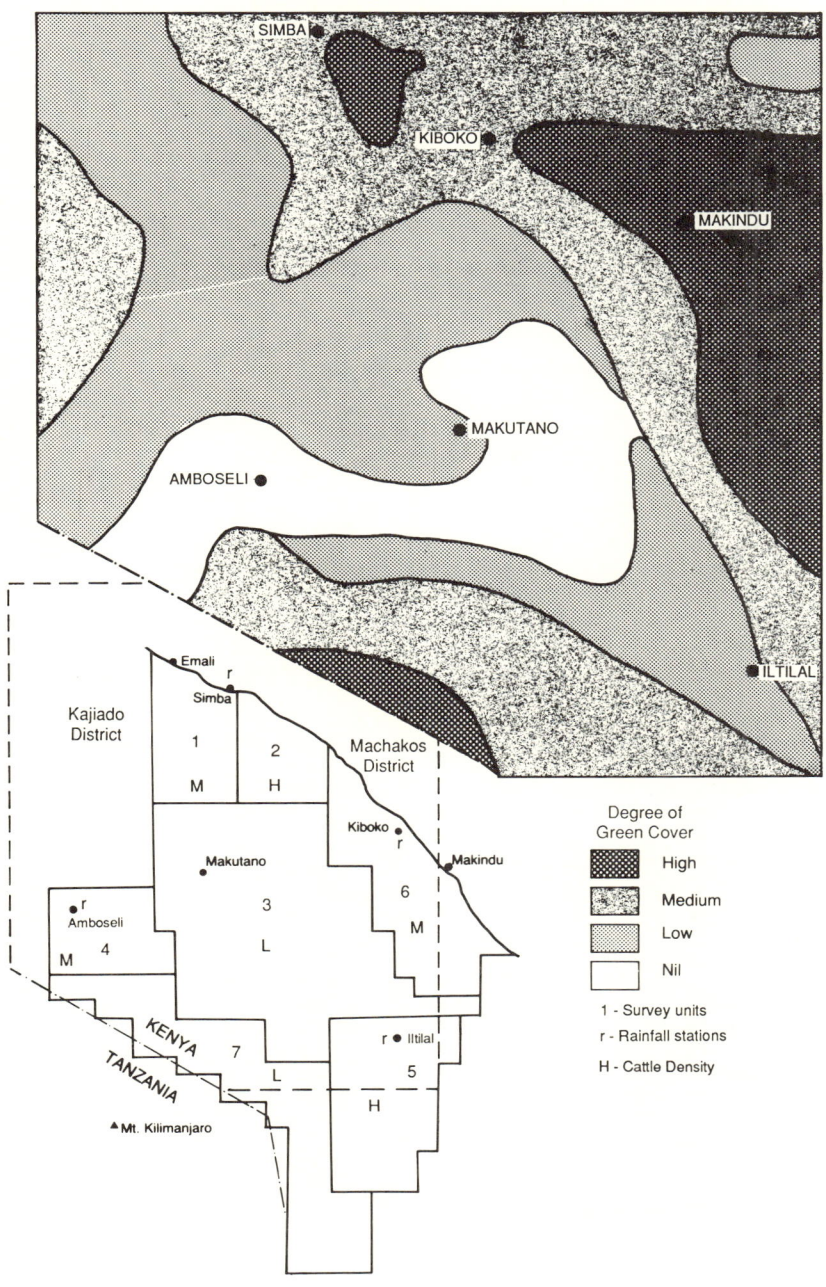

Table 15.1 Characteristics of Olkarkar and Mbirikani Group Ranches

	Olkarkar	Mbirikani
Year registered	1970	1981
Subtribe	Kaputiei	Kisongo
Size (ha)	10,200	135,000
No. households resident	40	200
Average annual rainfall (mm)	600	300–600
No. cattle (1981)	4,000	37,000
No. smallstock (1981)	4,000	22,000
Mobility/management	semisedentary	seminomadic
Households in joint residence (1983)	2	3.5
Herd splitting	rare	common in dry season

Notes: Cattle and livestock data are from census conducted by the International Livestock Centre for Africa (ILCA) in 1981.

Table 15.2 Seasonal Rainfall in Southeastern Kajiado, 1981–1984

Rainfall Stations	Simba	Kiboko	Amboseli	Iltilal
Nov/Dec 1981	200	160	70	90
April/May 1982	300	160	90	210
Total	500	320	160	300
Nov/Dec 1982	380	515	200	370
April/May 1983	240	110	200	110
Total	620	625	400	480
Nov/Dec 1983	340	175	120	170
April/May 1984	70	65	0?	80
Total	410	240	120	250

Source: Data from the Kenya Meteorological Department and Kiboko National Range Research Station.
Notes: Rainfall stations are marked on Figure 15.2. The zero rainfall amount for Amboseli in April to May 1984 is doubtful.

Table 15.3 Distribution of Cattle in Late September 1984

Units	Area (sq km)	Number (1,000)	Density (per sq km)
1. Poka-Olkarkar-Merueshi	575	15.0	26
2. Kiboko-N. Chyulu	450	22.8	51
3. Kisongo Ranches	2,625	17.4	7
4. Amboseli	550	17.3	31
5. Tsavo South	1,000	40.5	40
6. Makindu-Kibwezi-Tsavo N.	1,175	29.9	25
7. Kilimanjaro foothill-Taveta	1,375	20.7	15
Total	7,750	163.6	21

Note: Survey units are marked on Figure 15.2.

Table 15.4 Annual Livestock Inventory Change, 1981–1983

Livestock	Olkarkar			Mbirikani		
	Poor	Average	Rich	Poor	Average	Rich
Cattle						
Mean holding 1981	29	62	272	37	120	240
Inventory change (%)	+20	+13	+17	−2	−8	−5
Households with net loss (%)	0	10	0	75	100	66
Smallstock						
Mean holding 1981	51	132	232	53	106	108
Inventory change (%)	+5	+14	+19	−18	+8	+1
Households with net loss (%)	33	30	13	88	40	50

Source: Adapted from Grandin (1984). See also Grandin and Bekure (1982).
Notes: See text for definition of poor, average, and rich households. Mean holding is number of stock in June 1981. Inventory change are percent per year between June 1981 and May 1983. The increase in cattle by poor households in Olkarkar is largely due to gifts received.

Table 15.5 Livestock Inventory Change During Drought in Olkarkar Group Ranch

Livestock	Poor	Average	Rich
Cattle			
Inventory change (%)	−72	−17	−42
Households with net loss (%)	100	80	100
Smallstock			
Inventory change (%)	−23	−12	−22
Households with net loss (%)	100	60	75

Note: Period of censuses is May 1983 to January 1985.

· 16 ·
Food Acquisition by the Samburu Herders During the Drought of 1983/84

LOUISE SPERLING

In 1983 and 1984, drought spread across the northern rangelands of Kenya, and herders in lowland Samburu lost substantial portions of their livestock. Food aid arrived when 50 to 75 percent of the cattle had already died, and after poorer pastoralists were hungry enough to sell their remaining productive animals. No pastoralists died of the immediate effects of the drought, but many were so pauperized that their longer-term prospects for remaining herders look dim.

This chapter describes the difficulties of the Samburu in obtaining food during the drought itself. The more indigenous food strategies of herding, hunting, and gathering offered limited benefits. Equally, however, commercial channels for procuring food proved inadequate: animals often could not be sold, and grain and sugar staples were not always available, even when cash was on hand. Lacking means to provide for themselves, the Samburu came to depend on varied kinds of handouts.

THE SETTING

The Samburu are Maa-speaking, seminomadic pastoralists, who number about 67,000 (Ministry of Finance and Planning 1984a). They predominantly tend cattle, sheep, and goats, keeping donkeys for transport; some of the wealthier stock owners are also starting to adopt small numbers of camels (Sperling 1987a). Agriculture is practiced to a limited extent, largely by non-Samburu; fishing is nonexistent. The Samburu domain (roughly corresponding to Samburu District) is characteristic of many of the areas currently used by pastoralists. Dwarf shrub and bushed and wooded grassland are the predominant vegetation; soils are generally poor and volcanic; rainfall is erratic, highly localized, and unpredictable. While there are pockets of forest and evergreen bushland, 84 percent of Samburu District has been classified as low potential, indicating that it is primarily suitable for pastoralism (Ministry of Finance and Planning 1984a). This particular research was conducted in Wamba Division, a lowland area, where all land falls into the low-potential category (Figure 16.1).

Until the early 1960s, the Samburu were among the more successful and more specialized pastoralists in East Africa. They had been an important supplier of immature cattle to the Kenyan market (Perlov 1981) and had a consistently high cattle-to-people ratio of at least 8:1. In the last three decades, however, a series of crises have depleted the herds of all and left many families completely stockless. In 1980, government estimates suggested that 50 percent of the population was below the poverty line, with 10 percent being virtually destitute (Ministry of Economic Planning and Development 1980). The 1984 aggregate numbers of cattle (about 120,000) are similar to those of the late 1910s, despite a sixfold increase in human population; per capita cattle holdings have fallen to less than two (Table 16.1).

The recent economic decline of the Samburu can be traced to several sources. The widespread raiding conducted between 1964 and 1980, attributed to *shifta* (bandits) and *ngoroko* (cattle rustlers), resulted in losses of men and livestock. Foot and mouth disease in 1970 and 1976 and East Coast fever (starting in 1976) have swept through cattle herds. Other major misfortunes can be attributed directly to drought. In the last thirty years, there have been five droughts: 1960, 1965, 1971, 1980, and 1984. The Samburu recognize that droughts seem to be increasing in frequency and in the intensity of their effects. For the period 1900–1960, only two other droughts have been recorded: one in 1928 and one in 1944 (Fumagalli 1977). While there is little firm evidence of long-term change in rainfall patterns, the Samburu now must restrict their use of about 55 percent of the grazing land marked as officially theirs in 1947. Some land has been permanently lost to forest and wildlife reserves, town centers, and farming areas. Other land can be grazed only at great risk, due to banditry, raiding, and exposure to East Coast fever (Sperling 1987c).

Meanwhile, the human population has grown steadily, and overall livestock numbers have remained sufficiently high to put pressure on a dwindling resource base. Loss of land and intensified use of remaining tracts may be magnifying the effects of low-rainfall years to the levels of hardship usually associated with drought. Although drought is associated with a lack of rainfall, it must be linked to spatial and temporal parameters (Sandford 1979). Drought is not equated with a lack of rainfall per se, but rather the degree of rainfall that induces a shortage of some vital economic good (forage, for example).

The following discussion is based on research from April 1983 to November 1984, during which three sequential wet seasons fell far short of expected rainfall. The severity of the drought is evidenced in declining livestock holdings. For a sample of forty-six herd owners, livestock holdings decreased by 70 percent for cattle, 32 percent for smallstock (when, under average conditions, they would have *increased* about 30 percent [Dahl and Hjort 1976]), and 53 percent for donkeys. The 1984 drought followed on the heels of the 1980 drought, when herders in the lowland study area lost 50 to 75 percent of their cattle (Wamba Veterinary Department 1980, author's field notes).

FOOD PROCUREMENT DURING THE DROUGHT OF 1984

Like many other pastoral groups, the Samburu have three principal means of obtaining food. They can procure it directly through their herds, either with renewable products, such as milk and blood, or terminal products, such as meat. They can also forage, hunt wild game, or gather a variety of plant foods, or pastoralists may trade for, purchase, or even grow agricultural produce. Their relative dependence on these three sources of food changes seasonally, varying according to animal wealth, herd and flock demography, management practices, and dietary preferences. Figure 16.2 broadly suggests the degree to which Samburu rely on these three food sources during a wet season, dry season, and drought.

Several trends are worthy of note. For the wealthy herders (those possessing sixty or more Tropical Livestock Units, or TLU), livestock products supply a major portion of the diet in the wet season and a significant share in the dry. Their dependence on purchased foods, especially grain, varies markedly by season. The same can be said of herd owners with medium-sized holdings (twenty-six to fifty TLUs), but to a lesser degree; livestock products contribute greatly to their wet season diet, but purchased food (primarily grain) is of prime importance in the dry season. For the poorer Samburu (those with twenty-five or less TLUs), livestock products are a relatively small part of the diet all year long. Their dependence on purchased foodstuffs is substantial and constant. During a drought, however, all stock owners depend on purchased foodstuffs to meet the bulk of their dietary needs. Livestock products are limited, and direct access to livestock may be restricted when animals, particularly cattle, are led to far-off grazing camps.

Herders regard the three major sources of food as complementary, and shortages of one are to be compensated for by greater consumption of the others. During the 1984 drought, however, all three food sources were in scarce supply. This discussion focuses on the time after the third consecutive failure of a main rainy season, in May 1984, until the end of the drought in November 1984—a period of six months. Dry-season conditions were accentuated sufficiently to qualify as a drought episode.

Livestock Products

For the majority of the Samburu population, cattle provided food (particularly milk) only during the first month of the drought (that is, until June 1984), and quantities produced fell far below consumption needs. Herders generally retained only one or two animals (if any at all) at home settlements after May 1984. Milk measurements show that each animal was producing between 300 and 600 ml a day, enough to feed a small child for one or two meals and less than half the adult requirement for a single meal.

The larger livestock were sent to grazing camps 50 to 100 km from the main homestead for most of the critical period. Manning these outlying grazing camps, warriors potentially had access to milk, but women, young children, and elders were deprived of cattle products for at least five months preceding the rains.

It is not clear to what degree those engaged in tending cattle were able to consume animal products. The pattern of cattle mortality was uneven, and the most productive animals died first (that is, milking cows, sucking calves, and pregnant cows succumbed the most easily). Over 90 percent of the calves born during the drought soon died. Further, what little milk was produced was generally not saved for human consumption. In this time of stress, the Samburu fed most milk to calves (both the older *botor* and younger *lelerie*), as neither had alternate sources of food. After the failure of the third set of rains, cattle also became too weak to be bled for food, serving as a source of sustenance only after they died. While some herders may have eaten the meat of recently deceased cattle, many deemed the thin, fatless flesh (*sasin*) nauseating and unhealthy. Moreover, herders often lacked time to butcher the carcass when trekking the remaining animals to better pasture.

The first cluster of deaths occurred from June to mid-July 1984, when lowland animals were trekked long distances to highland areas in search of water and grass. The Samburu attribute the second cluster of deaths (from mid-July to October) to contact with East Coast fever in the more elevated areas. Remarkably, the proportions of cattle loss were comparable across all herd owners in the sample (46). That is, the wealthier herd owners did not lose proportionally less than did the poor.[1]

---

1. The regression of cattle holdings by family in 1984 with holdings in 1983 supports this conclusion:

$$\log_e Y = 1.088 \log_e X - 1.805$$
$$(t = 8.15 \; p < .001)$$

The slope does not differ significantly from 1, indicating that the proportional losses did not vary with the initial size of holdings. A more complete analysis of trends in Samburu livestock holdings during periods of drought and recovery is in preparation (Sperling and Loevinsohn). Double-logarithmic regressions are widely employed in analogous contexts in population ecology (see Southwood 1978).

Goats generally did not die directly of starvation during the drought. Two months before the onset of the rains, they were afflicted by several ailments and what herders say was a high rate of miscarriage. The Samburu consider hunger as the primary cause of smallstock death in only 14 percent of the cases recorded during the six-month period, although it was probably a complicating factor in many more. Ticks, severe worm infestation, and enterotoxemia were seen as the direct killers.

Overall, goats proved to be more reliable than cows as a source of drought food because of their spatial distribution and productive capacity. Except for a brief period in September 1984, they remained around home settlements. Goats produced milk for about two-thirds of the drought period, although quantities fluctuated greatly. In contrast, sheep produced so little milk that all of it was given to the lambs. Households with average herds (thirty to eighty goats) had access to about 0.5 to 1 litre of goat milk a day. Toward the end, quantities generally fell below the 0.5 litre mark. Such an amount of milk provides enough to lighten the tea of the smallest children, but it is an insignificant part of the caloric diet of a household. The poorest herders generally sold what little milk they had in order to buy grain. One glass of goat milk may feed one small child for one meal but, if exchanged for grain, it can feed the equivalent of 1 to 1.5 adults.

Goats were rarely slaughtered for meat. Very poor pastoralists did slaughter them when they had nothing else to eat; in such circumstances, the weaker animals were butchered first so as to save others for sale. A single goat carcass can make a stew last two or three days. The wealthier generally slaughtered to provide additional food for select individuals (for example, visitors, pregnant women, the sick, or warriors). Only the wealthy could afford to butcher an occasional sheep, whose fat is said to have unusual curing and fortifying properties. Within a subsample of thirteen households (of varying wealth), only 40 smallstock were slaughtered in total during the entire critical period, an average of less than 0.5 animals per household per month.

Additionally, some herders were willing to bleed their goats. The period of bleeding was short and coincided with an unusually healthy period for goats (mid-April to May 1984), due to the presence of *acacia* pods, which are used for forage. A goat can be bled about once every two to three weeks; depending on the goat's size, half a litre to one litre of blood can be taken at each session. However, many Samburu chose not to bleed their goats at all either because they feared weakening their animals at a precarious time or because they were inexperienced bleeders.

An analysis of smallstock decline shows that the wealthier stock owners lost more than those with initially smaller holdings. Further, records from the field subsample suggest that the cause of loss varied. The wealthy stock owners lost clusters of goats in localized epizootics, while declines among poorer herders were generally due to sales and consumption—transactions that register as losses of one or two animals at a time.[2]

Thus, Samburu procured relatively little food directly from their animals during the drought, with goats, not cows, carrying this burden of food provision. In terms of direct consumption of animal products, the wealthy did only marginally better than those less well-off.

Foraged Foods

Foraging (gathering and hunting) is cited here as a food strategy during the drought more in recognition of its former than due to its current importance. Plant foods have been used to supplement the Samburu diet in the dry, wet, and transitional (wet to dry) seasons. Before about 1940, the *acacia* pod was an important dry-season staple; it was consumed directly, or boiled and pressed. Shortly after the end of the rains, a spate of fruits and leaves were consumed (for example, *Grewia villosa, Cordia ovalis, Acalypha fruiticosa.*) Even during the rains, roots were gathered (such as *Commiphora sp.*) and leaves (*Cyphostemma maranguense*) boiled in order to help balance the dairy diet.

Gathering, however, has been on the wane in Samburu for several decades and in all seasons. The Samburu have lost access to some of their more extensive plant reserves, and plants that they once consumed, especially the *acacia* pods, are now vital for their cattle and goats. Herders also have some means to buy alternate foodstuffs, such as maize meal, and these have substituted for gathered plants. As a result, the younger generation of Samburu has lost the knowledge, as well as taste for, a wide range of potentially edible plants.

During the drought, gathering provided supplemental food for one-and-a-half months in at least one geographic area of Samburu territory (east of the Matthews Range at Sunya), and gathered fruits were also sold in one or two local trading centers (for example, at Archer's Post). It was primarily the elderly who retained the knowledge of where to obtain and how to prepare fruits, tubers, and leaves.

Hunting is more within the current technical repertoire of Samburu. It is also more socially acceptable than gathering, as killing a beast attests to a man's masculinity, bravery, and cunning. Warriors in grazing camps do most of the hunting, with buffalo and giraffe being favorite prey. Older men might spear or trap medium-sized animals that water near home settlements, such as

---

2. As with cattle, the regression of smallstock holdings by family in 1984 with those in 1983 results in:

$$\log_e Y = 0.754 \log_e X - 0.563$$
$$(t = 13.5\ p < .001)$$

The slope is significantly less than 1, indicating that those with initially large holdings suffered disproportionately greater losses through the drought.

antelope, gazelle, or impala. Boys club the smaller animals, such as dik-dik.

During the 1984 drought, many herders did resort to hunting furtively, but at great legal risk; hunting has been banned in Kenya since 1977, and penalties for poaching are severe. In June 1984, a Samburu man was sentenced to three years in jail for shooting a single giraffe. Still, on several occasions, one giraffe carcass was able to feed an entire pastoral settlement for two weeks.

Throughout the critical period, direct food procurement was limited. Domesticated animals gave insufficient amounts of milk and blood, and few were consumed directly. Hunting and gathering offered very restricted options.

Agricultural Products

Herders purchase maize meal, fat, tea, and sugar as staple foods. While the wealthy may also regularly buy maize kernels, beans, and even meat, the poor restrict themselves to essentials. The following discussion of agricultural products will be limited to maize meal, the core drought food, although one should note that sugar was in equal (if not more constant) short supply during the six-month period. The extent to which herders rely on grain has been previously described; the absence of grain leads to a critical food situation. Grain refers to a coarse maize meal that sells for Ksh 3/kg ($0.22). Few herders buy a higher grade of maize meal that sells for Ksh 4/kg ($0.30). In the dry season, a family of six may purchase 10 to 15 kg of grain per week, perhaps 60 percent of its calories, but, in a drought, purchases may rise to 15 to 20 kg, representing 80 percent of the calories consumed. During much of the drought, Samburu herders were unable to purchase maize meal since households had to obtain cash and locate a grain supply. Both stages proved difficult.

Obtaining cash. Samburu living in pastoral settlements generally obtain cash from sales of live animals (usually goats, but sometimes cattle). They receive small amounts from selling sheep and goat skins (Ksh 3 to 8). The poorest will sell milk (Ksh 1/cup) or firewood (Ksh 1/3 pieces, Ksh 3/bundle) in order to buy grain to satisfy immediate needs. As cattle die during a drought, hides also become a source of income. Some Samburu work as wage laborers, either regularly or in times of food stress. In the mid-1950s, adult men started to work on a limited basis; since the 1980 and 1984 droughts, warriors have sought wage work in large numbers (Sperling 1987b).

For the majority of herders, the sale of livestock provided their most constant income during the drought; those who had to rely exclusively on local markets (mainly the poor) were the most afflicted. Cash proved difficult to obtain because the local goat market could not absorb the supply, and prices tumbled. A local cattle market never really existed, and prices received for hides fell sharply.

Even in the best of times, the marketing of animals in lowland Samburu is a haphazard affair. There is little physical infrastructure, no price controls, and no marketing schedule to facilitate congregations of buyers and sellers. When cash needs arise, herders from pastoral settlements (up to 40 km away) trek their animals into local centers, one by one. They station themselves in a known open-sales yard and wait for a buyer, sometimes waiting for several days. The seller is at a disadvantage since he usually needs to make a sale and, with the passing of time, his merchandise gets weaker. While the prices are not formally regulated, local ken has a range of acceptable values for each category of animal according to age, sex, health, reproductive history, and other factors. Prices show marked seasonal variations; wet season prices are higher because animals may be healthier and the seller's need to make a sale is not as pressing.

It was difficult and not lucrative to sell goats during the drought, although the animals remained healthy and fat until the last few months. The livestock market was flooded as herd owners offered a constant stream of goats for sale. Local butchers could not absorb the supply, nor could those traders transporting smallstock out of the region. Government administrative reports indicate that during the critical period, average monthly legal sales in Wamba town totaled only 203 head of smallstock, with another 227 head being transported out of the division for sale or slaughter (Wamba Veterinary Department 1984). The magnitude of these figures is no different from smallstock sales during a plentiful wet season when herder cash needs are presumably lower.

The price received for goats also plummeted. The Samburu were selling goats prolifically, but so was a neighboring group, the Rendille, who came to make use of the already limited Samburu markets and who were also willing to sell more cheaply than the Samburu. Table 16.2 summarizes the goat prices for the animals most frequently put up for sale: a young uncastrated male goat (*loro kiti*) and a young female goat (*sipen*). The Samburu sold goats for about 50 percent of their dry-season value, while Rendille smallstock went for 20 to 35 percent of the local dry-season rate. During a normal dry season, the average Samburu can sell a goat and meet dry-season family expenses for about two weeks. During the drought, however, proceeds from a goat sale could only meet dry-season family expenses for about three days (Rendille price) to five days (Samburu price), as prices were down and maize meal consumption was up.

Several factors caused these terms of trade to disproportionately affect the poorer herders. First, they were the segment most directly tied to the goat market for cash. Few poorer herders were given the shop credit that was extended to the wealthy. Further, the poor did not have the capital to engage in entrepreneurial enterprise (such as livestock trading), and wage remittances could only partially cover their subsistence expenses. In order to buy food, poor herders usually needed to sell an animal. Many poorer herders sold a goat each week, versus the bimonthly or monthly sales made by the wealthier herders, if they sold any goats at all.

Because the poor had to sell, their bargaining position was a weak one. They were competing with the wealthy, and more importantly, with others like themselves who constantly put goats up for sale. The poorer Samburu did not necessarily receive lower prices than other people, but they had to increase the range of animals they would consider marketing. Only the poor put their valued pregnant or milking animals up for sale, and only the poor were willing to sell prized sheep. Certainly, it was only the very poor who tried to market goat kids, which fetch very little, and for a relatively high labor cost. Thus, those who could least afford to do so were selling more stock, their reproductive stock, and their highly valued male stock.

There is no formal local market for cattle. Butchers may buy ten to twenty head a month; among themselves, herders may occasionally barter or sell older male calves for female animals. Most of the cattle that is sold is bought by intermediary traders, who then take animals to larger regional centers (such as Isiolo or Nanyuki) or to the distant markets of Nairobi. Traders often take animals on credit, and the herder may wait six months or longer before receiving even a partial payment.

Cattle lost health relatively quickly during the drought. They were trekked off to distant grazing camps by the time herders realized that the cattle had to be sold, and that long trek back would have killed many. In the first half of 1984, a German development team (GTZ) helped to truck some cattle to Nairobi. The numbers transported, however, were minimal, and the more privileged herders made the greatest use of this service.

Theoretically, herders can procure a relatively large amount of money from the sale of hides. Returns are determined by weight and price. While a calf skin weighs 1 to 2 kg, cow and small steer hides range from 4 to 9 kg, with the bigger male animal hides weighing up to 10 kg. During most of the drought, prices remained around Ksh 12/kg in the lowland center of Wamba.

In practice, however, it proved difficult to retrieve money from hides. Many cattle died in the process of migration. Since it takes an hour or longer to skin an animal, the delay was a luxury few could afford. Further, hides are heavy, and the weakened remaining animals could not transport the extra weight on their backs. Some warriors waited until the end of the drought to cash in accumulated hides at once. However, in mid-October 1984, prices in lowland Samburu dropped from Ksh 12 to 5/kg within a day or two; local traders reported that the international hide market had fallen.

In general, during the drought period, Samburu herders had difficulty getting the money needed to buy food. Many had the resources (goats, cattle, and hides), but could not easily convert them into cash. The poor, in particular, had greater difficulty selling their goats and cattle. Those who did succeed in obtaining cash then had to face the challenge of finding maize meal for sale.

Buying Grain

From October 1983 through October 1984 (the period after the failure of second rains to the end of the drought), the supply of grain was monitored in the major center of lowland Samburu. Wamba (population of about 2,600) provides shopping facilities for an area with about a 40-km radius, an estimated 8,000 persons. During this period, maize meal could not be purchased in Wamba on ninety-seven days (sometimes for two or three weeks at a stretch), or, in an absolute sense, 25 percent of the time. Practically, for most herders, however, the absence was a more extended one. As soon as lorries were unloaded, grain would be purchased by the resident town population or hoarded by wealthier herders having accounts with specific shopkeepers and who could afford an entire 90 kg bag. Herders in pastoral settlements often received news of grain shipments only after supplies were depleted. At a conservative estimate, they could not buy grain 40 percent of the time. The extent of the shortage becomes even more apparent if one looks at the critical period after the failure of the third rains, from May through October 1984. For this half year, grain could not be purchased in Wamba 45 percent of the time in absolute terms and, practically, for the herder, over 60 percent of the time.

Although there was a shortage of grain nationwide during the latter part of this period, much of the earlier dearth in lowland Samburu was related to distribution problems. One could find basic commodities 100 km away (a walk of four days) in the district capital of Maralal, when they had already been absent in Wamba for periods of three weeks or more. As early as mid-June 1984, the district commissioner called together the eleven or twelve wholesalers to discuss "the erratic supply of commodities." Maize prices are strictly controlled by the state, and the local traders claimed they were losing money on maize sales. The allowed markup did not cover the costs of transport and loading to more remote areas. Even considerable government pressure to encourage traders to keep their shelves full did not result in an increase in the local availability of maize.

Again, the poor disproportionately suffered from these shortages. They could not afford to buy grain in bulk when it did arrive. Equally, they did not have the means to purchase alternative, more costly foodstuffs.

Outside Aid

For many Samburu, the above-mentioned means of obtaining food during the drought were insufficiently reliable to meet daily food needs. To augment their food supply, they became clients of outside agents. Sometimes herders enrolled in two or three different programs simultaneously. Several are briefly described below; the list is not exhaustive.

The most extensive source of immediate aid came from the German development team working in the lowland area of Samburu. Having arrived in Wamba Division in 1982, the team was well ensconced in the region long before the drought hit full force. By October 1984, when the rains arrived, the Germans had one thousand local people on their payroll who were involved in a variety of food-for-work projects, such as planting trees and digging shallow pans. Were their employees distributed throughout Wamba Division, one out of every three families would have had a member directly getting food for work. In practice, a greater percentage of employed family members lived in the vicinity of Wamba Town. The German team was largely responsible for what marketing and grain supplies did exist in lowland Samburu.

The local Catholic mission extended its aid beyond its normal charitable giving through programs to feed the elderly and providing supplemental food to underweight infants. The mission also purchased firewood far in excess of its immediate fuel needs.

The schools continued providing maize and beans lunches to pupils. During the drought, some children ate little beyond these single meals.

For two weeks, the World Food Programme exchanged weak and emaciated cattle directly for maize flour at a rate of 45 kg maize meal per carcass (the equivalent of Ksh 135, or about a tenth of the dry-season value of a smallish ox). A total of 266 cattle were slaughtered. Beginning in mid-July 1984, the German development team also exchanged hides for ground maize at a rate of 45 kg maize meal for a large hide and 15 kg for a small hide.

SUMMARY AND DISCUSSION

This chapter has described food procurement strategies of Samburu herders during the drought of 1984. They had difficulty obtaining food directly from livestock, while hunting and gathering, formerly important alternatives, are today limited. Equally, however, commercial avenues of food procurement proved inadequate. Insufficient marketing facilities made it difficult for herders to sell goats, cattle, and hides in order to obtain cash. Further, the basic maize meal staple could not be reliably purchased in these remote areas. With limited cash-generating possibilities and tight budgets, the poor were disproportionately affected.

Several observations emerge from this description. First, many herders had the potential to sustain themselves for extended periods, since they had goats to offer for sale, and all knew where and how to purchase foodstuffs. Second, food channels that function at acceptable levels in normal times lacked the capacity to withstand stress situations. In Samburu, goat markets and retail maize meal trade were two such channels. Some of the means of alleviating food stress in Samburu (both during a drought and more generally) lie in modifying these food channels; reforms in price structure, livestock marketing, and grain distribution are fundamental to shoring up food supplies.

However, short-term, more crisis-specific means of alleviating food shortages in Samburu were also only partially effective. Famine relief (maize, beans, and powdered milk) arrived in Samburu at the very end of the drought, just as the rains of November 1984 started to fall. It arrived at a time when there was little food from any other source and when the productive capacity of many to sustain themselves (or to recuperate swiftly) had been severely compromised. Many cattle were dead, goats were in ill health, and, among the poor, reproductive and prized animals had been sold. Famine relief was given when the least vulnerable and most vocal segment of the population—the wealthier group—was experiencing food shortages. Food stress for the poor had reached critical levels some four to five months earlier.

The recent literature on famine relief is replete with references to famine early warning systems. Governments, scientists, and aid organizations (among others) are concerned with detecting potentially severe food deficits before they reach damaging levels. The Samburu case can be used to illustrate several points on the general themes of famine relief and early famine indicators.

Famine Relief

Famine relief is almost universally equated with food aid. Some relief efforts have recently been expanded to include a rehabilitation component, with such programs being initiated after the population has endured significant stress. Famine relief is predicated on the assumption that people are hungry because of an absolute shortage of food. However, for many months in Samburu, food was not necessarily scarce, but access to it was blocked. Had famine relief been conceived of as support for existing food channels, herders may have survived the drought with fewer livestock losses, and a wider population may have had access to such aid. Some such institutional support has since been forthcoming, with positive results; in 1985 and 1986, the German development team supplied trucks to allow Samburu to move their animals to better markets. Assuring that maize meal supplies are available should be a second initiative. Many similar cases of failure of food channels, rather than food scarcity per se, can be described for a range of food-stressed areas. Thus, we return to the first point: Famine relief should be more than food aid. Before food transfers take place, local channels for obtaining food should be bolstered.

Early Warning Systems

An early warning system would ideally focus on those segments of the population that are most susceptible to famine. Those most at risk are often the poorer populations, and early warning indicators that differentiate between classes (or take account of differing levels of vulnerability) will be the most sensitive to food stress. To identify impending famine, those institutions or food channels on which the poor rely in times of food stress should be closely monitored. Thus, the second and third points emerge in terms of early warning systems: Rather than solely focus on only people, monitor food channels; rather than sample the whole population, focus on the most vulnerable. In the Samburu case, the availability of grain and the possibility of goat sales for the poorer herders would figure prominently in early warning assessments. One particularly sensitive stress indicator might be the terms of trade between goat sales and grain purchases. Local knowledge and established government policy should be able to determine both the thresholds beyond which aid is needed and potential, practicable relief measures. Such a trade indicator would probably be useful in many other pastoral areas, but other stress measures would need to be formulated for nonherding regions.

The development of stress indicators is a formidable task, not the least because of the particularism it may demand. A growing body of empirical research, however, indicates that failings of food channels, similar to those in Samburu, are encountered elsewhere (see other chapters in this book and, for example, Sen 1981). A clearer understanding of the causes of food shortage should suggest indicators that are more predictive of food stress. Their elaboration could proceed as follows:

1. Identify the means by which populations get food, with a focus on the most vulnerable groups
2. Identify critical levels below which the performance of food channels is considered inadequate
3. Prepare actions to alleviate immediate constraints

Such an approach might make interventions possible before local production capacity has been severely compromised, as well as enable affected peoples to participate actively in sustaining food supplies.

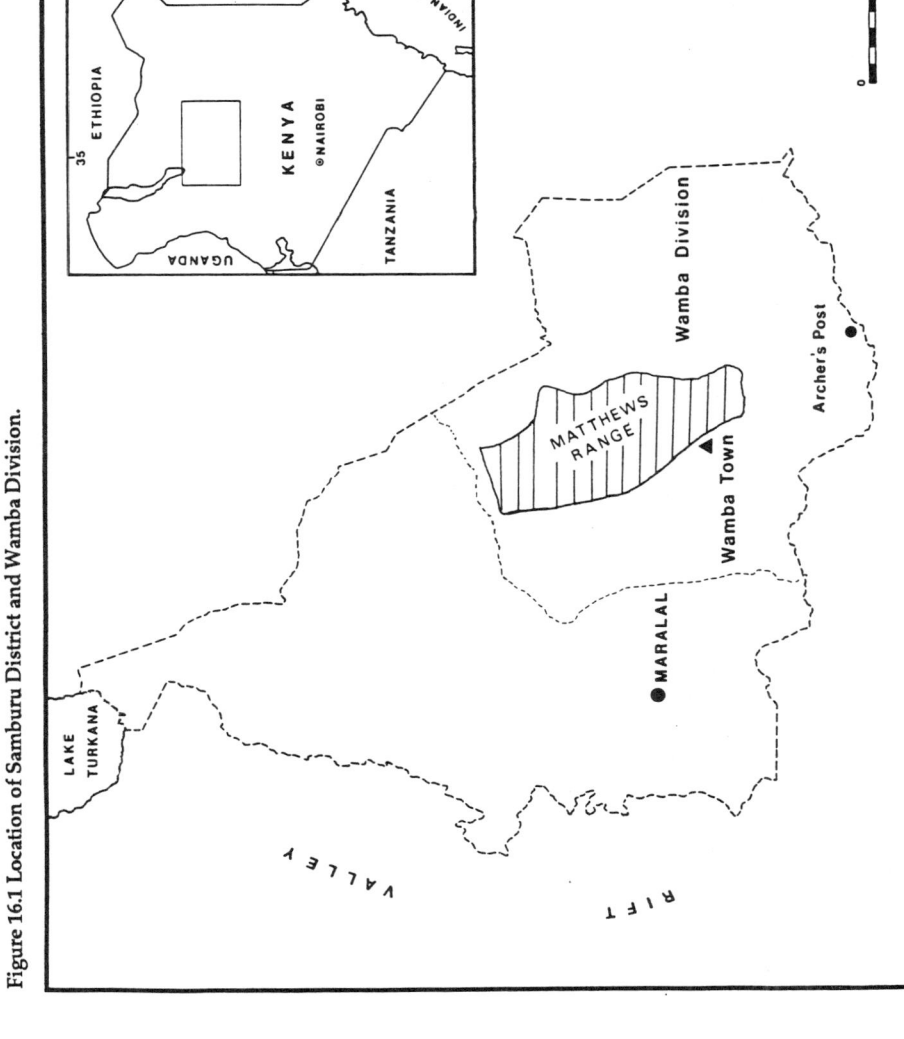

Figure 16.1 Location of Samburu District and Wamba Division.

278 • COPING WITH DROUGHT IN KENYA

Figure 16.2 Samburu food sources by season. The dry season and drought data are preliminary estimates from household budgets and food surveys collected during fourteen months of field work in 1983 and 1984. The estimates of wet-season consumption patterns come from interviews only. For ease of comparison, consumption patterns are not differentiated by age and sex, and a family size of six to seven persons has been used as a referent (two adults, two children under six years, and two or three older offspring, seven to eighteen years). The economic categories (e.g., wealthy) are relative. Tropical Livestock Unit equivalents are: Camel = 1.0, Cow = 0.7, sheep = 0.1, and goat = 0.1.

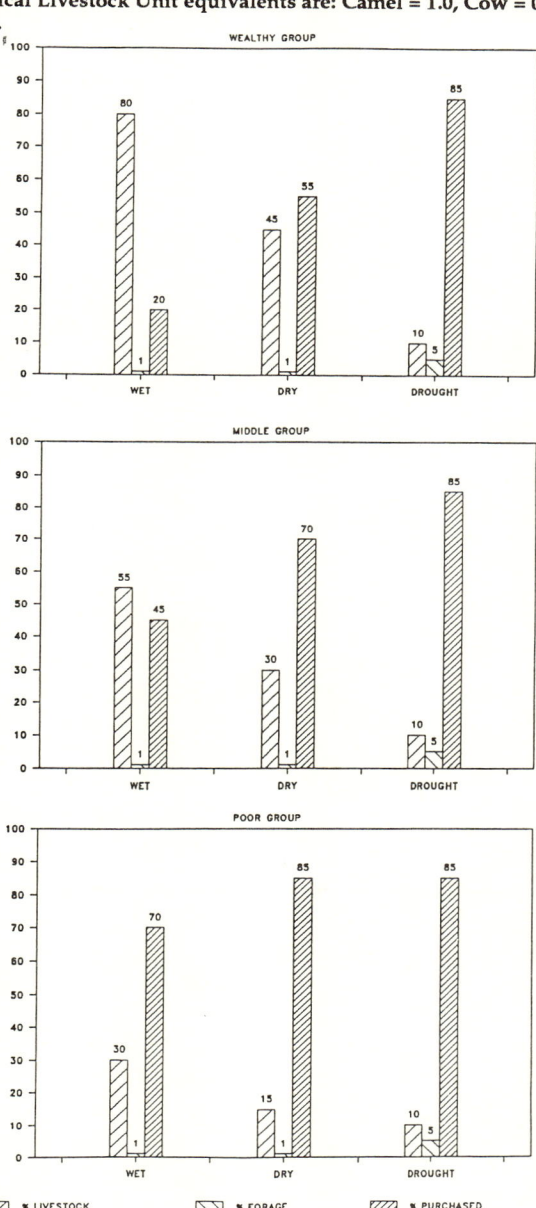

Table 16.1 Human and Cattle Populations in Samburu District, 1915–1984

Year	Human Population			Cattle Population	Cattle per Samburu Person
	Samburu	Others	Total		
1915	5,000	—	—	—	—
1917	10,000	—	—	100,000	10
1922	10,000	—	—	150,000	15
1925	—	—	—	102,569	—
1933	12,000	—	—	119,403	10
1938	18,816	—	—	—	—
1948	18,797	—	—	—	—
1950	—	—	—	253,850	—
1954	35,000	5,000	40,000	300,000	8.6
1955	36,000	—	—	350,000	9.7
1962	43,000	13,935	56,935	320,000	7.4
1969	51,503	18,016	69,519	420,000	8.2
1971	52,320	—	—	300,000	5.7
1977	—	—	—	241,120	—
1978	—	—	—	221,205	—
1979	57,653	19,255	76,908	—	—
1980	—	—	—	127,260	—
1982	—	—	—	109,094	—
1983	65,697	22,160	87,857	158,674	2.4
1984	67,300	—	—	117,483	1.7

Source: For complete references, see Sperling (1987c).
Notes: The tallies of both human and cattle populations are subject to inaccuracies. For instance, human population censuses are only made at pastoral settlements, not at grazing camps, and cattle figures represent only those animals brought to the crushes during vaccination campaigns. Further, the 1977–1983 animal censuses were prematurely halted due to vehicle and fuel shortages. The data have been amassed from census material, population projections, archival correspondence, and official colonial and post-colonial reports.

Table 16.2 Goat Prices at Wamba Town, 1984

Animal Sold	Samburu		Rendille Drought
	Dry Season	Drought	
Male goat	130–180	50–100	30–40
Female goat	120–140	50–70	40–55

Note: Prices in Kenyan shillings, Ksh 13.5 = U.S.$ 1.00.

·PART 4·
Institutional Experiences in Drought Management

Chapter 2 of this book has presented an overview of the national response to the 1984/85 food emergency, while Part 4 provides additional detail, in the form of specific case studies of individual institutions. The contributions are by members of the institutions who are writing in a personal capacity, rather than presenting official evaluations.

During the critical period in mid-1984 and before commercial imports arrived, the World Food Programme (Chapter 17) was instrumental in providing NGOs with food from the NCPB. Credited against future shipments of wheat, the maize enabled many NGOs to begin timely emergency relief programs. The expansion of the School Feeding Programme not only fed people, but it also prevented a more substantial decline in school enrollments (Chapter 19). The provision of transport funds from the U.S. Office of Foreign Disaster Assistance, coordinated by CARE, enabled NGOs to continue and expand emergency relief activities (Chapter 21). The grain-for-livestock exchange demonstrated the potential to support pastoralists' efforts to procure food from their traditional source of wealth, and the restocking projects assisted in the recovery from drought (Chapter 23).

Several issues arose in the drought. The inadequate health-monitoring system has since been expanded and improved to include nutritional assessments (Chapter 18). Agreement was never reached on appropriate rations. Many programs started late due to inadequate preparedness for drought responses (e.g., Chapter 22). While many NGOs distributed seed and other inputs following the drought, the amounts were often inadequate and distribution delayed.

To date, it appears that the emergency was treated as an isolated episode that required extraordinary responses. This is, of course, true. There is a need, however, to evaluate the emergency responses in light of continuing development problems. Questions that require answers include: What impact did the emergency responses have on the community and aid institutions? How many of the emergency projects were finished and are operational? What are the current plans to anticipate food crises and include emergency assistance as part of regular program planning?

In collaboration with national agencies, districts should be able to expand their preparedness. A model plan, currently being implemented in Turkana District, emphasizes using existing district resources and activities as a beginning in a process to expand preparedness, including a set of timely responses that would prevent the worst drought impacts (Chapter 20).

· 17 ·
World Food Programme Emergency Food Aid for Drought Victims in Kenya

WORLD FOOD PROGRAMME

On 19 June 1984, the government of Kenya (GOK) appealed to the international community for 0.9 to 1.1 million metric tons of maize, 126,000 mt of wheat, and 1,400 mt of dried skim milk in the form of concessional imports to cover anticipated production shortfalls resulting from drought conditions. In response to this request and in cooperation with other donors, the World Food Programme[1] (WFP), on 19 August 1984, approved an emergency project allocating 18,000 mt of maize and wheat valued at $3,694,600 (including freight) to Kenya's famine-relief program. The objective of the WFP project (number 1398) was to alleviate human suffering caused by hunger among the drought-affected population. The emergency aid went mainly to Machakos, Kitui, and Meru districts.

The emergency operation aimed to provide a ration of 400 grams of maize per day for 180 days to approximately 250,000 beneficiaries. In total, Kenya received 1,851 mt of maize and 15,133 mt of wheat through the WFP. The maize arrived in September 1984 and the wheat in March 1985 (Table 17.1). A special credit arrangement between the WFP and the National Cereals and Produce Board (NCPB) allowed for the exchange of imported wheat for domestically produced maize and beans. WFP imported wheat and delivered it to the NCPB depot in Mombasa. The wheat was then credited for a specified amount of maize (1 mt wheat = 1.1 mt maize), which could be drawn from local NCPB grain depots for distribution for school and emergency feeding programs and food-for-work projects. The WFP actually distributed maize to destitute people in advance of the wheat's arrival in Kenya. The wheat was sold at normal prices, and the money received went toward a special fund.

---

1. This chapter is based on a report by the World Food Programme, authored by Pascal T. Woldemariam.

DISTRIBUTION OF FOOD AID

The national distribution of food aid was coordinated by the Ministry of Finance and Planning, while day-to-day operations were administered by the Office of the President. Inland transportation of the maize from NCPB depots was covered through other donor assistance and the government's own resources. The NCPB was assigned responsibility for the receipt, storage, management, and interdepot transport of the cereals. Nongovernmental organizations (NGOs) assisted the government in food distribution through ongoing relief programs and food-for-work activities. Approximately 70 percent of the food aid was distributed by NGOs, while the GOK covered the remainder. Methods of distribution varied, yet cooperation and communication between these two channels was of utmost importance to the success of the project.

GOK DISTRIBUTION

The government administered the drought emergency relief program through a steering committee of permanent secretaries and the Task Force on Food Supply and Distribution, which implemented the program. The government emphasized the collection of information directly from the field concerning food availability, as well as the numbers of people in distress and their nutritional requirements. On the basis of this information, the WFP revised the original target population, which had been identified at the initial planning stages, and proceeded to allocate 6,300 mt (70,000 bags) of maize to the Office of the President for distribution in twenty-five locations (Table 17.2). This food was collected from the nearest NCPB depots and distributed by the appropriate district authorities.

The strength of the GOK and WFP coordination was the timeliness of the initial distribution of maize. The project was approved in mid-August 1984, and distribution through the government commenced in October, six weeks later. This proved to be a crucial period, as other major donors were still waiting the arrival of maize from outside Kenya. By January 1985, when large-scale distribution of USAID maize commenced, the WFP allocation of 6,300 mt was almost completely exhausted. Approximately 250,000 people received WFP rations for sixty days during the last quarter of 1984 through this channel.

NGO Distribution

In total, there were twenty NGOs cooperating with the WFP and the government in maize distribution. These ranged from major organizations, such as the World Vision, Kenyan Red Cross, AMREF, Oxfam,

Kenya Freedom from Hunger, CRS, CARE, and church groups, to smaller specialized organizations, such as the Children's Mercy Fund and Materi Girls' Center (Table 17.3). NGOs proved to be effective channels for food distribution because they were able to mobilize their staff quickly to identify food-deficit regions. They also were able to use the increased allocations in ongoing nutrition-intervention projects.

The Kenya National Council of Social Services coordinated the activities of the NGOs to avoid duplication of areas covered and to ensure that no needy area was ignored. Many NGOs that did not normally participate in food distribution altered their emphasis during the peak of the drought. Like the district authorities, the NGOs collected the maize from the closest NCPB depots and transported it in their own or hired transport. This facilitated delivery and eased the burden of transport and storage, which had, up to this point, been mainly the government's responsibility. The effective working relationship between the WFP, NGOs, and the government enabled the distribution of 13,050 mt (145,000 bags) of maize, most of which occurred between November 1984 and February 1985.

NGOs operated somewhat differently than the government in managing food distribution at the field level. Despite the different administrative techniques, personnel and information were shared by NGOs and government agencies. NGO field staff consulted closely with local chiefs, church authorities, and local government administrators in identifying beneficiaries of food aid. These consultations were later formalized as recognized famine-relief committees were established by the government. NGOs distributed food on either a weekly or monthly basis. NGOs reported rations ranging from a low of 133 g/person/day to a high of 500 g/person/day. Most NGOs combined food assistance with other activities, such as the establishment or maintenance of clinics and distribution of medicine (50 percent of the NGOs) and the construction of wells and water-transport networks (25 percent). Half of the NGOs distributed food through food-for-work activities, a departure from the more traditional food handouts. The achievements of food-for-work programs are notable: 3,173 workers built 264 km of roads; 1,173 workers planted 231,860 trees; 14,014 workers participated in soil-conservation activities; 6,913 worked on churches; 1,324 workers dug thirty-six wells; and 4,254 workers were involved in water harvesting, latrine building, or similar community projects. In addition to food for work, Oxfam and the Catholic mission in Marsabit were involved in a destocking program aimed at exchanging food with nomadic groups for goats and cattle (see Chapter 23). This program provided a market for dying animals and gave stock owners a dignified option for obtaining badly needed food for their families.

CONCLUSION

Through this emergency project, the government of Kenya and the WFP contributed significantly to alleviating malnutrition and starvation in the drought-affected areas of Kenya. Cooperation between the government, WFP, and NGOs led to the timely and efficient distribution of 22,590 mt (215,000 bags) of maize to over two million Kenyans during the critical drought period of 1984/85. About half of the food was distributed through food-for-work activities or exchanged for stock. The effective cooperation between all agencies involved in food distribution resulted in a well-organized and innovative famine-relief project. The World Food Programme played an important coordinating role throughout the emergency period. Valuable experience was gained in planning and implementing food aid programs during the 1984/85 drought. The government fully intends to capitalize on this experience to expand its preparedness for future droughts.

Table 17.1 World Food Programme Shipments and Distribution of Food Aid

Vessel	Bill of Lading	Landed	Arrival
Maize			
Dias	2,485.0	1,850.7	7/11/84
Wheat			
Pac City	10,986.0	10,886.0	31/3/85
Pac City	2,158.0	2,065.2	31/3/85
Coronia	2,181.8	2,181.8	5/3/85
Total	15,325.8	15,133.0	

Notes: Figures in mt. Landed weights are the nominal shipment less losses in transport. The landed wheat, 15,133 mt, plus 793 mt from a project extension, was converted to maize at a 1:1.1 rate. Thus, 15,926 mt of wheat resulted in a maize credit with the NCPB of 17,518 mt. The maize credit and actual maize shipments (1850.7 mt) totaled 19,369 mt of maize, which was distributed by the GOK (6,300 mt) and NGOs (13,069 mt).

Table 17.2 World Food Programme Emergency Food Assistance Distributed by the GOK

Region	No. of Beneficiaries	Quantity (mt)
Baringo	3,150	90
Meru	26,250	630
Embu	22,250	540
Marsabit	15,000	360
Isiolo	15,000	360
Kitui	45,000	1,080
Machakos	63,150	1,530
Samburu	7,500	180
Narok	3,150	90
W. Pokot	3,150	90
Nyandarua	3,150	90
Nyeri	1,815	45
Kirinyaga	1,875	45
Kiambu	1,875	45
Taita Taveta	1,875	45
Tana River	7,500	180
Lamu	1,875	45
Garissa	3,750	90
Wajir	7,500	180
Mandera	3,750	90
Laikipia	7,500	180
So. Nyanza	1,875	45
Turkana	7,500	45
Kajiado	7,500	180
Elgeyo Marakwet	1,875	45
Total	264,815	6,300

Notes: Number of beneficiaries is estimated. Quantities were processed in 90 kg bags; the total of 6,300 mt equals 70,000 bags. Period of distribution is mid-November 1984 to mid-January 1985, a total of 60 days.

Table 17.3 World Food Programme Emergency Food Assistance Distributed by NGOs

NGO	Districts	Beneficiaries	Days	Quantity (mt)	Period of Distribution
Materi Girls Center	Meru	16,000	60	180	Dec 84/Jan 85
Karaba Catholic Mission	Embu	4,000	180	135	Nov 84/Apr 85
Nutrition CRSP	Embu	12,800	180	180	Nov 84/Apr 85
CRS	25 districts	99,000	90	900	Nov 84/Jan 85
Children's Mercy Fund	7 districts	41,500	90	90	Dec 84/Feb 85
NCCK	7 districts	37,600	30	90	Dec 84
RC Marsabit	Samburu/ Marsabit	35,000	180 (ongoing)	900	Nov 84/Apr 85
Oxfam	Samburu	3,400	90	439	Dec 84/Apr 85
Kenyan Red Cross	Wajir	114,800	180	381	Nov 84/Apr 85
Freedom from Hunger	7 districts	98,500	180	2,350	Nov 84/Apr 85
Food for the Hungry	15 districts	90,700	180	1,738	Nov 84/Apr 85
RC Isiolo	Isiolo	13,000	180 (ongoing)	135	Nov 84/Apr 85
AMREF	Machakos	40,100	180 (ongoing)	918	Nov 84/Apr 85
World Vision	25 districts	1,295,000	120	3,652	Nov 84/Jan 85
RC W. Pokot	West Pokot	60	180 (ongoing)	16	Nov 84/Dec 85
RC Machakos	Machakos	11,200	60	270	Nov 84/Dec 85
CARE		12,100	60	291	Nov 84/Dec 85
CPK	Embu	11,200	60	270	
Nbi. Lutheran	Kajiado	3,000	30	73	
SDA	Machakos	8,000	60	52	Jan 85/Mar 85
Young Muslims	Garissa	750	30	9	
Total		1,947,650		13,069	

Note: Quantity, 13,069 mt, totals 145,209 bags (90 kg).

· 18 ·

Nutrition and Health Activities of the Ministry of Health

MONICA A. OKOTH
VALERIE S. WAMBANI

Some of the activities of the Ministry of Health in the areas of nutrition and child-growth monitoring are detailed in this chapter. The 1984 drought highlighted that extreme environmental conditions can exacerbate a prevalent situation of malnutrition and declining food production. In Kenya, the evidence indicates that long-term, chronic malnutrition is common, whereas acute wasting affects fewer people. A population that is malnourished, however, is extremely susceptible to acute malnutrition under conditions of environmental stress, such as crop failure. Given this awareness, the Ministry of Health, in cooperation with UNICEF, undertook to increase activities related to monitoring and improving child growth and nutritional health. These activities are administered under the Supplemental Feeding Programs and the Growth Monitoring Program, for which CHANIS (Child Health and Nutrition Information System) is the information-gathering facility.

NUTRITION IN KENYA

Reports from the Central Bureau of Statistics document a slight increase in the prevalence of malnutrition in Kenya between 1977 and 1982 (Table 18.1). An estimated one million households have undernourished children under normal conditions, and are thus susceptible to hunger under extreme conditions, such as during a drought (Wasonga 1985). Within households, the populations at greatest risk of incurring nutritional stress include pregnant and lactating women and young children. Children, in particular, are vulnerable to malnutrition, and are most susceptible to the conditions associated with chronic or acute malnutrition, such as stunted physical growth, wasting, sickness, and morbidity. Malnourished adults and children are thought to be less responsive to stimuli, and hence less likely to learn. They are also less productive in work due to sickness, lethargy, and lack of energy.

Children are in a high-risk population, and their growth patterns must be carefully monitored to discern problems of inadequate nutrition. Stunted growth reflects chronic, long-term malnutrition. It is measured by a height-for-age ratio, where less than 90 percent of the median height for a particular age group represents stunted growth. Height-for-age ratios are unaffected by seasonal fluctuations in food intake. Stunting is the more common form of malnutrition among children in Kenya. Wasting, which indicates acute malnutrition, or short-term, yet severe, food deprivation, is measured through a weight-for-height ratio, where 80 percent of the median weight-for-height is a critical threshold. A third measure of malnutrition is weight-for-age, which can indicate either acute or chronic malnutrition. The 1982 Child Nutrition Survey (Central Bureau of Statistics 1983b) revealed that 24 percent of Kenyan rural children between the ages of three to fifty-nine months exhibited stunted growth (chronic malnutrition), and 3 percent were wasted (acute malnutrition). This survey was conducted before the 1984 drought, when the number undoubtedly increased. The prevalence of malnutrition varies greatly by province and district, being highest in Coast, Nyanza, and Western provinces (Table 18.2).

Under normal climatic conditions malnutrition in Kenya can be attributed to the interaction of a number of causes. Agricultural productivity has been declining in the past years. Coupled with rapid population growth, this results, on average, in less food available per person. Marginalized, rural household producers are most apt to experience declining productivity on their lands. Thus, poverty is linked to low productivity and, in turn, to inadequate nutrition. The resultant vicious circle is difficult to break out of, given poor monetary returns on agricultural products, relative to production inputs, and declining crop yields due to land degradation. Malnutrition can also be attributed to the inadequate provision of basic needs and services, such as clean water, accessible health facilities, housing, and transport.

On a household level, there are several factors thought to affect the nutritional status of family members. These include the quality of household amenities (water supply, sewage disposal, cooking facilities, and type of floor), demographic characteristics of the mother (age, marital status, number of children born and surviving, and educational level), child feeding patterns (infant feeding and weaning practices), and child health immediately preceding and during periods of nutritional stress. The effects of these factors are interactive and complex, yet there seems to be a positive relationship between these elements, along with other socioeconomic indicators, and the nutritional status of children.

Agricultural practices are also directly related to household nutrition. In some cases, the incidence of malnutrition increases when farmers change the types and varieties of crops grown. This may also be true for a shift from food to cash crops, although the evidence is not conclusive in this regard. In many cases, however, farming households that diversify the crop mix and cultivate drought-resistant crops tend to fare better, from a nutritional point of view, than farming households that plant hybrid crops only. Studies conducted in the arid and semiarid regions of Eastern Province show that children from households that grow drought-resistant crops (such as millet, sorghum, and cotton), either alone or in combination with maize, have better nutritional status than children from households that grow maize alone. About 10 percent of the children from the former households were stunted, compared to 21 percent for households growing only maize and beans (Haaga et al., 1986). In the Rift Valley and Western provinces, there is a higher prevalence of chronic child malnutrition in households that have adopted hybrid maize varieties than in households that cultivate traditional local varieties. Local varieties are usually more drought-resistant than "improved" hybrid varieties, although they have lower yields. It is also possible that users of hybrid varieties are not able to adopt the whole technological package that accompanies hybrid seeds, including fertilizers, irrigation, and pesticides, because of insufficient capital or information about their use.

THE SUPPLEMENTARY FEEDING PROGRAM

The 1984 drought led to widespread hunger, particularly in Central and Eastern provinces. It became apparent that government assistance was necessary to address some of the immediate needs of those who had been hardest hit. There were indications that during the few months preceding the short rains harvest in early 1985, there would be a significant decline in the nutritional status of the population, especially children, in those drought-affected areas where the incidence of malnutrition was already relatively high.

In Eastern Province, the Cooperative Research Support Program (CRSP) team in Embu reported a shortage of food and that people were feeding on pawpaws and mangoes (see Chapter 14). Discussions with district health officials confirmed that the health of children was deteriorating.

In November 1984, UNICEF joined its efforts with the district health offices in Embu, Meru, Kitui, and Machakos to initiate a supplementary feeding program for children under five years of age. The government (Office of the President) provided food for general distribution to those affected. A famine-relief fund was also set up to which individuals and communities could donate money or food.

The objectives of the supplementary feeding program were twofold. The immediate task was to prevent a rapid decline in the nutritional status of the most affected children in the drought areas of four districts in Eastern Province during the time between planting and harvesting. The second goal of the program was to prepare district health officials for organizing a supplementary feeding program. This involved familiarization with:

1. Screening techniques to identify malnourished children
2. Planning and implementing a large scale-feeding program
3. Monitoring the recovery of malnourished children

The feeding program was financed by UNICEF. Organization and implementation of the program was in cooperation with government health officials in each district, except in Meru, where the Ministry of Health requested two church hospitals to take responsibility. In the other three districts, the missionary hospitals were integrated into the district program, where they covered areas not catered to by government services. The program was to be an integrated health program executed by the district health-management committee and all health workers involved. Since it is difficult to facilitate planning in a large committee, nutrition officers in each district and UNICEF personnel were given the mandate to organize the program. Target areas were selected from the known incidence of malnutrition in the area. A one-day training for the implementation team was held in all four districts. The feeding program incorporated health education, immunizations, simple treatment, and demonstrations on the use of oral rehydration solution.

Inputs were provided as follows:

1. Office of the President (food, with the district commissioners providing transport for food and personnel)
2. Ministry of Health (personnel and facilities)
3. UNICEF (funds for food and equipment)
4. World Food Programme (oil through UNICEF)
5. Volunteers identified by the local community (water, firewood, and transport to bring children in for screening)

The village chiefs were responsible for informing people about screening days. Children under five were invited to the various feeding sites. Weight-for-height measurements were taken alongside weight-for-age (Table 18.3). Each child was weighed, and the weight plotted on the Road to Health card (Figure 18.1). Children above 80 percent weight-for-age (considered healthy) were discharged, unless the child had underlying clinical disorders. Those below 80 percent weight-for-age were measured for weight-for-height on a color-coded card. Children less than 80 percent weight-for-height (in the red bands) were admitted into the feeding program. Children of 80 to 90 percent weight-for-height (yellow band) required follow-up to recover, were given a premix, and were to be reviewed two weeks later. Children over 90 percent weight-for-height (green) were discharged.

Additional activities at the feeding sites included immunization of children, treating sick children, and transferring referrals to the hospital for admission. Approximately 35,000 children were screened by health officers, and more than 10,000 (28 percent) received food assistance.

Take-home rations were given to last a week (2 kg of the premix). The ration per child per week was:

Maize flour (Unga)	100 g
Dried skimmed milk (DSM)	100 g (1,440 kcal)
Oil	60 ml (later 30 ml)
Sugar	50 g (later 30 g)
Total	310 g (later 260 g)

The cost of the premix averaged Ksh 4.50 per day. The amount of oil was later reduced, as it caused diarrhea in some children, and the amount of sugar was also reduced to make the mixture less sweet.

The majority of the children put on the premix gained 100 to 400 g, but a minority did not gain weight for the first week. Failure to gain weight was partly due to worms or because the premix was being fed to other family members (siblings). This situation warranted further steps in order for the premix treatment to be effective. All children who were suspected of having worms were dewormed on admission. The premix was also given to siblings of children enrolled in the program. As a result, the majority of the children gained 200 to 500 g weekly. Children discharged from the program with satisfactory weight gain were referred to the health units for further monitoring. In addition, home visits were made by nutrition officers.

LESSONS LEARNED

Many lessons were learned from the drought situation during the implementation of the feeding program:

1. Field staff and community members must be educated as to the use of new screening methods, such as the weight-for-height chart.
2. Growth monitoring should be a permanent procedure, with a focus toward the prevention of mild and moderate malnutrition. Nutritional surveillance is necessary as a routine information system on child health and nutrition, which can then be used to monitor the impact of the drought, identify specific locations in need of food aid, and quickly implement feeding programs.
3. Integrated planning is needed to coordinate all efforts of government ministries and NGOs in setting priorities and planning for the management of the program. Interministerial coordination should be strengthened in the areas of food production, storage, and utilization.
4. Community participation is crucial to the success of the program. When communities become more involved in monitoring the nutritional status of their children, the early signs of malnutrition and famine are perceived and responded to sooner. Communities should be involved in choosing feeding sites, determining the needs

and methods to use, and providing available inputs. At the feeding sites, those centers where chiefs and community volunteers were included were the best run. Communication should be improved at all levels through established groups, posters, and extension agent training and teaching sessions.
5. Provision of adequate training and supervision when a new system is being introduced is imperative. Training time should have been doubled to allow all variables to be well covered. Any system of data collection must be designed with the users in mind and should be integrated into the information system of the Ministry of Health. In some areas, problems were encountered with the data sheets in terms of accuracy.
6. Training in the preparation of premixed food and nutrition education is also necessary. Both health workers and parents learned how quickly their children's growth improved through the use of the premix. It would have been advantageous to translate the formula into locally available foods right from the start for parents to continue even after the program ended. Use of local foods is cheaper and can be sustained longer.
7. Communities are very responsive to collective education when there is a common problem. This provided an opportunity to educate more people on health issues, as well as to give them greater access to health services. Many parents were encouraged to take children to clinics as a result of the positive effects of the premix on malnourished children.

The constraints experienced during the implementation of the supplementary feeding program in Eastern Province can be alleviated with careful early planning and coordination between program participants. The main problems encountered were transport, personnel, and training.

Transport is a vital component of the program for the movement of personnel and food to various centers. Delays in getting food from Nairobi to the districts caused the cancellation or rescheduling of screening days. The shortage of personnel led to difficulties in coping with the magnitude of the crowd that turned out on screening and feeding days. Those persons involved in the program worked long hours. In addition, the training session was short, leading to inadequate personnel training.

In all four districts, various types of feeding programs were in operation. Some centers charged a few shillings for services, while others covered small sections of the district and had irregular food distribution. Government programs appear unique in that they unconditionally reach the poor in a large portion of their districts.

CHANIS: THE CHILD HEALTH AND NUTRITION INFORMATION SYSTEM

The Kenya Growth Monitoring Programme is included in the Nutrition Section of the Division of Family Health. The Growth Monitoring Programme (GMP) was initiated in 1985 by the Ministry of Health and UNICEF. The notion of preventative health care, with an emphasis on nutrition, is fundamental to the objectives of the program, which are twofold. First, through the study of and attention to child-growth patterns, the GMP seeks to improve the nutritional status of children. Second, information gathered on the nutritional status of children will be used in designing district and national policy relevant to health and nutrition. The Growth Monitoring Programme trains health officials and community residents in methods of monitoring child growth and interpreting results, and ways to change behavior toward better nutrition.

CHANIS, the Child Health and Nutrition Information System, is the information-gathering and interpretation branch of the GMP. CHANIS can be used as a guide and methodology for collecting and reporting data about children's nutrition in Kenya. Such data alone, however, are incomplete, since only children attending the health facilities are represented. Thus, such information is useful as a supplement to survey data, rather than as a replacement. The information gathered will be used as a database to analyze the Growth Monitoring Programme and to plan future health programs and policies. With a usable database, the Ministry of Health will be better able to prevent severe forms of malnutrition before they occur and also recognize and reduce the moderate forms of malnutrition before they become chronic.

CHANIS has published guidebooks that are used by health personnel. The booklets introduce the child-monitoring and information recording system to health workers, while also providing a means of reporting, consolidating, and interpreting data gathered from health facilities. The data from district headquarters is then sent to the Ministry of Health for statistical interpretation; at which point such information becomes useful for policy recommendations. At this time, however, data collection is inconsistent; it is therefore not suitable for a thorough analysis of the nutritional status of children in Kenya (Werner 1986).

296 • COPING WITH DROUGHT IN KENYA

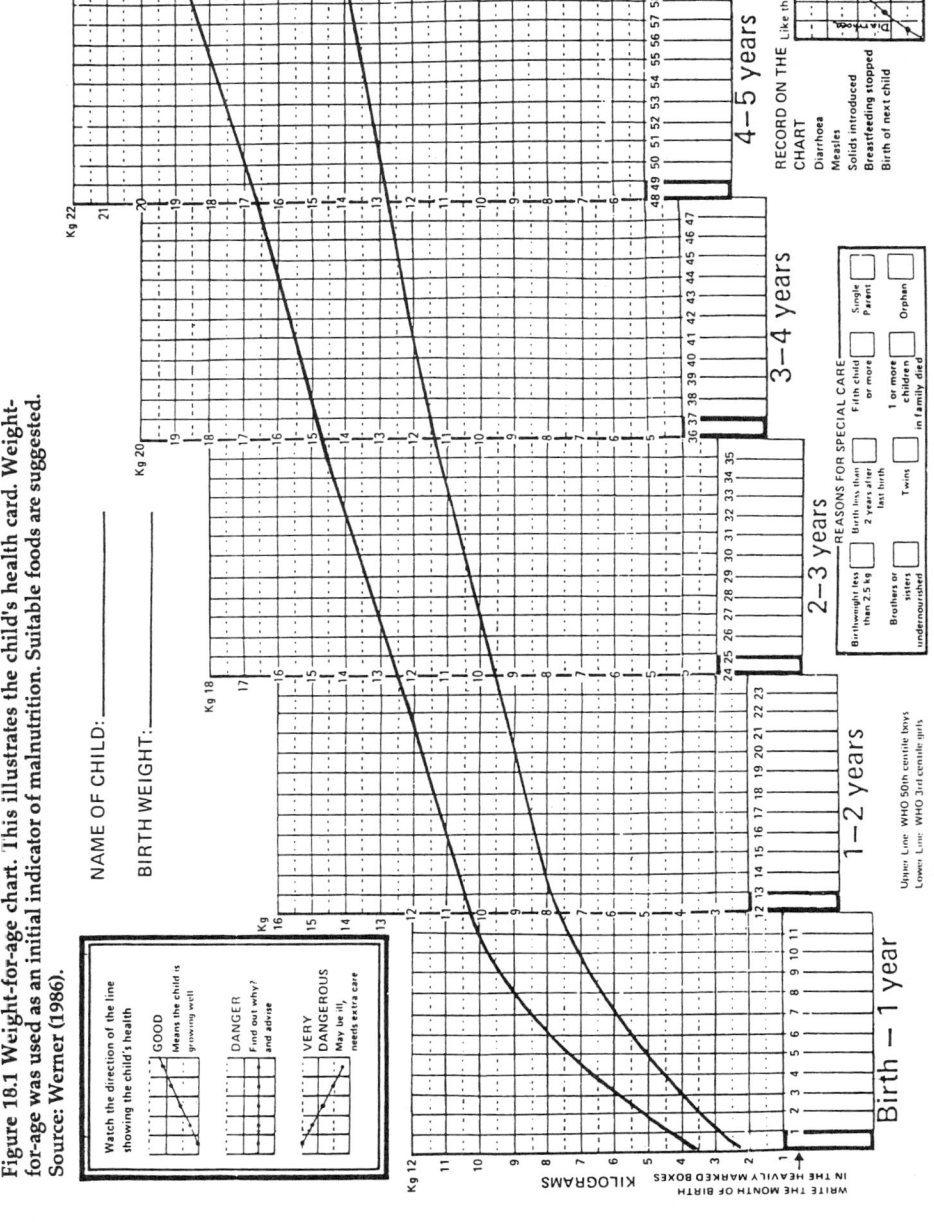

Figure 18.1 Weight-for-age chart. This illustrates the child's health card. Weight-for-age was used as an initial indicator of malnutrition. Suitable foods are suggested. Source: Werner (1986).

Table 18.1 Stunted Children in 1977, 1979, and 1982

	1977		1979		1982	
Province	Percent	Mean	Percent	Mean	Percent	Mean
Central	26	93.6	21	94.5	24	94.0
Coast	14 *	96.3	40	92.9	39	92.2
Eastern	34	92.8	24	94.6	27	93.3
Nyanza	21	94.7	34	93.6	33	93.4
Rift Valley	25	94.0	24	94.2	22	94.9
Western	16	95.0	24	94.0	30	92.9
National	24	94.1	27	94.5	28	93.7

Source: Central Bureau of Statistics (1983b).
Note: Percent is percent of children less than 80 percent of the height-for-age standard. Mean is the 50 percentile value for percent of the standard height for age.
* Data unreliable due to small sample size.

Table 18.2 Indicators of Childhood Health

Province	N	Stunted (%)	Mean HA	Wasted (%)	Mean WH	Mortality Census	Mortality Survey (%)
Coast	419	36.2	92.6	5.0	99.8	206	16.0
Nyanza	788	28.9	93.9	3.6	103.6	220	13.5
Western	787	25.7	93.7	2.0	103.1	187	14.8
Eastern	1,195	22.6	94.0	2.7	99.2	128	8.2
Central	907	20.4	94.6	2.8	99.1	85	6.5
Rift Valley	1,227	19.8	95.2	3.0	100.1	132	9.2
National	5,323	24.0	94.2	3.0	100.7	156	10.5

Province	Sick (%)	Mothers with no education (%)	Piped Water (%)	Without Sewage (%)	Persons per sq km Total	Persons per sq km Arable Land
Coast	54.3	77.4	79.3	61.9	12	87
Nyanza	58.8	51.6	97.5	37.8	211	211
Western	56.8	46.3	95.5	19.4	233	247
Eastern	43.4	45.9	88.2	37.6	64	133
Central	37.1	30.3	77.3	1.7	178	254
Rift Valley	39.1	55.1	88.7	49.6	34	101
National	46.5	48.6	88.2	33.5	61	138

Source: Central Bureau of Statistics (1983).
Notes: HA is less than 90 percent of height-for-age. WH is less than 80 percent weight-for-height. Census mortality is the proportion of children dying in the first five years of life, per 1,000, from the 1979 census. Survey mortality is calculated for each child as the number of siblings died/number of children of mother ever born, in percent.

Table 18.3 District Feeding Programs for Children Under the Age of Five

District	Feeding Sites	Children Screened	Children Fed	Children at Risk	Hospital Referrals	Immunizations
Embu	8	12,698	799	2,805	16	1,118*
Meru	10	5,813	1,480	1,600	40*	2,500*
Machakos	10	11,842	6,515*	1,102	92	na
Kitui	9	3,024	543	1,100	na	na
Total	37	33,377	9,337	6,607	148	3,618

Source: Ministry of Health data.
Note: Data as of 31 January 1985. Children fed were below 80 percent weight-for-height. Children at risk were between 80 and 90 percent weight-for-height.
* Estimated figures

· 19 ·

Effect of the 1984 Drought on Education

J. B. M. BUKUSI
SIMON K. MBARIRE

Kenya has a wide range of educational institutions, the majority of which are primary and secondary schools. Others are pre-primary (nursery) schools, village polytechnics, adult education centers, and colleges. Educational institutions are not evenly distributed spatially. They are concentrated in high-potential areas, which have more economic benefits, better infrastructure, and more dense population compared to low-potential areas.

Total school enrollment for 1980 to 1984 recorded by the Ministry of Education, Science, and Technology increased over the years. A large majority of the school-age population is already attending classes, a clear indication that people in Kenya attach great importance to formal education. In addition to the national curriculum, extracurricular activities, and clubs that promote environmental awareness (such as the 4-K Clubs, geographical clubs, wildlife clubs, scouting, and girl guides) are also offered, although they are not available in all schools. Tree nurseries have been developed in the schools, reflecting a growing awareness of the importance of trees in helping to conserve soil.

Most of the educational institutions have similar problems. Primary and *harambee* (self-help) schools are staffed by untrained teachers. Although the figures for untrained schoolteachers are not available, it is evident that they form a sizable portion of the teaching force. Each year, untrained teachers are taken for in-service training at teacher-training colleges. Though this helps to alleviate the teacher shortage, the availability of trained teachers continues to be a problem because of the increase in the school-age population. Overcrowding in the classroom is a related problem, which is especially severe in primary schools; there, a teacher may have over fifty pupils.

The government provides most primary school materials, although the provision of supplies may be delayed due to management and communication problems. Transport problems hinder the efficiency of school inspectors, who are supposed to visit the schools and check on the quality of education, instructional progress, and school needs. The district education officers have a few cars that they sometimes lend to the inspectors, but the inspectors do not have their own transport, which, of course, they should.

Another problem is the seasonal variation in school attendance. A large percentage of pupils, in both primary and secondary schools, are absent from schools during harvest seasons, especially in September and November, when coffee is picked in the high-potential areas of Murang'a and Kiambu districts. Families often require labor from their children, especially when household income does not allow for the hiring of sufficient laborers. Adult literacy classes are also affected during agricultural peak periods, as the students are often the family breadwinners. Seasonal labor demands affect the majority of educational institutions, including village polytechnics and colleges.

Educational institutions face many other problems. Students often must travel long distances to reach the nearest school. There are shortages of well-constructed classrooms, water, and access roads. Schools are plagued with a high dropout rate, especially in the low-potential areas.

EFFECTS OF THE 1984 DROUGHT

Educational institutions, like other institutions in Kenya, were affected by the 1984 drought, especially in July through December.

Most schools experienced a general shortage of water. In some cases, the water sources completely dried up. Students had to fetch water, often from great distances, for use in school. Some boarding institutions had to hire Ministry of Transport and Communications tankers or local carts to transport water.

Food was in short supply throughout the country, and schools could not afford to pay the high prices. As a result, they incurred debts, which remained unpaid by some schools over a year later. Students were fed an unbalanced diet; due to a shortage of beans in the country, students at times ate only maize. Most of the schools had to forgo some extracurricular activities, such as educational trips, to save money for food.

Most parents from low-potential areas could not afford school fees for their children. As a result, schools incurred heavy losses in outstanding fees for 1984, some of which had not been repaid over a year later. Wanguru Secondary School, for example, reported that in 1984 the school had an outstanding fees balance of Ksh 206,675.60, of which very little has been recovered.

A number of students left school due to household economic constraints, such as the lack of food or money to buy food. Some students left school to look for work to help their parents. The situation was exacerbated for adult literacy classes and village polytechnics. Day school students often looked dull in class because they had little to eat at home.

In areas badly hit by drought, the interruption of classes was common.

Children reported to school sporadically. A school in Siakago Division, Embu, recorded a large drop in attendance from August to December 1984 (Table 19.1). By the end of the year, over 20 percent of the class was absent. At least some of the students never returned to continue their education, a situation that may have been more common for secondary school students.

Since the procurement of food and water were the primary concerns of people during the drought, development projects, such as the expansion of educational facilities, were not given priority. As such, little or no building of educational facilities was recorded in the low-potential areas.

RESPONSES TO THE DROUGHT

In association with several nongovernmental organizations (NGOs), the government of Kenya responded well during the drought period. Assistance to educational institutions was coordinated by the Ministry of Education, Science, and Technology.

Government of Kenya

The Ministry of Education, Science, and Technology gave out special grants worth Ksh 10,760,000 to drought-stricken areas throughout the country (Table 19.2). Government-aided secondary schools received Ksh 80,000 (boarding schools) and Ksh 40,000 (day school) each. No financial assistance was given to *harambee* secondary schools.

The School Feeding Programme (SFP) was initiated in 1981 by the Ministry of Education, Science, and Technology, in collaboration with the World Food Programme (WFP), as a response to the 1979 drought in the arid and semiarid regions of Kenya. The program included fourteen districts: Turkana, West Pokot, Samburu, Marsabit, Isiolo, Garissa, Wajir, Mandera, Lamu, Tana River, and parts of Kajiado, Narok, Baringo, and Laikipia. These districts were most affected by food shortages in normal years as well as during the 1979 drought. The main objectives of the original program were to:

1. Provide food assistance to primary and pre-primary school children, thereby improving their nutritional and health status
2. Promote regular attendance and hence the enrollment of the children at school
3. Encourage and promote good health habits among children and, subsequently, the community at large

The provision of food at schools in these areas resulted in more regular attendance and a rise in school enrollment. Teachers also indicated that children's response to school improved. The original program was intended to last five years (from 1981 to 1985). It was later extended for an additional three years since the impact of the 1984 drought further hindered food production in the semiarid regions.

The 1984 drought affected more areas of the country than did the 1979 drought. The Ministry of Education, Science, and Technology, again in collaboration with the WFP, responded to the increased need by expanding the school feeding program on an "emergency basis" to four new districts in Eastern Province: Machakos (Makueni Division), Meru (Tharaka Division), Embu (Mbeere area), and Kitui District, where the program was initially planned to cover the whole district but, due to the large size of the district and overwhelming financial constraints, only pockets that were identified to be the hardest hit were served.

To implement the expanded program successfully, the ministry solicited funds from various sources. Trucks were needed to transport food from the National Cereals and Produce Board stores to schools, more stores had to be hired or constructed to store food, and utensils had to be bought. Not all schools requiring food had access to water, and either water tanks had to be installed or tankers hired to carry water to installed water tanks at the schools. Kitchens had to be constructed and cooks employed for feeding centers on the school grounds. To meet these needs, the World Food Programme, UNICEF, Australian High Commission, and others assisted the ministry. To assist in food distribution the WFP donated fifteen new trucks, while UNICEF donated seven.

Almost 2,000 schools (both pre-primary and primary) and over 400,000 children were assisted in 1984 under the expanded emergency relief program (Tables 19.3 and 19.4). Over 6,500 mt of food were distributed over the 1981 to 1985 period, with substantial increases in 1984 and 1985 (Table 19.5).

Nongovernmental Organizations

Nongovernmental organizations also contributed toward reducing the impact of the drought on educational institutions. The regional office of ActionAid in Kagio aided primary schools in Murang'a, Kirinyaga, and Embu districts in 1984. It gave furniture, meals (including the initiation of a feeding program), and agricultural inputs to five primary schools and two women's groups in Kirinyaga and six primary schools in Embu District. Donations of agricultural inputs were aimed either at improving agricultural education or given in the form of soft loans to 4-K club members to boost their agricultural activities (Table 19.6). These soft loans are usually repaid by individual members. In 1984, because of the drought, members were unable to repay the full loan, and ActionAid waived the balance due.

In 1984, in response to the drought and to improve education, Plan International raised "Disaster Funds" for drought victims in Embu District (Gachoka Division). It bought and distributed 153 mt (1,700 bags) of maize, 54 mt (600 bags) of beans, 72 mt (800) bags of sorghum, several kilograms of dried skimmed milk, and corn oil. In addition, it helped several primary schools in the district. In Gachoka Division, the Plan paid school fees for fifty needy Plan families, assisted 2,500 children with school uniforms, and supplied fifty-one schools with desks, forms, and furniture. In Karaba Location, Plan International constructed standard eight classrooms in two schools, repaired five classrooms, and completed four others. It also started a school feeding program in Gachoka and Igembe, feeding over 15,000 malnourished children in June 1984.

RECOMMENDATIONS

The Ministry of Water Development should provide schools with permanent water. Schools should be encouraged to have storage tanks or reservoirs constructed either for storing water from the main supplies or from trapped rain water.

Boarding schools should buy and store large quantities of food. They should grow crops that are resistant to drought. Parents and the community should participate in the initiation, management, and daily operation of school feeding programs.

Parents can be encouraged to pay school fees in advance. Education expenses should be lowered so that people do not have to sell food to raise school fees. Government grants should be distributed fairly to all institutions, depending on size and need, and should cover both government and *harambee* institutions.

Environmental stress can affect educational institutions in detrimental ways. The managers of educational institutions are responsible for alleviating these negative effects, should they occur. Through early planning for drought conditions and provision of food to school children, managers can raise enrollments and lower dropout rates.

In collaboration with NGOs involved in community development, the government should educate people on drought-coping strategies to improve education in drought-prone areas. This can be achieved through administrative circulars, or by hosting regional seminars or workshops for teachers and others involved in educational institutions.

Table 19.1 Enrollment at Kanyiri Primary School, Embu, in 1984

Month	No. of Pupils Present	No. Absent	Total No. Enrolled
August	186	9	195
September	186	9	195
October	169	26	195
November	154	41	195
December	154	41	195

Source: Ministry of Education data.

Table 19.2 Financial Aid to Government Secondary Schools in 1984/85

Province/District	Aid (Ksh)	No. of Students	No. of Schools
Central	600,000		
Kirinyaga		400	3
Kiambu		260	2
Eastern	5,920,000		
Embu		3,900	15
Kitui		4,130	18
Machakos		9,698	33

Source: Ministry of Education data.

Table 19.3 Schools Covered by the School Feeding Programme, 1981-1985

District	1981	1982	1983	1984	1985
Baringo	37	32	33	41	145
Embu	—	—	—	—	128
Garissa	35	30	31	30	35
Isiolo	53	63	51	50	51
Kajiado	84	133	133	158	160
Kitui	—	—	—	118	91
Laikipia	10	10	10	10	25
Lamu	67	60	39	39	44
Machakos	—	—	—	211	230
Mandera	27	24	21	25	27
Marakwet	—	—	—	—	76
Marsabit	55	72	73	83	92
Meru	—	—	—	169	165
Narok	60	39	34	50	50
Samburu	117	87	90	113	123
Tana River	88	81	80	100	113
Turkana	116	95	76	140	151
Wajir	32	30	31	30	35
West Pokot	261	111	119	135	207
Total	1,042	867	821	1,502	1,948

Source: Ministry of Education data.

Table 19.4 Pupils Covered by the School Feeding Programme, 1981–1985

District	1981	1982	1983	1984	1985
Baringo	4,194	4,214	5,085	4,851	44,088
Embu	—	—	—	—	36,412
Garissa	—	4,986	5,461	4,450	8,248
Isiolo	6,852	7,486	7,908	9,182	9,838
Kajiado	—	22,289	16,292	32,505	34,139
Kitui	—	—	—	41,378	35,214
Laikipia	—	—	1,005	1,058	4,023
Lamu	—	10,313	10,841	11,143	11,318
Machakos	—	—	—	48,320	56,531
Mandera	—	4,892	5,646	5,890	8,298
Marsabit	7,141	9,872	9,860	12,257	14,502
Meru	—	—	—	33,363	19,021
Narok	—	5,729	5,011	6,898	8,187
Samburu	11,317	11,945	14,935	16,772	17,818
Tana River	—	13,412	17,499	18,781	20,264
Turkana	16,957	17,687	19,781	31,549	36,094
Wajir	—	4,722	5,810	5,669	6,626
West Pokot	30,186	30,186	21,475	29,139	38,005
Total	76,647	147,733	146,609	313,205	408,626

Source: Ministry of Education data.
Notes: Kitui, Meru, Machakos, and Embu districts were added later in 1984 in an expansion of the emergency program.

Table 19.5 Food Distributed by the Supplementary Food Program

Year	Maize	Beans	Vegetable Oil	Peas
1981	540.9	108.2	73.1	—
1982	2,341.2	628.2	476.8	—
1983	2,248.7	636.8	246.8	—
1984	2,460.1	321.1	123.5	—
1984 (Sept)	4,557.7	—	241.0	1,970.4
1985	3,596.0	27.0	539.4	1,100.5
Total	15,744.6	1,721.3	1,700.6	3,070.9

Source: Ministry of Education data
Notes: Figures in mt. There was a shortage of beans in 1984/85, and the government distributed peas instead. 1984 (Sept) is for project Ken 1398/1; others are for project Ken 2502.

Table 19.6 Loans from ActionAid, Kagio

	Long Rains	Short Rains	Total
Total loans	86,169.90	71,491.05	157,660.95
Member repayment	8,731.70	15,455.75	24,187.45
Amount waived	77,438.20	46,035.30	123,473.50

Source: ActionAid data.
Notes: Figures in Ksh. Loans are from the Kagio regional office of ActionAid.

· 20 ·
Planning Against Drought and Famine in Turkana: A District Contingency Plan

JEREMY SWIFT

Although drought is a natural event that is beyond human control, such is not the case with famine. Policies and action at national and local levels can reduce or eliminate the risk of famine. The commitment by the government of Kenya to end the threat of famine is a credible policy objective, supported by the successful response to the 1984 drought. This chapter summarizes a report (Swift 1985) commissioned by Oxfam and the Turkana Rehabilitation Project (TRP), and carried out with the support and encouragement of the Turkana District and Nairobi authorities. The aim of the study was to assess the risk of drought and famine in Turkana District and to recommend measures to reduce the likelihood of a drought deteriorating into a famine. The government of Kenya, with its District Focus policy, has decentralized important aspects of development decisionmaking and action. This study, therefore, emphasizes policies and actions for Turkana District itself. The Turkana District authorities, who are in daily contact with development problems, are best placed to plan and implement a drought-contingency strategy. They have adopted the report and are beginning to implement a distict plan.

Three themes run through this chapter. First, although drought is inevitable, famine is not; quite simple measures can prevent it. Second, measures to prevent famine need not be expensive; much of what is proposed here merely involves the reorganization of already-existing priorities and work. Third, and perhaps most important, the Turkana rural people have been dealing with drought and famine for centuries. Rural development in Turkana should seek to encourage the responses already made by herders, farmers, and fisherfolk to the risk of drought and famine.

This chapter deals mainly with the specific responsibilities of district officials, missions, and nongovernmental organizations (NGOs) in response to drought and the threat of famine. The following section describes methods of estimating the probability of drought and the changing risk of famine in Turkana. The third and fourth sections outline preparedness plans and the operation of an early warning system, respectively. Brief conclusions are presented in the final section.

DROUGHT AND FAMINE IN TURKANA DISTRICT

Estimating the Probability of Drought and Famine in Turkana District

Two methods have been used to record the occurrence of drought in Turkana District. Ecological indexes include rainfall and vegetation data collected by the government of Kenya. Turkana oral chronologies, which may provide clues as to future drought frequencies, indicate the Turkana's own perception of drought (see the Chapter 11 for drought perceptions among the Gabbra).

Ecological indexes can be used to determine the probability of wet or dry years (Table 20.1). Probabilities are calculated, using a weighted ecological index that accounts for two years of rainfall in differing degrees (two-thirds for rain in year Y, one-third in year Y-1). Plant production in any one year is influenced by the previous year's rain, through the amount of soil moisture (which enables early germination), and by its effect on species composition, the degree of ground cover, and vegetative or seed stock from the previous year.

At all stations, periods wetter than normal are more frequent than drier periods. This is especially notable at Lokitaung and Todenyang, which are located in the extreme northeast of the district. According to the index, very dry years are unusual at Lokitaung and Lokichokio, and have not been recorded during the short period of observation at Kapedo; very dry years are, however, regular at Lodwar and Todenyang. Dry years occur once every five to eight years at all stations.

Like other farmers and herders, Turkana date years by important events. Although names and descriptions used for events vary by tribal section and place, there is usually agreement about the most important events, such as major droughts. Drought chronologies were collected in south, west, and north Turkana and from Father Joe Morris of Lokitaung (Erukudi 1985).

Turkana distinguish serious droughts as "years in which people died," or *eron*—a time when "everything dies and there is no way to turn." This is opposed to less important droughts in which vegetation or animals may be affected or people simply go hungry. Since 1955, according to the Turkana chronologies, famine did not occur in all years listed (Table 20.2). Other years, not recorded here, were especially bad in particular parts of Turkana but did not affect the entire district.

The chronology suggesting a Turkana-wide disaster that leads to human starvation has occurred about seven times since the chronologies began around 1913, or a frequency of about one every ten years (which does not, of course, mean it occurs at ten-year intervals). This confirms estimates made from rainfall records. The Turkana chronologies also indicate that drought alone has not been the only trigger for starvation; animal disease and security problems in 1979-1981 have been important. The chronologies suggest that large-scale famines are relatively recent, although starvation is well known in recent Turkana history.

Changing Famine Risk

In droughts or other disasters, Turkana herders depend on the exchange of animals for cereals. The effect of drought on the pastoral economy depends crucially on the relative value of livestock and of the cereals that herders must barter or buy. Anything that affects these relative values, including animal disease, security, or government pricing policy, can determine whether a drought has few long-term consequences or turns into a famine.

Changing social and economic conditions can also hamper the effectiveness of traditional responses to drought. The deteriorating security situation on Kenya's northern boundary, particularly the spread of automatic weapons from Uganda through Turkana, has increased the incidence and severity of cattle raiding and general banditry. Recent estimates suggest that nearly half of Turkana District is not grazed because of the risk of cattle raiding and banditry (Ministry of Energy and Regional Development 1985). Similarly, international migration of animal herds could become more precarious as state boundaries are increasingly controlled. The Turkana also rely on fallback activities during drought, such as fishing, hunting, or wage employment, which have become increasingly unsatisfactory. The lake ecosystem is now overpopulated, and overfishing has caused declining productivity. Wild animals for hunting are now scarce. High population growth rates in much of Kenya have led to fewer casual wage-employment opportunities for the Turkana during times of crisis.

DROUGHT AND FAMINE PREPAREDNESS

The Turkana District administration can prepare now for a more efficient response when a major drought threatens. Some of the measures proposed here are already contained in the District Development Plan, 1984–1988, and need only be given priority to be carried out rapidly; other proposed measures are new.

District Drought Policy

Effective preparedness hinges on prior planning; Lodwar authorities must draw up a district plan to guide the actions of technical services and nongovernmental organizations in the event of a major drought. The policy should be formulated by the district development committee and discussed in detail in order to ensure that it is consistent with sectoral development plans. The district drought policy should complement the district development policy set out in the District Development Plan (Ministry of Finance and Planning 1984b).

Among major objectives of a Turkana District drought policy are:

1. To encourage a substantial but orderly destocking of Turkana rangelands in the event of a major drought in such a way that the purchasing power of herders is maintained, massive animal deaths are avoided, and a reservoir of breeding females is preserved as the nucleus from which to restock herders after the crisis is over
2. To maintain adequate cereal availability, at controlled prices, at shops spread widely throughout the district
3. To maintain, as far as possible, a dispersed pattern of population distribution and avoid the creation of large famine-relief camps with their public health dangers
4. To provide employment on useful public works to destitute people in order to maintain their ability to buy food
5. To guarantee a minimum of emergency feeding and health and nutrition care to ensure that particularly vulnerable groups do not suffer
6. To ensure that the district administration has the ability to react early enough to prevent a drought from turning into a famine by implementing drought-preparedness measures, including cereal security stocks, infrastructure, and an early warning system
7. To turn relief rapidly into rehabilitation at the end of a crisis by equipping rural households with the means to resume an independent life as soon as possible

Plans, administration, funds, and staff. One of the main problems of contingency planning is how to prepare for the great increase in requirements for certain activities, especially for staff and funds. There are three main sources of additional staff and funds, and plans should be made in advance for all three to be mobilized in Turkana in such an eventuality:

1. Staff and funds can be switched from other uses within the district. This will be possible to some degree, especially within sectoral programs and individual ministries, but will be hard between ministries and sectoral programs. Each ministry representative in Lodwar should be asked to prepare a contingency plan, in line with the district drought policy, showing what activities are regarded as essential in a major drought and what funds and personnel could, if necessary, be switched to higher priority, drought-related tasks within that sector program.

2. The district can maintain spare capacity (underused staff and deposited

funds) in the expectation that they will be called upon periodically. This option would be costly in Turkana, as widepread drought will strike, on average, only one year in ten. Nevertheless, consideration should be given to the creation of a special drought contingency fund out of central government revenue, to be used at the district commissioner's discretion in response to information from the early warning system. The fund would meet two main needs: to finance public works undertaken for cash wages rather than for food (probably the early stages of a guaranteed employment scheme), and to finance the additional administrative expenses (such as extra fuel or transport costs) needed for the district to put into action its drought response measures. The lack of such funds was a constraint to the relief effort in 1984.

3. The district can rely upon substantial foreign aid in staff and funds in a crisis. Given the past record, it is reasonable to suppose that in a major drought, Turkana District will get substantial aid. The time bilateral and multilateral agencies, churches, and other NGOs need between a request for help and its arrival varies, but it may be quite long, with aid arriving too late to implement some of the strategies mentioned here. The proposed early warning system will provide a periodic, objective assessment of the threat to the district from drought and famine. As part of the district drought-contingency plan, Turkana and Nairobi authorities should negotiate, *in advance of a crisis*, commitments about the level and type of help (funds and food) that major donors can offer if the early warning system indicates that a serious crisis is likely.

While most of the proposed measures utilize existing district activities, the coordination of activities and administration of the early warning system will be essential. A district drought-contingency officer, recruited by the district commissioner's office or by the Ministry of Planning and National Development, would act as a liaison between district officers and other organizations in order to make the drought-contingency plan operational.

Cumulative experience and learning should guide the implementation of the district drought-contingency plan, but the regular turnover of district staff could hamper this process. The problem of rapid employee turnover can be alleviated through the preparation of a district drought-contingency manual. The manual would describe the strategy and plan, including the early warning system, instructions for administrative and technical officers responsible for implementing the plan, and the reasons for different programs. Lists and quantities of special equipment and supplies (such as drips and vaccines) needed in an emergency would be included within the manual so that essential supplies can be ordered when signals from the early warning system indicate the need. The manual should also include detailed instructions on types of food and rations needed for the emergency feeding of adults and children. The district drought-contingency officer, in cooperation with district technical services and NGOs, would be responsible for the compilation of this manual.

When the early warning system indicates a serious crisis, the suspension of cess taxes on the export of skins from the district would serve to encourage livestock sales. The Turkana County Council should be reimbursed the lost income, which will be important at such times. Agreements with donor agencies could include a revenue compensation fund in case of a major drought. A precedent for this policy was established when the EEC compensated the Niger government for the suspension of cattle taxes during the 1973 drought.

In the event of a major drought, the district administration may need reserve legal powers to guarantee quick and efficient response to the situation. A study should be made of the laws and stipulations regarding the district commissioner's ability to commandeer vehicles from technical services, NGOs, and private groups, and to move government staff between services. In a future crisis, it may also be desirable to suspend the legal ban on the movement of cereals into Turkana other than through official channels. Standby legal provision for extra powers during major droughts should be sought in Nairobi.

Physical infrastructure. The construction of a drought- and famine-related infrastructure during ordinary times will facilitate the district reaction to a crisis. It may be possible to use existing food-for-work programs through the TRP to build some of this. Where possible, such infrastructure should be designed so that it can also be used during normal times.

At present, cereals for Turkana are collected from the National Cereals and Produce Board (NCPB) store in Kitale. Cereals have to be brought over 300 km before distribution can even start within much of Turkana District. An NCPB cereal store, built at Lodwar, would eliminate the long-distance trucking of food supplies. This store should have a capacity of one normal year's supply of normal Turkana District requirements, of which a supply of six months would be considered a district strategic reserve, not to be used except in exceptional circumstances. Standby cereal-storage facilities at division and location levels are also necessary. These could consist of a concrete apron with a tarpaulin cover. Those stores already existing should be maintained.

If a strategy for the development of associations of Turkana herding families is followed, the associations should be encouraged (through food-for-work and credit at concessionary rates) to build a store and to buy their own cereal stocks for normal dry season use, with a reserve carried over from one year to the next against the danger of a more serious food shortage. Several associations might share storage facilities at the same site in order to benefit from economies of scale.

The road network plays a part in preparing for drought in Turkana, since better communications and transportation reduce the cost of cereal distribution, facilitate animal marketing, and improve the district administration's information about what is happening in remote places. Airstrips at the division and location level would also aid communications.

Water is a crucial development tool in a largely pastoral district such as Turkana, and it has to be planned with care as part of the overall land use. For the district drought strategy, three things are important. First, to avoid the danger of the failure of a borehole pump (as occurred in 1984) during a major drought, when large numbers of animals depend on it and cannot move elsewhere, all such boreholes should be fitted with backup pumps and reservoirs. Second, within the current district development plan, priority in the Rural Water Program should be given to places that are likely, on the basis of past experience, to become major population concentrations in the event of a drought or famine. The aim should be to have a good water supply at about half a dozen sites in order to adequately cope with the extra demands made by large relief camps so that hygiene and sanitation do not break down. Finally, boreholes at the three livestock holding grounds at Lotongot (first priority), Lokitaung, and Kakuma should be given high priority in the district development plan since they are essential to orderly animal destocking in a drought.

Economic Measures

Livestock marketing and maintenance. One of the chief features of a drought that threatens to lead to famine in pastoral areas such as Turkana is the collapse of the market for animals, animal products (such as skins), and other products of the rural economy. Turkana herders produce mainly high-value, high-protein produce, which is exchanged during part of the year for lower-value cereals. At normal prices, herders can get more calories by exchanging their meat and milk for cereals than by eating the milk and meat. The rate at which animal products can be exchanged for cereals is known as the pastoral terms of trade.

Experience in other African pastoral famines suggests that a dramatic decline in pastoral purchasing power, resulting from changes in pastoral terms of trade, is a main cause of famine (see Chapter 16 for a case study of the Samburu during the 1984/85 drought). Figure 20.1 shows the changing relative values of meat and cereals during the full cycle of a pastoral famine in such a place as Turkana. The vertical axis shows increasing prices of meat and maize per kg, compared to the cost of calories. The horizontal axis shows the changes in these values over time, dividing the pastoral famine cycle into five main periods.

In the normal situation, the pastoral terms of trade are generally favorable for herders. Since meat prices per calorie are higher than those for cereal, meat can be exchanged for more cost-effective cereal calories. Early in a drought, animal production declines and an increasing proportion of household animals are sent to market to maintain caloric consumption. Animals start to flood the market and meat prices fall, yet cereal prices remain unaffected. Pastoral terms of trade decline as meat prices spiral downward. During the drought, terms of trade deteriorate further, and cereal prices may rise and surpass the calorie equivalent meat price. At this time, herders are vulnerable to shortfalls in caloric consumption, or to famine. The immediate post-drought period is usually marked by rains and the fall of cereal prices in expectation of a good harvest. The downward spiral of meat prices reverses since meat is relatively scarce due to the ravages of the drought. Finally, during the recovery period, cereal prices return to normal levels, but meat prices remain high while the herds recover. Eventually, meat and cereal prices return to their pre-famine levels.

Due to insufficient water and forage in a major drought, large numbers of animals will have to leave the Turkana rangelands or be sold to purchase cereals. Orderly destocking is one key to effective control of drought in Turkana. A destocking policy can be implemented given the infrastructure to maintain it: improvement in animal health, feasibility studies (including one on the Kenya Meat Commission's [KMC] ability to increase its throughput), and a contingency fund to buy animals in order to keep prices up.

Animals bought by the district in a drought should be divided into three groups: the best reproductive females (to be kept on holding grounds), animals that will be slaughtered locally, and those that can be exported from the district to the KMC. Overall improvements in livestock and range management should include the construction of catchment ponds, shallow wells, cattle dips, and crushes; delineation of holding grounds; and better livestock vaccination. In view of the role proposed for the three holding grounds, provision for reliable water and supplementary fodder production and storage is necessary. Turkana District has been in quarantine for contagious bovine pleuropneumonia (CBPP) since the early 1960s. Improved animal vaccination would not only reduce animal mortality, but it would simplify and increase cattle marketing out of the district. The success of an emergency destocking exercise depends on lifting the CBPP quarantine, which would reduce the risk of a collapse of the livestock economy in a drought.

There will undoubtedly be a large rise in the number of weak and thin animals that die or have to be slaughtered. The district policy should encourage the most productive use of such animals for their meat, skins, and bone meal. This would be facilitated by simple processing in each division. Each site should include basic slaughter facilities (a concrete apron, metal frame, and running water) and tanning facilities.

An advance commitment by donors should be sought for fodder aid. The best female animals should be bought by the district authorities during a drought and kept on or around the three planned holding grounds as the nucleus of a post-drought restocking scheme for Turkana herders. These animals will need supplementary fodder. In the past, the World Food Programme has supplied fodder along with more conventional food aid. The fodder provided would supplement natural feed, especially browse.

Employment guarantee. One of the main causes of a famine is lost purchasing power; there may be food in the district, but without money or salable assets, people cannot buy it and therefore go hungry. One way to avoid this, without making many people dependent on famine-relief handouts, is to provide employment on useful public works, paid either in food or wages. Turkana District has considerable experience in administering food-for-work programs, and this experience should be put to use to develop food-for-work or guaranteed employment for wages as a central part of the district drought-response strategy.

Public works programs, which respond to increased rural demand for food and work, must be planned in advance of actual implementation. There should be a register of well-prepared projects to be executed, stockpiles of necessary tools and equipment, and a cadre of trained supervisors to carry out projects, set tasks, and measure work accomplished for payment. Possible public work programs for Turkana include water harvesting; construction of roads, tracks, airstrips, shallow wells, and terracing; planting trees around settlements for amenity, timber, and fuel; planting browse; watering and protecting trees; and small-scale, low-lift riverbank irrigation.

Turkana's recent experience with public works projects has been entirely through food-for-work since food aid was available. There is, however, no reason why future public works programs should not pay in cash rather than in food. Cash payments are a great deal simpler to administer than food payments, since there are none of the problems of procuring, transporting, storing, and handing out food. In a future drought or famine, it would make sense for initial public works programs to be for wages, which would be paid from the district drought-contingency fund. If laborers are paid in cash, the normal cereal trade networks should be able to meet the increased demand. If a major crisis develops, international food aid may be expected to reach the district through advance commitments. Some of the public works programs can then, if necessary, revert to food-for-work, especially if normal cereal trading networks have broken down.

Monitoring, Information, Research, and Training

An information system increases drought preparedness by giving district decisionmakers a clear idea of what is happening in a drought and what needs to be done. It will enable them to adjust their programs in the light of experience gained.

Monitoring nutritional status will contribute to the proposed district early warning system and provide useful information for hospital-, clinic-, and dispensary-based nutrition support programs. In a crisis, nutritional status measurement takes on added importance in identifying individuals and populations at risk and needing extra feeding or medical care. To do this, the district drought plan must first standardize and improve the nutritional status measurement techniques used in the district so that data from different sources are entirely compatible and give unambiguous results. Programs in Turkana tend toward mid-arm circumference (MAC) as the main measure. The reliability of this measure in Turkana must be established in comparison with other measures, especially weight-for-height, which is a proven indicator of acute malnutrition and short-term changes in nutrition. The baseline surveys should be designed to show seasonal variations in nutrition (at least two surveys in the year and perhaps even four). The pastoral population is in most urgent need of surveying, followed by farmers, fisherfolk, and people in food-for-work camps.

When large numbers of malnourished people gather in famine camps, nutrition and health care require special techniques that health staff do not encounter in normal routines. These include intravenous rehydration, treatment for famine camp diseases (such as typhoid and cholera), and the calculation and use of proper rations. As part of the district drought preparedness, an annual one-week training session should be held in Lodwar for district health personnel, including missions and NGOs, on emergency health and nutrition care techniques. UNICEF and international organizations, such as Oxfam and Save the Children Fund, that have experience in famine relief in neighboring countries would also be able to help in training.

EARLY WARNING SYSTEM

The measures outlined in the previous section are designed to lead Turkana District into a state of permanent preparedness for drought. The second part of a district contingency plan is an early warning system (EWS). The purpose of an EWS is to provide information about the development of a drought or famine to district and national authorities, local NGOs, and Turkana rural people. No single indicator of drought is totally reliable when taken alone; rather, a composite picture is required in which slow changes in several key indicators start to ring preliminary alarm bells, even if other indicators do not show unusual values. There must also be a learning period to determine relevant indicators. The first-generation early warning system should operate as an experiment, a tool to investigate how a more precise, more quantified system can be put in place. An adequate EWS can be activated in Turkana without time-consuming measurement or sophisticated mathematical analysis. In the first-generation EWS, no quantitative measurements are needed apart from rainfall figures. In addition, almost all the proposed indicators are either already collected (although reporting and synthesis of this data are uncoordinated between regions and national headquarters) or are common-sense questions that can be answered by anyone knowledgeable in that field. Each of the proposed indicators is intended to uncover unusual trends, which are readily observable, for the area and time of year concerned.

Proposed EWS Indicators

Government offices, research stations, and the TRP would be responsible for monitoring the proposed indicators, as presented below.

DISTRICT COMMISSIONER'S OFFICE, DISTRICT OFFICERS, AND LOCATION CHIEFS:
Famine relief list. People currently receiving assistance and probable numbers of relief recipients in the near future.
Availability of maize (whole and ground). Reflects unusual levels of purchases by herders.
Prices of noncontrolled cereals. Especially sorghum and millet.

LODWAR METEOROLOGICAL STATION:
Rainfall. Reports for all stations in Turkana (and perhaps several nearby stations) with a record of more than ten years (Lodwar, Lokitaung, Todenyang, Lokichokio, and Kapedo) when monthly, cumulative, and prior annual rainfall is less than half the median value.

DISTRICT VETERINARY OFFICER (DVO):
Animal production. Unusual trends in births, deaths, milk production, animal nutrition, or animal disease.

LIVESTOCK MARKETING ADVISOR:
Livestock marketing. Sales, purchases, barter, and prices for any species, including unusual changes in the number of animals offered, numbers offered but remaining unsold, numbers of females (especially pregnant females), or very young animals.

DISTRICT AGRICULTURAL OFFICER (DAO):
Agricultural situation. Unusual status of agricultural meteorology, especially soil moisture, area planted, crops, harvest, or village or settlement level food stocks in household granaries.

DISTRICT RANGE OFFICER (DRO):
Range condition and trend. The DRO already makes monthly reports to Nakuru, copied to Nairobi, on range conditions and trends, standing vegetation, rainfall, and animal condition. For the EWS, the DRO should provide, at the divisional level, estimates of the current situation compared to normal for seasonal stream flows, range conditions and trends, range and browse use, estimates of changing selection of browse species from the

most-to-least palatable species according to a predetermined sequence, animal nutrition condition, and animal disease.

KENYA ARID LANDS RESEARCH STATION (KALRES):

Ecological changes. KALRES is setting up three small field stations in Turkana District for ecological monitoring, demonstration sites, and experimental plots. The stations will include fenced control and experimental areas, as well as demarcated but open plots under normal Turkana herder use. Around twenty to thirty ha of land will be under intense observation at each site. Ecological trends will be monitored in detail using standard procedures to measure vegetation density, basal and canopy cover, biomass, and annual production at different animal feeding heights. Livestock performance monitoring and an animal disease and nutrition component will likely be added. KALRES could contribute to the EWS by providing estimates of the most important vegetation and animal production changes, including the primary production for the season; range condition and trend (including the effects of use); change in animal browse preferences from more palatable to less palatable species; livestock performance (milk production, liveweight gain, birth and death rates, and nutritional condition) compared to expected rates; and animal disease situation.

DISTRICT EDUCATION OFFICER (DEO):

Participation in school feeding programs and school-enrollment trends.

TURKANA REHABILITATION PROGRAM:

Systematic reconnaissance flights. Quarterly or semiannual flights estimating changes in numbers and distribution of animals and people, increases in the number of people at or around settlements, ecological parameters (percentage grass cover, biomass changes, and the extent of *laga* flows compared to expected levels).

Unusual jobs and incomes. The Turkana Rehabilitation Project/ Meteorological Station (TRP/MET) should report the following EWS indicators: unusual sales of jewelry, spears, household utensils, or other personal belongings; unusual sales of, or a decline in the price of, firewood or charcoal; unusual sales of wild fruits or other wild products; unusual increases in the number of herders seeking to enroll as fishermen; and herders in large numbers leaving to look for salaried work outside Turkana.

Food-for-work enrollment. TRP keeps records of the amount of food disbursed for food-for-work and the numbers of people enrolled in the program. The TRP logistics officer should report unusual changes in the number of people enrolled for food-for-work and increases in the ratio of people seeking food-for-work to those actually enrolled.

Health and nutrition. TRP is increasing its activities in health and nutrition through the seven dispensaries it presently operates. Dispensaries are staffed by patient attendants, who generally have some primary school education and are trained in a three-month course at the mission hospital. TRP staff in mobile units, responsible for immunizations, supervise the dispensaries on a weekly or monthly basis. The dispensaries and mobile teams serve mainly the settled population, especially those in food-for-work camps. TRP was scheduled to begin systematic nutritional surveillance in 1985, again mainly among the settled population. Although no final decision had been made, it is likely that mid-arm circumference will be the nutritional status measure. For the EWS, the TRP medical team should report the following indicators: unusual changes in the number of patients reporting at TRP dispensaries or in their general medical or nutritional status; unusual changes in the incidence of major diseases, especially measles, typhoid, diarrhea, and TB; and, when nutritional status measures are introduced, changes in the number of patients falling below the chosen nutritional standard.

MINISTRY OF HEALTH (MOH)/LODWAR HOSPITAL:

Health and nutrition. Through Lodwar Hospital, the MOH collects medical statistics monthly from dispensaries, clinics, and other medical facilities in Turkana; these data cover deaths and the incidence of the thirty most common diseases. The figures, however, are routinely passed to Nakuru and Nairobi, bypassing local analysis. The recent appointment of a community-based health care advisor will allow a more epidemiological approach to be followed. Basic analytic statistics on changes in disease incidence and prevalence would ideally be compiled in Lodwar, thus enabling direct feedback to the dispensaries and clinics furnishing the raw data.

The new program in primary health care will include training community health care workers, primarily traditional birth attendants with some recent training. These health care workers will be supervised by Lodwar Hospital and by Mother and Child Health (MCH) community nurses.

Through Lodwar Hospital, local dispensaries, and MCH clinics, the MOH can provide similar EWS indicators as mentioned above for the TRP medical team. The hospital should also report unusual changes in district death rates.

DIOCESE OF LODWAR AND OTHER MISSIONS:

Health and nutrition. The Catholic church runs a mission hospital at Kakuma, four health centers, and a number of small mission dispensaries. These activities are coordinated through the Lodwar Diocesan Development Office. Although their feeding programs are being reduced, the church still runs one nursery-school feeding program. Other church and missionary groups run small dispensaries and occasional feeding programs. The Diocese of Lodwar, like the MOH facilities, has direct contact with the settled population and can contribute to the EWS by monitoring the number of patients, disease frequency, nutritional status of children, and numbers of patients, disease frequency, nutritional status of children, and numbers of children enrolled in the nursery-school feeding program. Other missions and church groups should be requested to report the same information through the district officer in their division.

TURKANA COUNTY COUNCIL:

Cess tax. The Turkana County Council in Lodwar imposes a small cess tax on animals and animal products (such as skins) that are exported from the district. The Turkana Council should report any unusual changes in the numbers of animals or skins on which cess is paid, as an EWS indicator.

NATIONAL CEREALS AND PRODUCE BOARD (NCPB):

Cereal stocks. For the EWS, the NCPB should provide information regarding the level of uncommitted stocks at Kitale, together with an indication of how this compares with the normal situation at that time of year. The NCPB should estimate the level of demand for cereals from traders and others for sale in Turkana, compared to the normal situation.

Liaison with National and International Monitoring Systems

The relationship between Turkana and the rest of Kenya is important in determining what actions should be taken in Turkana District in response to a developing crisis. In order to facilitate integrated national planning, it is proposed that data from the Turkana EWS be sent to the Office of the President in Nairobi and to the provincial administration in Nakuru. This will ensure that central and provincial authorities are kept informed about events and prospects in Turkana and that this information is shared with the relevant services through interministerial committees.

Equally important is the flow of information in the other direction, from Nairobi to Nakuru and Lodwar. The central government has information about the food situation in neighboring regions and in the rest of Kenya, and the district authorities can use this to put events in Turkana into a larger perspective. If progress is made toward a national early warning system, this information would be especially valuable to districts, such as Turkana, that are trying to forecast their own prospects. Particular reports of benefit to Turkana planners include rainfall and agrometeorology, crop yields and forecasts, cereal stocks in storage and imported, remote sensing data of vegetation, and livestock conditions in Kenya, Karamoja (Uganda), southern Sudan, and southwestern Ethiopia.

Analysis and Reporting

Coordinators. Responsibility for collecting and reporting the Turkana District indicators lies with the organizations under which the indicators are listed. Sample indicators are listed in Table 20.3 in a proposed format for the

EWS report. In a number of cases, several similar indicators will be reported by different sources, e.g., the nutritional status indicators reported by the Lodwar Hospital, TRP, and mission clinics. In such cases, a single coordinator is needed in Lodwar to synthesize the indicators.

Food situation and EWS report. Like all districts in Kenya, Turkana submits a monthly food situation report to the Office of the President (OP) in Nairobi. These reports, submitted by the district commissioner and based on information gathered by the district food committee, go to the senior assistant secretary responsible for drought coordination in the Office of the President, who is responsible to the permanent secretary for administration. If a district report indicates a serious food shortage, decisions are taken by the interministerial food monitoring committee, which includes representatives of the main ministries concerned.

This food situation report is a key document in the food information system and should be the main focus for EWS indicators. In order to limit the administrative load, an expanded food situation report may be prepared quarterly, taking the place of the normal monthly report every three months. The best timing for this expanded report might be in June (after the main rains), September (before the short rains), December (after the short rains), and March (at the end of the main dry period). If the EWS indicators show that unusual conditions are developing, expanded food situation reports should increase in frequency.

An equally important channel of information is from the Lodwar administration downward to the district officers, location and sublocation chiefs, and directly to the Turkana herders. These are the people most directly affected by the threat of drought, food shortage, and famine; they are well placed to give relevant information if they are kept informed of the overall picture that the district administration is able to compile.

Warning stages. Indicators in the EWS must be assessed cumulatively to determine the extent and degree of a developing crisis in Turkana. In several cases, indicators may report the same event from different points of view, different respondents, or different ways of measurement. Reports from the various ministries and organizations will need to be scored to arrive at a simple categorization of a small number of warning stages. For example, these might be: (1) a *normal* stage, in which worse scores, indicating a deteriorating situation, do not exceed 20 percent of total scores; (2) an *alert* stage, in which worse scores are between 20 and 40 percent of total scores; (3) an *alarm* stage, in which worse scores are 40 to 60 percent of total scores; and (4) an *emergency* stage, in which worse scores are more than 60 percent of total scores. These figures will have to be changed in light of experience and are given as an illustration only.

Information channeled to the EWS can serve as a regular aid to the district development plans, in addition to ringing warning bells of the danger that serious food shortages or famine might be developing. Creating an informed demand for monitoring information at a time when the EWS does not indicate an impending food crisis, will sharpen up the gathering, analysis, and reporting of information. It will also avoid the danger that in a long period when the EWS does not signal any particular problem (which may be the case on average nine years out of ten), the EWS information will decline in quality due to lack of interest. Regular use of EWS indicators as a guide to district development planning will enable the identification of those indicators for which reliable measurement is difficult because of faulty technique, unreliable sampling, or inadequate training of respondents.

Improving EWS Indicators

A second-generation EWS should be devised on the basis of the experience of the first two to three years of operation of the EWS proposed here. The second-generation EWS should include more quantitative measurement of key indicators: (1) agrometeorology, especially soil-water balances; (2) plant production, especially measurement of changes in range and browse layer production, standing crop, and use at the three KALRES ecological monitoring sites; (3) animal production, especially measurements of animal births and death rates, nutrition condition, liveweight gain, and milk production; (4) animal marketing and prices, especially significant quantitative changes in the level of marketing, age, and sex composition of animals sold and bartered, and animal prices; (5) cereal availability and prices, especially rises in price of nongazetted cereals and declining availability of gazetted cereals; (6) air survey data, especially evidence of changes in numbers and distribution of animals and herding camps; and (7) human nutrition standards, especially significant increases in the proportion of children below standard.

Technical services and NGOs will be responsible for the provision of better quantitative data on these questions, and the district development committee will be responsible for coordinating this data into an improved, second-generation EWS. In conjunction with each of the responsible services and organizations, the proposed district drought contingency officer will play a key role in making sure that the quantitative indicators fit into the overall EWS and that there are no important gaps in the coverage.

One of the research tasks will be to look at the statistical correlations between different quantitative indicators. Experience elsewhere in Africa (for example, in Botswana, as reported in Mason et al., 1985) suggests that changes in key quantitative indicators, such as soil-water balance, cattle nutritional condition, and changes in relative prices of important foods and other commodities, can be correlated with a later decline in the nutritional status of children in a bad year. The expansion of the EWS should not be done at the expense of qualitative indicators which, because of their simplicity and way they are readily understood by herders and others, should always play an important role in the district EWS.

RESPONSES TO A DROUGHT

The preparedness measures and early warning system proposed here should ensure that Turkana District will be prepared for a major drought and potential famine. Taken alone, these measures will neither prevent nor contain drought. They are designed, in part, to provide the information, funds, resources, staff, plans, and infrastructure to make specific responses available to district officials. These responses, in turn, can be turned to policies and actions aimed at the rapid rehabilitation of the rural economy after the crisis is over. Most of the responses have been described above. A few notes are included here, along with a list of appropriate responses for each warning level (Table 20.4).

Emergency Drought Management Subcommittee

At a signal from the early warning system that the situation is deteriorating, the district development committee should activate its emergency drought-management subcommittee, composed of the district commissioner (chairman), DVO, DAO, MOH, livestock marketing advisor, TRP, Lodwar Diocese, a representative of the secular NGOs active in the district, and the district drought contingency officer (secretary). This subcommittee would be responsible for reviewing information, monitoring, and recommending major actions to the district development committee.

Cereal Availability and Storage

At the first signal from the early warning system, the NCPB should ensure that its Lodwar cereal store is filled to capacity, and as long as the overall district warning stage is other than normal, a particular effort should be made to keep the store filled. At signs from the early warning system that a serious food situation may be developing, the district administration should move cereals from Lodwar and Kitale into standby cereal storage facilities at division and location levels. The district commissioner would have the authority to release these cereals to the traders on behalf of the NCPB in the normal way, or to distribute them as food-for-work or emergency famine relief.

Animal Health, Grazing, and Destocking

Animals that are weak from undernutrition in a drought are especially susceptible to disease. When the early warning system indicates cause for alarm, the DVO should put his staff on special alert for signs of contagious animal diseases, such as contagious caprine pleuropneumonia (CCPP). The DVO should have a contingency plan for rapid laboratory analysis, disease-strain typing, vaccine production, and distribution. An increased petrol allocation paid from the district drought contingency fund may be needed to enable the officer to react immediately to any extreme situation.

A large part of Turkana is presently undergrazed because of security problems. Increased security in the affected areas would enable the extension of grazing in a drought. Turkana herders will probably use such areas anyway, putting themselves at risk from raiders from outside the district. The district commissioner should authorize an increase in the Turkana home guard, which would involve temporarily arming a cadre of Turkana herders in selected areas.

At the first signal from the early warning system, the district commissioner would alert Nairobi that the contingency fund and pledged fodder aid may be required soon. At a second signal, the DC would seek authorization from Nairobi to transfer a portion of the fund (perhaps a quarter) to a special account in Lodwar. Food and fodder pledges made under this program would also be activated at this time. No disbursements of cash, food, or fodder would be made until the early warning system passed into a third-stage alert. At such time and after discussion in the emergency drought-management subcommittee and the district development committee, the district commissioner would authorize the animal-purchase program to be started in a particular division or in the district as a whole. The DVO, livestock marketing staff, and perhaps TRP/MET would be responsible for carrying out the program. Animals of all species would be bought either at action markets or at guaranteed prices at special buying centers modelled after those operated by Oxfam/TRP for their restocking program. The prices would be on a fixed scale adopted by the services operating the scheme. An effort would be made to buy animals in reasonable condition and to spread purchases over households and areas.

Public Works Program

At the first signal from the early warning system, the TRP should contact potential public works site supervisors on its standing list to alert them of the possibility that they will be needed. They must also check and inventory stockpiles of tools and equipment, familiarizing themselves with projects on the public works register. At this stage, the TRP and the district commissioner should issue a preliminary alert to donors bound by contractual agreements for food or cash. At the second warning stage, the TRP, through the district commissioner, would issue a formal request to donors within the terms of the contract for food or cash aid, and start to hire additional public works site supervisors. At the third warning stage, TRP would start hiring laborers. At first, they would normally be paid cash wages from the district drought contingency fund, although they could also be paid in food from the emergency stocks that were by then in place at the division and location level. As emergency food aid starts to arrive in the district, an increased proportion of public works would be paid directly in food.

Relief Feeding

Regardless of how successful district efforts are in protecting rural purchasing power and maintaining job possibilities through public works programs, there will inevitably be some people (the very old, the very young, and the sick) who will not be able to work for cash or food; these are the people at greatest risk as a drought begins to turn into a famine. If a famine begins to develop, the number of destitute people may quickly exceed the administrative and supervisory capacity of the public works program. The district commissioner's famine relief list should be maintained as a mechanism to meet this need. Through the recommendation of location chiefs, a rapid enlargement of the list should be made possible when the number of destitute people rises too fast for the public works programs to accommodate them. The food for this purpose would be drawn from the district strategic reserve, dispersed in location level stores at an early stage of a crisis and subsequently increased through donor pledges and other food-aid commitments.

Alternative Fallback Activities

In major droughts, Turkana herders adopt an array of fallback strategies that include gathering wild plant foods, hunting, fishing, and labor migration out of the district. Fishing has been of great importance in the past; and in some earlier droughts, NGOs, including Oxfam, helped destitute herders by giving them fishing nets. There is some circumstantial evidence, however, backed up by the opinion of Turkana and other people knowledgeable about the district, that Lake Turkana is now so heavily exploited that fishing no longer offers a useful fallback activity for more than a few herders in a drought. This is an important reason for the increased vulnerability to drought in the district. If studies show that there is room for expansion, even at relatively low productivity, the drought contingency plan should include the rapid provision of fishing equipment, especially nets, boats, and perhaps motors in a crisis. There is probably little that can be done to help other fallback activities in a drought, especially hunting, gathering, or migrant labor.

CONCLUSIONS

Throughout this analysis, emphasis has been placed on preparedness for drought. When taken early at the district level, simple measures can prevent a drought from deteriorating into a famine. Government agencies, along with NGOs (local, national, and international), church groups, schools, and hospitals, can play a part in monitoring the local situation. Notice of several simultaneous drought early warning signals, reported by various agencies, would trigger planned drought responses. The organizations concerned would operate at all times under a situation of readiness to respond to extreme situations; thus, when the alarm is sounded, the steps are already delineated as to what actions should be taken. Crucial to this process is the unimpeded flow of information among all organizations in the region, as well as between centralized government agencies and Turkana District officials.

The implementation of initial drought-preparedness measures and an early warning system would be neither costly nor difficult. The staff and organizations are already in place; what is needed are improved coordination and communication among all involved in the region. Incremental improvements in the district's ability to respond to drought can be achieved through the gradual development of existing resources.

Figure 20.1 Cycle of pastoral terms of trade during drought conditions. Source: Swift (1985)

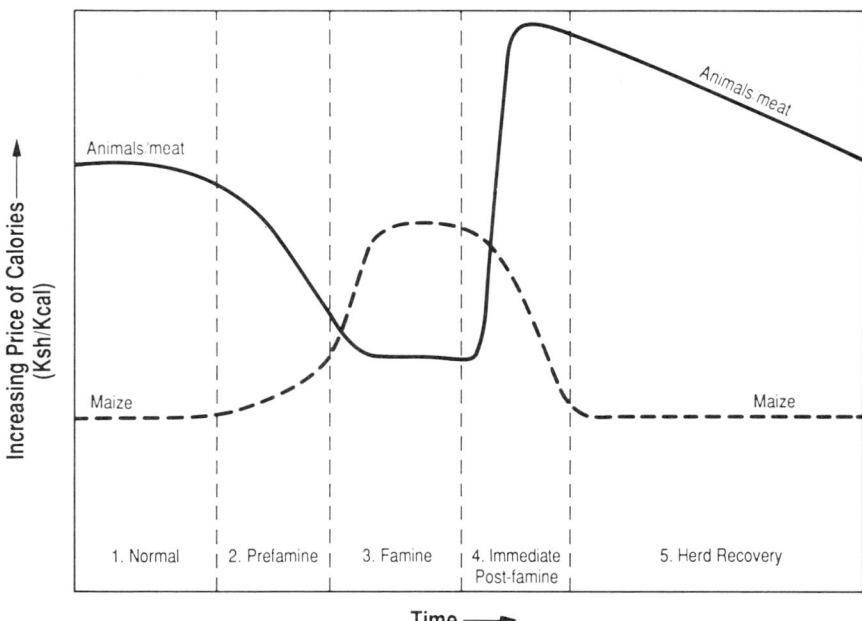

Table 20.1 Annual Probability of Wet and Dry Years According to a Weighted Ecological Index

Area	n	Annual Probability			
		Very Dry	Dry	Normal	Wet
Lodwar*	57	.11	.21	.32	.37
Lokitaung	41	.02	.12	.41	.44
Todenyang	18	.11	.22	.22	.44
Lokichokio	23	.04	.17	.52	.26
Kapedo	15	0.00	.20	.60	.20

Source: Swift (1985).
Notes: The ecological index weights the previous year by one-third and the current year by two-thirds. A very dry year is one whose weighted ecological index is less than half the median index at that station; a dry year is one with an index of 0.5 to 0.8 of the median. A normal year is 0.8 to 1.2 of the median, and a wet year is more than 1.2 of the median.
* Index and mean calculated separately before and after 1950.

INSTITUTIONAL EXPERIENCES IN MANAGEMENT • 327

Table 20.2 Main Disaster Years According to Turkana Chronologies

Year	Name	Type of Disaster
1925	*ekwakoit*	Bad hunger
Early 1930s	*abirikae*	Drought or bad hunger
1942	*lolewo*	Bad animal disease
1943	*ekuwam lonyang*	Drought and famine
1947	*ataa nachoke* or *awoyate*	Animal disease and famine
1949	*ngilowi*	Animal disease
1952	*lotira*	Animal disease, drought, and famine
1953–1954	*lokulit*	Bad years, famine continued
1960	*namotor*	Drought and famine
1966	*etop*	Serious but short drought
1971	*lolewo*	First cholera epidemic, many deaths
1979–1981	*loukoi* (CCPP), *lopiar*, *atanayanaye*	Animal disease (CCPP, anthrax), security problems, famine

Source: Swift (1985).

Table 20.3 Sample Checklists for the Turkana District Early Warning System

	Situation Compared to Normal for Time of Year		
Indicator (Source)	Worse	Normal	Better
Range condition (DRO)			
Lodwar central			
Lokitaung			
Kakuma			
Lorugum			
Lokori			
Katilu			
Area planted (DAO)			
Lodwar central			
Lokitaung			
Kakuma			
Lorugum			
Lokori			
Katilu			
Harvest (DAO)			
Lodwar central			
Lokitaung			
Kakuma			
Lorugum			
Lokori			
Katilu			
Level of animal sales and barter (Livestock Advisor, Ministry of Ag., Livestock Development, TRP/MET)			
Lodwar central			
Lokitaung			
Kakuma			
Lorugum			
Lokori			
Katilu			

Source: Swift (1985).

Table 20.4 Warning Stages and Planned Responses

Warning Stage	Action	Responsible Officer
ALERT	Activate emergency drought management subcommittee (EDM), which meets monthly.	DC/DDCO
	EWS reports monthly.	DDCO
	Alert NGOs.	DDCO
	Alert contractual donors for animal purchase and fodder contingency funds.	DC/DVO/Animal marketing
	NCPB fills and maintains Lodwar store at capacity. Alert contractual donors for cash and food pledges for public works.	NCPB DC/TRP
	Contact public works site supervisors; check inventory of stockpiled equipment; familiarization with public works register of projects.	TRP
	Alert contractual donors for cess tax remission.	DC/TDC
ALARM	EDM meets weekly.	DC/DDCO
	Three-month cereal supply is dispersed to locations from Lodwar NCPB; refill Lodwar NCPB store to capacity.	DC/NCPB
	NCPB monthly cereal stock report to EDM	NCPB
	DOs and chiefs report monthly to EDM on cereal availability and prices; increase Turkana home guard to improve security.	DC
	Special alert on animal disease.	DVO
	Activate donor animal purchase and fodder commitments; transfer first part to Lodwar.	DC/TRP
	Recall/recruit public works site supervisors.	TRP
	Activate donor pledges for cess tax compensation.	DC/TDC
EMERGENCY	Start emergency animal purchase; also purchase skins if necessary.	Animal/DVO marketing
	Export animals to KMC; hold best females, slaughter rest.	DVO/Animal marketing
	Start public works projects.	TRP
	Start purchase of firewood, gravel, and stones.	TRP
	Prepare new projects for register.	TRP
	Remit cess taxes.	DC/TDC
	Prepare emergency camp sites and equipment.	MOH

Source: Swift (1985)
Notes: Abbreviations are: EDM = Emergency Drought Management subcommittee; DC = District Commissioner; DDCO = proposed District Drought-Contingency Officer; EWS = early warning system; NGO = nongovernmental organization; NCPB = National Cereals and Produce Board; DO = District Officer; DVO = District Veterinary Officer; TRP = Turkana Rehabilitation Project; TDC = Turkana District council; MOH = Ministry of Health; KMC = Kenya Meat Commission

· 21 ·

Drought Assistance to NGOs Provided by CARE-Kenya

ROBIN NEEDHAM

Kenya historically suffers a serious drought affecting major parts of the country on the average of about once every ten years. In some parts of the country, these droughts usually persist for two or more growing seasons, leading to a considerable loss of agricultural production, livestock, and wildlife. As early as May 1983, there were reliable indicators that some of the arid and semiarid areas of the country would experience drought conditions after insufficient rains in March and April 1983. There was little reason at that time, however, to be unduly concerned since most of the affected areas were more dependent on the short rains of September to October for their food production. Local populations focused their efforts on maximizing food-production potential for the coming short rains rather than coping with the attendant period of food shortage.

The extent of the drought and the seriousness of the situation in the arid and semiarid areas was apparent with the failure of the expected short rains of 1983. The first requests for drought relief were received by the central government and the World Food Programme (WFP) from Isiolo District and the drier parts of Meru and Embu districts. Subsequently, aid was sought by the Catholic missions in Marsabit and Samburu and then by Kitui, Machakos, Kajiado, and Narok. As the rains failed in Northeastern Province, Tana River District, and parts of Rift Valley Province, similar appeals for assistance increased markedly.

Reports of grain and dairy-product shortages were received more and more frequently from these areas, yet the scarce food situation did not receive nationwide concern until after the failure of the March to April 1984 long rains throughout most of the country. Agriculture and livestock production had already been seriously affected by drought conditions. Three successive seasons were poor in Kitui, Machakos, Meru, and Embu districts. By June 1984, seed and food stocks, as well as ready cash, were nearly exhausted. Crop yields were estimated to be as low as 9 percent of normal years. As production declined, the gap between domestic consumption and production of basic foodstuffs increased. The government of Kenya was forced to import over one million tons of food. Food imports had negative repercussions on the balance of trade, external debt, and the development budget, but they were largely successful in keeping domestic demand satisfied in the more prosperous areas.

According to the Office of the President, approximately 11 percent of the total population was critically affected by the drought in that it had insufficient purchasing power to maintain reasonable nutritional standards. Virtually every farmer or livestock owner in the eastern part of the country and the pastoral areas suffered seriously from a loss of earnings, loss of inputs, and cattle deaths. Due to depleted stocks of grain for domestic consumption, higher rates of malnutrition and related problems, particularly among the vulnerable groups of children, women, and the elderly, were evident.

RESPONSE BY NONGOVERNMENTAL ORGANIZATIONS

A wide variety of nongovernmental organizations (NGOs) provide humanitarian assistance to Kenya. Interagency collaboration, both local and international, has been extensive, although informal. As a whole, NGOs possess considerable resources and skills that are of relevance and utility to the government in a drought situation. A number of NGO employees have extensive experience in emergency relief, nutritional surveillance, maternal and child health care, and institutional feeding, as well as in long-term capacity-building activities in agriculture, livestock development, and soil conservation. Many NGOs have a presence, either directly or indirectly, in the affected areas, and most have some access to relief commodities or emergency funds.

During the 1984/85 drought, the government felt NGOs could play an important role in moving significant amounts of the imported relief supplies to affected areas and in assisting the districts with distribution to targeted famine-relief recipients. The Kenya National Council for Social Services (KNCSS) was appointed as an agent for NGOs involved in food distribution. Relief activities would be coordinated through the KNCSS to avoid duplication of efforts or gaps in the relief program.

In the northern districts, the WFP, Oxfam, some Catholic missions, World Vision, and UNESCO implemented an innovative destocking project that entailed the exchange of grain for livestock in nomadic areas to provide a market for drought-stricken animals, reduce grazing pressure on the range, and distribute food without encouraging settlement (see Chapter 23).

In other areas, NGOs tackled the situation through expanded school feeding and Mother and Child Health (MCH) programs, food-for-work activities, mobile clinics, and regular free distribution of food to needy people.

LOGISTICS

The extra food imports for market support and drought relief required large-scale logistical management. The country's port, storage, rail, and transport capacities were heavily taxed to handle the imports. The Mombasa-Nairobi railway ran at half capacity (1,500 mt per day) because of engine breakdowns and insufficient rolling stock. Up to 3,000 mt per day were transported by road at double the price of railway haulage. USAID and the EEC greatly facilitated matters by allowing cash generated from market sales of their donated commodities to offset the costs of primary transport from Mombasa to National Cereals and Produce Board (NCPB) stores. Without this arrangement, the cost burden for the relief operations would have been too high for both the government and NGOs. A commodity exchange formula was also worked out with the NCPB whereby control of donated commodities (maize and wheat only) arriving at Mombasa was transferred from the donor agency to the NCPB. A credit was then established in the name of the donor agency so that cereals could be drawn by the agency from NCPB storage depots up-country.

Thus relieved of substantial primary transport costs, NGOs were able to undertake new projects or expand their ongoing relief programs. Secondary transport costs, however, were still a major financial burden for NGOs. Transport of relief supplies from NCPB depots to points of final distribution was very expensive due to the long distances, difficult road conditions, and dispersed populations. Financing such transport required increases in overall budget expenditures, particularly in the areas of personnel and operations, far above and beyond normal development programs. Many agencies were not in a position to meet the high costs of handling, transporting, and distributing additional food.

This particular bottleneck—reimbursement of in-country food transport costs incurred by NGOs—was addressed by the U.S. Office of Foreign Disaster Assistance (OFDA, grant No. ASB-000-G-SS-4207-00). The OFDA grant, effective from 26 September 1984 to 30 September 1985, totaled $1,940,952, of which over 90 percent was for the reimbursement of NGO food transport costs to drought- and famine-affected areas, with the remainder to be spent for administrative expenses incurred by CARE-Kenya.

The OFDA grant was made available on the basis of information provided by several NGOs about their anticipated or existing programs in August 1984. Letters of understanding were drawn up in October between CARE-Kenya and these NGOs, and a provisional allocation of funds to NGOs was made (Table 21.1).

During the first few months of the drought-relief program in Kenya, agencies drew food from NCPB stores that had been allocated to them by the World Food Programme. The amount of food allocated to NGOs totaled about 18,000 mt between early 1984 and early 1985. Most agencies, however, did not get their main drought-relief programs started until late 1984. The Catholic Diocese of Marsabit, the Kenyan Red Cross Society, the National Christian Council of Kenya (NCCK), and some of the smaller missions that were working actively from early 1984, particularly in the northern districts, were notable exceptions. The increase of NGO drought-relief programs toward the end of the year is clearly seen when month-by-month OFDA grant disbursements are compared (Table 21.2).

From March to June 1985, expenditures under the grant ran at a fairly consistent figure of between $179,000 and $243,000 per month. For most of 1984, little famine relief was distributed by the government. The government priority was to keep market demand satisfied. The first consignment of PL480 Title II food, for concessional distribution to drought-affected areas through the Office of the President, did not arrive until late October/early November. This began to reach districts in significant quantities by December. By this time, many agency drought-relief programs were operating at their highest level of activity. The district commissioners were hampered by transport shortages, and relief food began to stockpile at NCPB stores. An agreement was reached in late December between the Office of the President, NCPB, and USAID that permitted district commissioners to direct the NCPB trucks delivering relief food from Mombasa straight to the affected areas, instead of unloading them at the NCPB stores.

In mid-December, the WFP announced that the food it was allocating to NGOs for drought and famine relief was running low; henceforth, NGOs would have to make other arrangements to obtain food for their relief programs. At this point, an arrangement was made for NGOs to request food allocations directly from the district commissioners. This was considered a sound move for the following reasons:

1. District commissioners are well placed to coordinate relief efforts within the district. They can ensure that duplication of food relief does not occur, and they can also see that neglected areas receive attention.
2. District centralization of food allocation helps to improve cooperation, coordination, and information between NGOs and also between district officials and NGOs.
3. District control of food allocation is in line with the government policy of district focus for rural development and the decentralization of decisionmaking.

This arrangement, however, was not easily implemented. The situation regarding food allocations was very confusing and inconsistent in the first few months of the year. There was some conflict between the Office of the President and the district commissioners as to who actually had the authority to make food allocations to NGOs. The Office of the President claimed that the authority was vested in the district commissioners, yet the district commissioners felt that they needed formal authorization from the Office of the President. Inconsistencies in food policy management and implementation for different districts plagued NGOs. Some agencies were successful in obtaining allocations from the district commissioners for their programs, while other NGOs found they had to undertake the district commissioners' food-distribution program themselves. Some district commissioners claimed that they did not have any food for NGOs, and others attempted to sell the concessional food to NGOs.

The short rains in October and November of 1984 were widespread, and in many areas the general crop situation improved dramatically. There were still considerable difficulties; a large outbreak of army worm infestation destroyed large areas of maize, but beans and potatoes were not affected. There was also a severe shortage of seed for planting (particularly the popular Katumani maize variety) so that the crop harvested in February to March was not exceptional. In many areas, however, it was the first crop of any significance to be harvested in two years.

The long rains of 1985 were even better than the short rains of 1984; they were considerably above average over most of Kenya. Army worm infestation was less severe, and more seed was available than during the previous planting season. In the agricultural districts of Meru, Embu, and Machakos, NGO drought- and famine-relief measures were phased out in April and May.

In the pastoral areas, recovery from the drought was generally slower than in the central agricultural regions. The rains in the far north were good, but not as widespread as elsewhere. Livestock also takes longer than crops to recover from periods of stress. The herds in the arid and semiarid areas were severely depleted; in some areas up to 80 percent of cattle and smallstock had died during and after the drought (see Chapter 5). Those remaining were in poor condition, and females had stopped lactating and ovulating. Goats and sheep started giving birth in April and May, whereas cattle and camels did not have significant numbers of offspring until August to September. To compensate for the lag period in recovery, food assistance to these areas continued through the end of July, although on a reduced scale.

The OFDA grant was originally intended to expire the end of July 1985, but in March to April, it was apparent that an extension would be desirable. No additional money was requested since it appeared there would be a balance of about $200,000 at the end of the extended project period. The extension to the grant period was approved in Washington in mid-June. In June, however, the amount of reimbursements rose to about three times the normal monthly rate. Similarly, shipping costs for June ($59.12 per mt) were much higher than normal. There are several likely explanations for this rise in allocations:

1. Since some agencies thought there would be problems with the grant extension, they completed their claims procedure early to avoid potential shortfalls.

2. Some famine-relief food was ordered independently of USAID or WFP and dispatched several months later by NGOs. This food arrived some months into 1985 and was not cleared from the port until May to June (for example, an NCCK shipment of maize and beans). Consequently, there was a larger-than-usual amount of transport from Mombasa (rather than from local NCPB stores), which contributed to an increase in claims.
3. The areas that were still being served by NGO drought- and famine-relief programs in June were the more distant and inaccessible areas of the north (Marsabit, Turkana, and Samburu) rather than such areas of easier access as Embu, Meru, Machakos, and Kitui. In addition, rainfall increased the price of transport to some of the more marginal areas because roads had deteriorated, even washing away in some parts.
4. The two largest claims for June, amounting to a total of more than $250,000, were for cumulative expenses incurred for long periods prior to June (eight months or so each).
5. For some agencies (including CARE), the end of June is the end of the financial year. Thus, there was a rush to make claims and settle accounts.
6. Concerned about large reserves of famine-relief food (yellow maize) stockpiled in their stores, some district commissioners (notably in Baringo, Kitui, and Kajiado) called upon certain NGOs (World Vision and Food for the Hungry) to assist them in distributing the food before it became infested.

The combined effect of this unusual level of activity in June left only $129,750 of the grant money to cover the remaining three months of the period. Agencies still working in the pastoral areas were contacted, and each was given an allocation of money for the remaining period based on their past levels of expenditure and anticipated future needs.

CONCLUSION

In spite of the rather abrupt end of this project, the CARE-Kenya drought-relief program was an outstanding success on many counts:

1. More than 33,000 mt of food were distributed to famine- and drought-affected persons in Kenya due to the provision of grant money. This amount of food is several thousand more tons than was originally anticipated in the initial project proposal.
2. Twenty-eight NGOs were assisted in their efforts to distribute food. Had the transport aid not been available, the level of assistance provided by these agencies would have been much less.

3. CARE-Kenya was able to have a significant effect on the success of drought- and famine-relief efforts in Kenya with very little disturbance of regular activities. Only two extra staff members were employed for the project period.
4. Dispensing of the grant money kept CARE-Kenya at the forefront of drought- and famine-relief measures within the country.
5. Contacts with other NGOs were made and relationships cemented. This will benefit the long-term involvement of CARE-Kenya in development programs within Kenya.

Table 21.1 NGO Participation in the OFDA Grant for Transport Costs

NGO	Provisional Allocation ($)
World Vision	700,000
National Christian Council of Kenya	500,000
Kenya Freedom from Hunger Council	230,000
Adventists Relief and Development Agency	135,000
Kenyan Red Cross Society	130,000
African Medical Research and Education Foundation	100,000
Food for the Hungry	100,000
Diocese of Marsabit, Nanyuki	75,000

Smaller NGOs, not given specific allocations:

ActionAid	AIC Hurri Hills Project, Marsabit
Children's Mercy Fund	Chogoria Hospital, Meru District
Diocese of Garissa	Diocese of Kisii
Diocese of Kitui	Diocese of Machakos
Diocese of Mount Kenya East	Kacheliba Catholic Mission, Kapenguria
Karaba Catholic Mission, Embu	Lutheran Mission, Kajiado District
Maua Hospital, Meru District	Merti Catholic Mission, Isiolo District
Nutrition CRSP Project, Embu	Oxfam
Turkana Rehabilitation Project	UNESCO, Integrated Project in Arid Lands, Marsabit
UNICEF	
World Concern	

Table 21.2 CARE-Kenya Monthly Grant Dispursements for Transport

Month	Amount ($)	Food Moved (mt)
November 1984	51,149	869
December 1984	41,842	603
January 1985	105,625	2,491
February 1985	196,763	4,492
Total	395,379	8,455

Source: CARE-Kenya.

· 22 ·

Drought Relief Activities of the Kenya Freedom From Hunger Council

MOSES G. MBUGUA

The Kenya Freedom From Hunger Council (KFFHC) is a nongovernmental organization that focuses on the development of projects throughout Kenya. Its main objective is to alleviate hunger and malnutrition through such projects as water development, institutional assistance, women's groups, irrigation, and community food activities. The National Freedom From Hunger Walk is held every year to raise funds and bring attention to the problems of hunger and malnutrition in Kenya.

During the 1984 drought, it was apparent to the KFFHC staff that emergency drought assistance would be required and that food aid would be needed by July 1984. Due to a shortage of personnel and the lengthy process required to identify viable projects, however, the Emergency Food Aid Program was not initiated until September, and food was not distributed until December. This chapter chronicles the KFFHC effort and identifies important conclusions for future drought-assistance programs.

PROJECT ACTIVITIES

Food-for-work projects were identified by the local authorities, including district commissioners (DC), their officers, and the district development committees. The requests were sent to the KFFHC through the DC's office. KFFHC officers then visited the projects, discussed possible alternatives, and approved the final request if it was deemed viable. The project visits were conducted from October to December. The district and KFFHC staff also identified famine-relief projects, where food was distributed to schools, children's homes, homes for the disabled, dispensaries, village polytechnics, hospitals, and communities. When approved, food was dispatched every month according to an approved timetable. Table 22.1 lists the districts receiving assistance and the duration of food deliveries. Most of the projects began in December or January, although a few were delayed beyond the starting month indicated. A total of 1,043 mt (11,590 bags) of maize was distributed among thirty-nine famine-relief projects during the period of December 1984 to April 1985. The projects were stopped in April 1985, after the harvest from the November-December rains and the improved food situation. At this time, the government increased its deliveries of yellow maize.

During March and April 1985, the KFFHC distributed Katumani maize and bean seeds (Table 22.2). Seeds of all types, but especially Katumani maize and beans, were in short supply and therefore difficult to procure during the 1984 short rains. The KFFHC had difficulties purchasing seeds in preparation for the long rains. Katumani seed was available only after late March 1985; thus, the KFFHC found it difficult to distribute the seed in time for planting. Despite the shortage of seeds, a good crop was reported, except in the southern division of Kitui where the rains were poor (the January-to-May 1985 rainfall in southern Kitui was 102 mm). The KFFHC purchased seed for distribution in Kitui during the 1985 short rains, which are more reliable in that area.

During the months of February, June, and July, the KFFHC distributed tools to the food-for-work projects in six districts, with funds largely from the EEC. Tool distribution was intended to encourage continuation of community projects (Table 22.3). The projects also received wheelbarrows (471), axes (328), grinding mills (86), hand pumps for shallow wells (20), and a few other items. In Machakos and Kitui, it was felt that the projects would certainly continue. In Meru, however, the KFFHC thought the projects were less viable due to competition from growing *miraa*, a mild narcotic. The staff was hopeful of success for most of the other projects.

REPORTS BY DISTRICT

Kiambu

The most drought-affected areas in Kiambu were Ndeiya and Karai locations and Munyu and Ngoliba villages in Thika Division. The two villages requested support in December, and the two locations in January. Most of the projects identified for support in Karai Location were already being assisted by the Rural Development Fund's (cash-for-work) program. In Ndeiya Location, the KFFHC suggested that famine-relief food be sent to small-scale community development projects rather than to secondary schools. The chief and district officer adopted this approach, and new projects began in April. In March, food was sent in bulk to the chief's camp, from where it was distributed. The last food consignment was distributed in May 1985 in the two locations, at which time food supplies were normal. Munyu and Ngoliba received 8,313 kg of fat along with the maize.

The Munyu Self Help group received assistance from the KFFHC and other donors (Government of Kenya, DANIDA). The group has nearly one thousand members who operate a poultry project. In 1984, the project had 50,000 chickens, and 80,000 in 1985. Eggs were sold in Nairobi. During 1984–1985, one chicken house for 20,000 chickens was completed and another started. A water pipe was also installed. The last food aid was distributed in July 1985 since the group manager expected food supplies to be normal in August. All this was possible due to the KFFHC food assistance.

Machakos

The KFFHC supported thirty-one food-for-work projects and eleven famine-relief projects in Machakos. The famine-relief projects ended in May, as the food situation had recovered in most of the district. A mission in Makindu continued to get food assistance after July 1985 because rainfall in the area had been very poor. The farmers stored nearly all of the seeds sent by the KFFHC for planting in the November-December rains, which are more reliable than the rains in the March-May season. In addition to the maize, 1,530 kg of fat were delivered.

The self-help tradition of the Akamba people facilitated the organization and success of the community food-for-work projects. In particular, the people of Wamunyu and Masii achieved good results. Most of the earth dams supported by KFFHC were completed by the time food aid was suspended. After the tools were distributed, the people promised to finish the catchments for the next rainy season. Other soil-conservation projects required continued maintenance for the repair of eroded areas and the extension of the protection area.

Kitui

The KFFHC worked only in southern Kitui, the driest division, where it supplied food to the local unskilled laborers participating in the Mutomo Soil and Water Conservation project of the Ministry of Agriculture, with technical and financial support from DANIDA. The KFFHC project began in 1983 when the Ministry of Agriculture completed nine water-conservation projects (mostly rock catchments). By 1984, forty-two more projects were completed; between January and July 1985, forty additional projects were concluded. Project staff consider that the rapid progress is due to both an increase in the support facilities (staff, vehicles, and materials) and the incentive of the food-for-work. During the food-for-work program, 15,000 people (95 percent of whom were women) worked on the water-conservation projects. Each worker received 2 kg of maize per working day and was allowed to work a maximum of two days per week. When the KFFHC switched from yellow to the preferred white maize, the work force on the soil and water projects increased. In addition to the maize, 28,350 kg of beans and 44,557 kg of fat were distributed.

Soil-conservation projects are never finished; there is always more that could be done. Approximately six thousand people worked on more than one hundred soil-conservation projects in Mutomo. These included cut-off trenches, tree planting, and grass strips. From the beginning of the project until July 1985, 408 km of trenches had been dug and 1,500 trees planted.

Food was to be transported to Mutomo until September 1985, since the March to May rains were very poor. The seeds distributed in the November-December rains included Katumani maize, cow peas, green grams, sorghum, and *mwezi moja* beans.

Embu

The food-for-work projects were initiated in December 1984, but since most of them were not well developed or monitored, they were finalized in January 1985. After an inspection in January, the KFFHC remained with six famine-relief projects that were finalized in April. Two food-for-work projects were requested and approved in January for the Karaba mission. One involved five hundred people for three months, and the other involved one hundred people until the end of the program. Maize distribution was supplemented with 340 kg of fat. Seeds and tools were also distributed.

Nyeri

Kieni East and Kieni West divisions received assistance. Six famine-relief projects and eight food-for-work projects were undertaken. Five of the projects were to develop water sources on the slopes of Mt. Kenya. Most of the projects went well, although pipes were lacking. The government promised to assist in project completion. In Kieni West, the KFFHC agreed to construct a classroom at the Laburo primary school. During the first visit, the foundations had been dug and some stones delivered; four weeks later, the entire classroom had been constructed and pupils were inside. At the Mweiga tree nursery, a promising start stagnated. After food was delivered for 15,400 working hours, half of a plot was cleared and weeded, with ten new seed beds dug and planted. The reason for the lack of success was not determined.

Meru

The request for assistance in Maua Division consisted of nine small food-for-work projects (water, soil conservation, and cattle dips). Overall, the food-for-work projects were successful, partly because the Foster Parents Plan provided technical advice, materials, and close supervision for the water and irrigation projects. The other projects were self-help. The only project to fail was a water project in Ithima that never got off the ground. The cattle dip in Antubetue was hindered by a land dispute, which was not adjudicated because the local chief was ill for two months. The cattle dip at Amungenti was very successful. Construction started in December 1984; the dip was first used in June 1985. A veterinary officer, visiting the site weekly, reported that 70 percent (over 800) of the cattle of the area are dipped each week.

Famine relief was distributed between December 1984 and April 1985 in Maua Division and from January to April 1985 in Tharaka Division. In late December, cholera broke out in the area, and food supplies were even more essential. Along with the maize, 3,927 kg of fat were distributed.

Marsabit

The great distances within Marsabit District and to the district from Nairobi hindered regular monitoring of projects. Near Marsabit town, a relatively wet area, famine relief ended in April 1985, while the other projects received assistance until September. Agricultural projects were supported in Central Division and, along with soil-conservation programs, in the Moyale and Sololo areas. In the western part of the district, activities included shallow-well construction and some small afforestation projects. Seeds were distributed in mid-April, and crops did well in the long rainy season. In Moyale and Sololo, the seeds were distributed after the rains had begun, but the harvest was exceptional regardless of the late planting. Also, 21,650 kg of beans and 31,790 kg of fat were distributed. When the seeds were being distributed, the roads were impassable due to heavy rains, and the KFFHC was compelled to hire donkeys to deliver the seeds.

SUMMARY

There are several important lessons learned by the KFFHC in coping with the 1984 drought. The actual flow of food began in December or later, while it should have begun in July. The government closely monitored the food situation in the country, but there is a need for more timely reporting, particularly to the NGOs so they can begin their own planning of food-assistance projects in time. The need for a timely early warning system cannot be overemphasized. Together with the government, the KFFHC should continue to develop its monitoring capabilities.

In some areas of the country, food shortages are not caused only by low agricultural production. The shortage of suitable storage facilities thwarts food and seed storage for lengthy periods. For example, in Moyale and Sololo, most of the food and seed was stored in the office of the chief or other local offices. Some of the food may be destroyed by rain or insects before the next harvest, precisely when it is needed the most.

Follow-up to the projects was as close as possible, considering the distances between projects and the shortage of staff. Most projects were visited every month, yet this was far from sufficient. More frequent visits for longer periods of time would allow the KFFHC staff to actually participate in the work. The involvement of the chiefs, local extension workers, local leaders, other government staff, and local aid organizations varied from project to project, but it was crucial to the success of the food-aid emergency program. In a few places, the willingness and dedication of the people themselves overcame the lack of leadership and supervision from the outside.

The support from the government staff; our sister organization, The German Freedom From Hunger agency; CARE-Kenya; the EEC; DANIDA, and the spirit shown by our staff in administering the Emergency Food Aid Program were the pillars of the success of the program. In the nine districts where food aid was distributed, however, the success of the development programs was due to the support, understanding, and hard work of the communities involved.

Table 22.1 Duration of Food Assistance Provided by the KFFHC

District	Assistance Started	Food-for-Work Ended	Famine Relief Ended
Kiambu			
Ndeiya & Karai	Jan. 85	May 85	Apr. 85
Ngoliba & Munyu	Dec. 84	Jul. 85	Apr. 85
Machakos*	Dec. 84	May 85	Apr. 85
Kitui	Dec. 84	Dec. 85	Apr. 85
Embu	Dec. 84	Jan. 85	Apr. 85
Nyeri	Dec. 84	May 85	Apr. 85
Meru	Jan. 85**	Jul. 85	Apr. 85
Marsabit	Dec. 84	Sep. 85	Apr. 85

Notes: * Except for one project
** Famine relief began in December 1984.

Table 22.2 Seed Distribution by the KFFHC

District	Katumani Maize (mt)	Beans (mt)
Kiambu	28.8	14.4
Machakos	26.4	13.2
Kitui	44.2	22.1
Embu	6.0	3.0
Nyeri	18.6	9.3
Meru	6.3	3.2
Marsabit*	29.0	14.5
Samburu	25.1	22.5
West Pokot	15.0	12.5
Nakuru	0.5	0.3

Notes: Period of time involved is March to April 1985.
* In addition, 3.5 mt of sorghum and 2.0 mt of millet were distributed.

Table 22.3 Tool Distribution by the KFFHC

District	Pans	Hoes	Forked Hoes	Shovels	*Pangas*
Kiambu	563	935	578	422	155
Machakos	715	695	510	605	191
Embu	80	380	170	70	15
Nyeri	265	400	265	163	40
Meru	170	210	160	150	33
Marsabit	745	575	530	605	250

Note: *Pangas* are similar to *machetes*, used to clear brush.

· 23 ·

Relief and Recovery for Pastoralists: Oxfam's Experience

ELIUD NGUNJIRI

Beginning in 1983, Oxfam responded to the drought in Kenya in a variety of ways. It began a nutritional rehabilitation program in Wajir in early 1984, provided funds to hire aircraft used in the survey of the northern districts carried out by the Integrated Project in Arid Lands team in July 1984 (Field and Njiru 1985), supplied funds for the transport and administrative costs of the Kitui Inter-Church Emergency Programme (a consortium of church agencies responding to the drought in Kitui District), and provided small amounts of food and seed to a number of community groups around the country.

This chapter describes two innovative projects undertaken by Oxfam in the pastoral areas of Kenya. The grain-for-livestock exchange sought to provide food relief to pastoralists facing deteriorating terms of trade for their cattle. From 1983 to the present, Oxfam has been restocking pastoralists to assist them to recover from drought and reenter the pastoralist economy.

For centuries, pastoralism has been the dominant economy and way of life in Kenya's arid and semiarid lands. Pastoralists have relied on sheep, goats, cattle, and camels for subsistence, using mobility and herd dispersion to take advantage of the uneven distribution of moisture and to withstand drought. Pastoralism, however, is increasingly threatened as a sustainable way of life. Pastoral peoples and their herds have increased in number, while the wetter fringes of traditional pastoral lands have been converted to agriculture and national reserves. In addition, insecurity, particularly in border areas, reduces the available grazing area, and animals are lost from raiding. Overlaid on these processes, drought can severely deplete herds and force the poorer pastoralists out of the pastoral economy (see Chapter 16, and Fry 1988, Hogg 1985, 1987, Homewood and Lewis 1987, and Moris 1988a, 1988b).

GRAIN-FOR-LIVESTOCK EXCHANGE

The activity absorbing the greatest amount of staff time was the Grain-for-Livestock Exchange Scheme, which was implemented in Samburu District between July 1984 and January 1985. The concept of combining destocking with relief is not a recent one, but applications are few. The colonial government had implemented a similar effort using a mobile abattoir in the 1950s. Oxfam's experience is documented here to share it with other agencies working in pastoral areas of Kenya and elsewhere.

Pilot Phase

As a result of its involvement in projects with pastoral groups in northern Kenya, Oxfam was aware of the poor rains and the deteriorating situation during 1983. In early 1984, discussions were held internally on ways to assist pastoral groups. One idea was to move some of their breeding stock to areas where the grazing was in better condition, i.e., near the coast or around Kitale in the west. Unfortunately, all areas were equally badly affected by drought, so this idea was dropped. Another proposal was to improve the outreach of the livestock marketing system (poorly developed in many northern areas), with Oxfam and other groups acting as buying agents using cash and maize for the purchases. This idea was also dropped due to the build-up of cattle waiting to be slaughtered at the Kenya Meat Commission.

Another proposal was to purchase weakened livestock using grain as a means of exchange, and then to slaughter them and distribute the meat to people in need. Such a scheme was particularly attractive because it would simultaneously meet several objectives:

1. By providing fixed amounts of grain in exchange for the animals, it would help limit the deterioration in the terms of trade invariably experienced by pastoralists at times of drought, i.e., falling livestock prices at a time of rising grain prices.
2. It would enable stock owners with severely weakened animals to gain at least some income from their surviving animals.
3. It would provide a good source of protein to needy people at a time when all staple foods, but particularly beans, the normal protein source for many people, were virtually unobtainable in many areas.

The idea was discussed with, and received enthusiastically by, the staff of the Catholic Diocese of Marsabit and the World Food Programme (WFP) office in Nairobi. In order to test the idea, a pilot project was begun in May 1984 at North Horr in Marsabit District. It was implemented by the Catholic Diocese of Marsabit with assistance from Oxfam and the WFP. The project involved the purchase of 600 sheep and goats using 27 mt (300 bags) of maize donated by the WFP. The animals were then slaughtered and the meat given to local schools and destitute people, either as fresh meat or dried into strips of biltong.

Samburu District

Due to the success of the pilot project, Oxfam decided to implement a larger scheme in Samburu District for cattle, sheep, and goats (see also Chapter 16). The Catholic Diocese continued to implement the smallstock project in Marsabit District, using maize flour provided by the WFP.

Oxfam began to set up buying centers around Samburu District in early July 1984, and the first purchases and slaughtering began in the middle of the month. Between July 1984 and January 1985, when the project was wound down, a total of 2,000 cattle and 6,000 sheep and goats were slaughtered in exchange for around 360 mt (4,000 bags) of maize flour provided by the WFP.

Before embarking on the project, permission for this unusual type of intervention was obtained from the relevant authorities in Nairobi. The project was then explained to district administrators, from the district commissioner to subchief level, and their agreement to proceed obtained. A simple survey, which drew heavily on the views of local community leaders, was then carried out to identify the worst-hit areas and gain a clearer picture of such considerations as where the livestock was and who was particularly badly affected. On the basis of this survey, fourteen locations were selected to serve as buying centers. A West German development project operating in Wamba also set up buying centers on behalf of Oxfam, with Oxfam providing advice and money for the transport of the grain. Millers and transporters were then contracted to mill the WFP maize and deliver the maize flour from the NCPB store at Nyahururu to each of the centers.

In each location, the local community was asked to form a committee to be responsible for managing the project in that area. A recording clerk, who acted as secretary, was also selected. Under the committee's guidance, stones were piled to form a slaughtering slab, and the recording clerk compiled lists of those whose severely weakened animals were to be slaughtered. Care was taken to ensure that as many livestock owners as possible were included in the lists. The actual slaughtering conformed to Muslim ritual and the carcasses were inspected by local government meat inspectors. Oxfam supplied knives, poles, notebooks, wire, scales, and other equipment to each committee.

The exchange rate for smallstock was set at 1.5 kg of maize flour for each kg of liveweight. Therefore, weighing was necessary before slaughtering commenced. For cattle, there was a flat rate of 45 kg per head in order to spread assistance to as many as possible using scarce resources. Livestock owners who exchanged in this way were also returned a portion of the meat from their animal for their own use. The Muslim butcher and laborers helping in the work were paid 3 kg of maize flour per day. The clerk received a cash payment. Laborers were not employed permanently, but instead rotated on a daily basis to spread the benefits as widely as possible.

The hides were cured and sold, thereby raising cash to help cover

Oxfam's costs in milling and transporting the maize flour and administering the project. It was hoped that once demonstrated, the suspension method of curing the hides (as opposed to the traditional ground-drying method), would be adopted after the drought and help increase the value of hides sold to traders.

When the rains commenced in December 1984, owners immediately became less willing to sell their livestock and the project began winding down. Despite the rains, it was known that it would be six to twelve months before the surviving animals began to provide milk. Furthermore, many owners had lost their entire stock. Therefore, rehabilitation activities, introduced at nine of the fourteen centers, involved a restocking project to provide some of those who had lost all their stock with breeding stock with which to rebuild their herd (see Moris 1988b). In addition, food-for-work projects were implemented, involving tree planting and microcatchment activities.

Inevitably, the Grain-for-Livestock Exchange Scheme encountered some problems. For instance, local traders tended to see the project as competing with their own businesses, and some tried to interfere with the project's implementation.

Possibly a more fundamental problem resulted from the way in which stock owners tended to divide their herds into two in response to the drought. Women, children, and older members of the household were often left with the milk herd near centers where relief was likely to be provided. The men often moved the remainder of the herd in search of better grazing in areas distant from the centers. Though this meant that the project tended to reach the most vulnerable members of the household, it also meant that much of the stock put forward for slaughter was female stock, which would better have been retained for rebuilding the herd after the drought. This dilemma for the pastoralists worsened as grazing around the trading centers was inadequate, thereby increasing the vulnerability of female stock that then had to be slaughtered.

RESTOCKING PROJECTS

To facilitate rehabilitation of the pastoral economy, restocking projects were carried out in four districts. The objective was to reestablish families as nomadic pastoralists, allowing them to move away from market and administrative centers, to be self-sufficient and not depend on food for work, and to have a renewed sense of identity (see Fry 1988 and Moris 1988b, from which this discussion is drawn, for details). Projects were undertaken in Wajir, Samburu, Isiolo, and Turkana districts (Table 23.1). All of the projects were reasonably successful. The important lessons for future drought-recovery activities involve the selection and timing of recipients, herd characteristics, and the role of NGOs in pastoralist communities. While there are many details and unanswered questions, the singular consensus is that restocking is an innovative, viable way of assisting pastoralists.

Targeting and Timing

Families selected for restocking were destitutes unable to operate in the pastoralist economy. They were small families with few animals, who were willing and able to move away from the market center once restocked. The families headed by women (20 to 40 percent, except in Wajir) had to have a male relative to assist in keeping the livestock.[1] In the larger projects (Turkana and Samburu), families were selected by local groups of elders, government administration, and NGO staff. The Samburu project utilized the committees of elders formed during the earlier destocking project, resulting in a longer-term effort of assistance to the pastoralists. In Isiolo and the early activities in Wajir, local people familiar with the families made the selections. It is important to have a process of selection whereby the poorest pastoralists are selected first, providing they are capable of reentering the pastoralist economy, and that this is done in a way that precludes criticisms of favoritism. If stock is given to families that are unwilling or unable to move away, there will be increased destruction of vegetation around the urban center. This did not happen in the Oxfam projects. Even when a family's herds were decimated, the animals were left with relatives while the family stayed in town to work or seek food.

Pastoralists have a variety of means of acquiring livestock and restocking themselves after a drought, epidemic, or theft. Milk animals are loaned to relatives, animals are exchanged to balance a herd, and animals are begged, either as gifts or with a future obligation. These means of restocking are less successful after a widespread, severe disaster, when the entire clan is unable to spare livestock. Often families will send some of their members to relief centers until the herds recover. When NGOs restock the poor families, it may be best to wait until the drought emergency is over. This encourages the traditional restocking measures to assist some of the families and the rangelands to recover before stocking rates increase.

Herd Reproduction

The aim of the Oxfam restocking project was to enable the pastoralists to be self-sufficient. Sufficient animals have to be given to each family to give them a reasonable chance of building a viable herd. The actual number and

---

1. Women may keep the milk herds and own some of the livestock, but the majority of the livestock is traditionally owned by men and livestock trading is a male occupation. Some of the women-headed households were able to use their new position as self-sufficient pastoralists to remarry, furthering their reintegration into the pastoralist economy.

mix of animals depends on the ecology, prevailing rangeland conditions, traditional livestock management, and existing herds. A mix of thirty to seventy smallstock (sheep and goats), primarily female goats, seems the minimum requirement.

In addition, enough grain for a year, until the young females have matured and produced offspring, is required. Oxfam provided maize from the WFP, some tools and household goods, and a pack animal, usually a donkey. Veterinary assistance was also provided for the first year.

Smallstock reproduce more quickly than cattle or camels, are more easily traded, and are more cost-effective by producing milk quickly. Although under model conditions a smallstock herd can increase 50 percent per year, an average expectation in the four districts, based on the restocking experience, would be 8 to 10 percent per year. For example, in the beginning of the restocking project, growth rates were 43 to 96 percent (Table 23.1), but averaged about 10 percent per year over subsequent years.

Community Structures and NGO Assistance

A major issue involves the relationship between an NGO donor and the pastoralist community. At the simplest level, questions arise concerning monitoring the selection of families, the use of the animals, and the success of the project. Oxfam employed monitors in each area to keep track of the restocked families and to ensure the animals were not slaughtered, donated to relatives, sold, or used to meet local tax obligations. In each area, the livestock was given with an expressed condition that it was not to be sold, slaughtered, or given away. One clear benefit was that the government administration could not tap the restocked animals for local taxes for self-help projects.

In Wajir, Isiolo, and Turkana (in 1984), the livestock were gifts; in the subsequent Turkana project and in Samburu, however, the animals were loans that were to be repaid (in part in Turkana and in full in Samburu) in about two and a half years. In Samburu, loan returns have been remarkable, enabling a revolving system to restock additional families. However, the repayments and conditions on disposal of the animals hinder herd development and restrict the renewal of social networks of livestock exchange. The restocked families are self-sufficient in good or average years, which 1985–1987 have been, but they would not be able to withstand a moderate drought that might cause a mortality rate of 50 percent in their herds. They have had little surplus to sell for cash needs or to invest in maintaining traditional livestock entitlement relationships.

This issue raises the question of how involved an NGO, such as Oxfam, wants to be. A loan scheme requires a continued involvement in developing local committees and overseeing project implementation. On the one hand, it represents a community structure that is parallel with traditional clan decisionmaking. On the other hand, it may present an opportunity to integrate destocking and restocking, and to facilitate access by pastoralists to the national livestock markets through their local communities. In an environment of recurrent drought and increasing pressure to transform pastoralism into commercial ranching, this may provide a long-term benefit as pastoralists retain more control over their resources.

The project costs about $1,000 to $2,500 per family, including Oxfam's indirect staff costs. This is about a tenth of the cost of major irrigation schemes in the area, and about equal to minor water-harvesting techniques.

CONCLUSION

The food-for-livestock exchange seems to have been largely successful in providing food to the Samburu people through a difficult period, while maintaining their dignity, making use of animals that would otherwise have gone to waste (or provided much less food to each family), supported the terms of trade for pastoral people, and provided some relief food for schools and other groups in the area. The restocking efforts have been successful as well; they are an ongoing experiment in providing long-term assistance to pastoralists. Working through local committees contributed to the success of the projects and also formed the basis for continued, rehabilitation work; now the same committees are moving on to plans for community development. It is hoped they will also develop their own early warning and risk-spreading mechanisms, and may use grain for livestock exchanges and restocking as one part of their strategy, as appropriate. Part of Oxfam's intention in implementing these projects was to demonstrate an effective means of helping pastoralists survive and recover from drought. We believe it was a successful initiative, worth pursuing where the local community accepts the necessity and is willing to take control. Perhaps the best evaluation is by the pastoralists themselves, summarized by a family in Isiolo: "Before we were given Oxfam animals, no one would greet us; now we are happy because we are visited and greeted wherever we go" (Fry 1988, p.1).

Table 23.1 Oxfam's Restocking Projects

Area/Years	Families Aided (% Headed by Women)	Smallstock Given per Family[1]	% Herd Growth (Year)[2]	
			Early Phase	With Loan Repayment
Isiolo 1983	70 (21)	50	43 (1983)	na
Wajir 1984–1985	30 (100)[3]	30	63 (1984)	na
Turkana 1984–1987	380 (40)	70	78 (1984)	–15 (1987)
Samburu 1984–1987	186 (20)	30–70	96 (1985)	–12 (1987)

Source: Fry (1988).

Notes: [1]Smallstock were sheep and goats. Almost all families received a pack animal, usually a donkey. In the Turkwel-Kalemenyang area of Turkana, families received fifty smallstock.

[2]Growth rates are from the first year of the project to the year indicated in parentheses. In Turkana after 1984 and in Samburu, the smallstock were loans, and repayment was required after 2 1/2 years.

[3]The Wajir project targeted widows or women whose husbands were unable to support them after the 1983 drought.

· PART 5 ·
Drought and Food Policy

Part 5 extends the analysis of drought responses to issues of food policy in Kenya and places Kenya's experience in the context of African food policy and economic development.

Chapter 24 summarizes the current status of Kenyan food policy, and, drawing upon the drought experience, suggests urgent lessons for improving food production and food security. These include expanded storage; food-security planning in advance of food crises; coordinated early warning systems; a contingency plan for food imports, distribution, and logistics; planning recovery measures; and the reduction of long-term vulnerability.

Summarizing key aspects of the African food crisis of the 1980s, Chapter 25 brings this book to a close. In many respects, the Kenyan experience is a positive anomaly, an example of the direction in which effective drought-coping strategies might be pursued. Food production and development interact through the rising demand and alternative investments for capital and labor, among other factors. A food-aid strategy must consider numerous criticisms, including constraints on the use of food aid. The financial implications of droughts have been widely reported, but less so the impact of food surpluses and strategic reserves. While India's experience in preventing famine is important, it will not be easily transferred to Africa. Drought should be seen as a warning of the desperate African food crisis to come if research and policy fail to address the mix of economic, food-security, and population problems in Africa.

·24·

Drought and Food Policy in Kenya

J. B. WYCKOFF

THE SETTING

Kenya's food situation since independence has basically been sound. The transfer of land ownership from expatriate to African ownership and the success of smallholder agriculture, which now accounts for over half the total agricultural production, has been most gratifying. Agricultural production, which rose at an average rate of 4.7 percent between 1964 and 1972, dropped to an average of 2.9 percent between 1972 and 1981. Production was high in 1982 and 1983 but was followed by low output due to the drought of 1984. Improved weather conditions provided for a quick recovery in 1985. As such, the projected rate of increase in agricultural production of 4.3 percent during the current five-year plan, 1984 through 1988, now appears valid. Output increases of maize, rice, potatoes, pulses, fruits, vegetables, and bananas (for food crops), and of cotton, coffee, tea, and pineapple (for cash crops) are expected. Beef production is not expected to expand, but will be offset by more output from sheep and goats. There is potential for increased milk production should the present marketing system be altered to permit more milk-processing firms.

Demographic features are among the most important sources of change in the Kenyan food economy. Such issues as the targeting of food-policy instruments and the projection of food needs, for example, are influenced by the character of demographic change, including population growth and migration. Food production is expected to keep up with population growth in the near term, but the rate of population growth must be reduced if food self-sufficiency is to be realized in the longer term.

Kenya is presently thought to have the highest population growth rate in the world, with an annual increase of almost one million persons. Schools are graduating 300,000 students per year, of whom only about 10 percent are absorbed in the modern sector, leaving agriculture and the rural informal sector to absorb the rest. Consequently, Kenya's smallholdings, as well as many large farms and ranches, continue to be subdivided into smaller and smaller production units, as less than 20 percent of Kenya's land area is arable.

The average annual growth rate in the population between the 1969 and 1979 censuses was 3.43 percent (Central Bureau of Statistics 1981a). Studies of age cohorts relating to fertility indicate that growth is accelerating. In the last half of the period, the population was increasing at an annual rate that was close to 4 percent. Such growth portends a rapid increase in the demand for basic foods and increasing pressure on the land.

The significance of these changes is reflected in a projected rural population growth rate of 3 percent and an urban growth rate of 7.2 percent. Rural demand for food, given no changes in growth or settlement pattern, will double by 2010, while urban demand will double by 1995 and quadruple by 2004.

Fully 85 percent of the population in Kenya is rural. One implication of this large rural, land-based population is that food producers and food consumers are largely the same people. Thus, policies aimed at raising producer incomes, including pricing policies, may not conflict with the consumption objectives pursued by food-security policy. There is also great variation among producer/consumers as to the degree of their dependence on the market for food purchases, as well as the linkages with (and the degree of access to) the market economy.

This chapter outlines Kenya's current food-production policy, which emphasizes self-sufficiency in food production, food security, and distribution in times of shortage. Policy formulation and implementation, including food production, marketing, and pricing policies, are reviewed. Although Kenya's food production policy is functioning adequately, it is clear that improvements are necessary to cope with increased demand for food and extreme climatic fluctuations. An improved food-security policy would promote strategies to reduce vulnerability to food shortages, such as improved storage facilities. The 1984 drought, which tested the functioning of the food-security system, proved the importance of adequate planning and preparedness. Elements that should be improved include: early warning systems, weather monitoring, crop monitoring, planning for security, district level distribution of foodstuffs, drought-recovery measures, diversification of agricultural activities, irrigation, and livestock adjustments.

KENYA'S NATIONAL FOOD POLICY

Food Policy Objectives

The National Food Policy paper states (Government of Kenya 1981, p.1):

> The agricultural sector must continue to play the leading role in Kenya's development and nearly all of the nation's food requirements

will need to be met from domestic production. In addition, the agricultural sector must continue to generate foreign exchange earnings to pay for oil, capital equipment and other imports, and at the same time, it must be the major source of new jobs for the rapidly growing labor force.

The paper sets the following goals for food production and distribution in Kenya (p.2):

— to maintain a position of broad self-sufficiency in the main foodstuffs in order to enable the nation to be fed without using scarce foreign exchange on food imports;
— to achieve a calculated degree of security of food supply for each area of the country; and
— to ensure that these foodstuffs are distributed in such a manner that every member of the population has a nutritionally adequate diet.

Objectives for the livestock sector are (Ministry of Livestock Development 1980, p.1-2)

to help the nation avoid shortfalls in livestock production [through] the production of sufficient animal proteins to ensure adequate nutrition of our people; production of the necessary raw materials for our agro-industries; intensification in use of high potential land to ensure higher land and other resource productivity; [and] full development of our extensive rangelands.

The 1984–1988 national development plan, with the theme of "mobilizing domestic resources for equitable development," identified agricultural objectives, including (Government of Kenya 1983): (1) development of efficient agricultural and livestock marketing systems, characterized by ready access to all producers, prices that reflect quality, available supplies, and effective consumer demand, and prompt cash payment to producers for the quantities delivered; (2) ready access to appropriate production technology and required inputs, including management, credit, fertilizer, seed, chemicals, animal health care, feed, forage, fodder, and improved genetic resources; (3) sustainable use of land and water resources for crops and livestock production; and (4) development of a supportive institutional framework for pastoralists and smallholders that encourages soil, water, and wildlife conservation and environmental protection.

The Policy Formulation Process

Kenya food policy is formulated via the development of national policy papers and five-year development plans. The process of preparing the National Food Policy (Government of Kenya 1981) was described by Cohen (1984). The policy was drafted by the Development Planning Division (DPD) of the Ministry of Agriculture. An ad hoc committee was given a vague mandate to review food requirements and production potential, but it did not initially seek to produce an "action-oriented" food policy paper. An "action-oriented" policy was pursued only when the politics of the maize shortage crisis in 1980 to 1981 highlighted the need for a national food policy paper. Senior Kenyan officers made the central decision on which the paper was premised: that Kenya could and should aim to achieve self-sufficiency in basic food supplies. Hence, the most critical assumption was made early on, without analysis or consideration of alternative approaches. While overseen by an interministerial committee of Kenyan officers and given general guidance by an ad hoc committee of central planners, DPD economists were largely responsible for the analysis and writing of each draft. Throughout this process there was little of the "planner-decisionmaker dialogue" the planning literature idealizes (Killick 1976). Rather, draftsmen prepared the paper with no substantive direction or advice from the operations divisions at ministerial headquarters, field-level technicians, or other planners or economists elsewhere in the government.

The second instrument of food policy formulation is the five-year development plan. The responsibility for the actual drafting of the plan for the Ministry of Agriculture and Livestock Development[1] rests with the Strategy Section of the Development Planning Division. The process is initiated, however, by the Ministry of Planning and National Development via their appointment of an Agriculture and Livestock Development Sectoral Committee. Within the Ministry of Agriculture and Livestock Development, numerous subcommittees are assigned responsibility for examining development policies and strategies; programs for research, extension, irrigation, input supply, and land use; and food, cash, and export crop and livestock production and marketing. Development growth targets are rationalized, resource requirements projected, and shortfalls noted. The Strategy Section integrates the information and produces the final plan. It is recognized throughout this process that the agricultural food industry is but a part of the national economy. Thus, it must operate within the context of national policies.

Food Production

Twenty-five percent of the rural population resides on semiarid lands. Although almost 70 percent of the total rural population growth during the 1969–1979 period was absorbed in higher potential lands, the technological potential of this land is limited. With a population growth rate of 4 percent,

---

1. In the mid-1980s, the Ministry of Agriculture and Livestock Development existed as one ministry. Formerly and subsequently it was the Ministry of Agriculture and the Ministry of Livestock Development. The text uses the appropriate names for the contemporary reference.

migration to semiarid areas is a certainty, thus worsening national food security. The 1984/85 drought threatened the food security of as many as three million people.

The National Food Policy paper stresses the importance of policy design so that cash and export crop production do not detract from the achievement of food self-sufficiency goals. Food policy analysis in recent years, however, suggests that the most difficult economic trade-off is not between food and export crops, but among the food crops themselves. The major export crops, with coffee occupying 3 percent and tea 1.6 percent of cropped area, do not provide important competition for food crops. As a viable food policy can only be achieved in the context of a healthy general economy, a strategy for expanding export crop production, which has high labor-absorptive capacity and value generated per hectare, may be critical.

The trend growth rate of domestic maize production from 1971 through 1982 was about 3.8 percent (adjusting for abnormally high production at the end of the period). A continuation of this growth rate might enable the country to remain self-sufficient in maize in a normal production year. It is inevitable, however, that imports will be required during severe droughts.

There has been no upward trend in maize yields since 1975, although considerable technological potential remains to be exploited. The growth in domestic production has come entirely from area expansion, with maize substituting for wheat, cattle production, and other activities on small- and medium-sized farms. Unless there are improvements in output per hectare, competition between maize and other food-producing activities, particularly dairying, will increase under the pressure of rural population growth alone.

A maize research program must be accorded high priority. Research resources are scarce and must be allocated so as to obtain rapid productivity increases in high-potential zones of Central and Eastern provinces and in western Kenya. There has been no significant increase in fertilizer consumption in Kenya over the past decade. The levels of fertilizer use on maize are very low, even in regions where the use of hybrid maize seed is common. Current maize prices do not seem to offer enough incentive for smallholder producers to adopt a package of modern inputs.

While an adjustment of maize prices may be a precondition for input intensification, recent projections of world commodity prices show fertilizer prices rising over the next ten to twenty years, even as maize prices fall. This will result in lower incentives for the adoption of new inputs. If these projections are realized, it may be necessary either to offer higher maize prices or to subsidize fertilizer prices in order to maintain maize productivity. The latter policy may be more efficient in overall economic terms and more conducive to income distribution and welfare objectives. The costs of such a subsidy, however, could be large relative to the cost of supporting maize prices insofar as the country remains self-sufficient in maize. Adoption of productivity-increasing technology by medium and smallholders seems to be essential for success in the intensification of maize production.

As the major food crops compete for the same resources in production, it is important to assess the relative contribution of these commodities to development objectives and the cost of this contribution. For example, a shift away from the very costly policy of self-sufficiency in sugar to one where resources are employed in the production of a crop for which Kenya has a comparative advantage (such as white maize for export), might provide net economic benefits while adding a potential "buffer stock" for emergency food needs. Removal of the existing restrictions on the movement of food crops to permit free transfer from surplus to deficit areas would encourage the production of maize, as well as other crops, in areas where they have a comparative advantage in production. It may be economically viable to shift out of rice and wheat production in favor of vegetables and maize. Long-term contracts for the import of such commodities as sugar, rice, and wheat can be negotiated. This would minimize the effects of world price variations, while taking full advantage of concessionary programs presently available for the latter two commodities. Such policies could conceivably improve Kenya's net economic position with little impact on the country's food position.

Food Marketing

With rapid population growth and urbanization, the stress on the food economy will be led by demand. Food marketing will be one of the growth sectors in the economy. With properly designed policy, this sector can be instrumental in creating employment opportunities. Kenya's economy is mixed, founded on an environment where private participants can make profits while contributing to development. Competition among the major food crops can be modified through the creation of market incentives to channel demand toward substitute commodities that can be produced domestically by small farms in poorer agricultural regions. As such, potential resource conflicts may be converted to contribute both to economic growth and income redistribution.

Food Pricing

Gazetting agricultural prices began in Kenya in the 1940s. Originally, prices were set at levels that would encourage continued production for export to Europe and settlement by European farmers. Some two decades later, Kenya gained independence, and many of the large farms were converted to smallholder agriculture. Price gazetting of major corps and livestock products and exports of agricultural products continued. Another two decades have since passed, smallholder agriculture has become the norm, and imports of food commodities have largely ceased (although wheat is imported regularly, and maize is imported during drought years). Domestic demand for food has grown rapidly with population growth and urbanization. Major agricultural commodity prices are still gazetted at all levels of the market. The specific objectives for agricultural price gazetting is to stimulate production to achieve growth rates necessary to maintain broad self-sufficiency.

Noticeably missing in the price review process is any indication of the quantities of crop and livestock products needed to meet projected effective demand. Another serious omission is any attempt to determine the impacts of relative producer price changes on forthcoming supply. The fact that consumer prices are set separately from producer prices further confuses the issue.

Relative to consumer prices, the National Food Policy document (Government of Kenya 1981, p.16) states that "consumer prices will generally be set at levels which cover the domestic producer prices plus processing and distribution costs." Since price policy relates farm gate producer prices to import parity, food prices (should) reflect international price levels, plus domestic processing and distribution costs. Sugar is the only food commodity that is grossly subsidized in order to protect Kenya from the changing foreign-exchange requirements of fluctuating international sugar prices. Domestic rice production is also subsidized via government-operated irrigation schemes.

The other major incentive policy is the provision of agricultural credit. Not only have interest rates been less than those available commercially, but repayment has not been effectively policed. As such, the credit system is currently undergoing a thorough review.

Food Policy Implementation

The general responsibility for the implementation of the national food policy lies mainly with the Ministry of Agriculture and Livestock Development. However, the ministries of Water Development, Lands and Settlement, Cooperatives, and Planning and National Development all have complementary responsibilities. The ministries are all headquartered in Nairobi, with representatives at the provincial and district levels. The development process is now centered at the district level via the District Focus for Rural Development strategy initiated by the president. District development committees, representatives of the central ministries, and local elected leaders are responsible for designing and executing development initiatives. The ministry headquarters in Nairobi continue to exert control via budget allocations. Foreign donors also participate in policy design through the selection and funding of development projects.

Government agricultural parastatals and statutory boards play a large role in the implementation of food policy objectives. Parastatals traditionally have served large-farm agriculture; they have not yet adjusted to servicing smallholder agriculture, which is now the prevalent form of food production in Kenya. The government is working to upgrade the management and performance of these organizations.

ELEMENTS OF AN IMPROVED FOOD-SECURITY POLICY

Budget austerity and the recent drought have directed attention toward the rationalization of a lower-cost, more-effective food-security policy for Kenya. The government desires to reduce the cost of agricultural subsidies and food imports, while maintaining or improving food security, nutrition and public health levels, food-production incentives, consumer food purchasing power, and income levels and distribution.

The 1984 Drought

The 1984 drought was the most severe since 1930. Production from major grain-, horticultural-, and livestock-producing areas was sharply reduced. Nevertheless, in spite of the severity of the drought, the government responded with the necessary measures to prevent a widespread famine.

However, the overall success does not mean that there are not lessons to be learned to increase preparedness to cope with future droughts. These lessons can be divided into five main categories:

1. Storage and food-security planning
2. Early warning systems
3. Management of food imports, distribution, and logistics
4. Drought-recovery measures
5. Longer-term measures to reduce vulnerability to drought

All of these categories are interlinked, and any follow-up measures should treat them as a package.

Storage and Food-Security Planning

Food-security policies are designed to (Government of Kenya 1981, pp.19-20): increase food production in all areas of the country, including drought-resistant crops, such as sorghum and millet; establish a food commodity monitoring and reporting system; improve monitoring and forecasting of weather conditions in the main agricultural zones and widen the dissemination of information on expected weather trends; develop a drought-response strategy to minimize drought impact on producers and food production; rationalize food exports relative to domestic supplies and import food to meet nutritional requirements; and support a multicommodity strategic food reserve from domestic surpluses and grain supplied on concessional terms for use during periods of crop failure or other emergency situations.

A first step in developing a food-security policy is to determine a "safe minimum standard" (SMS) of stocks of storable commodities. This could be established equal to 1.0, 1.5, 2.0, or any other, standard deviation of average production variation, depending upon the degree of food security desired and the level of available financing.

A second step is to generate sufficient "loss free" storage capacity to handle the desired level of stocks. ("Loss free" is defined as being capable of effective control of access by rats, birds, insects, pilferage, and weather or moisture damage.) This storage capacity can be owned or leased by parastatals in production areas or urban centers, on-farm, or connected with private sector commercial processing facilities. All storage stocks would be rotated on a "first in, first out" basis to prevent deterioration.

A third component of food-security planning is to examine storage requirements and the management and distribution of stocks. This would define where stocks should be held, when and how accumulated stocks in surplus areas should be transferred to deficit areas, and what arrangements are necessary at the district level to ensure food security. The cost of additional storage and stock holding would need to be balanced against the savings to be made from a more effective utilization of available stocks through timely distribution.

The NCPB has the major capacity and responsibility for grain storage in Kenya. The government currently is committed to a strategic national reserve of four million bags. A policy to expand government grain storage capacity in various regions, with the help of donor funds, is now being implemented. The large stocks of maize and wheat held by NCPB in early 1984 reduced the impact of the 1984 drought. These stocks met national food needs until imports could be ordered, landed, and distributed.

Private sector ownership of grain storage would greatly lower the government's capital requirements. Both on-farm grain storage and storage in commercial milling and processing facilities would tend to buffer seasonal price variations and the absolute quantities needed to be held by the government to ensure their SMS of food security. The government recently authorized millers to purchase grain directly from farmers for processing and storage in their facilities. This may encourage the private sector to expand its storage capacity, particularly if it permits them to take advantage of seasonal price changes.

Another aspect of food-security planning focuses at the farm level. To the extent that farmers could be induced to hold larger food stocks, the NCPB storage requirements and trade fluctuations would be reduced. The physical aspects of on-farm storage should be examined, along with pricing and marketing measures that would give farmers an incentive to store grain. With the help of USAID, the government is sponsoring a pilot on-farm grain storage project, consistent with the policy of encouraging on-farm storage and the prevention of post-harvest grain losses. On-farm grain storage not only contributes to national food-security stocks, but it also provides farmers with an opportunity to exploit any seasonal price changes that may occur. For some commodities, adjusting producer prices more frequently would facilitate increased production in the short term. In the case of milk, the cost of dairy feed increased sharply at the time when the dry-season bonus ended in 1984. An extension of the bonus might have prevented some of the livestock losses that subsequently occurred.

A crisis element tends to emerge when exceptional food imports are required. A well-defined and workable food-security plan would remove this element and facilitate prompt and coordinated response to periodic food needs. Persons with inadequate purchasing power would be assisted directly (as in the case of famine relief) in order to ensure that all consumers have adequate access to the nation's food supplies.

Early warning systems. The 1984 drought illustrated that, in this particular case, the current systems for alerting the government to the need for food imports proved almost adequate to enable maize imports to be ordered, landed, and distributed before stocks ran out completely and before widespread food shortages occurred. Nevertheless, there was a period in September/October 1984 when a number of NCPB depots in deficit areas were empty and consumption appears to have been constrained by a lack of available food. Had maize stocks been lower than their high levels in early 1984, deficiencies in the early warning systems would have been more apparent.

Improvements in weather forecasting and information dissemination are desirable for two reasons. Reliable weather-forecasting systems allow farmers to adjust their behavior to limit the impact of impending drought by saving resources normally used for land preparation or seed, which is often wasted as a result of drought. If these losses can be avoided in the future, drought recovery will be quicker. Second, the earlier that reliable information on abnormal weather conditions can be obtained, the earlier critical decisions can be taken by the government, such as on the import of food. The existing state of meteorological knowledge of the weather systems affecting Kenya needs to be improved. Equally important is a review of the dissemination of information to the farming community via extension or other methods.

At a national level, there are a number of bodies that provide information of various kinds on area, yield, and output of major crops (see Part 2 of this book). In addition, the Meteorological Department has extensive agrometeorological data that could be used to give early warning of impending crop shortages or crop failure. The amount of effort put into data collection does not often yield the desired results. There is need for better coordination among the various organizations involved and for defining their respective responsibilities more clearly. While there remains room for improvement in the data available for the major crops (i.e., maize and wheat), it is also apparent that reliable data on other minor food crops (which are collectively important) are deficient.

Food Imports, Distribution, and Logistics

The 1984 drought illustrated the importance of good contingency planning and management. The Task Force on Food Supply and Distribution, set up by the government, functioned effectively, and the various components of the system, particularly the NCPB, performed the basic tasks of distributing food with considerable efficiency. It is appropriate to reflect on the methods used by the Task Force and to have a contingency plan to mobilize the same or a similar system when drought again threatens.

The importance of close cooperation between donors and government was evident during the 1984 drought. Donors were alerted early to the dimensions of the drought and the need for concessional food imports. This was instrumental in generating a favorable response by the donor community, which was better able to assess requirements because of the full and detailed information provided by the government.

During 1984, a number of problems occurred in the distribution of food and the organization of relief at the local level. The government famine-relief program was initially slow to meet the estimated requirements of those in need. There was some confusion over the exact number of people who required relief food. While some areas were oversupplied with food, others received insufficient amounts, pointing out the importance of identifying vulnerable groups.

The responsibilities of the district administration, church bodies, and NGOs need to be defined and coordinated for managing food distribution. A possible solution to the confusion in assessing when and where free food distribution should occur would be the production of a procedures manual for officials involved at all levels. A clarification of the rules would minimize unnecessary delays in food distribution to those in need.

Preparatory work is also required so that food-for-work programs can be initiated at an early stage. This would involve both identifying viable projects that can be implemented quickly and streamlining the provision of additional funds to finance these programs and to transport food. To the extent that rural works programs can be initiated at an early stage, the need for free food would be reduced in line with government policy. An effective mechanism is also needed to convey district food requirements to the NCPB and to ensure that imported grain from the port arrives in the correct quantities, at the appropriate depots, and at the required time.

Drought-Recovery Measures

The drought revealed more or less predictable consequences in respect to the availability of agricultural inputs for drought recovery. It is clear that planning by both the government and donors needs to be instituted at an earlier stage (i.e., as soon as the severity of the drought is established) in order to meet drought-recovery requirements satisfactorily.

Seed requirements, as a general rule, cannot be met from outside the country, and it is necessary to lay contingency plans for the emergency production of seeds (likely to be in deficit following a drought). Increasing the Kenya Seed Company seed reserves to meet drought-induced increases in demand should be considered.

In order to protect the livestock herd from unnecessary depletion, various short-term measures should be taken. These include: (1) making feedstuffs available during and following a drought (even if the raw materials have to be imported); (2) adjusting output prices on feedstuffs to thwart a possible price rise and thus ensure that farmers have an incentive to maintain their herds or to dispose of them via the market while their product value still exists; and (3) to have contingency plans in place for widespread destocking in pastoral areas and coordination of livestock marketing to prevent animals from dying while awaiting slaughter.

Longer-Term Measures to Reduce Vulnerability to Drought

In the longer term, vulnerability to drought can be reduced by promoting certain agricultural and livestock policies. Kenya's susceptibility to drought is increased by its extreme dependence on maize as the basic foodstuff. Moreover, as population pressure increases, maize is being grown in semiarid areas where yields are low and crop failure is frequent. In the short term, it is difficult to change consumption habits, yet demand for more drought-resistant food crops, such as sorghum, millet, sweet potato, and cassava, can be stimulated by appropriate emphasis on research, pricing, marketing, and extension. Efforts currently being made in this direction need to be strengthened by ensuring that a new agricultural research strategy takes these objectives into account. Pricing policies need to enhance farmer incentives in addition to improving market access and effectiveness and encouraging processing industries.

Irrigation is an obvious means to reduce drought susceptibility, but experience in Kenya has shown high development and operating costs, and management difficulties in large-scale irrigation schemes have absorbed a disproportionate share of the resources available for agricultural development. National policy gives priority to valley drainage and small-scale irrigation schemes, with farmer involvement and control. In some parts of the country, ground-water development for irrigation purposes may be desirable.

The 1984 drought also demonstrated deficiencies in livestock marketing. The arid areas of Kenya are distant from the main slaughterhouses, yet their residents depend almost totally on the sale of livestock products for income, and as a major portion of their subsistence during a drought. The existing parastatal system is unable to effectively market livestock from these areas. Thus, policies to disperse slaughter facilities and improve livestock transportation and market access for producers in these areas is necessary. The colonial practice of mobile slaughterhouses during droughts and the recent livestock-for-grain trades (see Chapter 23) are worthwhile examples.

Some diversification in livestock mix is beneficial, as sheep, goats, and free-range chickens suffered lower losses than cattle or confined broilers and layers during the drought. Both camels and goats tend to be browsers. As a consequence, their source of food is less affected by drought than the grasses and forbes that are the primary source of forage for cattle. Camels also have lower water requirements that permit the utilization of areas that cannot be grazed by cattle because of insufficient water availability. The goat's lower water requirement, ability to utilize browse, efficient forage conversion, lower susceptibility to some diseases, smaller size, shorter reproduction and growth cycles, and generally higher relative prices are now recognized. The promotion of these animals during drought and for speeding recovery following drought should be pursued.

CONCLUSION

Kenya's rapidly growing population and its limited quantity of arable land leaves it vulnerable to the impact of erratic rainfall patterns. Since the government has adopted a basic policy of food self-sufficiency, optimum patterns of food production, storage, and distribution are essential to ameliorate the effects of periodic local and regional droughts. The encroachment of cropping into traditional livestock grazing areas and the continuing subdivision of farm units into smaller entities make the task of achieving food self-sufficiency more and more difficult.

Cash crops provide little competition for food crop resources, generate a relatively high labor intensity, and provide foreign exchange that can be used to purchase foodstuffs when domestic production falls below the self-sufficiency level. Food crops and dairying, however, compete for many of the same resources, thus requiring the proper "balance" of gazetted prices to prevent distortions in available supply and effective consumer demand.

Maize provides the predominant share of the country's food; as such, the failure to increase maize yields during the last decade is a serious problem. Promotion of maize research and an increase in fertilizer use are imperative. The present policy of restricting free movement of food from areas with surplus supplies to deficit supply areas should be rescinded. The production of individual crops would then shift to those areas where there is a comparative production advantage.

Specific actions to be undertaken as a result of the lessons learned from the 1984 drought include improving drought early warning systems, including weather and crop monitoring, and increasing systematic food security planning. Finally, longer-term programs to encourage adequate seed availability following droughts, as well as enterprise diversification, irrigation, and adjustments in livestock mix designed to minimize drought impacts, need to be introduced. Kenya performed quite well during the serious drought of 1984. Nevertheless, implementation of suggested policy changes would guarantee even better performance in the next drought emergency.

· 25 ·

Drought and Food Policy in the African Context

PHILIP NDEGWA

The 1980s famine in Africa was one of the most serious calamities to have occurred this century. Apart from the loss of life, the extent of human suffering through widespread malnutrition, loss of livestock, physical dislocation, and losses of welfare, livelihood, and opportunity, is tragic. The drought is part of a more worrisome long-term decline in food availability in Africa. The drought has increased awareness of food-production and security issues by exacerbating them. In particular, the quantity and quality of discussion on the African food situation has taken a quantum advance. To a large extent, this has been due to the visibility of the consequences of drought, which have been graphically portrayed in virtually every part of the world. The danger is that a more relaxed attitude to the problem will be engendered now that food output has improved.

This chapter reviews the experience in coping with drought in Africa in the 1980s and suggests policies to reduce long-term vulnerability. While Kenya coped well with the food crisis in 1984/85, the disheartening performance elsewhere in Africa warrants closer attention.

There are two cutting edges in the crisis: the complexities of food production and excessive rates of population growth. Policies to deal with the food and population problems must be compatible with the social setting in which they operate. For example, they must recognize the prevalence of smallholders, who often are from different tribal backgrounds, utilize varying farming systems, and produce different commodities.

Overall trends in food production in Africa are easy to identify (Table 25.1). Dependence on imported cereal has increased (17 percent of requirements in sub-Saharan Africa in 1980-1982), corresponding to changes in consumption patterns and lagging agricultural production. Total agricultural output in sub-Saharan Africa grew by only 1.4 percent per year between 1970 and 1982. Sub-Saharan Africa is the only region in the world in which food production is growing less rapidly than its population, due, in part, to rapid population growth in the area (3.2 percent per year). In 1981, daily calorie supplies in sub-Saharan Africa averaged about 90 percent of the amount required to sustain normal activity and health.

DROUGHT IN AFRICA

The severe drought in much of sub-Saharan Africa was unusually harsh in its intensity, duration, and the number of countries affected. According to the FAO, of thirty-four drought-prone countries regarded as vulnerable to food shortages, twenty-four required emergency food imports in 1984 (FAO 1984b, Burki 1985). In some of the Sahelian countries, there have been two prolonged droughts in the last ten to fifteen years (the early 1970s and early 1980s). There were, of course, other droughts in Africa (in the 1910s and 1940s, for example). The recent drought, however, has had serious social, political, and economic consequences, including:

1. *Loss of human life.* In addition, malnutrition has meant reduced life expectancy for many and retarded the physical development of millions of children.
2. *Loss of livestock*, an important capital asset and means of livelihood that will take years to recover.
3. *Dislocation of societies.* There have been massive movements of people from their home areas in search of food, accelerating urban migration, internal social instability, and problems associated with refugees.
4. *Increased unemployment and poverty*, associated with reduced on-farm production and higher food prices.
5. *Loss of soil and vegetative cover*, which may either be irreversible or will take many years to overcome.
6. *Reduced underground water resources*, and increased electricity costs associated with switches from hydroelectric to other energy sources.
7. *Declines in foreign-exchange earnings*, resulting from reduced exports, increased imports, and reduced investment for future production of goods and services. Commodity prices of some export products collapsed, resulting in even less earnings.
8. *Loss of self-respect and political independence.* To ensure their survival, many countries have increased their dependence on foreign powers.

Lessons learned in coping with the drought can be applied toward the formulation of future development strategies and policies. The drought dramatized the downward trend in agricultural production, highlighted dependence on certain foods, and exposed the inadequacies of infrastructure and food aid. As such, the drought underlined the importance of diversification and expansion of agricultural production.

INTERACTIONS BETWEEN FOOD PRODUCTION AND DEVELOPMENT

Food-supply problems are inextricably interwoven with economic development issues (Mellor 1982, Mellor and Gavian 1986). The demand for food tends to rise more rapidly than supply as economic conditions and incomes improve. The growth in demand is influenced by a range of factors, including real-income levels and distribution, rate of population growth, and relative prices. Food types sought by consumers also change, including an increase in the demand for animal products, which gives rise to an increase in the demand for cereals for animal feed. The supply of food, on the other hand, depends on the availability of arable land and agricultural labor, investment and technological change in agriculture, pricing policy, and marketing.

The net outcome of the interplay among these factors is usually a rise in the relative price of food as development proceeds since demand normally exceeds supply. As the purchasing power of low-income groups suffers most, rising demand often results in a widening of income differentials and the deterioration of nutritional standards for low-income groups. The relative price of labor tends to rise, and with it the rate of unemployment. If governments attempt to contain food-price pressures by subsidy or additional imports, rising budgetary and/or external deficits may undermine macroeconomic stability and growth prospects.

These effects can be minimized if the development of the food-producing sector increases in step with (or ahead of) growth in the economy as a whole. The impact of rapid agricultural development on the food supply may be more or less matched by an increase in demand as income levels rise through the multiplier effects of higher agricultural incomes and expenditures.

If economic development in Africa accelerates over the next decade, an increasing number of countries will enter the medium-income range, in which food demand can be expected to exceed supply by the largest margin. Increases in food dependency, therefore, seem inevitable in the next decade or so. According to one estimate, based on projection of present trends, imports of basic food staples may reach 40 million tons by the end of the century, about four times the recent level. Problems of supply, transport, and balance-of-payments financing could stretch the financial and other capacities of many African countries beyond their limits, unless meaningful steps are taken to stem the incipient crisis.

FOOD AID

The amount of food aid to sub-Saharan Africa has increased enormously over the last two decades. Africa is the only area of the world in which food aid is rising; the total volume of food aid to all developing countries is on a declining trend, and food aid to Asia and Latin America has halved over the last two decades. Sub-Saharan Africa is now the recipient of a larger amount of food aid than any other region.

Food aid is a controversial subject. At the international level, food surpluses sometimes bring political and economic influence. Countries with an exportable surplus usually prefer to provide food to those deficient countries with whom they are on friendly terms. Perceptions and attitudes to food aid are complicated by the "institutionalization" of international imbalances in food supply. Agricultural-surplus countries have often sought to protect domestic markets through the subsidization of agricultural exports.

While food aid is desirable and essential in the short term simply to keep people alive, it has been rightly criticized:

1. Food aid may have an adverse effect on local production. Food aid often leads to lower food prices, thus reducing production incentives and increasing dependency on food aid. This problem may be exacerbated if food aid interferes with research and development efforts. Lower prices may also result in an increase in demand for food, furthering dependence on food imports and food aid. Food aid can also lead to a change in tastes in favor of crops that are not grown efficiently in the recipient country.
2. Food-aid programs may involve a reorientation of existing Official Development Assistance budgets by donor countries, rather than the provision of additional assistance.
3. The amount of food aid can be unpredictable, as it is often the subject of debate among officials and legislatures of donor countries, as well as among various donor agencies.
4. The effectiveness of aid may be negligible if not accompanied by financial or other support for inland transport to the points of need.
5. Like other types of Official Development Assistance, food-aid programs often are designed to serve the priorities and interests of the donor country or agency, which may be out of tune with the objectives of the developing country. Recipient countries may be required to accept certain conditions in domestic policies and programs, such as agricultural pricing and marketing, in order to receive food aid.
6. Donors often require that they be consulted about the use of counterpart funds that arise from sales of food given as aid.
7. Some food aid is given in the form of loans, which add to debt-service burdens.
8. Constraints may be placed on the way the food is used, such as prohibitions on use for animal feed or on subsequent export, although they may be the most efficient uses of the food aid.

Many of these problems may be eased or overcome by careful and sensitive management of food-aid programs. The overriding concern is the need for recipient countries to ensure that well-designed agricultural development efforts are not interrupted by adverse effects of food aid, which should be oriented toward improving self-sufficiency in food production.

Ideally, one way to ensure greater consistency between food aid and other development objectives would be to use food aid to help generate agricultural surpluses in the developing countries themselves. A number of African countries can produce substantial food surpluses, given financial resources to support such production and management of food stocks. A better food-aid strategy might be for donors to contribute the necessary resources for production of food surpluses in Africa and to use those surpluses as food aid. Unfortunately, this kind of "internalization" of food aid is unlikely to receive support from the present donors because of the political influence of their farmers and the leverage that food surpluses give to donor countries.

Regional food reserves within Africa would reduce the need for individual countries to maintain expensive stockpiles, which, in aggregate, might be greater than required on the continent as a whole (although it is unlikely that all African countries will produce surpluses at the same time). Regional mechanisms for the transportation, storage, and financing of food surpluses might ease the financial burdens on the poorer countries that arise from variability in food supplies by reducing food-financing requirements and introducing an element of intra-African cooperation in financing. Regional reserves would result in the quicker delivery of food to needy areas.

FINANCIAL ASPECTS

The financial impact of food deficiencies includes foreign-exchange costs and indebtedness from increased commercial imports of food grain and increased domestic costs from a substantially enlarged need to transport imported grain. The logistical problems and costs can be severe in times of drought, when enormous quantities of both commercially purchased grain and imports under aid programs suddenly start to arrive. Much of the grain provided under aid programs may not be sold. The financial commitments arising in these circumstances can strain government budgets and administrative capacity.

The financial implications of food surpluses are less widely recognized. Many nations in sub-Saharan Africa wish to maintain a food reserve, built up at times when local production exceeds demand, for use when demand exceeds supply. The domestic financing costs of a buildup of a food surplus can be comparable in magnitude to the costs arising from a deficit. It is expensive to purchase a grain stockpile and to finance the facilities necessary for storage and transportation.

IS THE ASIAN EXPERIENCE RELEVANT?

The largest proportion of international experience in dealing with food-supply problems has been in Asia. With some successes to their credit, international bodies concerned with food-supply issues are now focusing on African problems. The Asian experience, however, may not be easy to transfer to Africa, because conditions in the two continents are enormously different:

1. Labor-to-land ratios in Africa are on the average much lower than in Asia. The ratios vary considerably, and are rising rapidly in some areas.
2. Population growth and urbanization are more rapid in Africa. Furthermore, the diversity of ethnic groups, each with its own food-consumption patterns, is much greater in Africa than in Asia.
3. Farm technologies, both those actually in use and the most promising lines of development, differ between Africa and Asia; the relatively greater difficulty in developing irrigation schemes in Africa is a good example. One result of this is that agriculture in Africa is relatively more dependent on rainfall.
4. Environmental factors differ between the two continents. Rainfall is generally less reliable in Africa. In many parts of semiarid Africa, soils have lower natural fertility, organic content, and water-retention capacity than in semiarid areas of Asia.
5. Food tastes are very different. In Asia, rice is by far the most prevalent staple, and rice production has benefited from irrigation and the application of new technology. In contrast, a more diverse range of food grains and other staples is consumed in Africa; maize, wheat, potatoes, sorghum, millet, barley, rice, cassava, and yams, among other items. Food-consumption patterns are hard to change, so it is probably true that for many years to come African food-development efforts will have to be spread over a wide range of food items.
6. The human resource base and administrative talent are more developed in Asia than in Africa, facilitating the planning and implementation of food-development efforts. Asian countries have had greater experience in economic planning, policy formulation, and institution building. This experience is now being put to great use to ensure price flexibility and promote exports. On the other hand, many African countries are still experimenting with systems, institutions, and strategies.
7. Rural infrastructure, including such services as banking, is more developed in Asia. This facilitates delivery, transport, and storage of farm inputs. Marketing is better organized in Asia, and credit is more readily available. As Asian countries have larger industrial sectors, they are more self-sufficient in some agricultural inputs.

8. Food-related research efforts also differ between Africa and Asia. The diversity of ethnic groups, food tastes, and climatic and soil conditions make research problems more difficult in Africa. The number of scientists employed in food research is very low in Africa (Lipton 1985).

ELEMENTS OF THE RESEARCH AGENDA

Our understanding of the reasons for inadequate food output in sub-Saharan Africa must be improved. The reasons, no doubt, arise from the complex interrelationships existing among many factors, including rapid population growth; urbanization; labor shortages; land shortages; soil degradation; climatic factors; limited improvement in seed technologies; inadequate supply of fertilizer, credit, and other inputs; underdeveloped infrastructure; inappropriate pricing and other incentives; and political factors that impede production. Structural changes (including increasing the rural labor supply by reducing the pace of urbanization) may make an important contribution to increased agricultural output, while improvements in output prices may be relatively unhelpful as a way to increase output unless infrastructure and related factors also adjust (Delgado and Mellor 1984).

The appropriate role of government in agricultural development and food policy raises several questions. Governments usually play a large role in agriculture in Africa, regardless of ideological orientation. Some government involvement in agricultural development is necessary in order to provide public services and to ensure that the domestic terms of exchange for agriculture are conducive to increased output. Research on political and economic forces that influence agricultural policies is thus important.

Research on the interactions between food production and economic development would raise our understanding of the economic development process. Some of the many questions here include: how does the income elasticity of demand for food alter as per capita income grows and as the distribution of income changes? How does the composition of the demand for food (including the demand for animal feed) alter as incomes grow? What are the effects on income distribution and nutrition of changing food prices? What is the relationship between technological change and rural income levels? How does the demand for and supply of labor react to both changing food prices and the related matter of changing rural/urban wage differentials? How does food supply react to changes in the rural labor force? What role might food aid play in bridging the food supply/demand gap (as distinct, for example, from its role in famine relief)?

While food-aid and pricing policies have had an impact in influencing food-consumption patterns in African countries, the rapid urbanization process now taking place in the continent is another powerful force.

Life-styles and conditions in urban areas encourage the consumption of food items that are already processed, such as bread, or those that can be quickly prepared, such as rice. Wheat and rice are crops that Africa is not able to produce adequately and efficiently at present. Therefore, considering the rapid urbanization taking place in all African countries, it is clear that a most potentially fruitful area of research is how foods such as bananas, cassava, sorghum, and millet, which African countries are able to produce in large quantities, can be processed to meet the requirements of urban populations (for instance, sorghum can be mixed with wheat to produce bread).

More research needs to be done in the many areas of the natural sciences that affect agriculture, particularly smallholder production. Research should focus on such areas as seed types (high-yielding, drought-resistant), fertilizer types and their application (including the possibilities for increased use of natural products such as seaweed), ecological matters (including reversing the processes of soil degradation and erosion, and improving integration of forestry with agriculture), water management (including small-scale irrigation systems and water exploration), remedies for animal and plant diseases (control of the tsetse fly is probably the major target here), and improved storage technology (including the development of low-cost storage methods usable by smallholders). In all of these areas, the smallholder sector must be emphasized (McNamara 1985).

Cooperation in research, training, and education among African countries would provide benefits from economies of scale and sharing of costs and benefits of research.

CONCLUSION

The drought should be seen as the final warning of the desperate food crisis to face the African continent in the years to come unless appropriate actions, in all the necessary fields, are undertaken now. With the rapid increase in population and the increasing pressure on the available land, among other factors, vulnerability to future droughts will increase and resultant famines are likely to be severe.

Food policy in Africa must include economic cooperation among African countries. In the past, economic cooperation in Africa has been seen mainly in terms of industrialization, and occasionally in terms of development of large infrastructure facilities. It is now clear that cooperation is essential in agriculture, most certainly in food production. The economic weakness and fragility of African countries makes production of food surpluses on a sustained basis impossible in many countries. There is also a geographical consideration; many countries will not be able to efficiently produce some of their food requirements because of natural factors. Deliberately promoted intra-African trade is essential, especially to compete with industrial countries in food exports.

The food problem in Africa must be seen as an integral part of development processes. As such, efforts to deal with the problem should be designed in a way that facilitates the achievement of other development objectives. For example, food-production strategies should also promote employment and equitable distribution of income. African countries, however, must give agriculture higher priority in their development efforts (World Bank 1986b).

In the final analysis, policies to address the mix of economic, food-security, and population problems must be developed within Africa. An increase in the awareness of the crucial role to be played by agriculture in development, including smallholder agriculture, is necessary. Too much emphasis has been placed on industrialization, while agriculture has been starved of resources. An example is food-pricing policies that favor urban over rural communities.

Africa is gradually learning these important lessons. Improvements in institutional strength and increased commitment to improved policies are being made. Research has a critical role to play in the effort to improve food security by providing the knowledge necessary to ensure that aid and policy efforts are not misguided. Progress requires the participation of all parties, an improvement in coordination among them, and long-term commitments to ensure that the effort to improve food production is sustained long enough to cement in place an enduring framework for food security in Africa.

Table 25.1 Production and Imports of Cereals in Africa

	Africa				Sub-Saharan Africa	
	1970	1975	1980	1983	1969–1971	1980–1982
PRODUCTION (million mt)						
Total cereals	61.1	67.5	70.8	62.7	35.6	41.8
Wheat	8.0	9.7	8.9	9.0	1.2	1.4
Rice	7.3	7.8	8.4	8.6	4.7	6.2
Maize	21.7	24.9	27.2	22.4	12.1	13.8
Food production per capita	104	100	95	88	—	—
IMPORTS (million mt)						
Total Cereals	—	13.1	22.0	25.9	2.3	8.7
Wheat	—	10.4	15.7	17.4	1.0	3.3
Rice	—	0.7	2.4	3.2	0.7	2.5
Maize	—	1.4	3.4	3.5	0.4	1.7
IMPORTS (% of requirements)						
Total Cereals	—	16.3	23.7	29.2	6.2	17.2
Wheat	—	51.7	63.8	65.9	45.6	70.5
Rice	—	8.2	22.2	27.1	12.6	28.2
Maize	—	5.3	11.1	16.7	3.1	10.9

Sources: FAO (1977a, 1977b, 1982a, 1982b, 1984c, 1984d) and World Bank (1984).
Notes: Data for sub-Saharan Africa are average annual volume. Imports for total Africa are higher than for sub-Saharan Africa, reflecting the impact of north African countries that are substantial cereal importers (e.g., Algeria, Egypt, Morocco, and Tunisia).
Requirements are defined as production plus imports.

References

Agatsiva, J. L., Mwendwa, H., Ottichillo, W. K., Peden, D. G., and Pilloto, J. 1984. *Maize Harvest Forecast for 1984 in Bungoma, Kakamega, Nandi, Trans Nzoia and Uasin Gishu Districts.* KREMU Technical Report No. 111. Nairobi: Ministry of Finance and Planning.

Agricultural Sub-Committee. 1985. *Lessons from the Drought.* Nairobi: Office of the Delegate of the European Communities (Manuscript).

Agumba, F. O. 1984. *Fluctuation of the Long Rains in Kenya in Relation to Large Scale Circulations.* Research Report No. 1/85. Nairobi: Institute for Meteorological Training and Research.

Akong'a, J., Downing, T. E., Konjin, N. T., Mungai, D. N., Muturi, H. R., and Potter, H. L. 1988. The Effects of Climatic Variations on Agriculture in Central and Eastern Kenya. In *The Impact of Climatic Variations on Agriculture. Volume 2: Assessments in Semi-Arid Regions*, M. L. Parry, T. R. Carter, and N. T. Konijn, eds., pp. 122–270. Dordrecht, the Netherlands: Kluwer.

Ambler, C. H. 1988. *Kenya Communities in the Age of Imperialism: The Central Region in the Late Nineteenth Century.* New Haven: Yale University Press.

AMREF (African Medical Research and Education Foundation). 1985. *Report on Project No ID 06 - AMREF Famine Relief Programme.* Nairobi: AMREF (Manuscript).

Anyamba, E. K., and Ogallo, L. J. 1984. *Anomalies in the Wind Field over Africa during the East African Rainy Season 1983/84.* Nairobi: Institute for Meteorological Training and Research.

Bake, G. 1986. *Water Management as a Steering Factor of a Controlled Grazing System in a Nomadic Area: A Plan to Combat Desertification in Northern Kenya.* Nairobi: United Nations Educational, Scientific, and Cultural Organization (Manuscript).

———. 1984. *Water Resources and Water Management in Southwestern Marsabit District.* IPAL Technical Report B-4. Nairobi: United Nations Educational, Scientific, and Cultural Organization.

——— 1983. *An Analysis of Climatological Data from the Marsabit District of Northern Kenya.* IPAL Technical Report No. B-3. Nairobi: United Nations Educational, Scientific, and Cultural Organization.

Berry, L., Hunter, O., Seidman, A., Ford, R., Puffer, F., and Perritt, R. 1980. *Eastern Africa Country Profiles: Kenya.* Worcester, Mass: International Development Program, Clark University.

Borton, J. 1987. *The 1984/5 Drought Relief Programme in Kenya: A Provisional Review.* Discussion Paper No. 2. London: Relief and Development Institute.

Borton, J., and Stephenson, R. 1984. *Disaster Preparedness in Kenya.* London: Relief and Development Institute.

Braun, H. M. H. 1977. *The Reliability of the Rainy Seasons in Machakos and Kitui Districts.* Miscellaneous Paper M12. Nairobi: Kenya Soil Survey.

Burki, S. J. 1985. The African Food Crisis: Looking beyond the Emergency. Paper presented at the Conference on South-South Cooperation, November. Harare, Zimbabwe (Manuscript).

Campbell, D. J. 1984. Response to Drought among Farmers and Herders in Southern Kajiado District, Kenya. *Human Ecology* 12(1): pp. 35–64.

———. 1981. Kajiado District—Case Study. In *The Development of Kenya's Semi-Arid Lands,* D. J. Campbell and S. E. Migot-Adholla, eds., pp. 212–241. Nairobi: Institute for Development Studies, University of Nairobi.

CARE. 1985. *The Kenya Drought 1984/5: A Report on the NGO Response and the OFDA Grant ASB-0000-G-SS-4207-00.* Nairobi: CARE (Manuscript).

CBS (Central Bureau of Statistics). 1988. *Economic Survey 1988.* Nairobi: Government Printer.

———. 1986. *Economic Survey 1986.* Nairobi: Government Printer.

———. 1985. *Economic Survey 1985.* Nairobi: Government Printer.

———. 1984. *Economic Survey 1984.* Nairobi: Government Printer.

———. 1983a. *Statistical Abstract.* Nairobi: Government Printer.

———. 1983b. *Third Rural Child Nutrition Survey 1982.* Nairobi: Government of Kenya.

———. 1982. *Seasonal Variations in Food Crops: Evidence from IRS4.* Nairobi: Ministry of Economic Planning and Development (Manuscript).

———. 1981a. *Kenya Population Census, 1979.* Volume I. Nairobi: Government Printer.

———. 1981b. *Compendium to Volume I, 1979 Population Census.* Nairobi: Government Printer.

———. 1981c. *The Integrated Rural Surveys 1976–79.* Nairobi: Ministry of Economic Planning and Development.

———. 1970. *Kenya Population Census, 1969.* Volume 1. Nairobi: Government Printer.

———. n.d. *1979 Population Census.* Volume II: Analytical Report. Nairobi: Central Bureau of Statistics.

Cohen, J. M. 1984. Participatory Planning and Kenya's National Food Policy Paper. *Stanford Food Research Institute Studies* XIX, pp. 187–213.

Cohen, J. M., and Lewis, D. B. 1987. Role of Government in Combatting Food Shortages: Lessons from Kenya 1984/85. In *Drought and Hunger in Africa,* M. H. Glantz, ed., pp. 269–296. Cambridge: Cambridge University Press.

Dahl, G., and Hjort, A. 1976. *Having Herds: Pastoral Herd Growth and Household Economy.* Stockholm: University of Stockholm.

Davies, T. D., Vincent, C. E., and Beresford, A. K. C. 1985. July–August Rainfall in West-Central Kenya. *Journal of Climatology* 5: pp. 17–23.

Delgado, C. J., and Mellor, J. W. 1984. A Structural View of Policy Issues in African Agricultural Development. *American Journal of Agricultural Economics* 66: pp. 665–670.

Deloitte, Haskins and Sells Management Consultants (DH & SMC). 1985. *Final Report on the USAID/GOK Food Relief Monitoring and Evaluation.* Nairobi: USAID/Kenya (Manuscript).

Dennett, M. D., Elston, J., and Rodgers, J. A. 1985. A Reappraisal of Rainfall Trends in the Sahel. *Journal of Climatology* 5: pp. 353–362.

Development Planning Division, Ministry of Agriculture and Livestock and Development. 1984. *The Plan for Agriculture and Livestock Development 1984–1988.* Nairobi: Government of Kenya (Manuscript).

de Wilde, J. C. 1984. *Agriculture, Marketing, and Pricing in Sub-Saharan Africa.* Los Angeles: African Studies Center and African Studies Association, University of California.

Downing, J., Berry, L., Downing, L., Downing, T. E., and Ford, R. 1987. *Drought and Famine in Africa: 1981–1986.* Worcester, Mass.: Clark University (Manuscript).

Downing, T. E. 1988. *Climatic Variability, Food Security and Smallholder Agriculturalists in Six Districts of Central and Eastern Kenya.* Ph.D. dissertation. Worcester, Mass.: Clark University.

———. 1982. *Eastern Africa Regional Studies: Climate.* Worcester, Mass.: Clark University.

Downing, T. E., Akong'a J., Mungai, D. N., Muturi, H. R., and Potter, H. L. 1988. Introduction to the Kenyan Case Study. In *The Impact of Climatic Variations on Agriculture. Volume 2. Assessments in Semi-Arid Regions*, M. L. Parry, T. R. Carter, and N. T. Konijn, eds., pp. 129–148. Dordrecht, the Netherlands: Kluwer.

Downing, T. E., Lezberg, S., Williams, C., and Berry, L. 1988. *Population Change and Environment in Central and Eastern Kenya from 1969 to 1979.* Worcester, Mass.: Clark University (Manuscript).

Downing, T. E., Mungai, D. N., and Muturi, H. R. 1988. Drought Climatology of Central and Eastern Kenya. In *The Impact of Climatic Variations on Agriculture. Volume 2. Assessments in Semi-Arid Regions*, M. L. Parry, T. R. Carter, and N. T. Konijn, eds., pp. 149–174. Dordrecht, the Netherlands: Kluwer.

Downing, T. E. and Porter, P. W. 1987. *Potential Crop Productivity in Central and Eastern Kenya: Results from a Water Balance Model.* Paper presented at the First Technical Conference on Meteorological Research in Eastern and Southern Africa. Nairobi: Institute for Meteorological Training and Research.

East Africa Meteorological Department (EAMD). 1975. *Climatological Statistics for East Africa. Part 1: Kenya.* Nairobi: EAMD.

Economist Intelligence Unit (EIU). 1986. *Country Report: Kenya.* London: EIU.

———. 1985. *Country Report: Kenya.* London: EIU.

———. 1984. *Country Report: Kenya.* London: EIU.

EcoSystems Ltd. 1986. *Baseline Survey of Machakos District: 1985 and Land Use Changes in Machakos District: 1981-1985.* Report Number 4 for the Machakos Integrated Development Programme. Nairobi: EcoSystems Ltd.

Erukudi, C. 1985. *Akisitamunet (Remembrance).* Lodwar, Kenya: Lodwar Diocese (Manuscript).

FAO (Food and Agriculture Organization). 1986. *Early Agrometeorological Crop Yield Assessment.* Plant Production and Protection Paper 73. Rome: FAO.

———. 1984a. *Assessment of the Agriculture, Food Supply and Livestock Situation: Kenya.* Rome: FAO/Office for Special Relief Operations.

———. 1984b. *Food Supply in 24 African Countries Affected by Food and Agriculture Emergencies.* Special Task Force Report No. 3. Rome: FAO.

———. 1984c. *Production Yearbook 1983.* Rome: FAO.

———. 1984d. *Trade Yearbook 1983.* Rome: FAO.

———. 1982a. *Production Yearbook 1981.* Rome: FAO.

———. 1982b. *Trade Yearbook 1981.* Rome: FAO.

———. 1977a. *Production Yearbook 1976.* Rome: FAO.

———. 1977b. *Trade Yearbook 1976.* Rome: FAO.

———. 1972. *Production Yearbook 1971.* Rome: FAO.

———. 1969. *1968 Food Composition Table for Use in Africa.* Rome: FAO.

Farmer, G. 1988. Seasonal Forecasting of the Kenya Coast Short Rains 1901-84. *Journal of Climatology* 8(5): pp. 489-497.

———. 1987. *A Rainfall Database for Eastern Africa with some Kenyan Examples.* Proceedings of the First Technical Conference on Meteorological Research in Eastern and Southern Kenya. Nairobi: Kenya Meteorological Department.

———. 1981. *Regionalisation and Study of an Alleged Change in the Rainfall Climatology of East Africa.* Ph.D. dissertation. Sheffield: University of Sheffield.

Farmer, G., and Wigley, T. M. L. 1985. *Climatic Trends for Tropical Africa.* Research Report for the Overseas Development Administration. Norwich: Climatic Research Unit (Manuscript).

Field, C. R., Lamprey, H. F., and Masheti, S. M. 1976. *A Preliminary Report of Livestock Numbers and Distribution in Marsabit District.* Nairobi: United Nations Educational, Scientific, and Cultural Organization (Manuscript).

Field, C. R., and Njiru, G. K. 1985. *Conclusions and Urgent Recommendations Concerning Famine Relief Requirements in Six Districts of the Arid Zone of Kenya.* Marsabit: Integrated Project in Arid Lands (Manuscript).

Folland, C. K., Palmer, T. N., and Parker, D. E. 1986. Sahel Rainfall and Worldwide Sea Surface Temperatures. *Nature* 320: pp. 602-607.

Frere, M., and Popov, G. F. 1979. *Agrometeorological Crop Monitoring and Forecasting.* Plant Production and Protection Paper 17. Rome: Food and Agriculture Organization.

Fry, P. (with assistance from U. Herren). 1988. *Evaluation of Oxfam's Four Restocking Projects in Kenya.* Nairobi: Oxfam (Manuscript).

Fumagalli, C. 1977. *A Diachronic Study of Change and Sociocultural Processes among the Pastoral Nomadic Samburu of Kenya 1900-1975.* Ph.D. dissertation. New York: Buffalo University.

Gommes, R. 1985. *The Tanzanian Crop Monitoring and Early Warning Systems Project.* Dar es Salaam: Food and Agriculture Organization (Manuscript).
Government of Kenya. 1986. *Economic Management for Renewed Growth.* Sessional Paper No. 1 of 1986. Nairobi: Government of Kenya.
———. 1985. *Mali Yetu Ya Asili.* Volumes 1 and 2. Quarterly newsletter. Nairobi: Government of Kenya.
———. 1983. *Development Plan, 1984–88.* Nairobi: Government Printer.
———. 1981. *National Food Policy.* Sessional Paper No. 4. Nairobi: Government Printer.
Grandin, B. E. 1986a. Land Tenure, Sub-Division and Residential Changes on a Maasai Group Ranch. *Development Anthropology Bulletin* 4(2): pp. 9–13.
———. 1986b. *Wealth and Pastoral Dairy Production: A Case Study from Maasailand.* Internal Report. Nairobi: International Livestock Centre for Africa (Manuscript).
———. 1985. *Functions of Sheep and Goats in the Maasai Production System.* Paper presented at the SR-CRSP Kenya Workshop, Kakamega. Nairobi: International Livestock Centre for Africa (Manuscript).
———. 1984. *Livestock Offtake in Maasailand.* Paper presented at a seminar on Livestock Production Systems: The Masaai, sponsored by ILCA and the Ministry of Agriculture and Livestock Development. Nairobi: International Livestock Centre for Africa (Manuscript).
Grandin, B. E., and Bekure, S. 1982. *Livestock Offtake and Acquisition: A Preliminary Analysis of Livestock Transactions in Olkarkar and Mbirikani Group Ranches.* Internal Report. Nairobi: International Livestock Centre for Africa (Manuscript).
Grandin, B. E., and Lembuya, P. 1987. *The 1984 Drought: A Case Study from a Maasai Group Ranch in South-Eastern Kajiado District.* Pastoral Network Paper 23e. London: Overseas Development Institute.
Haaga, J., Mason, G. J., Omoro, F. Z., Quinn, V., Rafferty, A., Teft, K., and Wasonga, L. 1986. Child Malnutrition in Rural Kenya: A Geographic and Agricultural Classification. *Ecology of Food and Nutrition* 18: pp. 297–307.
Herlehy, T. J. 1984. *Historical Dimensions of the Food Crisis in Africa: Surviving Famines along the Kenya Coast, 1880–1980.* Working Paper No. 87. Boston: Boston University, African Studies Center.
Hogg, R. 1987. Development in Kenya: Drought, Desertification and Food Scarcity. *African Affairs* 34 (2): pp. 47–58.
———. 1985. The Politics of the Drought: The Pauperization of the Isiolo Boran. *Disasters* 9(1): pp. 39–43.
Homewood, K., and Lewis, J. 1987. Impact of Drought on Pastoral Livestock in Baringo, Kenya, 1983–1985. *Journal of Applied Ecology* 24: pp. 615–631.
Hounan, D. E., Burgos, J. J., Kalik, M. S., Palmer, W. C., and Rodda, J. 1975. *Drought and Agriculture.* Technical Note No. 138. Geneva: World Meteorological Organization.
Hutchinson, P. 1985. Rainfall Analysis of the Sahelian Drought in the Gambia. *Journal of Climatology* 5: pp. 665–672.

ILCA (International Livestock Centre for Africa). 1981. *Introduction to East African Range Livestock Systems Study/Kenya.* Working Document No. 23. Nairobi: ILCA (Manuscript).

———. 1979. *An Illustrated Rainfall Introduction to the Rainfall Patterns of Kenya.* Working Document No. 12. Nairobi: ILCA (Manuscript).

IPAL (Integrated Project in Arid Lands). 1984. *Integrated Resource Assessment and Management Plan for Western Marsabit District, Northern Kenya* (2 volumes). Nairobi: United Nations Educational, Scientific, and Cultural Organization (Manuscript).

Jaetzold, R., and Schmidt, H. 1983. *Farm Management Handbook of Kenya: Natural Conditions and Farm Management Information.* Nairobi: Ministry of Agriculture.

Kanamitsu, N., and Krishnamurti, J. N. 1978. Northern Summer Tropical Circulations during Drought and Normal Rainfall Months. *Monthly Weather Review* 106: pp. 331–347.

Kates, R. W., Chen, R. S., Downing, T. E., Kasperson, J. X., Messer, E., and Millman, S. R. 1988. *The Hunger Report: 1988.* Providence: World Hunger Program, Brown University.

Katz, R. W., and Glantz, M. H. 1986. Anatomy of a Rainfall Index. *Monthly Weather Review* 114: pp. 764–771.

Kenya Power and Lighting Co. 1985. *Annual Report and Accounts, 1984.* Nairobi: Kenya Power and Lighting Co.

Kidson, J. W. 1977. African Rainfall and its Relation to Upper Air Circulation. *Quarterly Journal of the Royal Meteorological Society* 103: pp. 441–456.

Killick, T. 1976. *The Economies of East Africa.* Boston: Hall.

King, J. M. 1983. *Livestock Water Needs in Pastoral Africa in Relation to Climate and Forage.* Research Report No. 7. Addis Ababa: ILCA.

Kinuthia, J. H., et al. 1984. *The Failure of the 1984 Long Rains in Kenya.* Nairobi: Institute for Meteorological Training and Research (Manuscript).

Kliest, T. 1985. *Regional and Seasonal Food Problems in Kenya.* Leiden, the Netherlands: Institute of African Studies.

KMD (Kenya Meteorological Department). 1984. *Climatological Statistics.* Nairobi: KMD.

KNCSS (Kenya National Council for Social Services). 1984–1985. *Minutes of the NGO Coordinating Committee.* Nairobi: KNCSS (Manuscript).

Konijn, N. T. 1988. The Effects of Climatic Variability on Maize Yields. In *The Impact of Climatic Variations on Agriculture. Volume 2. Assessments in Semi-Arid Regions,* M. L. Parry, T. R. Carter, and N. T. Konijn, eds., pp. 191–208. Dordrecht, the Netherlands: Kluwer.

Kufwafwa, J. W. 1985. *Numbers and Distribution of Livestock and Wildlife in Kenya: An Overview.* Paper presented to the Livestock/Wildlife Interface Conference, Taita Hills Lodge. Nairobi: Kenya Rangeland Monitoring Unit (Manuscript).

Lamb, P. J. 1982. Persistence of Subsaharan Drought. *Nature* 299: pp. 46–47.

———. 1978. Large Scale Tropical Atlantic Circulation Patterns Associated with Subsaharan Weather Anomalies. *Tellus* 30: pp. 240–251.

Lipton, M. 1985. *The Place of Agricultural Research in the Development of Sub-Saharan Africa*. Discussion Paper 202. Institute for Development Studies. Sussex, U.K.: University of Sussex.

Lough, J. M. 1981. *Atlantic Sea Surface Temperatures and Weather in Africa*. Ph.D. dissertation. Norwich: University of East Anglia.

Mason, J. B., Haaga, J. G., Marks, G., Quinn, V., Test, K., and Maribe, T. 1985. *Using Agricultural Data for Timely Warning to Prevent the Effects of Drought on Child Nutrition: An Analysis of Historical Data from Botswana*. Ithaca, NY: Cornell Nutritional Surveillance Program, Cornell University.

Mbugua, S. W. 1986. *Monitoring Livestock and Wildlife in Kenya*. Nairobi: KREMU (Manuscript).

McAlpin, M. B. 1987. Famine Relief Policy in India: Six Lessons for Africa. In *Drought and Hunger in Africa: Denying Famine a Future*, M. H. Glantz, ed., pp. 393–414. Cambridge: Cambridge University Press.

McNamara, R. S. 1985. *The Challenges for Sub-Saharan Africa*. Sir John Crawford Memorial Lecture. Washington, D.C.: World Bank.

Mellor, J. W. 1982. Third World Development: Food, Employment, and Growth Interactions. *American Journal of Agricultural Economics* (May).

Mellor, J. W., and Gavian, S. 1987. Famine: Causes, Prevention, and Relief. *Science* 235: pp. 539–545.

Ministry of Economic Planning and Development. 1980. *Samburu District Development Plan 1979–1983*. Nairobi: Government Printer.

Ministry of Energy and Regional Development. 1985. *Turkana District Resources Survey (1982–1984)*. Nairobi: EcoSystems, Ltd.

Ministry of Finance and Planning. 1984a. *Samburu District Development Plan 1984–1988*. Nairobi: Government Printer.

———. 1984b. *Turkana District Development Plan, 1984–88*. Nairobi: Government Printer.

Ministry of Livestock Development. 1980. *National Livestock Development Policy*. Nairobi: Government of Kenya (Manuscript).

Mitchell, J. M. J., Dzerdzeevskii, B., Flohn, H., Hofmeyr, W. L., Lamb, H. H., Rao, K. N., and Wallen, C. C. 1966. *Climatic Change*. WMO Technical Note 79. Geneva: World Meteorological Organization.

Moris, J. 1988a. Failing to Cope with Drought: The Plight of Africa's Ex-Pastoralists. *Development Policy Review* 6: pp. 269–294.

———. 1988b. *Oxfam's Kenya Restocking Projects*. Pastoral Development Network Paper 26c. London: Overseas Development Institute.

Mukhebi, A. W. et al. 1985. *Impact of the 1983/4 Drought on Cattle, Sheep and Goats in Kenya*. Technical Report No. 3. Nairobi: Ministry of Agriculture and Livestock Development.

Mungai, D. N., and Muturi, H. R. 1988. Agroclimatic Zones and Agricultural Production in Central and Eastern Kenya. In *The Impact of Climatic Variations on Agriculture. Volume 2. Assessments in Semi-Arid Regions*, M. L. Parry, T. R. Carter, and N. T. Konijn, eds., pp. 175–190. Dordrecht, the Netherlands: Kluwer.

Murage, F. 1985. *NCPB Maize Yield Survey, A Forecasting Tool in the Context of Food Policy*. Oxford: Oxford University, Food Studies Group (Manuscript).

Mutulu, P. M., Okoola, R. E., and Cheres, K. A. 1988. *Further Evidence of Periodic Fluctuations in Kenyan Rainfall Records.* Nairobi: Kenya Meteorological Department (Manuscript).

Mwaniki, H. S. K. 1975. *The Living History of Embu and Mbeere.* Nairobi: East African Literature Bureau.

Ndegwa, P. 1986. *The African Challenge.* Nairobi: Heinemann.

Newell, R. E., and Kidson, J. W. 1984. African Mean Wind Changes Between Sahelian Wet and Dry Periods. *Journal of Climatology* 4: pp. 27–33.

Nicholson, S. E. 1985. African Rainfall Fluctuations 1850 to Present: Spatial Coherence, Periodic Behavior and Long Term Trends. *American Meteorological Society Extended Abstracts*: pp. 62–63.

———. 1981a. The Historical Climatology of Africa. In *Climate and History*, T. M. L. Wigley, M. J. Ingram, and G. Farmer, eds. pp. 249–270. Cambridge: University Press.

———. 1981b. Rainfall and Atmospheric Circulation During Drought Periods and Wetter Years in West Africa. *Monthly Weather Review* 109: pp. 2,191–2,208.

Nicholson, S. E., and Entekhabi, D. 1986. The Quasi-periodic Behavior of Rainfall Variability in Africa and its Relationship to the Southern Oscillation. *Archiv für Meteorologie, Geophysik und Bioclimatologie* 34: pp. 311–348.

Nieuwolt, S. 1980. *The Interpolation of Rainfall in the Nairobi Area.* Research Report 8/80. Nairobi: Meteorological Department.

Njoka, T. J. 1979. *Ecological and Socio-cultural Trends of Kaputiei Group Ranches in Kenya.* Ph.D. dissertation. Berkeley: University of California.

Nkanata, J. 1985. *Workshop on Provision of Livestock Production Research Information for Use by Extension Workers in the Training and Visit Programme.* Muguga, Kenya: Kenya Agricultural Research Institute.

Norton-Griffiths, M. 1978. *Counting Animals.* Handbook 1. Nairobi: African Wildlife Leadership Foundation.

Odingo, R. 1986. A Study of the Causes, Consequences and Policy Recommendations on Drought in Kenya. In *Drought and Man: The 1972 Case Study*, Volume 3, R. Garcia and J. Escudero, eds. New York: Pergamon.

Office of the President. 1984. *Guidelines on Food Supply and Distribution.* Circular sent to District Officials, 21 August. Nairobi: Office of the President (Manuscript).

———. n.d. *Wind Up of the Food Distribution Exercise.* Notes for the Meeting of the National Food Steering Committee. Nairobi: Office of the President (Manuscript).

Ogallo, L. J. 1987. Relationship Between Seasonal Rainfall in East Africa and the Southern Oscillation. *Journal of Climatology* 8: pp. 31–43.

———. 1978. *Rainfall in Africa.* Research Report No. 5/78. Nairobi: East African Institute for Meteorological Training and Research.

Ogallo, L. J., and Anyamba, E. K. 1985. *Drought of Tropical Central and Eastern Africa, July–November, Northern Springs of 1983–1984.* Nairobi: Kenya Meteorological Department (Manuscript).

Ogallo, L. J., and Okoola, R. E. 1985. *Response of Seasonal Rainfall in East*

Africa to the Weather Changes Over Some Regions of the Indian Ocean. Nairobi: Kenya Meteorological Department (Manuscript).

Ojany, F., and Ogendo, R. 1973. *Kenya: A Study in Physical and Human Geography.* Nairobi: Longman.

Okoola, R. E. 1986. *The Role of Meteorology in the National Food System — a Management Perspective.* Technical Note No. 2. Nairobi: Kenya Meteorological Department.

Palutikof, J. P., 1986. Drought Strategies in East Africa: The Climatologist's Role. *Climatic Change* 9: pp. 67–78.

Palutikof, J. P., Farmer, G., and Wigley, T. M. L. 1982. Strategies for the Amelioration of Agricultural Drought in Africa. In *Proceedings of the Technical Conference on Climate—Africa,* World Meteorological Organization (WMO), eds., pp. 222–248. Geneva: WMO.

Parry, M. L., Carter, T. R., and Konijn, N. T., eds. 1988. *The Impact of Climatic Variations on Agriculture. Volume 2: Assessments in Semi-Arid Regions.* Dordrecht, the Netherlands: Kluwer.

Paul, A. A., and Southgate, D. A. T. 1978. *McCance and Widdowson's The Composition of Food.* 4th Revised and Extended Edition of MRC Special Report No. 297. New York: Elsevier/North-Holland Biomedical Press.

Peacock, C. P. 1984. *The Productivity of Smallstock in Three Group Ranches in Kajiado District, Kenya.* Ph.D. dissertation. Reading: University of Reading.

Peacock, C. P., de Leeuw, P. N., and King, J. M. 1982. *Herd Movement in the Mbirikani Area.* Internal Report. Nairobi: International Livestock Centre for Africa (Manuscript).

Pearson, R. L., Miller, L. D., and Tucker, C. J. 1976. Handheld Spectral Radiometer to Estimate Graminous Biomass. *Applied Optics* 15: pp. 416–418.

Peden, D. G., and Mwendwa, H. 1984. *Estimating Maize Yield Using Airborne Digital Photometers.* KREMU Technical Report No. 110. Nairobi: Ministry of Finance and Planning.

Peden, D. G., Mwendwa, H., Agatsiva, J. L., and Ottichillo, W. K. 1985. Experiments in Estimating Maize Yield in Kenya Using Airborne Digital Photometers. *ITC Journal* 1: pp. 9–13.

Perlov, D. 1981. *Livestock Marketing in Samburu Land, Kenya: An Investigation of the Sociocultural Context of Marketing Behaviour.* Working Paper 414. Nairobi: Institute for Development Studies.

Platt, B. S. 1962. *Tables of Representative Values of Foods Commonly Used in Tropical Countries.* Special Report Series 302 (Revised Edition of SRS 253). London: Medical Research Council.

Porter, P. W. 1976. Climate and Agriculture in East Africa. In *Contemporary Africa, Geography and Change,* C. G. Knight and J. L. Newman, eds. pp. 112–139. Englewood Cliffs: Prentice-Hall.

Potter, H. L. 1988. The Effects of Climatic Variability on Livestock Production. In *The Impact of Climatic Variations on Agriculture. Volume 2. Assessments in Semi-Arid Regions,* M. L. Parry, T. R. Carter, and N. T. Konijn, eds., pp. 209–220. Dordrecht, the Netherlands: Kluwer.

Radley, D. E., Brown, C. G. O., Burridge, M. J., Cunningham, M. P., Kirimi,

I. M., Purnell, R. E., and Young, A. S. 1975. East Coast Fever: Chemoprophylactic Immunization of Cattle against *Theileria Parva* (Muguga) and Five *Theilerial* Strains. *Veterinary Parasitology* 1: pp. 35–41.

Ray, R. T. 1984. *Drought Assessment: Kenya*. Nairobi: USAID/Kenya.

Robinson, P. W. 1985a. *Gabbra Historical Texts*. Evanston, IL: Northwestern University (Manuscript).

———. 1985b. *Gabbra Nomadic Pastoralism in Nineteenth and Twentieth Century Northern Kenya: Strategies for Survival in a Marginal Environment*. Ph.D. dissertation. Evanston, IL: Northwestern University.

Rodhe, H., and Virji, H. 1976. Trends and Periodicities of East African Rainfall Data. *Monthly Weather Review* 104: pp. 307–315.

Ropelewski, C. F., and Halpert, M. S. 1986. Global and Regional-Scale Precipitation Patterns Associated with the El Niño/Southern Oscillation (ENSO). *Monthly Weather Review* 114: pp. 2,352–2,362.

Rukandema, M., Mavua, J. K., and Audi, P. O. 1981. *Report on Survey Results from Mwala Location (Machakos)*. Katumani, Kenya: National Dryland Farming Research Station.

Rukandema, M., Muhammed, L., and Jeza, A. 1983. *The Farming Systems of Semi-Arid Lower Embu, Eastern Kenya*. Katumani, Kenya: National Dryland Farming Research Station.

Sandford, S. 1979. Towards a Definition of Drought. In *Symposium on Drought in Botswana*, M. T. Hinchey, eds., pp. 33–40. Gabarone: Botswana Society.

Schmidt, G. 1979. Effectiveness of Maize Marketing Controls in Kenya. In *Price and Marketing Controls in Kenya*, J. T. Mukui, ed., pp. 158–180. Nairobi: Institute of Development Studies, University of Nairobi.

Sen, A. 1981. *Poverty and Famine: An Essay on Entitlement and Deprivation*. Oxford: Oxford University Press.

Silverman, A. 1985. *Kenya Emergency Programme 1984/5: Reflections*. Nairobi: UNICEF (Manuscript).

Sombroek, W. G., Braun, H. M. H., and van der Pauw, B. J. A. 1982. *Exploratory Soil Map and Agroclimatic Zone Map of Kenya*. Nairobi: Kenya Soil Survey.

Southwood, T. 1978. *Ecological Methods*. 2nd edition. London: Chapman and Hall.

Sperling, L. 1987a. The Adoption of Camels by Samburu Cattle Herders. *Nomadic Peoples* 22.

———. 1987b. Wage Employment among Samburu Pastoralists of Northcentral Kenya. *Research in Economic Anthropology* 9.

———. 1987c. *The Labor Organization of Samburu Pastoralism*. Ph.D. Dissertation. Montreal: McGill University.

Stelfox, J. G., Kufwafwa, J. W., and Ottichillo, W. K. 1981. *Distribution and Population Trends of Elephants and Rhinoceros in Kenya, 1977–1980*. Report No. 43. Nairobi: Kenya Rangeland Ecology Monitoring Unit.

Stelfox, J. G., and Ngatia, M. 1979. *Grevy's Zebra Survey in Northern Central Kenya*. Report No. 13. Nairobi: Kenya Rangeland Ecology Monitoring Unit.

Survey of Kenya. 1970. *National Atlas of Kenya*. Nairobi: Survey of Kenya.

Swift, J. 1985. *Planning against Drought and Famine in Turkana, Northern Kenya*. Sussex: Institute of Development Studies (Manuscript).

Tablino, P. 1980. *I Gabbri del Kenya*. Bologna: E.M.I.

———. 1974. *Calculation of Time among the Gabbra*. Nairobi (Manuscript).

Tanner, C. 1987. Malnutrition and the Development of Rural Households in the Agreste of Paraiba State, North-east Brazil. *Journal of Development Studies* 23(2): pp. 242–264.

USAID (United States Agency for International Development). 1987. *Situation and Outlook Report for Maize and Wheat as of January 20, 1987*. Nairobi: USAID/Kenya.

Verma, V., Marchant, T., and Scott, C. 1988. *Evaluation of Crop Cut Methods and Farmer Reports for Estimating Crop Production: Results of a Methodological Study in Five African Countries*. London: Longacre Agricultural Development Centre, Ltd. (Manuscript).

Waghela, S., Ndarathi, C. M., Okello, O. J. A., Semenye, P. P., and Rugema, E. 1983. *Animal Health Component Report on Phase I—Extensive Studies*. Nairobi: Veterinary Research Laboratory and International Livestock Centre for Africa (Manuscript).

Wamba Veterinary Department. 1980. *Annual Report*. Folio 49, Volume 1/2. Wamba: Ministry of Livestock Development (Manuscript).

Wasonga, L. M. 1985. *Kenya Nutrition and Economic Development—Policies and Strategies*. Paper presented in the Seminar on Nutrition in Agriculture and Rural Development. Nairobi: Kenya Food and Nutrition Planning Unit (Manuscript).

Watt, B. K., and Merrill, A. L. 1975. *Composition of Foods*. Handbook No. 8. Washington, D.C.: United States Department of Agriculture.

Weg, R. F. van der, and Mbuvi, J. P. 1975. *Soils of the Kindaruma Area*. Reconnaissance Soil Survey Report No. R1. Nairobi: Kenya Soil Survey.

Werner, L. H. 1986. *Growth Monitoring Programme: Final Report*. Nairobi: United Nations Children's Fund (UNICEF) (Manuscript).

Wisner, B.G. 1986a. *Kenya: Policies and Prospects for Restoring Sustained Growth of Per Capita Income*. Washington, D.C.: World Bank (Manuscript).

———. 1986b. *World Development Report 1985*. Washington, D.C.: World Bank.

———. 1984. *Towards Sustained Development in Sub-Saharan Africa*. Washington, D.C.: World Bank.

———. 1977. *The Human Ecology of Drought in Eastern Kenya*. Ph.D. dissertation. Worcester, Mass.: Clark University.

World Vision. 1985. *Annual Report 1985*. Nairobi: World Vision Kenya Office.

Abbreviations and Units of Measure

These abbreviations refer to Kenyan agencies and programs unless otherwise specified.

$	Refers to US$, unless otherwise indicated
£	Refers to UK£ Sterling, unless otherwise indicated
AID	Agency for International Development (U.S.)
AMREF	African Medical Research and Education Foundation
AVHRR	Advanced very-high-resolution radiometers
bags	Commonly 90 kg of grain, although some of the U.S. yellow maize was distributed in 50 kg bags
BARAC	Black Americans in Response to African Crisis
CBPP	Contagious Bovine Pleuropneumonia
CBS	Central Bureau of Statistics
CCC	Commodity Credit Corporation (U.S.)
CCPP	Contagious Caprine Pleuropneumonia
CFS	Crop Forecast Survey
CHANIS	Child Health and Nutrition Information System
CMEWSP	Crop Monitoring and Early Warning Systems Project (Tanzania)
CPK	Church of the Province of Kenya
CRS	Catholic Relief Services (U.S.)
CRSP	Collaborative Research Support Program
DADO	District Agricultural Development Officer (Tanzania)
DANIDA	Danish International Development Agency
DAO	District Agricultural Officer
DC	District Commissioner
DDCO	District Drought-Contingency Officer (proposed)
DEO	District Education Officer
DI	Drought Index
DO	District office
DRO	District Range Officer

DSM	Dried Skim Milk
DVO	District Veterinary Officer
EAMD	East Africa Meteorological Department
ECF	East Coast Fever
ECU	European Currency Unit, a basket of European currencies. In 1984, 1 ECU = £ Sterling 0.59 = Kshs 11.2
EDM	Emergency Drought Management Subcommittee (proposed)
EEC	European Economic Community (Europe)
ENSO	El Nio/Southern Oscillation
EWS	Early Warning System
FAO	Food and Agriculture Organization (UN)
FFP	Food-for-Peace
FNPU	Food and Nutrition Planning Unit (Ministry of Planning and National Development)
FSG	Food Studies Group (Oxford University, U.K.)
g	Gram
GDP	Gross Domestic Product
GHT	Gabbra Historical Texts
GMP	Growth Monitoring Programme
GOK	Government of Kenya
GTZ	German Agency for Technical Cooperation (FRG)
ha	Hectare
hPa	Hectopascal; 1 hPa = 100 Pa = 1 mb
ICO	International Coffee Organization
IDS	Institute for Development Studies, University of Nairobi
ILCA	International Livestock Centre for Africa
ILRAD	International Laboratory for Research on Animal Diseases
IMF	International Monetary Fund
IMFFC	Interministerial Food Forecasting Committee
IPAL	Integrated Project in Arid Lands
IRS	Integrated Rural Survey
ITCZ	Intertropical Convergence Zone
KALRES	Kenya Arid Lands Research Station
KANU	Kenya African National Union
K£	Kenya pound (= Ksh 20)
KFFHC	Kenya Freedom From Hunger Council
kg	Kilogram
KILIMO	Ministry of Agriculture and Livestock Development (Tanzania)
KMC	Kenya Meat Commission
KMD	Kenya Meteorological Department (Ministry of Transport and Communications)
KNCSS	Kenya National Council of Social Services
KP&L	Kenya Power and Lighting Co.
KRCS	Kenyan Red Cross Society

KREMU	Kenya Rangeland Ecology Monitoring Unit. Subsequently renamed the Department of Resource Surveys and Remote Sensing (Ministry of Planning and National Development)
Ksh	Kenya Shilling: Ksh 20 = K£ 1. In 1984, US $1 = Ksh 16, £ Sterling 1 = Ksh 19.
KTA	Kenya Transport Association
LU	Livestock Unit, 1 LU = 250 kg liveweight
MAC	Mid-Arm Circumference
MALD	Ministry of Agriculture and Livestock Development. Subsequently divided into separate ministries
mb	Millibar
MCH	Mother and Child Health
mm	Millimeter
MOA	Ministry of Agriculture
MOH	Ministry of Health
MOLD	Ministry of Livestock Development
mt	Metric ton
NASSEP	National Sample Survey and Evaluation Programme
Nbi	Nairobi
NCAR	National Center for Atmospheric Research (U.S.)
NCCK	National Christian Council of Kenya
NCPB	National Cereals and Produce Board
NES	National Environment Secretariat (Ministry of Environment and Natural Resources)
NGO	Nongovernmental Organization
NMC	National Milling Corporation (Tanzania)
NOAA	National Oceanic and Atmospheric Administration (U.S.)
ODA	Overseas Development Administration (U.K.)
OFDA	Office of Foreign Disaster Assistance (U.S.)
OP	Office of the President
Pa	Pascal
PEM	Protein Energy Malnutrition
PSU	Primary Sampling Unit
RC	Roman Catholic Church
SDA	Seventh-Day Adventists
SEN	S. E. Nicholson
SFP	School Feeding Programme
SMS	Safe Minimum Standard
TDC	Turkana District Council
TLU	Tropical Livestock Unit; same as LU, livestock unit
TRP	Turkana Rehabilitation Project
TRP/MET	Turkana Rehabilitation Project Meteorological Station
Tsh	Tanzanian Shilling; Tsh 19.85 = US $1.00 in 1986 at the official rate

UNEP	United Nations Environment Programme
UNESCO	United Nations Educational, Scientific and Cultural Organization
UNICEF	United Nations Children's Fund
USAID	U.S. Agency for International Development
USDA	U.S. Department of Agriculture
UTM	Universal Transverse Mercator grid
WFP	World Food Programme
WHO	World Health Organization

Contributors

George J. Anyango, National Environment Secretariat (P.O. Box 67839, Nairobi, Kenya), is concerned with the conservation of natural resources.

Gernot Bake (P. O. Box 30677, Nairobi, Kenya) was formerly the hydrologist with the Integrated Project on Arid Lands (IPAL) based in Marsabit, Kenya. He is a consulting hydrologist with experience throughout the arid lands of Africa and the Middle East.

M. Baksh, assistant researcher, UCLA School of Public Health, and visiting assistant professor of anthropology, UCLA (Los Angeles, CA 90024, U.S.), was formerly the field director of the Nutrition CRSP project in Embu District.

John Borton, senior research associate, Relief and Development Institute (1 Ferdinand Place, London, NW1 8EE, U.K.), worked as the planning officer for drought relief for the government of Botswana in the 1980s. He has since been involved in research into aspects of relief operations and in evaluations of the response to emergencies in Africa by nongovernmental and donor organizations.

J. B. M. Bukusi, assistant director of Education (Ministry of Education, P.O. Box 30040, Nairobi, Kenya), is in charge of the school milk program in Kenya and helped in general coordination of responses by the ministry during the drought.

N. O. Bwibo, principal, College of Health Sciences, and professor of pediatrics, University of Nairobi Faculty of Medicine, Kenya, was co-principal investigator of the Nutrition CRSP project in Embu District.

E. Carter is now a medical resident in post-graduate training at the University of North Carolina School of Medicine (Chapel Hill, NC 27514, U.S.). He was the first field director for the Nutrition CRSP project in Embu and was instrumental in informing local and central government about the 1984 food crisis in Embu and in mobilizing food aid for the study area.

D. Cattle, assistant professor, Miami University (East High St., Oxford, OH 45056, U.S.), was the field anthropologist for the Nutrition CRSP project in Embu District.

A. H. Coulson, epidemiologist, UCLA School of Public Health (Los Angeles, CA 90024, U.S.), was an investigator for the Nutrition CRSP project in Embu District.

Thomas E. Downing, National Center for Atmospheric Research (P. O. Box 3000, Boulder, CO 80307-3000, U.S.), spent four years in Kenya with the National Environment Secretariat assisting the government of Kenya in documenting the impacts of and responses to the 1984/85 drought.

Graham Farmer, senior research associate, Climatic Research Unit, University of East Anglia (Norwich, NR4 5TJ, U.K.), works on issues of climate change and climate-impact assessment, with a special interest in tropical climatology in Africa.

Carolyn Getao, National Environment Secretariat (P.O. Box 67839, Nairobi, Kenya), is concerned with the conservation of natural resources.

M. Gitahi, National Environment Secretariat (P.O. Box 67839, Nairobi, Kenya), is concerned with the conservation of natural resources.

Kangethe W. Gitu, Ministry of Finance and Planning (P.O. Box 30005, Nairobi, Kenya), was formerly with the Long Term Strategy Section of the Ministry of Agriculture. He is an agricultural economist and has reviewed development policy in Kenya and contributed to planning efforts since 1981.

Barbara E. Grandin, International Laboratory for Research on Animal Diseases (ILRAD) (P.O. Box 30709, Nairobi, Kenya), is an anthropologist specializing in livestock development. She participated in the International Livestock Centre for Africa's multidisciplinary study of Maasai livestock production from 1980 to 1986.

A. A. J. Jansen, Fiji School of Medicine (Private Mail Bag, Suva, Fiji, South Pacific), was co-investigator of the Nutrition CRSP project in Embu District and former assistant professor of community health, University of Nairobi, Faculty of Medicine, Nairobi.

Charity Kabutha, National Environment Secretariat (P.O. Box 67839, Nairobi, Kenya), is a planner with experience in rural surveys and the evaluation of development projects. She also contributed to the Women's Decade with research on women's access to health services.

Crispin M. Kamau, Ministry of Education, Science, and Technology (P.O. Box 30040, Nairobi, Kenya), was formerly with the National Environment Secretariat. He is active in environmental assessments, land use, and planning issues.

Mary Karanja, National Environment Secretariat (P.O. Box 67839, Nairobi, Kenya), is a planner with interests in resource conservation and environmental management.

D. A. R. Kashasha, Crop Monitoring and Early Warning Systems Project (P.O. Box 5384, Dar es Salaam, Tanzania), is an agrometeorologist with experience in monitoring crop production in East Africa.

A. K. Kiriro, director, National Environment Secretariat, Ministry of Environment and Natural Resources (P.O. Box 67839, Nairobi, Kenya), has extensive experience in the government of Kenya, including the Ministry of Agriculture and Ministry of Health. He directs a variety of programs at the National Environment Secretariat on district environmental assessment, pollution control, conservation, and human settlements.

Peter N. de Leeuw, International Livestock Centre for Africa (ILCA) (P.O. Box 46847, Nairobi, Kenya), is an ecologist with widespread experience in remote sensing, rangeland evaluation, and livestock productivity.

P. Lembuya (P.O. Box 10807, Nairobi, Kenya) was a research assistant and fieldwork supervisor with the International Livestock Centre for Africa Maasai research project from 1980 to 1988.

Michael W. Macodras, Kenya Meteorological Department (P.O. Box 30259, Nairobi, Kenya), is a meteorologist with an interest in rainfall climatology and data management.

B. F. Maganda, Central Bureau of Statistics (P.O. Box 30266, Nairobi, Kenya), is a statistician working on crop monitoring and food policy.

Sabina W. Maghanga, National Environment Secretariat (P.O. Box 67839, Nairobi, Kenya), is a planner concerned with issues of resource management.

Simon K. Mbarire, National Environment Secretariat (P.O. Box 67839, Nairobi, Kenya), is an environmental officer in the Environmental Education and Information Division.

Moses G. Mbugua, general secretary, Kenya Freedom From Hunger Council (P.O. Box 30762, Nairobi, Kenya), is responsible for field projects on water, health, livestock, and afforestation to ensure increased food production and a Kenya free from hunger and malnutrition. Development programs are implemented throughout Kenya.

Simeon Munene, National Environment Secretariat (P.O. Box 67839, Nairobi, Kenya), is an officer in the Resource Management Division, concerned with conservation policy.

F. G. Murage, chief statistician, National Cereals and Produce Board (P.O. Box 30586, Nairobi, Kenya), is responsible for compiling and reporting statistics on crop yields, expected volume of purchases and sales, and current stocks within the NCPB.

Wycliffe Mutero, National Environment Secretariat (P.O. Box 67839, Nairobi, Kenya), is in the Human Settlements Division, with training in data base management and resource assessment.

Harun R. Muturi, National Environment Secretariat (P.O. Box 67839, Nairobi, Kenya), is a geologist with interests in climate change, climate-impact assessment, and drought management.

B. Mwangi, National Environment Secretariat (P.O. Box 67839, Nairobi, Kenya), is an agriculturalist with interest in soil conservation.

Duncan N. Mwanjila, Ministry of Agriculture (P.O. Box 30028, Nairobi, Kenya), is a crop specialist and assists the government in monitoring the stage and progress of crop production thoughout the country.

H. Mwendwa, senior ecologist, Department of Resource Surveys and Remote Sensing, formerly KREMU (P.O. Box 47146, Nairobi, Kenya), has worked on numerous studies of rangeland and crop forecasting using remote sensing, with special emphasis on resource assessment for development planning.

John Mwikya, Kenya Meteorological Department (P.O. Box 30259, Nairobi, Kenya), is an agrometeorologist responsible for reporting the farming weather throughout the country.

Philip Ndegwa, governor, Central Bank of Kenya (P.O. Box 60000, Nairobi, Kenya), is an economist. He has served the government of Kenya in various senior positions, is active in several international organizations, and has contributed to numerous publications.

Robin Needham, assistant country director, CARE Bangladesh (GPO Box 226, Dhaka, Bangladesh), was formerly the drought relief coordinator for CARE Kenya (P.O. Box 43864, Nairobi).

Charlotte G. Neumann, professor of public health and pediatrics, UCLA (Los Angeles, CA 90024, U.S.), co-directed the Nutrition Collaborative Research Support Program (CRSP) in Kenya and was part of a three-country study of the impact of malnutrition on human function.

D. Ngare, UCLA School of Public Health (Los Angeles, CA 90024, U.S.), is a medical sociologist with the Kenya Medical Research Institute in Kenya, now pursuing a doctoral degree at UCLA.

Eliud Ngunjiri, Oxfam (P.O. Box 40680, Nairobi, Kenya), is a projects officer. He has extensive experience in the rangelands of Kenya and with the administration of development projects.

Philip N. Nthusi, Kenya Meteorological Department (P.O. Box 30259,

Nairobi, Kenya), is a meteorologist, with interest in synoptic climatology of Eastern Africa.

M. A. Okoth, Ministry of Health (P.O. Box 20723, Nairobi, Kenya), is a public health officer.

M. Paolisso, International Center for Research on Women (1717 Massachusetts Ave., NW, Suite 501, Washington, D.C. 20036, U.S.), was field anthropologist with the Nutrition CRSP in Embu District.

Paul W. Robinson, field director, St. Lawrence University (P.O. Box 43759, Nairobi, Kenya), wrote his dissertation after several years of fieldwork among the Gabbra.

Louise Sperling, Rockefeller post-doctoral fellow with the Center for International Tropical Agriculture (B.P. 259, Butare, Rwanda), is an anthropologist who has spent several years, including the 1984 drought, in Samburu District studying labor organization of Samburu pastoralists.

Jeremy Swift, Institute of Development Studies (University of Sussex, Brighton, BN1 9RE, U.K.), is an anthropologist researching pastoral systems, monitoring, disaster response, and food-security issues throughout Africa.

Margaret Wainaina, National Environment Secretariat (P.O. Box 67839, Nairobi, Kenya), is an officer in the Human Settlements Division with interest in energy development and improving human habitats in Kenya.

V. S. Wambani, Ministry of Health (P.O. Box 20723, Nairobi, Kenya), is a public health officer.

S. Weinberg, in Gothenberg, Sweden, was a field nutritionist with the Nutrition CRSP project in Embu District.

F. Were, National Environment Secretariat (P.O. Box 67839, Nairobi, Kenya), has experience in data processing and resource assessment.

Pascal T. Woldemariam, World Food Programme (P.O. Box 30218, Nairobi, Kenya), was deputy regional representative during the 1984/85 drought.

J. B. Wyckoff, chairman, Department of Agricultural Economics, University of Hawaii at Manoa (Honolulu, HI 96822, U.S.) was with the Ministry of Agriculture in Kenya during the 1984/85 drought, working on issues of long-range agricultural planning and development.

Index

Aberdares, 170–171, 174, 177, 212
ActionAid-Kenya, 222, 302, 305, 336
Adano, M., 156
Ade, S., 156
Administrative Boundaries, 14
Advanced Very High Resolution Radiometers (AVHRR), 250, 261
Africa, 82–83, 86–88, 369–378
African Inland Church (AIC), 222
African Medical Research and Education Foundation (AMREF), 39, 42–44, 57, 60, 284, 288, 336
Agatsiva, J.L., Mwendwa, H., Ottichillo, W.K., Peden, D.G., and Pilloto, J., 95
Agricultural Prices, *see* Markets
Agricultural Production; Africa, 369, 378; agroecological zones, 5–6, 15, 170–172, 174–176, 192, 199, 226, 231, 240; constraints to, 137, 176–177, 187–189, 210; drought impacts, 4–7, 23, 179–189; estimates, 7, 23; inputs and investment, 15, 61, 220–221, 291, 359; low productivity, 355; monitoring, 94–97, 100–101, 122–130, 202; research and policy, 358–362; comparative advantage, 360; *see also* specific crops
Agricultural Sub-Committee, *see* Government/Donor Agricultural Sub-Committee
Agriculturalists, 139–140
Agumba, F.O., 69, 70
AID, *see* U.S. Agency for International Development
Akong'a, J., Downing, T.E., Konijn, N.T., Mungai, D.N., Muturi, H.R., and Potter, H.L., 201, 210
Alle, B., 156
Ambler, C.H., 22

Amboseli, 249, 254–255, 262–263
American Council of Learned Societies, xix
Andere, D.K., xviii
Anyamba, E.K. and Ogallo, L.J., 69–70
Anyango, G.J., 3, 169, 211
Army Worms, 179, 333
Aronson, D., xix
Athi River, 170, 176
Australia, 53–54, 56, 61
Australian High Commission, 302

Bake, G., 3, 141, 142, 143, 150, 156
Baksh, M., 231
Baringo, 7, 55, 60, 97–102, 115–118, 130, 287, 301, 304–305, 334
Baringo Pilot Semi-Arid Area Project, 7
Beans, 7, 23, 34, 40, 52, 59, 61, 114, 117–118, 120, 122, 171, 175–176, 179, 181–182, 202, 205–207, 212–215, 218–222, 226, 228, 230–231, 235–236, 270, 275, 291, 300, 302, 305, 333, 338–343, 355
Berry, L., Hunter, O., Seidman, A., Ford, R., Puffer, F., and Perritt, R., 15, 22, 190
Black Americans in Response to African Crisis (BARAC), 236
Borana, 141, 143, 160
Borton and Stephenson, xvii, 25
Borton, J., xvii, 3, 24, 52, 62
Botswana, 245
Braun, H.M.H., 174
Browdy, B., xviii
Bukusi, J.B.M., 299
Bungoma, 94–97, 101, 106, 115–118, 128, 130
Bura Irrigation Scheme, 38, 121
Burki, S.J., 370
Burundi, 32, 55

400

Busia, 115–118, 130
Bwibo, N.O., 231

Campbell, D.J., 246, 249, 256
Canada, 53, 56
CARE, 2, 11–12, 39, 41, 44–45, 47, 281, 284, 288, 329–336, 342
Carter, E., 231
Cash Crops, 175, 367; *see also* specific crops
Cassava, 176, 212, 218, 231, 239, 366, 374
Catholic Diocese, Missions, Orders, 39, 219, 221–222, 274, 288, 330; Garissa, 336; Isiolo, 288; Karaba, 336; Kitui, 35, 329, 336; Lodwar, 318–319, 322; Machakos, 288; Maikona, 153; Marsabit, 35, 285, 288, 329, 332, 336, 345–346; Mount Kenya East, 336; Nanyuki, 336; West Pokot, 288
Catholic Relief Services (CRS), 35, 42, 57–58, 219, 221, 284
Cattle, D., 231
Central (Province), 7–8, 22, 34, 59, 72, 107, 130, 139, 169–210, 211–230, 291–293, 297, 304, 359
Central Africa, 70, 174
Central Bank of Kenya, 19, 57
Central Bureau of Statistics (CBS), xviii, 5–6, 11, 14–26, 37, 49, 57–58, 60–61, 63–67, 96, 101, 106–118, 123, 126–127, 172, 180, 183, 185, 200–201, 203, 226, 289–290, 297, 356
Central Bureau of Statistics/National Environment Secretariat (CBS/NES) Survey of Drought Responses, 180–210
Cereals and Sugar Finance Committee, 29
Chalbi (Desert, Lowlands), 141, 155, 159–160, 162
Chara, P., xix
Cherangani Hills, 95
Child Health and Nutrition Information System (CHANIS), 109–110, 289, 295–298
Child Nutrition Survey, 183, 290
Children's Mercy Fund, 285, 288, 336
Christian Children's Fund, 221
Church of the Province of Kenya (CPK), 219, 221, 288
Chyulu Hills, 246, 248–249, 252–254, 263
Clark University, xv–xvi
Climate Change 67; *see also* Rainfall, Cycles
Climatic Research Unit, University of East Anglia, xvii
Coast (Province), 6, 22, 34, 83–87, 89–93, 128, 130, 297
Coffee, 8, 23, 57–58, 171, 174–177, 189, 202, 212–216, 226, 238, 355
Cohen, J.M., 357
Cohen, J.M. and Lewis, D.B., 28–30, 33, 62
Collaborative Research Support Program (CRSP), 34, 59, 231–244, 288, 336
Commodity Credit Corporation (CCC) (U.S.), 30, 36–37, 48, 54, 62; *see also* Food Aid
Congo, 72, 75
Contagious Bovine Pleuropneumonia (CBPP), 313
Contagious Caprine Pleuropneumonia (CCPP), 323, 327
Corn, *see* maize
Cotton, 171, 174–175, 202, 214, 226, 291, 355
Coulson, A.H., 231
Cove Trader, 37, 54, 62
CPC Industrial Products, 60
Crop Forecast Survey (CFS), *see* Food Monitoring
Crop Monitoring and Early Warning Systems Project (CMEWSP) (Tanzania), 131–137
Currency; conversion rates, 392–393; foreign exchange reserves, 19, 46, 58, 62
Cycles; Gabbra calendar 151–168; rainfall and climate, 85–86, 93

Dadu, M., 156
Dahl, G. and Hjort, A., 266
Danish International Development Agency (DANIDA), 60, 221–222, 338–339, 342
Davies, T.D., Vincent, C.E., and Beresford, A.K.C., 84
de Leeuw, P., xviii, 245
de Wilde, J.C., 188
Delgado, C.J. and Mellor, J.W., 375
Deloitte, Haskins and Sells Management Co. (DH and SMC), 20, 39, 54–55, 62, 207
Denmark, 56
Dennett, M.D., Elston, J., and Rodgers, J.A., 86

Dependency, 370–373
Development, 353; community structures, 349–350; food aid, production, 371–373, 375
Development Planning Division (DPD), Ministry of Agriculture, 357
Didiru, B., 156
Directorate of Meteorology (Tanzania), 132
District Agricultural Development Officer (DADO) (Tanzania), 132–133
District Agricultural Officer (DAO), 316, 322, 327
District Commissioner (DC), 316, 322, 328, 337
District Drought-Contingency Officer (DDCO), 328
District Education Officer (DEO), 317
District Focus for Rural Development, 224, 306, 361
District Office (DO), 328
District Range Officer (DRO), 316
District Relief Committees (District Food Security Committees), 29
District Veterinary Officer (DVO), 316, 322–323, 328
Donors; appeal to, 26, 58, 283; responses and donations, 38–42, 56, 61; see also specific agencies
Downing, J., Berry, L., Downing, L., Downing, T.E., and Ford, R., 62
Downing, T.E., xvii, 3, 22, 169, 186–192, 208, 210–211
Downing, T.E., Akong'a, J., Mungai, D.N., Muturi, H.R., and Potter, H.L., 22
Downing, T.E. and Porter, P.W., 177
Downing, T.E., Lezberg, S., Williams, C., and Berry, L., 6, 172, 200
Downing, T.E., Mungai, D.N., and Muturi, H.R., 195–196, 237, 244
Dried Skim Milk (DSM), see Milk, Food Aid
Drought; Africa, 370; chronology, 57–62, 307–308, 327; definition, indices and probability, 3–4, 141–142, 146, 150, 201, 244, 307–308, 326; forecasting and monitoring, 11, 65–67; geography and hazard, 3–5, 21, 48; history, 22, 158, 237, 246–247; household coping strategies, 12, 139–140, 186–189, 202, 205, 209–230, 237–239; impacts, 6–9, 214–230, 232–233: on coffee and tea, 8–9, on the economy, 9, on education, 300–301, on food production, 7, on livestock, 7–8, 97–99, 102–105; institutional responses, 281–351; lessons learned, 1–2, 46–50, 223–225, 293–294, 362; migration, 185–186; national responses, 9–13, 20, 24–56; vulnerability, 4–5, 6, 11–12, 139–140, 169–210, 366–368; water supply, 142–144
Drought-Resistant Crops, 209–210, 225, 290, 366; see also specific crops

Early Warning System (EWS), 10, 46–48, 57–58, 67; early warning phase of national response, 25–32; indicators, 316–319, 321; improvements to, 364–365; Turkana, 282, 315–325, 327–328; liaison with other systems, 319; Samburu, 275–276; warning stages, 320–321, 328; see also specific agencies
East Africa, 22, 72;
East Africa Meteorological Department (EAMD), 226
East Coast Fever (ECF), see Livestock
Eastern (Province), 6–7, 22, 33–34, 47–48, 57, 59, 72, 107–108, 130, 139, 141, 169–210, 211–230, 231, 290–294, 297, 304, 359
Economist Intelligence Unit (EIU), 62
Economy, 46; growth, 6; impact of drought, 9; smallholder participation, 140
EcoSystems, Ltd., 188, 255
Education, 214–217, 229, 294; educational institutions, 299–300, 304; school feeding programs, 273, 301–305
El Niño/Southern Oscillation (ENSO), 85
Elgeyo Marakwet, 35, 55, 94–96, 101, 115–118, 130, 287, 304
Elgon, Mt., 95
Elliott's Bakeries, 61
Eluaai, 252
Embu, 34, 40, 55, 59–60, 109, 115–118, 128, 130, 140, 169–210, 231–244, 287, 291–293, 298, 301–302, 304–305, 329, 333–334, 340, 343
Emergency Drought Management Subcommittee (EDM), 328
Employment, 50, 59, 181, 209–210, 217–224, 308, 314, 323–324
Entitlements, 4, 67, 349
Erukudi, 307

Ethiopia, 22, 98, 143, 151–168, 319
Europe, 360
European Economic Community (EEC), 30, 44, 53–54, 56, 311, 331, 342

Famine, *see* Drought, Food Aid, Food Security
Farm Management Handbooks (FMH), *see* Jaetzold and Schmidt
Farmer, G., 82, 84–86
Farmer, G. and Wigley, T.M.L., 82–85, 88, 174
Field, C.R. and Njiru, G.K., 7, 62, 344
Field, C.R., Lamprey, H.F., and Masheti, S.M., 98
Fishing, 308, 324
Folland, C.K., Palmer, T.N., and Parker, D.E., 86
Food Aid, Food Distribution, and Food Relief; appeal to donors, 26–27; Asian experience, 374–375; central and eastern Kenya, 183–184, 188–189, 206–210, 217–223, 230; concessionary, 46; contingency and preparedness planning, 48; GOK distribution, 27, 34–35, 55, 207, 284, 287; Ministry of Education, 301–302; Ministry of Health Supplementary Feeding Programme, 291–293, 298 NGOs 11, 27, 41–47, 160, 234–236, 264, 273–275, 283–288, 302–303, 329–336, 338–343; national organization and policy, 27–29; rations, 35, 234, 281, 283, 292–293; CRSP project area, 234–235; recipients, 20, 34–35, 47, 54, 59, 60; seed, 235–236; sub-Saharan Africa, 371–373; targeting, 234, 292, 348, 365; Titles I and II, 34–37, 43, 45–47, 53–55, 332; Turkana, 324; *see also* specific agencies, districts, Food Imports
Food and Agriculture Organization (FAO), 5, 7–8, 26, 31–33, 39, 41, 44, 51, 56, 59, 62–64, 108, 131, 186, 232, 370, 378
Food and Nutrition Planning Unit (FNPU), 111
Food Availability, 20
Food Consumption, 232–233, 240
Food Crops, 175–176; *see also* specific crops
Food Crops, Minor (green grams, pigeon peas, cow peas, vegetables, fruits), 48, 175–176, 179, 187–188, 206, 212–214, 218–222, 226, 228, 230, 305, 355, 365, 374
Food for the Hungry, 288, 334, 336
Food Imports; commercial and concessionary, 20, 27, 30–34, 53–54, 56, 61, 62; distribution and logistics, 331–335, 365; requirements 5, 27, 52; *see also* Food Aid, specific crops
Food Interventions, 20
Food Losses, 63–64
Food Monitoring System, 10, 65–67, 106–118; agrometeorological crop forecasting, 108–109, 131–137; Area Planted Survey (CBS), 25; collaboration between agencies, 10–11, 65–67; crop codes 137; Crop Forecast Survey, 37, 57, 60–61, 106–109, 111, 114–118 entitlement approach, 67; food crop monitoring, 119–121; health and nutrition information, 109–110; Large Farms Survey, 107, 123; Market Price Survey, 109; monthly food situation report, 320; Tanzanian model, 67, 131–137; use and processing of food-sector monitoring information, 110–112
Food Policy, 13, 353; drought in Africa, 369–378; drought in Kenya, 355–368; marketing and pricing, 360; objectives and improvements to, 356, 362
Food Security; food deprivation, 170, 183–187; food poverty, 170, 180–183, 186; food shortage, 169, 173–180, 186, 214–217; food-for-work projects, 323; marketing and storage, 218–223, 362–364; national policy, 363–368; planning, 48
Food Storage and Stocks; financial aspects, 373; household, 209–210, 222–225, 230, 233, 238, 363–364; national, 46, 61, 63–64, 362–363; private, 63–64; *see also* National Cereals and Produce Board
Food Studies Group (FSG), Oxford University (U.K.), 106
Food-for-Peace (FFP), *see* U.S. Agency for International Development
Food-for-Work, 34, 42, 60, 230, 283–286, 314, 317–318, 337–343, 365; *see also* specific agencies
Foods, wild, 221, 233, 237, 269–270

Ford Foundation, xv, xvii, xviii
Foreign Exchange, *see* Currency
Foster Parents Plan, 340
France, 53, 56
Frere, M. and Popov, G.F., 131
Friends of McGill, xix
Fry, P., 344, 347, 350–351
Fulbright Hays, xviii
Fumagalli, C., 265

Gabbra, 141, 151–168
Gabbra Historical Texts (GHT), xvii, 151, 153–157, 166
Galaty, J., xix
Garissa, 7, 41, 55, 97–98, 103, 287, 301, 304–305
Gatab, 142
Gearing-up Phase, 27–32, 58–61
German Agency for Technical Cooperation (GTZ) (FRG), 272–273, 346
German Freedom From Hunger Agency, 342
Germany (FRG), 54, 56
Getao, C., 169
Gitahi, M., 169, 211
Githunguri, 125–126, 128, 211–230
Gitu, K.W., 3
Goma, B., 154
Gommes, R., 131, 133, 135–136
Government/Donor Agriculture Sub-Committee, 35, 48
Government of Kenya (GOK) (publications only), 30, 122, 162, 283, 356–357, 362; *see also* specific agencies
Grandin, B.E., xviii, 245–246, 252, 257, 263
Grandin, B.E. and Bekure, S., 263
Grandin, B.E. and Lembuya, P., 245
Gross Domestic Product (GDP), 6, 9
Growth Monitoring Programme (GMP), 295
Guyo, H., 156

Haaga, J., Mason, G.J., Omoro, F.Z., Quinn, V., Rafferty, A., Teft, K., and Wasonga, L., 291
Herlehy, T.J., 22
Highlands, 83–87, 89–93
Hogg, R., 25, 344
Homewood, K. and Lewis, J., 344
Hounan, D.E., Burgos, J.J., Kalik, M.S., Palmer, W.C., and Rodda, J., 3
Hunger; coping strategies, 187–189; prevalence, 215–217; vulnerability, 186–187, 208; *see also* Drought, Vulnerability
Hurri, G., 153
Hurri Hills, 141, 158–160
Hutchinson, P., 86

Idho, D., 156–157
Ildalalakutuk, 252
Ilmao Hills, 254
Iltilal, 249, 254, 262
Implementation Phase, 32–35, 61–62
Income, 180–183, 204, 224; distribution 256–258, 263, 266, 278, 371
India, Asia, 8, 54, 353, 374–375
Indian Ocean, 5, 70–75, 77, 86, 173
Indigenous Knowledge, 151–168, 218–223, 229
Institute for Development Studies (IDS), University of Nairobi, xix
Integrated Project in Arid Lands (IPAL), UNESCO, 7, 141, 344
Integrated Rural Survey, (IRS) 203
Interministerial Food Forecasting Committee (IMFF), 106, 108, 110
International Coffee Organization (ICO), 8, 58
International Laboratory for Research on Animal Diseases (ILRAD), xix
International Livestock Center for Africa (ILCA), xviii, 150, 245, 254, 256, 262
International Monetary Fund (IMF), 5, 57
Intertropical Convergence Zone (ITCZ), 69–75
Irrigation, 176, 179–180, 215, 224, 366
Isiolo, 7, 35, 55, 97–98, 102–103, 130, 287, 301, 304–305, 329, 347–351

Jaetzold, R. and Schmidt, H., 171, 192–194, 198–199, 226
Jansen, A.A., 231

Kaambo Hills, 248, 254
Kabutha, C., 169
Kajiado, 8, 22, 43, 55, 60, 115–118, 130, 245–263, 287, 301, 304–305, 329, 334
Kakamega, 22, 94–96, 101, 106, 115–118, 128, 130
Kakuma, 327
Kalacha, 160–161
Kamau, C.M., 3, 169, 211
Kamba, 22, 172, 247, 257

Kanamitsu, N., and Krishamurti, J.N., 70
Kapedo, 316, 326
Karanja, M., 169
Kashasha, D.A.R., 131
Kates, R.W., Chen, R.S., Downing, T.E., Kasperson, J.X., Messer, E., and Millman, S.R., 169
Katilu, 327
Katz, R.W. and Glantz, M.H., 83
Kawelu, 211–230
Kenya African National Union (KANU), 211
Kenya Arid Lands Research Station (KALRES), 317, 321
Kenya Cooperative Creameries, 23, 60
Kenya Freedom From Hunger Council (KFFHC), 39, 284, 288, 336, 337–343
Kenya Livestock Development Project, 246
Kenya Meat Commission (KMC), 8, 23, 59, 180, 313–314, 328, 345
Kenya Meteorological Department (KMD), xvii, 11, 17–18, 20, 57, 62, 65, 69–70, 75–81, 83, 86, 90–92, 108, 110–111, 262, 364
Kenya, Mt., 6, 170–171, 174, 177, 212
Kenya National Archives, xviii
Kenya National Council of Social Services (KNCSS), 29, 41, 43–45, 58–60, 285, 330
Kenya Ports Authority, 28
Kenya Power and Lighting Co. (KP&L), 59, 61–62
Kenya Railways, 28, 32, 58
Kenya Rangeland Ecology Monitoring Unit (KREMU), renamed Department of Resource Surveys and Remote Sensing, xviii, 11, 49, 65–66, 94–105, 110–111, 127
Kenya Seed Company, 121
Kenya Soil Survey (KSS), 171, 176, 192, 198; see also Sombroek et al.
Kenya Transport Association (KTA), 32–33, 60
Kenyan Red Cross Society (KRCS), 41, 44, 57, 284, 288, 332, 336
Kericho, 106, 115–118, 128, 130
Kerio Valley, 22, 95
Kerugoya, 125–126, 128, 176, 197
Kiambu, 55, 115–118, 128, 130, 169–210, 287, 300, 304, 338–339, 343
Kibirigwi, 176
Kiboko, 247–248, 250, 252–255, 262–263

Kibwezi, 42–43, 60, 248, 263
Kidson, J.W., 70
Kikuyu, 22, 172
Kilifi, 115–118, 130
Kilimanjaro, Mt., 249, 255, 263
Killick, T., 358
Kilonyeti, 248, 251
King, J.M., 141
Kinuthia, J.H., et al., 69
Kinyanjui, K., xix
Kirega, S.W., xvii
Kirinyaga, 115–118, 128, 130, 169–210, 211–230, 287, 302, 304
Kiriro, A.K., xvii
Kisii, 115–118, 128, 130
Kisumu, 5, 115–118, 130
Kitui, 22, 34–35, 40, 55, 59–60, 95, 115–118, 126, 128–130, 169–230, 283, 287, 291–293, 298, 304–305, 329, 334, 339–340, 343–344
Kitui Inter-Church Emergency Programme, 344
Kliest, T., 62
Kombuini, 211–230
Konijn, N.T., 176, 197
Kufwafwa, J.W., 98
Kulal, Mt., 142
Kwale, 115–118, 130
Kyeni South, 231

Laikipia, 35, 55, 98, 102, 104, 115–118, 130, 287, 301, 304–305
Lake Turkana, 141, 143, 159
Lake Victoria, 5, 6, 22, 72, 75, 173
Lamb, P.J., 86, 174
Lamu, 55, 115–118, 130, 287, 301, 304–305
Land Ownership and Use, 15, 188, 243, 245
Larick, R., xix
League of Red Cross, 41
Legesse, A., 153
Lekutai, S., xix
Lembuya, P., xviii, 245
Lipton, M., 375
Livestock, 23, 188, 212–217, 238; destocking/restocking projects, 322–323, 347–351; diseases, 247–249, 253, 257–259, 267; drought impacts, losses, and mortality, 7–8, 60, 102–105, 160, 177–180, 203, 214–217, 223, 256–258, 263, 267–268; feed, 54, 63–64, 313–314, 323, 366; grain-

for-livestock exchange scheme, 59, 281, 344–347; health, grazing and destocking during a drought, 322–323, 344–347; hides, 270–272; marketing, prices, maintenance, 182, 216, 228, 256–257, 270–272, 279, 312–314, 366; mobility and distribution, 250–255, 263; monitoring, 97–105; populations, 265, 267, 279; zone in central and eastern Kenya, 171–210; *see also* Pastoralists
Livestock Unit (LU), 256
Lodwar, 316, 318–319, 323, 326–327
Lodwar Hospital, 318, 320
Loevinsohn, M., xix, 267
Lokichokio, 316, 326
Lokitaung, 307, 316, 326–327
Lokori, 327
Longonot, 95
Lorugum, 327
Lough, J.M., 86
Lutheran Church, 288

Maasai, 22, 245–263
McAlpin, M.B., 49
Machakos, 8, 22, 34–35, 40, 44–45, 55, 59–60, 95, 107, 115–118, 126, 128–130, 169–230, 247–248, 252, 255, 283, 287, 291–293, 298, 304–305, 329, 333–334, 339, 343
McNamara, R.S., 376
Macodras, M.W., 69
Madagascar, 71
Maganda, B.F., 96, 106
Maghanga, S.W., 169
Maikona, 161
Maize, 4, 7, 23, 25–28, 30–37, 39–40, 45–47, 49, 50–56, 57–63, 65, 101–109, 114–116, 120–130, 133, 171, 174–177, 179, 181–184, 187–189, 193, 202–203, 205–207, 212–215, 218–226, 228, 230–231, 233–236, 270, 272–276, 291, 293, 300, 302, 305, 311–313, 319, 326, 338–343, 345–346, 355, 359–360, 363–364, 374, 378; husbandry, 124–125, 129; monthly average price, 114; policy, 35, 367; phenology and condition, 135–136; procurement in lowland Samburu, 273; imports, production, stocks, trade and use, 63, 202, 283–288; seed (Katumani, hybrid), 38, 120, 175, 333; yellow maize surplus, 36, 47; yields, 94–97, 101, 118, 122–130, 197
Makindu, 176, 197, 263
Mandera, 7, 55, 97–98, 102, 104, 287, 301, 304–305
Maralal, 98, 273
Marginal, (Low-Potential) Lands 6, 264, 300, 334
Markets; food crops, 23, 222–224, 360; government regulation, 4, 140; hoarding, 59; local markets, 12, 140, 180–183, 188, 203, 209–210, 212–214, 224–225, 228, 238, 273; prices, 57, 61, 109, 114, 205, 360–361; Turkana, 308; yellow maize, 223
Marsabit, 7, 35, 42, 55, 97–98, 102, 105, 130, 141–168, 287, 301, 304–305, 329, 334, 341, 343, 345–346
Martin, R.M., xviii
Mason, J.B., Haaga, J.G., Marks, G., Quinn, V. Test, K., and Maribe, T., 321
Matapato, 252–253
Materi Girls' Center, 285, 288
Mau, 95
Maua Hospital, 336
Mauritius, 71
Mbarire, S.K., 169, 299
Mbilin, 251
Mbirikani Group Ranch, (Kisongo Maasai), 246–263
Mbiuni, 211–230
Mbugua, M.G., 337
Mbugua, S.W., 97–98
Mellor, J.M. and Gavian, S., 371
Mellor, J.W., 371
Meru, 22, 34–35, 40, 55, 59–60, 98, 115–118, 128, 130, 283, 287, 291–293, 298, 304–305, 329, 333–334, 340–341, 343
Merueshi, 252, 263
Mid-Arm Circumference (MAC), 184–185, 315
Migot-Adholla, S., xix
Milk, 23, 34, 42, 52, 56, 58–61, 120, 177–179, 207, 219, 230, 235–236, 267–270, 275, 283, 293, 302, 312
Millet, 122, 171–172, 175, 179, 188–189, 202, 206, 213–214, 220–222, 225–226, 228, 231, 235, 239, 291, 361, 366, 374
Ministry of Agriculture (MOA) and Ministry of Agriculture and Livestock Development (MALD), 11, 25, 28, 57,

60, 63–66, 96, 101, 110–111, 119–121, 122, 202, 327, 339, 357–358, 361
Ministry of Agriculture and Livestock Development (KILIMO) (Tanzania), 132
Ministry of Cooperative Development, 361
Ministry of Economic Planning and Development, 265
Ministry of Education, Science and Technology, 299–305
Ministry of Energy and Regional Development, 308
Ministry of Environment and Natural Resources, 60
Ministry of Finance and Planning, 7, 25–26, 28–29, 40, 43, 56–58, 122, 264, 284, 309
Ministry of Health (MOH), 41, 109–110, 289–298, 318, 322, 328
Ministry of Lands and Settlement, 361
Ministry of Livestock Development (MOLD), 60, 357
Ministry of Planning and National Development, 310, 358, 361
Ministry of Transport and Communications, 28, 60
Ministry of Water Development, 303, 361
Ministry of Works, 60
Miraa, 338
Mitchell, J.M.J., Dzerdzeevskii, B., Flohn, H., Hofmeyr, W.L., Lamb, H.H., Rao, K.N., and Wallen, C.C., 86
Mombasa, 5, 31–33, 60, 130, 170, 331, 334
Moris, J., 344, 347
Morris, Father Joe, 307
Morzaria, S., xix
Mother and Child Health (MCH), 42, 318, 330
Moyale, 156, 167
Mozambique, 72, 74
Mukhebi, A.W., et al., 8
Munene, S., 169
Mungai, D.N. and Muturi, H.R., 240
Murage, F., 96, 122, 128
Murang'a, 55, 115–118, 128, 130, 169–230, 300, 302
Mutero, W., 169
Mutomo, 222
Mutomo Hospital, 217
Mutomo Soil and Water Conservation Project, 339
Mutulu, P.M., Okoola, R.E., and Cheres, K.A., 85
Muturi, H.R., 169
Mwangi, B., 169
Mwaniki, H.S.K., 237
Mwanjila, D., 96
Mwea, 176
Mwendwa, H., 94
Mwikya, J., 69
Mwingi, 182

Nairobi, 5–6, 57, 170, 294, 316, 319–320, 323, 331, 339
Nakuru, 94–96, 101, 106, 115–118, 128, 130, 316, 319
Nandi, 94–96, 101, 106, 115–118, 130
Narok, 43, 55, 60, 115–118, 130, 287, 301, 304–305, 329
National Aeronautics and Space Administration, 250
National Center for Atmospheric Research (NCAR), xvi, 83, 88–92
National Cereals and Produce Board (NCPB), 1–2, 10–12, 20, 25–26, 28–29, 30–31, 33, 35–36, 38, 51–52, 55, 57–58, 60, 63–64, 65–66, 96, 106, 110–111, 122–130, 139, 182, 281–286, 302, 311, 319, 322, 328, 331, 346, 363–365
National Child Health Survey, 233
National Christian Council of Kenya (NCCK), 44, 288, 332, 336
National Dryland Farming Research Station, 175
National Environment Secretariat (NES), xv, xvii–xviii, 139, 169, 180–183, 200, 211; NES Survey of Household Coping Strategies, 226–229
National Famine Relief Fund, 26, 38, 58, 120
National Food Policy paper, 30, 120, 356–361
National Freedom From Hunger Walk, 337
National Irrigation Board, 121
National Milling Corporation (NMC) (Tanzania), 132
National Oceanic and Atmospheric Administration (NOAA) (U.S.), 250, 261
National Range Research Station, 8, 248, 262
National Sample Survey and Evaluation Programme (NASSEP), 106–107, 113
Ndegwa, P., xix, 369

Ndoto and Njiru Mountains, 141
Needham, R., 329
Netherlands, 53, 56, 131
Netherlands Embassy, 234
Neumann, C.G., 231
Newell, R.E. and Kidson, J.W., 70
Ngare, D., 231
Ngunga River, 216
Ngunjiri, E., 344
Nicholson, S.E. (SEN), 70, 83, 85, 88–92, 174
Nicholson, S.E. and Entekhabi, D., 85
Nieuwolt, S., 173
Niger, 311
Njeru, E.K., xviii
Njoka, T.J., 246
Nkanata, J., 178
Nongovernmental Organizations (NGOs), 29, 41–46; community structures and assistance, 349–350; coordination, 43–44, 50, 59; distribution of WFP food, 284–288; Relief Coordinating Committee, 43–44, 60; schools, 302–303; *see also* specific organizations
Normao, 248–252
North Horr, 154–155, 161, 165
Northeastern (Province), 22, 34, 57, 329
Norton-Griffiths, M., 97
Nthusi, P.N., 69
Nutrition; changes in diet, 183; food deprivation, 183–186; food intake, 232–233; mortality, 48, 298; status 140, 184–185, 208, 217, 233, 241–244, 289–291, 297, 315; supplementary feeding program, 291–294; surveillance, growth monitoring, 281, 289–298, 314–315, 318–319; *see also* Collaborative Research Support Program
Nyahururu, 346
Nyamindi River, 170
Nyandarua, 55, 115–118, 128, 130, 287
Nyanza (Province), xv 22, 128, 130, 297
Nyeri, 55, 115–118, 128, 130, 287, 340, 343

Odingo, R., 22
Office of Foreign Disaster Assistance (OFDA) (U.S.), *see* U.S. Agency for International Development
Office of the President (OP), xix, 25, 27–30, 33–40, 44–46, 48–49, 54, 57, 60, 111–112, 234, 284, 291–292, 319–320, 330, 332
Ogallo, L.J., 85–86
Ogallo, L.J., and Okoola, R.E., 69–70
Ogallo, L.J., and Anyamba, E.K., 69–70
Oil and Fat, 34, 42, 56, 206, 222, 230, 235–236, 270, 292, 293, 302, 305, 338–341
Ojany, F. and Ogendo, R., 22, 25
Okoola, R.E., 69
Okoth, M.A., 289
Oldoinyo Sampu, 249, 252–254
Ole Maki, M., xix
Olkarkar Group Ranch (Kaputiei Maasai), 246–263
Oltiasika, 249, 254
Oltorot, 142
Overseas Development Administration (ODA) (U.K.), xvii, 38–39
Oxfam, 39, 41, 57, 59, 284–285, 288, 306, 315, 323–324, 330, 344–351

Palutikof, J.P., 86
Palutikof, J., Farmer, G., and Wigley, T.M.L., 86
Paolisso, M., 231
Parry, M.L., Carter, T.R., and Konijn, N.T., xv
Pastoralists; coping strategies, 11–12, 139, 144–145, 151–168, 245–263, 266–270, 278–279; fallback areas, 247–249; food acquisition, 264–279; group ranches, 246–249; integration into economy, 25; location, 5; recovery from drought, 333; terms of trade, 271, 312, 326, 345; *see also* Livestock
Paul, A.A. and Southgate, D.A.T., 232
Peacock, C.P., 249
Peacock, C.P., de Leeuw, P.N., and King, J.M., 249, 250
Pearson, R.L., Miller, L.D., and Tucker, C.J., 95
Peden, D.G. and Mwendwa, H., 95, 97
Peden, D.G., Mwendwa, H., Agatsiva, J.L., and Ottichilo, W.K., 95
Perlov, D., 265
Plan International, 302
Planning not Panic, 59
Platt, B.S., 232
Population; age and sex, 201; agroclimatic zone, 200; density, 171–172, 200, 226; distribution, 6, 16, 200; food consumption, 63–64; growth, 172–

173, 200, 279, 355–356, 367, 369; migration, 185–186, 215; projections, 200
Porter, P.W., 173
Potatoes (English and Sweet), 7, 23, 171, 175, 202, 212–213, 218, 226, 231, 333, 366, 374
Potter, H.L., 178
Preparedness, 10, 306–328
Pressure Patterns, Tropical Cyclones, and Streamlines, 72–75, 77–81
Primary Sampling Unit (PSU), 123
Private Voluntary Organizations, *see* Nongovernmental Organizations
Protein Energy Malnutrition (PEM), 233

Quebec Ministry of Education, xix

Radley, D.E., Brown, C.G.O., Burridge, M.J., Cunningham, M.P., Kirmi, I.M., Purnell, R.E., and Young, A.S., 259
Rain Gauges, 135
Rainfall; drought, 6–7, 76, 142, 250, 262; indigenous forecasting, response farming, 218–223, 229; monitoring, 69–70, 85–87; rainfall data and graphical methods, 83; reliability, 193–194, 226; seasonal patterns and trends, 6, 17, 18, 20, 37, 71–72, 82–85, 88–93, 141–142, 146–150, 156, 165, 167, 173–174, 195–196; synoptic features, 70–71; Turkana, 326; variability, 82–93, 142, 146–150, 196; *see also* Drought
Ranches; group ranches, 245–263; range quality, 261
Rassa, Y., 156
Ray, R.T., 6, 28–29, 43, 62
Recovery Phase, 35–38, 49, 62
Red Crescent Societies, 41
Rehabilitation, 37–38, 62, 365–366; availability of agricultural inputs, 366; grain-for-livestock exchange, 344–347; measures to reduce vulnerability to drought, 366–368; National Famine Relief Fund; 37; Oxfam project in Wajir, 344; restocking projects, 347–351; seed distribution, 41, 61, 235–236, 281, 338, 343, 366
Relief and Development Institute, xvii
Relief Strategy; Government/Donor Agricultural Sub-Committee, 48–49; Kenyan government, 27–38, 283; lessons, 50–51; Task Force on Food Supply and Distribution, 70, 284, 365; Turkana, 308–314; *see also* Food Aid
Rendille, 271
Research; agenda, 375–377; livestock, 258–259; vulnerability, 140
Rice, 122, 179–180, 219, 355, 360–361, 374, 378
Rift Valley (Province), 5–7, 22, 34, 59, 72, 107, 114, 130, 290, 297, 329
Risa, 249, 254–255
Roba, K., 159
Robinson, P.W., xviii, 151, 154, 163–168
Rodhe, H. and Virji, H., 85
Roman Catholic Church (RC), *see* Catholic Relief Services, Catholic Diocese
Ropelewski, C.F. and Halpert, M.S., 85
Rukandema, M., Mavua, J.K., and Audi, P.O., 187
Rukandema, M., Muhammed, L., and Jeza, A., 187
Rural Development Fund, 60
Rwanda, 32

Sabarei, 154–155, 165
Safe Minimum Standard, (SMS) 363
Sagana, 182
Sahara, 71
Sahel, 82, 88
Samburu, 7, 42, 55, 98, 102, 105, 130, 139, 141, 264–280, 287, 301, 304–305, 329, 334, 343–351
Save the Children Fund, 315
Schmidt, G., 188
School Feeding Programme (SFP), 40–41, 57, 59, 60, 281, 301–302, 304–305
Self-help, 216, 228, 299, 338, 339–341
Sen, A., 4, 276
Seventh-Day Adventists (SDA), 288, 336
Siaya, 115–118, 130
Silverman, A., 41
Silverman, T., xviii
Simba, 262
Social Science Research Council, xix
Soils, 170–171, 174; conservation, 218–219, 222, 339–340; water-holding capacity, 176–177, 198
Sombroek, W.G., Braun, H.M.H., and van der Pauw, B.J.A., 171, 198–199, 226
Sorale, Y., 156–157, 159
Sorghum, 122, 172, 175–177, 179, 188–189, 202, 206, 212–214, 218–222,

225–226, 228, 230–231, 239, 291, 302, 340, 361, 366, 374, 376
South Africa, 71
South Atlantic, 73
South Nyanza, 6, 106, 115–118, 130, 287
Southwood, T., 267
Spatial Compensation Zones, 85–87
Sperling, L., 264–265, 279
Steering Committee, 28–29, 58
Stelfox, J.G. and Ngatia, M., 98
Stelfox, J.G., Kufwafwa, J.W., and Ottichillo, W.K., 98
Sudan, 32, 82, 245, 319
Sugar, 182, 216, 270, 293, 360–361
Survey of Kenya, 191
Sweden, 54
Swift, J., 306, 326–328

Tablino, P., 153
Taita Taveta, 55, 115–118, 130, 287
Tana River, 22, 55, 97–98, 115–118, 121, 170, 176, 287, 301, 304–305, 329
Tanner, C., 173
Tanzania, 67, 131–137
Task Force on Food Supply and Distribution, 28–29, 43, 58, 70, 111–112, 284
Tea, 8–9, 23, 57–58, 171, 174–177, 182, 202, 270, 355
Thailand, 9, 30–32, 36, 46–47, 53–54, 61
Thiba River, 170
Tiva River, 216
Tobacco, 174–175
Tocha, Y., 151, 156–157
Todenyang, 316, 326
Trans Nzoia, 94–97, 101, 106, 109, 115–118, 128, 130
Transportation; logistics, 31–34, 44, 58, 214, 284, 302, 329–336; infrastructure, 46, 50, 311–312
Tropical Livestock Unit (TLU), 266, 278
Trostle, R.M., xviii
Tsavo National Park, 212, 249, 254–255, 263
Turkana, 22, 40, 55, 139, 287, 301, 304–328, 334, 347–351
Turkana District (or County) Council (TDC), 311, 319, 328
Turkana Rehabilitation Project Meteorological Station (TRP/MET), 317, 327
Turkana Rehabilitation Project (TRP), 57, 60, 306, 311, 316–318, 320, 322–323, 328, 336

Uashin Gishu, 94–96, 101, 106, 115–118, 128, 130
Uganda, 22, 32–33, 61, 308, 319
United Kingdom, 38, 56
United Nations Children's Fund (UNICEF), 40–41, 43–44, 56, 59–61, 233, 289–295, 302, 315, 336
United Nations Educational, Scientific and Cultural Organization (UNESCO), 7, 59, 330
United Nations Environment Programme (UNEP), xv–xvi
United States Agency for International Development (USAID), xviii, 20, 28–29, 35, 37–40, 42, 47, 49, 53–54, 56–60, 63–64, 222, 232, 284, 363; Office of Foreign Disaster Assistance (OFDA), 12, 42, 44, 47, 60, 281, 331–336; Food-for-Peace, 59, 63–64
United States Department of Agriculture (USDA), 63–64
Universal Transverse Mercator Grid (UTM), 95, 123
University of California at Los Angeles, 232
University of Nairobi, 232
Urban Sector; service center strategy, 224; effect on food system, 375–376

Verma, V. Marchant, T., and Scott, C. 107
Vulnerability; drought, 4, 6, 169–210, 366–367; hunger, 186–187, 208

Waghela, S., Ndarathi, C.M., Okello, O.J.A., Semenye, P.P., and Rugema, E., 248
Wainaina, M., 169, 211
Wajir, 7, 42, 55, 97–98, 102, 104, 287, 301, 304–305, 347–351
Wamba, 265–279, 346
Wamba Veterinary Department, 266, 271
Wambani, V.S., 289
Wasonga, L.M., 289
Water Supply; conservation projects, 222, 339–340; development, 312; domestic, 215, 290; drought, 139, 141–150, 312; pastoralists, 247–251, 254–255; restrictions in Nairobi, 57; schools, 300, 302
Watt, B.K. and Merrill, A.L., 232

Weeda, A. and Mungai, D.N., 176
Weg, R.F. van der and Mbuvi, J.P., 176
Weinberg, S., 231
Wenner-Gren Foundation for Anthropological Research, xix
Were, F., 169
Werner, L.H., 295–296
West Africa, 88
West Pokot, 55, 94–97, 101–102, 105, 115–118, 130, 287, 301, 304–305, 343
Western (Province), xv, 6, 130, 290, 297
Wheat, 4, 7, 23, 26–28, 33, 36, 39–40, 42, 52–56, 58–59, 61–62, 64, 120, 122, 171, 360, 363–364, 374, 376, 378; imports, production, stocks, trade, and use, 63, 202, 283–288
Wigley, T.M.L., xvii
Wildlife, 97–105, 253

Wisner, B.G., 22
Women; food deprivation 140, 183, 187, 232–233, 236, 241–243; livestock economy, 251–253, 267, 348
World Bank, 8, 36, 44, 56, 377, 378
World Concern, 336
World Food Programme (WFP), 2, 11–12, 32, 38–45, 47, 54, 56–57, 59–60, 62, 222, 234, 274, 281–288, 292, 301–302, 329–336, 345, 349
World Health Organization, 185
World Vision, 42, 57, 222, 236, 284, 288, 330, 334, 336
Wyckoff, J.B., 355

Yatta, 176
York, S., xvii
Young Muslims, 288

Zaire, 32

FEB 2 2 1990